SECOND EDITION

CIVIL RIGHTS
AND LIBERTIES

Provocative Questions
and Evolving Answers

Harold J. Sullivan

John Jay College/The City University of New York

PEARSON

Prentice
Hall

Upper Saddle River, New Jersey 07458

Library of Congress Cataloging-in-Publication Data

SULLIVAN, HAROLD J. (HAROLD JOSEPH)
   Civil rights and liberties: provocative questions and evolving answers /
HAROLD J. SULLIVAN.
     p. cm.
   Includes bibliographical references and index.
   ISBN 0-13-117435-5
   1. Civil rights—United States.   I. Title.
   KF4749.S85   2005
   342.7308'5—dc22

Editorial Director: *Charlyce Jones Owen*
Acquisitions Editor: *Glenn Johnston*
Assistant Editor: *John Ragozzine*
Editorial Assistant: *Suzanne Remore*
Marketing Manager: *Kara Kindstrom*
Marketing Assistant: *Jennifer Lang*
Editorial/Production Supervision: *Edie Riker*
Prepress and Manufacturing Buyer: *Sherry Lewis*
Cover Art Director: *Jayne Conte*
Cover Designer: *Bruce Kenselaar*
Cover Art: *Stuart Westmorland/Corbis*

Pearson Education LTD.
Pearson Education Singapore, Pte. Ltd
Pearson Education, Canada, Ltd
Pearson Education–Japan
Pearson Education Australia PTY, Limited

Pearson Education North Asia Ltd
Pearson Educación de Mexico, S.A. de C.V.
Pearson Education Malaysia, Pte. Ltd
Pearson Education, Upper Saddle River, NJ

10 9 8 7 6 5 4 3 2 1

ISBN 0-13-117435-5

To my wife, Joan, who will always remain my love and best friend.

CONTENTS

CHAPTER TWO

The First Amendment and Freedom of Expression   21

CHAPTER THREE

Freedom of Religion   65

CHAPTER FOUR

Equality Under the Constitution   97

PREFACE

Since the first edition of this book appeared in the Fall of 2000, there have been significant developments in constitutional law concerning civil rights and liberties. In this second edition I continue to hope to stimulate readers into thinking critically about both new and continuing issues in the civil rights/civil liberties field.

In order to stimulate such thinking, each section of this book is introduced with a question. The questions are followed by responses which present the variety of "answers" justices of the United States Supreme Court have given to such questions in actual cases which have come before the Court. The questions are phrased simply and directly, and each answer is an essay designed to make constitutional interpretation accessible to readers even if they have no background in constitutional law. I expect that when such readers see many of the questions, they will think to themselves: "I've always wondered about that." When they read the "answers," they will be exposed to various constitutional tests and doctrines. I hope as well that when they read the questions and the variety of answers to them, they will be stimulated to explore in greater detail the U.S. Supreme Court decisions from which these answers were derived.

The subtitle of this book refers to "provocative questions/evolving answers." The answers provided by the United States Supreme Court justices have in fact been constantly evolving as the justices have sought to apply the principles of the Constitution to changing circumstances and new questions, some of which could not have been anticipated by the authors of the Constitution. Indeed some of the answers concerning questions relating to cross burning and racial intimidation, diversity and affirmative action, sexual privacy, pornography over the Internet, and government support for religious institutions, to name a few, have "evolved" significantly since the publication of the first edition of this book. This second edition, then, preserves what is still relevant from the first edition while incorporating more recent developments in constitutional law.

Having discussed both traditional and new issues throughout, in the end I hope to provoke readers into thinking about some questions that may become increasingly important in the future. These are issues with which the U.S. Supreme Court has only begun to grapple. I hope my discussion of them will stimulate readers to help evolve some new solutions on their own.

ACKNOWLEDGMENTS TO SECOND EDITION

Although the first edition of this book was published in the Fall of 2000, I still owe an enormous debt to those whose support helped make it possible and to others who have provided encouragement to me as I have prepared this revised edition. I will begin by acknowledging colleagues at the City University of New York and others who have provided ideas and encouragement. I have had the privilege of chairing an extraordinarily dynamic and committed Government Department at John Jay College / CUNY for almost 15 years. Two Government colleagues in particular, Barry Latzer and Roger McDonald, provided constructive criticism. Other John Jay colleagues whose friendship and encouragement continue to be invaluable include Jim Cohen, Anna Goldoff, Karen Kaplowitz, and Robert Sullivan. Outside of CUNY, Stephen K. White of the University of Virginia with whom I first discussed the idea for this project while we were still graduate students; Glenn Tinder whose book *Political Thinking* (Boston: Little Brown, 1970) gave me the idea for the question-and-answer format of this book, and my mentor and friend from college, George Goodwin, deserve acknowledgment and thanks. It is to the inspiration of George Goodwin, in particular, that I owe my career and the opportunity to teach so many wonderful John Jay students. In addition I owe thanks to

Judith Baer of Texas A&M University; as well as to Beth Mejia, Jayme Heffler, Glenn Johnston, John Ragozzine, and Edie Riker of the editorial staff at Prentice Hall; to the reviewers for the first edition: Richard Hardy, University of Missouri, Columbia; Gregory Scott, University of Central Oklahoma; as well as to the reviewers who helped shape this second edition: Robert G. Seddig, Allegheny College; Alex Landi, Spring Hill College; and James Renneker, Francis Marion University.

While acknowledging that I owe much to professional friends and colleagues, I am most in debt to family members and very close friends without whose help and support nothing would be possible. My wife Joan Kross, to whom I again dedicate this book, continues to supply seemingly limitless love and inspiration. My late mother, Margaret (Shine) Sullivan and my late sister Evelyn always supported me in everything I did as my brother Kenneth continues to do today. Although my father, Michael, died when I was 10 years old, I remain influenced by his impatience with injustice. My stepsons, John and Edward Noble, have been generous in welcoming me into their family. John is an admirable model of passionate commitment to worthwhile values, and his younger brother, Edward, a promising writer himself, is finding his own distinct path. My wife's mother, Irene Kross, continues to show a keen interest in my work. I am happy again to be in position to acknowledge as well my unofficial family, Deb, Stephen, A. J. and Eric Devaux. It was through Deb and Stephen that I met my wife, Joan. For many years before I had a family of my own, Stephen and his two awesome sons, AJ and Eric, always made me feel like part of their family. I have been close to AJ and Eric since they were born, and I shared in the joy of watching them grow into remarkable young men. Shortly after this edition actually appears in print AJ will be on his way to college where he is sure to impress all with his intellectual curiosity and quick wit. The always considerate Eric will continue earning deserved respect and winning friends in middle school and beyond. I look forward to them both being, like their dad, my friends for life. They are part of a larger coterie of very close friends, "the Group," many of whom I have known for over 35 years.

Together family, personal friends, and professional colleagues have contributed to whatever is worthwhile in this book. I will accept sole "credit" only for any errors.

CHAPTER ONE

INTRODUCTION
Judicial Defense of Civil Liberties and Civil Rights

The proper relationship of the individual to the state and society has always been a central question to political thinkers. The question becomes especially complicated in a society that claims to be governed by democratic principles. Probably the principal element in all the many competing definitions of democracy is the notion of majority rule. If, indeed, the government represents the will of the majority of the citizens, then perhaps we need not worry so much about protecting individuals from government. If we choose the government, what do we have to fear?

Most of us, however, are uneasy about giving power over our lives to others—even others like ourselves. Most of us often feel we want to be left alone. On the other hand, most of us do readily conform to societal norms with little complaint, and we may have little patience for people who insist on being different. Especially in a society in which we are forced to live close to each other and to interact with others on a daily basis, many may long for order.

In America the Constitution determines the rules for the relationship of the individual to the state. Broadly speaking, it defines the areas in which government may act and places restrictions on the power of government to interfere with or restrain our individual or collective choices.

When we speak of constitutional protections for us as individuals, we are speaking broadly of **civil liberties** and **civil rights.** Although many of us use the terms interchangeably, they really define two somewhat distinct aspects of our relationship to the state and society. *Civil liberties refer to those restrictions on government which leave the individual free to think and sometimes to act as he or she chooses without interference from government. Civil rights, on the other hand, refer to those affirmative protections that government owes to each individual as a citizen or participant in the society.*

A classic example of a civil liberty is freedom of religion. In its most elemental sense we understand this to be our right to believe (or disbelieve) whatever we want without the threat of retaliation from government. Government is restricted from interfering with our religious beliefs. When we think of civil rights, the first example that comes to mind is our expectation that we must be free from discrimination based on our race or gender. The realization of civil rights, however, can often require government action on our behalf, preventing other citizens from disadvantaging us solely because of something we cannot control. While civil liberties usually require that government leave us alone or keep its hands off, civil rights often require government action to protect our interests or rights from interference from others. Protection of civil rights, then, often requires government to act; protection of civil liberties usually just requires that government do nothing.

Even when we understand the differences between the terms "civil rights" and "civil liberties," we have barely begun to come to some understanding of civil rights and liberties in the United States. The practical meaning of these terms here is determined first of all by the Constitution. But what is the Constitution? The Constitution is the legal document that assigns and distributes government powers. In assigning power, however, it both explicitly and implicitly limits government powers. Once a society decides to have a constitutional government, by giving some powers it implicitly withholds those not given or assigned. The purpose of the Bill of Rights in our Constitution was to put additional explicit limits on the powers of the national (or federal) government and the purpose of the Fourteenth and Fifteenth Amendments was to place additional restrictions on the powers of the individual states which collectively make up the United States.

Every liberty we may want may not be protected by the Constitution; every right upon which many of us might want to depend may not have been a concern of those who drafted and approved those sections of the Constitution that restrict government powers or give government a command to protect our rights. The principal sources of our constitutional rights and liberties are the first ten amendments to the Constitution, usually referred to as the Bill of Rights, and the Thirteenth, Fourteenth, and Fifteenth Amendments. It is important to notice that it was in the amendments or changes to the Constitution as originally drafted by the framers that our rights and liberties are most explicitly addressed. When the Constitution was submitted to the original 13 states for ratification or acceptance as the governing charter of the United States, many felt it did not protect civil liberties enough. There was considerable sentiment expressed calling for more explicit limitations on federal government power. These were added by constitutional amendment almost immediately following ratification of the Constitution. Constitutional protections for civil rights really came only after the Civil War.

Any understanding of civil rights and liberties in America, then, begins with an understanding of the Constitution. But an understanding of the meaning of the Constitution requires an understanding of the role and significance of the courts, especially the United States Supreme Court. Although many sections of the Bill of Rights seem clear on the surface, for example, the First Amendment command that "Congress shall make no law . . . abridging the freedom of speech, or of the press," on reflection we may realize that this may not be as clear as it first appears. What does "abridge" mean? Is a law that regulates the places where we may speak, a law "abridging" our freedom of speech? What is encompassed by the phrase "the freedom of speech"? Does the freedom of speech include the freedom to interrupt others while they are speaking? Does it mean we may speak about the relative merits of the New York Yankees or the Boston Red Sox, about any subject we please, while a court of law is considering a tax case? Does it mean we may deliberately lie so as to damage the reputation of others? Does it mean we may make unwanted verbal sexual advances to an employee?

In the United States answers to questions such as these, as well as answers to the questions that make up the body of this book, are provided by the courts. To understand the role of the courts in defining civil rights and liberties we must begin by trying to understand the concept known as **judicial review.** *Judicial review is the power that American courts claim to decide on the constitutionality of actions of other parts of government.* It is the power they exercise to declare actions of other branches and levels of government unconstitutional and therefore not binding on the courts. When a court rules that a law or other government action is unconstitutional, generally all it is really saying is that the court will refuse to apply that law in the cases before it. If the courts consistently refuse to follow a law as they adjudicate disputes, then the law will cease to have practical effect.

Although there is substantial evidence that the framers of the Constitution intended the courts to exercise the power of judicial review, the Constitution does not explicitly and unambiguously give this power to the courts. All who exercise power under the U.S. Constitution are sworn to uphold and defend it. When the courts claim an action of another branch of government violates the Constitution, they are in effect second-guessing other government officials and challenging their fidelity to their oaths. In trying to understand the courts' exercise of the power of judicial review, we must view their claim in the context of an understanding of the nature of the judicial process.

WHAT COURTS DO

It is the responsibility of courts to resolve disputes by applying the law in individual cases or controversies. The case in which the U.S. Supreme Court first expressly claimed the right to refuse to give effect to the actions of another branch of government was *Marbury v. Madison,* in 1803. The actual dispute in *Marbury* was rather trivial, involving a dispute over a presidential appointment to a relatively insignificant judgeship. Marbury was a judicial candidate; Madison, in his capacity of secretary of state, in effect represented the president. But as has often been true historically, cases which in the immediate sense seem trivial become the vehicle for important legal rulings and interpretations of the Constitution.

In *Marbury v. Madison* the U.S. Supreme Court was confronted with the question of what happens if in making laws the Congress of the United States, *in the view of the Court,* disregards the distribution of powers established by the Constitution and substitutes its own judgment for how governmental powers should be allocated. The Court recognized that in the ordinary course of deciding cases, courts virtually everywhere are required to apply general laws passed by legislatures to individual cases. The first task before a court is to discover which laws are relevant to the case, in other words, which laws provide guidance.

In a country with a constitution a court would naturally look to it to see whether it provides guidance. Then it would look to statutes, laws passed by legislatures carrying out powers given to them by the constitution. Of necessity, however, in applying these laws, courts have to interpret their meaning.

In *Marbury v. Madison,* however, the Supreme Court confronted an additional question that has proved pivotal: What if there are two laws which both give guidance for deciding a case and those two laws appear to the court in question to be in conflict? If you follow one law, you will decide the case one way. If you follow the second law, you will decide the case differently. What is a court to do? Which law should the court apply to the case before it?

According to Chief Justice John Marshall writing for a unanimous Supreme Court in *Marbury v. Madison,* because the courts owe their very existence to the Constitution, because all government power in the

United States is limited by the Constitution, when the Court determined in *Marbury v. Madison* that the Constitution was at odds with a law passed by Congress, the justices determined that it is only natural that in the case of such conflict they should follow the Constitution and disregard the law approved by Congress. In support of this position, Chief Justice Marshall cited the language of the Constitution itself. Article III gives to the federal courts the responsibility to decide cases or controversies arising under the Constitution and the laws of the United States. The Supremacy clause of Article VI states: "This Constitution, and the laws of the United States which shall be made in pursuance thereof; . . . shall be the supreme law of the land; and the judges in every state shall be bound thereby, any thing in the . . . laws of any state to the contrary notwithstanding."

Chief Justice Marshall argued that the Supremacy clause means only laws of the United States passed in *pursuance of the Constitution* are "supreme." From this he concluded that in deciding cases to which a provision of the Constitution and a law both apply, the courts must determine if the law is "in pursuance of the Constitution" or contrary to it. If the courts are bound in deciding cases to laws made in pursuance of the Constitution, they are then not bound by those contrary to the Constitution. If they must decide a case by applying a law contrary to the Constitution or by applying the Constitution itself, the Supremacy clause, in listing the Constitution first, means they must follow the Constitution.

Although the Court's justification for its power of judicial review was not always universally supported, it has today become a fundamental element of American life. How is the power of judicial review exercised in the ordinary course of adjudication?

When any case is brought before a court, the parties to the case expect the court to apply existing law to their dispute in order to determine whose claim will succeed. In a criminal case, for example, a prosecutor representing the government seeks to persuade a judge and/or jury to decide that the accused has violated a criminal statute, a law passed by some state legislature or by Congress. In order to decide whether an accused is guilty a judge must first decide what the law means before either he or she or the jury decides whether the accused has violated the law. Any time a law is applied in an individual's case, the meaning and scope of the law must be understood. This requires interpretation.

When in the course of adjudication a party to the case contends that the law being applied to him or her violates the Constitution, the court must decide on the legitimacy of that claim. This requires the judge to interpret the law in question and the relevant section of the Constitution to determine whether there is a conflict. If in the judge's view the conflict exists he or she will declare the law or government action in question "unconstitutional" and refuse to give it effect.

Consider a hypothetical example. What if Congress, in response to the controversy aroused by the scandal surrounding former President Clinton's relationship with Monica Lewinsky, were to pass a criminal law making it a crime punishable by a year in prison for anyone to discuss in word or print the personal life of the president or any other high government official. Suppose that a reporter, subsequent to the law's enactment, were to learn that the majority leader of the Senate had, himself, had an illicit sexual liaison with an administrative aide. The reporter decides to publish an article in the *New York Post* detailing this relationship, including lurid details obtained from interviews with the now dismissed aide. Following the publication, the United States Attorney for New York prosecutes the author of the article, and a trial is scheduled for the U.S. District Court for the Southern District of New York.

It is clear from the facts of this fictional case that the author in question has violated the statute passed by Congress. He has openly published an article including intimate details of a sexual relationship involving a high official in the U.S. government. What would the reporter's lawyers do? Clearly, they would ask the federal district court judge to throw out the case and dismiss the indictment on the grounds that the law in question violates the First Amendment to the Constitution, which states in part that "Congress shall make no laws abridging the freedom of speech or of the press. . . ." What would the federal district court judge do? No doubt she would review the precedents, prior Supreme Court rulings interpreting the First Amendment, to decide whether she could apply the law in question against the accused without violating the First Amendment. She would, in other words, have to decide whether two laws, which both seem to apply to the case before her, are in conflict. If so, following *Marbury v. Madison,* she would decide to disregard the law passed by Congress.

Although there would probably be little doubt today that such a law violates the First Amendment, one can imagine another result. The court would first have to ask itself whether commentary on the personal lives of politicians is part of "the freedom of speech." We are so accustomed to such exposés today that we may think the answer to this question is obvious, but certainly this has not always been the case. Is such reporting one of the great purposes for which the amendment was added to the Constitution in the first place? Would banning such reporting seriously jeopardize the values intended to be protected by the First Amendment? In many other countries where freedom of speech is also highly valued, articles such as the one described here would clearly not be permitted.

We might ask ourselves if the likely result in this hypothetical case would be different in the United States had the law in question banned only "false" reporting on the personal lives of high public officials. If so, the result would clearly not have been as obvious. (See Chapter 2, Question 7.)

HOW DO WE KNOW WHAT THE CONSTITUTION MEANS?

Whenever a court declares the action of some government agency unconstitutional, the judge explains his or her decision. The government agency in question will almost invariably appeal such an action to an **appellate court.** An *appellate court is a court that reviews the actions of trial courts to determine whether they have properly interpreted and applied applicable law in an individual case.* Appellate court judges issue "opinions," or *written explanations of their rulings or interpretations of the law.* Those interpretations in turn serve as **precedents,** *court decisions in prior cases which provide guidance to other courts called upon to decide similar cases in the future.* Generally court decisions overturning laws passed by Congress or a state legislature on constitutional grounds will be appealed by the government all the way to the United States Supreme Court. Usually, the Supreme Court is considered obligated to make the ultimate determination as to the constitutionality of state legislative or congressional actions which have been overturned by a lower court. When the U.S. Supreme Court interprets the Constitution in the course of coming to a decision in a case in which a law has been challenged on constitutional grounds, its decisions interpreting the Constitution are considered controlling on lower courts. Those decisions provide precedents to guide the lower courts in similar cases. The parties in similar cases which arise in the future will know that if the trial court in their case disregards the Supreme Court interpretations, they too can appeal the decision up to the Supreme Court and, barring some change of mind, the Court will interpret the Constitution the same way again.

If we want to know what a specific provision of the Constitution means in practice, we must look to U.S. Supreme Court decisions interpreting the Constitution. By reading the Court opinions in cases that have previously arisen, we can usually determine what the Court is likely to do in a future case raising similar issues. Courts generally consider themselves bound by precedents. The rule of precedents, or *stare decisis,* however, in cases interpreting the Constitution is not considered as important as in cases interpreting ordinary statutes. Changing the Constitution itself is very difficult. If a court misinterprets an ordinary statute or law, a legislature can correct the decision simply by changing the law. A change in the Constitution, however, is much more difficult. Generally a constitutional amendment requires a two-thirds majority of both houses of Congress and the ratification of the legislatures of three-fourths of the states. A misinterpretation of the Constitution by the courts, then, is very difficult to correct or change. Because of this, courts are more willing to reinterpret the Constitution to correct perceived errors themselves. Such overturning of constitutional interpretations by the courts, however, although not exceptionally rare, is still unusual.

Often the Supreme Court itself is divided in its interpretation of the Constitution in the cases it decides. The very fact that a case reaches the Supreme Court tells us that it involves controversy. Different justices on the Court can have very different views concerning what a constitutional provision means, and even when they agree concerning its basic meaning, they may disagree concerning its application to the controversy before the Court.

The Supreme Court, like most appellate courts, makes its decisions by majority vote. A justice representing the majority view of the Court is designated to write an **Opinion of the Court,** *which sets forth the legal rationale behind the majority's decision in the case.* The Opinion of the Court explains to the parties in the case, to concerned others, and to future courts hearing comparable cases why the Court ruled as it did and what that ruling means. When the chief justice votes with the majority, he or she either writes the Opinion of the Court or decides who will draft the Opinion of the Court. When the chief justice disagrees with the decision of the majority in the case, the senior associate justice voting with the majority decides who is to draft the Opinion of the Court. When justices on the Court disagree with the Opinion of the Court, they often express their disagreements by writing what are known as **separate opinions.** If a justice approves of the decision in the specific case but disagrees with elements of the reasoning justifying it used by the author of the Court's opinion (or simply wants to add something), he or she may write what is know as a **concurring opinion,** *an opinion that explains the rationale used by the concurring justice or justices to justify their agreement with the decision of the majority as well as any differences concerning the rationale behind that decision.* A justice or justices who disagree with the decision made by the Court will often write **dissenting opinions,** *opinions which explain the grounds for their disagreement with the majority's decision.*

Although the reasonings in court opinions not attracting the support of an actual majority of the Court are not considered precedents binding future cases and lower courts, they often point the way to other litigants in the future who are looking for grounds to challenge existing interpretations of the Constitution. Sometimes dissents ultimately serve as the foundation for new interpretations of the Constitution. Some dissents in the end have more lasting significance in American constitutional interpretation than opinions of the Court which society comes to reject on reflection.

Together, Opinions of the Court, concurring opinions, and dissents provide authoritative views as to the meaning of the Constitution. Because the variety of opinions also alerts us to the variety of possible interpretations of the meaning of various constitutional provisions, these opinions can provide a window to the controversies arising over civil rights and civil liberties in American life. Judicial opinions in actual cases will then provide the raw material for discussing controversial questions relating to civil rights and liberties throughout this book. As the reader will soon see, there are a variety of interpretations of most sections of the Constitution, especially those sections of the Constitution pertaining to civil rights and liberties.

THE FOURTEENTH AMENDMENT AND THE "INCORPORATION" OF THE BILL OF RIGHTS

Because the United States has a federal system of government which divides government authority between a strong central government (usually referred to as the federal government) and the 50 state governments, potential and actual threats to civil rights and liberties can come from either or both levels of government. Today, according to contemporary interpretation by the U.S. Supreme Court, the United States Constitution restrains both the federal government and the states in precisely the same way with regard to almost all the civil liberties recognized by the Bill of Rights of the United States Constitution. The application of the same standards to both state and federal governments, however, is largely a twentieth-century development. In order to understand United States constitutional standards for contemporary issues in civil rights and liberties it is, therefore, no longer important to distinguish between threats to those rights and liberties emanating from state or federal government. Nonetheless it is useful briefly to survey how, in spite of the federal system, the states came to be covered by constitutional guidelines initially developed to restrain principally the national government.

The Bill of Rights, as noted above, was added to the Constitution because some feared that the Constitution as drafted might enable the national government to interfere with important liberties. The Bill of Rights was not intended to bind the states. Each of the original states had its own constitution which to varying degrees limited the state's powers to interfere with individual liberties. When some sought the protection of the federal Bill of Rights from claimed invasion of individual liberties by state governments, the Supreme Court, emphasizing the framers' original purpose, concluded in *Barron v. Baltimore* (1833) that the Bill of Rights restricted only Congress and the national government. The state governments were restrained only by their own constitutions and by the few limited restrictions on them included in the body of the unamended Constitution of 1787.

Following the Civil War, however, in order principally to assure protections for African Americans from hostile legislation within the former "slave states," additional protections for rights and liberties were added to the Constitution through the Thirteenth, Fourteenth, and Fifteenth Amendments. These restrictions, especially the Fourteenth and Fifteenth Amendments, provided a basis for forcing the state governments to conform to some national constitutional standards for civil rights and liberties and served to alter somewhat the relationship between state and national governments. Very quickly, however, conflict arose within the Supreme Court over whether the Fourteenth Amendment subjected state governments to the national standard of the Bill of Rights in the same way as the national government or whether the scope of its protections for individual liberties in the states was far more limited.

Today, as a result of many court decisions spread over decades, virtually all the protections for individual liberties included in the Bill of Rights restrict state and local governments in the same way they restrict the national government. Because the focus of this book is on central substantive issues concerning fundamental civil rights and civil liberties, we will not survey in detail the complex arguments for and against applying the protections for civil liberties included in the Bill of Rights to state governments through the Fourteenth Amendment. We will, however, briefly explore how the Bill of Rights became substantially "incorporated" under the Fourteenth Amendment as its liberties became restrictions on the powers of state and local governments.

Because the Fourteenth Amendment does not explicitly provide that state governments be subject to the protection for civil liberties included in the Bill of Rights, the case for their inclusion required interpretation of two sections of Section 1 of the Fourteenth Amendment. Section 1 of the Fourteenth Amendment states that

> All persons born or naturalized in the United States, and subject to the jurisdiction thereof, are citizens of the United States and of the State wherein they reside. No State shall make or enforce any law which shall abridge the privileges or immunities of citizens of the United States; nor shall any State deprive any person of life, liberty, or property, without due process of law; nor deny to any person within its jurisdiction the equal protection of the laws.

When the U.S. Supreme Court was called upon to interpret the meaning of the Privileges and Immunities clause in the *Slaughterhouse Cases* of 1873, it rejected by a 5 to 4 vote the argument that the clause was designed to apply the Bill of Rights to the states. Instead the Court confined the interpretation of this clause to rights, such as the right to travel from state to state—rights of a national character—which had existed before the adoption of the Fourteenth Amendment. The Court came to this conclusion in part through its determination that the primary purpose of the amendment was to extend existing constitutional protections to African Americans who had previously been granted no rights by the states of the Confederacy and few rights even by states that had long banned slavery. Though the amendment declared that all, including formerly enslaved African Americans, were to be citizens both of the United States and of the state where they resided, the Court argued that they must be accorded all the rights held by other citizens but only those grounded in their national citizenship. Such national rights, according to the Supreme Court decision in *Barron v. Baltimore,* never included protection from state government infringements of rights protected by the Bill of Rights against infringement by the national government.

The Court majority's narrow interpretation of the Privileges and Immunities clause was challenged by four of the nine justices on the Court, who argued in dissents that privileges and immunities of citizens of the United States included all the protections for fundamental liberties included in the Bill of Rights. Despite the dissents, the U.S. Supreme Court has never yet overturned its initial narrow interpretation of the Privileges and Immunities clause. The protections for individual liberties which now apply to the states as well as the federal government were applied to them through the Due Process clause of the Fourteenth Amendment. In effect the Court has gradually come to interpret the word "liberty," which is protected against state infringement "without due process of law," to include most of the liberties encompassed by the Bill of Rights and more.

This process of "incorporation" of the protections of the Bill of Rights into the liberties protected by the Fourteenth Amendment against infringement by the states has been gradual, selective, and the subject of great controversy on the Court. First of all it is important to remember that almost any liberty or right, including even the right to life, can be restricted by government as a punishment for crimes. So initially when we read that "life, liberty, or property" may not be taken away without "due process of law," we understand that following proper procedural protections included under the concept of due process of law, liberty or property or even life may be taken away. But liberty means more than simply being free from imprisonment or other physical constraint. The term "liberty" must be given content or meaning through interpretation.

In interpreting the Fourteenth Amendment Due Process clause, then, the Court has had many occasions when it has had to define what liberty means. To some this term means simply and exclusively the specific liberties outlined in the Bill of Rights (referred to in constitutional interpretation as "total incorporation"); to others it has meant only those liberties included in the Bill of Rights, which are fundamental liberties traditionally respected within Anglo American legal-political traditions ("selective incorporation"); to others it has been an evolving concept including even more rights and liberties than those expressly recognized in the Bill of Rights ("total incorporation plus" or "selective incorporation plus"). Finally, to some the meaning of liberty and of due process in the Due Process clause of the Fourteenth Amendment are not directly tied to any of the specific provisions of the federal Bill of Rights.

In the twentieth century the argument in support of incorporation of the Bill of Right has been best exemplified by Justice Hugo Black. Justice Black argued that the history of the enactment of the Fourteenth Amendment made it clear that its authors and principal supporters intended that the Privileges and Immunities clause would itself apply the Bill of Rights to the states (see the Appendix to his dissent in *Adamson v. California,* at 93–123, 1946). But recognizing that this interpretation had been rejected by the Court in the *Slaughterhouse Cases,* he for a time supported the applications of the Bill of Rights to the states through the Due Process clause, arguing that the liberties protected by the Fourteenth Amendment were nothing more, or nothing less, than those included in the Bill of Rights. Justice Black argued against those (discussed below) who would substitute some other standard for determining which liberties are to be protected:

> I cannot consider the Bill of Rights to be an outworn 18th century "straight jacket." . . . Its provisions may be thought outdated abstractions by some. And it is true they were designed to meet ancient evils. But they are the same kind of human evils that have emerged from century to century whenever excessive power is sought by the few at the expense of the many. . . . I fear to see the consequences of the Court's practice of substituting its own concepts of decency and fundamental justice for the language of the Bill of Rights. . . . If the choice must be between the selective process of the Palko decision applying some of the Bill of Rights to the states or the Twining rule applying none of them, I would choose the Palko selective process. But rather than accept either of these choices, I would follow what I believe was the original purpose of the Fourteenth Amendment—to extend to all people of the nation the complete protection of the Bill of Rights (*Adamson v. California,* 1946, Black, J., dissenting, at 89).

According to Justice Black, any other interpretation of the Fourteenth Amendment allows Supreme Court justices to substitute their own judgments for those of the framers of the Bill of Rights and the Fourteenth Amendment.

One of the chief proponents of viewing the Due Process clause of the Fourteenth Amendment as being entirely independent and distinct from the Bill of Rights was Justice Felix Frankfurter, a contemporary of Justice Black on the Court. In the same case, *Adamson v. California,* he rejected both Black's "total incorporation" and the Court standard of "selective incorporation," derived in part from Justice Benjamin Cardozo in *Palko v. Connecticut* (1937). Instead he would substitute a case-by-case approach for determining whether state actions challenged under the Fourteenth Amendment adequately protect liberties on the whole.

The *Adamson* case concerned the question of whether the privilege against self-incrimination from the Fifth Amendment precluded a comment within a trial on a defendant's failure to respond at trial to charges against him. Had this been a federal criminal case, this practice would have been prohibited by the Fifth Amendment. The question then was whether the Fourteenth Amendment Due Process clause imposed this same restriction upon the states. In interpreting the Fourteenth Amendment Due Process clause, Justice Frankfurter, in direct contradiction to Justice Black, argued:

> The [Fourteenth] Amendment neither comprehends the specific provisions by which the founders deemed it appropriate to restrict the Federal government nor is it confined to them. . . . And so, when, as in a case like the present, a conviction in a State court is here for review under a claim that a right protected by the Due Process clause of the Fourteenth Amendment has been denied, the issue is not whether an infraction of the specific provisions of the first eight Amendments is disclosed in the record. The relevant question is whether the criminal proceedings which resulted in conviction deprived the accused of the due process of laws which the United States Constitution entitled him. Judicial review of the guaranty of the Fourteenth Amendment inescapably imposes upon this Court an exercise of judgment upon the whole course of the proceeding in order to ascertain whether they offend those canons of decency and fairness which express the notions of justice of English-speaking peoples even toward those charged with the most heinous offenses (*Adamson v. California,* 1946, Frankfurter, J., concurring, at 66–68).

In reply to the position of Justice Black, who argued that the Bill of Rights alone provides the meaning of liberty and due process under the Fourteenth Amendment, Justice Frankfurter argued:

> These standards of Justice are not authoritatively formulated anywhere as though they were prescriptions in a pharmacopoeia. But neither does the application of the Due Process clause imply that judges are wholly at large. The judicial judgment in applying the Due Process clause must move within the limits of accepted notions of justice and is not to be based upon the the idiosyncrasies of a merely personal judgment (at 66–68).

When there is any doubt that a state action contradicts such "accepted notions of justice," Justice Frankfurter argued that respect for federalism and the state courts required the Supreme Court to defer to their judgments (at 67–68).

In effect the middle ground on whether the protections accorded by the Bill of Rights applies to the states is provided by those justices who adopt what is termed "selective incorporation" of the Bill of Rights under the umbrella of the Fourteenth Amendment. In this view some of the provisions of the Bill of Rights are more central to the preservation of liberty than others. Where the line is to be drawn between rights and liberties encompassed by the Due Process clause of the Fourteenth Amendment has been a moving target throughout the twentieth century. The movement, however, has been toward increasing the breadth of coverage as more and more provisions of the Bill of Rights have been viewed as "fundamental."

Justice Benjamin Cardozo's opinion in *Palko v. Connecticut* (1937) has provided a principal rationale for selectively applying particular provisions of the Bill of Rights to the states through the Due Process clause of the Fourteenth Amendment. Although he rejected the argument that the "liberty" protected by the Fourteenth Amendment was precisely tied to the specific liberties listed in the Bill of Rights, Justice Cardozo did argue that some of those liberties were of such fundamental importance to a free society that, in effect, we would not have liberty if they were to be disregarded.

The question before the Court in *Palko* was whether granting the state a new trial of a defendant because of errors, detrimental to the prosecution at a first criminal trial, amounted to unconstitutional "double jeopardy." Under the Fifth Amendment it was clear that a second trial would not be permitted in federal cases. Because this case involved a state prosecution, the question became whether subjecting a defendant to punishment following conviction at a second trial, or "double jeopardy," would deprive him of "liberty without due process of law" contrary to the Fourteenth Amendment.

In determining which rights and liberties derived from the Bill of Rights are applicable to the states through the Due Process clause of the Fourteenth Amendment, Justice Cardozo in effect asks whether the specific liberties in question ". . . have been found to be implicit in the concept of ordered liberty." According to this view and summarizing Court precedents established at the time of the *Palko* decision, Justice Cardozo found that, for example, the right of free speech is included under the liberties protected by the Fourteenth Amendment. On the other hand, "[t]he right to trial by jury and the immunity from prosecution except as a result of an indictment [although they] may have value and importance . . . are not of the very essence of a scheme of ordered liberty. To abolish them is not to violate a 'principle of justice so rooted in the traditions and conscience of our people as to be ranked as fundamental'" (at 324–325).

The justices who have in effect supported selective application of the Bill of Rights to the states through the Fourteenth Amendment have not relied on the specific provisions of the Bill of Rights in determining the outer limits of the liberty protected by the Due Process clause of the Fourteenth Amendment. Both in drawing lines to include some provisions of the Bill of Rights and not others, and in discovering and defining liberties nowhere specifically mentioned in the Constitution (see discussion of right to privacy in Chapter 5), these justices have demonstrated the crucial role played by the Supreme Court in defining the meaning of civil liberties and civil rights in America. They not only interpret for us what specific provisions of the Constitution mean; they also decide which provisions are more fundamental than others and which liberties, nowhere specifically mentioned in the Constitution, are nonetheless part of constitutional protected liberty.

As a result of Court decisions interpreting the scope of Fourteenth Amendment protections for civil rights and liberties against state governments, all rights and liberties discussed in this book restrict the national (federal) and state governments in the same ways and to the same degree. It will therefore not be necessary generally for us to distinguish between the levels of government involved as we discuss the varying interpretations found in Court decisions of our rights and liberties.

A HIERARCHY OF RIGHTS AND LIBERTIES

Implicit in the debate within the Court over the application of the Bill of Rights to the states through the Fourteenth Amendment was the notion that not all constitutional rights and liberties are of equal significance and as deserving of special judicial protection. The Court has from time to time given explicit recognition to the argument that some of the protections in the Bill of Rights are "preferred freedoms." Similarly the Court has found that some alleged denials of the right to equal protection of the laws are more constitutionally "suspect" than others. Although the Court's opinions gradually extending the protections of the Bill of Rights to the states gave implicit recognition to a hierarchy of rights and liberties, perhaps the most explicit statement of this argument can be found in a footnote to what at first would appear to be a rather insignificant Court decision. In *U.S. v. Carolene Products Co.* (1938), a decision upholding federal regulations of artificial additives to milk products, in his famous Footnote No. 4, Justice Harlan Stone argued that all rights and liberties may not be created equal. When, for example, a liberty has been explicitly stated in the text of the Constitution, laws which can be viewed as restricting that liberty are not due the deference normally given to enactments of a democratically elected legislature. As Justice Stone argued, "[t]here may be narrower scope of operation of the presumption of constitutionality when legislation appears on its face to be within a specific prohibition of the Constitution, such as those of the first ten amendments, which are deemed equally specific when held to be embraced within the Fourteenth."

In a related sense Justice Stone speculated that legislative actions not readily correctable through the operation of normal political processes in society (because the legislation itself limits or restricts the openness or potential responsiveness of those processes) may require more searching judicial analysis. If open government decision-making processes are not open and responsive enough to correct mistakes, then the courts may have special justification for stepping in.

Finally, legislation which targets a minority within society for discriminatory treatment also calls for more robust judicial intervention simply because a minority, because of insufficient potential voting strength, may well be unable to protect its interests in a political system governed by majority rule. ". . . [S]tatutes directed at particular religious . . . or national, . . . or racial minorities. . .; prejudice against discrete and insular minorities may be a special condition, which tends seriously to curtail the operation of those political processes ordinarily to be relied upon to protect minorities . . . [and] may call for a correspondingly more searching judicial inquiry" (at 152). While we are all at some point or another in a minority with relation to some specific issue, some, such as racial minorities, may have their vital concerns indefinitely ignored. Because of their relatively permanent excluded minority status, their ability to assemble sufficient votes to bring change may be virtually nonexistent. For them the courts may be their only recourse.

THE CHECKERED HISTORY OF JUDICIAL DEFENSE OF RIGHTS AND LIBERTIES

Before beginning our exploration of the Supreme Court's protections for our rights and liberties and of the great variety in interpretation given even some of our more fundamental freedoms, it is important to recognize that the Supreme Court through much of our history has not been in the forefront of extending protection of our civil liberties and civil rights. In part because the selection process for Supreme Court justices is itself part of the political process, the same pressures that can from time to time influence democratically elected leaders to give inadequate protection to civil rights and liberties can influence our unelected, yet politically appointed, Supreme Court justices to reflect the dominant views of their times. If society is in a repressive mood, so too can be the

U.S. Supreme Court. If politicians can sometimes be dismissive of individual liberties or the rights of minorities, so too can Supreme Court justices, who tend to be selected from among the more privileged sectors of society. It is important to remember as we survey the variety of views on the Court concerning some of the more important rights and liberties, that the Court has from time to time provided the constitutional cover for what many consider some of our government's more regrettable actions.

A few examples might help us keep the Court in perspective. It took the U.S. Supreme Court to state explicitly what the founders of our country no doubt intended but nonetheless left unstated: America as founded rested on profoundly racist ideas of white supremacy. In *Dred Scott v. Sandford* (1857) Chief Justice Roger Taney argued that even "freed slaves" had "no rights which the white man was bound to respect." African Americans, according to Taney's Opinion for the Court, could, under the Constitution of 1789, never be citizens. Only the Civil War and a Constitution revised by the Thirteenth, Fourteenth, and Fifteenth Amendments could change the results of the Court's interpretation. Subsequently later Court interpretations, even of these amendments, had for generations permitted federal and state governments to disregard their clear purpose of mandating racial equality under the law.

In the periods following both the First and Second World Wars the U.S. Supreme Court gave judicial sanction to constitutional interpretations of our free speech protections which permitted punishment of people espousing views that the majority found threatening. In cases such as *Gitlow v. New York* (1925) and *Dennis v. United States* (1951), the Court read into the First Amendment exceptions to our free speech protections that are today widely rejected. In ruling as it did, the Court reflected the fears of its time.

On the other hand there have been moments in our history where the Supreme Court has taken positions that extended rights and liberties. At some of these moments the Court has been well ahead of the political leadership of society and probably the desires of most citizens, but it has taken stands that it felt were dictated by its duty to interpret the Constitution. In *Brown v. Board of Education* (1954) the U.S. Supreme Court in effect overturned its own ruling in *Plessy v. Ferguson* 58 years earlier, which had said that the Equal Protection clause of the Fourteenth Amendment permitted state-imposed separation of citizens in public places on the basis of race. In declaring state-imposed racial segregation in the schools unconstitutional in *Brown,* the Court set in motion a legal and political struggle that would last a generation or more to undo the entrenched system of racial segregation found in the American South. In this decision the Court was ahead of much of society. In the area of free speech in the later part of the twentieth century the Court protected free expression even of those despised by society.

Following the terrorist attacks of September 11, 2001, civil rights and liberties again have been threatened. While most of the targets of government restrictions under the so-called USA PATRIOT Act of 2001 have been noncitizens and foreign nationals in the United States, it does not take much imagination to anticipate how future terrorist attacks could precipitate a political crackdown on dissent or discriminatory actions against those who share the ethnic and religious origins of the "terrorists." Whether the Supreme Court would stand up against such pressures during a time of crisis or reflect the fears of the people and the government must for the moment remain a matter for speculation.

In reviewing the performance of the Court on pivotal civil liberties and civil rights issues, it is important to keep a sense of perspective. The Court rarely speaks with one voice; the Court can sometimes be a conscience for the nation and at other times merely a temporary legitimizer of its more selfish and destructive instincts.

LEGISLATIVE PROTECTIONS FOR RIGHTS AND LIBERTIES

This book explores civil rights and civil liberties issues through judicial decisions and opinions enforcing constitutional provisions; it is important, however, to remember that judicial decisions are not the only source of protection for our rights and liberties. Both the Congress and the state legislatures can, and do, approve laws that provide protections beyond those required by the Constitution. Through its Article I, Section 8 powers to "regulate commerce . . . among the . . . states," for example, Congress has chosen to prohibit private persons from interfering with the ability of people to participate in the economic life of the country on account of race, color, creed, national origins, or disability.

The ability of Congress in particular to pass laws such as the Civil Rights Act of 1964 and the Americans with Disabilities Act depends on the reach of its commerce power. Supreme Court interpretations of this power of Congress have shifted dramatically over the course of American history. The question of the limit of Congress's commerce power is, however, beyond the scope of this book. Our focus is on constitutional provisions that in and of themselves directly define and give meaning to constitutional safeguards for civil rights and liberties.

Because the Constitution itself restricts only government action, however (see Chapter 6, Question 4), these additional statutory protections for civil rights are not a matter of constitutional "right." They are given to us largely at the discretion of Congress and the state legislatures as they exercise their regulatory power over commercial activity and other private conduct. We do not discuss the specific provisions of these federal and state laws except where necessary to explain how the Constitution places limitations upon them. (See discussion of affirmative action, Chapter 4, Question 4.)

CONTINUING CONTROVERSY: WHY SO MANY QUESTIONS?

Any book that seeks to explore the rich territory of civil liberties and civil rights in America cannot avoid being selective in its coverage. This book is no different. Our focus is on those fundamental rights and liberties that have been at the core of controversy in American constitutional history and politics. These are rights and liberties at the core of the American political system—those which determine most centrally the nature of our political institutions. First of all, in Chapter 2 we explore core First Amendment issues relating to freedom of thought and expression. The ability of citizens to be part of the political process requires their ability to become informed concerning options available to society and the ability to make themselves heard in decision-making counsels. In selecting questions we have attempted to highlight core First Amendment principles and explore continuing controversies concerning the limits, if any are appropriate, on the expression of ideas.

Freedom of religion has long been considered a core value in American political life. Because of the nation's increasing diversity and the history of persecution of peoples throughout the world over issues of conscience, the definition of this freedom and any limits to it will no doubt continue to be one of the leading agenda items for the Supreme Court. In selecting questions in Chapter 3, we have also attempted to highlight basic principles guiding freedom of religion litigation and to explore ongoing controversies in this field.

No issue has divided American society more than the question of race. Slavery and racial discrimination marked America from its very beginnings and have had a direct impact on the original design of the Constitution and its revision. Conflict over race has led us to decide how important equality is and what equality demands—even beyond race to issues of gender and unequal distribution of wealth and opportunity. Developing an understanding of how the justices of the U.S. Supreme Court in the contemporary era have addressed these issues through interpretation of the Fourteenth Amendment is the purpose of Chapter 4.

The most controversial decisions of the Supreme Court in the latter part of the twentieth century have no doubt been those concerning the right to privacy—especially issues related to abortion rights, homosexual rights, and the right to die. None of these rights are explicitly discussed in the Constitution, yet all are crucial to determining the fate of individuals and individual autonomy in contemporary society. All too have been the subject of some of the more heated and emotional political controversy that has engaged the United States Supreme Court. Each of these issues will be explored in Chapter 5 as well as the core question behind all of them: How does the Court identify rights and liberties which are not explicitly mentioned in the Constitution?

Finally in Chapter 6 we move away from what have historically been core issues of civil liberties and civil rights to an exploration of emerging new issues. The contemporary communications environment presents some newer threats to what Justice Oliver Wendell Holmes termed the "free marketplace of ideas." Are First Amendment standards which were designed to keep that marketplace of ideas open and competitive threatened by new technologies and/or by concentrated economic power? Another issue is the government's ceding increasing aspects of our lives to private groups. Are our constitutional protections adequate to deal with possible new threats from some private sources?

Finally in Chapter 7 we explore some of the implications of current court interpretations of core constitutional issues for the future in an effort to invite the readers to think about possible emerging threats to civil rights and liberties.

Throughout, questions are posed that should help the reader think through historic and continuing controversies that have engaged the attention of American courts as they attempt to give practical meaning to the relatively few words included in the Constitution of the United States.

REFERENCES

Adamson v. California, 332 U.S. 469 (1946).

Barron v. Baltimore, 32 U.S. 243 (1833).

Brown v. Board of Education, 347 U.S. 483 (1954).

Dennis v. United States, 341 U.S. 494 (1951).

Dred Scott v. Sandford, 60 U.S. 393 (1857).

Gitlow v. New York, 268 U.S. 652 (1925).

Marbury v. Madison, 5 U.S. 137 (1803).

Palko v. Connecticut, 302 U.S. 319 (1937).

Plessy v. Ferguson, 163 U.S. 537 (1896).

The Slaughterhouse Cases, 83 U.S. 36 (1873).

U.S. v. Carolene Products Co., 304 U.S. 144 (1938).

CHAPTER TWO

THE FIRST AMENDMENT AND FREEDOM OF EXPRESSION

INTRODUCTION

Freedom of speech and freedom of the press are core constitutional values in American democracy. Without open public debate and discussion about issues that touch at the foundations of society, it is impossible for the people effectively to control the direction of our political institutions. This chapter begins, therefore, with a basic question: *What is "freedom of speech"?* It introduces the idea that from its inception the idea of freedom of speech may have included some limits on our ability to say what we want when we want. It seeks to explain the difference between censorship or "prior restraint," the stopping of speech or publication deemed threatening to some important societal value, and punishment for speech after it has occurred.

The second question addressed in this chapter is: *How has the Court justified limits on the expression of ideas?* Despite the clear command of the First Amendment that "Congress shall make no law . . . abridging the freedom of speech, or of the press," the United States Supreme Court throughout our history has to varying degrees and under varying circumstances argued that the Constitution does permit punishment for speech and publication. This section reviews some of the central "doctrines" of First Amendment adjudication such as "clear and present danger," "balancing," "preferred position," and "bad tendency." It begins, however, with a discussion of Justice Hugo Black's "absolutist" position, which argues that no limits on speech are justifiable.

Because to all of us from time to time some speech seems clearly offensive and even dangerous, the third question addressed in this chapter is: *Shouldn't we ban dangerous ideas?* This section focuses on the difference between mere advocacy and action. It assesses the often-cited example of dangerous speech, "falsely shouting fire in a crowded theater and causing a panic," in order to see when, if ever, mere words are dangerous. It will investigate the possible value of even "dangerous" speech.

One particular form of speech that many find extremely disturbing is the phenomenon known as "hate speech." In light of America's troubled history of racial tension and conflict, "racist speech" seems particularly dangerous. This section, then, seeks to answer Question 4: *May the government punish those who engage in "hate speech"?*

As the discussion following Question 1 should make clear, the Supreme Court has long held the view that obscenity is not included in the categories of expression protected by the First Amendment. Nonetheless what many people consider obscene still exists. This section therefore seeks to answer the question: *Why must society tolerate obscenity?* Question 5 explores the difficulty which the Court has faced in trying to define obscenity. We discuss the various standards the Court has used to distinguish obscenity from "protected" expression. Finally, we will discuss the efforts by some feminists to ban obscenity as "sex discrimination."

The development of the Internet, which brings all kinds of expression into the homes of citizens who own a computer and modem, raises a new issue for those concerned about obscenity. Question 6 asks: *Why does government permit sexually explicit material to invade our homes over the Internet?* In exploring the Court's approach to the issues raised by this question, we will begin our exploration of the implications of the Internet for freedom of expression, a topic to which we will return in Chapter 6, Question 2.

Many citizens are justifiably disturbed by the tenor of our public discussion and debate. There seems to be little concern for truth as charges are hurled back and forth and as the lives of public officials and celebrities are dissected in the media. This section, therefore, seeks answers to Question 7: *Why not require that people in public debate tell the truth?* This section discusses issues surrounding libel and slander cases. It will focus on the *New York Times* standard, the conflict between protecting individual reputations and robust public debate, the different treatment given by the courts to public figures and private citizens, and the question of upon whom should the burden of proving "truth" fall.

A form of expression which has stirred much political controversy has been "flag burning." Because of the reverence which most Americans hold for the flag, people react, sometimes violently, to its desecration. This section, therefore, seeks to answer Question 8: *How is burning the American flag a form of free speech?* In answering this question, this section reviews the Court's approach to so-called symbolic speech and discusses the First Amendment requirement that regulations of speech must be "content neutral."

While burning the American flag may be deeply offensive to many, a burning cross has become a symbol of hate and intimidation. Question 9 asks: *If flag burning is protected by the First Amendment, why is cross burning sometimes not protected?* In this section we explore possible bases for distinguishing between these two controversial modes of expressing unpopular ideas.

Finally, although freedom of speech is widely held to be an essential precondition for democracy, some find it hard to understand why a democratic society should tolerate free speech for enemies of democracy and even of free speech itself. This section then seeks to answer Question 10: *Why should a democratic society tolerate the expression of views that are offensive to the majority?* This section discusses the fundamental role of free debate in a democratic society. It discusses difficult cases, such as that of the Nazis in Skokie, Illinois. Finally, the topic of this section should allow for a summing up of and conclusion to the entire chapter, providing an assessment of the role played by free speech in a society that considers itself to be democratic.

Question 1   *What is "freedom of speech"?*

The First Amendment to the United States Constitution commands that "Congress shall make no law . . . abridging the freedom of speech, or of the press." Since the U.S. Supreme Court decision in *Gitlow v. New York* in 1925, the Fourteenth Amendment has been interpreted as applying this same restriction to the states. Although the language of the First Amendment is more direct and emphatic than probably in any other part of the Constitution, there has always been considerable debate concerning precisely what the First Amendment Free Speech/Free Press clause protects.

When children speak in class out of turn or when they are expected to be silent, limits are placed on their freedom *to* speak. When a member of the United States House of Representatives speaks without having been recognized by the presiding officer, he is silenced. If you visit a courtroom to watch a trial and decide to tell the court you don't like what you see, you will at best be removed and more likely, if you refuse to be silent, found in contempt of court and sent to jail. None of these examples is thought to raise any First Amendment problems. No reputable First Amendment scholar or Supreme Court justice has ever seriously argued that freedom of speech means you can say whatever you want wherever or whenever you please.

The First Amendment really concerns open debate, the ability to express and to hear a variety of points of view. Although on the surface the First Amendment would seem to prohibit any governmental interference with the verbal or written expression of ideas, most Supreme Court justices have argued that certain forms of expression are completely outside constitutional protection. They would argue that the First Amendment does not protect all speech; rather it protects what has been understood historically as "the freedom of speech." Certain categories of speech are included in that phrase; others are not included (see Meikeljohn, pp. 16–19).

In a famous passage from his decision in *Chaplinsky v. New Hampshire* (1942), Justice Frank Murphy argued:

> There are certain well-defined and narrowly limited classes of speech, the prevention and punishment of which have never been thought to raise any Constitutional problem. These include the lewd and obscene, the profane, the libelous, and insulting or "fighting" words—those which by their very utterance inflict injury or tend to incite an immediate breach of the peace. It has been well observed that such utterances are no essential part of any exposition of ideas, and are of such slight social value as a step to truth that any benefit that may be derived from them is clearly outweighed by the social interest in order and morality. "Resort to epithets or personal abuse is not in any proper sense communication of information or opinion safeguarded by the [Constitution]." *Cantwell v. Connecticut,* 310 U.S. 296 (1940).

Although this passage might appear to provide clear guidance to anyone seeking to understand the limits of freedom of speech, in reality it has not held up under scrutiny. Even those who generally accept the premise that the First Amendment protects only those expressions that contribute to the "exposition of ideas" and "the search for truth" have had to confront the questions concerning, for example, precisely what is "obscene" or "libelous." Attempts to limit either can in some circumstances spill over into limits of the exposition of ideas and the search for truth.

Prior Restraint

Demand for the protection of freedom of speech emerged against a historical backdrop of censorship, the need to obtain prior approval of some government agency before speaking or publishing. The historical rejection of any right of government to silence us *before* we speak or write has led to a broad consensus among Supreme Court justices that "prior restraint" on the press is the least acceptable form of government inter-ference with free expression. As the British legal philosopher William Blackstone put it: "Every freeman has the undoubted right to lay what sentiments he pleases before the public; to forbid this, is to destroy the freedom of the press" (*Near v. Minnesota,* at 713, 1931).

The consensus against prior restraint, however, does not extend to a belief that no one should be or can be punished for what he or she says or prints. Although you generally do not need prior government approval to express any ideas you desire, should what you say or print offend some important government interest, you may be subject to some form of punishment *after* you speak.

The distinction between prior restraint and punishment after you speak could be stated as follows: The First Amendment protects your right to say what you feel you must, but it does not always free you from suffering adverse consequences for what you say. Obviously fear of seri-ously negative consequences would keep most people quiet, but, at least in the absence of prior restraint, the ultimate decision concerning what the public may hear is left to potential speakers and not to the govern-ment. The fear of the consequences will certainly discourage most from expressing ideas punishable by law, but in the absence of effective prior restraint, it is at least possible that someone will inform society about information which the government might want suppressed.

As Chief Justice Warren Burger observed in *Nebraska Press Associ-ation v. Stuart* (1976), before one can be punished for something he has already said or written, he has the opportunity to appeal to the highest courts to protect First Amendment values. "A prior restraint . . . [how-ever,] has an immediate and irreversible sanction." Even if the censor's order is ultimately lifted, while it remains in effect, society is denied in-formation. Contrasting prior restraint with the threat of punishment after speech, Chief Justice Burger went on to argue: "If it can be said that the threat of criminal or civil sanctions after publications 'chills' speech, prior restraint 'freezes' it at least for a time" (at 559).

Although the U.S. Supreme Court has never upheld a government attempt at prior restraint, most on the Court have claimed that there are limited circumstances in which even prior restraint would be approved. The Supreme Court decision in which the broad prohibition against "prior restraints," *Near v. Minnesota* (1931), was first proclaimed recog-nized certain potential "exceptional cases" relating to protecting the pub-lic from obscenity and incitement to riot. In the area of what today we term "national security," the *Near* Court argued that "[No] one would question but that a government might prevent actual obstruction of its recruiting service or the publication of sailing dates of transports or the number and location of troops" (at 716). It was this "national security" exception that provided the focus of the debate within the Supreme Court in the famous Pentagon Papers cases, *New York Times Co. v. United States* (1971).

Beginning June 13, 1971, the *New York Times* published an until-then secret government study, "History of U.S. Decision-Making Process on Viet Nam Policy," better known as the "Pentagon Papers." Almost immediately the U.S. government went to court and obtained an injunction blocking further publication of the classified study. Within a matter of days the U.S. Supreme Court heard the arguments of the parties in the case and on a 6 to 3 vote overturned the injunction. The Court's action reflected the "heavy presumption against . . . [the] constitutional validity" of prior restraints (per curium, at 714). Simply, the government did not come up with a sufficiently weighty justification for overcoming the presumed right of the press to print whatever it wants.

Although the justices on both sides differed concerning the details of the appropriate standard to be applied in a case such as this, there was broad agreement that if the government could ever win, it must show that publication would result in ". . . direct, immediate, and irreparable damage to our Nation or its people" (Stewart, P., concurring at 1088). Most of the justices referred to the troopship example from *Near* as providing the standard. In the words of Justice William Brennan, "only government allegation and proof that publication must inevitably, directly and immediately cause . . . " harm comparable to that which would flow from publishing the location of troopships in time of war and thus aiding enemy submarines to sink the ships and kill the men would be of sufficient weight to justify prior censorship of the press (at 726–27).

Perhaps because he doubted that such an extreme example would ever arise or perhaps out of deeply held principle, Justice Black argued that prior restraint was never constitutionally permissible. In assessing the very limited circumstances when most justices would permit a prior restraint, Black wrote: "In my view it is unfortunate that some of my Brethren are apparently willing to hold that publication of the news may ever be enjoined. Such a holding would make a shambles of the First Amendment" (at 715).

Generally where the Court divided in this case was over the question of the actual severity of the danger posed by the publication of the Pentagon Papers. While the dissenters in the case were more willing to trust the executive's assessment of the danger, doubting the Court's ability to weigh and understand foreign policy matters, Justices William Brennan, Byron White, and Potter Stewart argued that the government had not sufficiently proved that the harm caused by publication would be irreparable. Justice Hugo Black, one of the justices in the majority, however, argued that prior restraint was never acceptable arguing that the First Amendment protected the press precisely ". . . so that it could bare the secrets of government and inform the people."

As a result of the *New York Times* decision, the secret government history of the Vietnam War was published. This report certainly embarrassed the government because it revealed that the war from its beginning had its foundation in misjudgments and a general pattern of deception.

The government did attempt to prosecute Daniel Ellsberg, a former Defense Department official, for turning the classified report over to the press, but his prosecution was thrown out on the grounds of government misconduct unrelated to the First Amendment's free speech protections. Although we cannot know how Ellsberg's prosecution would have been received by a trial jury or by the appellate courts had he been convicted, we are free to speculate. Would a jury have been willing to convict him knowing what his action revealed? Wouldn't some jurors have voted not guilty simply because they were pleased that someone had at last provided them with the "truth" about a war which many found either unjust or stupid?

Had the government's attempt at prior restraint been successful, we might have waited many years to learn what the publication of the Pentagon Papers revealed. The threat of prosecution did not deter Ellsberg or suppress the truth. Even had the prosecution run its course, Ellsberg's apparent law violations might have been excused by jurors or his conviction could have been overturned on appeal. If you doubt that prior restraint is any greater a threat to free speech than the threat of criminal prosecution after publication, consider that Ellsberg was willing to risk prosecution in order to tell his story, and in the end he was not punished. Had the government won in *New York Times v. United States,* to this date the true story about the Vietnam War might not be known.

Although there are some who historically have argued that the First Amendment does no more than to forbid censorship and the routine resort to prior restraint, the consensus today is that the First Amendment also limits the government's power to punish people for what they say or print. Particularly in the twentieth century the Supreme Court struggled constantly to identify the limited circumstances when people might be punished merely for what they said or printed.

Question 2 *How has the Court justified limits on the expression of ideas?*

Although the justices on the Court have sometimes been willing to permit the punishment of speech simply because the words themselves were false or offensive and contributed nothing to the "exchange of ideas," often when the Court has permitted government limits on speech, it has been precisely because the words might stimulate thoughts that will (or might) produce unacceptable actions.

Generally in free speech cases we must understand the distinction between mere words and actions. No one, for example, seriously argues that the First Amendment protects your right to *do* anything you want. Some, however, argue that it does protect your right to *say* anything you want. The majority on the Supreme Court, however, have justified sometimes punishing words that could lead people to engage in illegal actions. The speaker then is being punished not simply for what he says but rather for the acts that his or her speech could produce.

On the other hand, one Supreme Court justice, Hugo Black, argued that a sharp line should be drawn between speech and action. In effect he argued that the First Amendment protects your right to say anything you please. The government may never punish you for your words or for the ideas you express. Should you or someone else act on those words, the government may then step in. But until the line between speech and action is actually crossed, the government must keep hands off.

This view of Justice Black is known as First Amendment "absolutism." To the absolutist, the First Amendment means exactly what it says: Congress shall make *no* law abridging freedom of speech. *No* means *none,* not *some.* As long as all one does is speak or write, the government may not step in to restrain or punish. If one acts, however, the First Amendment provides no protection.

Most on the Court have not accepted Black's absolutist interpretation of the First Amendment. Although today the justices on the Supreme Court find little room under the First Amendment for limits on speech, the Court generally holds to the view that under some circumstances even mere words are not constitutionally protected from punishment. Over the years, however, there has been much difference of opinion concerning precisely under what circumstances speech loses its constitutional protection.

To begin to understand why most of the Court argues that sometimes speech or press is not protected even by the emphatic words of the First Amendment, we must understand, in the words of Justice Blackmun, that the "First Amendment, after all, is only one part of an entire Constitution" (*New York Times v. United States,* at 761). Articles I and II of the Constitution give to the government much power to accomplish many important and sometimes vital ends. Clearly the First Amendment is meant to restrict the exercise of those powers. Those who reject First Amendment absolutism ask, however, whether speech should be allowed to defeat the purposes of legitimate exercises of government power.

Government officials take oaths to "preserve, protect and defend the Constitution." What if someone or some group advocates the violent overthrow of that Constitution? Does the Constitution protect the speaker's right to try to convince others to destroy it? Local authorities have the plain duty to protect the public safety. What if a speaker attempts to incite to riot? Clearly, sometimes a speaker's unlimited right to speak can threaten legitimate government concerns.

When should a speaker's First Amendment rights give way in the face of a government's claim for the necessity of regulation? In answering a question such as this, some justices have argued for a "balancing" of First Amendment rights on the one hand against the government interests calling for limiting speech or press on the other. Such justices would themselves attempt to measure the relative value of each claim in light of the specific circumstances in which the case arose. They attempt to measure the potential costs to government or society in leaving a particular speech unpunished against the benefits derived from allowing it. Other justices argue that such weighing of competing "interests" is best left to the democratic process. Trust legislatures elected by the people and not judges isolated from the people.

A problem that some observers find in such balancing is that it can produce inconsistent results. Different judges (or legislators) will judge the significance of competing claims differently. Some will give great weight to the values served by free speech; others will see order and security as more important.

Beginning in the early part of this century, the Court began the effort to identify standards to be used to judge circumstances when protections for speech and press give way to protections for other governmental interests or social values. In several important cases, Supreme Court justices attempted to develop standards which they could use to decide when a speaker's free expression can be limited by government.

During World War I some were prosecuted for distributing pamphlets and making speeches in apparent violation of laws meant to forbid obstruction of military recruitment, interference with war production, or inciting insubordination within the armed forces. In one such case which reached the Supreme Court, *Schenck v. United States* (1919), Justice Oliver Wendell Holmes developed a standard for judging when speech might be punished. According to Holmes:

> [the] question in every case is whether the words used are used in such circumstances and are of such a nature as to create a *clear and present danger* [emphasis added] that they will bring about the substantive evils that Congress has right to prevent. It is a question of proximity and degree. When a nation is at war many things that might be said in time of peace are such a hindrance to its effort that their utterance will not be endured so long as men fight (at 52).

The "clear and present danger" doctrine, which emerged from this case, has survived several decades and a variety of interpretations (see Question 3 below). What in essence it amounts to is a statement that under some circumstances government interests can outweigh First Amendment freedoms. Because only a clear and present danger that speech will actually precipitate illegal action justifies limiting speech, however, the doctrine gives some priority to First Amendment rights over routine government interests.

The reasoning behind the Court's decision in *Gitlow v. New York* (1925), six years after *Schenck,* provided even less protection to speech than that seemingly provided by the clear and present danger doctrine. While the clear and present danger doctrine seemed to require a court to measure carefully the seriousness of a threat and its "proximity" or closeness in time, the so-called "bad tendency" standard announced by the Court's majority in *Gitlow* explicitly rejected judicial calculation of dangers posed by speech. In discussing the potential consequences of a publication advocating "revolutionary mass action" as a prelude to the establishment of a "Communist" regime, Justice Edward Sanford for the Court majority wrote: "The State cannot reasonably be required to measure the danger from every such utterance in the nice balance of a jewelers scale" (at 669). Once the legislature itself has determined that such revolutionary advocacy poses a danger, all the courts are permitted to do is determine if a specific statement's "natural tendency and probable effect was to bring about the substantive evil which the legislative body might prevent" (at 671).

Although debate over the adequacy of the clear and present danger doctrine continues to this day, the bad tendency standard announced in *Gitlow* has generally been rejected as providing too little protection for speech. Today almost any government effort to punish political speech is presumed unconstitutional. Since *Brandenburg v. Ohio* (1969), when the Supreme Court unanimously struck down the convictions of Ku Klux Klan members for advocating violence, the Court has held that the First Amendment does not permit "a State to forbid or proscribe advocacy of the use of force or of law violation except where such advocacy is directed to inciting or producing imminent lawless action *and* [emphasis added] is likely to incite or produce such action" (at 447). If there is time for speech to have the opportunity to counteract speech, if the forces in society urging lawful conduct have time at least to attempt to dissuade those who might engage in illegal conduct, then government may not resort to criminal sanctions to punish advocates of illegal conduct.

In his concurring opinion in *Brandenburg* Justice William O. Douglas joined ranks with Justice Black in attacking even this version of the clear and present danger doctrine and rejecting virtually any limits on speech:

> I see no place in the regime of the First Amendment for any "clear and present danger" test, whether strict and tight as some would make it, or free-wheeling as the Court . . . [has sometimes] rephrased it. When one reads the opinions closely and sees when and how the "clear and present danger" test has been applied, great misgivings are aroused. . . . [T]he threats were often loud but always puny and made serious only by judges so wedded to the status quo that critical analysis made them nervous (at 454).

When one reviews the periods in history when the Court upheld government restrictions on speech, it does appear that a factor present was near public hysteria over threats that in retrospect appear much more imaginary than real. Fears that speeches or pamphlets by little-known people during World War I would lead to the crippling of our war effort or fears of Communist subversion or revolution in the periods following both world wars seem rather silly now. These fears, however, were enough to lead legislatures and the Supreme Court to justify repression of open public debate.

Today, as during the tense period of the Vietnam War, the Court remains relatively vigilant in its protection of the free speech rights of even generally despised groups. Although all justices have not adopted the specific language, most now view the First Amendment and the values it protects as warranting special judicial protection. The justices seem to recognize what some have termed the "preferred position" of First Amendment rights. While in most areas of constitutional adjudication deference is shown to legislative judgments, and those challenging a law carry the burden to demonstrate its unconstitutionality, in First Amendment adjudication the Court subjects legislation limiting free expression to very careful scrutiny. Before permitting any limit on speech or press the Court generally demands evidence that some "compelling governmental interest" requires restrictions on free expression. This special treatment for the freedom of expression is justified in part because of the emphatic language of the First Amendment itself and in part because of the vital role free debate plays in the democratic political process.

In the wake of the events of September 11, 2001, and in the midst of "the War on Terrorism" we can only speculate concerning how forthright the Court will remain in its protection for even threatening ideas should speech and illegal advocacy be perceived as posing an immediate threat. What if extremists identified with Middle Eastern factions hostile to

America should use the Internet to rally supporters and stimulate sympathizers to action. What if, for example, a website should appear that praises suicide bombers and suggests that Americans should emulate their behavior. If Congress were to pass a law providing for criminal penalties for such speech, might not such advocacy of illegal conduct or justification for terrorist acts instantly accessible to a potentially fanatical audience be viewed by the Court as posing the kind of "imminent" and "likely" threat that even the *Brandenburg* Court would have deemed sufficient to warrant the punishment of speech?

Question 3   *Shouldn't we ban dangerous ideas?*

When arguing that "dangerous" speech should be limited, people often bring up the example of shouting "fire" in a crowded theater. According to Justice Holmes in *Schenck v. United States* (1919), "The most stringent protection of free speech would not protect a man in falsely shouting fire in a crowded theatre and causing a panic." It might be useful to analyze the reasons why this example is so frequently mentioned as a justification for punishing dangerous speech. What is it about falsely shouting "fire" that causes us to recoil?

To falsely shout "fire" can directly and immediately produce physical injury as a result of panic. Almost inevitably, it produces an immediate reaction, flight, without occasion for thoughtful reflection.

In deciding whether we should punish or restrict dangerous ideas, shouldn't we first ask if there are really any ideas that have an effect comparable to falsely shouting "fire"?

In the Supreme Court decision from which the fire example and the "clear and present danger doctrine" come (see Question 2 above), the expression punished was a pamphlet that urged resistance to military conscription during World War I. Might the response to such a pamphlet have been comparable to the response to shouting "fire," that is, one that is immediate and possibly catastrophic?

How might we distinguish the circumstances in *Schenck* and other cases in which the clear and present danger doctrine has been applied, from the circumstances surrounding shouting "fire" in a crowded theater? First, although the danger might arguably be real, the danger was not immediate in the sense that some instantaneous and irreversible response would result. To put it simply, there was time for people to reflect on the consequences of their actions. Having heard or read the words, the audience had time to weigh engaging in illegal actions in light of the likely consequences, that is, going to jail for violating the law.

Indeed, Justices Oliver Wendell Holmes and Louis Brandeis eventually attempted to restrict the clear and present danger doctrine to circumstances where the danger was both real and immediate. In their dissent in *Abrams v. United States* (1919), they wrote: "Only the emergency that makes it immediately dangerous to leave correction of evil counsels to time warrants making any exception to the sweeping command, 'Congress shall make no law . . . abridging freedom of speech'" (at 630). To the argument that some ideas might incite others to commit illegal acts, Holmes responded in *Gitlow v. New York* (1925): "Every idea is an incitement. It offers itself for belief and if believed it is acted on unless some other belief outweighs it or some failure of energy stifles it at birth" (at 673).

Fear of going to jail is not the only thing that might outweigh dangerous ideas and prevent us from acting in response to them. Far more important is the fact that we are all subject to arguments on the other side. Certainly the dominant opinions in society that we hear every day do not support "dangerous" ideas. If they did, no law restricting the actions advocated would be passed in the first place. In sum, we are not just victims of dangerous ideas. We are also able to weigh alternatives and consequences. Such weighing of alternatives by citizens is at the heart of freedom of speech and of democracy.

When we consider how society should deal with those who advocate ideas that to us appear dangerous, perhaps we should ask what causes them to speak as they do. Before we would condemn someone for shouting fire in a crowded theater wouldn't we first ask whether he felt there really was a fire? If you are in a theater and you think there is a fire, should you wait until you actually see flames before you alert others? If signs of fire are not apparent to most in the audience, they might panic simply because you say there is a fire. They might instead, however, take prudent precautions without running headlong toward the exit.

Hearing a speaker say that a "war is evil," "the draft is unjust," "the police are your enemies," or "the government should be overthrown"— hearing any dangerous idea—will not cause most of us to act. It may, however, cause some of us to consider why others feel that way. Although we will shun the illegal course of action advocated, our attention may be drawn to the grievances that cause others to speak angrily or forcefully.

The value, then, of extreme or dangerous speech is that it can rivet our attention far better than measured scholarly dissertations on injustice. It does not force us to act, but it can entice us to listen to the grievances of those who speak dangerous words. If it does that, it can contribute to the free exchange of ideas.

In the "free marketplace of ideas," just as in a supermarket, a new product may have to be garishly displayed to attract our attention. If the consequences of a mistaken judgment are slight (i.e., the product is inexpensive), we may sample it. If the product is expensive, however, we are likely to read the label carefully and ask others for advice before risking too much of our hard-earned money. The same is true with new ideas. We are not likely to follow ideas that pose risks. Knowledge that certain actions that may be advocated are illegal will cause us to hold back. It is one thing to talk, to listen, and to think; it is quite something else to act. The distinction between mere speech and action is essential to understanding the role of speech and freedom of the press.

Question 4   *May the government punish those who engage in "hate speech"?*

In light of America's ongoing problem of racial division, hostility, and even racist violence, it seems perfectly natural for us to want to remove the idea of racial hatred at the root of such violence from public debate. Although for much of our early history notions of white racial supremacy had been in effect written into our Constitution, following the Civil War the Thirteenth, Fourteenth, and Fifteenth Amendments removed the constitutional foundations for racial discrimination. Nonetheless racial hostility and violence remain a problem and racial tensions periodically explode in our communities. In good-faith efforts to remove racism from our society and to protect citizens from the emotional (and perhaps worse) harm caused by racist epithets, many states have enacted "hate speech" statutes. Many of these statutes also address crimes motivated by religious intolerance and gender discrimination as well. Some forbid crimes motivated by homophobia, or hatred of people because they are homosexual.

In 1992 the U.S. Supreme Court in *R. A. V. v. St. Paul* had to decide on the constitutionality of a St. Paul, Minnesota's Bias-Motivated Crime ordinance. The ordinance was challenged by one of several teenagers who were prosecuted for placing a burning cross on the lawn of a black family in their neighborhood. Burning crosses had long been a symbol of Klu Klux Klan intimidation of African Americans. The ordinance provided:

> Whoever places on public or private property a symbol, object, appellation, characterization or graffiti, including, but not limited to, a burning cross or Nazi Swastika, which one knows or has reasonable grounds to know arouses anger, alarm or resentment in others on the basis of race, creed, religion, or gender commits disorderly conduct and shall be guilty of a misdemeanor (at 580).

The teenager who challenged the statute did so on the basis that it violated his First Amendment rights. His assertion was that the statute was "substantially over broad and impermissibly content based" (at 580). The "overbreadth" claim was founded on the argument that the statute's definition of punishable expression swept too broadly, encompassing speech that is in fact constitutionally protected. For example, the statute prohibited speech that "arouses to anger, alarm or resentment in others on the basis of race. . . ." The Supreme Court has long held that merely provoking "anger" in others cannot be sufficient grounds for punishing speech (see *Terminiello v. City of Chicago,* 1949). After all, almost any provocative idea can provoke someone to anger or resentment. Certainly many statements by conventional politicians cause the blood in some citizens to boil!

Justice Scalia's Opinion of the Court, however, found that the Minnesota courts had solved the obvious overbreadth problem in the statute by construing (or interpreting) it to apply only to speech addressing the prohibited subjects that amount to "fighting words." Ever since its decision in *Chaplinsky v. New Hampshire* (1942), the U.S. Supreme Court has held that some categories of speech are simply outside First Amendment protection. In *Chaplinsky,* Justice Murphy wrote:

> There are certain well-defined and narrowly limited classes of speech, the prevention and punishment of which have never been thought to raise any Constitutional problem. These include the lewd and the obscene, the profane, the libelous, and the insulting or "fighting words"—those which by their very utterance inflict injury or tend to incite an immediate breach of the peace. It has been observed that such utterances are no essential part of any exposition of ideas, and are of such slight social value as a step to truth that any benefit that may be derived from them is clearly outweighed by the social interest in order and morality" (at 572).

Although the definition of each of these prohibitable categories of speech has been significantly refined since *Chaplinsky,* it remains true that these "categorical exceptions" to free speech protections cited remain today.

Justice Antonin Scalia agreed that the Minnesota court's confining the speech prohibited by the ordinance to actual fighting words saved the ordinance from an overbreadth challenge. It did not, however, save the ordinance from a challenge on the grounds that it violated "content neutrality." According to Justice Scalia's opinion, "[t]he First Amendment generally prevents government from proscribing speech . . . because of disapproval of the ideas expressed. Content-based regulations are presumptively invalid" (at 382). The problem with the Minneapolis ordinance according to the opinion of Justice Scalia was that it selected certain fighting words for prohibition not solely because they were fighting words but also because they expressed viewpoints and attitudes that the majority of society rejects and condemns. The content "bias" that Justice Scalia found in the statute is that it prohibited fighting words directed at some favored targets (for example, race or gender) but did not address fighting words directed toward others (homosexuals, union members, etc.). Although not explicitly stated, what may have troubled Justice

Scalia and those who joined his opinion is that the ordinance in question appears to condemn those whose views are not "politically correct," views which many of society's opinion leaders find taboo.

Although under the fighting words doctrine and other categorical exceptions there is a presumption that they are not really included in the concept of "the freedom of speech," they are not wholly noncommunicative. They, like actions, can express ideas or at least intensity of emotion associated with ideas. Like symbolic actions, they are not wholly protected by the First Amendment, but neither, according to Justice Scalia's interpretation, may they be restricted in particular instances because of government's or society's hostility to the underlying message they may rather crudely convey. As Justice Scalia himself wrote: "Fighting words are . . . analogous to a noisy sound truck: each is, as Justice Frankfurter recognized, a 'mode of speech' (citation omitted); both can be used to convey an idea; but neither has, in and of itself, a claim upon the First Amendment. As with the sound truck, however, so also with fighting words: the government may not regulate use based on hostility—or favoritism—towards the underlying message expressed" (at 386).

Other justices, while agreeing on "overbreadth" grounds that the ordinance was unconstitutional, contended that under Justice Scalia's approach, in order for Minneapolis to overcome Justice Scalia's constitutional objection to the ordinance, it would have had simply to ban all fighting words without exception. Since, however, in the words of Justice Byron White's concurring opinion "the government may proscribe an entire category of speech [fighting words,] because the content of that speech is evil," it may also ban only a subset of that category because "the content of that subset is, by definition, worthless and undeserving of constitutional protection" (at 401).

Justice White rejects Justice Scalia's contention that fighting words are "quite expressive indeed, "arguing instead that "[f]ighting words are not means of exchanging views, rallying supporters, or registering a protest; they are directed against individuals to provoke violence or to inflict injury. *Chaplinsky,* 315 U.S., at 572. Therefore, a ban on all fighting words or a subset of the fighting words category would restrict only the social evil of hate speech, without creating the danger of driving viewpoints from the marketplace" (at 401).

Justice Scalia, in his opinion, rejected Justice White's characterization of his views. He responded that the state does remain free to prohibit some fighting words and not others, but that its basis for distinguishing between the prohibited and the permitted must be something other than hostility to the speaker or his underlying message or point of view. He argued, for example, that because obscenity is also a category of speech not protected by the Constitution, government may prohibit some obscenity while ignoring other obscene expressions.

When the basis for the content discrimination consists entirely of the very reason the entire class of speech at issue is proscribable, no significant danger of viewpoint discrimination exists. Such a reason, having been adjudged neutral enough to support the exclusion of the entire class of speech from First Amendment protection, is also neutral enough to form the basis of distinction within the class. To illustrate: a State might choose to prohibit only that obscenity which is most patently offensive in its prurience—i.e., that which involves the most lascivious displays of sexual activity. But it may not prohibit, for example, only that obscenity which includes offensive political messages (citation omitted) (at 388).

Although Justice Scalia does not provide an example directly relating to fighting words, we might wonder whether he would be willing to uphold a "hate speech" statute that forbade only speech calling for the death or extermination of any class of citizens. Such speech when addressed to a member of any particular group would no doubt satisfy the fighting words category. Such a statute would address a most extreme manifestation of hate speech, and it would not seem to favor any particular segment of society.

In its decision in *Virginia v. Black* in 2003 (see fuller discussion below in Question 9) a majority of the Court, with the agreement of Justice Scalia, indeed indicated a willingness to uphold a statute that specifically singled out cross burning with intent to intimidate for particular punishment. The Court majority did not feel that the statute in question ran afoul of the *R. A. V. v. St. Paul* decision even though it did not treat all intimidating speech or symbolic action alike. The Court upheld this cross burning ban ". . . because burning a cross is a particularly virulent form of intimidation. Instead of prohibiting all intimidating messages, Virginia may choose to regulate this subset of intimidating messages in light of cross burning's long and pernicious history as a signal of impending violence" (at 554). Although many associate cross burning with racial or religious bigotry, the Court noted that in fact cross burnings had been used by the Klan and others to intimidate a wide variety of people. Because of this fact the Virginia cross burning statute did not focus its protections on certain favored groups or causes. Unlike the Minnesota statute at issue in *R. A. V. v. St. Paul,* therefore, the Virginia statute did not incorporate "viewpoint discrimination."

Although the Supreme Court was unanimous in condemning the Minneapolis ordinance in *R. A. V. v. St. Paul,* four of the nine justices rejected at least in part Justice Scalia's approach. The other justices were not so troubled by Minneapolis's singling out only some hate speech for punishment. In light of the history of racial conflict in America and of the victimization of racial minorities, they felt that it was reasonable for the city to focus on this most damaging form of hate speech. In Justice White's words: "This selective regulation reflects the city's judgment that harms based on race, creed, religion, or gender are more pressing public concerns than the harm caused by other fighting words. In light of our Nation's long and painful experience with discrimination, this determination is plainly reasonable" (at 407).

Justice White did not, however, respond to an argument implicit in Justice Scalia's approach, that is, that others, not included in those mentioned in the Minneapolis statute, have been and are subjected to hate speech also. Homosexuals, for example, are frequently victimized by verbal assaults akin to those suffered by racial minorities, yet such fighting words were not covered by the ordinance's prohibitions. Could it be that homosexuals are not as favored by the majority of the Minneapolis City Council or the majority of that city's population? Would their inclusion have stimulated the opposition of antigay religious conservatives to the hate speech ordinance? If the exclusion of antigay hate speech from the ordinance had been the result of the antigay bias of the majority, was Justice Scalia wrong to condemn the ordinance for failing to be "content neutral"?

Despite their vigorous disagreement with Justice Scalia's Opinion of the Court, the remaining four justices also found the ordinance unconstitutional. Their grounds, however, was "overbreadth." According to their reading of the Minnesota Supreme Court's construction of the ordinance, it permitted punishment of words "which inflict injury or tend to incite an immediate breach of the peace." Because that Court appeared to equate "injury" with words or displays "that one knows or should know will create anger, alarm or resentment based on racial, ethnic or religious bias," Justice White's concurrence found it still to suffer from "overbreadth." "Although the ordinance reaches conduct that is unprotected, it also makes criminal expressive conduct that causes only hurt feelings, offense, or resentment, and is protected by the First Amendment. . . . The ordinance is therefore fatally over broad and invalid on its face" (at 414).

Those who either have been or fear being victimized by racist or sexist speech may find the Court's refusal in this instance to permit punishment of that which causes them such discomfort disturbing, but to insulate all of us from expression that causes someone distress could at some point silence almost all of us. Most of us, however, can think of words or phrases which we know to be extremely hurtful and provocative to racial minorities, women, or homosexuals, to name just a few. Could a statute be designed which would just single out those particularly offensive phrases or epithets which cause such obvious pain? If we think about such a potential statute, however, we might also recognize that sometimes members of the very groups "victimized" by such epithets use those same words themselves. Even others, who may not themselves be in the same racial group, might in fun or as part of good-natured banter use the same words without producing a hurtful reaction. Can the law fairly and clearly distinguish between what are fighting words if used by one person, but mere lighthearted banter if used by another? There is probably no offensive phrase or word in or out of the dictionary that has not been exchanged between teenage boys in the course of playful "conversation" without any participant taking offense. We may think we can discern the difference between fighting words and loose or vulgar talk, but can we safeguard free speech if the government tries to do so?

Question 5   *Why must society tolerate obscenity?*

Ever since its decision in *Chaplinsky,* the Supreme Court majority has argued that obscenity is not protected by the First Amendment. Obscenity was included in those categories of speech given no constitutional protection because they ". . . are no essential part of any exposition of ideas, and are of such slight social value as a step to truth that any benefit that may be derived from them is clearly outweighed by social interest in order and morality" (571–72). When the question before the Court is obscenity, there is no need for the government to prove that a particular magazine or movie, for example, poses some "clear and present danger" of producing some unlawful action. Obscenity in itself is considered harmful enough to forfeit constitutional protection.

Then why does what many people consider obscenity survive?

The Supreme Court's claim that the Constitution does not protect obscenity does not help us identify what obscenity is. Over the years the Court has attempted time and time again to identify obscenity. After its decision in *Roth v. United States* (1957), that "presumed obscenity to be '*utterly* without redeeming social value,'" a plurality on the Court argued that for material to be found obscene it must be proved to be "utterly without redeeming social value." This, according to the Court in *Miller v. California* (1973), amounted to a burden that was "virtually impossible to . . . [prove]" (at 22).

The Court has been concerned that any limits on material that is obscene not "spill over" onto material that deserves constitutional protection. Many works considered obscene in the past, James Joyce's *Ulysses,* for example, are today considered great works of literature. Although their sexually explicit content may offend some, to others it is "central to the story." Scientific and even political information may include material that to some appears vulgar or even obscene. To forbid any material containing such content, however, could interfere with communication on matters central to society's interests.

In order to avoid punishing expression that is constitutionally protected, the Court has attempted to define obscenity as clearly as possible.

If it fails to define obscenity precisely, a citizen could be punished for publishing material that he or she could not have known with certainty was obscene (and, therefore, not constitutionally protected). Or alternatively, a person might refrain from writing a story or showing a film that deserves constitutional protection because he or she fears prosecution.

Miller v. California (1973) represents the Court's most recent attempt to define obscenity. According to the Court, state obscenity statutes must limit only

> . . . works which depict or describe sexual conduct. That conduct must be specifically defined by the applicable state law, as written or authoritatively construed. A state offense must also be limited to works which, taken as a whole, appeal to the prurient interest in sex, which portray sexual conduct in a patently offensive way, and which, taken as a whole, do not have serious literary, artistic, political, or scientific value (at 24).

Of course, this *Miller* standard in defining obscenity does not automatically help us identify obscenity. What precisely appeals to "prurient interests"? What is "patently offensive"? Whose "prurient interests"? To deal with questions such as these, the majority of the Court in *Miller* would rely on the judges and juries ("triers of fact") within the states.

> The basic guidelines for the trier of fact must be: (a) whether "the average person, applying contemporary community standards" would find that the work, taken as a whole, appeals to the prurient interest . . . (b) whether the work depicts or describes, in a patently offensive way, sexual conduct specifically defined by the applicable state law, and (c) whether the work, taken as a whole, lacks serious literary, artistic, political, or scientific value (at 24).

According to Chief Justice Burger: "It is neither realistic nor constitutionally sound to read the First Amendment as requiring that the people of Maine or Mississippi accept public depiction of conduct found tolerable in Las Vegas, or New York City. . . . People in different States vary in their tastes and attitudes, and this diversity is not to be strangled by the absolutism of imposed uniformity" (at 33).

The standard for obscenity then depends on the values and standards that will vary from place to place. On its surface, however, the Court's guidelines do not leave communities free to suppress sexually explicit speech at will. Their discretion is constrained by the requirements of this *Miller* decision.

Did these *Miller* guidelines end the debate or resolve the uncertainty?

According to the dissenters in *Miller,* concepts such as "prurient interests," "patent offensiveness," and "serious literary value" are inherently vague. "The meaning of these concepts necessarily varies with experience, outlook, and even idiosyncrasies of the person defining them" (at 84). To permit the state to interfere with speech or press on the basis of such vague concepts seriously endangers First Amendment freedoms.

Although Justice Douglas, and earlier Justice Black, felt that the First Amendment permitted no interference with written, spoken, or filmed depiction of sexually oriented material, Justice Brennan would not go quite that far. In his dissent in *Paris Adult Theatre I v. Slaton* (1973) he, however, weighed what possible interests might justify limiting such expression in the absence of any precise standard for distinguishing the obscene from the constitutionally protected. In the end he argued that only an interest in protecting children and unconsenting adults from exposure to such materials justified the risks posed by limits on expression that might inevitably sweep too broadly.

On this basis the state might regulate the distribution of sexually oriented material to only those who want such material and/or to adults who are mature enough to make the decision for themselves. As Chief Justice Burger, the author of the *Miller* standard, noted, however, Brennan's approach does not provide guidelines for distinguishing with any precision between sexually oriented materials that might be distributed to children or unconsenting adults from those that might not (at 27).

It is only on the question of withholding constitutional protection from "child pornography" that the Court has come close to unanimity on an issue relating to obscenity. In effect, in *New York v. Ferber* (1982), the Court decided that sexually oriented material depicting children engaged in sexual acts deserves no constitutional protection. In identifying such material a majority of the Court did not feel constrained to weigh possible "serious" literary or scientific value of such material or to find that it appeals to the average person's prurient interests. The Court felt that the likely physiological and emotional harm inflicted on children who participate in production of such material far outweighs any interference with First Amendment freedoms. "The prevention of sexual exploitation and abuse of children constitutes a government objective of surpassing importance" (at 757).

Punishing distribution of such sexually explicit depictions of children is justified as the only effective means of preventing the harm caused by employing children in such production. To stop the exploitation of children, the state must "dry up" the market. To avoid long-term "emotional" harm the distribution of a "permanent record" of a child's participation in such production must be punished (at 759). The Court's approach in *Ferber,* focusing as it did on the harm that making pornography has on participants (in that case children), seemed to some to open the door for an assault on pornography because of the harm it does to women.

Because many feminists believe that pornography contributes to male attitudes that demean women and foment sex discrimination and even violence, some have advocated banning pornography as a form of sex discrimination. In this effort they have sought to control sexually explicit materials not necessarily on the grounds of morality but rather in the interests of fighting sex discrimination. Under an ordinance adopted in Indianapolis, Indiana, pornography was defined in part as "the graphic sexually explicit subordination of women, whether in pictures or in words . . ." (*American Booksellers Association, Inc., v. Hudnut,* at 324, 1985).

When this statute was challenged in court, Circuit Judge Frank A. Easterbrook in effect accepted the argument put forward by its supporters that "men who see women depicted as subordinate are more likely to treat them so. Pornography is an aspect of dominance. . . . Depictions of subordination tend to perpetuate subordination" (at 328–29). Yet despite his listing of the doleful consequences for the status of women that may be attributed to men's attitudes shaped by pornography, Judge Easterbrook struck down the Indianapolis statute as violative of the First Amendment.

The problem which the statute attempted to address was the possibility, and even likelihood, that pornography might effectively persuade, that it might succeed in influencing the attitudes of men in particular and society in general. The statute clearly discriminated "on the grounds of the content of speech. Speech treating women in the approved way—in sexual encounters 'premised on equality'—is lawful no matter how sexually explicit. Speech treating women in the disapproved way—as submissive in matters sexual or as enjoying humiliation—is unlawful no matter how significant the literary, artistic, or political qualities of the work taken as a whole" (at 328). It was this preference for one point of view over another that led to the invalidation of the statute. In the words of Judge Easterbrook, "The Constitution forbids the state to declare one perspective right and silence opponents" (at 325, judgment affirmed *American Booksellers Association, Inc., v. Hudnut,* (1985)).

While the lesson of the *Miller* decision is that efforts to restrict "hard core" pornography have sometimes withstood constitutional challenge, uneasiness remains. It is hard to believe that the Court has succeeded in defining obscenity in a manner that can readily be understood by all. Many believe that leaving the definition of such terms as "prurient interests" and "patently offensive" to varying community values violates the notion that the Constitution applies to all government conduct throughout the United States. While the rural South may well have different notions of what is acceptable than the streets of Manhattan, much of the press and film production today is for national and international audiences. A magazine that may be sold in New York under its "contemporary community standards" might lead to prosecution in Tuscaloosa under that community's standards. Can we, consistent with the First Amendment applicable throughout the United States, punish a publisher or distributor for selling in Alabama what the First Amendment protects in New York? On the other hand, unless we argue that the Constitution forbids all interference with obscenity, is it fair to subject the people of rural Maine to the standards of Las Vegas? Perhaps many agree with Justice Stewart when he wrote: "I don't know what obscenity is, but I know it when I see it" (*Jacobellis v. Ohio,* 1964, Stewart, J., concurring at 197). Whether a government or a Supreme Court's acting on the basis of such an observation provides adequate protection for First Amendment freedoms is one of those questions that still needs to be answered.

Question 6   *Why does the government permit sexually explicit material to invade our homes over the Internet?*

Today a vast computer network, the Internet, is available to bring an ever-growing stream of information and entertainment into the homes of all who possess a computer and access to the World Wide Web. Almost anyone has the capacity to disseminate information, ideas, and images to a worldwide audience. And as many parents know, an increasing number of children are even more adept than their parents at accessing that information at any time any day or night.

The Internet has created an entirely new communications environment, one never envisioned by the authors of the First Amendment. This new channel of communications has enormous potential for advancing the exchange of information and ideas. However, because it facilitates those of like mind reaching others who share particular ideas, it also opens up the possibility of the increasing fragmentation of communication. Rather than ideas clashing with ideas in the "free marketplace of ideas," like minds may speak only to like minds (for further discussion of this point, see Chapter 6, Question 2). One thing that is clear, however, is that the Internet offers us the opportunity easily to seek and obtain information on almost any topic.

Parents are naturally afraid of the potential influences that might reach their children. They are afraid of the many hours that children spend unsupervised at their computer monitors seeking out new information and cyberadventure. In an effort to protect children and in a natural response to parental concerns about their own ability to monitor everything their children might view, Congress passed the Communications Decency Act (CDA) of 1996. The act was designed to punish "knowing" transmission of "obscene or indecent" messages to anyone under 18 years old (*Reno v. American Civil Liberties Union,* 1997 at 2338).

Promptly following the law's passage, the American Civil Liberties Union, joined by other interested parties, filed a lawsuit challenging the act's constitutionality under the First Amendment.

The Supreme Court has long held that obscenity is not protected by the Constitution (see Question 5 above). The Court has unanimously upheld laws that punish obscenity aimed at children. Adult entertainment, involving explicit sexual conduct, however, has received at least limited constitutional protection. The government is not permitted to censor all speech, movies, video, or other communication simply because it might inadvertently be encountered by sensitive audiences, including children. The Court has, however, allowed restrictions on the time, place, or manner of dissemination of sexually explicit adult entertainment in the interest of assuring that only mature audiences who seek to view or read such material are likely to come in contact with it.

In both *Young v. American Mini Theatres, Inc.* (1976) and *City of Renton v. Playtime Theatres, Inc.* (1986) the Court upheld zoning ordinances that restricted the locations in which even adult entertainment facilities can be located. In these cases the Court claims to have upheld the ordinances in question not because of societal disapproval for the sexually explicit nature of the entertainment in question, but rather because of the "secondary effects of such theaters on the surrounding community." According to Justice Lewis Powell in *American Mini Theatres*, ". . . the ordinance by its terms is designed to prevent crime, protect the city's retail trade, maintain property values, and generally 'protec[t] and preserv[e] the quality of [the city's] neighborhoods, commercial districts, and the quality of urban life. . . .' If the City had been concerned with restricting the message purveyed by adult theaters, it would have tried to close them or restrict their number rather than circumscribe their choice as to location" (at 82, n. 4).

In light of these precedents, proponents of keeping sexually explicit adult material off the Internet argued in effect that the Internet was an inappropriate location for the dissemination of sexually explicit materials. Because of ready access to the Internet by children, Congress felt justified in declaring the Internet in effect a nonadult entertainment zone, free of indecent materials which might fall into children's hands.

When the issue reached the United States Supreme Court, however, the justices found the government's position unpersuasive. The Court took note of the unique characteristics of the Internet, the difficulty that would be encountered by "speakers" who would legally be required to either remain "silent" or keep their messages exclusively in the hands of adults. The Court recognized that the Internet provided a new and promising forum for the exchange of ideas and was loathe to permit restrictions on this new public forum.

Unlike an adult entertainment theater or zone, Justice John Paul Stevens, writing for the Court in *Reno v. American Civil Liberties Union* (1997), recognized that "[o]nce a provider posts its content on the Internet, it cannot prevent its content from entering any community." While a child entering an adult theater can easily be recognized and turned away, there is as yet no reliable technique for age identification of Internet users who may enter an adult "chat room." Realistically the only way a user of the Internet can be sure his or her message will not reach a child is to refrain from speaking entirely. To punish one who posts a message on the Internet if his or her message reaches an underage user will lead to only child-appropriate messages being posted. The Court, however, has never permitted restricting adult communication to levels appropriate for children.

The Court came to its decision despite its ruling in *Federal Communications Commission v. Pacifica Foundation* (1978) upholding a Federal Communications Commission (FCC) regulation of "indecent" material on the radio. In that case, George Carlin, a famous comedian, did a monologue using what he termed "filthy words," "the words you couldn't say on the public, ah, airwaves, um, the ones you definitely wouldn't say ever" (at 729). The broadcast of this monologue at 2 P.M. on October 30, 1973, led to a complaint being filed by the father of a young son. The commission in turn ruled that the station's conduct in broadcasting the "indecent" material "would be associated with the station's license file, and in the event that subsequent complaints are received, the Commission will then decide . . . " what punitive measures it might then take.

In deciding whether broadcast of "patently offensive words dealing with sex and excretion may be regulated because of its content," the Court argued that it had "long recognized that each medium of expression presents special First Amendment problems." Because broadcasting was considered by the Court at the time to have "established a uniquely pervasive presence in the lives of all Americans," the Court justified more restrictions on it than would be permitted for the print media, for example. "Patently offensive, indecent material presented over the airwaves confronts the citizen, not only in public, but also in the privacy of the home, where the individual's right to be left alone plainly outweighs the First Amendment rights of the intruder. . . . Because the broadcast audience is constantly tuning in and out [or channel surfing, to use a more contemporary phrase] prior warnings cannot completely protect the listener or viewer from unexpected program content" (at 748).

The Court in *Pacifica* also emphasized the fact that "broadcasting is uniquely accessible to children, even those too young to read. Although . . . an [indecent] written message might . . . [be] incomprehensible to a first grader, Pacifica's broadcast could have enlarged a child's vocabulary in an instant" (at 749).

The Court in *Reno v. American Civil Liberties Union* found the differences between the Internet and the CDA, and broadcast media and FCC regulation to be significant enough to justify the apparently conflicting results in the two cases. First, the FCC order in *Pacifica* in effect regulated "when—rather than whether—it would be permissible to air such a program in that particular medium. . . . Second, unlike the CDA, the [FCC] Commission's declaratory order was not punitive; . . . [the Court] expressly refused to decide whether the indecent broadcast 'would justify criminal prosecution.' Finally, the Commission's order applied to a medium which as a matter of history had 'received the most limited First Amendment protection' in large part because warnings could not adequately protect the listener from unexpected program content. The Internet, however, has no comparable history" (at 2342).

In contrast to the broadcast media, the Court concluded that the sexually explicit and/or indecent material on the Internet is usually accompanied by advanced notice of its nature and content. Those viewing, therefore, are generally only those who elect to see such material. According to the Court, the district court specifically found that "communications over the Internet do not 'invade' an individual's home or appear on one's computer screen unbidden. Users seldom encounter content 'by accident'" (at 2343).

The Court was evidently not yet familiar with the emergence of graphic "pop-up" advertising for pornographic websites that does appear unsolicited on many computer screens. The reasoning behind the Court's opinion at least leaves open the possibility that legislation banning such pop-ups (or at least requiring that "pop-up blockers" be made available by Internet service providers) might survive a constitutional challenge.

The refusal of the U.S. Supreme Court to uphold the Communications Decency Act of 1996 did not mark the end of congressional efforts to "protect" children and others from inappropriate content over the Internet. In 2003 the U.S. Supreme Court decided a challenge to the Children's Internet Protection Act (CIPA), which denied federal funds for Internet access to public libraries that fail to install software which would filter out obscene or pornographic materials. The Act did permit, but not require, libraries to disable the software upon request of adult patrons seeking access to constitutionally protected adult materials. Although the Court was somewhat divided on the appropriate rationale behind its decision, the Court by 6 to 3 upheld the Children's Internet Protection Act. Chief Justice Rehnquist, in an opinion, joined by Justices O'Connor, Scalia, and Thomas likened the use of filtering software to decisions traditionally made by libraries concerning which books to buy and place on their shelves and which not to buy. Just as those decisions are treated deferentially by the Court even though they limit the store of potential information available to customers at any particular public library, so too is Congress's decision not to fund Internet access for libraries providing access to websites containing materials Congress also deems inappropriate. As Chief Justice Rehnquist noted,"[m]ost libraries already exclude pornography from their print collections because they deem it inappropriate for inclusion. We do not subject these judgments to heightened scrutiny; it would make little sense to treat libraries' judgments to block online pornography any differently, when these judgments are made for just the same reasons" (at 4469).

No one on the Court had any problem in principle with protecting children from pornography. The principal grounds for disagreement concerned the impact of the legislation on adult access to materials that are constitutionally protected. All of the justices recognized that existing filtering software has a tendency to "overblock" constitutionally protected materials; that is, they erroneously label and remove materials that are in fact not pornographic while at the same time fail to block some materials that are indeed pornographic. To some on the Court this technological flaw renders the imposition of such software a violation of rights of the user of the library. To the chief justice, however, any possible constitutional problems presented by such "erroneous blocking . . . are dispelled by the ease with which patrons may have the filtering software disabled. When a patron encounters a blocked site, he need only ask a librarian to unblock it . . ." (at 4470).

The principal points of disagreement between the majority and the dissenters concerned the adequacy and certainty of the provision allowing the filtering software to be overridden at the request of an adult library patron and, even more importantly, on the accuracy of the plurality's attempt to equate a librarian's use of discretion in purchasing and shelving some books and not others with the filtering software's blocking access within the library of patrons to some Internet sites and not others. According to Justice Souter's dissent, the principal justification for the librarian selectivity in purchasing books and making them available in the library is the question of scarcity.

> There is only so much money and so much shelf space, and the necessity to choose some material and reject the rest justifies the effort to be selective with an eye to demand, quality, and the object of maintaining the library as a place of civilized inquiry by widely different sorts of people. . . . At every point, however, the Internet blocking here defies comparison to the process of acquisition. Whereas traditional scarcity of money and space require a library to make choices about what to acquire, and the choice to be made is whether or not to spend the money to acquire something, blocking is the subject of a choice made after the money for Internet access has been spent or committed. Since it makes no difference to the

cost of Internet access whether an adult calls up adult material or the Articles of Confederation, blocking (on facts like these) is not necessitated by scarcity of either money or space. In the instance of the Internet, what the library acquires is electronic access, and the choice to block is a choice to limit access that has already been acquired. Thus, deciding against buying a book means there is no book (unless a loan can be obtained), but blocking the Internet is merely blocking access purchased in its entirety and subject to unblocking if the librarian agrees. The proper analogy therefore is not passing up a book that might have been bought; it is either to buying a book and then keeping it from adults lacking an acceptable "purpose," or to buying an encyclopedia and then cutting out pages with anything thought to be unsuitable for all adults (at 4477–78).

According to the dissenters, therefore, the actions of the libraries in response to the requirements imposed by Congress amount to a classic case of censorship of what adult citizens may read or see. Rather than being treated with deference, such actions should be upheld only if they satisfy the requirements of strict scrutiny. They must be a "narrowly tailored remedy" to accomplish what is a "compelling state interest." Although the Court unanimously agrees that protecting children from pornography is such an interest, the means chosen sweep too broadly, preventing as they do even adults from having access to sexually explicit, but not always pornographic, materials. The availability of alternative means to protect children (e.g., permitting them to have access only to computers with filtering software, while allowing adults unimpeded access to other unblocked computers) means that the Children's Internet Protection Act (CIPA) violates the First Amendment. Justice Souter, then, ". . . would hold in accordance with conventional strict scrutiny that a library's practice of blocking would violate an adult patron's First and Fourteenth Amendment right to be free of Internet censorship, when unjustified (as here) by any legitimate interest in screening children from harmful material" (at 4479).

Despite the concerns voiced by the dissenters the threat to First Amendment interests posed by the Children's Internet Protection Act is distinguishable from the Communications Decency Act in a two ways: (1) The CIPA applied only to public libraries and restricted only such libraries if they accepted federal funds to assist in buying access to the Internet; (2) the CIPA permitted even recipients of federal funds to provide unimpeded access to the Internet to adults. The Communications Decency Act, on the other hand, prevented adults even in their own homes from having access to and disseminating material inappropriate for children because such materials might reach children.

Although the Court's decision which struck down the Communications Decency Act may leave parents feeling vulnerable, nothing in the Court's opinion appears to preclude Congress eventually from passing less sweeping legislation that might in effect create "adult zones" on the Internet. As technology advances it should become increasingly possible to "tag" sexually explicit materials to enable parents to acquire software that will block access to them by their children. As the debate within the Court concerning *United States v. American Library Association, Inc.* (2003) makes clear, however, foolproof software that will remove *all* pornography (and that will remove *only* the targeted offensive materials) is not yet here. As many parents have learned, existing software for home computers allows much that is obscene to get through, and purveyors of pornography are creative in developing ways around the latest software innovations. At least until much improved filtering software is developed, however, the Court's decisions make it clear that the government may not restrict adults (at least in their own homes or on private computers) from taking advantage of the Internet to access only materials suitable for viewing by children.

Question 7   *Why not require that people in public debate tell the truth?*

That people should not lie seems like a pretty simple proposition. That people should not attempt to influence the decisions of others with lies, especially when those decisions concern the future of a whole society, seems indisputable. But lies, or at least half-truths and exaggeration, are a common part of everyday political debate. Many media outlets, especially such tabloids as the *National Enquirer* or the *National Star,* are known for their wild stories. Reports of aliens from outer space landing in Detroit may do no harm, but stories about the private lives of politicians or other celebrities can damage reputations and potentially destroy careers. Because the tabloids are known for their unreliability, few take them seriously, but the same cannot necessarily be said for the more "responsible" press. When should First Amendment protections hinge on the truthfulness of the expression?

In 1964 in *New York Times Co. v. Sullivan* the Supreme Court was called upon to decide whether the First Amendment protects a newspaper or citizens from libel actions brought by public officials. Libel is a written or published false statement damaging to the reputation of another. At the height of the civil rights movement in the South, an advertisement sponsored by supporters of the civil rights movement and Dr. Martin Luther King, Jr., appeared in the *New York Times.* The advertisement criticized actions of the Montgomery, Alabama police department in suppressing civil rights demonstrations and arresting Dr. King.

The advertisement contained some factually inaccurate statements that were deemed by the Alabama courts to have damaged the reputation of the Montgomery, Alabama police commissioner.

The Supreme Court was confronted with the question of whether the First Amendment provides protection for libelous statements criticizing the official conduct of government officials. In approaching this question Justice Brennan's Opinion of the Court noted our "... profound national commitment to the principle that debate on public issues should be uninhibited, robust, and wide-open, and that it may well include vehement, caustic, and sometimes unpleasantly sharp attacks on government and public officials" (at 270).

In political debate concerning emotionally charged issues, exaggeration and false statements are inevitable. To require that only statements that can be proved to be true be made would deny the freedom of expression essential "breathing space" (at 272). If defendants in libel suits were required to prove that all they have written is true, this might deter "would-be critics of official conduct ... from voicing their criticism, even though it is believed to be true and even though it is in fact true, because of doubt whether it can be proved in court or fear of the expense of having to do so" (at 279).

To some these negative consequences flowing from insisting on the truth may not seem so terrible. What, you might ask, do we lose if people hold their tongues until they know for sure what they are saying? After all, many of us are sick of the charges and countercharges and the "backbiting" that have become a central part of political debate today.

Perhaps a brief review of what happened during the Watergate scandal might put these ideas in perspective.

During the 1972 presidential election campaign, agents of the Nixon White House broke into the Democratic National Committee office apparently to install electronic listening devices. To this date we are uncertain about what they expected to learn, and we really do not know exactly who ordered the break-in. What did eventually become clear, however, was that high administration and campaign officials participated in a coverup, and several were eventually convicted of obstruction of justice and other serious offenses. Because of President Nixon's role in the coverup, impeachment proceedings were initiated against him. Nixon resigned from office shortly before an impeachment vote was scheduled to take place in the House of Representatives.

Public knowledge about the Watergate scandal emerged very slowly. When the charges first appeared in the press, no one had sufficient evidence to prove that either Nixon or his aides had participated in the planning of the break-in or, more importantly, in the obstruction of justice which followed it. To put it simply, many made charges and printed accusations which they could not then prove to be true. Those charges, however, brought denials from government officials. Subsequent debate about the credibility of those denials and continued press accusation led to investigations and the eventual emergence of evidence that would establish much of the truth.

If the slightest misstatement by the press could have led to a libel suit, would reporters have had the temerity to print accusations which they could not prove? If Nixon had not been forced by public opinion to respond to unproven accusations, would the obvious holes in his story and the subsequent damning evidence have ever emerged?

In its decision in *New York Times v. Sullivan* the Court in the end decided that the threats to free public debate posed by resort to libel actions by public officials were too great. Today, as a result of the *Times* decision, a public official may not recover ". . . damages for a defamatory falsehood relating to his official conduct unless he proves that the statement was made with 'actual malice'—that is, with knowledge that it was false or with a reckless disregard for whether it was false or not" (at 279–80). The public official in effect has to prove that the person making accusations against him or her was knowingly and deliberately telling a lie. This is a very difficult standard to meet.

At the beginning of the Watergate scandal, it is unlikely that those who accused Nixon and high officials in his administration with an illegal "coverup" could have proved their charges true. It is equally clear, however, that Nixon or his aides could not have met the standard for proving "actual malice" on the part of their accusers. Their grounds for suspicion were substantial enough to make any charge of a "reckless disregard for the truth" insupportable.

Public officials are, of course, not the only targets for damaging stories in the press. Celebrities, from sports figures to movie stars, are the constant subject of accusations and seemingly outrageous stories. While the *New York Times v. Sullivan* decision argued for the need for vigorous and uninhibited debate about the official conduct of public officials, what standard should apply to the activities of those who are famous but who are not part of government?

Sometimes, of course, the line between public officials and other celebrities gets quite blurred. Many celebrities, especially movie stars, involve themselves directly in public debate. One, Ronald Reagan, even got himself elected president!

During the early 1980s a freeze on the production and deployment of nuclear weapons as a first step toward arms reductions was advocated by many. When formal debates on this subject were held on television, however, it was not just politicians who participated. The actors Paul Newman (pro-"freeze") and Charlton Heston (anti-"freeze") debated each other on network TV. Similarly, during the Vietnam War actors and other participants in the performing arts often led protests both at home and abroad. Later in the mid-1990s the actor Charlton Heston became a leader in the National Rifle Association, an organization that vigorously opposes most gun regulation.

Recognizing that "public figures," like "public officials," often play an influential role in ordering society, the Court in *Curtis Publishing Co. v. Butts* and *Associated Press v. Walker* (1967) decided that both should be treated alike when they attempted to sue for libel. According to then Chief Justice Earl Warren, ". . . 'public figures' have as ready access as 'public officials' to mass media. . . , both to influence policy and to counter criticism of their views and activities. Our citizenry has a legitimate and substantial interest in the conduct of such persons, and the freedom of the press to engage in uninhibited debate about their involvement in public issues and events is as crucial as it is in the case of 'public officials'" (at 164).

Usually when we think of politicians and celebrities, we assume that they have many more privileges than do ordinary citizens. We think of ourselves as vulnerable while they always get their way. In dealing with the question of how to treat libel of "ordinary" citizens, the Court has taken our relative vulnerability into account. When it comes to our ability to protect our reputations from unfair injury, the Court's interpretation of the First Amendment permits average citizens to use legal remedies now generally unavailable to the famous and powerful. In this area of law, at least, the greater your obscurity, the greater your legal protections.

The distinction made between public officials and figures on the one hand and private citizens on the other is based on two advantages public personalities have over the rest of us. First, because of being more accessible to the media, public figures are better able to respond to charges and accusations made against them; and second, public figures generally have sought notoriety and have benefited from their celebrity status. Public criticism, even unfair attacks, come with the territory. Since private citizens generally cannot easily command media attention to state their side of the story when they are attacked and because they have neither sought nor benefited from public notice, they are ". . . not only more vulnerable to injury than public officials and public figures; they are also," according to the Court, "more deserving of . . . [compensation for injury.]" (*Gertz v. Robert Welch, Inc.,* 1974 at 345).

The differences in the treatment of libel against public figures or officials and private citizens have not ended the debate concerning how the law should deal with untrue charges and statements. Are politicians and celebrities truly able to protect themselves from unfair and untrue attacks? Do private citizens need special protection?

Justice Brennan, the author of the *New York Times* decision that made it difficult for public officials to win libel suits, doubts that the distinction between people in public life and those in private life adequately protects legitimate public debate. The *New York Times, Curtis Publishing Co.,* and *Walker* decisions all emphasized to varying degrees the roles played by public officials and public figures in "ordering society." The stress was on their "public" role. Today, however, many of the more damaging attacks on famous people concern their "private" lives rather than their public performance.

As the campaign for the 1988 presidential election began, Gary Hart was clearly the leading contender for the Democratic presidential nomination. He was forced to withdraw from the race, however, after allegations surfaced about alleged extramarital affairs. Although the charges against him did not concern his positions on political issues, his voting record in the Senate, the breaking of any laws, or using his political office for financial gain, his chances of becoming president evaporated.

In the end Mr. Hart came close to admitting that some of the charges of sexual misconduct were true, but in considering the significance of his case for the Court's position concerning libel, we might speculate about what might have happened had the charges been untrue. Because he was a public official, to win a libel judgment he would have had to have proved that those who made the charges told knowing lies or that they had shown a "reckless disregard for the truth." Even if the charges had been untrue, the likelihood that he could have won is slight indeed. The charges alone might well have been sufficient to have cast enough doubt on him to have fatally damaged his campaign. The time taken in publicly responding to such charges would surely have distracted his and the public's attention from real debate on vital political issues.

More recently, even before his involvement in the Lewinsky scandal, President Bill Clinton had to contend with a variety of charges and scurrilous attacks, many of which concerned his private life. Can anyone seriously say that he was less vulnerable to injury than a private citizen? Isn't it his very public status that invites damaging attacks, many of which are no doubt untrue?

Because in part he doubted that public officials and public figures can always command media attention to respond to reckless attacks on their purely private conduct, Justice Brennan argued that the heightened protection of First Amendment rights provided by the *New York Times* standard concerning libel should apply in all debate about matters of public interest whether or not the persons caught up in the debate were public officials or public figures. "The public's primary interest is in the event; the public focus is on the conduct of the participant and the content, effect, and significance of the conduct, not the participant's prior anonymity or notoriety" (*Rosenbloom v. Metromedia, Inc.,* at 43, 1971).

In its decision in *Chaplinsky* (see above) the Court argued that libel was among those limited categories of speech not protected by the First

Amendment because ". . . such utterances are no essential part of any exposition of ideas, and are of such slight social value as a step to truth. . . ."
The Court's decision in *New York Times,* however, recognized that the
best method for finding the truth is to encourage free, open, and "robust"
debate. Except in the instance of the deliberate lie designed purely to inflict injury, the Court in effect adopted the view expressed by Justice
Holmes in a very different kind of case: "That the best test of truth is the
power of the thought to get itself accepted in the competition of the market" (*Abrams v. United States,* 1919, Holmes, dissenting at 630).

Isn't the danger posed by silencing or punishing views and even offensive personal attacks greater than the damage potentially inflicted by
such attacks?

Question 8   *How is burning the American flag a form of free speech?*

Drawing a sharp line between speech and action can be difficult. Some, as
we have seen, justify punishing people simply for advocating ideas that
could possibly cause others to engage in illegal actions. Others are loathe
to accept any limits on mere words, arguing instead that government
should focus directly on actions. There is, however, another side to the
sometimes fuzzy distinction between words and actions. Sometimes ideas
are expressed not in speech, in the press, or on film, but rather through
actions; such nonverbal expression has been termed "symbolic speech." In
symbolic speech cases, the question before the courts is: When do actions
equal speech? When does punishing certain actions interfere with the exchange of ideas?

Although one might want to argue that the First Amendment protects any action designed to express an idea, on reflection no one could
support such a position. For example, one might choose to express one's
opposition to the president by burning down the White House. Some actually do burn or bomb abortion clinics to show their opposition to abortion.
As the cliché goes: "Actions speak louder than words." Few miss the message in such actions, but virtually everyone recognizes that the framers of
the First Amendment did not intend to authorize arson.

What if the target for burning is not the White House or an abortion
clinic, but an American flag, a cross, or a draft registration card? On such
questions the courts are, sometimes, sharply divided.

In its decision upholding the constitutionality of a law punishing
those who burned their draft registration cards, the Court devised a formula to aid it in deciding when the Constitution protects symbolic
speech.

During the Vietnam War, the law required men of draft age to carry
their draft cards on which was listed their degree of eligibility for the

draft. Burning these documents in public became a popular form of protest among those opposed to the war. In apparent response to such actions, Congress made destruction of such records a crime. Although the Court admitted that the First Amendment sometimes protected actions designed to express ideas, it upheld government regulation of such conduct under the following circumstances:

> . . . a government regulation is sufficiently justified if it is within the constitutional powers of the government; if it furthers an important or substantial governmental interest, if the governmental interest is unrelated to the suppression of free expression; and if the incidental restrictions on alleged First Amendment Freedoms is no greater than is essential to the furtherance of the interest (*United States v. O'Brien,* at 377, 1968).

Since the government had the right to require draft registration, and since, the Court argued, the information printed on the registration cards facilitated communication between the draft board and the individual registrant permitting the "smooth and proper functioning of the system that Congress has established to raise armies" (at 381), the Court upheld the law.

Although it was obvious to any observers at the time that Congress passed the law primarily to punish a particular form of protest—to stifle this dramatic communication—the Court argued it was not its duty to assess the congressional motives. In banning the burning of draft cards, Congress had successfully stifled one form of symbolic speech, but as Justice Harlan's concurring opinion argued, other channels of communication involving "pure speech" remained open. People were still free to speak and write against the war.

Perhaps more than any other example of symbolic speech, burning the American flag in protest elicits anger and controversy. To many the flag borders on a sacred symbol. They are profoundly offended when others treat it disrespectfully. The offense comes, however, not because a piece of striped cloth has been burned, but because the action expresses ideas that are offensive; for example, contempt for the country. However offensive this idea may be, few constitutional scholars would doubt that the First Amendment protects such ideas. The issue, then, is whether the First Amendment also protects this mode of expression.

Old flags are properly burned when they are being discarded or replaced by new flags. It is, therefore, not the act of burning but the thought behind it that offends.

In his dissent from a Court decision striking down the conviction of a flag burner, Justice Abe Fortas argued: "If a state statute provided that it is a misdemeanor to burn one's shirt or trousers on the public thoroughfare, it could hardly be asserted that the citizen's constitutional right is violated. . . . If as I submit it is permissible to prohibit burning of personal property on the public sidewalk, there is no basis for applying a different rule for flag burning" (*Street v. New York,* 1969, Fortas, dissenting, at 616).

Fortas seems to focus simply on the conduct in question. The problem with his approach, however, is that, generally, states do not pass laws carrying stiff penalties for burning your shirt. They do pass such laws for burning the American flag. Could it be that their fear is not of arson or smoke pollution, but of ideas? If so, are such laws permissible under the First Amendment?

It was not until 1989 that the Supreme Court in *Texas v. Johnson* confronted this First Amendment question directly. Johnson was convicted for burning an American flag in protest outside the Republican National Convention in Dallas in 1984. Under the Texas flag desecration statute he was sentenced to one year in prison.

In his Opinion of the Court in *Texas v. Johnson,* Justice William Brennan acknowledged the "expressive element in conduct relating to flags. . . . The very purpose of a national flag is to serve as a symbol of our country; it is, one might say, 'the one visible manifestation of two hundred years of nationhood'" (at 405). It is precisely because of its primarily expressive significance that conduct relating to the flag is in most instances protected by the First Amendment. As is the case with any exercise of free speech, the Constitution does not permit the state to "prohibit the expression of an idea simply because society finds the idea itself offensive or disagreeable . . . " (at 414). While acknowledging the fact that society in general is deeply offended by flag desecration, Justice Brennan and a majority of the Court concluded that if we were to punish those who desecrate the American flag, "we [would] dilute the freedom that this cherished symbol represents" (at 420).

The dissenters on the Court as well as the Court's critics in society focused on the flag's unique role in society. It is that role, they contend, that justifies limits on its physical desecration. While acknowledging that the Texas law did interfere with one form of symbolic expression, amounting, in Chief Justice William Rehnquist's words, to "an inarticulate grunt or roar that, it seems fair to say, is most likely to be indulged in not to express any particular idea, but to antagonize others. . .," it still left undisturbed "a full panoply of other symbols and every conceivable form of verbal expression to express . . . deep disapproval of national policy."

In response to the Court's decision in 1989 striking down the Texas flag desecration statute, then President George Bush and countless others called for a constitutional amendment to permit the states and the federal government to pass laws punishing flag desecration. In pressing their objections, the dissenters on the Court and the critics outside argued in effect that the flag symbolizes only good. In the words of Justice Stevens: "It is a symbol of freedom, of equal opportunity, of religious tolerance and good will for other people who share our aspirations." Others, however, might sometimes view the flag differently. To the Klu Klux Klan members and sometimes to African Americans alike it has sometimes been a symbol of white supremacy and intolerance. The flag was carried by soldiers who liberated Europe from the Nazis, but it was also carried by soldiers who "exterminated" native Americans. Many of the loudest proponents of a constitutional amendment permitting bans on flag desecration to this day celebrate Civil War "rebel" heroes who fired cannon against it.

Whatever happens to proposals for constitutional amendments banning flag desecration or laws meant to circumvent the Supreme Court's decision upholding this form of free expression, those in society who are offended by flag burning still have the recourse provided by the First Amendment. In the words of Justice Brennan: "The way to preserve the flag's special role is not to punish those who feel differently about these matters. It is to persuade them that they are wrong."

Question 9   *If flag burning is protected by the First Amendment, why is cross burning sometimes not protected?*

Except perhaps for the Nazi swastika, a burning cross is probably the most commonly recognized symbol for racial and ethnic hatred and religious bigotry in the United States. In its decision in *Virginia v. Black* (2003) the U.S. Supreme Court recited much of the sorry history of this symbol and its role in racist and religious intimidation. Some legislators would punish cross burning because of the hateful and often intimidating nature of the message it communicates. Nonetheless the Supreme Court found that in many circumstances cross burning is constitutionally protected. Like flag burning, cross burning is expressive conduct meant at least in some instances to express ideas, however offensive.

To understand the Court's treatment of cross burning it might be useful to look first at what flag burning or desecration and cross burning have in common. As already discussed above in Question 8 American flags are sometimes burned as a dramatic form of protest against government policies. There is no question that both burning a cross and burning an American flag generally are designed to send a message. In *Virginia v. Black* the justices on the Supreme Court discussed at length the message conveyed by cross burning in American history. In her Opinion of the Court Justice Sandra Day O'Connor surveyed the history and role of cross burning in the evolution of the Ku Klux Klan (KKK). Although the Klan began as a "social club, it soon changed into something far different.

The Klan fought Reconstruction and the corresponding drive to allow freed blacks to participate in the political process. . . . The Klan employed tactics such as whippings, threatening to burn people at the stake, and murder (internal citations omitted)" (at 548).

Although the first KKK was successfully suppressed during the 1870s, its successor emerged early in the twentieth century. According to Justice O'Connor's opinion,

> [f]rom the inception of the second Klan, cross burnings have been used to communicate both threats of violence and messages of shared ideology. . . . For its own members, the cross was a sign of celebration and ceremony. . . . To this day, regardless of whether the message is a political one or whether the message is also meant to intimidate, the burning cross is a symbol of hate." *Capitol Square Review and Advisory Bd. v. Pinette,* 515 U.S., at 771 (Thomas, J., concurring). And while cross burning sometimes carries no intimidating message, at other times the intimidating message is the *only* message conveyed. For example, when a cross burning is directed at a particular person not affiliated with the Klan, the burning cross often serves as a message of intimidation, designed to inspire in the victim a fear of bodily harm. Moreover, the history of violence associated with the Klan shows that the possibility of injury or death is not just hypothetical. The person who burns a cross directed at a particular person is often making a serious threat, meant to coerce the victim to comply with the Klan's wishes unless the victim is willing to risk the wrath of the Klan (at 548–50).

In her opinion, therefore, Justice O'Connor, while deploring what cross burning has stood for throughout American history, nonetheless argued that as a symbol the burning cross has had multiple meanings. Although she accepted that the state may legitimately punish cross burnings which are designed to intimidate, it may not punish cross burnings designed to rally supporters or symbolize the white supremacist viewpoints of Klan members and sympathizers. In this she treated cross burning as the equivalent of pure speech. Consistent with the dominant view on the Court, Justice O'Connor argued that the First Amendment is not absolute and that some limited categories of speech are not protected. Of most direct relevance here is the Court's position that "the First Amendment permits a state to ban a 'true threat.' *Watts v. United States,* 394 U.S. 705, 708. . . ." 'True threats' encompass those statements where the speaker means to communicate a serious expression of an intent to commit an act of unlawful violence to a particular individual or group of individuals. . . . The speaker need not actually intend to carry out the threat. Rather, a prohibition on true threats 'protects individuals from fear of violence' and 'from the disruption that fear engenders,' in addition to protecting people 'from the possibility that the threatened violence will occur' (citation omitted). Intimidation in the constitutionally proscribable sense of the word is a type of true threat . . . " (at 552).

When a cross burning is designed to intimidate and amounts to a true threat, it, like speech which constitutes a true threat, is not protected by the First Amendment. When, on the other hand, a cross burning is designed merely (however offensively) to express white protestant supremacist ideology, it is protected by the Constitution.

The issue before the Court in *Virginia v. Black* was the constitutionality of a Virginia law banning cross burning with "an intent to intimidate a person or group of persons." While the majority of the Court upheld the constitutionality in principle of a law punishing cross burning with "an intent to intimidate," it struck down the statute in the form presented to the Court because of a provision in the statute that stated that "[a]ny such burning of a cross shall be prima facie evidence of an intent to intimidate . . . " (at 541). Although the Court was sharply divided over the meaning and significance of this "prima facie" evidence provision, Justice O'Connor and the Court majority argued that it would permit a jury to convict in some circumstances even when there was in fact no direct proof presented that a cross burning was intended to intimidate. The prima facie evidence provision permits a jury to infer the necessary intent to intimidate in circumstances where a defendant exercised his or her constitutional right not to put on a defense. Under such conditions, according to the Court majority, under the statute as written, a jury might convict a defendant even in the absence of a true threat.

In arguing against the presumption in the statute that any cross burning is designed to intimidate, Justice O'Connor observed: "The act of burning a cross may mean that a person is engaging in constitutionally proscribable intimidation. But the same act may mean only that the person is engaged in core political speech. The prima facie evidence provision in this statute blurs the line between these two meanings of a burning cross. . . . It does not distinguish between a cross burning at a public rally or a cross burning on a neighbor's lawn. It does not treat the cross burning directed at an individual differently from a cross burning directed at a group of like-minded believers . . . " (at 556).

Nothing communicated by flag burning is outside the sphere of protected speech. However offensive flag desecration is to most Americans, the message sent is protected by the Constitution. Similarly the white protestant supremacist message sent by cross burning is, according to the Court in *Virginia v. Black,* also protected speech. When, however, the message conveyed by cross burning is not just an offensive belief system but instead is aimed at particular individuals or groups designed to intimidate them, cross burning loses its constitutional protection. True threats like fighting words are in the narrow categories of speech for which the Constitution provides no protection. Although flag burning can make people angry, it can never really be said to be directed personally at any individual. Flag desecration carries a political message not a personal one.

In *Texas v. Johnson* (1989), however, the Court did acknowledge one possible hypothetical circumstance when flag desecration could be punished. If flag desecration were to threaten a breach of the peace or provoke "imminent lawless action," Justice Brennan acknowledged it might be punished. One can imagine a circumstance in which a protestor might almost inevitably provoke a violent reaction during a Memorial Day observance by burning an American flag in front of veterans who were honoring their recently fallen comrades. Such a provocative action might be punishable even under the Court's ruling in *Texas v. Johnson*.

The Court's decision in *Virginia v. Black* argues that cross burning, which is meant to intimidate, may be punishable even when there is no proof that violence may be imminent. The fear engendered by the threatening nature of the message sometimes contained in cross burning is enough to sometimes deprive this dramatic communicative action of its constitutional protection. Cross burning that poses a true threat, like genuinely threatening speech, loses its constitutional protection. For flag burning to lose its constitutional protection additional evidence showing that the flag burning is likely to produce imminent lawless action, a breach of the peace, is required.

Question 10 *Why should a democratic society tolerate the expression of views that are offensive to the majority?*

Majority rule is the most fundamental tenet of democracy. Only the majority has the right to put its will into law, and all are expected to obey the majority's will expressed in law. In the United States there is a consensus on many fundamental ideas concerning how society should be ordered. There is, as well, very broad agreement that some philosophies and ideas are unacceptable. One need only think of the near universal condemnation of Nazism to understand this point. Yet despite the consensus opposed to Nazism, Nazis are still permitted to express their views. Similarly, despite the fact that the civil rights revolution has produced widespread popular rejection of open racism, the Ku Klux Klan (KKK) still exists and still stages marches under the protection of the law.

If virtually all of us reject and despise the views espoused by such groups, why must we tolerate them? Isn't permitting them to continue publicly to express their opposition to the values the vast majority of us share contrary to the principle of majority rule? Isn't it a threat to democracy itself?

The answers to such questions are complex, but they concern the very heart of the values meant to be protected by the First Amendment. If the vast majority of us "know" that the Nazis and the KKK represent ideas that are evil, what possible purpose is served by giving them a chance to attract others to their cause? The answers involve an exploration of the meaning of democracy and the search for truth. In his dissent in *Abrams v. United States* (1919), Justice Holmes confronted the issues raised by questions such as these:

> Persecution for the expression of opinions seems to me perfectly logical. If you have no doubt of your premises or your power and want a certain result with all your heart, you naturally express your wishes in law and sweep away all opposition. To allow opposition by speech seems to indicate that you think speech impotent, as when a man says that he has squared the circle, or that you do not care wholeheartedly for the result, or that you doubt either your power or your premises. *But when men have realized that time has upset many fighting faiths, they may come to believe even more than they believe the very foundations of their own conduct that the ultimate good desired is better reached by free trade in ideas—that the best test of truth is the power of the thought to get itself accepted in the competition of the market, and that truth is the only ground upon which their wishes safely may be carried out.* That at any rate is the theory of our Constitution. It is an experiment, as all life is an experiment. Every year if not every day we have to wager our salvation upon some prophecy based upon imperfect knowledge. While the experiment is part of our system I think that we should be eternally vigilant against attempts to check the expression of opinions that we loathe and believe to be fraught with death, unless they so imminently threaten immediate interference with the lawful and pressing purposes of the law that an immediate check is required to save the country [emphasis added] (*Abrams v. United States,* 1919, Holmes, dissenting, at 630).

The idea expressed by Holmes was not new. It adopts a position previously taken by both John Milton's *Areopagitaca* and John Stuart Mill's *On Liberty.* Simply, we can be confident that we have found the truth, that we know the truth, only if we are willing to let our "truth" be tested in competition against other ideas. If our beliefs attract the support of society after being subjected to open challenge, then our ideas are probably correct. If, however, our ideas win out through silencing opposition, because other ideas are either not expressed or not heard, then we have no right to have confidence in them.

In a democratic society the decision-making process is like the search for truth. Obviously what the majority decides is what the majority believes is the best policy among the alternatives. If society is prevented by laws or by its own prejudices from hearing all possible alternatives, then it is acting out of at least partial ignorance.

Holmes, however, addresses the issue of whether a democratic society can tolerate the expression of views which directly challenge democratically made decisions. Isn't permitting defiant challenges the same as an admission of doubt, a belief that you have made an error? Isn't tolerance for rejected ideas a sign of weakness or uncertainty?

As Holmes argued, we can look back at history and see that "time has upset many fighting faiths." New information and experiences have often shown that beliefs firmly held by virtually all society were simply wrong. Witches were burned at the stake. Galileo was threatened with a similar fate when he denied that the earth was the center of the universe. Despite the firmly held beliefs of the vast majority for most of human history, the earth is not flat!

We can have little doubt that Milton, Mill, and Holmes are correct. Generally, acting on information is preferable to ignorance. But no doubt many of us are left uneasy when confronted by those who express beliefs we "know" are evil or at least just plain wrong. Don't we have to choose? Don't we have to sometimes make final decisions and simply reject outrageous alternatives?

When a group of American Nazis announced plans to march in Skokie, Illinois during the late 1970s even many long-time advocates of civil liberties and freedom of speech felt things had gone too far. Skokie was a town which had a large Jewish population, including a substantial number of survivors of World War II Nazi extermination camps. Permitting American Nazis to march in such a town would force many victims of Nazi atrocities to relive their horrible experiences and might as well cause them to fear that it could happen again.

To those who opposed permitting the Nazi march, the Nazis were not simply expressing an alternative point of view to those shared by most of society. The Nazi were not simply wrong; they were the personification of evil in the world. To tolerate even this small march could once again cause their hateful ideas to become acceptable. It is one thing to believe that the best way to find the truth is through the unrestricted competition of ideas, but most of us know that most people do not listen with an open mind. Some, possibly a majority, might hear the Nazi lies and for a time at least believe them and act on them. After all, even as Lincoln argued that "you can't fool all of the people all of the time," he acknowledged that "you can fool all of the people some of the time." Do we have enough confidence in the majority to take the chance that they might be seduced by Nazi ideology. Why take the risk?

If we could be certain that the majority would silence only those espousing genuinely evil ideas, perhaps little would be lost by silencing Nazis. But experience has shown that often the majority finds the "truth" sufficiently troubling to silence those who speak it. In the Skokie case the ideas expressed by the Nazis were profoundly shocking and frightening to the majority in that community. Because they found those ideas so terrible, they attempted to use the law to ban the public expression of Nazi beliefs. If, however, the measure of what can be said and what cannot be said is a function of the level of revulsion or hostility the potential "speaker" or marcher evokes in the community, then Martin Luther King, Jr., and other civil rights advocates could have been silenced in many American communities during the 1950s and 1960s. Dr. King challenged the deeply ingrained beliefs and prejudices of a majority in many communities. A review of old television tapes and newsreels from that era would show the extreme emotion and hostility directed against King and other demonstrators by very average-looking white Americans. Perhaps they felt King challenged their whole way of life. When Dr. King led an open housing march in Cicero, Illinois, in 1968, he and his fellow marchers had to be protected by National Guard troops from a mob determined to keep blacks from living in "their" community.

Although today we "know" that Dr. King was right and the Nazis are wrong, the majority everywhere clearly has not always known this. If the majority can silence opinions which they find intolerable, then at varying times in our history it would have been those who speak the truth who would have been silenced.

When free speech is vigorously safeguarded, will the truth always prevail? Certainly not. Without protection for freedom of speech, however, we have no right to expect that the truth will ever prevail. The best anecdote for bad speech is, in Justice Brandeis's words, "more speech, not enforced silence" (quoted in Meikeljohn, p. 56).

REFERENCES

Abrams v. United States, 250 U.S. 616 (1919).

American Booksellers Association, Inc. v. Hudnut, 771 F.2d 323 (7th Cir., 1985).

Association Press v. Walker, 388 U.S. 130 (1967).

Brandenburg v. Ohio, 395 U.S. 444 (1969).

Capitol Square Review and Advisory Bd. v. Pinette, 515 U.S. 771 (0000).

Cantwell v. Connecticut, 310 U.S. 296 (1940).

Chaplinsky v. New Hampshire, 315 U.S. 568 (1942).

City of Renton v. Playtime Theaters, Inc., 476 U.S. 41 (1986).

Curtis Publishing Co. v. Butts and *Associated Press v. Walker,* 388 U.S. 130 (1967).

Federal Communications Commission v. Pacifica Foundation, 483 U.S. 726 (1978).

Gertz v. Robert Welch, Inc., 418 U.S. 323 (1974).

Gitlow v. New York, 268 U.S. 652 (1925).

Jacobellis v. Ohio, 378 U.S. 184 (1964).

Meikeljohn, Alexander, *Free Speech and Its Relation to Self-Government* (New York: Harper & Row, 1948).

Miller v. California, 413 U.S. 15 (1973).

Near v. Minnesota, 283 U.S. 697 (1931).

Nebraska Press Association v. Stuart, 427 U.S. 539 (1976).

New York v. Ferber, 485 U.S. 747 (1982).

New York Times Co. v. Sullivan, 376 U.S. 254 (1964).

New York Times Co. v. United States, 403 U.S. 713 (1971).

Paris Adult Theatre I v. Slaton, 413 U.S. 49 (1973).

R. A. V. v. St. Paul, 505 U.S. 377 (1992).

Reno v. American Civil Liberties Union, 117 S. Ct. 2329 (1997).

Rosenbloom v. Metromedia, Inc., 403 U.S. 29 (1971).

Roth v. United States, 354 U.S. 476 (1957).

Schenck v. United States, 249 U.S. 47 (1919).

Street v. New York, 394 U.S. 576 (1969).

Terminiello v. City of Chicago, 337 U.S. 1 (1949).

Texas v. Johnson, 491 U.S. 397 (1989).

United States v. American Library Association, Inc., 71 USLW 4465 (2003).

United States v. O'Brien, 391 U.S. 367 (1968).

Virginia v. Black, 155 L. Ed. 2d 535 (2003).

Watts v. United States, 394 U.S. 705 (1968).

Young v. American Mini Theatres, Inc., 427 U.S. 50 (1976).

CHAPTER THREE

FREEDOM
OF RELIGION

INTRODUCTION

The ancestors of many Americans came here to escape religious persecution in their homelands. The quest for religious liberty, therefore, has always been an important element in American life. If public opinion surveys and the rhetoric of politicians are to be believed, today religion continues to play an important role in the lives of most Americans. In order to protect religious liberty and religious expression, the First Amendment to the Constitution provides for the separation of church and state. Over two centuries after the adoption of the First Amendment the Supreme Court's understanding of the requirements of the religion clauses continues to stir controversy and continues to evolve. Vigorous debate continues concerning what separation of church and state means. This chapter explores central questions relating to religion and the Constitution.

One of the core issues regarding the First Amendment is to what degree it demands strict separation of government from religion. Some argue for a "wall of separation" between church and state, while others assert the Constitution mandates accommodation between church and state. Question 1 asks: *Why can't government help advance the religious values that the majority of Americans share?* This section begins with a brief description of the Establishment and Free Exercise clauses of the First Amendment and then explores in greater depth the variety of understandings on the Court of what in particular the Establishment clause forbids. It reviews the so-called *Lemon* test frequently used by justices on the Court in recent decades to judge the constitutionality of government programs that in some way affect religion or religious institutions.

While the Establishment clause focuses on the propriety of government support for religion, the Free Exercise clause concerns the freedom of people to practice their religion without government restriction. Question 2 asks: *Are there limits on a person's right to practice his or her religion?* Here we explore deep divisions within the Court in recent years concerning the degree to which government must provide exemption from laws and other regulations when compliance with them would conflict with a person's religious beliefs. The issue is whether the Free Exercise clause of the First Amendment protects merely one's right to believe or whether it protects as well one's right to act in accordance with his or her beliefs.

Sometimes the right to free exercise of religion appears to run into conflict with the prohibition against establishment of religion. The controversy over religion in the public schools highlights this conflict. Question 3 asks: *Doesn't banning "voluntary prayer" in public schools interfere with children's freedom of religion?* Here we explore the highly controversial Supreme Court decisions concerning government-sponsored prayer in public schools. Concerning a related issue Question 4 asks: *If secular groups are allowed access to the schools, shouldn't religious groups have the same rights?* This question forces us to explore the issue of whether the Establishment clause forces government to discriminate against religious expression in our public institutions. The Court has been forced to weigh the relationship between free speech and religious expression and whether the Constitution mandates or forbids equal access by religious groups to public forums.

Controversy about the teaching of evolution in the public schools has existed since early in the twentieth century. In 1999 the curriculum guidelines for the state of Kansas for a time removed discussion of evolution from the state's approved scientific curriculum. Fundamentalist religious groups have long denounced evolution as contrary to literal interpretation of the origins of the human species as described in Genesis. This section explores Question 5: *Doesn't teaching evolution in the public schools amount to the establishment of secular religion?*

Finally, in light of President George W. Bush's push for increased governmental support for "faith-based-initiatives," Question 6 asks: *Isn't government funding for social services provided by religious organizations endangering the constitutional separation of church and state?* This section explores the evolution of the Court's interpretations of both the Establishment and Free Exercise clauses away from the strict separation philosophy adopted by the Court in the mid-twentieth century and, in particular, the implications of the Supreme Court's acceptance of government aid to religious schools. Our discussion of this question will serve to summarize the current status of the church/state relationship in America.

Question 1   *Why can't government help advance the religious values that the majority of Americans share?*

A larger proportion of the American population attends church on a regular basis than in most other countries, and surveys of the population show that most Americans consider themselves religious. When questions concerning religion and government arise, it is natural that many are confused. Even people who consider themselves tolerant of the feelings and beliefs of others have a difficult time understanding why prayer in the schools, for example, is controversial. Many when told that some object to school prayer respond: "It won't do them any harm, and it might do them some good." Whenever former President Ronald Reagan hit the campaign trail, he was always guaranteed cheers from the crowd when he called for the restoration of "voluntary prayer" in the public schools.

If we look beyond America, however, we can readily see the divisive role played by religion in many countries throughout the world. Calls are heard periodically in some "fundamentalist" Islamic countries for "holy war." Persecution of minority religious sects is found almost everywhere. Ancient nationalist political conflicts, such as those in the north of Ireland or Kosovo, take on religious overtones. Virtually every nation has at one time or another felt confident that "God is on our side."

The history of the relationship between church and state in America is often distorted and easily misunderstood. Many early Americans came here to escape religious persecution, but once here many practiced religious intolerance themselves. Most of the original colonies had an "established" state church or churches and/or provided tax support for favored churches. From the beginning there was dissent from minority religions and warnings from leaders such as Jefferson and Madison of the dangers of links between church and state.

Today some churches still seek state support for religious schools and other sectarian institutions. Religious and political leaders frame the struggle for civil rights, for helping the poor, for and against capital punishment, or for laws forbidding abortion in religious terms. Clergymen sometimes endorse candidates for office, and in 1988 two Protestant ministers, Jesse Jackson and Pat Robertson, actually ran for president of the United States.

Legal debate concerning religion and the state in America revolves around the meaning of the First Amendment Establishment and Free Exercise clauses. The First Amendment religion clauses state: "Congress shall make no law respecting an establishment of religion, or prohibiting the free exercise thereof." There is no doubt that the Establishment clause at minimum prohibits the government from setting up a single recognized state church. There has, however, been considerable controversy concerning whether this clause commands a complete separation between church and state. Some see the Establishment clause as mandating simply "no preference" on the part of government for one church over another. They rely on the historic understanding based on European experience that "establishment" refers to state support for a single recognized church. A respected constitutional scholar, Leonard Levy, has argued, however, that the "establishments of religion" found in most of the American colonies and original states involved state support for churches in general. In some of the first states citizens were forced to pay taxes to support their own churches. The state was in effect a collection agency for many churches. When Madison and Jefferson opposed established religions, they opposed not only state preference for particular religions but also such state tax support for any religions. They considered religion to be a purely private matter.

Many, however, argue that the Constitution does permit accommodation between government and religion in general. Some would go so far as to argue that government's failure to aid all religion amounts to a preference for irreligion, or what some have termed "secular humanism."

The dominant view on the Supreme Court during much of the twentieth century had been, however, that the Constitution mandates a "wall of separation" between church and state. The Court majority generally in effect has argued that the First Amendment not only forbids a preference for any particular religion, but it also forbids a preference for religion in general over irreligion. It bans any entanglement between government and religion.

In a much quoted passage from the Supreme Court's decision in *Everson v. Board of Education* (1947) Justice Hugo Black summed up the meaning of the Establishment clause as follows:

> Neither a state nor the Federal Government can set up a church. Neither can pass laws which aid one religion, aid all religions, or prefer one religion over another. Neither can force or influence a person to go to or remain away from church against his will or force him to profess a belief or disbelief in any religion. No person can be punished for entertaining or professing religious beliefs or disbeliefs, for church attendance or non-attendance. No tax in any amount, large or small, can be levied to support any religious activities or institutions, whatever they may be called, or whatever form they may adopt to teach or practice religion. Neither a state nor the Federal Government can, openly or secretly, participate in the affairs of any religious organization or group and vice versa.

In the words of Jefferson, the clause against the establishment of religion by law was intended to erect a "wall of separation between church and state" . . . (at 15–16).

When Justice Black wrote these words, he was writing for a Court majority that actually upheld a very limited government program to pay for transportation to schools for all students, including those attending religious schools. The four justices who dissented in *Everson* called for an even stricter and more total separation of church and state. Black's words endorsing a wall of separation, however, clearly reflect the unanimous view of the Supreme Court at the time, one mandating a nearly complete separation of church and state.

The issue of the proper relationship between church and state will not, however, go away. Since the *Everson* decision, the Court has been forced to decide a number of cases, and its decisions have not always been consistent. In a decision upholding government support for the display of a Christmas crèche on public land, Chief Justice Warren Burger dismissed the concept of a " 'wall' of separation" as "a useful figure of speech." But he went on to argue that ". . . the Constitution [does not] require complete separation of church and state; it affirmatively mandates accommodation, not merely tolerance, of all religions, and forbids hostility toward any . . . " (*Lynch v. Donnelly,* 1984).

In support of this position, Chief Justice Burger and other advocates of accommodation cite the long history of official recognition of religious themes and religious observances in American public life. Acts of Congress have placed "In God We Trust" on our coins and "one Nation, under God" in the pledge of allegiance. Presidents as far back as Washington have proclaimed Thanksgiving Day and days of prayer and fasting. Congress begins each session with prayers offered by chaplains on the public payroll, and chaplains are provided for the armed forces as well. The list could go on. Clearly, our practice has not always corresponded to the proclaimed principle of a wall of separation.

Separation of church and state, however, cannot mean a total denial of the role of religious values in American life. Many who opposed America's sad history of racial oppression did so citing religious grounds. Prohibitions against murder, stealing, or lying are found both in secular law and in the Ten Commandments. Surely the prohibition against an "establishment of religion" found in the First Amendment does not mean that the state may not pursue policies that happen to be consistent with religious values.

The Supreme Court on a number of occasions has attempted to delineate when it is permissible for state or federal laws to parallel religious laws or commands. In *Lemon v. Kurtzman* (1971), Chief Justice Burger attempted to summarize the Court's evolving understanding of the Establishment clause. He argued that the framers of the Establishment clause

> did not simply prohibit the establishment of a state church or
> state religion. . . . Instead they commanded that there should be
> "no law *respecting* an establishment of religion." A law may be one
> "*respecting*" the forbidden objective while falling short of total
> realization. A law "respecting" the proscribed result, that is, the
> establishment of religion, is not always easily identifiable as one
> violative of the Clause. A given law might not *establish* a state
> religion but nevertheless be one "respecting" that end in the sense
> of being a step that could lead to such establishment and hence
> offend the First Amendment . . . (at 612).

From this analysis Chief Justice Burger went on to develop guidelines that have come to be known as the *Lemon* test:

> Every analysis in this area must begin with consideration of the
> cumulative criteria developed by the Court over many years. Three
> such tests may be learned from our cases. First, the statute must
> have a secular legislative purpose; second, its principal or primary
> effect must be one that neither advances or inhibits religion; finally,
> the statute must not foster "an excessive government Entanglement
> with religion" (at 612, 613).

Thinking about the "purpose prong" of the *Lemon* test, one can understand that although prohibitions against murder are found in the Bible, the state does not necessarily prohibit murder *because* it is prohibited in the Bible. People's natural instinct to live provides quite ample secular motivation in itself, even to those who have neither read nor even heard of the Bible.

On the other hand when the Supreme Court was confronted with a challenge to a Kentucky statute requiring the posting of the Ten Commandments in every public school classroom, the Court majority found no "secular purpose" behind the action and therefore struck it down as a violation of the Establishment clause. In so ruling the Court dismissed the state's contention, noted in small print at the bottom of each display of the Ten Commandments in the schools, that "[t]he secular application of the Ten Commandments is clearly seen in its adoption as the fundamental legal code of western Civilization and the Common Law of the United States" [citations omitted,] (*Stone v. Graham,* at 41, 1980).

According to the per curium opinion in *Stone v. Graham,*

> The preeminent purpose for posting the Ten Commandments on
> schoolroom walls is plainly religious in nature. . . . The Command-
> ments do not confine themselves to arguably secular matters, such

as honoring one's parents, killing or murder. . . . Rather, the first
part of the Commandments concerns the religious duties of
believers: worshiping the Lord God alone, avoiding idolatry, not using
the Lord's name in vain, and observing the Sabbath Day . . . (at 42).

When the Court was confronted with a constitutional challenge to
"Sunday closing laws," however, it chose to downplay the fact that "[t]here
is no dispute that the original laws which dealt with Sunday labor
were motivated by religious forces" (*McGowan v. Maryland,* at 431, 1961),
arguing instead that today such laws ". . . have become part and parcel" of
the increased government concern in this century for "improvement of
the health, safety, recreation and general well-being of our citizens."
Today, then, according to the Chief Justice Warren's Opinion of the Court,
"[t]he present *purpose and effect* of most of them is to provide a uniform
day of rest for all citizens; the fact that this day is Sunday, a day of particular significance for the dominant Christian sects, does not bar the State
from achieving its secular goals" (at 445).

In applying the *Lemon* test to various state programs to aid
parochial schools, the Court acknowledged the possibility, as asserted by
the states, that their "purpose" was secular; that is, assuring that all children, including those in church schools, are provided with good educations in secular subjects. But in applying these principles to a particular
Rhode Island program supplementing the salaries of teachers in certain
secular subjects, the Court concluded that assuring that the teachers
would *not* inculcate religious doctrines at state expense would require a
level of state supervision of practices within church schools as to amount
to "excessive entanglement" between church and state. In effect the chief
justice argued that it is simply too difficult to keep religious teachings
separate from secular ones in religious schools founded on religious principles. Because the Court majority believed that assuring that state
funds would not be used for religious teaching would require an intrusive
state regulatory supervision of the schools, there would inevitably be an
excessive entanglement between church and state.

In *Zelman v. Simmons-Harris* (2002), however, Ohio, with the
Supreme Court's approval, found a different way around the "entanglement" issue caused by the need to prevent government from supporting
religion. By giving the money instead to parents in the form of a school
voucher, the state isolated itself from the ultimate decision concerning who
would receive the funds. Since it was not the state directly that gave the
money to the religious school, there was no need for the state subsequently
to police the uses to which the money was put (for a fuller discussion of
Zelman, see Question 6 below).

Another and somewhat different manifestation of what the *Lemon*
test terms "excessive entanglement" can be found in *Larkin v. Grendel's
Den, Inc.* (1982). Grendel's Den was a restaurant in Harvard Square

in Cambridge, Massachusetts. Under Massachusetts law "[p]remises . . . located within a radius of five hundred feet of a church or school shall not be licensed for sale of alcoholic beverages if the governing body of such church or school files written objection thereto." Because of the objection by the adjoining Holy Cross Armenian Catholic parish, an application by Grendel's Den for a liquor license was denied. Although the courts below the U.S. Supreme Court did not deny the existence of a secular purpose behind limiting liquor establishments near churches or schools, they did find that the "veto" authority given to churches conferred "a direct and substantial benefit upon religions" (at 120). In other words it had in the words of Chief Justice Burger's Opinion of the Court, "a 'primary' and 'principal' effect of advancing religion." In addition, however, the Court expressed concern about "the entanglement implications of a statute vesting significant government authority in churches." Chief Justice Burger concluded that "[t]his statute enmeshes churches in the exercise of substantial government powers contrary to our consistent interpretation of the Establishment Clause; '[t]he objective is to prevent, as far as possible, the intrusion of either [Church or State] into the precincts of the other.' *Lemon v. Kurtzman,* 403 U.S., at 614" (at 126).

The Court's frequent reliance upon the *Lemon* test for determining when government actions violate the Establishment clause has produced considerable controversy on the Court. Justice Antonin Scalia dismisses the *Lemon* test, arguing that "[o]ur religion-clause jurisprudence has become bedeviled (so to speak) by reliance upon formalistic abstractions that are not derived from, but positively conflict with, our long-accepted constitutional traditions" (*Lee v. Weisman,* at 644, 1992). He argues instead that the Constitution "affirmatively mandates accommodation [in the Free Exercise Clause (see below, Question 2)], not merely tolerance of all religions . . . " (*Lamb's Chapel v. Center Moriches Union Free School District,* at 402, 1993).

Certainly in some of its decisions such as that upholding prayer at the beginning of legislative sessions, the Court has conveniently ignored the *Lemon* test. But except under circumstances where the Court finds historic practice mandates some limited accommodation of religious practices, the *Lemon* test remains a frequently used guidepost for distinguishing unconstitutional establishment of religion from policies promoting secular values which find parallels in religious principles.

Question 2   *Are there limits on a person's right to practice his or her religion?*

The meaning of the First Amendment Free Exercise clause has been the subject of only slightly less dispute than that of the Establishment clause. Clearly the state cannot make it a crime for anyone to profess any religious belief. But though it is one thing to profess, it is quite something else to practice. When the line is crossed between mere expression of belief to actual practice (the performance of some act or the refusal to perform some action for religious reasons), the consensus within the courts about freedom of religious exercise breaks down.

As was true of the other principal First Amendment freedom, freedom of speech, when there is agreement over the definition of what is encompassed by free exercise of religion, the Court in recent years has been nearly unanimous in denying the government the right to restrict that freedom except for some narrowly defined "compelling state interest." But some on the Court argue that free exercise protects only the right to believe or profess while others argue it includes the right to practice.

In 1963 in *Sherbert v. Verner,* the Supreme Court seemed to extend to the right to practice religion its most stringent protection. In that case a member of the Seventh Day Adventist religion was denied unemployment benefits because she had refused a job which would have required her to work on Saturday, her sabbath. By a 7 to 2 vote the Supreme Court ruled that the denial of benefits amounted to an unconstitutional abridgment of her right to exercise her religion freely. In other words the Court ruled that the state had impermissibly conditioned her right to a benefit upon her agreement to ignore a central tenet of her religious beliefs.

Even though the unemployment compensation regulations placed no explicit or direct limitation on the free exercise of religion, Justice Brennan, writing for the Court majority argued that

> Sherbert's ineligibility for benefits derive[d] solely from the practice of her religion. . . , [and] the pressure upon her to forego that practice . . . [was] unmistakable. The ruling forces her to choose between following the precepts of her religion and forfeiting benefits, on the one hand, and abandoning one of the precepts of her religion in order to accept work, on the other hand. Governmental imposition of such a choice puts the same kind of burden upon the free exercise of religion as would a fine imposed against appellant for her Saturday worship" (at 737–38).

Because of the Court's ruling Ms. Sherbert would receive unemployment benefits even though she had in effect refused work. In his dissenting opinion Justice Harlan argued that this in effect amounted to requiring the state to show preference for those asserting religious reasons for refusing work over other reasons for refusing to accept a job. A single mother who refused a job because she could not find a baby-sitter would be denied benefits by the state, but a woman who refused work because of religious scruples would receive benefits. In Justice John Harlan's words as a result of the majority's ruling, "[t]he state . . . must *single out* for financial assistance those whose behavior is religiously motivated, even though it denies such assistance to others whose identical behavior (in this case inability to work on Saturdays) is not religiously motivated." As Justice Potter Stewart asserted in his separate concurring opinion, such preference for religion runs counter to the Court's precedents interpreting the Establishment clause. Stewart himself was not troubled by that conflict because he felt the Court had gone too far in mandating strict separation of church and state. He believed that "the guarantee of religious liberty embodied in the free exercise clause affirmatively requires government to create an atmosphere of hospitality and accommodation to individual religious belief or disbelief" (at 740).

Sherbert v. Verner demonstrates that sometimes there is a tension between the Establishment clause and the Free Exercise clause. Sometimes treating everyone the same will penalize those whose religions require that they act differently from the majority. But to provide exceptions to rules applicable to all for those motivated by religious principles can be interpreted as giving special privileges to those belonging to certain religions. If the state gives special treatment to the religious, isn't it guilty of violating the Establishment clause?

The majority opinion written by Justice Brennan had in effect held that only a "compelling state interest" could justify the government's refusal to carve out exceptions to generally applicable law when applying a law to a particular individual would compel him to act in a way contrary to his religion. This decision gives special status to religious beliefs over other interests and beliefs, but the Court majority in *Sherbert* felt such special treatment is required by the Free Exercise clause.

In a subsequent case in 1990, *Employment Division of Department of Human Resources of Oregon v. Smith* (1990), a narrow Supreme Court majority appears to have abandoned Justice Brennan's approach to free exercise challenges to laws which do not single out religion for special discriminatory treatment but which nonetheless have the effect of penalizing action motivated by religion. This case involved the denial of unemployment benefits to two native Americans who had been fired from a privately operated drug rehabilitation program because they had smoked peyote. Ingesting peyote was an integral part of their particular native American religious ceremonies, but peyote is an illegal drug. Because they were fired for cause, they were denied unemployment benefits as would other workers who were fired for misbehavior. Because the behavior for which they were fired was required by their religion, however, they claimed that to penalize them by denying unemployment benefits would amount to a state punishment of them for freely exercising their religion.

The principal conflict within the Supreme Court over this case concerned the applicable standard by which the Court should judge government conduct under the Free Exercise clause. In his Opinion of the Court, Justice Antonin Scalia in effect rejected the compelling state interest test applied by Justice William Brennan in *Sherbert v. Verner*. To Justice Scalia, "[t]he free exercise of religion means, first and foremost, the right to believe and profess whatever religious doctrine one desires" (*Employment Division . . . v. Smith,* at 877). But it does not immunize religiously motivated conduct from generally applicable laws which apply equally to the religious and nonreligious. Unless the law singles out a religious practice for special punishment, there is no basis for a free exercise challenge and no need for the government to show some compelling state interest to justify applying the law even to those who raise a religious objection. To challenge the application of a law to you as a violation of your free exercise of religion, you must first show that the government treated you differently from others who do not share your religious conviction.

An example of a government policy that could not survive even the less sweeping approach of Justice Antonin Scalia arose in the case of the *Church of the Lukumi Babalu Aye v. City of Hialeah* (1993). In response to the announced plans of believers in Santeria, a church that believed in and engaged in ritual animal sacrifice, to build a church in Hialeah, Florida, the Hialeah City Council passed an ordinance which among other things banned the killing of animals for ritual sacrifice when the killing was not for "the primary purpose of food consumption" (at 527).

While under the *Smith* test a law banning killing of animals could no doubt survive constitutional challenge even if it did serve to ban religious ceremonies involving animal sacrifice, to survive constitutional challenge the law could not single out religious sacrificial killings for special prohibition. According to the Court in *Church of the Lukumi,* this is precisely what the law did. In his Opinion of the Court, Justice Anthony Kennedy acknowledged that even though the law referred directly to "sacrifice" and "ritual," this alone did not suffice to find that it singled out religious killing for special prohibition because such terms can have secular applications. Taken as a whole, however, in light of the history surrounding the law's enactment, it was clear that the law was designed to target the practices of a disfavored religion. The city council resolution accompanying the enactment of the statute referred to the practices of "certain religious groups . . . " (at 534, 535).

Significantly, according to Justice Kennedy's opinion, the city defended its ordinance in court as designed to protect public health and to prevent cruelty to animals. If such were indeed the goals, however, according to Justice Kennedy, the ordinance was "under inclusive," in that "[t]hey fail to prohibit non-religious conduct that endangers these interests to similar or greater degree than Santaria sacrifice does" (at 543). He noted that both fishing and extermination of mice and rats are permitted by the statute. In addition "[t]he health risks posed by the improper disposal of animal carcasses are the same whether Santaria sacrifice or some nonreligious killing preceded it. The city does not, however, prohibit hunters from bringing animal kill to their houses, nor does it regulate disposal after their activity" (at 544).

In sum it appears clear that it was the religious motivation for animal destruction that offended the majority of the community and not the destruction of animals itself. For this reason the Court concluded that the ordinance in question was one that targeted a religion for discriminatory treatment.

The controversy within the Court over the appropriate constitutional standard for protecting the free exercise of religion has been extended to Capitol Hill. Religious leaders of many denominations were troubled by the threat potentially posed to free exercise of religion by the Court's approach announced in *Employment Division . . . v. Smith* (1989). An odd coalition of liberal and conservative clergy and civil libertarians succeeded in persuading Congress in 1993 to pass the Religious Freedom Restoration Act of 1993 (RFRA), which was designed to restore the constitutional protections for minority religions provided by *Sherbert v. Verner.* Because Section 5 of the Fourteenth Amendment gives to Congress the power to "enforce, by appropriate legislation . . ." the provisions of the amendment, Congress asserted that it could advance the free exercise of religion by restoring "the compelling state interest test" from *Sherbert* in challenges to even generally applicable or "neutral" government actions which "substantially burden religious exercise" (*City of Boerne v. Flores,* at 515, 1997). Although at that time in the area of "affirmative action" in race and gender discrimination cases there was precedent for Congress to define rights and liberties more broadly than the Court felt the Constitution required (see *Fullilove v. Klutznick,* 1980), the Court in *City of Boerne v. Flores* (1997) argued that the power to enforce is different from the power to define a right or liberty. "Legislation which alters the meaning of the Free Exercise clause cannot be said to be enforcing the clause. Congress does not enforce a constitutional right by changing what that right is. It has been given the power 'to enforce, not the power to determine what constitutes a constitutional violation'" (at 519).

Although the Court in effect focused not on the definition of free exercise but rather on the limits of congressional power to revise constitutional interpretations announced by the Court, the effect of the *City of Boerne* case was to leave in place for now at least the interpretation of the Free Exercise clause adopted in *Employment Division . . . v. Smith.* One's right to exercise freely one's religion is largely confined to the right to believe as one pleases and to be free from discriminatory treatment by government because of one's religious beliefs. Society is free, however, to make it difficult for those in minority religions to practice what they believe as long as the restrictions on conduct apply in the same way to all believers and nonbelievers. Whether this provides enough protection for those of us whose beliefs dictate ways of living different from those approved by society in general will no doubt continue to be debated within the U.S. Supreme Court and beyond.

Question 3   *Doesn't banning "voluntary prayer" in public schools interfere with children's freedom of religion?*

Images of religious persecution and sectarian violence throughout the world seem to many Americans far removed from the simple innocent act of little children invoking God's blessings on their activities as they embark on their school day. Many, perhaps most of us, find little danger in a child being exposed to a simple prayer. Many believe such an act of quiet reverence, as long as it is not coerced, can set a tone of respect and reflection for young children. If nothing else it can quiet them down and ready them to learn. For these reasons many find it very difficult to understand why prayer is not permitted in public schools. Indeed, many find the absence of prayer to be an affront to their deeply held religious convictions.

In 1962 in *Engel v. Vitale,* however, the U.S. Supreme Court, in one of its more controversial decisions, declared even formally voluntary prayer in the public schools to be a violation of the Establishment clause of the First Amendment. This Court decision has provoked much debate and repeated efforts to amend the Constitution in order to overturn the Court's decision and restore "voluntary prayer" to the public schools.

Engel overturned a "non-denominational prayer" written by the State Board of Regents for use at the beginning of the school day in all the public school classrooms in New York. The prayer was a simple one: "Almighty God, we acknowledge our dependence upon Thee, and we beg Thy blessings upon us, our parents, our teachers and our country" (at 422).

Although this prayer may seen innocuous to most, it was the contention of Steven Engel and other parents of children in a New York school district, that the state policy requiring or permitting use of the Regents' prayer "must be struck down as a violation of the Establishment clause because that prayer was composed by government officials as a part of a governmental program to further religious beliefs" (at 425). Justice Hugo Black writing for the Court majority agreed because under the Establishment clause "it is no part of the business of government to compose official prayers for any group of the American people to recite as a part of a religious program carried on by government" (at 425).

Justice Black recited the history of religious persecution in England and its continuation in early America as the previous victims of persecution used their new power here to impose their religious beliefs on others. It was in part that history, he contended, that led to the First Amendment Establishment and Free Exercise clauses. The First Amendment religion clauses state that "Congress shall make no law respecting an establishment of religion, or prohibiting the free exercise thereof."

Because the New York school prayer law in question had been limited by the New York Court of Appeals to requiring recitation of the prayer only by "voluntary" participants, Justice Black acknowledged the possibility that it did not run afoul of the Free Exercise clause of the First Amendment applied to the states through the Due Process clause of the Fourteenth Amendment. He asserted, however, that even so-called "voluntary" public school prayer clearly violated the Establishment clause of the First Amendment.

> The Establishment Clause, unlike the Free Exercise Clause, does not depend upon a showing of direct governmental compulsion and is violated by enactment of laws which establish an official religion whether those laws operate directly to coerce nonbelieving individuals or not. . . . The purposes underlying the Establishment Clause go much further than that. Its first and most immediate purpose rested on a belief that a union of government and religion tends to destroy government and to degrade religion (at 431).

To understand Justice Black's contention that a union between religion and government tends to degrade religion, consider how many Americans feel about public officials. Is it really good for religion to be closely associated with them? At a more serious level Justice Black contended that in both England and in America "whenever government had allied itself with one particular form of religion, the inevitable result had been that it incurred the hatred, disrespect and even contempt of those who held contrary beliefs" (at 431).

Although Justice Black's opinion noted that the prayer was in the strictest sense voluntary and therefore not violative of the Free Exercise clause of the First Amendment, he nonetheless questioned whether any school prayer can be truly voluntary. "When the power, prestige and financial support of government is placed behind a particular religious belief, the indirect coercive pressure upon religious minorities to conform to the prevailing officially approved religion is plain" (at 431). While one might doubt the significance of that pressure on adults, a point made by the Court in its decision permitting prayers in legislative chambers (see *Marsh v. Chambers,* 1983), pressure on children not to appear "different," and, even more so, pressure not to offend their teachers, could well prove overwhelming.

It was the coercive nature of such indirect pressure that led in part to the Supreme Court's decision striking down a public school graduation prayer in *Lee v. Weisman* (1992). Distinguishing the circumstances of a public school graduation from a prayer at a legislative session, Justice Kennedy wrote:

> The atmosphere at the opening of a session of a state legislature where adults are free to enter and leave with little comment and for

any number of reasons cannot compare with the constraining potential of the one school event [graduation] most important for the
student to attend. The influence and force of a formal exercise in a
school graduation are far greater than the prayer exercise we con-
doned in *Marsh*. . . . At a high school graduation, teachers and prin-
cipals must and do maintain a high degree of control over the
precise contents of the program, the speeches, the timing, the movements, the dress, and the decorum of the students. In this atmosphere the state imposed character of an invocation and benediction
by clergy selected by the school combine to make the prayer a state-
sanctioned religious exercise in which the student was left with no
alternative but to submit . . . (at 597).

Justice Scalia's dissent vigorously challenges this notion of coercion
as a basis for rejecting the constitutionality of school-sponsored voluntary prayer. Since no one in *Lee* is being forced to actually recite the
prayer, he sees no coercion. All, in fact, students are required to do is
maintain a respectful silence while those who choose to pray, do so.

The Court's notion that a student who simply sits in "respectful
silence" during the invocation and benediction (when all others are
standing) has somehow joined—or would somehow be perceived as
having joined is nothing short of ludicrous. We indeed live in a vulgar age. But surely "our social conventions," have not coarsened to
the point that anyone who does not stand on his chair and shout
obscenities can reasonably be deemed to have assented to everything said in his presence. Since the court does not dispute that
students exposed to prayer at graduation ceremonies retain
(despite "subtle coercive pressures") the free will to sit, there is
absolutely no basis for the Court's decision (at 637).

Others in the Court majority placed less emphasis on coercion than
did Justice Kennedy. They emphasized rather the need for the state to
maintain neutrality on religious matters. For the state to sponsor prayer
at public events, is for the state to send a message favoring or endorsing
religion. To the nonreligious or to religious minorities, such sponsorship
lessens their relative standing or status in the community.

Because the Court in its school prayer cases has emphasized government authorship, endorsement, and even coercion in support of particular
prayers, some have sought to blunt this argument by proposing that students themselves be permitted to initiate, select, or compose prayers for
school use. Rather than the state mandating a prayer or prayers, which is
viewed by many as "establishment" of religion, if students themselves
compose and lead the prayers, this could be viewed as their engaging in

the "free exercise" of religion. To prevent students from voluntarily pray-
ing as they please is viewed by some as suppressing religious belief and
expression.

One can, however, anticipate a host of possible problems with this
approach. Who, for example, would decide who is to lead others in prayer?
What if the student composing the prayer would choose to pray in a manner profoundly offensive to others? Some Christians might want to pray
for the conversion of Jews. Some Islamic students might pray for victory
in a "holy war." Might not some atheistic students reasonably demand
"equal time" and offend the deeply held religious convictions of some of
their classmates?

To the argument that not permitting organized prayer interferes
with the free exercise of the religious convictions of a majority of students, supporters of the Court's school prayer decisions sometimes respond that all are free to pray whenever they please quietly to
themselves. To those desiring public devotion and dedication to God, this
enforced silence concerning what they view as the most important part of
their lives is an affront.

In its decisions concerning religious exercises in the public schools,
the Court has not contended that the public schools must be blind to the
role of religion in American society and in the people's lives. Just one year
after its decision in *Engel v. Vitale* the Court applied the same reasoning
to strike down a Pennsylvania law mandating that verses of the Bible be
read in the public schools, without comment by teachers or administrators, at the opening of each school day. *School District of Abington township, Penn., et al. v. Schemp et al.,* 374 U.S. 203, at 205 (1963).

In rejecting a claim that forbidding Bible reading at the beginning
of the school day or the recitation of a prayer establishes "a religion of
secularism," Justice Clark wrote:

> We agree of course that the State may not establish a "religion of
> secularism" in the sense of affirmatively opposing or showing hostil-
> ity to religion, thus "preferring those who believe in no religion over
> those who believe. . . . " We do not agree, however, that this decision
> in any sense has that effect. In addition, it might well be said that
> one's education is not complete without a study of comparative reli-
> gion or the history of religion and its relationship to the advance-
> ment of civilization. It certainly may be said that the Bible is worthy
> of study for its literary and historic qualities. Nothing we have said
> here indicates that such study of the Bible or of religion, when pre-
> sented objectively as part of a secular program of education, may not
> be effected consistently with the First Amendment (at 225).

The Court has made it clear that the Establishment clause does not
permit government to sponsor religious devotions in the public schools. It

has, however, left the door open to public schools educating students concerning the role played by religion in our society and history. To the devotedly religious this walling off of an important part of their children's day from public devotion to God may be deeply troubling. Although the Free Exercise clause permits them to educate their children in a religious environment, the Establishment clause forbids the state to provide such an environment for them.

Question 4   *If secular groups are allowed access to the schools, shouldn't religious groups have the same rights?*

When the United States Supreme Court decided that the Constitution forbids government-sponsored prayer in the schools, it did so in part because of the particular vulnerability of children to pressure to conform from both peers and school authority figures, such as teachers. When on the other hand the Court found no constitutional impediment to prayer at the beginning of legislative sessions, it emphasized the fact that adults are not forced to participate and indeed are free to absent themselves from the chamber during the brief prayer.

Among the issues that must be considered as we look at religious use of public schools is the question of whether the constitutional prohibition of an "establishment of religion" actually places religions at a disadvantage compared to other private groups when it comes to access to public facilities. Are religious viewpoints actually discriminated against in public debate? Does barring religious groups from public expression in public schools or other government facilities violate the free speech rights of such groups? On the other hand does the Free Exercise clause, which guarantees the right of all to their religious beliefs without fear of persecution by government, place religions and religious expression in a privileged position relative to other viewpoints in society?

In 1984 Congress passed the Equal Access Act, which was designed in particular to prohibit discrimination against religious groups who seek to hold meetings and form clubs within public schools when such opportunity was open to other "noncurriculum related" groups. According to the Act,

> It shall be unlawful for any public secondary school which receives Federal financial assistance and which has a limited open forum to deny equal access or a fair opportunity to, or discriminate against, any students who wish to conduct a meeting within the limited open forum on the basis of religious, political, philosophical, or other content of speech at such meetings. *Westside Community Board of Education v. Mergens,* at 235 (1989).

Under the Equal Access Act's provisions, "a limited open forum" exists whenever a public secondary school "grants an offering or opportunity for one or more non-curriculum related student groups to meet on school premises during non-instructional time . . ." (at 235).

This act of Congress had the effect of extending to secondary schools the results of a Supreme Court decision in *Widmar v. Vincent* (1981), which on free speech grounds invalidated a state university policy excluding "student use of facilities 'for purposes of religious worship or religious teaching'" (*Widmar* at 235). School policies both here and in *Widmar* were no doubt designed to avoid running afoul of the Supreme Court's Establishment clause rulings, which in the school area in particular had been concerned with the need of avoiding any union between government and religion. In considering a challenge to the *exclusion* of religion from the schools on free speech grounds, the Court was careful to be sure that the establishment of religion line was not crossed. In pressing in the university setting what the Court in *Widmar* itself termed an "equal access policy," the Court found no violation of the Establishment clause, but it noted that "[u]niversity students are, of course, young adults. They are less impressionable than younger students and should be able to appreciate that the University's policy is one of neutrality toward religion" (*Widmar,* at 274, n. 14).

In judging the application of the Equal Access Act to a public high school, the Court had to consider whether Congress was correct in assuming that permitting religious groups to use public school facilities would not be misunderstood by high school students as amounting to a government "endorsement" of religion or of particular religious beliefs. In part to assure that this misunderstanding would not occur, the Equal Access Act specifically forbade school authorities or teachers from "promoting, leading or participating in a [religious] meeting." Their involvement had to be confined to merely a "custodial role" (*Widmar,* at 237). By merely permitting religious groups, like other groups, to take advantage of the "limited public forum" provided by after-school activities, the Equal Access Act, in the Court's view, does not endorse religion in violation of the Establishment clause. As Justice Sandra Day O'Connor wrote in her Opinion of the Court,

> There is a crucial difference between *government* speech endorsing religion, which the Establishment Clause forbids, and *private* speech endorsing religion, which the Free Speech and Free Exercise clauses protect. We think that secondary school students are mature enough and are likely to understand that a school does not endorse or support student speech that it merely permits on a nondiscriminatory basis.
>   . . . Under the Act, a school with a limited open forum may not lawfully deny access to a Jewish students' club, a Young Democrats club, or a philosophy club devoted to the study of Nietzsche. To the extent that a religious club is merely one of many different

student-initiated voluntary clubs, students should perceive no message of government endorsement of religion (at 253).

The Equal Access Act, however, does not tell us what the Constitution requires. In upholding the application of the Equal Access Act, the Court of necessity had to interpret the act itself. In deciding whether it conforms to the Constitution, it had to interpret the Constitution.

In his dissenting opinion, Justice John Paul Stevens expressed concern that the Court majority misconstrued the Equal Access Act as requiring opening of schools to religious and controversial groups whenever it permits noncourse-related clubs to exist on campus. Justice Stevens argued that there is a fundamental difference between a chess club, for example, and a Young Republican or Young Socialist club. Congress, he contended, did not mean that the presence of a chess club or a scuba diving club would trigger the requirement that virtually all groups, however controversial, would be permitted. On the other hand, to permit a religious club to form in a setting, such as the one before the Court, where the religious organization in question would be the only "advocacy" group actually on campus, could impermissably lead to the perception of endorsement of its religious message by students. Precisely because there were not in fact a broad array of advocacy groups and clubs at Westside High School, forcing this school to permit a Christian club to form might well send a message of state endorsement and support of particular religious beliefs.

More recently in *Lamb's Chapel v. Center Moriches Union Free School District* (1993) the Court again addressed the question of when or whether religious viewpoints can be banned from schools and other public institutions. This case squarely addressed the constitutional issue and, unlike *Westside Community Board of Education v. Mergens,* did not require interpretation of the Equal Access Act. The question in this case was, when may government forbid use of school facilities after school by a religious organization? In this case a religious group sought to use the public school during after-school hours to show a film series on family values and child rearing. Under New York State law school facilities can be used by private groups for 10 different purposes, which do not include religious purposes. Discussion by private groups of child rearing and other family issues would be permitted, but because the school district viewed the proposed film series as church related, it was barred. The issue according to the Court was whether this restriction on the use of the facilities to express a religious viewpoint on a subject matter for which the school facility may be used violated the Free Speech clause of the First Amendment.

Although the Court argued that government may decide that certain subject matter are not suitable topics for discussion in fora that are not fully open to the public, ". . . access to a nonpublic forum can be based on subject matter and speaker identity [only] so long as the distinctions drawn are reasonable in light of the purposes served by the forum and are viewpoint neutral (citations omitted)" (*Lamb's Chapel*). Although the Court acknowledged that under New York State policy all religions and religious views are treated alike, this does not answer the question ". . . whether it discriminates on the basis of viewpoint to permit school property to be used for the presentation of all views about family issues and child rearing except those dealing with the subject matter from a religious standpoint" (at 394).

In other words in opening the schools to a discussion of family values in after-school hours when students were no longer required to attend, could the state bar the expression of religious perspectives? To the Court the answer was no. According to Justice O'Connor's Opinion for the Court, "[t]he principle that has emerged from our cases 'is that the First Amendment forbids the government to regulate speech in ways that favor some viewpoints or ideas at the expense of others'" (*City Council of Los Angeles v. Taxpayers for Vincent,* at 495, 1984).

Unlike the State of New York, the Court was not concerned that opening the school during after-school hours to this expression of a religious viewpoint might amount to an unconstitutional establishment of religion. The position adopted by the Court was one of neutrality. The school would be available to all points of view concerning relevant subject matters. To open the schools in this context to church groups, as well as others, could not be seen as government "endorsement" of religion.

So long as government itself does not advance a religious perspective, it appears that the constitutional requirement of separation of church and state permits access to public facilities by church groups on the same basis as other groups to express their points of view. So long as government permits private groups to use public facilities to express their points of view, it appears that the constitutional protection of freedom of speech requires access be given to religious as well as secular groups.

Providing "equal access" to religious groups to noninstructional after-class fora, however, requires that access be provided to nonreligious groups as well. Gay, lesbian, bisexual, transsexual and other groups have points of view on family values and child rearing as well as do religious groups. Nazi groups can have views on the meaning of patriotism as well as the Boy Scouts can. What both the Equal Access Act passed by Congress and upheld as constitutional by the Court and Court decisions interpreting the Free Speech and Free Exercise clauses of the First Amendment themselves now mean is that no group with a point of view on issues open for discussion after hours in our public schools or other public fora may be barred. In theory at least, it may well be that in seeking an audience for religious messages in the public schools religious groups and their supporters in government may have opened the door to less popular groups as well. On the other hand, because in many communities religious perspectives dominate, we have to wonder whether equal access can turn into special privilege with the public forum becoming dominated by religious expression. If religious advocacy does come to dominate the after-school activities within our public schools, have we jeopardized the separation of church and state?

Question 5 *Doesn't teaching evolution in the schools amount to the establishment of secular religion?*

The Scopes Trial, the subject of the popular movie *Inherit the Wind,* made in 1960, pitted two giants of American history, William Jennings Bryan and Clarence Darrow, in a courtroom battle over science and religion in America. On one side were those who accepted conventional scientific teaching concerning evolution of the human species; on the other were those who believed in a literal interpretation of the story of Genesis in the Bible. To those who revere the Bible as literal historical truth, Darwin's theory of evolution is blasphemous in that it denies that the story of Adam and Eve in Genesis actually describes the origins of the human species. Because such teaching challenges the deeply held religious convictions of many, state legislatures in some states have banned the teaching of evolution in science classes.

Even in the last decade of the twentieth century many felt so strongly that evolution was antireligious that they succeeded in persuading some textbook publishers to omit discussion of evolution in scientific textbooks and in the state of Kansas succeeded for a time in removing discussion of evolution from the state-mandated science curriculum. Although legislative efforts to actually ban teaching evolution in the schools were rejected by the U.S. Supreme Court in *Epperson v. Arkansas* (1968), efforts to influence school scientific curriculum to better conform to "fundamentalist" religious teaching did not stop.

From a constitutional law perspective, cases involving conflicts between science and religion present difficult problems. To people having a deeply held religious conviction that evolution is not true and contrary to God's law, having the state nonetheless teach this in the school can be seen as a threat to their religious freedom. Are not their children being indoctrinated by government command in a belief system that attacks fundamental religious principles? On the other hand, to the scientist or the student of science, isn't omitting the dominant scientific explanation for human origins and biological development from science classes, because it conflicts with religious beliefs, the same as an unconstitutional establishment of religion?

Epperson v. Arkansas concerned a constitutional challenge to an Arkansas law passed in 1928 which ". . . [made] it unlawful for a teacher in any state-supported school or university 'to teach the theory or doctrine that mankind ascended or descended from a lower order of animals,' or 'to adopt or use in any such institution a textbook that teaches' this theory" (at 99). Despite the fact that there was no record of any person actually being prosecuted for offending the statute in question, the Court accepted a case from a teacher who felt under the threat of prosecution because she assigned a text which included a discussion of evolution.

The Supreme Court decided that the state ban on teaching evolution ran afoul of the First Amendment. In the words of Justice Abe Fortas in the Opinion of the Court,

> . . . the law must be stricken because of its conflict with the constitutional prohibition of state laws respecting an establishment of religion or prohibiting the free exercise thereof. The overriding fact is that Arkansas' law selects from the body of knowledge a particular segment which it proscribes for the sole reason that it is deemed to conflict with a particular religious doctrine; that is, with a particular interpretation of the Book of Genesis by a particular religious group" (at 103).

Having failed to ban completely the teaching of evolution in the public schools, those who were deeply troubled on religious and perhaps other grounds sought other means to lessen the threat they perceived coming from teaching children evolution. In 1987 the Supreme Court, in *Edwards v. Aguillard* (1987), heard a challenge to the Balanced Treatment for Creation-Science and Evolution-Science in Public School Instruction Act passed by the Louisiana legislature in 1982. According to Justice Brennan's Opinion of the Court, "[t]he Creationism Act . . . [forbade] the teaching of the theory of evolution in the public schools unless accompanied by instruction in 'creation science.'" The Act did not require the teaching of either evolution or so-called creation science. It did, however, require "[i]f either is taught . . . the other must also be taught . . ." (at 581).

In a sense this Balanced Treatment Act responded to the Court's decision in *Epperson*. Rather than banning evolution outright from the classroom, this new law merely required that so-called "creation science" receive equal attention. This case placed the Court in the difficult position of judging what is and what is not a legitimate scientific theory. It also placed the Court in the position of challenging the stated rationale of the legislation before it. The legislature could claim that it was merely responding to genuine controversy within the community by requiring that both sides be heard. The legislature in fact asserted that its purpose was to advance "academic freedom."

In deciding whether or not the act violated the Establishment clause of the First Amendment, the Court majority applied what has come to be called the *Lemon* test. Although the *Lemon* test is discussed at greater length above (see Question 1), we must briefly look at it now to see how it was applied in this case. According to Chief Justice Burger's opinion in *Lemon v. Kurtzman* (1971),

> Every Analysis . . . [applying the Establishment Clause] must begin with consideration of the cumulative criteria developed by the Court over many years. Three such tests may be learned from our cases. First, the statute must have a secular legislative purpose; second, its principal or primary effect must be one that neither advances nor inhibits religion; finally, the statute must not foster "an excessive government entanglement with religion" (at 612–13).

In *Edwards* Justice Brennan applied the so-called "purpose prong" of the *Lemon* test to invalidate the Louisiana Balanced Treatment statute. Under this test the Court asks whether there is a secular legislative purpose or whether the purpose of the statute is to advance religion in general or some particular religious belief. In Justice Brennan's words,

> In this case, the purpose of the Creationism Act was to restructure the scientific curriculum to conform with a particular religious view point. Out of the many possible science subjects taught in the public schools, the legislature chose to affect the teaching of the one scientific theory that historically has been opposed by certain religious sects. . . . [T]he Creationism Act is designed *either* to promote the theory of creation science which embodies a particular religious tenet by requiring that creation science be taught whenever evolution is taught *or* to prohibit the teaching of a scientific theory disfavored by certain religious sects by forbidding the teaching of evolution when creation science is not also taught. The Establishment Clause, however, "forbids *alike* the preference of a religious doctrine *or* the prohibition of theory which is deemed antagonistic to a particular dogma." (Citing *Epperson,* at 106–07, in *Edwards,* at 593.)

Justice Brennan rejected the State's contention that its purpose was to promote academic freedom by exposing students to both sides of the evolution debate. He noted that the Balanced Treatment Act provided funding for the development of curriculum guides for creation science without providing comparable guides for evolution (at 588). Further the act specifically forbade school authorities from discriminating ". . . against anyone who 'chooses to be a creation-scientist,' but fails to protect those who choose to teach evolution . . ." (at 588). In further support of his rejection of the academic freedom purpose advanced by the state, Justice

Brennan cited evidence from the legislative history, including statements by leading advocates of creation science, that their religious views must be included in the curriculum.

If advancing academic freedom had been the real purpose behind the act, then Brennan argued it would ". . . enhanc[e] the freedom of teachers to teach what they will" (at 586). Instead the act forbids teachers to teach evolution unless they also teach creation science. In so doing it restricts the freedom of teachers rather than enhances it.

Although Justice Brennan's view of academic freedom more closely conforms to conventional understanding of the term than does the state's emphasis on "balanced" presentation of contending viewpoints, the position of the state cannot simply be dismissed as wholly without merit. Would a law requiring that students be exposed to both Northern and Southern perspectives concerning the causes of the Civil War be consistent with academic freedom? It would restrict a teacher's freedom to teach what he or she pleases, but wouldn't such a law be better than simply allowing teachers who hold a purely regional perspective to "indoctrinate" students? Are not all teachers restricted in what they can teach by course descriptions or in lower grades by school board or administration imposed "lesson plans"?

From the religious perspective the banning of their understanding of the origins of human beings amounts to the adoption of an alien and purely secular orthodoxy. Many now contend that the courts have imposed a quasi-religion, "secular humanism," on the schools. But if public institutions are permitted to teach religiously founded perspectives, the Court majority in effect asks, how are we to maintain the separation of church and state mandated by the First Amendment? According to the Court's decisions, public schools may teach science, but the Constitution requires that the teaching of beliefs based on faith be left to others.

Question 6   *Isn't government funding for social services provided by religious organizations endangering the constitutional separation of church and state?*

One of the principal campaign themes of George W. Bush, as he sought the presidency, was a claim that private groups and charities, especially those based on religious principles, could deliver social services better than government bureaucracies. President Bush pursued his "faith-based-initiatives" once in office but these proposals proved highly controversial. Opponents believed that assisting religious organizations in helping others violated the separation of church and state. Giving taxpayer funds to religious groups, they argued, was precisely the kind of program which the Establishment clause of the First Amendment was designed to prevent (see Question 1 above). Proponents, on the other hand, pointed to a long list of existing programs in which public money has long been channeled both directly and indirectly to and through religious organizations. Many students, for example, have used their federal government Pell grants to help pay for their educations at church-sponsored or -affiliated universities. Hospitals owned and operated by religious organizations provide vital medical care in many American cities for which they are reimbursed by Medicare and Medicaid. Government-funded research is carried out at both religiously affiliated hospitals and universities. Tracing how and why the Court has come to accept such connections between church and state will help us come to an understanding of the current status of separation of church and state in America.

The 1980s brought movement away from the relatively simple concept of a "wall of separation" between church and state. More conservative justices on the Court argued that accommodation between church and state does not violate the Establishment clause. On the other hand, in applying the Free Exercise clause these same justices, in many instances, made it more difficult for citizens successfully to assert a constitutional exemption from laws when compliance would conflict with religious principles.

While the prohibition against an establishment of religion primarily restrains any attempt by the majority to use government power to advance its purely religious values, the protection for free exercise primarily protects religious minorities from state oppression and coercion. The potential threat to separation of church and state presented by trends in the judicial interpretation of the religion clauses of the First Amendment from the 1980s through today may be one of increased links between religion and government and possibly decreased need to accommodate those whose religious beliefs (or disbeliefs) deviate far from the views of the mainstream of American society. Of course, as we saw above in Question 2, a willingness to accommodate religious beliefs by giving people the right to disregard certain laws which may conflict with their religions can, itself, be viewed as unconstitutional preferential treatment of religion.

It is important, however, to remember that insistence on a strict separation is a relatively recent development in American constitutional interpretation. The first case cited in Question 1 of this chapter calling for a wall of separation, *Everson v. Board of Education* (1947), actually permitted a very limited program of state support for student transportation to religious schools. The case probably most frequently cited in the popular press as a sign of the rigid separation of church and state, *Engel v. Vitale* (1962), which forbade state-sponsored prayer in public schools, still holds today and was reinforced by *Wallace v. Jaffree* (1985), which forbade a state-sponsored moment for silent prayer in the schools, and *Lee v. Weisman* (1992), which banned state-sponsored prayer at public high school graduation ceremonies.

While the school prayer decisions and many others serve as symbols of the separation of church and state, there have been many other decisions, particularly in recent years, which have permitted state assistance to religious institutions when the primary purpose and effect of that assistance has been considered by the Court to advance a secular purpose. In 1988, for example, in *Bowen v. Kendrick,* the Supreme Court upheld the expenditure of public funds to aid churches and other private institutions counseling against premarital sex. Earlier in *Meek v. Pittenger* (1973) the Court had upheld the loan of secular textbooks to parochial schools. In *Mueller v. Allen* (1983) the Court upheld an annual tax deduction for parents of children attending religious schools to help defray the costs of private education. In *Zobrest v. Catalina Foothills School District* (1993) the Court upheld a publicly funded sign language interpreter for a deaf child attending a religious school, even though the interpreter would inevitably be conveying religious messages. And in 1997 in *Agostino v. Felton* the Supreme Court reversed itself and overturned its prior ruling in *Aguilar v. Felton* (1985), which had declared unconstitutional a federal program that paid to send public school teachers into parochial schools to provide remedial educational assistance to poor and disadvantaged students. As a result of *Aguilar* it had been necessary for states to provide such educational assistance in separate buildings or portable classrooms physically removed from the religious institution. The Court had feared that sending public school teachers into religious schools would require such careful supervision of their work to assure that they were not participating in religious instruction as to require "an excessive entanglement" between church and state. In 1997, however, the Court in effect argued that its concern about excessive entanglement had itself been excessive. Now the Court was willing to trust publicly funded teachers not to engage in religious education, so very close monitoring of what happened within the confines of the church school was no longer necessary. If close monitoring of what goes on in the remedial education classes is not necessary, then any entanglement between church and state associated with such monitoring need not be "excessive."

The Court's ruling in *Agostino v. Felton,* then, can serve as a symbol of the somewhat relaxed concern for strict maintenance of the separation of church and state. Together this and many other accommodations to religion and religious institutions approved by the Court have taken us far beyond the "wall of separation" encouraged by Jefferson and cited approvingly by the late Justice Hugo Black in the *Everson* decision. Perhaps the biggest step, however, was taken by the Court in its decision in *Zelman v. Simmons-Harris* (2002). This decision opened the door to government funding for religious schools and may have paved the way for the Court's giving its constitutional blessings to other faith-based-initiatives in the delivery of publicly funded services.

Zelman concerned an Ohio state government program that provided so-called "scholarship vouchers" for students in "failed" public school districts which could be used at the parents' discretion to pay tuition at private or religious schools or for tutorial services for their children. In practice, of the parents electing to use their tuition vouchers for enrollment in nonpublic schools, 96 percent of them enrolled their children in parochial (religious) schools (at 620). The effect of these "private choices" was to direct public money to the religious schools which their children attended. Unlike most other programs approved by the Court in the past, the public money finding its way into the hands of religious schools was not restricted to, for example, pay for secular textbooks or computers. The religious schools receiving public funds through the parents' choices under the voucher program could spend that money for any part of their educational endeavors including teachers' salaries or even for religious instruction.

The Court justified this assignment of taxpayer funds to potentially clearly religious purposes because the choice to spend the vouchers this way was at the unfettered discretion of the parents seeking better education for their children. Under the voucher program it was the parent and not the state who made the determination on how the funds would be spent. The role of government, according to the Court majority, was one of strict neutrality. Chief Justice Rehnquist, writing for the Court's majority, emphasized that the state in establishing the voucher system was pursuing "the valid secular purpose of providing educational assistance to poor children in a demonstrably failing school system." Under the Court's existing test, however, it was still necessary to determine whether the Ohio program had "the forbidden 'effect' of advancing or inhibiting religion" (at 614). Even though the vast majority of the funds under the voucher program ended up in religious schools, this "effect" of the program was not a result of actions of the state, but rather the result of the choices made by parents. Nothing in the program, according to Chief Justice Rehnquist, "deliberately skewed incentives toward religious schools" (at 614). On the contrary the chief justice argued that government provided greater aid to public magnet schools to which students could also transfer than it provided to private or parochial schools (at 617–18).

In effect the chief justice's position is that the state is no more responsible for the taxpayer money going to a religious institution in this instance than it is, to cite just two examples, when a police officer or public employee elects to spend part of her publicly funded salary on religious school tuition for her children or even when she tithes a portion of her salary to her preferred church. In both instances the money in question is raised from taxpayers; in handing that money (salary or voucher) over to a citizen, the government does not assume responsibility for the way it is spent.

To the dissenters on the Court, however, the issue in the case is simply whether the Establishment clause permits governments to pay for religious indoctrination (Stevens, dissenting, at 637). Although the precedents cited above had significantly eroded the wall of separation, according to another dissenter, Justice Souter, until this case the Court had at least attempted to assure that public money would not be diverted for directly religious purposes and the Court had shown concern as well for the "substantiality of aid," or the scope or size of the government contribution.

What are the implications of the school voucher decision for so-called faith-based-initiatives? It appears clear that if, for example, government funding for drug rehabilitation programs were channeled through addicts in the form of vouchers with which the addicts could pay for rehabilitation, the money could be given to church-based programs. Approval of such uses of public money would in all probability depend on the availability of non-church-based alternatives. To provide only a religious rehabilitation program at public expense would be comparable to the state funding attendance only at religious schools. Even the majority in *Zelman* would have no doubt found that unacceptable. But what if the nonreligious private rehabilitation centers and their public counterparts had long waiting lists or obviously inferior programs or facilities; might not addicts have little choice other than to attend the religious programs? Would heroin addicts seeking methodone to ease their craving have a genuine choice of avoiding religious indoctrination if the faith-based-program could treat them more quickly? Wouldn't such limited "choices" violate the constitution?

Justice Souter's dissent in *Zelman* argued that practically speaking the voucher system in Ohio favored Catholic schools because the vouchers covered most, if not all, of the costs of attending Catholic schools, which are subsidized by parishes, but would not cover the full costs of other private alternatives. Could not the same issue arise in other faith-based programs?

Another potential issue relating to faith-based-initiatives that was raised by Justice Souter's dissent in *Zelman* is the potential intrusion by the state into the affairs of religion. A concern of the Court since *Lemon v. Kurtzman* has been a requirement that there not be "excessive entanglement" between church and state. The possibility of state inquiry into the doctrines of particular churches might cross the boundary between church and state and amount to an "excessive entanglement." On the other hand, state regulations of potential government fund recipients to assure that money taken from all taxpayers is not spent in a discriminatory manner or in support of beliefs that the majority finds offensive might also be interpreted as either excessive entanglement or as actual establishment of preferred religious doctrines. Might not conditioning public aid on renunciation of core beliefs of a religion also violate free exercise? (See Question 2 above.)

The school voucher program upheld by the court majority in *Zelman,* for example, required that schools receiving state funds ". . . not . . . teach hatred of any person or group on the basis of . . . religion." This provision, according to Justice Souter's dissent, "could be understood (or subsequently broadened) to prohibit religions from teaching traditionally legitimate articles of faith as to the error, sinfulness, or ignorance of others, if they want government money for their schools" (at 655). Is it not likely that government bureaucrats distributing funds or the courts will be drawn into controversies within and among religions concerning the "correct" interpretation of dogma? Might this not be legitimately viewed as excessive entanglement? Is not a preference for religions preaching tolerance of others, itself, an unconstitutional establishment of preferred religious beliefs? On the other hand, in the absence of such restrictions on the use of public money, will we not be forcing citizens to pay taxes to support religious doctrines that many find repugnant? As Justice Souter points out:

> Not all taxpaying Protestant citizens, for example, will be content to underwrite the teaching of the Roman Catholic Church condemning the death penalty. Nor will all of America's Muslims acquiesce in paying for the endorsement of the religious Zionism taught by many religious Jewish schools. . . . Nor will every secular taxpayer be content to support Muslim views on differential treatment of the sexes, or for that matter, to fund the espousal of a wife's obligation of obedience to her husband, presumably taught in any school adopting the articles of faith of the Southern Baptist convention . . . " (at 657).

All government policies, of course, are the product of choices, some of which correspond to the religious preferences of some citizens and not others. As we saw above in Question 1 the simple fact of an agreement between a religious belief and a public policy is not grounds for overturning that policy. If it were, government programs for feeding the hungry or sheltering the homeless might be challenged. Are they not consistent with the beliefs of many religions? Isn't the support for them by some legislators at least a product of their personal religious convictions?

There is no question that today the Supreme Court remains sharply divided over church/state issues. On the one hand there are justices who largely remain faithful to the so-called *Lemon* test discussed several times in this chapter. On the other hand, there are justices who largely ridicule that standard or who believe it goes much further than the framers intended in insisting on isolating the state from religion and vice versa.

The most controversial element of the so-called *Lemon* test is the requirement that any government statute in any way affecting religion must first have "a secular legislative purpose." In *Edwards v. Aguillard,* Justice Antonin Scalia resorted to ridicule in his dissent:

> Our cases interpreting and applying the purpose test have made such a maze of the Establishment Clause that even the most

conscientious governmental officials can only guess what motives will be held unconstitutional. We have said essentially the following: Government may not act with the purpose of advancing religion except when forced to do so by the Free Exercise Clause (which is now and then); or when eliminating existing governmental hostility to religion (which exists sometimes); or even when accommodating governmentally uninhibited religious practices, except that at some point (it is unclear where) intentional accommodation results in the fostering of religion, which is of course unconstitutional. . . .

But the difficulty of knowing what vitiating purpose one is looking for is as nothing compared with the difficulty of knowing how or where to find it. For while it is possible to discern the objective "purpose" of a statute (i.e., the public good at which its provision appear to be directed), or even the formal motivation for a statute where that is explicitly set forth. . . , discerning the subjective motivation of those enacting the statute is, to be honest, almost always an impossible task. The number of possible motivations, to begin with, is not binary, or indeed even finite. In the present case, for example, a particular legislator need not have voted for the Act either because he wanted to foster religion or because he wanted to improve education. He may have thought the bill would provide jobs for his district, or he may have wanted to make amends with a faction of his party he had alienated on another vote, or he may have hoped the Governor would appreciate his vote and make a fund raising appearance for him . . . [O]r he may have been mad at his wife who opposed the bill, or he may have been intoxicated and utterly *un*motivated when the vote was called, or he may have accidentally voted "yes" instead of "no," or, of course, he may have had (and very likely did have) a combination of some of the above and many other motivations. To look for *the sole purpose* of even a single legislator is probably to look for something that does not exist (at 637).

This problem is compounded further by the question of whose purpose or motivation is relevant. Should one legislator's impermissible motivation be sufficient to condemn a statute? Must the majority who voted for the statute share the impermissible purpose? If Justice Scalia is correct that it is impossible to know even the complete motivation of one legislator, how he asks, are we to know the collective purpose of the entire legislature?

Although Justice Scalia's attack on the *Lemon* test has not yet succeeded in getting it fully rejected, today, despite that standard, a Court majority finds no constitutional problem with far-ranging support by government for educational programs within religious schools. Whether then the separation of church and state is threatened by recent developments depends in good measure on whether one believes the Court in some of its rulings has taken this separation too far.

We began our discussion of religion by citing Justice Black's opinion for the Court in the *Everson* case. That opinion itself has been criticized for its reliance upon Jefferson's metaphor of a "wall of separation between church and state." In his dissenting opinion in *Wallace v. Jaffree* (1985) then Associate Justice Rehnquist roundly criticized the *Everson* decision as being inconsistent with the history of the First Amendment and of the intent of its framers. According to Justice Rehnquist,

> The framers intended the Establishment Clause to prohibit the designation of any church as a "national" one. The Clause also was designed to stop the Federal Government from asserting a preference for one religious denomination or sect over others. Given the "incorporation" of the Establishment Clause as against the States via the Fourteenth Amendment in *Everson,* States are prohibited as well from establishing a religion or discriminating between sects. As its history abundantly shows, however, nothing in the Establishment Clause requires government to be strictly neutral between religion and irreligion, nor does that Clause prohibit Congress or the States from pursuing legitimate secular ends through nondiscriminatory sectarian means (at 113).

In light of such cited historical practices as the proclamation of a day of national Thanksgiving by almost all of our presidents at the behest of Congress, Justice Rehnquist concludes that the Court's overturning of a moment of silence in Alabama schools because the state wished to "characterize prayer as a favored practice" would come as a "shock to those who drafted the Bill of Rights . . . " (at 113).

If one agrees with Chief Justice Rehnquist, the continued separation of church and state most certainly is not in danger. On the contrary the separation of church *from* state and state *from* church has gone much too far. Nonetheless there is little doubt that the changing personnel on the Court since the 1980s has eroded somewhat the vision of a strict separation envisioned in the *Everson* decision. At least as of today, however, there appears to be little threat that persecution of religious minorities or of those having no religion will result from the "accommodations" of religion sanctioned by the Court. Nor is there much threat that the power of government will be wielded exclusively in support of any particular religion. But there appears to be a real likelihood that religions and religious institutions could play a larger role in our public life. Whether this actually threatens the values behind the First Amendment is a judgment we will all need to make for ourselves.

REFERENCES

Agostino v. Felton, 521 U.S. 203 (1997).

Aguilar v. Felton, 473 U.S. 402 (1985).

Bowen v. Kendrick, 487 U.S. 589 (1988).

Church of the Lukumi Babalu Aye v. City of Hialeah, 508 U.S. 520 (1993).

City Council of Los Angeles v. Taxpayers for Vincent, 446 U.S. 789 (1984).

City of Boerne v. Flores, 521 U.S. 507 (1997).

Edwards v. Aguillard, 482 U.S. 578 (1987).

Employment Division of Department of Human Resources of Oregon v. Smith, 494 U.S. 872 (1990).

Engel v. Vitale, 370 U.S. 421 (1962).

Epperson v. Arkansas, 393 U.S. 97 (1968).

Everson v. Board of Education, 330 U.S. 1 (1947).

Fullilove v. Klutznick, 448 U.S. 448 (1980).

Lamb's Chapel v. Center Moriches Union Free School District, 508 U.S. 398 (1993).

Larkin v. Grendel's Den, Inc., 459 U.S. 116 (1982).

Lee v. Weisman, 505 U.S. 577 (1992).

Lemon v. Kurtzman, 403 U.S. 602 (1971).

Lynch v. Donnelly, 465 U.S. 668 (1984).

Marsh v. Chambers, 463 U.S. 783 (1983).

McGowan v. Maryland, 366 U.S. 420 (1961).

Meek v. Pittenger, 413 U.S. 349 (1973).

Mueller v. Allen, 463 U.S. 388 (1983).

School District of Abington Township, Penn. et al. v. Schemp et al., 374 U.S. 203 (1963).

Sherbert v. Verner, 374 U.S. 398 (1963).

Stone v. Graham, 449 U.S. 39 (1980).

Wallace v. Jaffree, 472 U.S. 38 (1985).

Westside Community Board of Education v. Mergens, 496 U.S. 226 (1989).

Widmar v. Vincent, 454 U.S. 263 (1981).

Zelman v. Simmons-Harris, 153 L. Ed. 2d 604 (2002).

Zobrest v. Catalina Foothills School District, 113 S. Ct. 2463 (1993).

CHAPTER FOUR

EQUALITY
UNDER THE
CONSTITUTION

INTRODUCTION

In the Declaration of Independence the founders of the United States proclaimed their belief that "all men are created equal." While Americans from the beginning have consistently rejected the notion of a hereditary nobility and today assert their fidelity to equality of opportunity, many of us celebrate the wealthy and vigorously oppose any attempts to limit through taxation wealth we can leave our children. Most incongruous in light of our proclaimed belief in the equality of all people has been our tragic history of racial oppression. The author of the Declaration of Independence "owned" slaves. For most of our history we have struggled with slavery and its legacy.

In order to understand equality under the Constitution we must understand the Equal Protection clause of the Fourteenth Amendment. Question 1 asks: *How does the Constitution make us equal?* This section begins by noting that the Constitution provides for "equality" in only the limited sense of "equal protection of the laws." It then proceeds to look at various applications of the Equal Protection clause of the Fourteenth Amendment and the justification for applying different standards in cases of racial, gender, and other forms of discrimination.

The most obvious manifestation of inequality in America has been its treatment of African Americans even after the abolition of slavery. Question 2, therefore, asks: *If the Constitution commands "equal protection of the laws," why was racial segregation permitted for so long?* This section discusses *Plessy v. Ferguson* and the rise of the "separate but equal doctrine"; and, finally, the relationship between societal trends and values and constitutional standards concerning race.

Once our society began to take the command of the Equal Protection clause seriously in the twentieth century, it had to confront how practically to undo the effects of racial discrimination. Question 3 asks: *Why did the courts order "forced busing"?* and discusses the difficulties encountered in removing the effects of past discrimination and the role of school busing. It first, however, reviews *Brown v. Board of Education* (1954), the Court decision that declared segregation unconstitutional, and the evolution of the remedies for school segregation.

Today probably the most controversial issue relating to equality under the law is "affirmative action" because affirmative action is broadly perceived as permitting preferential treatment of those of a race or gender that had been victim to racial or gender discrimination. Question 4 asks: *Isn't "affirmative action" just another form of racial or sexual discrimination?* This section reviews the controversy surrounding affirmative action, with special attention paid to the arguments of its proponents and opponents concerning when it is necessary for government to take race or gender into account in decision making. In reviewing recent Supreme Court decisions it shows how the Court has moved away from affirmative action and toward a "colorblind" approach to equal protection. In doing so, however, the Court has in effect placed limits on the capacity of Congress and the state legislatures to use their powers to regulate the economy to advance the interests of Americans who may have been left behind. As was noted in Chapter 1, civil rights laws have sometimes been used to broaden the promise of equality promised by post–Civil War amendments to the Constitution. These civil rights laws themselves are subject to the restraints in the Constitution when, in the Court's view, advancing the interests of disadvantaged minority groups might be perceived as coming at the expense of equal treatment for members of the majority racial group.

One area in which the Court has clearly rejected an inflexible requirement for "color blindness" is in public university admissions. Question 5 asks: *May government "discriminate" on the basis of race in order to advance the cause of racial diversity?* In two decisions in 2003 the Court found justification for government to take race into account as it pursues the goals advanced by racial and ethnic diversity in educational institutions.

While to many the struggle for an Equal Rights Amendment to the Constitution may appear to be a fading memory of the distant past, Question 6 asks: *Do we still need a new Equal Rights Amendment (ERA) to secure gender equality?* Although the Court has used the Fourteenth Amendment to attack gender discrimination in the twentieth century, it has not interpreted it to ban gender discrimination to the degree that it bans race discrimination. If we had the ERA, however, the Constitution would treat race discrimination and sex discrimination alike. With a review of the Court's most recent decisions relating to gender discrimination, this section should assist the reader in deciding for him or herself whether an Equal Rights Amendment is in fact needed.

Finally, having reviewed the Court's varying interpretations of the Equal Protection clause, this chapter concludes by asking Question 7: *How do you know if you are a victim of unconstitutional discrimination?* This section discusses the so-called "intent" requirement in both racial and gender discrimination cases. It covers the reasons why the Court demands evidence of intentional discrimination and will not accept evidence of unequal results alone as sufficient to prove a violation of the Fourteenth Amendment requirement of equal protection of the laws. It also discusses the Court's shifting interpretation of the "intent standard" itself as demonstrated in the Court's decision in *McCleskey v. Kemp* (1987), the race and capital punishment case. Together this discussion should allow the reader to come to some judgments concerning equality under the Constitution.

Question 1   *How does the Constitution make us equal?*

A visit to any large American city should quickly demonstrate the limits of America's commitment to equality. In New York City, for example, garish displays of wealth exist side by side with signs of extreme poverty. If the guards are not looking, homeless people might pass through the lobby of Trump Tower, but none can hope to afford even temporary shelter in the floors above.

Such stark reminders of inequality exist despite the Fourteenth Amendment's command that "No State shall . . . deny to any person within its jurisdiction the equal protection of the laws." Although this important constitutional command does provide us with some protection from some kinds of state-imposed inequality, it leaves untouched inequalities which are not directly attributable to government policies.

"Equal protection of the laws" does not even require that the state treat all people alike. Tax laws, regulatory policies, laws designed to protect the health, safety, and welfare of people all make distinctions among people. Laws permitted under the Fourteenth Amendment routinely place us in different classifications based on our income, age, education, and/or demonstrated qualifications without serious constitutional challenge. Laws or government policies which make distinctions among people based on race, ethnicity, and gender, however, lead to serious constitutional disputes. Why are some classifications of people permitted by the sweeping language of the Equal Protection clause while others are forbidden? To answer this question we must look beyond the language of the Fourteenth Amendment to its history.

The Fourteenth Amendment, like the Thirteenth and Fifteenth, was a product of the Civil War. As the Supreme Court in its early decisions interpreting the scope of the Fourteenth Amendment Equal Protection clause made clear, all of these amendments together were designed with the "common purpose . . . [of] securing to a race recently emancipated [all] the civil rights" that whites enjoyed (*Strauder v. West Virginia,* 1880). The Court majority in the *Slaughterhouse Cases* (1873), only five years following the adoption of the Fourteenth Amendment, stated: "We doubt very much whether any action of a State not directed by way of discrimination against Negroes as a class, or on account of their race, will ever be held to come within the purview of the . . . [Equal Protection Clause]" (at 81).

That the original intent behind the Equal Protection clause of the Fourteenth Amendment was to protect the African American population that had been denied the most basic rights cannot be disputed. But since its adoption the amendment has gradually through judicial interpretation been given broader scope. While the Constitution implicitly argues that differences of race cannot justify different government treatment of peoples, other differences may justify and even demand different treatment. In deciding when the Constitution tolerates classifying people in order to provide different treatment, the Court has often used this society's treatment of African Americans as a yardstick. It has sometimes attempted to compare the situation of a population group claiming to be disadvantaged by some distinction written into law with the historic condition of blacks. In deciding whether to treat "discrimination" against a particular population group in the same way as discrimination against blacks under the Equal Protection clause, the Court has often inquired whether the group in question is "'a discrete and insular minority' requiring extraordinary protection from the majoritarian political process" (*Caroline Products,* n. 4 in *Regents of the University of California v. Bakke,* at 288). The "majoritarian political process," of course, refers to the power to elect and remove government officials according to how well they protect a group's interests. This power is of little use to a group that, because of its minority status (relatively small numbers), lacks the voting power to elect people representing its interests.

It did not take the Court long to extend the reach of the Fourteenth Amendment Equal Protection clause to other racial and ethnic minorities. In *Strauder v. West Virginia* (1880), the case in which the Court found that exclusion of blacks from jury service violated the Equal Protection clause, the Court noted that the exclusion of "naturalized Celtic Irishmen," for example, would also be inconsistent "with the spirit of the Amendment." Other cases that followed extending the protection of the amendment to Chinese and Mexican Americans rested on similar foundations; that is, discrimination against minorities who had historically been victims of discrimination and who were unable to protect themselves through the ballot box.

In recognizing that the abolition of racial discrimination was the primary purpose behind the Fourteenth Amendment, the Court nonetheless has recognized that sometimes considerations of race may be permissible under the Constitution. In light of the history of the grossest forms of racial oppression in the United States, however, the Court has decided not to trust government claims that the use of racial criteria or classifications in the law is justifiable.

In *Korematsu v. United States* (1944) the Court provided the standard still used today to judge government policies which treat people of different races differently. *Korematsu* was one of a series of cases that came to the Court challenging various restrictions, ranging from curfews to confinement in concentration camps, placed upon Americans of Japanese ancestry living on the West Coast following the start of World War II. In his opinion for the Court Justice Black declared that "all legal restrictions which curtail the civil rights of a single racial group are *immediately suspect*. That is not to say that all such restrictions are unconstitutional. It is to say that courts must subject them to the *most rigid scrutiny*. Pressing public necessity may sometimes justify the existence of such restrictions; racial antagonism never can [emphasis added]" (at 216).

Despite applying what has now come to be called "strict scrutiny," the Court found that the fear of the military authorities that an invasion of the West Coast was imminent and that there was no time to judge the loyalty of individual Japanese living there, justified the "exclusion" and confinement of people on the basis of their race. Although this result today is almost universally condemned and in 1988 Congress authorized reparations to Japanese Americans who were victimized, the strict scrutiny standard applied to *suspect classifications* survives. Since *Korematsu*, legislation or government action that subjects racial and ethnic minorities to discriminatory treatment has generally been struck down by the Court. Except for the limited area in which racial classifications are used to overcome past racial discrimination against minorities (see Question 4 below), the strict scrutiny standard has presented a barrier in the way of legislation based on racial classifications that legislatures have been unable to surmount.

Racial classifications are only upheld in Court if the government can prove some "compelling state interest"—some "pressing public necessity"—that cannot be accomplished without drawing racial distinctions.

Although strict scrutiny is the standard by which the Court judges racial and ethnic classifications, other types of classifications in the law are generally not subject to such rigorous review by the courts. Although no one can seriously doubt that sex discrimination has historically been a part of our society and of government policy, government policies that discriminate on the basis of sex have not generally been seen as impossible to justify under the Constitution.

On the surface this lesser concern for sex discrimination might seem puzzling. The words of the Fourteenth Amendment after all refer to "persons" and not simply to men. It is clear, however, that the male framers of the Fourteenth Amendment and the male legislators who ratified it had no interest in abolishing or restricting sex discrimination. Despite this clear record, the Supreme Court has gradually read "women's rights," or more broadly, gender equality, into the Fourteenth Amendment. The Court has done this in part by recognizing the odious history of sex discrimination in American history and by seeing similarities between our society's treatment of all women and its treatment of black men and women.

These parallel patterns of discrimination led four justices on the Supreme Court to argue in *Frontiero v. Richardson* (1973) that for purposes of constitutional adjudication "classifications based upon sex, like classifications based upon race, alienage, and national origin, are inherently suspect and must therefore be subjected to close judicial scrutiny" (at 682). Justice Brennan supported this conclusion by citing our nation's

> . . . long and unfortunate history of sex discrimination. Traditionally, such discrimination was rationalized by an attitude of "romantic paternalism" which, in practical effect, put women, not on a pedestal, but in a cage. As a result of notions such as these, our statute books gradually became laden with gross, stereotyped distinctions between the sexes and, indeed, throughout much of the 19th century the position of women in our society was, in many respects, comparable to that of blacks under the pre–Civil War slave codes. Neither slaves nor women could hold office, serve on juries, or bring suit in their own names, and married women traditionally were denied the legal capacity to hold and convey property or to serve as legal guardians of their own children (at 685).

Despite the logic of Justice Brennan's argument the Court as a whole has not been willing to go quite so far. In his concurring opinion in *Frontiero* Justice Powell argued that the Court should not on its own treat sex discrimination as a "suspect classification" subject to "strict scrutiny." At the time of *Frontiero* the proposed Equal Rights Amendment was before the country (see discussion of Question 6 below). If it were to be approved, sex discrimination would be given the same status as race discrimination under the Constitution. In its absence, however, treating sex discrimination exactly as race would have amounted to a "judicial amendment" to the Constitution.

If sex classifications are not to be subject to strict scrutiny, then how should they be treated? Generally, classifications in the law based on criteria other than race or ethnicity have been subjected to "deferential analysis." Under this approach the actions of a legislature will be upheld so long as "[t]he distinctions drawn by a challenged statute bear some rational relationship to a legitimate state end and will be set aside as violative of the Equal Protection clause only if based on reasons totally unrelated to the pursuit of that goal" (*McDonald v. Board of Election Commissioners,* at 809, 1969). Under this rational basis test the Court will not use its own judgment for what is fair or wise policy. It defers to legislative judgments as long as they are not clearly arbitrary or capricious. When, for example, states set 16 as the minimum age requirement for a driver's license, they clearly classify people according to age. Reasonable people might argue the wisdom of that particular age classification, but few could argue that setting such an age limit has no rational basis. According to the Court, classifications of this sort do not offend the Equal Protection clause of the Fourteenth Amendment even though they deny to 15-year-olds privileges granted to 16-year-olds. Clearly the two age groups are not treated equally, but abolishing such unequal treatment was not the purpose of the Equal Protection clause.

Although for much of our history sex discrimination was subjected to this "rationality test," the Court today has developed what has been called an "intermediate" level of review for sex discrimination cases. Although sex discrimination cases are not treated precisely the same as race cases, such cases are no longer subjected to only the rational basis test. While not subjecting sex classifications to "strict scrutiny," the Court has devised a new test, sometimes referred to as "heightened scrutiny," to be applied in sex discrimination cases. Under this test "classifications by gender must serve important governmental objectives and must be substantially related to achievement of those objectives" (*Craig v. Boren,* 429 at 197, 1976).

Although we generally think of women as the victims of sex discrimination, *Craig v. Boren,* the case in which the Supreme Court adopted the heightened scrutiny standard, concerned a claim of discrimination against men. Under Oklahoma law, 3.2 percent beer could not be sold to men until the age of 21; women, on the other hand, could purchase such beer at the age of 18. The state justified this "discrimination" on the basis of evidence that young men had significantly more alcohol-related driving accidents and arrests for "driving under the influence" than did young women. In the interests of traffic safety, therefore, young men were denied access to beer which could be purchased by women of similar age.

Although the evidence in question would probably have been significant enough to survive scrutiny by the Court under "deferential analysis," using the the rational basis test, it was not considered sufficient proof that the gender-based distinction was "substantially related to the achievement" of the admittedly "important objective" of assuring highway safety (at 204). In sum because a small but admittedly larger proportion of men than women drink and drive, you cannot discriminate against all men.

Under the Fourteenth Amendment's Equal Protection clause we do not all have to be treated alike in all things. The Court recognizes that the Fourteenth Amendment was added to the Constitution primarily to prevent the states from continuing to oppress African Americans after the formal institution of slavery was abolished. Discrimination based on race was the principal target of the amendment, and the Court in adopting the "strict scrutiny" standard for cases involving racial and ethnic classifications has today made it extremely difficult for government to treat people differently because of their race, something over which the individual has no control. Because sex, like race, is an "immutable characteristic" (*Frontiero,* at 686), the Court has come to see sex classifications, too, as difficult to justify under the Fourteenth Amendment. No doubt in large part because of the Court's recognition that the Fourteenth Amendment was not initially intended to abolish legal distinctions based on sex, the heightened scrutiny standard makes it somewhat easier for government to justify treating men and women differently. After all there are real differences based on gender; there are few, if any, real natural differences between people based on race. For a law or policy to survive strict scrutiny in a race case, the government must show a "compelling state interest." To survive heightened scrutiny in a sex discrimination case, the government must show that the policy is justified by some "important governmental objective." The difference is one of degree.

Generally, when the government classifies people for purposes unrelated to such "immutable characteristics" as race, ethnicity, or sex, all that the Fourteenth Amendment requires is that similarly situated people be treated alike. Whether it is a good idea to tax people of different incomes differently or to set any particular age as a qualification for a driver's license or for some other "privilege" or benefit is left to legislative discretion. All the Fourteenth Amendment requires is that the classification in question not be clearly arbitrary.

Question 2 *If the Constitution commands "equal protection of the laws," why was racial segregation permitted for so long?*

Prior to the late 1960s and early 1970s Americans throughout the South and some border states were rigidly segregated (separated) in schools and places of public accommodation on the basis of race. Although segregation affected all facets of life, it was most obviously present in the public schools. Black children were forbidden by law from attending school with white children. Therefore, Southern communities had "dual school systems," separate schools for black and white children.

Before the Civil War, when African Americans lived in slavery, laws generally forbade blacks from becoming educated at all. Whites recognized that education, the ability to read and write, would make it easier for blacks to communicate and organize to resist the slave system. Following the Civil War attempts were made to keep blacks in subservient positions. One reason for the approval of the Fourteenth Amendment was to forbid the emerging pattern of legal discrimination against those who had been slaves.

Despite the Fourteenth Amendment, segregation, both privately practiced and legally enforced, continued to exist following the Civil War. The Fourteenth Amendment, however, provided a tool to use to challenge the continuing forced racial separation and exclusion of African Americans. Segregation, however, raised a somewhat different issue from other forms of discrimination. On the surface at least, segregation treated blacks and whites alike. Each was kept apart from the other.

In *Plessy v. Ferguson* (1896) the Supreme Court faced the question of whether the Equal Protection clause of the Fourteenth Amendment permitted state-enforced racial separation. *Plessy* involved a challenge to an 1890 Louisiana law that required "equal but separate accommodations" for white and black railroad passengers. Although the Court recognized that "[t]he object of the Fourteenth Amendment was undoubtedly to enforce the absolute equality of the two races before the law," it nonetheless argued that "it could not have been intended to abolish distinctions based upon race."

The Court contended that segregation of blacks from whites was permitted by the Fourteenth Amendment because it did not deny the equality of blacks. In effect the Court said that if blacks chose to interpret segregation laws as branding them as inferior, that was their problem. Nothing in the law declared them to be inferior.

In accepting this particular form of segregation, however, the Court denied that it would be ". . . authorizing . . . [state legislatures, if they chose, to require separate railway cars for] people whose hair is a certain color, or who are aliens, or who belong to certain nationalities, or to enact laws requiring . . . [blacks] to walk upon one side of the street, and white people upon the other, or requiring white men's houses to be painted white, and . . . [black] men's black, or their vehicles or business signs to be of different colors, upon the theory that one side of the street is as good as the other, or that a house of one color is as good as another color." Rather the Court argued that only "reasonable" laws would be upheld. Only practices that conformed to the "established usages, customs, and traditions of the people, and with a view to the promotion of their comfort, and the preservation of the public peace and good order" (at 549–50) would be permitted.

In deciding that the segregation of blacks from whites met these criteria the Court referred to the existence of racially segregated schools in Massachusetts, a state that had banned slavery long before the Civil War, for support. In citing a Massachusetts court decision upholding such segregation in 1850, the Court failed to note, however, that this decision came nearly 20 years before the Fourteenth Amendment was added to the U.S. Constitution. The 1850 Massachusetts court that upheld segregation did not have to enforce the Equal Protection clause, because it did not yet exist.

Clearly the established "customs" upon which the Court relied to justify segregation in the post–Civil War period were products of the very institutions and practices that the Thirteenth, Fourteenth, and Fifteenth Amendments were designed to overturn. What the Court reflected in *Plessy* was the climate of racism that had marked American society from the beginning.

Only Justice Harlan dissented from the *Plessy* decision. He knew that the so-called "separate but equal doctrine" which emerged from this case was a sham that would fool no one. He wrote that everyone understood that the true purpose behind the segregation was ". . . not so much to exclude white persons from railroad cars occupied by blacks, as to exclude colored people from coaches [assigned] to white persons" (at 557). Harlan recognized the harm that would flow from such a policy of exclusion. Because "the destinies of the two races [are] indissolubly linked together, . . . the interests of both require that the common government of all shall not permit the seeds of race hate to be planted under the sanction of law" (at 560).

It did not take long for the mask of "equality" that might have obscured the true significance of the so-called separate but equal doctrine to fall away. In *Cumming v. County Board of Education* (1899) only a few years after *Plessy,* the Supreme Court decided unanimously that the separate but equal doctrine did not require a Southern community to provide a public high school to educate black children even though it provided one for white children. So much for equality.

These Court decisions can be explained only through an understanding of racism. People who had for hundreds of years held others in slavery had to convince themselves that their actions were justified by their natural superiority. Rather than admit that they pursued their personal profit through the total oppression of others like themselves, they denied the full humanity of those whom they had enslaved. Although the Civil War could wipe out the formal institution of slavery, it could not so quickly banish the attitudes of white supremacy that had served as the foundation for African slavery in North America for centuries.

Although for a brief time following the Civil War blacks obtained some political power and social privileges in the South, most of these advances quickly vanished once the Southern white majority regained control of their affairs from federal authorities. *Plessy v. Ferguson* did not cause segregation, but it did provide the "legal" justification for it. In words that proved prophetic, the lone dissenter in *Plessy,* Justice Harlan, warned that the Court's decision would "in time, prove to be quite as pernicious as the decision made . . ." in *Dred Scott,* the decision that had declared that Congress lacked the power even to restrict the expansion of slavery under the pre–Civil War Constitution (at 559). In assessing the separate but equal doctrine, Harlan correctly observed that "[t]he thin disguise of 'equal accommodations' [will] not mislead any one, nor atone for the wrong this day done" (at 562).

Question 3   *Why did the courts order "forced busing"?*

Under the system of segregation, black children were educated separately from white children throughout the Southern and border states. This system of segregation was kept in place through the force of law. While today most Americans condemn the system of segregation known as "apartheid" which until recently was practiced in South Africa, many of us forget that only a generation ago America had its own version of apartheid. Despite the clear command of the Fourteenth Amendment requiring "equal protection of the laws," children were classified according to their race and forcibly separated into separate educational systems. Despite the so-called "separate but equal doctrine" announced in the *Plessy v. Ferguson* decision (see Question 2 above), few seriously argued that the education given black children was equal to what whites, using their dominant position in government, provided for themselves.

Despite the Supreme Court's 8 to 1 endorsement of segregation in *Plessy v. Ferguson,* the leadership of the black community did not abandon efforts to get government to enforce the Equal Protection clause of the Fourteenth Amendment. The NAACP (National Association for the Advancement of Colored People) Legal Defense Fund financed and led a series of court cases designed to eat away at the foundations of segregated education. Because it is difficult to get the Supreme Court directly to overturn its own prior decisions, the NAACP at first attempted to get the Court not to reject the separate but equal doctrine but rather to enforce it. If states forced blacks to attend separate educational facilities, then they must assure that such facilities are equal.

Although segregation had its greatest impact in the public school system, the legal assault on segregation in schools began at the professional school level. Every state provided at least some public education to black children, but many states provided no places for blacks in their graduate and professional schools. In a series of cases beginning in the late 1930s dealing with such schools, the Supreme Court in effect chipped away at the foundations of the separate but equal doctrine.

At first its decisions invalidated obviously unequal educational opportunities for blacks and whites seeking graduate and professional school educations. When states requiring segregation began to recognize that the Court would demand equality in professional education, some took rather bizarre steps designed to maintain segregation. Oklahoma, for example, did admit a black to its state graduate school of education, but school regulations required that he be separated by barriers from whites within classrooms as well as in the library and cafeteria. Although such practices made communication between whites and blacks difficult or impossible, it did on the surface provide the black student exposure to the same instructors and facilities as whites.

The Supreme Court, however, decided in effect that segregation itself interferes with equal educational opportunity. In striking down the practices which physically separated black and white students, the Court argued that "such restrictions impair . . . [the student's] ability to study, to engage in discussion and exchange views with other students, and in general, to learn his profession." The Court had in effect rejected "restrictions imposed by the State which prohibited the intellectual commingling of students . . ." (*McLaurin v. Oklahoma State Board of Regents,* at 641, 1950). In effect the Court had struck down a form of segregation.

Finally, the stage was set for a direct assault on segregated public school education. In 1954 the U.S. Supreme Court heard together appeals from lower court decisions in five separate challenges to segregation of the public schools. This time, however, the NAACP did not focus on the unequal facilities or instruction provided to black children. Instead it challenged the forced separation of minority black children from the dominant majority in the society, whites. For purposes of its decision in *Brown v. Board of Education* (1954), the Court assumed that "tangible factors," such as facilities, teacher salaries and qualifications, supplies, and so on had been either "equalized or were being equalized" (at 492). The question then presented by the case was: "Does segregation of children in public schools solely on the basis of race, even though the physical facilities and other 'tangible' factors may be equal, deprive the children of the minority group equal educational opportunities?" (at 493).

In deciding that forced racial segregation did deny blacks the equal protection of the laws, the Court considered a number of factors. Probably the most significant influence on the Court, however, was the recognition of the central role played by education in contemporary American society. Attendance at school is after all compelled by the state today, and "education is perhaps the most important [and most expensive] function of state and local governments" (at 493). Education is not simply designed to provide students with skills necessary for future employment, rather it is "a foundation of good citizenship, . . . awakening the child to cultural values, . . . and . . . helping him to adjust normally to his environment" (*Brown,* at 493).

Segregation in education sends to the minority child an unmistakable message that he is excluded from the mainstream of American life. In the words of Chief Justice Warren, "[t]o separate . . . [black children] from others of similar age and qualifications solely because of their race generates a feeling of inferiority *as to their status in the community* [emphasis added] that may affect their hearts and minds in a way unlikely ever to be undone." (at 494).

Although the Court based its decision in part on evidence produced by psychological studies, no amount of social science evidence was required to explain the impact of segregation on those whom it was designed to exclude. Blacks knew that the white majority kept them apart in order to keep them down. Segregation told black children that they had no ". . . status in the community." It took no personal sense of inferiority for an excluded black child to know that his opportunities for success in a society dominated by a group that wanted to exclude him were few indeed.

For reasons such as these, the Supreme Court in *Brown* took the extraordinary step of finally explicitly repudiating its decision in *Plessy v. Ferguson* 58 years earlier. The Court ". . . conclude[d] that in the field of public education the doctrine of 'separate but equal' has no place. Separate educational facilities are inherently unequal" (at 495).

The Court's rejection of state-imposed segregation, although crucial, still left open the question of how desegregation might be accomplished. For decades school systems had been structured on the basis of segregation. School buildings were located and constructed to serve one-race populations. Teachers were hired and assigned on the basis of race. School bus routes were drawn to transport white children to white schools and black children to black schools. To undo what had been built up over generations would not be a simple task. Recognizing these facts, the Court in its first decision implementing its ruling in *Brown,* instructed the lower court at first to rely on the "good faith" efforts of local school authorities to make "a prompt and reasonable start" toward desegregation. The district courts were authorized to issue the orders "as are necessary and proper to admit [the students in whose name *Brown* was brought] to public schools on a racially nondiscriminatory basis *with all deliberate speed* [emphasis added] . . . " (*Brown v. Board of Education* (II), 1955).

During the decade immediately following *Brown* "massive resistance" on the part of whites throughout the South stood in the way of any significant progress toward desegregation. As late as 10 years after *Brown* "only 1.2 percent of the black students in the eleven Southern states attended schools with whites" (U.S. Commission on Civil Rights, p. 10). Faced with this record of resistance and defiance the Supreme Court in a 1961 decision proclaimed that "the time for 'deliberate speed' has run out." As Justice Black observed by then "[t]he original [*Brown*] plaintiffs ha[d] doubtless all passed high school age. There ha[d] been entirely too much deliberation and not enough speed in enforcing constitutional rights . . ." (*Griffin v. County School Board of Prince Edward County,* at 229–31, 1964). Despite these words of impatience, however, progress toward desegregation remained slow.

The Court was right in 1955 when it recognized how complex the task would be to do away with a deeply entrenched "dual" school system. Although in 1968 it decided to judge desegregation efforts by the results they produced (*Green v. New Kent County,* 1968), it was not until 1970 that the Court clearly endorsed the only policy capable of ending the separation of black and white children in many school districts where it continued.

When segregation was legal, both black and white children were "bused," often past schools near where they lived to more distant schools assigned to their particular race. In large metropolitan school districts, however, schools were naturally deliberately designed and built to serve the race that predominated in a particular area. Schools intended to serve black children only were built where mostly blacks lived. Schools serving only whites were built in predominantly white areas. If a particular section of a city had only 200 black children living within it, a small school designed to accommodate those students might be built. If a nearby area had 1,000 white children, then a larger school was built convenient to that particular concentration of one racial group.

In the years before *Brown* when segregation was legally required the system was designed to accommodate segregation. Once segregation became illegal, however, the system had to be redesigned. School buildings once constructed, however, cannot simply be moved.

In many communities school authorities changed their announced policy of segregation, but the system designed to accommodate segregation kept blacks and whites apart. Instead of requiring that all blacks must attend one school and all whites another, the school boards now said all children will be assigned to "neighborhood schools." But the Supreme Court eventually recognized that a decision to open a school to all regardless of race in a particular area will have little meaning if the school's location was chosen in the first place to serve one race which predominates in the area. "All things being equal, with no history of discrimination, it might, [according to Chief Justice Burger], be desirable to assign pupils to schools nearest to their homes. But all things are not equal in a system that has been deliberately constructed and maintained to enforce racial segregation" (*Swann v. Charlotte-Mecklenburg Board of Education*, at 28, 1971).

In response to what the Court termed such a "loaded game board" (at 29), students might have to be assigned to schools distant from their homes in order to bring about an end of state-imposed segregation. Just as school bus transportation had been used to deliver students to segregated schools, it would now be used to dismantle segregation.

In ordering busing for the purpose of integration, the Court used "a normal and accepted tool of educational policy" (at 29). Transporting students was the only practical means available to produce desegregation in areas where residential segregation was closely associated with school segregation. An unlimited use of "busing" could produce whatever degree of desegregation that the Court might feel was desirable. But the Court recognized that there were practical and legal limits. Although there is much racial isolation throughout the United States, the Court could only order remedies when racial segregation was a product of deliberate government action (see discussion of Question 7 below). In addition, transportation of students would be ordered only as long as it did not risk the health or safety of children or significantly impinge on the education process.

Court-ordered busing, like desegregation itself, was extremely controversial from the day it began. Many of those who claimed to favor desegregation vigorously opposed busing. Yet busing was ordered because as a practical matter no other means appeared to be available to undo the effects of generations of decisions imposing segregation. Students throughout suburban and rural America were routinely bused to school every day because schools are far away from home. When this routine measure was used to end segregation, however, busloads of children were sometimes attacked with stones. In the days of legal segregation buses were routinely used to separate children. When they were used to try to end separation, they became controversial. As Jesse Jackson once said: "It ain't the bus, it's us." Opposition to busing had in many instances become a socially acceptable way to oppose integration itself.

Question 4   *Isn't "affirmative action" just another form of racial or sexual discrimination?*

The term "affirmative action" refers to many different policies, all of which have in common the goals of abolishing the lingering effects of past discrimination and assuring that discrimination does not reoccur. Affirmative action programs range from simple requirements that, for example, open job opportunities be widely advertised so that minorities and women will be alerted to apply, to "preferential hiring policies" designed to assure that a certain minimum percentage of jobs or contracts will actually be filled by minority or women applicants.

Employment discrimination in America has in the past taken many forms. Often certain racial and ethnic groups were openly told that they were not wanted. Most of the better positions in society were routinely reserved for men. Some institutions such as police and fire departments would simply not even allow women to apply. Probably more common than open announced policies of racial discrimination was the simple practice of racial exclusion. If blacks applied, they would simply never be hired. Having gotten the unmistakable message, after a while other members of the excluded racial or ethnic groups would learn there was no point in even applying.

With the passage of the Civil Rights Act of 1964, generally racial and sexual discrimination in most places of private employment became illegal. Lawsuits under the Fourteenth Amendment's Equal Protection clause led to court orders banning discrimination in employment by state and local governments as well. Old habits and attitudes, however, were not easily swept away by words written in a statute book or court decision. To put into practice what had been written into law, legislatures and the courts began to require employers, especially those found to have discriminated against minorities and/or women in the past, to take certain steps to assure that minorities and women would in fact have access to opportunities long denied to them.

To white males who had not been forced to compete with minorities and women for jobs or contracts, affirmative action appeared to limit their opportunities. Sometimes these new programs assaulted the traditionally privileged position of white males, and such sudden loss of what had been theirs produced resentment.

Consider the story of a firefighter in a Massachusetts community. He had been a firefighter all his adult life. He lived in a town that had traditionally given preference in hiring to the sons of firefighters. Now his son was of age and ready to follow in his father's footsteps. There was a problem, however. There had never been a black hired as a firefighter in this community, so naturally there were no black sons who could claim the privilege of following their fathers into the fire department.

When the courts or an Equal Employment Opportunities Commission stepped in to ban the practice of giving preference to the sons of firefighters, the family of this white male firefighter was deeply resentful. Something they had come to expect was no longer theirs. When the position no longer reserved for their son goes to a black applicant, it is easy for the white who has been passed over to blame his fate on affirmative action. If the black applicant obtained the position in open competition with white applicants, however, this was not really affirmative action; it was simple nondiscrimination. The old policy which gave special advantage to the sons of firefighters was not based upon individual merit but rather on accident of birth.

If, however, the black applicant obtained the position over "better qualified" whites in order to give blacks representation within a fire department in which few or no blacks had served before, then this is a form of affirmative action. It would represent the kind of "preferential hiring" that has produced the most controversy and led to charges of "reverse discrimination," that is, discrimination against the white majority instead of against a minority.

The Supreme Court's view of affirmative action programs involving "preferential treatment" of minorities or women has not always been clear. Until its 1995 decision in *Adarand Constructors Inc. v. Pena,* the Court had generally been tolerant of affirmative action programs involving "preferences," which are in effect ordered by Congress under its power to regulate business through it power to "regulate commerce among the states" and through its powers to enforce the provisions of the Fourteenth Amendment against state and local governments. It had, however, generally only approved state- and local-government-initiated or court-ordered "preferences" for minorities when they were designed to remedy proven instances of past discrimination against minorities or women. According to Court decisions, removing the lingering effects of past deliberate discrimination is a "compelling state interest" sufficient to overcome the general constitutional prohibition against racial classifications (see Question 1). In effect the Court recognizes that we must sometimes consciously consider race if we are to undo past racial discrimination.

When, however, state governments attempt to use preferential treatment or quotas in order to assure some given percentage of minority employment or inclusion in some benefit without having first made a specific finding of actual discrimination against minorities by the agency in question, the Supreme Court has ruled that such racial policies violate the Fourteenth Amendment Equal Protection clause. In effect, under such circumstances the Court has determined that discrimination against whites in the name of benefiting previously disadvantaged minorities is as constitutionally suspect as discrimination against minorities.

In 1989 the U.S. Supreme Court weighed the constitutionality of a Minority Business Utilization Plan developed by the city of Richmond, Virginia, in order to assure participation by Minority Business Enterprises (MBEs) in construction contracts awarded by the city. Although the record showed that minority-owned businesses had in the past obtained only a minute portion of the contracts awarded by the city in which blacks constituted approximately 50 percent of the population, "[t]here was no direct evidence of race discrimination on the part of the City in letting contracts" (*City of Richmond v. J. A. Croson Co.,* at 485,

1989). Because of the wide gap between the proportion of blacks in the city's population and the share of contracts awarded to blacks and because of evidence elsewhere in the country of widespread discrimination in the construction industry, the city decided that 30 percent of all construction contracts would be awarded to businesses over which minorities had dominant control. This policy, according to the Court, had the effect of excluding whites from competing for "a fixed percentage of public contracts based solely upon race."

The central question for the Court as it considered the constitutionality of such policies was whether it should treat policies designed to benefit groups that had historically been victimized by discrimination throughout our society the same way as it treats policies that discriminate against such groups today. If "discrimination" in favor of blacks is as bad as discrimination against blacks, then "strict scrutiny" must be applied and only policies justified by some "compelling state interest" may be upheld.

The issue of how the Court should view alleged discrimination against members of the majority racial group, whites, had previously been debated on the Court in *Regents of the University of California v. Bakke* (1978). While recognizing that the original purpose behind the Fourteenth Amendment was to protect those who had been enslaved, blacks, from hostile government action, Justice Powell argued that the meaning of the amendment had evolved over time. For generations beginning with *Plessy v. Ferguson* (1896) (see Question 2 above), the Fourteenth Amendment's Equal Protection clause had for all intents and purposes been ignored. By the time the Court "rediscovered" the Equal Protection clause, Justice Powell argued, ". . . it was no longer possible to peg the guarantees of the Fourteenth Amendment to the struggle for equality of one racial minority. . . . [By then], the United States had become a nation of minorities . . . most of which can lay claim to a history of prior discrimination at the hands of the State and private individuals" (at 295). In light of this history, Powell concluded that the "guarantee of equal protection cannot mean one thing when applied to one individual and something else when applied to a person of another color" (at 290).

The Court in effect adopted Powell's view when in the *Richmond* case, it, for the first time, unambiguously decided that allegations of unconstitutional discrimination against any racial or ethnic group will be subject to the same level of judicial review. In the view of Justice O'Connor writing for the Court majority:

> Absent searching judicial inquiry into the justification for . . . racially based measures, there is simply no way of determining what classifications are "benign" or "remedial" and what classifications are in fact motivated by illegitimate notions of racial

inferiority or simple racial politics. Indeed, the purpose of strict scrutiny is to "smoke out" illegitimate uses of race by assuring that the legislative body is pursuing a goal important enough to warrant use of a highly suspect tool (at 493).

Resolving what had been an inconsistency in its treatment of racial "set asides" or preferences by states and by the federal government, Justice O'Connor writing for a divided court (5 to 4) in *Adarand Constructors, Inc. v. Pena* (1995) decided that the standard for judging all racial classifications, without regard for whether they benefit or harm minorities, must be the same. According to O'Connor, ". . . all racial classifications, imposed by whatever federal, state or local actor, must be analyzed by a reviewing court under strict scrutiny. In other words, such classifications are constitutional only if they are narrowly tailored measures that further compelling governmental interests" (at 227). In layman's language, government policies may treat people of different races differently only when such policies are essential to accomplishing some goal of paramount importance, and those policies must be designed so as to affect adversely only those necessary to accomplish that goal.

On the issue of racial set asides or preferences, the Court has been and remains today sharply divided. Most of its decisions which have gone against racial preferences or set asides for minorities whom society has historically discriminated against have produced vigorous dissents. The dissenters, however, have not simply urged blanket approval for affirmative action programs. Their opinions have recognized the possibility that such a program might be abused. They have, however, urged greater tolerance for government efforts to help those whom society has long discriminated against, even when doing so might jeopardize the interests of some members of the majority racial group.

In his dissent in *Adarand,* Justice John Paul Stevens, for example, accused the majority of the Court of

> . . . [assuming] that there is no significant difference between a decision by the majority to impose a special burden on the members of a minority race and a decision by the majority to provide a benefit to certain members of that minority notwithstanding its incidental burden on some members of the majority. In my opinion that assumption is untenable. There is no moral or constitutional equivalence between a policy that is designed to perpetuate a caste system and one that seeks to eradicate racial subordination. Invidious discrimination is an engine of oppression, subjugating a disfavored group to enhance or maintain the power of the majority. Remedial race-based preferences reflect the opposite impulse: a desire to foster equality . . . (at 243).

In support of his argument, Justice Stevens discussed a part-real–part-hypothetical example. Justice Stevens first noted that many Japanese Americans were subjected to "exclusion" from certain areas on the West Coast during World War II, many being placed in what most would term "concentration camps" solely because of their race, while at the same time other Japanese Americans were recruited and drafted into the military and "exhibited exceptional heroism." In light of this history, Stevens asked how the Court would treat a hypothetical program designed to "reward that service with a federal program that gave all Japanese-American veterans an extraordinary preference in Government employment." Such a program, he noted, would have been based on the same racial and ethnic characteristics that had led to the discriminatory treatment against Japanese Americans. Were the Court to follow its insistence on similar treatment for all racial classifications announced in *Adarand,* it would no doubt have condemned the program designed as compensation for victims of discrimination. "The consistency the Court espouses," according to Justice Stevens, however, "would disregard the difference between a 'no trespassing' sign and a welcome mat. It would treat a Dixiecrat Senator's decision to vote against Thurgood Marshall's confirmation in order to keep an African-American off the Supreme Court as on a par with President Johnson's evaluation of his nominee's race as a positive factor . . ." (*Adarand,* at 245).

The debate over affirmative action is in many ways a debate over how far our society has come in giving African Americans, in particular, the same rights and status as are enjoyed by European Americans. If by simply outlawing discrimination we have succeeded in doing away with discrimination against blacks, then affirmative action, or at least those forms involving racial preference, is probably unnecessary. If, however, blacks and other victims of discrimination continue to suffer the effects of discrimination practiced throughout our society for centuries, then racial preference in employment, in the awarding of contracts, or in school admissions might be necessary to assure that they have the opportunities they would have enjoyed except for the long history of discrimination against them.

The differing views in the Supreme Court over the constitutionality of affirmative action programs and how society should deal with the continuing effects of discrimination were most directly expressed in the *Richmond* case in the separate opinions of Justices Thurgood Marshall and Antonin Scalia. In arguing against all programs based on race, except those specifically and narrowly designed to undo a state's own racially discriminatory actions, Justice Scalia wrote:

> It is plainly true that in our society blacks have suffered discrimination immeasurably greater than any directed at other racial groups.

But those who believe that racial preferences can help "even the score" display, and reinforce, a manner of thinking by race that was the source of the injustice and that will, if it endures within our society, be the source of more injustice still . . . (at 527, 28).

To Justice Scalia, then, affirmative action programs designed to assure representation of blacks and others in positions from which they have long been excluded are themselves racially discriminatory. For him the Constitution requires government to be "colorblind."

From the perspective of Justice Marshall, however, the views espoused by Justice Scalia and indeed similar views shared by a majority of the Court are not so much colorblind as they are blind to the

. . . tragic and indelible fact that discrimination against blacks and other racial minorities . . . has pervaded our nation's history and continues to scar our society. . . . In concluding that . . . [considerations of race designed to remedy past discrimination] warrant no different standard of review under the Constitution than the most brutal and repugnant forms of state-sponsored racism, [Marshall argued,] a majority of . . . [the] Court signals that it regards racial discrimination as largely a phenomenon of the past. . . . In constitutionalizing its wishful thinking, the majority . . . does a grave disservice . . . to those victims of past and present racial discrimination in this nation whom government has sought to assist (at 552).

Although Justice O'Connor's opinion asserted that even under strict scrutiny racial classifications might sometimes be justified, the *Adarand* decision appeared to set the stage for the demise of preferential policies for minorities. When it comes to using "racial preferences" to compensate for general societal discrimination, it does indeed appear that affirmative action as a compensatory measure is, at least for now, dead. Except for in the rare circumstances where it is used to remedy specific proven instances of deliberate discrimination by some government agency (see, for example, *United States v. Paradise* 1987), the deliberate use of racial criteria to expand opportunities of racial minorities has been virtually ruled out. There is, however, one instance in which race-conscious government action has been approved by the Court. That is in the pursuit of "racial diversity" in educational settings.

Question 5 *May government "discriminate" on the basis of race in order to advance the cause of racial diversity?*

Although the U.S. Supreme Court has proved resistant to arguments that society's debt to racial and ethnic minorities for years of oppression and discrimination justifies "discrimination" against members of the relatively privileged white majority, the Court has been open to constitutional interpretations which allow government to promote racial and ethnic diversity in some limited contexts through race-conscious government action. Although government may not treat individual whites and individual blacks differently in order to realize the goal of promoting greater equality in society as a whole, government may apply different standards to judging the qualifications of black and white applicants to universities in order to promote the goal of a diverse student body. Why does the pursuit of "diversity" justify using race as a criterion of decision making by government when the pursuit of social equality does not?

In the case of *Regents of the University of California v. Bakke* (1978) while arguing that racial classification beneficial to minorities had to be treated as skeptically by the Court as those oppressing minorities, Justice Powell argued that in the educational context pursuit of a "diverse" student body amounted to a sufficiently "compelling state interest" to justify taking race into account in medical school admissions decisions. Central to the mission of a university or professional school, according to Powell, is the exchange of ideas. Powell cited approvingly the Court's opinion in *Keyishian v. Board of Regents of the University of the State of New York* (1967):

> Our Nation is deeply committed to safeguarding academic freedom which is of transcendent value to all of us and not merely to the teachers concerned. That freedom is therefore a special concern of the First Amendment. . . . The Nation's future depends upon leaders trained through wide exposure to that robust exchange of ideas which discovers truth "out of tongues [rather] than through any kind of authoritative selection (internal citation omitted)." The atmosphere of "speculation, experiment and creation"—so essential to the quality of higher education—is widely believed to be promoted by a diverse student body. As the Court noted in *Keyishian,* it is not too much to say the "nation's future depends upon leaders trained through wide exposure" to the ideas and mores of students as diverse as this Nation of many peoples (*Bakke,* at 312, 13).

To facilitate the exchange of ideas, universities with selective admissions policies had long sought students from a variety of backgrounds. Scores on the SAT, LSAT, or medical school admissions tests had for many elite institutions never been the sole criterion determining admissions. Differing backgrounds and exceptional artistic and athletic abilities, for example, have long been considered positive factors influencing admissions committees in addition to grades and test scores. Now, according to Justice Powell, adding racial diversity to the "mix" is not only appropriate, but can even be a compelling interest if a university is to fulfill its mission.

Under the specific circumstances of the *Bakke* case, however, Powell, nonetheless condemned a University of California at Davis "special admissions program" because it reserved a specific minimum number of seats in its class for racial and ethnic minorities, seats for which members of the racial "majority" could not compete no matter what contribution they as individuals might bring to the overall diversity of the student body. Powell's Opinion for the Court in *Bakke,* then, while making the case that race could be considered in admissions, actually struck down the specific program at issue in that case.

It was not until the U.S. Supreme Court's decision in *Grutter v. Bollinger* (2003) that the Supreme Court actually upheld a race-conscious university admissions program designed to promote diversity. The differences between the program upheld in *Grutter* and another university admissions policy simultaneously struck down in *Gratz v. Bollinger* should serve to clarify where the Court stands concerning the circumstances under which racial diversity may be a factor in government decision making under contemporary interpretations of the Equal Protection clause of the Fourteenth Amendment.

Grutter v. Bollinger (2003) concerned a challenge to the University of Michigan Law School's admissions policy. According to testimony presented to the district court which initially heard the case, as summarized by Justice Sandra Day O'Connor in her Opinion of the Court:

> The hallmark of that policy is its focus on academic ability coupled with a flexible assessment of applicants' talents, experiences, and potential "to contribute to the learning of those around them." The policy requires admissions officials to evaluate each applicant based on all the information available in the file, including a personal statement, letters of recommendation, and an essay describing the ways in which the applicant will contribute to the life and diversity of the Law School. In reviewing an applicant's file, admissions officials must consider the applicant's undergraduate grade point average (GPA) and Law School Admissions Test (LSAT) score because they are important (if imperfect) predictors of academic success in law school. The policy stresses that "no applicant should be admitted unless we expect that applicant to do well enough to graduate with no serious academic problems."
>
> The policy makes clear, however, that even the highest possible score does not guarantee admission to the Law School. Nor does a low score automatically disqualify an applicant. Rather, the policy requires admissions officials to look beyond grades and test scores to other criteria that are important to the Law School's educational

objectives. So-called "'soft' variables" such as "the enthusiasm of recommenders, the quality of the undergraduate institution, the quality of the applicant's essay, and the areas and difficulty of undergraduate course selection" are all brought to bear in assessing an "applicant's likely contributions to the intellectual and social life of the institution."

The policy aspires to "achieve that diversity which has the potential to enrich everyone's education and thus make a law school class stronger than the sum of its parts." The policy does not restrict the types of diversity contributions eligible for "substantial weight" in the admissions process, but instead recognizes "many possible bases for diversity admissions." The policy does, however, reaffirm the Law School's longstanding commitment to "one particular type of diversity," that is, "racial and ethnic diversity with special reference to the inclusion of students from groups which have been historically discriminated against, like African-Americans, Hispanics and Native Americans, who without this commitment might not be represented in our student body in meaningful numbers." By enrolling a "'critical mass' of [underrepresented] minority students," the Law School seeks to "ensure their ability to make unique contributions to the character of the Law School" (at 4499, 4500).

A central point of debate within the Court concerns the legitimacy of the law school's policy that a "critical mass" of minority students be admitted. On the surface the term "critical mass" appears to be another way of saying "quota" or set percentage. Justice Powell's Opinion in the *Bakke* case had rejected racial quotas. As explained by the university here and accepted by the Court majority the term "critical mass" was a flexible guideline designed to realize the full benefits allegedly flowing from a diverse student body. Eric Munzel, a director of admissions for the law school, testified at the district court trial of the case that "'critical mass' means 'meaningful representation,' which he understood to mean a number that encourages underrepresented minority students to participate in the classroom and not feel isolated" (at 4500).

Others testified that a critical mass of traditionally underrepresented minorities advances the educational benefits flowing from diversity because when a critical mass is present "racial stereotypes lose their force because nonminority students learn there is no "minority viewpoint" but rather a variety of viewpoints among minority students" (at 4501).

Although the exact percentage of "minority" students admitted during each year of the program varied somewhat, clearly the policy was designed to assure there would be sufficient minority students so that their presence would be felt in the classroom. That the Court emphasized the benefits flowing from diversity to the educational process over any notion of compensation to minorities for the long history of racial discrimination in American society, however, was reinforced by the Court's decision in *Gratz v. Bollinger* (2003). The *Gratz* case concerned a challenge to the undergraduate admissions policy at the University of Michigan.

At the undergraduate level the University of Michigan had used a variety of formulas for determining admission. Beginning in 1998, however, the University developed a "'selection index,' on which an applicant could score a maximum of 150 points. . . . Each applicant received points based on high school grade point average, standardized tests scores, academic quality of the applicant's high school, strength or weakness of high school curriculum, in-state residency, alumni relationship, personal essay, and personal achievement and leadership. Of particular significance here, under a 'miscellaneous' category, an applicant was entitled to twenty points based upon his or her membership in an underrepresented racial or ethnic minority group" (at 4482).

In his Opinion of the Court, Chief Justice William Rehnquist found that in distributing 20 points to every underrepresented minority applicant, the university in effect gave too much weight automatically to one variable, race, in the pursuit of the goal of diversity. The chief justice in this case did not dispute the position of Justice Powell in *Bakke* and Justice O'Connor in *Grutter* that the pursuit of diversity in an educational institution can be sufficiently compelling to take race into account in admissions. What was wrong with the undergraduate admissions program at Michigan was the automatic (and perhaps disproportionate) weight assigned to race in the admissions process. In citing a number of hypothetical examples of student profiles, for example, the chief justice noted that under the university's program even a student whose "'extraordinary artistic talent' rivaled that of Monet or Picasso" would receive "at most, five points," while every member of an underrepresented racial minority would receive 20 (at 4488).

In her concurring opinion in the case Justice Sandra Day O'Connor, the author of the Opinion of the Court in *Grutter*, emphasized the automatic quality of the point system in the undergraduate admissions program. The flaw in the program is in its failure to assess each applicant's contribution to diversity as an individual (at 4489). In acknowledging in *Grutter* the legitimacy of the University of Michigan Law School's concern for achieving a critical mass of minority students in order to reap the benefits of a diverse student body, the Court seemed to accept the special importance of racial and ethnic diversity. The Court, after all, did not indicate that equal consideration should be given to achieving a critical mass of poets or cricket players or cellists. On the other hand in *Gratz* the Court rejected any mechanistic formula for accomplishing the goal of racial and ethnic diversity.

The Court justified considering race in university admissions while rejecting considering race in the award of benefits, such as government contracts, on the grounds that in the university setting diversity promotes the free exchange of ideas—a core First Amendment concern. Advancing First Amendment values is of sufficiently paramount importance to reach the high threshold required before race may become a factor in decision making.

It may seem strange that in light of the long history of discrimination in American society against racial and ethnic minorities that a concern for equality in society itself should not be of sufficient weight to justify considering race. Indeed in her dissent in *Gratz v. Bollinger* (2003), Justice Ruth Bader Ginsburg, like Justice John Paul Stevens in *Adarand* (see Question 4 above), argued that considering race to remove the effects of oppression is quite different from using race as an engine of oppression.

> Our jurisprudence ranks race a "suspect" category, "not because [race] is inevitably an impermissible classification, but because it is one which usually, to our national shame, has been drawn for the purpose of maintaining racial inequality." But where race is considered "for the purpose of achieving equality," no automatic proscription is in order. For, as insightfully explained, "the Constitution is both color blind and color conscious. To avoid conflict with the equal protection clause, a classification that denies a benefit, causes harm, or imposes a burden must not be based on race. In that sense, the Constitution is color blind. But the Constitution is color conscious to prevent discrimination being perpetuated and to undo the effects of past discrimination." . . . Contemporary human rights documents draw just this line; they distinguish between policies of oppression and measures designed to accelerate *de facto* equality (at 4496).

To Ginsburg, then, awarding minority students 20 points in an admissions scale can be justified as a measure to advance their participation in the benefits of society. Achieving equality justifies this measure independent of any concern for how much of a contribution to "diversity" individual minority students might make. Because advancing such equality was the very purpose for which the Equal Protection clause of the Fourteenth Amendment was written, policies designed with that end in mind should not have to meet the same high constitutional threshold, strict scrutiny, that policies designed to perpetuate inequality have to surmount.

Taken together the Court's decisions concerning racially conscious government decision making prohibit most government decisions which discriminate in favor of minorities in the pursuit of a more equal society in the same way as they prohibit government decisions designed to oppress minorities. At least in the educational context, however, government may to some degree discriminate in favor of minorities in order to reap the presumed educational benefits that flow from the exchange of ideas from among peoples of diverse experiences and backgrounds. What remains unclear is whether an interest in diversity can justify considering race in other contexts beyond university admissions. Is it permissible to base employment decisions in universities at least in part on race on the assumption that faculty from diverse backgrounds will contribute to the free exchange of ideas in the same way as racial and other diversity among students contributes? May a police force give extra points to minority applicants on the assumption that a force made up of people of diverse backgrounds is more likely to understand the needs of a city population made up of people of many races?

While First Amendment values were relied upon to justify taking race into account in university admissions, there may be nothing of comparable constitutional significance to justify the use of the generally proscribed racial classifications in other settings. Time will tell whether the Court reaffirmation of the significance of diversity as a value of constitutional stature in educational settings will translate into a broader affirmation of diversity in society as a whole. If the pursuit of greater societal equality was not sufficiently compelling to justify racially conscious government decision making (see Question 4 above), then it may be doubtful that an interest in diversity outside of the special context of education will be enough.

Question 6 *Do we still need a new Equal Rights Amendment (ERA) to secure gender equality?*

During the early 1970s it looked very likely that an Equal Rights Amendment, guaranteeing that "[e]quality of rights under the law shall not be denied or abridged by the United States or by any State on account of sex," would become part of the United States Constitution. The proposed amendment, which easily obtained the necessary two-thirds vote in the United States House of Representatives and Senate, failed to obtain the approval of the legislatures of three-quarters of the states to become part of the Constitution. The reasons for this failure were many. Many religious and other conservatives opposed the notion of gender equality in principle, some believing it contrary to the Bible. Others worried that it would end special privileges and exemptions enjoyed by women, such as exception from compulsory military service when conscription is in place. Others, felt that it would end all distinctions between men and women, forcing the end of separate restroom facilities in public places and so forth. Many others, however, felt that the Supreme Court's decisions relating to the Fourteenth Amendment had already provided sufficient protections for the rights of women, the gender presumed to require protection from discrimination.

Clearly whether we need or want an Equal Rights Amendment to the Constitution depends in part on the accuracy of some of the fears expressed by opponents to the amendment and in part on your position on many of these disputed questions.

Although in Question 1 we have already briefly addressed contemporary Supreme Court treatment of gender discrimination under the Fourteenth Amendment, it is best to begin with a somewhat more detailed analysis of the current legal status of gender discrimination under the Constitution. As was noted above in Question 1, current judicial interpretation of the Fourteenth Amendment gives government somewhat more leeway in drawing legal distinctions between men and women than is permitted between and among racial and ethnic groups. Partly because of the fact that the Fourteenth Amendment was initially clearly intended to outlaw state government discrimination based on race and was silent on the question of gender, a Supreme Court majority has never held that gender distinctions in the law are constitutionally impermissible unless justified by some compelling state interest (the standard in race discrimination cases). Rather the Court has evolved a standard for judging gender discrimination that falls somewhat short of the "strict scrutiny" stand it has adopted for judging the constitutionality of racial classifications.

First in *Craig v. Boren* (1976) and consistently since, the Court unambiguously elevated gender discrimination to a special status under the Fourteenth and Fifth Amendments, a status not quite as suspect as racial distinctions, but still one requiring a "heightened" level of judicial scrutiny. Although until the Court's decision in *Reed v. Reed* (1971) the Court routinely upheld legal distinctions between men and women founded on gender stereotypes and the traditionally subordinate role of women in society and in the marketplace, in *Reed* the Court set the stage for the more explicit rejection of such stereotypes as the foundation for legislation which *Craig* made controlling.

The *Reed* decision struck down an Idaho law which required an automatic male preference in designating executors of estates between equally qualified males and females. Although the Court decision rejected the male preference provision as having no rational foundation, the state contended it served to avoid the necessity and expense of administrative hearings. The Court, however, considered this justification inadequate, contending that the male preference provision was "the very kind of arbitrary legislative choice" (at 76) forbidden by the Fourteenth Amendment.

Following the *Reed* case the Court began to define the special constitutional status of gender discrimination under the Fifth and Fourteenth

Amendments. Four justices in the *Frontiero* case (see above, Question 1) argued that gender discrimination is indistinguishable from race discrimination under the Constitution. According to them only a compelling state interest could justify gender distinctions in the law. The Court majority subsequent to *Frontiero* has with increasing consistency adopted the standard from *Craig*. The settled character of the "heightened scrutiny" standard from *Craig* is evidenced by the fact that in his concurring opinion in *United States v. Virginia* (1996), Chief Justice Rehnquist, the author of a vigorous dissent in *Craig,* himself relies on *Craig*. He wrote: "Two decades ago in *Craig v. Boren. . .* , we announced that 'to withstand constitutional challenge, . . . classifications by gender must serve important governmental objectives and must be substantially related to the achievement of those objectives.' We have adhered to that standard ever since" (at 2288).

In *United States v. Virginia* the Court majority further amplified the heightened scrutiny applied in gender discrimination cases and provided some explanation of why race and gender cases are not treated exactly alike. A review of that decision should aid us in beginning to come to an answer for the question of whether an Equal Rights Amendment promoting gender equality under the Constitution is either necessary or desirable today.

The basic issue in *United States v. Virginia* was the constitutionality of the exclusion of women from the Virginia Military Institute (VMI). In response to a legal challenge to VMI policy excluding women, a federal appeal court found that a single-gender military training program of the type in existence at VMI was constitutionally permissible if a comparable program were created elsewhere to serve women. If no such program were created, then women would have to be admitted to VMI.

Virginia responded to this Court ruling by creating Virginia Women's Institute for Leadership, an institution that lacked much of the vigorous "adversative" military training found at VMI, emphasizing instead the cultivation of leadership skills among the women cadets.

According to Justice Ruth Bader Ginsburg's Opinion of the Court, the case as it came to the Supreme Court presented two issues:

> First, does the exclusion of women from the educational opportunities provided by VMI—extraordinary opportunities for military training and civilian leadership development—deny to women "capable of all the individual activities required of VMI cadets," the equal protection of the laws guaranteed by the Fourteenth Amendment? Second, if VMI's "unique" situation—as Virginia's sole single-sex public institution of higher education—offends the Constitution's equal protection principle, what is the remedial requirement? (at 2274).

According to Justice Ginsburg any defense of a gender-based classification must have an "exceedingly persuasive justification" to survive what she termed the Court's "skeptical scrutiny" (at 2274). Her decision, which repeated the *Craig* requirement that the state must bear the burden of showing that any gender-based classification serves "important government objectives and that the discriminatory means employed are substantially related to the achievement of those objectives," nonetheless refused to go so far as to equate racial discrimination with gender discrimination.

As we consider the question of the need for a new Equal [gender] Rights amendment, this distinction between the Court's treatment of race and gender may be crucial. For as Justice Ginsburg noted under the strict scrutiny standard applied in race cases today, "[s]upposed 'inherent differences' are no longer accepted as a ground for race or national origin classifications. . . . Physical differences between men and women, however, are enduring: 'The two sexes are not fungible; a community made up exclusively of one [sex] is different from a community composed of both'" (*Ballard v. United States,* at 2276, 1946).

Acknowledging then that all distinctions among men and women in the law and public policy need not necessarily flow from invidious discrimination, but rather reflect natural and inevitable differences, Justice Ginsburg acknowledged that gender will sometimes serve as a legitimate basis for different treatment in the law without offending the Constitution. In applying this principle to the case of Virginia Military Institute, Justice Ginsburg argued that at least some women have shown that they are indeed capable of participating in training as physically rigorous as that of men. At least for such women, then, excluding them from VMI did constitute unconstitutional discrimination.

The implications of this decision for the debate over a new Equal Rights Amendment are not certain. On the one hand, if a new ERA were to become part of the Constitution, then the legal distinction between the treatment of gender and race discrimination would likely disappear. Just as racial classifications are now subject to strict scrutiny and can survive challenge only on a showing that they serve a "compelling state interest and are narrowly tailored to serving that interest," so too would gender classifications. While now under the *Craig* test, gender classifications are not held to quite such a strict test in that the interests that must be advanced by them need be "important" but not quite "compelling," after ERA gender classifications would have to be justified by the "stricter" standard applied to race if they were to survive challenge.

But Justice Ginsburg's opinion does provide a foundation for gender classifications surviving even after ERA. If the gender classification were in fact based on real differences between men and women, they might then be deemed sufficient under some circumstances to survive strict scrutiny. Today, on the other hand, racial differences are never considered sufficiently real to meet the compelling state interest test. Although it is quite conceivable to imagine legal distinctions meant to protect women of childbearing age, for example, from physical injury affecting their potential children or their ability to reproduce, it is also quite reasonable to treat men differently as a class because they cannot bear children. Even under the compelling state interest test, real differences justified by such a paramount interest could serve as the basis for different legal treatment. What Justice Ginsburg provides, therefore, is a reasoned foundation for understanding and acting on genuine differences that are more likely to exist in a gender than in a racial context. With such an understanding the application of the strict scrutiny standard to gender cases, which would almost certainly follow the adoption of an ERA, would still permit distinctions in law based upon physical distinctions that are real and not merely the reflection of stereotype and/or prejudice.

There is, however, one area in which an ERA might have what people concerned about women's rights might view as a detrimental effect on women's interests. In the area of affirmative action, programs designed to compensate women and minorities for past discrimination against them as groups, an ERA might serve to remove a current advantage which women enjoy over racial and ethnic minorities. Today the Supreme Court treats all racial classifications in the law the same. Even so-called "benign discrimination"—discrimination designed to benefit previously disadvantaged racial groups—is subjected to strict scrutiny and is therefore very difficult to defend against constitutional challenge. Only programs designed to make up for proven instances of deliberate racial discrimination against specific individuals and identifiable groups have survived application of strict scrutiny in the racial context. The Court has rejected making up for general societal discrimination against African Americans, for example, as sufficient justification for different treatment of whites and blacks to be considered a "compelling" state interest. Today because there is no ERA and gender discrimination is subjected to the lesser standard of "heightened scrutiny," different treatment of men and women is more easily defended if the purpose is to compensate women generally for historic discrimination against all women. As Justice Ginsburg noted in her opinion in *United States v. Virginia,* today still "[s]ex classifications may be used to compensate women 'for particular economic disabilities [they have] suffered' *Califano v. Webster,* at 313 (1977) . . . to promote equal employment opportunity . . ." (at 2276). Under current Supreme Court application of the strict scrutiny test to *all* racial classifications, however, such amorphous justifications would not be sufficient to justify a racial classification. To the degree an ERA would lead to equal treatment of racial and gender classifications under the law, women might lose an advantage they now have as society confronts its history of both racial and gender discrimination.

As Justice John Paul Stevens noted in his dissent in the *Adarand* case, it is indeed ironic that the Fourteenth Amendment, which was designed to undo our legacy of racial oppression, has now been used to make it more difficult for government to take steps to make up for past societal racial discrimination, while on the other hand, this same Fourteenth Amendment which ignored gender discrimination now permits such steps to make up for society's history of past gender discrimination.

Without an ERA, of course, it is always possible for courts to return to their past tolerance of vast gender discrimination against women. With women now constituting a majority of the electorate and a very substantial portion of the workforce and even the professions, it seems unlikely that legislatures will again pass discriminatory legislation against women. Discrimination in favor of women, however, such as in the exemption from military service, still survives in some areas. Perhaps men would benefit more from an ERA than would women.

Question 7   *How do you know if you are a victim of unconstitutional discrimination?*

You visit a community and observe that a neighborhood is entirely white while another is entirely black. You see a schoolyard filled with children all of the same race. You visit a state medical school and find that 98 percent of those enrolled are white or you watch a fire and see that all of the firefighters are men. We look at the death rows across America and find a much higher percentage of blacks there than we find in the population as a whole. We all know that this list could go on indefinitely. Whether we focus on race or sex, we can see that one race or sex often receives an apparently disproportionate share of society's benefits while another carries a disproportionate share of the burdens. Many of us are led to ask: If this isn't proof of discrimination, what is?

The Constitution commands that "No State shall . . . deny to any person . . . the equal protection of the laws." Although the examples cited above illustrate differences in our society's treatment of people on the basis of race or sex, they may not all represent unconstitutional denials of equal protection. Before condemning all of these illustrations as signs of unconstitutional discrimination, we must first ask: Who is responsible for the apparent differences? Are any of them a reflection of the genuine choices of different people? Are some of them a simple reflection of differences in economic status which many in society believe either is or should be beyond the control of government?

Recognizing in part that the Constitution does not expect uniformity and that Americans expect and even respect differences, the Court has argued that the Constitution prohibits only intentional government-imposed discrimination. Even government policies which themselves have the effect of producing differences among people of different races are not considered unconstitutional unless they were selected with that specific racial purpose in mind.

Consider the Social Security system. Everyone of working age pays into the Social Security trust fund. Once a person reaches 65, he or she collects benefits loosely based on the amount of his or her contribution. Although individual white and black men both pay Social Security taxes, a far smaller proportion of black men live to the age of 65 than do white men. Is the Social Security system discriminatory?

There is no doubt that the system has a discriminatory effect on the black male population as a whole, but individual blacks who live to 65 are treated the same as individual whites. Were the disproportionate burdens the Social Security system places on the overall black population intended by those who designed the system? Is it a reflection of the desires of the Congresses that continue the system?

Were black Americans to challenge the racially discriminatory impact of the Social Security system in court, there is little doubt that the U.S. Supreme Court would find it to be perfectly constitutional. When confronted with a government policy that has a *racially disproportionate effect,* the Court demands evidence that the policy is a result of *discriminatory intent.* When only evidence of a disproportionate racial effect is presented, the Court will presume discriminatory intent only when the effect ". . . is very difficult to explain on non-racial grounds" (*Washington v. Davis,* at 242, 1976).

Since a neutral nonracial justification for the Social Security system, providing income for people who live beyond working years, could be advanced, the Court would find the evidence of discriminatory effect insufficient to establish a constitutional violation. Before finding unconstitutional discrimination, the Court has ruled that proof must be presented that the ". . . decision maker . . . selected or reaffirmed a . . . [policy] at least in part 'because of,' not merely 'in spite of,' its adverse effects upon an identifiable group" (*Personnel Administrator v. Feeney,* at 279, 1979). Although Congress should be aware of the differences between the life expectancies of blacks and whites, it seems likely that Congress designed the Social Security system in spite of those differences not because of them.

While in the past racial criteria for government actions were written into statutes and regulations, today few government officials or agencies would be so foolish as to openly admit a discriminatory purpose. To prove discriminatory intent, therefore, we must look into ". . . such circumstantial and direct evidence of intent as may be available." As a start we must look to see whether policies that have had racially disproportionate effects have been singled out by policy makers for special treatment. Have they been handled differently from policies that have no racial impact? More specifically, in his opinion in *Arlington Heights v. Metropolitan Housing Authority* (1977), Justice Lewis Powell suggested review of racially suspect governmental decision making in an attempt to find some deviation from the norm in such aspects as the "specific sequence of events leading up to the challenged decision," "departures from normal procedures," or "substantive departures" (at 266–68).

What the Court looks for in such inquiries are signs that the potential racial impact of a decision has led decision makers to act in some unusual way. If, as is likely, decision makers will not admit that their actions were racially motivated, evidence must be developed by studying their behavior. If, for example, following normal procedures would have led to a result from which blacks might have benefited, but the officials for no apparent reason disregard normal procedures and act in an unusual way resulting in a decision detrimental to black interests, the courts might then be willing to demand some explanation for the decision under challenge. If no neutral (nonracial) explanation is available, then the courts are generally willing to presume that an action which produced a "discriminatory effect" resulted from unconstitutional discriminatory intent.

Although race seems still to make a difference in almost all aspects of life, debate over the role of race in the administration of criminal justice is probably the most intense. Blacks and other minorities often feel the least protected by the forces of law and order and at the same time the most likely to be treated severely by them.

For much of American history there was little doubt that racism influenced decisions concerning the death penalty. Belief that the death penalty was administered in a racially discriminatory manner influenced in part the Supreme Court's decision declaring then existing death penalty laws unconstitutional in 1972 (*Furman v. Georgia*). Today the death penalty is back and the controversy concerning its racially discriminatory application continues.

In 1987 a challenge to existing death penalty laws was mounted which raised a new question about how race enters into the criminal justice system. A black man, Warren McCleskey, challenged his death sentence claiming in essence that had he and others like him killed black people rather than white people, they would not have been sentenced to death. In support of this argument his lawyers presented a statistical study that showed that persons who were convicted of murdering whites were 11 times more likely to be sentenced to death than were persons who killed blacks. The data they presented reflected not only the apparent impact of race upon the sentencing decisions of juries in the state of Georgia where the study was done, but also the decision of prosecutors to even request the death penalty. While prosecutors requested death penalties in 70 percent of the cases where the defendant was black and the victim was white, they sought the death penalty in only 15 percent of the cases where the defendant was black and the victim was black (at 286–87).

Recognizing that differences in the specific nature of crimes committed might explain some of the differences in sentencing, the statistical analysis presented to the Court sought to take into account explanations other than race that might have accounted for the skewed result. In the end after extensive analysis of the data, even after accounting for the impact of 39 nonracial variables or explanations, the study concluded that "defendants charged with killing white victims were 4.3 times as likely to receive a death sentence as defendants charged with killing blacks" (at 287).

When the Supreme Court was confronted with these data, it did not dispute their accuracy; it did, however, refuse to accept them as proof of unconstitutional discrimination. Although the Court had ruled in *Washington v. Davis* that when a pattern exists "that is unexplainable on grounds other than race . . ." it would find sufficient proof of discriminatory intent, the Court in *McCleskey* concluded that "[w]here the discretion that is fundamental to our criminal justice system is involved, we decline to assume that what is unexplained is invidious [or discriminatory]" (at 313).

Prosecutors, judges, and juries make choices—exercise discretion—every day. In deciding on appropriate punishment for crimes within the limits set by law, they are left to their human judgment. Such discretion is designed to adjust the broad impact of the law to individual circumstances. It is considered essential to justice. While the Court majority in the *McCleskey* case apparently believed that sufficient safeguards are built into the criminal justice process to rule out improper motivation in the exercise of discretion, others, including the four justices who dissented, had severe doubts. They believed that racial discrimination is a continuing problem in this society, and they believed that the evidence assembled on McCleskey's behalf should have been enough to strike down capital punishment laws that produce such dramatically different results apparently depending upon the race of the victim of the crime.

While the rules of evidence, constraints on the jury selection process, and routine appellate court review all make decision making in the criminal justice system different from other kinds of government decision making, the *McCleskey* case raises the question of whether those differences are significant enough to justify treating evidence of racial discrimination differently. The dramatic differences in the application of the death penalty against those killing whites over those killing blacks were not explained by the Court on grounds other than race. Had this been a state employment discrimination case or a school segregation case there is little doubt that the type of statistical evidence presented in

McCleskey's behalf would have been sufficient to prove unconstitutional discrimination.

Justice Brennan, one of the four dissenters from the Court's decision upholding McCleskey's death sentence, felt that the Court's decision disregarded the history of race relations in America:

> At the time our Constitution was framed 200 years ago this year, blacks "had for more than a century been regarded as beings of an inferior order, and all together unfit to associate with the white race, either in social or political relations; and as so far inferior, that they had no rights which the white man was bound to respect." *Dred Scott v. Sandford* (1857). . . .
>
> In more recent times, we have sought to free ourselves from the burden of this history. . . . These have been honorable steps, but we cannot pretend that in three decades we have completely escaped the grip of an historical legacy spanning centuries. Warren McCleskey's evidence confronts us with the subtle and persistent influence of the past. His message is a disturbing one for a society that has formally repudiated racism, and a frustrating one to a Nation accustomed to regarding its destiny as the product of its own will. Nonetheless, we ignore him at our peril, for we remain imprisoned by the past as long as we deny its influence in the present (at 343–44).

While not challenging the fact that blacks often benefit less and suffer more from government actions than do whites, the Court refuses to presume that such measurable differences in results reflect any denial of "equal protection of the laws." Rather than acknowledging that racism may be a routine feature of American life, the Court treats racism as something unusual. No matter how obvious your predicament may seem, you are not a victim of unconstitutional discrimination unless you can satisfy the courts that government has intentionally discriminated against you. The equal protection of the laws does not guarantee that all will equally share in this society's benefits or burdens.

REFERENCES

Adarand Constructors, Inc. v. Pena, 515 U.S. 200 (1995).

Arlington Heights v. Metropolitan Housing Authority, 429 U.S. 252 (1977).

Ballard v. United States, 397 U.S. 187 (1946).

Brown v. Board of Education, 347 U.S. 483 (1954).

Brown v. Board of Education (II), 349 U.S. 294 (1955).

Califano v. Webster, 430 U.S. 313 (1977).

City of Richmond v. J. A. Croson Co., 488 U.S. 469 (1989).

Craig v. Boren, 429 U.S. 190 (1976).

Cumming v. County Board of Education, 175 U.S. 528 (1899).

Dred Scott v. Sandford, 60 U.S. 393 (1856).

Frontiero v. Richardson, 411 U.S. 677 (1973).

Furman v. Georgia, 408 U.S. 238 (1972).

Gratz v. Bollinger, 71 USLW 4480 (2003).

Green v. New Kent County, 391 U.S. 430 (1968).

Griffin v. County School Board of Prince Edward County, 337 U.S. 218 (1964).

Grutter v. Bollinger, 71 USLW 4498 (2003).

Keyishian v. Board of Regents of University of State of New York, 385 U.S. 589 (1967).

Korematsu v. United States, 323 U.S. 214 (1944).

McCleskey v. Kemp, 481 U.S. 279 (1987).

McDonald v. Board of Election Commissioners, 394 U.S. 802 (1969).

McLaurin v. Oklahoma State Board of Regents, 339 U.S. 637 (1950).

Personnel Adminstrator v. Feeney, 442 U.S. 256 (1979).

Plessy v. Ferguson, 163 U.S. 537 (1896).

Reed v. Reed, 402 U.S. 71 (1971).

Regents of the University of California v. Bakke, 438 U.S. 265 (1978).

The Slaughterhouse Cases, 83 U.S. 36 (1873).

Strauder v. West Virginia, 100 U.S. 303 (1880).

Swann v. Charlotte-Mecklenburg Board of Education, 402 U.S. 1 (1971).

United States v. Paradise et al., 480 U.S. 149 (1987).

United States v. Virginia, 116 S. Ct. 2264 (1996).

U.S. Commission on Civil Rights, *Twenty Years after Brown: Equality of Educational Opportunity.* (Washington, D.C.: Government Printing Office, 1975).

Washington v. Davis, 426 U.S. 229 (1976).

CHAPTER FIVE

PRIVACY AND INDIVIDUAL AUTONOMY

Probably no issue of constitutional rights continues to produce as much controversy as the debate over the right to privacy. To this point we have discussed conflicts within the Court over the precise meaning of liberties and rights protected by the Constitution. With the right to privacy, however, the first debate concerns whether the Constitution includes any such right at all. Question 1 introduces this controversy by asking: *How much privacy do we have a right to expect?* This section discusses the debate over just what aspects of privacy are protected by the Constitution. This discussion focuses on the Supreme Court's decision in *Griswold* in which Justice Douglas argued that privacy finds its roots in the First, Third, Fourth, Fifth, Ninth, and Fourteenth Amendments. Conversely, this section reviews Justice Black's dissenting argument that there is no constitutional right to privacy as such. In discussing the concurring opinions of Justices Harlan and Arthur Goldberg, however, this section lays the foundation for broader discussions that follow concerning how the Court identifies constitutionally protected rights and liberties not specifically mentioned in the Constitution.

The most controversial issue under the heading of the right to privacy has no doubt been a woman's right to choose abortion. Question 2 asks: *How did the "right to privacy" lead to a woman's right to have an abortion?* This section discusses the U.S. Supreme Court's decision in *Roe v. Wade* and the argument that a woman's control over her body and over the decision to have children flows from the general "right to privacy." *Roe v. Wade* and other cases dealing with competing claims of husbands or a minor girl's parents are discussed.

Much of the controversy over abortion concerns the competing claim of a fetus's "right to life." In light of Supreme Court rulings continuing to uphold a woman's right to choose abortion, Question 3 asks: *Does a fetus's "right to life" ever count more than a woman's right to privacy?* This section discusses the viability standard from *Roe v. Wade* and subsequent cases. It reviews the Court's decision in *Planned Parenthood v. Casey,* which gave somewhat greater latitude to government to protect "potential life."

Because early Supreme Court decisions relating to privacy concerned issues regarding intimate associations surrounding family life and reproduction, it was inevitable that other questions relating to sexual intimacy would arise. Question 4 asks: *May the state regulate private sexual relationships between consenting adults?* This section begins with a discussion of the limits on sexual privacy raised in Justice Harlan's concurring opinion in *Griswold v. Connecticut.* It focuses primarily on the Supreme Court's decision in *Lawrence v. Texas,* which overturned the Court's 1986 ruling in *Bowers v. Hardwick,* the "homosexual sodomy" decision. It explores the deep division that remains on the Supreme Court over the meaning of the right to privacy and the right of the state to regulate personal conduct.

The Court's birth control and abortion decisions in very important ways concern a person's right to control his or her own body and destiny. No issue is more central to such concerns as the decision of when and how we might end our lives. Question 5 asks: *Why doesn't the "right to privacy" include the right to decide to end our lives?* This section reviews the issues surrounding the right to die or the right to assisted suicide. It reviews the Supreme Court's decision upholding state government bans on assisted suicide, even for the terminally ill. It will discuss the debate concerning whether how long each of us lives is itself a profoundly private question that should be beyond society's control.

The questions explored in this chapter concern deeply personal decisions ranging from reproduction and sexual intimacy to circumstances surrounding the end of life itself.

Question 1　*How much privacy do we have a right to expect?*

To most of us "privacy" means being left alone. When we say, "I wish you would mind your own business," or "Keep out of my personal affairs," we are expressing the expectation that some matters concern no one but ourselves. When we direct such comments to government, we are saying that some things are solely personal concerns and, therefore, of no concern to government or society in general. How we handle such matters concerns only ourselves and those in whom we choose to confide.

The word "privacy" does not appear in the Constitution. When the Court has recognized a "right of privacy," some have argued that it is implicit in other rights which are mentioned. Some elements of privacy, according to the Court, predated the Constitution. They are so obvious that the framers felt no need even to mention them. The fact that certain rights exist which are not explicitly mentioned in the Constitution is recognized in the Ninth Amendment, which states: "The enumeration in the Constitution, of certain rights, shall not be construed to deny or disparage others retained by the people." In other words, the fact that certain rights are mentioned and explicitly recognized by the Constitution does not mean that these are the only rights we have. Although the Ninth Amendment recognizes the existence of rights beyond those listed, it gives us no help in identifying what those rights might be.

Other sections of the Bill of Rights, however, provide a basis for an expectation of privacy in certain spheres of life. The First Amendment, for example, protects our freedom of association, that is, our freedom to join with others to advance our views and express our opinions. When our opinions, or associations based on them, might cause us embarrassment or worse, the Court has recognized our right to keep such associations private (*NAACP v. Alabama,* 1958).

Probably the most private sphere of all is what goes on in our minds. In striking down a law punishing private possession in one's home of obscene materials, Justice Marshall wrote: "If the First Amendment means anything, it means that a state has no business telling a man, sitting alone in his home, what books he may read or what films he may watch. . . ." In sum, Marshall argued, the First Amendment forbids the state from ". . . controlling a person's private thoughts" (*Stanley v. Georgia,* at 565, 566, 1969).

It was from cases such as these that the right to privacy emerged. In his opinion in *Griswold v. Connecticut* (1965), which upheld the right to privacy and argued it included the right to decide for oneself whether to use birth control devices, Justice Douglas wrote:

> . . . that specific guarantees in the Bill of Rights have penumbras, formed by emanations from those guarantees that help give them life and substance. . . . Various guarantees create zones of privacy. The right of association contained in the penumbra of the First Amendment is one. . . . The Third Amendment in its prohibition against quartering of soldiers "in any house" in time of peace without the consent of the owner is another facet of privacy. The Fourth Amendment explicitly affirms the "right of the people to

be secure in their persons, houses, papers, and effects against unreasonable searches and seizures." The Fifth Amendment in its Self-Incrimination Clause enables the citizen to create a zone of privacy which government may not force him to surrender to his detriment. The Ninth Amendment provides: "The enumeration in the Constitution, of certain rights, shall not be construed to deny or disparage others retained by the people" (at 479).

When Douglas speaks of "penumbras," he likens the Bill of Rights to the sun. Just as an eclipse reveals a vast array of gases emanating from the sun not usually visible to the naked eye, close inspection of the provisions of the Bill of Rights seen together reveals zones of privacy. While the First and Fifth Amendments protect us from exposing our private thoughts when those thoughts could subject us to harm, the Third and Fourth Amendments provide protection for our homes and personal papers. They, in effect, codify the notion that "your home is your castle." Finally, the liberty protected by the Fifth and Fourteenth Amendments has been interpreted at times as protecting us from government intrusion into our "private" affairs.

Although Douglas found the right to privacy to be rooted firmly in the Bill of Rights itself, others in the Court majority emphasized the broad protection of "liberty" in the Due Process clause of the Fourteenth Amendment. The specific issue in *Griswold* concerned the constitutionality of a Connecticut statute that banned the use of birth control devices even by married persons; it also forbade anyone, including physicians, from counseling others in the use of contraceptive devices. According to Justice Goldberg's concurring opinion, this ban on birth control violated rights to liberty rooted in the "traditions and [collective] conscience of our people" (at 493). Goldberg found support in the Ninth Amendment for the notion that some rights and liberties are so fundamental that the framers saw no specific need to mention them directly. Surely the right to marital privacy and control over the decision to have a family rank among such fundamental rights.

As the discussion of incorporation in Chapter 1 demonstrates, giving specific content to the Due Process clause of the Fourteenth Amendment raises difficult issues. "Liberty" can mean different things to different people and certainly to different justices of the U.S. Supreme Court. The justices defending the right of privacy in marital relationships in *Griswold* argued, however, that their decision reflected their reading of history and the established customs and values of society as a whole and not merely their personal predilections.

The idea that the Constitution protects privacy " . . . at certain times and places with respect to certain activities" (Black, J., dissenting, at 508) is not really controversial. Rather, the controversy over privacy arises over the broad sweep given its protection by the Court. Justice Black's dissent argued that the only privacy protected by the Constitution are those elements of privacy covered specifically by the provisions of the Constitution discussed above. He wrote: "I like my privacy as well as the next one, but I am nonetheless compelled to admit that government has a right to invade it unless prohibited by some specific constitutional provision" (at 507). If parts of several amendments to the Constitution provide some element of privacy, Black felt obligated to confine the right of privacy to the sum of those parts. To the majority of the Court, however, the right of privacy implicit in a number of amendments extends beyond the specifics of those amendments; the whole right of privacy is, therefore, greater than the sum of its parts. To them the right of privacy has provided grounds for limits on government power in a number of spheres, the most controversial of which has been abortion.

Question 2   *How did the "right to privacy" lead to a woman's right to have an abortion?*

Although in *Griswold v. Connecticut* (1965) (discussed in Question 1) the Court first explicitly recognized a constitutional right of privacy, that decision did not clearly define its limits. *Griswold,* after all, only directly concerned the right of married persons to use birth control devices. The Supreme Court's decision in *Eisenstadt v. Baird,* 405 U.S. 438 (1972), however, extended that right to unmarried persons as well. Because most states at the time of *Griswold* allowed access to contraceptives, it might reasonably be argued that the decision in *Griswold* reflected a broad consensus in society concerning the question of the use of contraceptives; no such consensus existed on the question of access to abortion. In most states until the U.S. Supreme Court decided in *Roe v. Wade* (1973) that the right to privacy "is broad enough to encompass a woman's decision whether or not to terminate her pregnancy," having an abortion was a crime (at 153).

In striking down state laws banning abortion, Justice Blackmun, writing for the majority of the Supreme Court, justified his decision by surveying both the nature of the privacy cases decided to that date and the conflicting historical attitudes concerning abortion. In his decision he noted that the Court had recognized a close link between privacy and activities relating to marriage, procreation, contraception, family relationships, and child rearing. In effect Blackmun argued that decisions concerning the size of one's family and control over one's reproductive function are fundamentally personal. Summing up a woman's interest in being free to decide with medical advice on abortion, Justice Harry A. Blackmun wrote:

> The detriment the State would impose upon the pregnant woman
> by denying this choice altogether is apparent. Specific and direct

harm medically diagnosable even in early pregnancy may be involved. Maternity, or additional offspring, may force upon the woman a distressful life and future. Psychological harm may be imminent. Mental and physical health may be taxed by child care. There is also the distress, for all concerned, associated with the unwanted child, and there is the problem of bringing a child into a family already unable, psychologically and otherwise, to care for it. In other cases, as in this one, the additional difficulties and continuing stigma of unwed motherhood may be involved (at 153).

Against these interests of the mother, the Court weighed the interest in "life" of the fetus. In arguing that a woman does have genuine interests in being free to terminate a pregnancy, Justice Blackmun recognized that in some instances the state has interests in regulating, and sometimes prohibiting, abortion as well. The two state interests recognized were protecting the health of the pregnant woman and protecting the potential human life in her womb. Although the interest in safeguarding maternal health presented no great problem for the Court in confronting the question of abortion, the issue of the rights of potential human life is at the heart of the abortion debate.

In dealing with abortion as with any other medical procedure the state has broad latitude to assure through regulation that proper health and safety standards are followed. The issue in abortion, however, really is safety for whom? Obviously, if the "safety" of the fetus were the primary concern, abortion would not be permitted at all. If the interests of the fetus were more important than those of the mother, then every effort would have to be made to protect the life of the fetus even at the expense of the mother's life. If, on the other hand, the safety of the mother is always the primary concern, then abortion would also be permitted when continued pregnancy jeopardizes the mother's life. Before deciding what medical regulation of abortion would be permitted, the Court had to decide the prior question of whether the mother's or the fetus's potential interests were paramount. Of course, had the Court determined that the Constitution provided no guidance, this decision could have been left to legislatures.

If the interest in protecting the woman's health is a state's alleged concern, then some regulation of abortion procedures may be appropriate when abortion poses a real risk to the mother's health. This point is reached, according to Justice Blackmun's opinion in *Roe,* when the risk posed by abortion procedures is greater than the risk posed by remaining pregnant. The point where the risk shifts against unregulated abortion was, at least in 1973, at the end of the first trimester of pregnancy. "This is so because of the now established medical fact . . . that until the end of the first trimester mortality in abortion is less than mortality in normal childbirth" (at 163). Simply, a state's claim that it is restricting abortion procedures before this point in order to protect the mother would fall in the face of the medical reality that having an abortion is safer for a pregnant woman than staying pregnant.

In deciding the more difficult question of the competing "claims" of a woman desiring an abortion and of the fetus, Justice Blackmun was forced to address the question of just when life begins. If a developing embryo or later a fetus is recognized as a human life, a person, then it has legal interests which the Court would have to consider. If only an infant after birth is considered a person, then the Court could disregard any "claims" on behalf of the fetus.

For guidance concerning the legal status of the fetus, Justice Blackmun looked to the language of the Constitution and to historic tradition. After citing all references to "persons" in the Constitution, Justice Blackmun observes that the ". . . use of the word is such that it has application only postnatally" (at 157). In general he noted that "[i]n areas other than criminal abortion, the law has been reluctant to endorse any theory that life, as we recognize it, begins before live birth or to accord legal rights to the unborn except in narrowly defined situations and except when the rights are contingent upon birth . . ." (at 161).

On the more difficult question of when human life begins, although Blackmun concludes that the Court "need not resolve the . . . question," he in effect decides that life begins at the point of "viability," that is, the point at which sustaining life independent of the mother outside the womb is possible (albeit with technological assistance). Before choosing the point of viability over the claim of Texas that life begins at conception, Blackmun reviews the variety of approaches to this question found in religious and philosophical tradition. Although he identifies no clear precise consensus, he does find that the dominant views in religion, philosophy, medicine, and the law tend to focus on some stage of development substantially later than conception. He concludes, therefore, that before the stage when independent life outside the mother's womb is at least technically feasible, the fetus has no legal standing independent of the mother.

Question 3   *Does a fetus's "right to life" ever count more than a woman's right to privacy?*

The legal status of a fetus in light of the Supreme Court's abortion decisions remains somewhat unclear. Obviously as long as the Court recognizes a woman's right to choose to terminate her pregnancy, it is safe to say that the right to life of a fetus is significantly limited. In *Roe v. Wade* (1973) the Court in effect argued that a fetus has no right to life until at least the point of viability, the point at which it can be maintained independent of the mother outside the womb. Since its initial determination of this question in *Roe v. Wade,* however, legal recognition of the right to life of the fetus may have increased. What changes have taken place have occurred because of changes both in technology and in the Supreme Court's constitutional interpretation.

The viability standard from *Roe v. Wade* permitted the states to outlaw abortions, if they so chose, once fetal development had reached the stage when independent life outside of the mother's womb could be sustained. At the time when *Roe* was decided technology had advanced to the point that a fetus born prematurely could realistically survive only after the onset of the third trimester of pregnancy. Since then, however, the ability of medicine to sustain a baby born prematurely has begun to move earlier in the pregnancy cycle. If, therefore, fetal viability is the point at which abortion can be banned, then abortion may be banned earlier in the pregnancy today than it could in 1973.

In *Planned Parenthood v. Casey* (1992) the Supreme Court gave explicit recognition to the changes technological developments have worked on the trimester framework that emerged from *Roe v. Wade.*

> We have seen how time has overtaken some of *Roe*'s factual assumptions: advances in maternal health care allow for abortions safe to the mother later in the pregnancy than was true in 1973, and advances in neonatal care have advanced viability to a point somewhat earlier. But these facts go only to the scheme of time limits on the realization of competing interests, and the divergencies from the factual premises of 1973 have no bearing on the validity of *Roe*'s central holding, that viability marks the earliest point at which the State's interest in fetal life is constitutionally adequate to justify a legislative ban on nontherapeutic abortions. The soundness of that constitutional judgment in no sense turns on whether viability occurs at approximately 28 weeks, as was usual at the time of *Roe,* at 23 to 24 weeks, as it sometimes does today, or at some moment even slightly earlier in the pregnancy, as it may if fetal respiratory capacity can somehow be enhanced in the future. Whenever it may occur, the attainment of viability may continue to serve as the critical fact, just as it has done since *Roe* was decided . . . (at 860).

The simple answer then to the question of whether the fetus's right to life ever outweighs a mother's right to privacy therefore is yes. According to the Court when a fetus reaches the point of development where a prematurely born infant can be medically sustained, then the mother may legally be prevented from jeopardizing its right to live by terminating her pregnancy. In *Planned Parenthood v. Casey,* however, the Court majority appears to have given the interest of the fetus in life even greater recognition than the evolving viability schedule might imply. That case concerned attempts by the state of Pennsylvania to discourage abortion without directly outlawing it. If because of *Roe* the state could no longer ban abortion outright, could it by lesser means still take steps to advance its asserted interest in protecting "potential life"? If it could advance an interest in potential life, then how far could it go before the woman's right of privacy becomes paramount?

In the late 1980s Pennsylvania enacted a number of restrictions on women's access to abortions. Together these restrictions appeared designed to discourage women from having abortions and to place impediments in the path of an easy abortion decision. All appeared designed to highlight the state's interest in potential life, and thus to elevate the independent interest of a fetus in its life. Before an abortion could take place the law required that women (1) be provided with information by doctors on the stage of fetal development; (2) give their consent to the abortion and, if they were minors, obtain parental consent for the abortion; (3) wait at least 24 hours after giving their informed consent before the abortion can actually be performed; and (4) if married, inform their husbands of their intention to have an abortion. Finally, the law imposed various paperwork requirements on doctors performing abortions relating to reporting abortions and public disclosure.

When, in 1992 a challenge to these Pennsylvania restrictions finally reached the U.S. Supreme Court, the Court decided that

> [t]hough the woman has the right to choose to terminate her pregnancy before viability, it does not follow that the State is prohibited from taking steps to ensure that this choice is thoughtful and informed. Even in the earliest stages of pregnancy, the State may enact rules and regulations designed to encourage her to know that there are philosophic and social arguments of great weight that can be brought to bear in favor of continuing the pregnancy to full term and that there are procedures and institutions to allow adoption of unwanted children as well as a certain degree of state assistance if the mother chooses to raise the child herself (at 872).

In deciding how to measure which state regulations to uphold and which might impermissably interfere with the women's right to choose, the Court applied what it called an "undue burden analysis." According to Justice O'Connor's opinion, "An undue burden exists, and therefore a provision of law is invalid, if its purpose or effect is to place a substantial obstacle in the path of a woman seeking an abortion before the fetus attains viability" (at 878).

To understand what the Court's undue burden analysis means in practice, we may see how the Pennsylvania restrictions on abortion fared when subjected to this test. All restrictions, except for the requirement of the husband's notification, survived the Court's scrutiny. The fact that a woman would have to listen to arguments against abortion before exercising her right to an abortion was deemed by the Court not to pose an undue burden. The same was true of the requirement of a 24-hour waiting period, presumably to allow the woman to reflect fully on the consequences of her choice. When confronted with the requirement of spousal notification, however, the Court recognized that for many women this could pose a significant hardship. "There are millions of women in this country who are victims of regular physical and psychological abuse at the hands of their husbands." And as the Court noted, "[s]hould these women become pregnant, they may have very good reasons for not wishing to inform their husbands of their decision to obtain an abortion" (at 893).

In support of the Court majority's conclusion, one can just imagine what the consequences might be for a woman whose pregnancy results from an extramarital relationship, or even from a failure to use contraceptives, which an abusive husband might consider to be the woman's responsibility.

On the other hand, many men might view with dismay the Court's refusal to see their stake in their wives' pregnancy to be worth even a simple notification that the wife is considering abortion. Might it not sometimes be true that a wife might incorrectly anticipate her husband's response to a pregnancy? Although the Court's decision recognizes the right of the state to attempt to persuade a woman not to have an abortion, it denies the right of a husband and would-be father.

Whatever one thinks of the particulars of the Court's application of its undue burden analysis in *Planned Parenthood v. Casey,* what is clear is that we are left up in the air as to precisely what would constitute an undue burden. Would, for example a 72-hour waiting period amount to an undue burden? Even a 24-hour waiting period could prove burdensome to the less well off. Consider that in many states abortion providers are located in few places. Abortion services may well be far from home. To obtain an abortion one might have to travel hundreds of miles. If required to wait 24 hours from first visit to actual abortion, an overnight stay might be necessary. Hotels can be expensive. If that overnight stay were to stretch to 72 hours, the cost could be even more prohibitive. Would the Court agree that a 72-hour waiting period poses an undue burden? Answers to questions such as these must await further adjudication.

In upholding restrictions on access to abortion that do not actually prohibit abortion, the Court acknowledges what it terms the state's legitimate interest in potential life. This places slightly more weight on the side of the fetus in any balancing of interests between a mother's right to privacy and an asserted fetus's right to life. In assessing the relative weight given to the "interest" in life of the fetus versus the privacy interest of the mother, it is important to remember that nothing in any of the Court's opinions concerning privacy *requires* the government to protect even a viable fetus from abortion. All that the Court has now said is that the state is not forbidden by the Constitution from deciding to ban abortion in order to protect a viable fetus, and as a result of *Planned Parenthood v. Casey* the states *may,* if they choose, place restrictions on abortion as long as those restrictions do not pose an undue burden. Nothing the Court has said prevents the states from permitting totally unrestricted abortion.

Question 4   *May the state regulate private sexual relationships between consenting adults?*

There can be little doubt that most of us assume that our private consensual sexual conduct is not the business of government. Society has, however, not always been as tolerant as today. Concern for public morality has always influenced law making and the regulation of sexual behavior has long been a concern of governments. When the Supreme Court in 2003 in *Lawrence v. Texas* overturned its 1986 decision *Bowers v. Hardwick,* which had upheld the right of states to prohibit and punish certain consensual sexual conduct, it brought in sharp relief the debate over the right to privacy that the Court had generally expanded since its decision in *Griswold v. Connecticut* in 1965 (see Questions 1 and 2 above).

Many states had long had laws forbidding sodomy for both heterosexual and homosexual relationships. Prosecutions for sodomy, at least in the modern era, were, however, exceedingly rare. Even in the case that gave rise to the Supreme Court's decision in *Bowers,* the prosecution was dropped before the case ever went to court. The case came to the Supreme Court because the person against whom the initial charges were made successfully contended that he was always under threat of prosecution because he had no intention of ceasing the forbidden sexual conduct in the future.

The violation of the sodomy statute which led ultimately to Hardwick's challenging Georgia's sodomy law was actually stumbled upon by the police inadvertently. They had gone to Hardwick's apartment to arrest him for another matter, were admitted by a roommate, and directed to Hardwick's room, where they observed him engaging in sexual conduct forbidden by the antisodomy statute with another man. The prosecutor subsequently decided against going forward with the prosecution.

When this case ultimately reached the U.S. Supreme Court, the Court had to decide whether its precedents relating to privacy rights justified its striking down state antisodomy statutes. The debate between the Court majority and the dissenters was over the definition and scope of the liberty interests protected by the Due Process clause of the Fourteenth Amendment.

According to Justice White's opinion for the Court, the issue in the *Bowers* case was "whether the Federal Constitution confers a fundamental right upon homosexuals to engage in sodomy" (at 190). Viewed from this perspective, the answer according to Justice White was quite simply no.

When a claim is brought to Court that a state law violated a right protected against the states by the federal Constitution, many on the Court look first to the Bill of Rights to see whether that liberty is protected against infringement by Congress. As we saw in Chapter 1, virtually every liberty included in the Bill of Rights has through Supreme Court interpretation been incorporated by the Court into the Due Process clause of the Fourteenth Amendment as among the liberties protected against infringement by the states. When the asserted liberty interest is not among those explicitly recognized by the Constitution, most justices over the years have sought to determine whether the liberty in question is among those fundamental, but unstated, liberties, protected by the Due Process clause. The fact that there are unstated liberties protected by the Constitution is implicit in the Ninth Amendment, which states that "[t]he enumeration in the Constitution, of certain rights, shall not be construed to deny or disparage others retained by the people."

Attempts by the Court to identify and give effect to unstated liberties, however, as we saw in our discussion of *Griswold* above, have been controversial. In approaching the *Bowers* case, therefore, Justice White discussed how many on the Court have approached this issue:

> Striving to assure itself and the public that announcing rights not readily identifiable in the Constitution's text involves more than the imposition of the Justices' own choice of values upon the States and the Federal Government, the Court sought to identify the nature of the rights qualifying for heightened judicial protection. In *Palko v. Connecticut,* 302 U.S. 319 (1937) it was said that this category includes those fundamental liberties that are "implicit in the concept of ordered liberty," such that "neither liberty nor justice would exist if they were sacrificed." A different description of fundamental liberties appeared in *Moore v. East Cleveland,* 431 U.S. 494 (1977) (opinion of Powell, J.) where they are characterized as those liberties that "are deeply rooted in this nation's history and tradition" . . . (at 194).

Citing ancient legal and moral condemnations of homosexual conduct, including criminal prohibitions in the original 13 states and in most states at the time the case was before the Court, Justice White asserted that "[a]gainst this background, to claim that a right to engage in such conduct is 'deeply rooted in this Nation's history and tradition' or 'implicit in the concept of ordered liberty' is, at best, factitious" (at 194). Justice White asserted, largely correctly, that most of the Court's precedents relating to the right to privacy concerned marriage, family, and/or procreation, two interests obviously not at issue in homosexual relationships at least at the time the case was decided (the case preceded the as yet largely unsuccessful efforts to win legal recognition for gay marriages).

The Supreme Court in *Bowers* was sharply divided. The division itself was fundamentally over the definition of the controversy before the Court itself. While Justice White asserted that the issue was whether the Constitution conferred on homosexuals a "fundamental right" to engage in sodomy, Justice Blackmun in his dissent saw the issue quite differently. "This case is no more about 'a fundamental right to engage in homosexual sodomy,' as the Court purports to declare, than *Stanley v. Georgia* was about a fundamental right to watch obscene movies, or *Katz v. United States* (1967) was about a fundamental right to place interstate bets from a telephone booth. Rather, this case is about 'the most comprehensive of rights and the right most valued by civilized men, namely, the right to be left alone.'" *Olmstead v. United States* (1928) (Brandeis, J., dissenting) (*Bowers* at 199).

In making this argument Justice Blackmun asserts that many if not most of the Court's privacy cases do not assert fundamental rights to engage in any specific conduct. Rather they protect areas of personal autonomy, the right of all to decide for themselves how they will conduct certain aspects of their lives and/or certain places or circumstances within which people have a right to be free from government scrutiny or surveillance. He asserts in this instance that ". . . what the Court really has refused to recognize is the fundamental interest all individuals have in controlling the nature of their intimate associations with others" (at 206).

This debate within the Court concerning how far the state may intrude into personal decisions concerning intimate sexual relations was rejoined in 2003 in *Lawrence v. Texas*. There were many similarities between the *Lawrence* and *Bowers* cases and important differences as well. In *Lawrence* as in *Bowers* the police stumbled upon two men engaging in sexual acts in the course of investigating another complaint. A potentially important point of difference between the two cases, however, was the fact that the Texas statute focused its prohibition specifically on homosexual conduct. The Georgia statute applied in *Bowers,* on the other hand, forbade certain sexual behaviors whether engaged in by heterosexuals or homosexuals.

Although the differences between the statutes could have provided a basis for the Court to overturn the Texas statute and still leave the *Bowers* case standing (the different treatment of homosexuals and heterosexuals engaging in the same type of conduct did provide the basis for Justice O'Connor's concurring opinion based on denial of "equal protection of the laws" in *Lawrence*), the Court majority decided instead to revisit *Bowers*. In *Lawrence* in a sweeping ruling the Court majority decided that *Bowers* had been wrongly decided and laid the foundation for broad recognition that private sexual conduct, at least between consenting adults, is generally immune from government regulation. In doing so the Court challenged the fundamental assumptions underpinning the *Bowers* Court's ruling.

First, Justice Kennedy, like Justice Blackmun in his dissent in *Bowers,* rejected the majority's characterization of the issue presented to the Court in the case.

> To say that the issue in *Bowers* was simply the right to engage in certain sexual conduct demeans the claim the individuals put forward, just as it would demean a married couple were it to be said marriage is simply about the right to have sexual intercourse. The laws involved in *Bowers* and here are, to be sure, statutes that purport to do no more than prohibit a particular sexual act. Their penalties and purposes, though have more far-reaching consequences, touching upon the most private human conduct, sexual behavior, and in the most private places, the home. The statutes do seek to control a personal relationship that, whether or not entitled to formal recognition in the law, is within the liberty of persons to choose without being punished as criminals (at 4576).

Second, Justice Kennedy challenged the historical accuracy of the *Bowers* Court's assessment of society's traditional treatment of homosexual conduct. While the *Bowers* Court, as we saw above, emphasized traditional condemnations of homosexual conduct, Justice Kennedy claimed that "there is no longstanding history in this country of laws directed at homosexual conduct as a distinct matter. . . . [E]arly American sodomy laws were not directed at homosexuals as such but instead sought to prohibit nonprocreative sexual activity more generally" (at 4577). The specific focus on homosexuals and homosexual conduct, according to Justice Kennedy's analysis, was more a product of the mid-twentieth century. While Justice Kennedy did not deny widespread religious and moral disapproval in society of homosexual conduct throughout history, he did in effect deny that the law and legal tradition afforded homosexuals significantly less protection for nonprocreative sexual intimacy than it afforded heterosexuals. The Court's increasing recognition of the privacy interests associated with sexual conduct were a product of the mid- to late twentieth century. This period ". . . show[s] an emerging awareness that liberty gives substantial protection to adult persons in deciding how to conduct their private lives in matters pertaining to sex. 'History and tradition are the starting point but not in all cases the ending point of the substantive due process inquiry'" (at 4578).

In effect Justice Kennedy argued that neither history nor tradition justifies affording to homosexuals any less protection for their intimate behavior than heterosexuals. If, as the Court has found in a number of cases, the liberty protected by the Due Process clauses of the Fifth and Fourteenth Amendments protects heterosexual intimate conduct, it protects homosexual conduct as well and for the same reasons. Quoting from the Court's opinion in *Planned Parenthood v. Casey* (1992), "These matters, involving the most intimate and personal choices a person may make in a lifetime, choices central to personal dignity and autonomy, are central to the liberty protected by the Fourteenth Amendment. At the heart of liberty is the right to define one's own concept of existence, of meaning, of the universe, and of the mystery of human life." Beliefs about these matters could not define the attributes of personhood were they formed under compulsion of the State" (at 4578). In citing what Justice Scalia's dissent dismissed as the "famed sweet-mystery-of-life passage" from *Planned Parenthood v. Casey* (see Question 3 above), Justice Kennedy in effect equated one's private choices of sexual partners and practices with one's choices about reproduction and family.

As a result of the *Lawrence* decision private sexual relationships among consenting adults appear largely to be beyond the reach of law. This does not mean, however, that all sexual behavior is beyond the reach of the law. As Justice Kennedy made clear the scope of the Court's decision had limits:

> The present case does not involve minors. It does not involve persons who might be injured or coerced or who are situated in relationships where consent might not easily be refused. It does not involve public conduct or prostitution. It does not involve whether the government must give formal recognition to any relationships that homosexual persons seek to enter. The case does involve two adults who, with full and mutual consent from each other, engaged in sexual practices common to a homosexual lifestyle. The petitioners are entitled to respect for their private lives. The state cannot demean their existence or control their destiny by making their private sexual conduct a crime. Their right to liberty under the Due Process Clause gives them the full right to engage in their conduct without intervention by government (at 4579, 80).

The ability of the state to protect children or other vulnerable persons from sexual predators, whether heterosexual or homosexual, is left untouched by the decision. What is less certain, however, is the fate of other related government policies that give special recognition to heterosexual relationships and perhaps others that regulate sexual conduct. While in her concurring opinion Justice Sandra Day O'Connor asserts that state interests "beyond mere moral disapproval of an excluded group" exist to justify "the traditional institution of marriage" (at 4582), Justice Antonin Scalia in his dissent asserts that "[s]tate laws against bigamy, same-sex marriage, adult incest, prostitution, masturbation, adultery, fornication, bestiality, and obscenity are likewise sustainable only in light of *Bowers* validation of laws based on moral choices" (at 4583).

Justice Scalia's catalog of "moral choices" incorporated into law certainly contains some examples that are no doubt mere remnants of laws that *Lawrence* and other Court decisions such as *Griswold* and *Eisenstadt* have already made highly questionable. Even before *Lawrence,* attempts to enforce laws against fornication and masturbation would have likely been viewed as encroaching upon territory already deemed beyond the scope of government regulation. Laws relating to same-sex marriage or bigamy, on the other hand, reflect the historic understanding of an ancient legally sanctioned and regulated social compact of marriage. Although *Lawrence* makes it clear that the state may not regulate private consensual sexual behavior (by people old enough and in a position genuinely to consent), it is less clear that the state may not continue to deny same-sex couples a legally recognized civil marriage. Because the Court majority in *Lawrence* rested its decision on the Due Process clause protections for liberty rather than the Equal Protection clause it tells the state it must not interfere with private intimate behavior affecting those who freely consent. The liberty protected is "freedom from" state interference. *Lawrence* does not necessarily, however, carry with it an obligation to treat all relationships equally. If the state chooses to continue to restrict the legally recognized public *institution* of marriage to heterosexual relationships, there appears to be nothing in the Opinion of the Court that would necessarily prevent the state from doing so. Whether maintaining such a restriction is wise is, of course, another matter.

Near the end of 2003 the Supreme Judicial Court of Massachusetts in fact ruled that under the Massachusetts Constitution the State could not deny to same-sex couples the benefits of marriage (*Goodridge et al. v. Department of Public Health,* 2003). Although the Massachusetts Court explicitly acknowledged that the U.S. Supreme Court had not yet definitively ruled on the implications of the *Lawrence* decision for same-sex marriage, it argued that under the Massachusetts Constitution at least denying gays the benefits that flow from marriage violated both Massachusetts state due process and equal protection guarantees. This ruling produced considerable controversy and proposals for overturning it through both state and federal constitutional amendments defining marriage as a union of a man and a woman. The ultimate impact of the Massachusetts decision remains uncertain.

Question 5 *Why doesn't the "right to privacy" include the right to decide to end our lives?*

Modern medical care often seems to make it possible to sustain human life long past the point where it seems to many to be meaningful. Diseases such as some cancers and AIDS can take a terrible toll in human suffering sometimes bringing excruciating pain as death approaches. Some linger in such a condition for weeks and months. The prospect of death brings the only promise of relief.

In the 1990s the issue of a "right to die" was brought most starkly to public consciousness by a physician in Michigan, Jack Kevorkian. Dr. Kevorkian, or "Doctor Death," as he came to be known, assisted dozens of terminally ill patients to hurry their deaths. While Dr. Kevorkian in very public ways asserted the right of patients to end their suffering and hurry their deaths through the active intervention of physicians, others earlier had to fight for the right of the terminally ill to refuse medical intervention which served to prolong life. Physician-assisted suicide involved medical intervention to terminate life more quickly than would occur through natural causes. Withholding treatment or medical intervention is designed to allow nature to take its course.

The Court had long recognized the right of a competent person to refuse medical treatment, even when doing so would hasten death. In his Opinion of the Court in *Cruzon v. Director, Missouri Department of Health* (1990), ". . . the first case in which . . . [the Court] has been squarely presented with the issue of whether the United States Constitution grants what is in common parlance referred to as a "right to die" (at 277), Chief Justice Rehnquist asserted that a person's liberty interest extends so far as to refuse "lifesaving hydration and nutrition" (at 276). Rehnquist based this right in part on the assumption in common law that "even the touching of one person without consent and without legal justification" amounted to a battery. Quoting from *Union Pacific Railroad Company v. Botsford* (1891), Rehnquist argued that "[no] right is held more sacred, or is more carefully guarded, by the common law, than the right of every individual to the possession and control of his own person, free from all restraint or interference of others, unless by clear and unquestionable authority of law" (at 269).

The recognition of an individual's right to refuse treatment in *Cruzon*, however, did not resolve the specific issue in that case. There the right was asserted on Ms. Cruzon's behalf by her parents. Because Ms. Cruzon, as a result of an accident, was in a persistent vegetative state and unable to assert her wishes herself, her parents sought removal of feeding tubes on her behalf. Because, however, Missouri required evidence "by clear and convincing evidence" that the incompetent person would have wished the withdrawal of treatment, evidence unavailable in the instant case,

Ms. Cruzon's parents were denied the right to withdraw the feeding tubes and the United States Supreme Court found nothing in the Constitution of the United States that would supersede Missouri's judgment.

The issue then in *Cruzon* was not really the right to die. It was rather what limits the Constitution places on a state's insistence on a clear statement of an incompetent person's wishes. *Cruzon* left in place the rights of a competent person to refuse medical intervention against her will to prolong her life. The claim of a constitutional right of patients to select the time of their deaths, however, through physician-assisted suicide is considered by the Court to raise different issues. In *Washington v. Glucksberg* (1997) the Supreme Court faced a challenge to the State of Washington's ban on physician-assisted suicide. "The Plaintiffs asserted the existence of a liberty interest protected by the Fourteenth Amendment which extends to a personal choice by a mentally competent, terminally ill adult to commit physician-assisted suicide" (at 708).

Since there was no question of any specific constitutional prohibition on governmental restraint on suicide, the question in this case, as in all other cases asserting a liberty interest under the Fourteenth Amendment, was whether society had long assumed the existence of such a right even though it was not explicitly codified. As Chief Justice Rehnquist wrote in his Opinion of the Court: "We begin, as we do in all due-process cases, by examining our nation's history, legal traditions and practices. In almost every state—indeed in almost every western democracy—it is a crime to assist a suicide. The States' assisted suicide bans are not innovations. Rather they are longstanding expressions of the States' commitment to the protection and preservation of all human life" . . . (at 710).

Chief Justice Rehnquist recognized that advances in medical technology have had the effect of prolonging both life and the often painful process of death. As he observed, "public concern and democratic action are therefore sharply focused on how best to protect dignity and independence at the end of life" (at 716). But although legislatures have authorized "living wills" and health care proxies to assist citizens in having a say over which medical procedures they may want to refuse to prolong the end of life, they have also almost everywhere rejected proposals to legalize physician-assisted suicide. Were the Court to extend constitutional protection to this newly asserted right to physician-assisted suicide, it would ". . . place the matter outside the arena of public debate and legislative action" (at 720). This to Chief Justice Rehnquist would be an abuse of judicial authority.

> Here. . . . we are confronted with a consistent and almost universal tradition that has long rejected the asserted right, and continues to reject it today, even for the terminally ill, mentally competent adults. To hold for respondents, we would have to reverse centuries

of legal doctrine and practice, and strike down the considered policy
choice of almost every State . . . (at 723).

Even as he rejected the notion that physician-assisted suicide was a
fundamental right protected by the Fourteenth Amendment from infringement from the state, he still had to consider whether a restriction on
the practice was "rationally related to legitimate government interests"
(at 728). The Court interprets the Due Process clause of the Fourteenth
Amendment to require that any restraints placed on individual liberty or
autonomy be at minimum supportable by some understandable justification. The state's chosen policy need not be considered the best; it need only
be one supportable by some reasonable arguments.

When using this lenient and permissive standard as a measure, the
Court found little difficulty discovering legitimate concerns that might
prompt government decision makers to opt to forbid physician-assisted
suicide. The first asserted state interest recognized as reasonable by
Rehnquist was the state's general interest in preserving human life. Although abortion rights were not specifically mentioned by Rehnquist, the
state's interest in protecting human life was recognized even in the Court's
most recent decision upholding abortion rights. While in the abortion decision this interest had to give way to the "fundamental right" of privacy, the
foundation for abortion rights (see Question 2 above), in this case the
Court found no such fundamental right to physician-assisted suicide.

In considering the state's generalized interest in human life, Chief
Justice Rehnquist noted the prevalence of mental health disorders, especially depression, in people attempting suicide and the state's strong interest in protecting such vulnerable groups from themselves. The chief justice
noted that "[r]esearch indicates . . . many people who request physician-
assisted suicide withdraw that request if their depression and pain are
treated." Because physicians and others often do not respond adequately to
seriously ill patients' needs, however, the State has a legitimate interest in
stepping in to protect such patients from their "suicidal impulses" (at 730).

This concern for vulnerable citizens extends further than concern
for those suffering from depression or other mental or emotional illnesses. The "poor, elderly, and disabled" may need state protection from
abuse and neglect. Among the fears of those opposing physician-assisted
suicide is the possibility that financial pressures on individuals, concern
for the impact of the costs of lengthy medical treatments on families, including concern that one's estate will be eaten away by the high costs of
medical care, could induce a terminally ill person to opt for suicide because of either a misplaced sense of guilt about being a burden or even of
pressures being placed on the terminally ill to move on, and save their
families the expense and continued emotional distress potentially caused
by a loved one's serious illness.

To these concerns the Chief Justice added: "The State's interest here goes beyond protecting the vulnerable from coercion; it extends to protecting disabled and terminally ill people from prejudice, negative and inaccurate stereotypes, and 'societal indifference.' The state's assisted-suicide ban reflects and reinforces its policy that the lives of terminally ill, disabled and elderly people must be no less valued than the lives of the young and healthy, and that a seriously disabled person's suicidal impulses should be interpreted and treated the same way as anyone else's."

Another interest mentioned by Chief Justice Rehnquist, which arguably is advanced by state bans on physician-assisted suicide, is protecting individuals and society from both voluntary and potentially coerced euthanasia. Although not mentioned by Rehnquist, at a time when managed care has assumed an ever larger role in medicine, it is not difficult to imagine heath insurance providers openly encouraging physician-assisted suicide as a cost-saving measure. Many health plans, including Medicare, already pay the costs of "hospice care," designed as relatively inexpensive end-of-life care for those rejecting more extraordinary measures to temporarily extend life (or the process of dying.) Physician-assisted suicide could become another, even much less costly, way to manage and lessen the costs of death and dying. One can imagine a health plan waiving deductibles and/or co-pays for the costs of physician-assisted suicide as an incentive. Certainly many would think the state would have a rational interest in closing off such options.

Finally, Chief Justice Rehnquist asserted that the state has a legitimate interest in ". . . protecting the integrity and ethics of the medical profession." His decision took note of the expressed opposition to physician-assisted suicide of the American Medical Society, which views the practice as ". . . fundamentally incompatible with the physician's role as healer" (at 731).

Although the chief justice's opinion can be read as total rejection of physician-assisted suicide, all it did in practice is refuse to declare a constitutional restraint on the states as they consider the issue. His opinion and the Constitution as interpreted by him leave open the option for the states to authorize the practice if they choose.

The Court in *Washington v. Glucksberg* was unanimous in its decision that nothing in the Constitution precluded the states from banning physician-assisted suicide, at least under the circumstances of the case before them, but five justices wrote concurring opinions which may in varying degrees have signaled that the Court may not have spoken its last word on the issue.

Justice O'Connor and Justice Stephen Breyer, in their separate concurring opinions, stressed that nothing in the Court's opinion prevents physicians from taking steps to alleviate the pain of dying patients even when a secondary effect might actually be to speed the dying process. In the cases before the Court the states in question did not attempt to limit a physician's latitude in alleviating pain. If they had, Justice O'Connor's concurrence clearly implies that the Court might view the issue differently. Overall she expresses confidence that the delicate concerns involved can and will be addressed through the democratic political process. Nothing in the decision in this case, nor in the opinion of the Court, precludes the states from addressing the concerns of the dying while protecting the vulnerable among us from abuse. If the states were, however, to address this issue by denying even palliative care that alleviates excruciating pain but might hasten death, then she together with Justice Breyer indicates the Court might be forced to revisit this issue.

Recognizing that individuals do have a "liberty interest" that in some instances ". . . may outweigh the state's interest in preserving life at all costs," Justice Stevens argued that "[t]he liberty interest at stake in a case like this differs from, and is stronger than, both the common-law right to refuse medical treatment and the unbridled interest in deciding whether to live or die. It is an interest in determining how, rather than whether a critical threshold shall be crossed . . ." (at 745). In recognizing that the individual has a stake in determining the circumstances of his or her death, Justice Stevens leaves open the question of how far the state may go to advance its interest in limiting suicide.

Clearly, despite its clear rejection of a constitutionally imposed restraint on the states' ability to forbid physician-assisted suicide, the issue of the right to die has not been left entirely to the changing passions of popular majorities. While rejecting an unfettered interest of individuals to determine the time and circumstances of their deaths, the Court has made it clear individuals may refuse medical treatments and even necessary nourishment to prolong the life of those near death. Where the Court will ultimately strike the balance between individual autonomy and the state's traditional opposition to suicide remains to some degree an open question.

REFERENCES

Bowers v. Hardwick, 478 U.S. 186 (1986).

Cruzon v. Director, Missouri Department of Health, 497 U.S. 261 (1990).

Eisenstadt v. Baird, 405 U.S. 438 (1972).

Goodridge et al. v. Department of Public Health, 440 Mass. 309, 798 N.E. 2d 941 (2003).

Griswold v. Connecticut, 381 U.S. 479 (1965).

Katz v. United States, 389 U.S. 347 (1967).

Lawrence v. Texas, 71 USLW 4574 (2003).

Moore v. East Cleveland, 431 U.S. 494 (1977).

NAACP v. Alabama, 354 U.S. 449 (1958).

Olmstead v. United States, 227 U.S. 438 (1928).

Palko v. Connecticut, 302 U.S. 319 (1937).

Planned Parenthood v. Casey, 505 U.S. 833 (1992).

Roe v. Wade, 410 U.S. 113 (1973).

Stanley v. Georgia, 394 U.S. 557 (1969).

Union Pacific Railroad Company v. Botsford, 141 U.S. 250 (1891).

Washington v. Glucksberg, 521 U.S. 702 (1997).

CHAPTER SIX

Contemporary Issue of Equality and Freedom

INTRODUCTION

Civil liberties may be of little value to those struggling for mere survival. If one cannot find food, the liberties protected by the Constitution may appear empty promises. Certainly the relative value of rights and liberties to individuals may be dependent at least in part on their capacity to enjoy them, and that capacity is at least in part related to economic well-being. This chapter explores a few questions concerning constitutional liberties in which contemporary developments bring into sharp relief the relationship of equality to freedom. While the Supreme Court justices have in some instances attempted to grapple with these questions, their answers to date may appear inadequate to many of us. These questions in particular remain open for further debate as we judge the adequacy of our constitutional rights and liberties.

Our first question asks: *What use are rights and liberties if you lack the resources to take advantage of them?* This section opens with a discussion of the most visible recent controversy concerning the relationship of wealth and rights, that concerning the refusal of government to provide Medicaid funding for abortions. Then it explores the broader question by explaining the grounds used by the Supreme Court to justify requiring government to provide counsel and psychiatrists for poor people accused of crime while failing generally to fund the exercise of other rights and liberties. In the end the answer to this question is left to the judgment of the reader. The purpose of this section is to engage the reader in the exploration of what will remain a troubling question to many.

In Chapter 2 we explored traditional issues relating to the nature and limits of freedom of expression under the First Amendment. Here we explore the limits of those rights in a society marked by significant economic inequality. Our second question, then, asks: *What use is freedom of speech if no one can hear you?* This section discusses the problems posed for the "free marketplace of ideas" by the contemporary communications environment. Although television amplifies the voices of the powerless who become "newsworthy," it can also drown out the voices of those unable to gain access to it. This section discusses First Amendment issues raised by television and other electronic media of communications, the different treatment given by the courts to the electronic and print media, the potential impact of cable television and the Internet, and the continuing problems caused by the disparity in the ability of different interests to reach the audience.

Our third question focuses on the role of economic inequality in our political contests. Question 3 asks: *Is it possible for the wealthy few to dominate public debate and stifle the "free marketplace of ideas"?* This section explores the issues surrounding our system for financing our election and referenda campaigns. In effect, it asks, "if money talks," is spending money to spread one's ideas constitutionally protected free speech? Must the value of viewpoints in the marketplace of ideas be inevitably linked to the financial resources mobilized behind them?

Finally, Question 4 focuses on the capacity of private actors to restrict our freedom. It asks: *Does the Constitution protect us from private institutions which interfere with our liberties and rights?* This section explores whether private corporations and others can restrict our freedom. It discusses how employers limit our freedom of speech and invade our privacy. Because the Court interprets the Constitution as protecting us only from government infringement of our liberties and rights (state action doctrine), even protection against private race and sex discrimination is not mandated by the Constitution. The civil rights protections that we do enjoy result from legislation passed by Congress or state legislatures; as such, they are always potentially vulnerable to changing public sentiment. This section discusses the reasons why our rights and liberties are subject to private attack.

Question 1 *What use are rights and liberties if you lack the resources to take advantage of them?*

Although the Constitution places limits on the power of government to interfere with many of our choices, it does not generally require the government to provide us with the means or opportunities necessary to act on our choices. No one familiar with the First Amendment could seriously argue that government can stop you from printing an article critical of the president. If you lack the resources to purchase a printing press, however, that right may well appear meaningless to you. Similarly, the government cannot stop you from sending your children to a church school, but government need not (and, indeed, may be forbidden to) pay your child's tuition.

Controversy over the question of when government should aid citizens in the exercise of their liberties has recently focused on the question of access to abortion. In a case challenging the government's failure to provide Medicaid funding for poor women seeking abortions, Justice Stewart, writing for the Supreme Court majority, argued that "although government may not place obstacles in the path of a woman's exercise of her freedom of choice, it need not remove those not of its own creation" (*Harris v. McRae,* at 317, 1980). The state need not help a poor woman exercise her right to choose an abortion even if without such help access to safe abortion is unavailable to a poor woman.

The abortion funding controversy sharply divided the Supreme Court not only because poverty makes exercise of a right impossible for some but also because government policy concerning Medicaid funding provides an inducement for women to give up their freedom of choice. Although government will not fund abortion, it will pay the costs of childbirth. To Justice Brennan, a dissenter on the Court in the abortion funding cases, the state's paying for childbirth but not for abortion "clearly operates to coerce indigent pregnant women to bear children they would not otherwise choose to have, and just as clearly, this coercion can only operate upon the poor" (*Maher v. Roe,* at 483, 1977). The core of the majority's argument in the abortion funding cases, however, is that it is the woman's poverty and not some state regulation that has narrowed a woman's choice. The state's policy imposes "no restriction on access to abortion that was not already there" (at 482).

This basic rejection by the Court of any government obligation to fund the exercise of rights was reaffirmed its 1991 decision in *Rust v. Sullivan.* In *Rust* the Court upheld a Department of Health and Human Services regulation that denied federal funding to any family planning program that advised clients concerning even the availability of abortion as a family planning option. Not only was any family planning agency receiving federal funds forbidden to perform abortions; they were also forbidden in effect from informing clients of their right to have an abortion.

When confronted with the argument that this regulation forbidding abortion counseling in federally funded family planning programs limited a physician's freedom of speech as well as a woman's freedom of choice, Justice Rehnquist replied that the Constitution does not require the government to pay for the expression of views that it does not like. "When Congress established a National Endowment for Democracy to encourage other countries to adopt democratic principles, it was not constitutionally required to fund a program to encourage competing lines of political philosophy such as Communism or Fascism" (*Rust v. Sullivan,* at 194, 1991).

Clearly, to a poor woman dependent on direct government assistance or on government-financed programs, the right to choose an abortion is no right at all.

Despite the rather bleak picture painted so far of the opportunities for the poor to take advantage of rights and liberties, there are exceptions. When government assistance is necessary to provide the poor a reasonable opportunity to take advantage of constitutional protections afforded to those accused of crimes, the Court recognizes a positive government duty to help.

The Sixth Amendment to the Constitution provides those accused of crimes with a right to counsel, and the Court in *Gideon v. Wainwright* (1963) recognized that the right is meaningless for a poor defendant if the government does not pay for a lawyer. Similarly, where the state allows appellate court review of criminal convictions, it must provide counsel and necessary documents free to those unable to pay; and where a state allows an insanity defense, it must provide the poor with the aid of a psychiatrist.

Clearly in the criminal justice arena, the Court recognizes that rights mean nothing to one who lacks the ability to exercise them. According to Justice Hugo Black, "there can be no equal justice where the kind of trial a man gets depends on the amount of money he has" (*Griffin v. Illinois,* at 19, 1956). In another decision which required that counsel be appointed to assist the poor in preparing a criminal appeal, Justice Douglas wrote: "The indigent, where the record is unclear or the errors are hidden, has only the right of a meaningless ritual, while the rich man has a meaningful appeal" (*Douglas v. California,* at 358, 1963).

There were some on the Supreme Court who dissented from these decisions which required government help for the poor accused of crimes. Their arguments were very similar to those used by the Court majority in the abortion funding cases many years later. Since, they argued, poverty was not imposed by the state, the state is not required to remove or lessen the effects of poverty. As Justice Harlan wrote in his dissent in *Douglas v. California,* the Constitution ". . . does not impose on the states the affirmative duty to lift the handicaps flowing from differences in economic circumstances. To so construe it would be to read into the Constitution a philosophy of leveling that would be foreign to many of our basic concepts of the proper relations between government and society. The state may have a moral obligation to eliminate the evils of poverty, but it is not required . . . to give to some whatever others can afford" (at 362).

Despite such views, the Court majority requires the state to assist the poor in the exercise of some rights. Although the bases used for distinguishing between those rights requiring government assistance and those which do not is not always clear, two factors appear to be important. First, the Court considers the degree to which the government is responsible for the fate of the person needing help to exercise his or her rights or take advantage of his or her liberty. Second, the Court weighs whether the failure to provide assistance will lead to a complete inability to exercise a right or merely an unequal opportunity. Where the deprivation of rights is absolute, the Court is more likely to find a government obligation to help. Where the deprivation is only relative, the Court keeps hands off.

Although the lack of adequate resources may, for example, interfere with the effectiveness of one's free speech or may prevent a woman from obtaining an abortion, neither of those consequences, however serious, is a direct result of a government action. If, however, a person who is accused of a crime cannot obtain a lawyer to properly defend him, he may, as a result, lose his liberty or even his life. What ultimately happens to the poor person accused of a crime will be a direct result of government action taken against him. The government prosecutes, and if found guilty, the government punishes. However serious the consequences faced by a woman with an unwanted pregnancy may be, it was not the government that made her pregnant.

Finally, even though the Court requires counsel and psychiatric help to aid in the defense of indigent persons accused of crimes, it does not require that the counsel provided to the poor be of a quantity or quality equal to those the rich are able to purchase for themselves. Rather, it requires only "adequate counsel" and a "competent psychiatrist." "Adequate" and "competent" do not mean equal.

Certainly, those who are poor are not in the same position to take advantage of their constitutional rights and liberties as those who are rich. For the majority of us who are neither poor nor rich, our rights are also important. Whether they are adequate is a question which we must answer for ourselves.

Question 2 *What use is freedom of speech if no one can hear you?*

If anything can be said to be a hallmark as we enter the twenty-first century, it is the explosion of means and opportunities for the communication of ideas. First Amendment freedoms, which were designed to safeguard freedom of thought, conviction, and communication, have historically been ranked first among our freedoms as necessary preconditions for the maintenance of other freedoms and the possibility for democracy and majority rule. Traditionally the best safeguard for those freedoms has been a government policy of "hands off." Faith in an unfettered marketplace for the communication of ideas in the search for truth has probably been even stronger than faith in free economic competition as the best road to economic progress and prosperity.

If we are to understand new challenges to civil liberties in the contemporary era, however, we must first understand what makes the contemporary communications environment different from that known to the framers of the First Amendment and to the Supreme Court throughout much of our history as it has interpreted the meaning of the First Amendment in the face of ongoing challenges.

When the First Amendment was written, the only means of communication available were the unamplified human voice and the printing press. Pamphlets and newspapers were the means used by the framers of the Constitution themselves and by their contemporaries to rally support for American independence and later for the Constitution itself.

Through the nineteenth century newspapers became increasingly important. Control over great newspapers sometimes gave a few the capacity to influence millions, but still the local pamphleteer and even soapbox orator could have some hope to appeal to the consciences and attention of large numbers of citizens. During the twentieth century increasingly electronic means of communications came to supplant newspapers and replace the unamplified human voice as means of rallying political support and affecting popular attitudes.

At least until the emergence of television and radio whenever the Supreme Court sought to protect the values of the free marketplace of ideas, it simply restrained government and let voices, even "dangerous" voices, be heard. When television and radio emerged as the leading organs of public communication, however, the Court came to accept that regulation of them was sometimes necessary to keep the marketplace open for competition among ideas. Because television and radio as initially developed went over a limited band of communication channels, someone had to decide who would have the privilege of controlling those limited channels.

In *Red Lion Broadcasting Co., Inc. v. Federal Communications Commission* (1969) the Supreme Court provided its rationale for treating the broadcast media differently from traditional print media. In reply to the broadcast media's contention that they had the same right as the print media to communicate whatever they chose or to refuse to provide access to whomever they chose, Justice Byron White, for a unanimous Court, wrote:

> Where there are substantially more individuals who want to broadcast than there are frequencies to allocate, it is idle to posit an unabridgeable First Amendment right to broadcast comparable to the right of every person to speak, write or publish. If 100 persons want broadcast licenses but there are only 10 frequencies to allocate, all of them may have the same right to a license; but if there is to be any effective communication by radio, only a few can be licensed and the rest must be barred from the airwaves. . . .
>
> There is nothing in the First Amendment which prevents the Government from requiring a licensee to share his frequency with others and to conduct himself as a proxy or fiduciary with obligations to present those views and voices which are representative of his community and which would otherwise, by necessity, be barred from the airwaves. . . . Otherwise, station owners and a few networks would have unfettered power to make time available only to the highest bidders, to communicate only their own views on public issues, people and candidates, and to permit on air only those with whom they agreed. There is no sanctuary in the First Amendment for unlimited private censorship operating in a medium not open to all . . . (at 388–92).

In his opinion for the Court Justice White was defending from a First Amendment challenge the fairness doctrine, a Federal Communications Commission's requirement that broadcasters permit individuals airtime to reply to personal attacks and to political editorials. A similar requirement was rejected by the Court for the print media in *Miami Herald Publishing Co. v. Tornillo* (1974) in which the Court found a "right to reply" law unconstitutional on the grounds that it ran ". . . afoul of the elementary First Amendment proposition that government may not force a newspaper to print copy which, in its journalistic discretion, it chooses to leave on the newspaper floor." The differing treatment was justified simply by the differences he outlined between traditional and modern communications methods.

Several years later, however, Congress did away with the fairness doctrine. The advent of cable television with potentially hundreds of competing channels had made the scarcity argument, upon which the special treatment afforded broadcast media was based, largely obsolete. Theoretically, with cable almost everyone could find some outlet for expressing his or her views.

With the advent of the Internet and World Wide Web, upon which everyone with computer access and a modem can readily find outlets to express his or her views, it would seem that the need for government intervention to assure an open marketplace of ideas would have evaporated. But is this so clear? Both cable and the Internet make it possible for virtually anyone to find some niche within which they might be heard. But heard by whom? The very variety of cable channels and Internet "chat rooms" and Web pages of every description, rather than increasing the competition of ideas in a free marketplace of ideas, may instead lead to increasing isolation of people with contending points of view from each other. Instead of being exposed to a variety of conflicting points of view, we are instead drawn to communicate only with those sharing our own prejudices.

In Chapter 2 we learned that one of the principal arguments in support of allowing even those who advocate violence the opportunity to be heard was that airing such views in the public forum would invite vigorous debate and refutation by others. Through such vigorous debate, it was argued, society would learn of the weaknesses in the arguments of those purveyors of hate or other "dangerous ideas," and truth and tolerance would triumph.

In today's increasingly fragmented communications environment, however, isn't it possible that open debate will be replaced by each of us increasingly seeking out only cable channels or websites where others who already share our outlook and prejudices can be found? Rather than being confronted with views that make us uncomfortable, might not many seek out only views that reinforce their preexisting prejudices? The ideal of a free marketplace of ideas by which all views are heard and forced to compete for society's support might be replaced by a smorgasbord of ideas from which we select only those familiar ideas which suit our tastes, leaving unsampled those ideas that seem alien or challenging.

Of course, to a substantial degree in the days when newspapers were the principal means for obtaining news and observing public debate, many, perhaps most of us, read only those newspapers whose editorial outlook we shared. Even then, however, an effort was often made to present the "news" in a neutral way to inform the public. The most influential leading newspapers were often those that kept their most biased presentations on the editorial page.

If the preeminent purpose of free speech is to permit society to govern itself intelligently having witnessed an open exchange of views on important issues, it may be that the contemporary communications environments of cable TV and the Internet detract more than they add. If, however, the principal value we find in free speech is free expression itself, the opportunity for more and more people to vent their rage or advertise their ideas, then we may be entering a golden age of freedom of speech. As with so many other issues before, the reader is invited to draw his or her own conclusions.

Question 3   *Is it possible for the wealthy few to dominate public debate and stifle the "free marketplace of ideas"?*

In its determination to safeguard free speech in the contemporary era, the Supreme Court has struck down a variety of legislative efforts to lessen the advantages of those with substantial financial resources from dominating our election campaigns. Two Court decisions in the 1970s, *Buckley v. Valeo* (1976) and *First National Bank of Boston v. Bellotti* (1978), established the limits on government's capacity to level the playing field in political debate.

Following the scandals accompanying the Nixon presidential reelection campaign in 1972, Congress passed sweeping campaign finance legislation designed to diminish the corrupting influence of big money contributions to the electoral political process and designed at least in part to diminish the advantages of wealthy candidates in electoral competition. In its decision in *Buckley,* however, the Supreme Court overturned the provisions in the law that limited the amounts that candidates could spend in the pursuit of public office. The Court majority in *Buckley* reasoned that the nearly unfettered ability to spend money to spread your point of view to the widest possible audience was an essential element of First Amendment freedoms. In the words of the per curium opinion:

> A restriction on the amount of money a person or group can spend on political communication during a campaign necessarily reduces the quantity of expression by restricting the number of issues discussed, the depth of their exploration, and the size of the audience reached. This is because virtually every means of communicating ideas in today's mass society requires the expenditure of money (at 19).

Attempts by Congress to place limits on a candidate's ability to spend a candidate's own money to advertise his or her positions on the issues and to attack his or her opponents, according to the Court, struck at First Amendment freedoms. As a result the Court invalidated limits on a candidate's campaign expenditures, except for candidates who agreed to accept such limits in exchange for receiving federal financing of their presidential election campaigns. In doing so, however, the Court rejected the arguments that limits on expenditures were essential to maintain genuine competition in the electoral arena. Unlimited campaign expenditures might enable the wealthy and those supported by the wealthy to dominate the electoral arena, perhaps drowning out in effect the voices of the poorer candidates or candidates unable to accumulate a huge campaign war chest. But the Court's opinion rejected ". . . the concept that government may restrict the speech of some elements of our society in order to enhance the relative voice of others . . . [as] wholly foreign to the First Amendment, which was designed 'to secure the widest possible dissemination of information from diverse and antagonistic sources' . . ." (at 49).

Against the Court's view, Justices Marshall and White both argued that removing the advantages of money can enhance the exchange of ideas and thus serve fundamental First Amendment values. In Justice White's words:

> It is critical to obviate or dispel the impression that federal elections are purely and simply a function of money, that federal offices are bought and sold or that political races are reserved for those who have the facility—and the stomach—for doing whatever it takes to bring together those interests, groups, and individuals that can raise or contribute large fortunes in order to prevail at the polls (at 65).

Justice Thurgood Marshall shared this view, arguing that the interest advanced by expenditure limits on campaigns and by individual wealthy candidates is the "interest in promoting the reality and appearance of equal access to the political arena" (at 287).

In *Federal Election Commission v. National Conservative Political Action Committee* (1985) Justice White, joined again by Justice Marshall, elaborated further on his disagreement with the Court position in *Buckley*. In support of limitations on campaign spending, Justice White argued:

> The First Amendment protects the right to speak, not the right to spend, and limitations on the amount of money that can be spent are not the same as restrictions on speaking. I agree with the majority that . . . expenditures "produce" core First Amendment speech. . . . But that is precisely the point: they produce speech; they are not speech itself. At least in these circumstances, I cannot accept the identification of speech with its antecedents. Such a house-that-Jack-built approach could equally be used to find a First Amendment right to a job or a minimum wage to "produce" the money to "produce" the speech. . . . The burden on actual speech imposed by limitations on the spending of money is minimal and indirect. . . . The restrictions, to the extent they do affect speech, are viewpoint-neutral and indicate no hostility to speech itself or its effects.

In *Buckley* the Court did, however, permit Congress to place limits on the size of political contributions to candidates' election campaigns.

The Court accepted the argument that allowing unlimited contributions to candidates could serve to corrupt the electoral process, allowing wealthy contributors to "buy" candidates through such contributions. Although such contribution limits in the Court's view did close off one potential channel for contributors to express their viewpoints, they did not prevent contributors from expressing their views independently of the candidates' campaign organizations. For example, the contribution limit upheld by the Court prevents someone with the wealth of a Donald Trump from giving unlimited amounts to candidates who support casino gambling. They would not prevent Mr. Trump, however, from producing his own advertisements extolling the benefits of casino gambling and thus assisting candidates for public office who share his views; nor would they prevent him from spending unlimited amounts of his own money were he to seek public office himself.

The Court then accepted limits on the amount anyone can give directly to a candidate, accepting the argument that direct contributions can be corrupting and that stopping such corruption and the appearance of such corruption is a sufficiently "compelling state interest" to justify the limited infringement on free speech that such contribution limits entail. But the Court rejected limits on either how much a candidate can spend on his or her own campaign or how much a noncandidate may spend independently of the candidate's campaign organization in support of a particular candidate as not justified. The Court rejected the argument that the expenditure of vast sums of money for one side of a political campaign itself endangers the open competition of ideas. The justices opted instead to view the right to spend whatever one pleases to advance one's ideas as a core First Amendment freedom. They in effect endorsed the cliché that "money talks."

Similarly, in *First National Bank of Boston v. Bellotti* (1978) the Court rejected an effort by the state of Massachusetts to forbid corporations from spending corporate funds to pay for campaign advertising in referenda campaigns. Massachusetts had felt that corporations were permitted by law to accumulate vast sums of money, far outstripping the ability of individuals to compete. The state enacted a limit on corporate participation in campaigns in response to large corporate-sponsored advertising to defeat attempts by the state to amend its state constitution to permit a progressive income tax. Such a tax taxes those earning large incomes at a higher rate than those earning low incomes. Presumably corporate executives found such a tax system contrary to their interests, and they therefore used their control over corporate accounts to attempt to defeat it. Those lower-income groups favoring the progressive income tax did not have ready access to such large amounts of money and could, in effect, be drowned out by corporate advertising. Here too, however, the Supreme Court rejected any efforts to place limits on the expenditure of money to advance particular points of view.

The fund-raising practices surrounding the 1996 and 2000 presidential campaigns led to renewed efforts within Congress to reign in the influence of big money on the political process. Although the so-called McCain-Feingold law which was upheld by the Supreme Court in 2003 (*McConnell v. FEC*), attempted to plug some loopholes in existing campaign finance laws to lessen in particular the role of corporations and organized labor in funding election campaigns through large so-called "soft money" contributions to political party organizations rather than to specific candidates, no significant effort was made to restrain the ability of wealthy candidates themselves or candidates who can attract vast campaign contributions totals to spend almost unlimited amounts in seeking public office. One provision, however, would allow candidates facing wealthy self-financed opponents to raise larger amounts in individual contributions (up to $12,000 instead of the general contribution limit of $2,000). Clearly this provision is designed to attempt to level the playing field and to limit the capacity of wealthy self-financed candidates to overwhelm their opponents. Although this provision still does not limit how much a wealthy candidate may spend, it does make it somewhat more possible for less wealthy candidates to compete IF they can attract a large number of large contributions.

Whether Court decisions, which have stymied legislative efforts to equalize the resources potentially available to contending sides in political debate, actually stifle genuine competition of ideas is a matter of judgment. The candidate who spends the most does not always win, but the availability of vast amounts of money to one side in a political contest can discourage others from even attempting to compete. When it comes to the clash of candidates and ideas in the electoral process, the Supreme Court has in effect rejected the arguments promoting a "fair fight" between equally armed combatants. As long as the Supreme Court equates the spending of money for the dissemination of ideas with free speech itself, the free marketplace of ideas may be in danger of the equivalent of monopoly control. As long as regulation of campaign expenditures applies equally to all sides in a debate it may be difficult for some of us to understand how such regulations can be seen as suppressing free speech.

Question 4 *Does the Constitution protect us from private institutions which interfere with our liberties and rights?*

Among the most common political phrases in everyday American speech is "They can't do that to me; that's unconstitutional." Many of us believe that every perceived injustice from whatever source must violate the Constitution. In fact this is very often not true. The Constitution protects us only from certain kinds of abuse and only from abuse that is directly attributable to government. Many threats to our personal autonomy and freedom of action today, however, arise from nongovernmental sources. At a time when corporate power stretches across continents, far beyond the jurisdiction of any government, we can expect to be subject to potentially arbitrary decisions limiting our choices from a variety of actors. It is important, therefore, to understand the limited reach of our constitutional protections.

The protections for rights and liberties included in the United States Constitution restrict only government. The Constitution was designed initially to allocate and assign power to the national or federal government and to limit the capacity of that government to oppress citizens. Following the Civil War and the adoption of the Thirteenth, Fourteenth, and Fifteenth Amendments, new restrictions were placed on the state governments (and by necessary implication on local governments which are viewed as subordinate to state governments.) In addition new powers were given to the national government to protect individual rights and liberties from state encroachment. With the exception of the Thirteenth Amendment's prohibition on "involuntary servitude" throughout the United States, nothing in the Constitution limits the capacity of individuals or purely private institutions from practically interfering with our ability to exercise rights or liberties we might assume we have.

For example, what if your private employer were to decide to hire only Republicans as employees? You could be denied employment, in effect punished, for holding a political belief disapproved of by your employer. Although today Congress and the states have generally, through civil rights laws, forbidden private employers from discriminating against employees or potential clients on the basis of race, ethnicity, gender, or disability, the Constitution itself has not been interpreted by the Supreme Court as forbidding such conduct. In other words the Constitution in permitting Congress to regulate business through its power to regulate commerce among the states has allowed Congress, when it so chooses, to forbid private discrimination within and by businesses engaged in interstate commerce. The Constitution did not force Congress or the states to forbid such discrimination. In fact for decades the Supreme Court argued that the Constitution did not permit Congress to interfere with so-called private discrimination. The states were always free in the exercise of their so-called "police powers," their powers to regulate morality and protect public safety and welfare, to outlaw private discrimination, but for most of our nation's history the states chose to do nothing about it.

To understand how, when, and why most private conduct practically interfering with what we might think of as basic liberties and rights remains free from constitutional restraint requires us to review what is known as the state action doctrine.

A review of the Bill of Rights should make it clear that the restrictions involved are directed at government action. The First Amendment, for example, begins with the words: "Congress shall make no law respecting an establishment of religion, or prohibiting the free exercise thereof." Clearly this restriction is addressed to Congress. The Fourteenth Amendment, which was designed principally to assure that those who had been held in slavery would have the same rights as other citizens, contains the phrase "No state shall. . . ."

When, following the Civil War and the adoption of the Fourteenth Amendment, Congress attempted to assure that former slaves and other African Americans would be free from some manifestations of private discrimination in the use of such "public accommodations" as privately owned hotels, theaters, and railroads, the U.S. Supreme Court was called upon to decide whether Section 5 of the Fourteenth Amendment authorized Congress to restrict or punish such privately initiated discrimination.

Section 5 gave to Congress the "power to enforce [this article] by appropriate legislation." In deciding what this phrase meant, the Supreme Court in the *Civil Rights Cases of 1883* analyzed in detail the actual language of the Fourteenth Amendment.

> The first section of the Fourteenth Amendment . . . after declaring who shall be citizens of the United States and of the several states, is prohibitory in it character, and prohibitory upon the states. . . . It is state action of a particular character that is prohibited. Individual invasion of individual rights is not the subject matter of the amendment. . . . It nullifies and makes void all state legislation, and state action of every kind, which impairs the privileges and immunities of citizens of the United States, or which injures them in life, liberty, or property without due process of law, or which denies to any of them the equal protection of the laws (at 11).

In the words of Justice Joseph P. Bradley, writing for all but one of the justices then on the U.S. Supreme Court, the amendment then goes on to authorize Congress to enforce its provisions through "appropriate legislation." But, he asks, "[t]o enforce what"? His answer:

> To enforce the prohibition. To adopt appropriate legislation for correcting the effects of such prohibited state law and state acts, and thus to render them effectively null, void and innocuous. . . . And so . . . until some state law has been passed, or some state action through its officers or agents has been taken, adverse to the rights of citizens sought to be protected by the Fourteenth Amendment, no legislation of the United States under said amendment. . . , can be called into activity, for the prohibitions of the amendment are against state laws and acts done under state authority (at 11–12).

Although in his dissenting opinion Justice Harlan argued that the Court had misread the intent behind the Fourteenth Amendment, the fundamental principle that only actions attributable to government are restricted by the Constitution has remained virtually unchallenged since. There has, however, been considerable dispute within the Court over the years concerning exactly how much state involvement there must be in a challenged action to trigger constitutional protections. In the contemporary world there are very few activities about which it can be said that government has absolutely no role or responsibility. The line between what is "public" and what is purely "private" is often blurred.

In 1948 in *Shelley v. Kraemer* the Supreme Court showed in an unusual case one way the state action doctrine can work. It was very common in the past for deeds to property to include "racially restricted covenants" which prohibited sale of the property to nonwhites and often to non-Christians as well. When Shelley, a black man, purchased some land in Missouri in 1948, a white neighbor, Kraemar, objected, contending the sale violated a racially restrictive covenant barring sale to members of "the Negro or Mongolian" race. When the case eventually reached the United States Supreme Court, the Court found the covenant itself to be constitutionally unobjectionable. The Fourteenth Amendment, according to the Court "erect[ed] no shield against merely private conduct, however discriminatory or wrongful. . . . [T]herefore . . . the restrictive agreement standing alone cannot be regarded as a violation of any rights guaranteed . . . by the Fourteenth Amendment" (at 13).

Private contracts, however, are not always self-executing. If both parties to the contract follow their obligations, then even racially discriminatory agreements are permitted by the Constitution. If someone seeks to ignore the contract, however, then the usual recourse is to the courts to seek enforcement of the private agreement. When Kraemer went to the state courts to seek enforcement of the racially restrictive covenant, the Supreme Court ruled that "the action of state courts and judicial officers in their official capacities is to be regarded as action of the State within the meaning of the Fourteenth Amendment . . ." (at 14). Through judicial enforcement what had been immune from constitutional challenge had now become unconstitutional. The involvement of the state courts had triggered constitutional protections.

Although many "state action" cases have concerned efforts to overcome racial discrimination through the Equal Protection clause of the Fourteenth Amendment, actually all efforts to enforce constitutional rights, when private persons or institutions are affected, must first face the hurdle of the requirement that some level of state action be found.

Today the Supreme Court insists on a high level of state involvement in an actual decision challenged on constitutional grounds before it will rule that constitutional requirements applicable to government must be followed by ostensibly private institutions.

Under the Fourteenth Amendment, whenever a government agency makes a decision depriving you of some benefit or privilege, it must meet elemental requirements of due process. This is because the Due Process clause of the Fourteenth Amendment says that "No state shall . . . deprive any person of life, liberty, or property, without due process of law." While what is involved in "due process" can vary depending on the circumstances and the nature of the deprivation in question, due process at least requires that the person suffering some loss at the hand of government have an opportunity to be heard before a decision is final and have some opportunity to appeal the decision made against him or her.

When the deprivation in question comes not from government directly but from some private source, the state action doctrine forces the courts to determine first whether the action of some apparently private institution "may be fairly treated as that of the state itself" (*Jackson v. Metropolitan Edison,* at 351, 1974). Many services upon which even life itself may sometimes depend are provided not by government but by private companies, such as electric utilities, which are, however, generally highly regulated by government. Until recently electricity in most communities was provided by government-regulated but privately owned monopolies. The Supreme Court's decision in *Jackson v. Metropolitan Edison* concerned the decision of a Pennsylvania electric power monopoly to terminate electric service to a customer without what she considered to be adequate notice and the opportunity for a hearing. Despite the fact that the specific termination procedures of the company were "allowed by a provision of its general tariff filed with the [Pennsylvania Public Utility] Commission," the Supreme Court held that Metropolitan Edison was not subject to the Fourteenth Amendment due process requirements that would have applied to a state-owned and operated utility. State acceptance of a utility's policies even when accompanied by heavy and detailed state regulation is not enough to trigger constitutional protections. Before applying constitutional restraints the Court asks "whether there is a sufficiently close nexus between the State and the challenged action of the regulated entity so that the action of the latter may be fairly treated as that of the State itself" (at 351). Because the termination of service practices at issue in the case were initiated by the utility and simply accepted by the state rather than initiated by the state, the Court found insufficient connection to attribute the service termination to state action.

Following the *Jackson* decision, a series of other Supreme Court decisions made it increasingly difficult to subject private institutions to constitutional restraints even when those private institutions were implementing government policies and programs at public expense. For example, Medicaid, the government health care program for the poor, requires different levels of care at government expense in privately owned and operated nursing homes. Patients are reassigned to different levels of care according to guidelines issued by the government. Nonetheless, in

Blum v. Yaretsky (1982) the Supreme Court said private nursing home decisions implementing these guidelines requiring transfer of patients to lower levels of care were not subject to due process requirements.

Because the decision to transfer a specific patient was made by a nursing home committee rather than by a government official, the Court ruled that Fourteenth Amendment due process procedural protections did not apply. Similarly in *Rendell-Baker v. Kohn* (1982) the Court ruled First Amendment free speech protections and Fourteenth Amendment due process requirements did not restrain a privately owned, yet nearly totally publicly funded, school for maladjusted students, which issued diplomas certified by a public school committee, from firing teachers who had publicly criticized the school's administration. According to the Court, "[t]he core issue presented in the case is not whether [the teachers] were discharged because of their speech or without adequate procedural protections, but whether the school's action in discharging them can fairly be seen as state action" (at 839). To put it simply they have no free speech protections against the school administration unless their action is "attributable to the state." And, according to the Court, "the State can be held responsible for a private decision only when it has exercised coercive power or has provided such significant encouragement either overt or covert, that the choice must in law be deemed to be that of the State" itself (at 840).

The lesson then for anyone concerned about the growing power over our lives exercised by nongovernmental institutions is that unless there is direct collusion between a private decision maker and government in a particular decision affecting our liberties, the actions of the private decision maker are not subject to constitutional guidelines. At a time when governments across America are increasingly "privatizing" government services—that is turning over to private institutions decision-making power about who gets services and benefits—the potential for a shrinking of the areas of our lives protected by constitutional rights and liberties is significant.

There has long been one area where it was thought that government could not escape constitutional protections for rights and liberties by giving government authority to private institutions. These are activities covered by what the Court has termed the public functions doctrine.

Some activities are so closely associated with government and the power of the state that they keep their governmental character no matter who carries them out. Because throughout most of the world, and even in parts of the United States, government has been responsible for the provision of electric power, the party suing in *Jackson v. Metropolitan Edison* asserted that electric utilities should be considered public functions under the state action doctrine. In rejecting this argument, Chief Justice Rehnquist limited the category of public functions to the "exercise by a private entity of powers traditionally exclusively reserved to the state" (at 352–53). Applying this reasoning to the *Jackson* case itself, he argued that because electric power production did not involve government authority delegated to Metropolitan Edison by the state "which is traditionally associated with sovereignty, such as eminent domain . . . [,the power of government to seize private property for public use]," it could not be considered for constitutional purposes a "public function."

Because in America virtually every activity imaginable from the running of schools to prisons has at some point in our history been exercised by private institutions, it is difficult to think of any contemporary activity, except perhaps the running of elections, that has been recognized as both traditionally and exclusively the prerogative of the state. This being the case it is possible for government to lessen the scope of our constitutional protections by turning over to private institutions ever-increasing aspects of our lives. We, of course, can hope that the democractic political process will prevent government from allowing private entities to threaten our liberties. But we must remember that we rely on the Constitution already to protect us from disregard by our elected governments for the rights and liberties of each of us as individuals. If democracy and majority rule cannot always be trusted to assure us that our liberties will not be threatened *by government,* can we count on democracy alone to be sure that government will protect us from abuses by the private sector? The time could come when government itself may not be the greatest threat to our liberties. If that happens, then the significance of our constitutional rights and liberties could significantly erode.

REFERENCES

Blum v. Yaretsky, 457 U.S. 991 (1982).

Buckley v. Valeo, 424 U.S. 1 (1976).

Civil Rights Cases of 1883, 109 U.S. 3 (1883).

Douglas v. California, 372 U.S. 353 (1963).

Federal Election Commission v. National Conservative Political Action Committee 470 U. S. 480 (1985).

First National Bank of Boston v. Bellotti, 435 U.S. 765 (1978).

Gideon v. Wainwright, 372 U.S. 335 (1963).

Griffin v. Illinios, 351 U.S. 512 (1956).

Harris v. McRae, 448 U.S. 297 (1980).

Jackson v. Metropolitan Edison, 419 U.S. 345 (1974).

Maher v. Roe, 432 U.S. 464 (1977).

McConnell v. FEC, 1245 Ct. 619; 72 U.S. L. W. 4015 (2003).

Miami Herald Publishing Co. v. Tornillo, 418 U.S. 241 (1974).

Red Lion Broadcasting Co., Inc. v. Federal Communications Commission, 395 U.S. 367 (1969).

Rendell-Baker v. Kohn, 447 U.S. 830 (1982).

Rust v. Sullivan, 500 U.S. 173 (1991).

Shelley v. Kraemer, 334 U.S. 1 (1948).

CHAPTER SEVEN

CONCLUSION
What Is the Future of Civil Rights and Civil Liberties in America?

Civil rights and liberties are always insecure. Every period in our history has produced new challenges and setbacks, but at the same time much progress has been made in the over two centuries during which the Constitution has served as the governing charter of America. The degree to which our liberties are under threat is, like every other question concerning the Constitution, a matter of opinion and differing interpretation. While protections for the freedom of speech and of the press have probably never been as extensive in the past as they are today, the strict "wall of separation" of church and state that emerged from Court rulings from the 1940s through the 1980s appears to be showing some cracks. This erosion in separation of church and state can of course be seen as a pulling back by the Court from rulings which some have seen as jeopardizing the freedom of religion and religious expression also guaranteed by the First Amendment. But Court rulings in the 1990s have also limited our ability to challenge successfully government actions that make it difficult for individuals to follow their consciences.

The right to privacy, first clearly enunciated by the Supreme Court in the *Griswold v. Connecticut* (1965) decision protecting the right of married couples to use birth control without state interference, later led to the right of women to elect to have an abortion. Court rulings related to privacy from the 1980s through the end of the twentieth century had, however, been marked by an increasing reluctance by the U.S. Supreme Court to extend that right of privacy or personal autonomy to other areas, such as protection for homosexual relationships from state regulation and guaranteeing a right to physician-assisted suicide to the terminally ill. In a remarkable turnaround in 2003 the Court extended the right to privacy to protect intimate homosexual relationships. Whether any further extension of this right is likely is uncertain. At the same time as the Court was recognizing some claimed new rights as it rejected others, it also permitted increasing limits on a woman's right to choose abortion, first enunciated in *Roe v. Wade* (1973).

In the area of civil rights the Court has also been moving away from some of its more expansive rulings of the 1960s through the 1980s. Increasingly the Court has rejected affirmative action programs designed to assist racial minorities in favor of a colorblind approach that subjects any racial classifications to the same strict scrutiny. Today when considering whether a challenged government policy allegedly disadvantages a member of a racial minority or of the white majority, the Court generally approaches it with the same level of extreme skepticism. Whether this Court view is a step backward in civil rights or is simply a maturing of our understanding of what racial equality requires is for all of us to judge for ourselves. As was the case with privacy, however, the Court at the beginning of the twenty first century took a surprising turn. In giving clear recognition to the right of the state openly to pursue racial diversity in higher educational institutions, the Court signaled that racially conscious government action is not always forbidden by the Fourteenth Amendment. Whether the Court will find other areas where it is permissible to consider race may be unlikely, but it is not a closed question.

Because what the Constitution means at any time is determined by the Supreme Court justices who interpret it, the changes we have seen in constitutional interpretation reflect to a significant degree the changes in the personnel on the U.S. Supreme Court. During the period when the Court began to place limits on the expansion of civil rights and civil liberties protections during the 1970s to the end of the twentieth century, the Court has been increasingly dominated by justices appointed by Republican presidents. Although those justices were largely responsible for the general direction of the Court which had showed less sympathy for civil rights and liberties concerns than some of their immediate predecessors, some of them were, nonetheless, the authors of the Court decisions that extended some privacy protection and permitted consideration of race in the pursuit of diversity. Should President George W. Bush have the opportunity to fill any Supreme Court vacancies, he has indicated a preference for justices in the mold of Clarence Thomas and Antonin Scalia, two justices who dissented from the Court's 2003 decisions both extending the right of privacy and approving the pursuit of racial diversity in higher educational institutions. These same justices also opposed the Court's recent decision in *Planned Parenthood v. Casey* reaffirming the right of women to choose abortion. The election of 2004 may well prove pivotal in determining the future of a closely divided Supreme Court and of civil rights and liberties.

The level of protections for civil rights and liberties has often in American history been influenced by trends in the society as a whole. The events of September 11, 2001, may yet have a profound influence upon our rights and liberties. Although noncitizens in the United States were the first to feel the brunt of security concerns following the terrorist attacks, we can only speculate what further might happen should security threats become even greater. Will a climate of suspicion of foreigners, especially those from nations associated with the events of September 11, 2001, become an excuse for racial, ethnic, or religious discrimination?

Future threats to civil liberties and civil rights may, however, be even more profound than just those traditionally caused by the changing political fortunes of the political parties, shifting personnel on the courts, or even periods of international crisis. Technological trends and broader cultural trends in how we view government may pose even more fundamental threats to civil liberties and civil rights.

As was noted in Chapter 6 the Internet and other technological innovations affecting communication may pose significant challenges to our understanding of how we protect the values protected by the First Amendment freedom of expression. The proliferation of hate groups advocating violence and terrorist organizations, possibly mobilizing their supporters over the Internet, will tempt many to wonder about the viability of free speech doctrines which permit advocacy of violence. The fact that such groups are encountered only by those who seek them out and stay largely isolated from the persuasion of competing ideas and values can subject the value of the free marketplace of ideas to doubt. Today and in the future those advocating dangerous ideas may not subject themselves to the competition of the marketplace as each of us becomes more isolated from social forces which we elect to avoid. At the same time fear that such advocacy can now easily reach receptive nationwide and international audiences in an instant may increase pressures for punishing such speech. As already noted in Chapter 2 such punishment in this context may be seen as more acceptable even under the Supreme Court decision in *Brandenburg v. Ohio* (1969), under which only speech "directed to inciting or producing imminent lawless action" which is also "likely to produce such action" is subject to punishment (at 447). The Internet may be viewed as increasing the potential efficacy of such speech. If so the power of the Internet may be used to justify increasing suppression of free speech.

Constitutional safeguards against government oppression ironically may also become less valuable as government itself shrinks because of ideological suspicion of "big government." As government is increasingly replaced by private arrangements and enterprises, constitutional safeguards for privacy, liberty, and even civil rights become inoperable. As we saw in Chapter 6 for constitutional protections to be triggered there must be some state action jeopardizing rights and liberties protected by the Constitution from only government infringement. Private retaliation for our exercise of our political or religious freedoms is not restricted by a Constitution which was designed to constrain government tyranny. The less we are dependent on government, then, the less we are protected by constitutional constraints on government. The more dependent we are on the private sector and corporate power, the more our freedom of expression and action can be restrained. Should the move toward privatization lead to a loosening of civil rights laws which regulate business and now protect us from discrimination on grounds of race, gender, religion, or disability from private employers and service providers, the Constitution, under current Court interpretations of the state action doctrine, will provide us no legal recourse. Such a repeal of civil rights laws seems unlikely, but equally unlikely is an effort to extend to the private sector protections for our liberties which today restrain only government. A government that governs least may indeed threaten our liberties less, but a private sector which grows to fill any power vacuum left by a weakened government can threaten our individual freedoms too. If the Supreme Court has the will, an abusive government can be restrained by the Constitution, but an abusive private sector can be restrained only by democratic government. Before we weaken government too much, we should consider how private power centers can themselves threaten liberty free from constitutional restraints.

REFERENCES

Brandenburg v. Ohio, 395 U.S. 444 (1969).

Griswold v. Connecticut, 381 U.S. 479 (1965).

Planned Parenthood v. Casey, 505 U.S. 833 (1992).

Roe v. Wade, 410 U.S. 113 (1973).

Rust v. Sullivan, 500 U.S. 173 (1991).

APPENDIX

The Constitution of the United States

THE PREAMBLE

We the People of the United States, in Order to form a more perfect Union, establish Justice, insure domestic Tranquility, provide for the common defense, promote the general Welfare, and secure the Blessings of Liberty to ourselves and our Posterity, do ordain and establish this Constitution for the United States of America.

ARTICLE I

Section 1 All legislative Powers herein granted shall be vested in a Congress of the United States, which shall consist of a Senate and House of Representatives.

Section 2 The House of Representatives shall be composed of Members chosen every second Year by the People of the several States, and the Electors in each State shall have the Qualifications requisite for Electors of the most numerous Branch of the State Legislature.

No Person shall be a Representative who shall not have attained to the Age of twenty five Years, and been seven Years a Citizen of the United

States, and who shall not, when elected, be an Inhabitant of that State in which he shall be chosen.

Representatives and direct Taxes[1] shall be apportioned among the several States which may be included within this Union, according to their respective Numbers, *which shall be determined by adding to the whole Number of free Persons, including those bound to Service for a Term of Years, and excluding Indians not taxed, three fifths of all other Persons.*[2] The actual Enumeration shall be made within three Years after the first Meeting of the Congress of the United States, and within every subsequent Term of ten Years, in such Manner as they shall by Law direct. The Number of Representatives shall not exceed one for every thirty Thousand, but each State shall have at least one Representative; and until each enumeration shall be made, the State of New Hampshire shall be entitled to chuse three, Massachusetts eight, Rhode-Island and Providence Plantations one, Connecticut five, New-York six, New Jersey four, Pennsylvania eight, Delaware one, Maryland six, Virginia ten, North Carolina five, South Carolina five, and Georgia three.

When vacancies happen in the Representation from any State, the Executive Authority thereof shall issue Writs of Election to fill such Vacancies.

The House of Representatives shall chuse their Speaker and other Officers; and shall have the sole Power of Impeachment.

Section 3   The Senate of the United States shall be composed of two Senators from each State, *chosen by the Legislature thereof,*[3] for six Years; and each Senator shall have one Vote.

Immediately after they shall be assembled in Consequence of the first Election, they shall be divided as equally as may be into three Classes. The Seats of the Senators of the first Class shall be vacated at the Expiration of the second Year, of the second Class at the Expiration of the fourth Year, and of the third Class at the Expiration of the sixth Year, so that one third may be chosen every second Year; *and if Vacancies happen by Resignation, or otherwise, during the Recess of the Legislature of any State, the Executive thereof may make temporary Appointments until the next Meeting of the Legislature, which shall then fill such Vacancies.*[4]

No person shall be a Senator who shall not have attained to the Age of thirty Years, and been nine Years a Citizen of the United States, and who shall not, when elected, be an inhabitant of that State for which he shall be chosen.

The Vice President of the United States shall be President of the Senate, but shall have no Vote, unless they be equally divided.

[1] Modified by the 16th Amendment
[2] Replaced by Section 2, 14th Amendment
[3] Repealed by the 17th Amendment
[4] Modified by the 17th Amendment

The Senate shall chuse their other Officers, and also a President pro tempore, in the Absence of the Vice President, or when he shall exercise the Office of President of the United States.

The Senate shall have the sole Power to try all Impeachments. When sitting for that Purpose, they shall be on Oath or Affirmation. When the President of the United States is tried, the Chief Justice shall preside: And no Person shall be convicted without the Concurrence of two thirds of the Members present.

Judgment in Cases of Impeachment shall not extend further than to removal from Office, and disqualification to hold and enjoy any Office of honor, Trust or Profit under the United States; but the Party convicted shall nevertheless be liable and subject to Indictment, Trial, Judgment and Punishment, according to law.

Section 4 The Times, Places and Manner of holding Elections for Senators and Representatives, shall be prescribed in each State by the Legislature thereof; but the Congress may at any time by Law make or alter such Regulations, except as to the Places of chusing Senators.

The Congress shall assemble at least once in every Year, *and such Meeting shall be on the first Monday in December, unless they shall by Law appoint a different Day.*[5]

Section 5 Each House shall be the Judge of the Elections, Returns and Qualifications of its own Members, and a Majority of each shall constitute a Quorum to do Business; but a smaller Number may adjourn from day to day, and may be authorized to compel the Attendance of absent Members, in such Manner, and under the Penalties as each House may provide.

Each House may determine the Rules of its Proceedings, punish its Members for disorderly Behaviour, and, with the Concurrence of two thirds, expel a Member.

Each House shall keep a Journal of its Proceedings, and from time to time publish the same, excepting such Parts as may in their Judgment require Secrecy; and the Yeas and Nays of the Members of either House on any question shall, at the Desire of one fifth of those Present, be entered on the Journal.

Neither House, during the Session of Congress, shall, without the Consent of the other, adjourn for more than three days, nor to any other place than that in which the two Houses shall be sitting.

Section 6 The Senators and Representatives shall receive a Compensation for their Services, to be ascertained by Law, and paid out of the Treasury of the United States. They shall in all Cases, except Treason, Felony and Breach of the Peace, be privileged from Arrest during their Attendance at the Session of their respective Houses, and in going to and

[5]Changed by the 20th Amendment

returning from the same; and for any Speech or Debate in either House, they shall not be questioned in any other Place.

No Senator or Representative, shall, during the time for which he was elected, be appointed to any civil Office under the Authority of the United States, which shall have been created, or the Emoluments whereof shall have been encreased during such time; and no Person holding any Office under the United States, shall be a Member of either House during his Continuance in Office.

Section 7 All Bills for raising Revenue shall originate in the House of Representatives; but the Senate may propose or concur with Amendments as on other Bills.

Every Bill which shall have passed the House of Representatives and the Senate, shall, before it becomes a Law, be presented to the President of the United States; if he approve he shall sign it, but if not he shall return it, with his Objections to that House in which it shall have originated, who shall enter the Objections at large on their Journal, and proceed to reconsider it. If after such Reconsideration two thirds of that House shall agree to pass the Bill, it shall be sent, together with the Objections, to the other House, by which it shall likewise be reconsidered, and if approved by two thirds of that House, it shall become a Law. But in all such Cases the Votes of both Houses shall be determined by yeas and Nays, and the Names of the Persons voting for and against the Bill shall be entered on the Journal of each House respectively. If any Bill shall not be returned by the President within ten Days (Sundays excepted) after it shall have been presented to him, the Same shall be a Law, in like Manner as if he had signed it, unless the Congress by their Adjournment prevent its Return, in which Case it shall not be a Law.

Every Order, Resolution, or Vote to which the Concurrence of the Senate and House of Representatives may be necessary (except on a question of Adjournment) shall be presented to the President of the United States; and before the Same shall take Effect, shall be approved by him, or being disapproved by him, shall be repassed by two thirds of the Senate and House of Representatives, according to the Rules and Limitations prescribed in the Case of a Bill.

Section 8 The Congress shall have Power To lay and collect Taxes, Duties, Imposts and Excises, to pay the Debts and provide for the common Defence and general Welfare of the United States; but all Duties, Imposts and Excises shall be uniform throughout the United States.

To borrow Money on the Credit of the United States;

To regulate Commerce with foreign Nations, and among the several States, and with the Indian Tribes;

To establish an uniform Rule of Naturalization, and uniform Laws on the subject of Bankruptcies throughout the United States;

To coin Money, regulate the Value thereof, and of foreign Coin, and fix the Standard of Weights and Measures;

To provide for the Punishment of counterfeiting the Securities and current Coin of the United States;

To establish Post Offices and post Roads;

To promote the Progress of Science and useful Arts, by securing for limited Times to Authors and Inventors the exclusive Right to their respective Writings and Discoveries;

To constitute Tribunals inferior to the supreme Court;

To define and punish Piracies and Felonies committed on the high Seas, and Offences against the Law of Nations;

To declare War, grant Letters of Marque and Reprisal, and make Rules concerning Captures on Land and Water;

To raise and support Armies, but no Appropriation of Money to that Use shall be for a longer Term than two Years;

To provide and maintain a Navy;

To make Rules for the Government and Regulation of the land and naval Forces;

To provide for calling for the Militia to execute the Laws of the Union, suppress Insurrections and repel Invasions;

To provide for organizing, arming, and disciplining, the Militia, and for governing such Part of them as may be employed in the Service of the United States, reserving to the States respectively, the Appointment of the Officers, and the Authority of training the Militia according to the discipline prescribed by Congress;

To exercise exclusive Legislation in all Cases whatsoever, over such District (not exceeding ten Miles square) as may, by Cession of particular States, and the Acceptance of Congress, become the Seat of the Government of the United States, and to exercise like Authority over all Places purchased by the Consent of the Legislature of the State in which the Same shall be, for the Erection of Forts, Magazines, Arsenals, dock-Yards, and other needful Buildings;—And

To make all Laws which shall be necessary and proper for carrying into Execution the foregoing Powers, and all other Powers vested by this Constitution in the Government of the United States, or in any Department or Officer thereof.

Section 9   The Migration Importation of such Persons as any of the States now existing shall think proper to admit, shall not be prohibited by the Congress prior to the Year one thousand eight hundred and eight, but a Tax or Duty may be imposed on such Importation, not exceeding ten dollars for each Person.

The privilege of the Writ of Habeas Corpus shall not be suspended, unless when in Cases of Rebellion or Invasion the public Safety may require it.

No Bill of Attainder or ex post facto Laws shall be passed.

No Capitation, or other direct, Tax shall be laid, unless in Proportion to the Census or Enumeration herein before directed to be taken.[6]

No Tax or Duty shall be laid on Articles exported from any State.

No Preference shall be given by any Regulation of Commerce or Revenue to the Ports of one State over those of another; nor shall Vessels bound to, or from, one State, be obliged to enter, clear, or pay Duties in another.

No Money shall be drawn from the Treasury, but in Consequence of Appropriations made by Law; and a regular Statement and Account of the Receipts and Expenditures of all public Money shall be published from time to time.

No Title of Nobility shall be granted by the United States; And no Person holding any Office of Profit or Trust under them, shall, without the Consent of Congress, accept of any present, Emolument, Office, or Title, of any kind whatever, from any King, Prince, or foreign State.

Section 10 No State shall enter into any Treaty, Alliance, or Confederation; grant Letters of Marque and Reprisal; coin Money; emit Bills of Credit; make any Thing but gold and silver Coin a Tender in Payment of Debts; pass any Bill of Attainder, ex post facto Law, or Law impairing the Obligation of Contracts, or grant any Title of Nobility.

No State shall, without the Consent of the Congress, lay any Imposts or Duties on Imports or Exports, except what may be absolutely necessary for executing its inspection Laws: and the net Produce of all Duties and Imposts, laid by any State on Imports or Exports, shall be for the Use of the Treasury of the United States; and all such Laws shall be subject to the Revision and Controul of the Congress.

No State shall, without the Consent of Congress, lay any Duty of Tonnage, keep Troops, or Ships of War in time of Peace, enter into any Agreement or Compact with another State, or with a foreign Power, or engage in War, unless actually invaded, or in such imminent Danger as will not admit of Delay.

ARTICLE II

Section 1 The executive Power shall be vested in a President of the United States of America. He shall hold his Office during the Term of four Years and, together with the Vice President, chosen for the same Term, be elected as follows:

Each State shall appoint, in such Manner as the Legislature thereof may direct, a Number of Electors, equal to the whole Number of Senators and Representatives to which the State may be entitled in the Congress:

[6]Modified by the 16th Amendment

but no Senator or Representative, or Person holding an Office of Trust or Profit under the United States, shall be appointed an Elector.

The Electors shall meet in their respective States, and vote by Ballot for two Persons, of whom one at least shall not be an Inhabitant of the same State with themselves. And they shall make a List of all the Persons voted for, and of the Number of Votes for each; which List they shall sign and certify, and transmit sealed to the Seat of the Government of the United States, directed to the President of the Senate. The President of the Senate shall, in the Presence of the Senate and House of Representatives, open all the Certificates, and the Votes shall then be counted. The Person having the greatest Number of Votes shall be the President, if such Number be a Majority of the whole Number of Electors appointed; and if there be more than one who have such Majority and have an equal Number of Votes, then the House of Representatives shall immediately chuse by Ballot one of them for President; and if no person have a Majority, then from the five highest on the List the said House shall in like Manner chuse the President. But in chusing the President, the Votes shall be taken by States, the Representation from each State having one Vote; A quorum for this Purpose shall consist of a Member or Members from two thirds of the States, and a Majority of all the States shall be necessary to a Choice. In every Case, after the Choice of the President, the person having the greatest Number of Votes of the Electors shall be the Vice President. But if there should remain two or more who have equal Vote, the Senate shall chuse from them by Ballot the Vice President.[7]

The Congress may determine the Time of chusing the Electors, and the Day on which they shall give their Votes; which Day shall be the same throughout the United States.

No Person except a natural born Citizen, or a Citizen of the United States, at the time of the Adoption of this Constitution, shall be eligible to the Office of President; neither shall any Person be eligible to that Office who shall not have attained to the Age of thirty five Years, and been fourteen Years a Resident within the United States.

In Case of the Removal of the President from Office, or of his Death, Resignation, or Inability to discharge the Powers and Duties of the said Office, the same shall devolve on the Vice President, and the Congress may by Law provide for the Case of Removal, Death, Resignation, or Inability, both of the President and Vice President, declaring what Officer shall then act as President, and such Officer shall act accordingly, until the Disability be removed, or a President shall be elected.[8]

The President shall, at stated Times, receive for his Services, a Compensation, which shall neither be encreased nor diminished during the

[7]Changed by the 12th and 20th Amendments
[8]Modified by the 25th Amendment

Period of which he shall have been elected, and he shall not receive within that Period any other Emolument from the United States, or any of them.

Before he enter on the Execution of his Office, he shall take the following Oath or Affirmation:—"I do solemnly swear (or affirm) that I will faithfully execute the Office of President of the United States, and will to the best of my Ability, preserve, protect and defend the Constitution of the United States."

Section 2   The President shall be the Commander in Chief of the Army and Navy of the United States, and of the Militia of the several States, when called into the actual Service of the United States, he may require the Opinion, in writing, of the principal Officer in each of the executive Departments, upon any Subject relating to the Duties of their respective Offices, and he shall have the Power to grant Reprieves and Pardons for Offences against the United States, except in Cases of Impeachment.

He shall have Power, by and with the Advice and Consent of the Senate to make Treaties, provided two thirds of the Senators present concur; and he shall nominate, and by and with the Advice and Consent of the Senate, shall appoint Ambassadors, other public Ministers and Consuls, Judges of the supreme Court, and all other Officers of the United States, whose Appointments are not herein otherwise provided for, and which shall be established by Law: but the Congress may by Law vest the Appointment of such inferior Officers, as they think proper, in the President alone, in the Courts of Law, or in the Heads of Departments.

The President shall have Power to fill up all Vacancies that may happen during the Recess of the Senate, by granting Commissions which shall expire at the End of their next Session.

Section 3   He shall from time to time give to the Congress Information of the State of the Union, and recommend to their Consideration such Measures as he shall judge necessary and expedient; he may, on extraordinary Occasions, convene both Houses, or either of them, and in Case of Disagreement between them, with Respect to the Time of Adjournment, he may adjourn them to such Time as he shall think proper; he shall receive Ambassadors and other public Ministers; he shall take Care that the Laws be faithfully executed, and shall Commission all the Officers of the United States.

Section 4   The President, Vice President and all civil Officers of the United States, shall be removed from Office on Impeachment for, and Conviction of, Treason, Bribery, or other High Crimes and Misdemeanors.

ARTICLE III

Section 1   The judicial Power of the United States, shall be vested in one supreme Court, and in such inferior Courts as the Congress may from time to time ordain and establish. The Judges, both the supreme and inferior Courts, shall hold their Offices during good Behaviour, and shall, at stated Times, receive for their Services, a Compensation, which shall not be diminished during their Continuance in Office.

Section 2 The judicial Power shall extend to all Cases, in Law and Equity, arising under this Constitution, the Laws of the United States, and Treaties made, or which shall be made, under their Authority;—to all Cases affecting Ambassadors, other public Ministers and Consuls;—to all Cases of admiralty and maritime Jurisdiction;—to Controversies to which the United States shall be a Party;—to Controversies between two or more States; *between a State and Citizens of another State;*[9]—between Citizens of different States;—between Citizens of the same State claiming Lands under Grants of different States, and between a State, or the Citizens thereof, and foreign States, Citizens, or Subjects.

In all Cases affecting Ambassadors, other public Ministers and Consuls, and those in which a State shall be Party, the supreme Court shall have original Jurisdiction. In all the other Cases before mentioned, the supreme Court shall have appellate Jurisdiction, both as to Law and Fact, with such Exceptions, and under such Regulations as Congress shall make.

The Trial of all Crimes, except in Cases of Impeachment, shall be by Jury; and such Trial shall be held in the State where the said Crimes shall have been committed; but when not committed within any State, the Trial shall be at such Place or Places as the Congress may by Law have directed.

Section 3 Treason against the United States, shall consist only in levying War against them, or in adhering to their Enemies, giving them Aid and Comfort. No Persons shall be convicted of Treason unless on the Testimony of two Witnesses to the same overt Act, or on Confession in open Court.

The Congress shall have Power to declare the Punishment of Treason, but no Attainder of Treason shall work Corruption of Blood, or Forfeiture except during the Life of the Person attainted.

ARTICLE IV

Section 1 Full Faith and Credit shall be given in each State to the public Acts, Records, and judicial Proceedings of every other State. And the Congress may by general Laws prescribe the Manner in which such Acts, Records and Proceedings shall be proved, and the Effect thereof.

[9]Modified by the 11th Amendment

Section 2   The Citizens of each State shall be entitled to all Privileges and Immunities of Citizens in the several States.

A person charged in any State with Treason, Felony or other Crime, who shall flee from Justice, and be found in another State, shall on Demand of the executive Authority of the State from which he fled, be delivered up, to be removed to the State having jurisdiction of the Crime.

No person held to Service or Labour in one State, under the Laws thereof, escaping into another, shall, in Consequence of any Law or Regulation therein, be discharged from such Service or Labour, but shall be delivered up on Claim of the Party to whom such Service or Labour may be due. [10]

Section 3   New States may be admitted by the Congress into this Union; but no new State shall be formed or erected within the Jurisdiction of any other State; nor any State to be formed by the Junction of two or more States, or Parts of States, without the Consent of the Legislatures of the States concerned as well as of the Congress.

The Congress shall have Power to dispose of and make all needful Rules and Regulations respecting the Territory or other Property belonging to the United States; and nothing in this Constitution shall be so construed as to Prejudice any Claims of the United States, or of any particular State.

Section 4   The United States shall guarantee to every State in this Union a Republican Form of Government, and shall protect each of them against Invasion; and on Application of the Legislature, or of the Executive (when the Legislature cannot be convened) against domestic Violence.

ARTICLE V

The Congress, whenever two thirds of both Houses shall deem it necessary, shall propose Amendments to this Constitution, or, on the Application of the Legislatures of two thirds of several States, shall call a Convention for proposing Amendments, which, in either Case, shall be valid to all Intents and Purposes, as Part of this Constitution, when ratified by the Legislatures of three fourths of the several States, or by Conventions in three fourths thereof, as the one or the other Mode of Ratification may be proposed by the Congress; Provided that no Amendment which may be made prior to the Year One thousand eight hundred and eight shall in any Manner affect the first and fourth Clauses in the Ninth Section of the first Article; and that no State, without its Consent, shall be deprived of its equal Suffrage in the Senate.

[10]Repealed by the 13th Amendment

ARTICLE VI

All Debts contracted and Engagements entered into, before the Adoption of this Constitution, shall be as valid against the United States under the Constitution, as under the Confederation.

This Constitution, and the Laws of the United States which shall be made in Pursuance thereof; and all Treaties made, or which shall be made, under the Authority of the United States, shall be the supreme Law of the Land; and the Judges in every State shall be bound thereby, any Thing in the Constitution or Laws of any State to the Contrary notwithstanding.

The Senators and Representatives before mentioned, and the Members of the several State Legislatures, and all executive and judicial Officers, both of the United States and of the several States, shall be bound by Oath or Affirmation, to support this Constitution; but no religious Test shall ever be required as a Qualification to any Office or public Trust under the United States.

ARTICLE VII

The Ratification of the Conventions of nine States, shall be sufficient for the Establishment of this Constitution between the States so ratifying the Same.

Done in Convention by the Unanimous Consent of the States present the Seventeenth Day of September in the Year of our Lord one thousand seven hundred and Eighty seven and of the Independence of the United States of America the Twelfth *In Witness whereof We have hereunto subscribed our Names.*

AMENDMENTS: THE BILL OF RIGHTS

[The first ten amendments were ratified on December 15, 1791, and form what is known as the "Bill of Rights."]

AMENDMENT 1

Congress shall make no law respecting an establishment of religion, or prohibiting the free exercise thereof; or abridging the freedom of speech, or of the press; or the right of the people peaceably to assemble, and to petition the government for a redress of grievances.

AMENDMENT 2

A well regulated Militia, being necessary to the security of a free State, the right of the people to keep and bear Arms, shall not be infringed.

AMENDMENT 3

No Soldier shall, in time of peace be quartered in any house, without the consent of the Owner, nor in time of war, but in manner to be prescribed by law.

AMENDMENT 4

The right of the people to be secure in their persons, houses, papers, and effects, against unreasonable searches and seizures, shall not be violated, and no Warrants shall issue, but upon probable cause, supported by Oath or affirmation, and particularly describing the place to be searched, and the persons or things to be seized.

AMENDMENT 5

No person shall be held to answer for a capital, or otherwise infamous crime, unless on a presentment or indictment of a Grand jury, except in cases arising in the land or naval forces, or in the Militia, when in actual service in time of War or public danger; nor shall any person be subject for the same offence to be twice put in jeopardy of life or limb; nor shall be compelled in any criminal case to be a witness against himself, nor be deprived of life, liberty, or property, without due process of law; nor shall private property be taken for public use, without just compensation.

AMENDMENT 6

In all criminal prosecutions, the accused shall enjoy the right to a speedy and public trial, by an impartial jury of the State and district wherein the crime shall have been committed, which district shall have been previously ascertained by law, and to be informed of the nature and cause of the accusation; to be confronted with the witnesses against him; to have compulsory process for obtaining Witnesses in his favor, and to have the Assistance of Counsel for his defense.

AMENDMENT 7

In Suits at common law, where the value in controversy shall exceed twenty dollars, the right of trial by jury shall be preserved, and no fact tried by a jury shall be otherwise re-examined in any Court of the United States, than according to the rules of the common law.

AMENDMENT 8

Excessive bail shall not be required, nor excessive fines imposed, nor cruel and unusual punishments inflicted.

AMENDMENT 9

The enumeration in the Constitution, of certain rights, shall not be construed to deny or disparage others retained by the people.

AMENDMENT 10

The powers not delegated to the United States by the Constitution, nor prohibited by it to the States, are reserved to the States respectively, or to the people.

AMENDMENT 11

[Ratified February 7, 1795]

The Judicial power of the United States shall not be construed to extend to any suit in law or equity, commenced or prosecuted against one of the United States by Citizens of another State, or by Citizens or Subjects of any Foreign State.

AMENDMENT 12

[Ratified June 15, 1804]

The Electors shall meet in their respective states, and vote by ballot for President and Vice-President, one of whom, at least, shall not be an inhabitant of the same state with themselves; they shall name in their ballots the person voted for as President, and in distinct ballots the person voted for as Vice-President, and they shall make distinct lists of all persons voted for as President, and of all persons voted for as Vice-President, and of the number of votes for each, which lists they shall sign and certify, and transmit sealed to the seat of the government of the United States, directed to the President of the Senate;—The President of the Senate shall, in presence of the Senate and House of Representatives, open all the certificates and the votes shall then be counted;—The person having the greatest number of votes for President, shall be the President, if such number be a majority of the whole number of Electors appointed; and if no person have such majority, then from the persons having the highest numbers not exceeding three on the list of those voted for as President, the House of Representatives shall choose immediately, by ballot, the President. But in choosing the President, the votes shall be taken by states, the representation from each state having one vote; a quorum for this purpose shall consist of a member or members from two-thirds of the states, and a majority of all states shall be necessary to a choice. And if the House of Representatives shall not choose a President whenever the right of choice shall devolve upon them, *before the fourth day of March next following,* then the Vice-President shall act as President, as in the case of the death or other constitutional disability of the President.[11] The person having the greatest number of votes as Vice-President, shall be the Vice-President, if such a number be a majority of the whole numbers of Electors appointed, and if no person have a majority, then from the two highest numbers on the list, the Senate shall choose the Vice-President; a quorum for the purpose shall consist of two-thirds of the whole number of Senators, and a majority of the whole number shall be necessary to a choice. But no person constitutionally ineligible to the office of President shall be eligible to that of Vice-President of the United States.

AMENDMENT 13

[Ratified December 6, 1865]

Section 1   Neither slavery nor involuntary servitude, except as a punishment for crime whereof the party shall have been duly convicted, shall exist within the United States, or any place subject to their jurisdiction.

Section 2   Congress shall have power to enforce this article by appropriate legislation.

[11]Changed by the 20th Amendment

AMENDMENT 14

[Ratified July 9, 1868]

Section 1   All persons born or naturalized in the United States, and subject to the jurisdiction thereof, are citizens of the United States and of the State wherein they reside. No State shall make or enforce any law which shall abridge the privileges or immunities of citizens of the United States; nor shall any State deprive any person of life, liberty, or property, without due process of law; nor deny to any person within its jurisdiction the equal protection of the laws.

Section 2   Representatives shall be apportioned among the several States according to their respective numbers, counting the whole number of persons in each State, excluding Indians not taxed. But when the right to vote at any election for the choice of electors for President and Vice President of the United States, Representatives in Congress, the Executive and Judicial officers of a State, or the members of the Legislature thereof, is denied to any of the male inhabitants of such State, being twenty-one[12] years of age, and citizens of the United States, or in any way abridged, except for participation in rebellion, or other crime, the basis of representation therein shall be reduced in the proportion which the number of such male citizens shall bear to the whole number of male citizens twenty-one years of age in such State.

Section 3   No person shall be a Senator or Representative in Congress, or elector of President and Vice President, or hold any office, civil or military, under the United States, or under any State, who, having previously taken an oath, as a member of Congress, or as an officer of the United States, or as a member of any State legislature, or as an executive or judicial officer of any State, to support the Constitution of the United States, shall have engaged in insurrection or rebellion against the same, or given aid or comfort to the enemies thereof. But Congress may by a vote of two-thirds of each House, remove such disability.

Section 4   The validity of the public debt of the United States, authorized by law, including debts incurred for payment of pensions and bounties for services in suppressing insurrection or rebellion, shall not be questioned. But neither the United States nor any State shall assume or pay any debt or obligation incurred in aid of insurrection or rebellion

---

[12]Changed by the 26th Amendment

against the United States, or any claim for the loss or emancipation of any slave; but all such debts, obligations and claims shall be held illegal and void.

Section 5   The Congress shall have power to enforce, by appropriate legislation, the provisions of this article.

AMENDMENT 15

[Ratified February 3, 1870]

Section 1   The right of citizens of the United States to vote shall not be denied or abridged by the United States or by any State on account of race, color, or previous condition of servitude.

Section 2   The Congress shall have power to enforce this article by appropriate legislation.

AMENDMENT 16

[Ratified February 3, 1913]

The Congress shall have power to lay and collect taxes on incomes, from whatever source derived, without apportionment among the several States, and without regard to any census or enumeration.

AMENDMENT 17

[Ratified April 8, 1913]

The Senate of the United States shall be composed of two Senators from each State, elected by the people thereof, for six years; and each Senator shall have one vote. The electors in each State shall have the qualifications requisite for electors of the most numerous branch of the State legislatures.

When vacancies happen in the representation of any State in the Senate, the executive authority of such State shall issue writs of election to fill such vacancies: *Provided,* That the Legislature of any State may empower the executive thereof to make temporary appointment until the people fill the vacancies by election as the legislature may direct.

This amendment shall not be so construed as to affect the election or term of any Senator chosen before it becomes valid as part of the Constitution.

AMENDMENT 18

[Ratified January 16, 1919. Repealed December 5, 1933 by Amendment 21]

Section 1   After one year from the ratification of this article the manufacture, sale, or transportation of intoxicating liquors within, the importation thereof into, or the exportation thereof from the United States and all territory subject to the jurisdiction thereof for beverage purposes is hereby prohibited.

Section 2   The Congress and the several states shall have concurrent power to enforce this article by appropriate legislation.

Section 3   This article shall be inoperative unless it shall have been ratified as an amendment to the Constitution by the legislatures of the several states, as provided in the Constitution, within seven years from the date of the submission hereof to the States by the Congress.[13]

AMENDMENT 19

[Ratified August 18, 1920]

The right of the citizens of the United States to vote shall not be denied or abridged by the United States or by any State on account of sex.

Congress shall have power, by appropriate legislation, to enforce the provision of this article.

AMENDMENT 20

[Ratified January 23, 1933]

Section 1   The terms of the President and Vice President shall end at noon on the 20th day of January, and the terms of the Senators and Representatives at noon on the 3rd day of January, of the years in which such terms would have ended if this article had not been ratified; and the terms of their successors shall then begin.

Section 2   The Congress shall assemble at least once in every year, and such meeting shall begin at noon on the 3rd day of January, unless they shall by law appoint a different day.

Section 3   If, at the time fixed for the beginning of the term of the President, the President elect shall have died, the Vice President elect shall

---

[13]Repealed by the 21st Amendment

become President. If a President shall not have been chosen before the time fixed for the beginning of his term, or if the President elect shall have failed to qualify, then the Vice President elect shall act as President until a President shall have qualified; and the Congress may by law provide for the case wherein neither a President elect nor a Vice President elect shall have qualified, declaring who shall then act as President, or the manner in which one who is to act shall be selected, and such person shall act accordingly until a President or Vice President shall have qualified.

Section 4   The Congress may by law provide for the case of the death of any of the persons from whom the House of Representatives may choose a President whenever the right of choice shall have developed upon them, and for the case of the death of any of the persons from whom the Senate may choose a Vice President whenever the right of choice shall have devolved upon them.

Section 5   Sections 1 and 2 shall take effect on the 15th day of October following the ratification of this article.

Section 6   This article shall be inoperative unless it shall have been ratified as an amendment to the Constitution by the legislatures of three-fourths of the several States within seven years from the date of its submission.

AMENDMENT 21

[Ratified December 5, 1933]

Section 1   The eighteenth article of amendment to the Constitution of the United States is hereby repealed.

Section 2   The transportation or importation into any State, Territory, or Possession of the United States for delivery or use therein of intoxicating liquors, in violation of the laws thereof, is hereby prohibited.

Section 3   This article shall be inoperative unless it shall have been ratified as an amendment to the Constitution by conventions in the several States, as provided in the Constitution, within seven years from the date of the submission hereof to the States by the Congress.

AMENDMENT 22

[Ratified February 27, 1951]

Section 1   No person shall be elected to the office of the President more than twice, and no person who has held the office of President, or acted as

President, for more than two years of a term to which some other person was elected President shall be elected to the Office of the President more than once. But this Article shall not apply to any person holding the office of President when this article was proposed by the Congress, and shall not prevent any person who may be holding the office of President, or acting as President, during the term within which this Article becomes operative from holding the office of President or acting as President during the remainder of such term.

Section 2　This Article shall be inoperative unless it shall have been ratified as an amendment to the Constitution by the legislatures of three-fourths of the several states within seven years from the date of its submission to the States by the Congress.

AMENDMENT 23

[Ratified March 29, 1961]

Section 1　The District constituting the seat of Government of the United States shall appoint in such manner as the Congress may direct:

A number of electors of President and Vice President equal to the whole number of Senators and Representatives in Congress to which the District would be entitled if it were a State, but in no event more than the least populous State; they shall be in addition to those appointed by the States, but they shall be considered, for the purposes of the election of President and Vice President, to be electors appointed by a State; and they shall meet in the District and perform such duties as provided by the twelfth article of amendment.

Section 2　The Congress shall have power to enforce this article by appropriate legislation.

AMENDMENT 24

[Ratified January 23, 1964]

Section 1　The right of citizens of the United States to vote in any primary or other election for President or Vice President, for electors for President or Vice President, or for Senator or Representative in Congress, shall not be denied or abridged by the United States or any State by reason of failure to pay any poll tax or other tax.

Section 2　The Congress shall have power to enforce this article by appropriate legislation.

AMENDMENT 25

[Ratified February 10, 1967]

Section 1   In case of the removal of the President from office or his death or resignation, the Vice President shall become President.

Section 2   Whenever there is a vacancy in the office of the Vice President, the President shall nominate a Vice President who shall take the office upon confirmation by a majority vote of both houses of Congress.

Section 3   Whenever the President transmits to the President pro tempore of the Senate and the Speaker of the House of Representatives his written declaration that he is unable to discharge the powers and duties of his office, and until he transmits to them a written declaration to the contrary, such powers and duties shall be discharged by the Vice President as Acting President.

Section 4   Whenever the Vice-President and a majority of either the principal officers of the executive departments, or of such other body as Congress may by law provide, transmit to the President pro tempore of the Senate and the Speaker of the House of Representatives their written declaration that the President is unable to discharge the powers and duties of his office, the Vice President shall immediately assume the powers and duties of the office as Acting President.

Thereafter, when the President transmits to the President pro tempore of the Senate and the Speaker of the House of Representatives his written declaration that no inability exists, he shall resume the powers and duties of his office unless the Vice President and a majority of either the principal officers of the executive departments, or of such other body as Congress may by law provide, transmit within four days to the President pro tempore of the Senate and the Speaker of the House of Representatives their written declaration that the President is unable to discharge the powers and duties of his office. Thereupon Congress shall decide the issue, assembling within forty-eight hours for that purpose if not in session. If the Congress, within twenty-one days after receipt of the latter written declaration, or, if Congress is not in session, within twenty-one days after Congress is required to assemble, determines by two-thirds vote of both houses that the President is unable to discharge the powers and duties of his office, the Vice President shall continue to discharge the same as Acting President; otherwise, the President shall resume the powers and duties of his office.

AMENDMENT 26

[Ratified July 1, 1971]

Section 1   The right of citizens of the United States, who are eighteen years of age, or older, to vote shall not be denied or abridged by the United States or by any State on account of age.

Section 2   The Congress shall have power to enforce this article by appropriate legislation.

AMENDMENT 27

[Ratified May 7, 1992]

No law, varying the compensation for the services of the Senators and Representatives, shall take effect, until an election of Representatives shall be intervened.

INDEX

NAMED ONE OF THE BEST BOOKS OF THE YEAR

GOLF DIGEST • THE FINANCIAL TIMES • THE GUARDIAN

"I have been trying to write about Tiger since he was a teenager. I thought he was unknowable. This book proves me wrong. Here, finally, is Tiger Woods." **—MICHAEL BAMBERGER,** senior writer for *Golf* magazine and author of *Men in Green*

"An ambitious 360-degree portrait of golf's most scrutinized figure . . . The book features fresh reporting on almost every significant element of Woods's story. . . . It is a book brimming with revealing details." **—SAM WEINMAN,** *Golf Digest*

"When you read *Tiger Woods*, you realize these are not just high-level reporting gotchas. This is Tiger's life laid bare." **—BRYAN CURTIS,** *The Ringer*

"A storytelling feat born of unfathomable toil. Benedict and Keteyian culled crumbs from numerous journalists and from a heap of Woods books by Earl Woods (Tiger's father), Hank Haney (former swing coach), Steve Williams (former caddy), Woods himself, and others, and they performed their own excellent reporting for what feels like a book of record. . . . Benedict and Keteyian have turned out a book of surpassing quality against untold odds." **—CHUCK CULPEPPER,** *The Washington Post*

"Meticulously reported, scrupulously fair, endlessly interesting, Jeff Benedict and Armen Keteyian's *Tiger Woods* reveals the human being long-hidden behind the golf genius. The story of Tiger's passage from driven prodigy to lonely hero to disgraced celebrity is compelling, and often poignant, from first page to last." **—JEFFREY TOOBIN,** author of *American Heiress* and *The Nine*

"If *King Lear* had been about golf, or if the great Russian novelists had turned their lens toward modern expectations and fame, toward the most American of fathers and sons, the result would be this book. The rise and fall and return of Tiger Woods in these pages is both mythic and poignantly small and human." **—WRIGHT THOMPSON,** senior writer, *ESPN The Magazine*

Jeff Benedict (*left*) and Armen Keteyian are the *New York Times* bestselling authors of *The System: The Glory and Scandal of Big-Time College Football*. Benedict, a special-features writer for *Sports Illustrated*, is the author of fifteen previous books. He lives in Connecticut. Keteyian, the Anchor and Executive Producer at *The Athletic* and a longtime contributing correspondent to *60 Minutes*, is an eleven-time Emmy Award winner and the author of ten previous books. He lives in Connecticut and California.

TIGER
WOODS

Jeff Benedict and Armen Keteyian

SIMON & SCHUSTER PAPERBACKS

NEW YORK   LONDON   TORONTO   SYDNEY   NEW DELHI

Simon & Schuster Paperbacks
An Imprint of Simon & Schuster, Inc.
1230 Avenue of the Americas
New York, NY 10020

First Simon & Schuster trade paperback edition April 2019

SIMON & SCHUSTER PAPERBACKS and colophon are registered
trademarks of Simon & Schuster, Inc.

For information about special discounts for bulk purchases,
please contact Simon & Schuster Special Sales at 1-866-506-1949
or business@simonandschuster.com.

The Simon & Schuster Speakers Bureau can bring authors to your live event. For
more information or to book an event, contact the Simon & Schuster Speakers
Bureau at 1-866-248-3049 or visit our website at www.simonspeakers.com.

Interior design by Carly Loman

Manufactured in the United States of America

10 9 8 7 6 5 4 3 2 1

Library of Congress Cataloging-in-Publication Data is available.

ISBN 978-1-5011-2642-0
ISBN 978-1-5011-2644-4 (pbk)
ISBN 978-1-5011-2647-5 (ebook)

To Lydia, best of wives, best of women.

To Dede, my amazing wife, who endured, inspired, believed—and, best of all, loved.

CONTENTS

TIGER
WOODS

PROLOGUE

Standing between two gravestones, Mike Mohler drove a posthole digger deep into the dirt, twisting it like a corkscrew. It was Friday, May 5, 2006, and warm temperatures had softened the earth at Sunset Cemetery in Manhattan, Kansas. Clump by clump, the balding forty-four-year-old sexton meticulously dug a grave, piling the dirt beside it. In twenty-four hours, the ashen remains of the city's most famous son would be laid to rest there. Hardly anyone knew the burial was happening, and Mohler aimed to keep it that way.

The night before, Mohler had been home watching television when his phone rang. It was about nine p.m., and the caller didn't identify herself. "We have a burial coming your way," she said.

An odd way to begin a call, thought Mohler. Especially one made to his home at such a late hour.

"What's the name of the deceased?" he asked.

"I can't tell you that," the woman said.

"Well, I can't help you if you won't give me a name," he told her.

"I can't do that unless you sign confidentiality papers," she said.

Mohler told her that wouldn't be necessary. The state had required him to sign documents promising confidentiality when he became a sexton seventeen years earlier.

"I need to know who I'm burying to even know if they have a plot here," he said.

She assured Mohler that the deceased had a burial plot. Then Mohler heard a male voice in the background say: "Just tell him who he's burying."

"I'm calling on behalf of Tiger Woods," the woman told Mohler. "His father has passed."

Lieutenant Colonel Earl Dennison Woods died of a heart attack at his home in Cypress, California, on May 3, 2006. He was seventy-four years old and had been in failing health, his body weakened by cancer and his longtime affection for alcohol and cigarettes. A Green Beret who served two tours in Vietnam, Earl achieved worldwide acclaim for his almost mythical role in raising the most famous golfer of all time. He was notorious for making outlandish statements, like the time he predicted in *Sports Illustrated* that his then twenty-year-old son would have more influence on the world than Nelson Mandela, Gandhi, or Buddha. "He is the Chosen One," Earl told the magazine. "He will have the power to impact nations."

Those were overwhelming expectations. Yet Tiger repeatedly said that no one in the world knew him better than his father, the man he frequently referred to as his "best friend" and "hero." Together they shared one of the most memorable moments in sports history. Immediately after Tiger sank his final putt to win the 1997 Masters by a record twelve strokes, Earl gave him an iconic bear hug. In what was the most-watched golf broadcast in US history, an estimated forty-three million viewers—almost 15 percent of all American households—witnessed father and son sobbing in each other's arms as Earl said, "I love you, son." Dozens of golf telecasts had similarly ended with the two of them embracing and Earl whispering those same four words.

But Mike Mohler didn't watch golf tournaments. He just wasn't a fan of the game. He'd never even picked up a club. Still, he admired Tiger Woods, and he took great pride in digging the elder Woods's grave. Using a cemetery map, Mohler had located Earl's burial lot—block 5, lot 12, grave 02—right between his parents, Miles and Maude Woods. Since taking over as sexton in 1989, Mohler had dug more than two thousand graves. Earl's would be a lot smaller than most: he had been cremated. Tiger and his mother, Kultida, were flying from Southern California with a shallow ten-inch-by-ten-inch square wooden box that contained Earl's ashes. Mohler was ready for them. After nearly an hour of digging, he had fashioned a grave that resembled a miniature elevator shaft. It was twelve inches long by twelve inches wide, and forty-two inches deep. Using a shovel, he scraped away the loose dirt from the sides, making the edges ruler-straight.

The next day, at around noon, two limousines pulled up to an old section of the cemetery. Tiger; his wife, Elin; and Tiger's mother got out of the first car, and Earl's three children from his first marriage exited the second. Mohler and his wife, Kay, met them. Near the end of the twenty-minute ceremony, Kultida handed Mohler the wooden box containing her husband's ashes. He placed it in the hole and added cement. With the family looking on, Mohler carefully packed the hole with dirt, leveled off the top, and covered it with a piece of sod. The family then filed back into the limousines and—after a brief stop at Earl's childhood home—returned to the airport.

Days later, when word got out that Earl Woods had been interred, the local business that produced headstones and gravestones—an outfit called Manhattan Monuments—anticipated an order for a large granite monument. They called Mohler, but he had no information. Neither Tiger nor his mother had left any instructions for a headstone.

At first, Mohler thought the family just needed time to figure out what they wanted. Everyone grieves differently, he knew. But five and then ten years passed, and the family still had not ordered a grave marker.

"There is no gravestone," Mohler said in 2015. "Not for him. His grave isn't marked at all. The only way to tell where Earl Woods is buried is to know where to look for the corner markers buried in the earth. You have to have a map to find them."

In the end, Earl Dennison Woods was buried in the Kansas dirt in an unmarked grave. No stone. No inscription. Nothing.

"It's like he's not even there," said Mohler.

Tiger Woods was the kind of transcendent star that comes around about as often as Halley's Comet. By almost any measure, he is the most talented golfer who ever lived, and arguably the greatest individual athlete in modern history. For a fifteen-year span—from August 1994, when he won his first of three consecutive US Amateur Championships as an eighteen-year-old high school senior, to the early-morning hours of November 27, 2009, when he crashed his SUV into a tree and effectively ended the most dominant run in the history of golf—Woods was a human whirlwind of heart-stopping drama and entertainment, responsible for some of the most memorable moments in the history of televised sports.

Woods will forever be measured against Jack Nicklaus, who won more major championships. But the Tiger Effect can't be measured in statistics. A literary comparison may be more fitting. Given the full spectrum of his awe-inspiring gifts, Woods was nothing less than a modern-day Shakespeare. He was someone no one had ever seen or will ever see again.

Woods's golfing legacy borders on the unimaginable. He was both the first golfer with African American heritage and the youngest golfer in history to win a major championship. He won fourteen majors overall on his way to seventy-nine PGA Tour victories (second all-time behind Sam Snead) and more than one hundred worldwide. He holds the record for most consecutive cuts made (142, covering nearly eight years) and number of weeks ranked no. 1 in the world (683). In addition, he was honored as Player of the Year a record eleven times, captured the annual scoring title a record nine times, and won more than $110 million in official prize money—another record. The tournaments he played in shattered attendance marks throughout the world and consistently set viewership records on television, his charismatic presence and two decades of dominance the driving forces in the stratospheric rise in official PGA Tour purses from $67 million in 1996, his first year as a pro, to a record $363 million in 2017–18, and the rise of the average Tour purse from $1.5 million to $7.4 million during the same period. In the process, he helped make multimillionaires of more than four hundred Tour pros. Pure and simple, Woods changed the face of golf—athletically, socially, culturally, and financially.

At the height of Tiger's career, golf beat the NFL and the NBA in Nielsen ratings. As a spokesman for Nike, American Express, Disney, Gillette, General Motors, Rolex, Accenture, Gatorade, General Mills, and EA Sports, he appeared in television commercials, on billboards, and in magazines and newspapers. He was mobbed by fans wherever he went—France, Thailand, England, Japan, Germany, South Africa, Australia, even Dubai. Kings and presidents courted him. Corporations wooed him. Rock stars and Hollywood actors wanted to be him. Women wanted to sleep with him. For the better part of two decades, he was simply the most famous athlete on earth.

Tiger wasn't just alone atop the world of golf. In a very literal sense, he was alone, period. Despite his killer instinct on the course, he was an introvert off it, more comfortable playing video games, watching television, or practicing and training in solitude. As far back as childhood, he spent far more time by himself in his bedroom than playing outside with other children. An only child, he learned early on that his parents were the only ones he should truly trust and rely on. They more or less programmed him that way. His father took on the roles of golf mentor, sage, visionary, and best friend. His mother, Kultida, was Tiger's disciplinarian and fearsome protector. Together, his parents proved an impregnable force that never let anyone trespass on the tightly guarded path to success they had paved for their son. In their Southern California home, where life revolved around Tiger and golf, the mantra was clear: *Family is everything.*

The Woods family dynamic made Tiger the most mysterious athlete of his time, an enigma obsessed with privacy who mastered the art of being invisible in plain sight, of saying something while revealing virtually nothing. On one hand, he grew up before our eyes, appearing on television shows as early as age two and being photographed and chronicled throughout his childhood. On the other hand, so much of his true family history and personal life remains shrouded in conditional interviews, carefully constructed press releases, mythical tales, half-truths, sophisticated advertising campaigns, and tabloid headlines.

So we were not surprised when Woods, through his chief spokesman, Glenn Greenspan, declined to be interviewed for this book. (Or, to be more precise, we were told that before any interview would be "considered" we needed to disclose whom we spoke to, what they said, and the specific questions we would be asking, conditions that we were not willing to meet.) Woods's mother, Kultida, in turn, did not respond to our request for an interview. Woods did, however, authorize his longtime chiropractor to provide a comprehensive statement about his treatment of Woods and the issue of performance-enhancing drugs.

In an effort to be comprehensive, we began by reading every book of significance about Woods—more than twenty in all—authored by him, his father, former coaches, a former caddie, Earl's first wife (Barbara Woods Gary), and more. Included on that list were the often outstanding efforts of journalists such as Tom Callahan, John Feinstein, Steve Helling, Robert Lusetich, Tim Rosaforte, Howard Sounes, and John Strege. We would be remiss if we failed to single out two invaluable sources of information: *The 1997 Masters: My Story* by Tiger Woods with Lorne Rubenstein, published in 2017 on the twentieth anniversary of Woods's historic win at Augusta, and *The Big Miss: My Years Coaching Tiger Woods* by Hank Haney. We mined virtually every page of both books for insight, facts, and reflections that kept our narrative true and on track. In addition, we read books on Buddhism, Navy SEALs, gifted children, success, the business of golf, sex addiction, compulsive behavior, infidelity, and performance-enhancing drugs. Simultaneously, we spent months constructing a comprehensive 120-page time line of Woods's life, detailing every significant moment or event dating back to the birth of his parents. We also reviewed the transcripts of more than 320 official press conferences at which Tiger spoke between 1996 and 2017, as well as dozens of transcripts of interviews he granted on a wide range of topics with news organizations and television programs. With the help of a researcher at *Sports Illustrated*, we compiled and read thousands of newspaper, magazine, and journal articles about Tiger. And with assistance from CBS, NBC, Golf Channel, and the PGA Tour, we looked at more than a hundred hours of footage of Tiger on and off the course.

Over a three-year period, we also conducted more than four hundred interviews with over 250 people from every walk of Woods's life, from teaching professionals and swing coaches who once occupied a place in his inner circle to close friends on and off the Tour, to his first true love. But some of our greatest insights came from the scores of people in Tiger's past who have never been interviewed previously—those who helped finance his amateur career, the owner of the Augusta home where Tiger stayed during the Masters year after year, a close female confidant, former employees, business partners, his scuba-diving instructor, his neighbors in Isleworth, and those who worked with him behind the scenes at IMG, Nike, Titleist, EA Sports, NBC Sports, and CBS Sports.

Early on we discovered that two of the qualities Woods values most are privacy and loyalty. As to the former, many of the individuals we approached—from Tiger's former agent J. Hughes Norton III to past employees of Tiger's ETW Corp.—had signed nondisclosure agreements that prohibited them from speaking to us. "I was, as most others in his circle were, sworn to contracts and other legal documents," one former employee told us in an email. It's not unusual for public figures to require those around them—especially those with access to family members and personal information—to sign confidentiality agreements. But Tiger took extraordinary steps to protect even the most mundane information about his past. For example, he personally requested that his high school yearbooks not be shared with anyone. Remarkably, the public school district granted his wish, telling us we were not allowed to look at them. (We ended up viewing his yearbooks at the local library instead.) As for loyalty, individual after individual told us they would "have to check with Tiger" before agreeing to speak. One former high school classmate of his whom we approached in hopes of simply learning about Anaheim's Western High School said he would first need permission from Tiger. We told him not to bother.

All of this begs the question: Why tackle this project in the first place? Our answer is simple: Very few individuals are known throughout the world by one word. Tiger reached that exclusive club by being the greatest golfer—some would argue the greatest athlete—in modern history. But his story transcends golf, and his influence reached around the globe. Yet there has never been a comprehensive biography that offers a 360-degree look at Tiger's entire life to date, one that closely examines his roots and the vital role his parents played in his epic rise, fall, and return. After writing *The System*, a deep dive into the complex world of big-time college football, we were searching for another mountain to climb. We could think of none more imposing or exhilarating than Mount Woods. Our objective from the beginning was to deliver something fresh and revealing, and in the process construct a complete human portrait of a true, albeit reluctant, American idol.

This book is that portrait.

CHAPTER ONE

THE END

Barefoot and groggy, the most powerful athlete on the planet hid behind a locked bathroom door. For years, like an escape artist, he had been able to cover the tracks of his secret life. Not this time. His wife was finally on to him. But there was so much more she didn't know—so much more that no one knew. It was around two a.m. on Friday, November 27, 2009, the day after Thanksgiving. His mind likely clouded by prescription drugs, the man so obsessed with privacy couldn't have foreseen that his next move would shatter his picture-perfect image and lead to the steepest fall from grace in the history of modern sport. Tiger Woods opened the door and fled.

Two days earlier, the *National Enquirer*, hot on his trail for months, had published a bombshell story—"Tiger Woods Cheating Scandal"—with pictures of a stunning thirty-four-year-old New York nightclub hostess by the name of Rachel Uchitel. The supermarket tabloid accused Tiger of orchestrating a racy rendezvous with Uchitel a week earlier in Melbourne during the Australian Masters. Insisting it was just another lie, Woods had taken the extraordinary step of putting Uchitel on the phone with his wife, but after thirty excruciating minutes, Elin still wasn't buying her husband's story. She might have been blond and beautiful, but she wasn't stupid. And after Tiger returned to the house Thanksgiving evening after playing cards with some of the boys down at the club in their gated Isleworth community outside Orlando, Elin waited until he had taken an Ambien and drifted off to sleep. It was well after midnight when she took Tiger's phone and started scrolling. A single text from Tiger to a mysterious recipient cut her heart in two: "You are the only one I've ever loved."

Elin stared at those words, then used Tiger's phone to send a text of her own to the unknown person. "I miss you," Elin typed. "When are we seeing each other again?"

Within seconds a return text appeared, expressing surprise that Tiger was still awake.

Elin dialed the number. A woman answered in the same smoky voice that she had heard professing innocence the day before. Uchitel!

"I knew it," Elin shouted. "I knew it!"

"Oh, fuck," Uchitel said.

Moments later, Elin's shouting roused Woods from his slumber. Stumbling half-dazed out of bed, he took his phone and retreated to the bathroom. "She knows," he texted Uchitel.

But in truth, Woods didn't fear the woman standing on the other side of the bathroom door. He'd been cheating on her for years with dozens of women, feeding an insatiable appetite for sex that had spiraled into an out-of-control addiction. No—the only woman he had ever truly feared was the one sleeping in a guest room in another part of the mansion: his mother, who was visiting for the holiday. Now a widow for more than three years, Kultida Woods had endured what was at times a humiliating marriage that included verbal abuse, neglect, and adultery. Tiger worshiped his father, but he hated how he'd broken his mother's heart. For Tiger's sake, Kultida never divorced Earl, choosing instead to preserve the family name and dedicate her life to raising her only child to be a champion. Reputation and Tiger: nothing mattered more than those two things to Kultida.

When Tiger was young, his mother had laid down the law: "You will never, ever ruin my reputation as a parent," she told him, "because I will beat you."

When he was a boy, the fear of her hand had helped keep Tiger in line. Now that he was a man, there was nothing more terrifying than the prospect of his mother learning that he had followed in his father's footsteps. Looking her in the eye would be brutal.

Wearing nothing but shorts and a T-shirt, Woods emerged from the house into the forty-degree air. Elin reportedly gave chase with a golf club in hand. In an attempt to get away, Tiger hustled into his Cadillac Escalade and sped out of the driveway, immediately crossing over a concrete curb and onto a grass median. Swerving hard to his left, he crossed Deacon Circle, jumped a curb, grazed a row of hedges, swerved back across the road, and collided with a fire hydrant before plowing into a tree in his next-door neighbor's yard. Swinging the club, Elin shattered the rear driver's side and rear passenger's side windows.

Kimberly Harris woke to the knocking sound of a sputtering engine. Looking out the window, she saw a black SUV at the bottom of her driveway. The front end was crumpled against a tree, and the lone remaining headlight was shining at the house. Worried, she woke her twenty-seven-year-old brother, Jarius Adams. "I don't know who's outside," she told him, "but I think you need to go out there and find out what's happening."

Adams walked cautiously out the front door, trying to process what he was seeing. Woods was lying flat on his back on the pavement. He was shoeless, unconscious, and bleeding from the mouth. There was broken glass on the driveway and a bent golf club beside the vehicle. Sniffling, Elin hovered over her husband.

"Tiger," she whispered, gently shaking his shoulders. "Tiger, are you okay?"

Crouching down, Adams observed that Tiger was asleep, snoring. His lip was cut. His teeth were bloodstained.

"Please help me," Elin said. "I don't have a phone with me. Will you call someone?"

Adams ran back inside and yelled to his sister to get blankets and pillows. "Tiger is down," he told her.

Then he ran back outside and called 911.

Dispatcher: 911, what's your emergency?

Adams: I need an ambulance immediately. I have someone down in front of my house.

Dispatcher: Sir, is it a car accident?

Adams: Yes.

Dispatcher: Now, are they trapped inside of the vehicle?

Adams: No, they're lying on the ground now.

Dispatcher: Medical is on the line sir, okay?

Adams: I have a neighbor. He hit the tree. And we came out here just to see what was going on. I see him and he's laying down.

Dispatcher: Are you able to tell if he's breathing?
Adams: No, I can't tell right now.

Suddenly, Kultida Woods emerged from Tiger's house and ran toward the scene. "What happened?" she yelled.

"We're trying to figure that out," Adams told her. "I'm on the phone with the police right now."

Tears in her eyes, Kultida turned to Elin. Soon they heard a siren and saw blue lights approaching. A Windermere Police Department cruiser pulled up, followed by an ambulance, a sheriff, and a Florida Highway Patrolman. Paramedics checked Tiger's vital signs and started testing for paralysis, attempting to generate movement by stimulating his left foot. Groaning, Tiger opened his eyes, only for his pupils to roll back in his head while his eyelids remained open. All that was visible were the whites of his eyes.

As the paramedics hoisted Tiger's gurney into the ambulance and sped off, Kultida's question lingered in the air: *What happened?* Why had Tiger Woods fled his home in the middle of the night? And how did the most celebrated athlete of our time end up looking lifeless on the side of the road? Within days, the world would be asking far more troubling questions. The answers, much like the man, proved to be complicated. And when retracing a twisted journey, the best place to start is the beginning.

CHAPTER TWO

FAMILY MATTERS

On September 14, 1981, five-year-old Tiger Woods entered a kinder-garten classroom at Cerritos Elementary School that had been carefully decorated to help put children at ease. It was the first day of school. Pic-tures of animals and nature were tacked to a couple of bulletin boards. Hand-colored drawings—one of fluffy white clouds against a blue sky, and another of a bright yellow sun with beams radiating from it—were taped to a side wall. Numbers and the letters of the alphabet ran along the top of the chalkboard. But none of it diminished the fact that Tiger felt different from all the other kids. Vastly different. Instead of toys, his prized possession was a custom-made set of golf clubs. Besides his par-ents, his closest friend was his golf instructor, a thirty-two-year-old man with a mustache named Rudy. Tiger had already appeared on national television a couple of times, performed in front of millions of people, and rubbed shoulders with Bob Hope, Jimmy Stewart, and Fran Tarkenton. His golf swing was so smooth that Tiger looked like a pro in a miniature body. He had even signed autographs, printing "TIGER" in block letters to compensate for the fact that he had yet to learn cursive. He was a whiz with numbers too. When he was two years old, his mother taught him how to add and subtract. He was three when his mother created a mul-tiplication table for him. He worked on it every day, over and over. The more she drilled him, the more he developed a love of numbers. In math he was performing at a third-grade level. Yet no one in his kindergarten class knew any of this. Not even his teacher.

Tiger quietly found a chair among nearly thirty other kindergartners. Only three things were discernible about him: His skin was a little darker than everyone else's. He was painfully shy. And he had a very peculiar first name—Eldrick. But when kindergarten teacher Maureen Decker played a song written to help the children introduce themselves that first day, he referred to himself as Tiger. Throughout the remainder of the class, he resisted Decker's gentle attempts to get him to talk. It wasn't until class was over that he gingerly approached his teacher and tugged at her.

"Don't call me Eldrick," he stammered. "Call me Tiger."

Kultida Woods gave the same instructions—address her son by his nickname, not his given name.

Tiger lived one-tenth of a mile from the school. Each morning his mother dropped him off, and each afternoon she picked him up. Then she would drive him to a nearby golf course, where he practiced. It didn't take long for Decker to recognize that Tiger had an unusually structured routine that left little to no time for interacting with other children outside of school. Academically, he was way ahead of the other kids in his class, especially when it came to anything related to numbers. He was also unusually disciplined for a five-year-old. But he seldom spoke, and he looked lost on the playground, as if he were gun-shy when it came to playing with others.

As an adult, Tiger reflected back on his childhood and the fact that he focused solely on golf. In a 2004 "Authorized DVD Collection," Tiger said that he liked to run and play baseball and basketball as a kid, but he didn't love it. "Golf was my decision," he said. But his elementary school teachers have a different recollection. At the first parent-teacher conference, Decker diplomatically raised her concerns and suggested involving Tiger in some after-school activities. Earl instantly dismissed the idea, making it clear that Tiger played golf after school. When Decker tried explaining the benefits of letting Tiger make friends with kids his own age, Earl cut her off. He knew what was best for his son. Kultida remained quiet, and the conference ended awkwardly.

Decker decided she wouldn't bring it up again. But one day, Tiger approached her during recess. "Ask my mom if I can go play soccer," he said softly. Decker talked to Kultida privately. The two of them had developed a friendly rapport, and Kultida agreed with Decker that it would be good for Tiger to play soccer with the other children. She pleaded with Tiger's teacher to continue encouraging Earl to allow Tiger to participate in after-school activities. So at the next parent-teacher conference, Decker raised the subject again. This time Earl got animated. While he pontificated about knowing what was best for his son, Kultida again kept silent. The bottom line: No soccer. It was golf and nothing else.

"I felt sorry for the child, because he wanted to interact with others," Decker said.

At a time when very few fathers attended parent-teacher conferences at Cerritos Elementary, Earl Woods was known for always showing up. Sometimes he even arrived without Kultida. School administrators got used to seeing more of him than they did of any other father. He even came for show-and-tell. Ann Burger, Tiger's first-grade teacher, said she would never forget that day, because it was the most unusual show-and-tell in her thirty-year teaching career. Earl walked in with a bag of miniature golf clubs, and Burger ended up taking her entire class outside, where Tiger put on a show, blasting golf balls all over the playground.

"He was good," Burger recalled. "He had special clubs. They were little clubs. But they were *his* clubs."

Tiger was the show and Earl did the telling, explaining to the children how his son had become so accomplished through hard work and practice. The six-year-olds were in awe, but the performance was just one of a series of observations that raised questions in the minds of some of Tiger's teachers. *What is this child going through? What goes on in his home? What is the family dynamic?*

Part of Tiger Woods's family tree is rooted in Manhattan, Kansas, a hardscrabble, windblown city that was segregated when Earl Woods was born there on March 5, 1932. His father, Miles Woods, a fifty-eight-year-old stonemason whose health was already in decline at the time of Earl's birth, was affectionately described by his children as an "old, fussy, cussy man." A faithful Baptist who avoided alcohol and cigarettes, Miles nonetheless had a legendary habit of using foul language. "My father taught me discipline and how to swear," Earl would later say. "He could swear for thirty minutes and never repeat himself."

Earl's mother, Maude, a mixed-race woman of African, European, Chinese, and Native American ancestry, had earned a college degree in home economics from Kansas State University. She taught Earl to read and write in a cramped, 1,300-square-foot home. The family had no car and no television, and Earl spent a lot of time outdoors with his father. Together, they built a stone wall between the family home and the street. "He showed me how to mix the mortar," Earl said. "He had his own way. He'd say, 'You've got to have the right amount of spit in it.' He'd spit in the bucket and say, 'Yeah, that's about right.'"

Earl also spent a lot of time with his father at Griffith Park, a new minor league baseball stadium in town, where Miles was a scorekeeper. Miles could recite the names, batting averages, and pitching statistics of every future major leaguer who came through Manhattan. He scored his final game in August 1943; hours after the final pitch, Miles died from a stroke at age seventy. Earl was eleven at the time and recalled watching his grieving mother sit in a rocking chair, repeatedly humming the words from the gospel hymn "What Are They Doing in Heaven?" Four years later, Maude also suffered a stroke and died. Earl, just a few months shy of turning sixteen, was suddenly an orphan who ended up in the care of an older sister, who ran the house like "a little dictator."

Earl's father had one obsession when he died: he wanted Earl to become a professional baseball player. Nothing would have made him prouder. Knowing this, Earl set his heart on joining the big leagues. It was a dream that got a boost in 1947 when Jackie Robinson broke the color barrier and joined the Brooklyn Dodgers. That summer, Earl was working as a batboy at Griffith Park, and many of the best players in the Negro Leagues were barnstorming across the Midwest. Earl met Roy Campanella, Josh Gibson, and Monte Irvin. He also said that one afternoon during batting practice he caught for legendary pitcher Satchel Paige, whose fastball was believed to hit one hundred miles an hour.

After graduating from high school in 1949, Earl enrolled at Kansas State and joined the baseball team as a catcher. He would also pitch and play first base. By his junior year, he was one of the best players on a very bad team. As an adult, Earl published a best-selling memoir in which he claimed to have earned a baseball scholarship and broken the color line as the first black athlete in the Big 7 (later the Big 8, and now the Big 12) Conference. Both statements were exaggerated.

"He didn't get a scholarship from me," former Kansas State baseball coach Ray Wauthier told journalist Howard Sounes in 2003. "I think he put that in the story to make it sound a little better."

Nor was Earl the first black athlete to play in the Big 7; Harold Robinson and Veryl Switzer, who later played for the Green Bay Packers, preceded him. But Woods was the first black player to make the American Legion all-state team in Kansas, which prompted Wauthier to offer him a spot on the K-State roster, earning Earl the distinction of breaking the Big 7 color line in baseball.

Woods's baseball career would never advance beyond college, but his views on race were strongly influenced by his experience as the only black player on the roster. Once, while the team was on a spring-training trip to Mississippi, an opposing coach saw Woods warming up and told Coach Wauthier that his catcher would have to remain on the bus and not play. Wauthier responded by telling all his players to get back on the bus. The team left without participating. On another occasion, in Oklahoma, a motel manager informed Wauthier that his lone black player would not be allowed to stay, suggesting instead that Woods spend the night at a different motel three miles away. Wauthier canceled the reservation for his entire team.

These experiences were hardly Earl's first encounters with racism. Back at Manhattan High School, he had had his eye on an attractive white girl. He had always wanted to dance with her, but he didn't dare ask. In Kansas in the late forties, a relationship with a white girl was out of the question. Instead, he kept to himself, storing in his mind an inventory of taunts, snubs, and personal roadblocks that came his way because of the color of his skin.

During his junior year of college, Earl joined the ROTC. The first time he put on a military uniform, he felt an unfamiliar sense of pride and self-worth—unfamiliar because he'd never quite gotten over the fact that he wasn't talented enough to make it as a pro ballplayer the way his father had wanted.

One year after graduating from K-State with a degree in sociology, Earl enlisted in the army and got engaged to Barbara Ann Hart, a local girl he'd known since they were kids. She had moved to San Francisco to attend college, but at Earl's urging she dropped out in her second year and moved back to Kansas. On March 18, 1954, they were married at the courthouse in Abilene during a thunderstorm. She was twenty, and he was twenty-two.

The storm was an omen of things to come.

———

Barbara Hart believed that Earl Woods was a man who was going places. He owned a 1936 Chevy he called Jitney. He listened to jazz. He had a college degree. And his first serious military assignment was in Germany, where he quickly advanced to platoon leader. Their first child—Earl Woods Jr.—was born at an army hospital near the small village of Zweibrücken. It all seemed so romantic.

Over the next few years, Earl and Barbara had two more children—Kevin Woods, born June 1, 1957, in Abilene, Kansas, and Royce Woods, born June 6, 1958, in New York. By the time Royce came along, Earl was stationed at army headquarters in Fort Hamilton, Brooklyn, and the family was living nearby.

That's when Earl started to disappear. With three children under the age of four, he enrolled in a master's degree program at New York University. His days were spent on the base, and his nights were spent at school. When he wasn't working or studying, he stayed out with his army buddies, all of whom called him by his nickname, Woody. His marriage had already begun to disintegrate when he received orders to go to Vietnam in 1962. Barbara packed up the children—ages seven, five, and four at that point—and moved to San Jose, California, settling into a tiny three-bedroom home.

With Earl in Vietnam, Barbara's resentment toward him festered. She felt abandoned. And when Earl returned from a year overseas, he felt like a stranger in his own home. He described arriving at the house in California late at night and finding the door locked. He knocked loudly enough to wake Barbara.

"Who's there?" she said from behind the door.

"It's me," he said.

Long pause. "Who is 'me'?" she said.

"Open the damn door!" he yelled.

Moments later, their little girl stumbled out of bed and entered the room. "Mommy," she said, "who is that man?"

Earl later acknowledged that his children suffered from his long absences. In his memoir, he wrote, "I admit that I am to blame for that."

Yet his military career was advancing at an impressive rate. Upon returning from his first of two tours in Vietnam, he was assigned to the army's John F. Kennedy Special Warfare Center and School, and then to the 6th Special Forces Group at Fort Bragg in North Carolina. He went from there to Ranger School to Airborne School. At thirty-two, against all odds, he became a Green Beret and went off to the Alaska wilderness for advanced survival-training exercises. Then one day in the summer of 1966, he went home and informed Barbara that he had received orders to go to Thailand. She instantly became excited about the prospect of taking the family overseas, but Earl informed her that his orders were for an *unaccompanied tour*, meaning his wife and children had to stay behind.

In the spring of 1967, Lt. Col. Earl Woods showed up at a US Army office in Bangkok, where he planned to conduct job interviews with civilians who were applying for jobs on a local army project that he was overseeing. With an assistant at his side, Woods approached the reception desk. A young Thai woman looked up and said in English: "May I help you, sir?"

She addressed the question to Woods's assistant, a white man who she assumed was in charge. Woods didn't bother correcting her as she escorted him and his assistant to a private office that was separated from the reception area by a large glass window. Earl took a seat, put his feet up on the desk, and started issuing orders. Through the glass, he noticed that the secretary had returned to her desk and was looking at him.

"I was drawn to her immediately," he later wrote. "She was a stunningly attractive woman."

Woods turned to his assistant and said, "I'm going to go and talk to this fine little thing."

In his memoir, Woods described what happened next:

> I was so drawn to the striking woman with the expressive eyes. I approached her and, boy, did she blush. She had figured out by then that I was the colonel, not the assistant.
>
> As she started to apologize, I said, "No, no. Don't worry about that." That seemed to make it easier for us to talk on a more personal level. We chatted, made small talk, and she laughed easily. Her face was aglow and her eyes sparkled. I immediately felt a bond with her.
>
> Walking away, I was smiling like hell. I had me a date.

Kultida Punsawad was born in 1944 outside Bangkok, the youngest of four children in a well-to-do family. Her father was an architect, her mother a teacher. Kultida, known as Tida (pronounced TEE-da), was five when her parents divorced. If that wasn't jarring enough, she was placed in a boarding school until she was ten. "After they divorced, it was hard for me," she said in 2013. "When I was put in the boarding school, for five years I almost never went back to any of my family, just stayed at the school. Every weekend I'd hope my father or mother would visit me, or my older brothers or sisters, but no one ever came. I felt abandoned."

As an adult, Tida confided to a friend that her childhood was "traumatic" and "lonely." Well educated and conversant in English, she took a job in her early twenties as a civilian secretary and receptionist at a US Army office in Bangkok. When Lt. Col. Earl Woods showed up there in 1967, she had no idea that he was married with children. She simply liked the fact that he paid attention to her. Their entire first date, which took place on a religious holiday, was spent in church. It was a humble beginning to a relationship that would ultimately result in her giving birth to one of the greatest athletes in history. But at that moment in Bangkok, the prospects that anything would develop from her encounter with a US serviceman likely seemed remote. They lived eight thousand miles apart. She was twelve years younger than he was and had never left her homeland. He was an experienced world traveler with a family of his own. Plus, they were so different. She was a practicing Buddhist; he was a lapsed Baptist. Nevertheless, talk of Kultida's joining Earl in America happened fast, but not without a warning about racism.

"I know you are from Thailand," Earl told her. "I know you are Thai. But in the United States, there are only two colors—white and non-white. Whites will let you know without a doubt you are non-white; you'll see it in their actions and reactions to you. So don't think you can ever be a full-fledged citizen here in the United States."

When his tour in Thailand ended, Woods was assigned to Fort Totten, near Bayside, Queens, New York. Barbara and the children joined him there. He soon took a part-time position at City College of New York as an assistant professor of military science, teaching ROTC students psychological warfare studies. Barbara felt as though he were using his psychological warfare training on her. She recounted the following exchange as an example of his verbal and emotional manipulation:

> **Barbara:** *I don't understand. What did I do wrong?*
> **Earl:** *You don't know?*
> **Barbara:** *I don't know what you're talking about.*
> **Earl:** *Girl, you're losing it. You need help.*

After enough of these kinds of exchanges, Barbara started to question whether she was, in fact, losing it. Once a confident, self-assured woman, she telephoned her sister in tears, telling her, "I know I'm not crazy." But Earl's mind games were having an effect. "Maybe Earl is right," she told her sister. "Maybe I do need help."

A short time later, on May 29, 1968, Earl came home with his friend Lawrence Kruteck, an up-and-coming New York attorney. Barbara was in the bedroom watching television when Earl asked her to join them in the living room. Barbara noticed that Kruteck was carrying a briefcase.

"This is undoubtedly the hardest thing I've ever had to do," Kruteck told her.

He opened his briefcase, pulled out a legal document, and started reading the first paragraph: "Whereas, the parties hereto are now Husband and Wife, having been married on the eighteenth day of March 1954 at Abilene, Kansas—"

"Wait a minute," she interrupted. "What is this?"

"Woody wants a legal separation," Kruteck said.

Blindsided, she turned to Earl, who was sitting in the corner of the room.

"Yes," Earl said, not uttering another word.

Kruteck handed Barbara the document and encouraged her to read it.

She could hardly focus, but she read, "Whereas, by reason of certain unfortunate differences that have arisen between the parties hereto as the result of which they are desirous of living separate and apart . . ." She couldn't get past *separate and apart*. What did that even mean? What was happening?

The agreement stipulated that Earl and Barbara Woods would live apart for the rest of their lives "as if sole and unmarried." Barbara would have custody of the children, and Earl would have the right to visit them. He would also pay her $200 per month "for her support and for the support and maintenance of the said children."

Reeling, Barbara signed the document without consulting a lawyer.

That summer, Earl and Barbara drove with the children from New York to their little home in San Jose. They turned the road trip into a rare family vacation, stopping at landmarks such as the Liberty Bell and the Lincoln Memorial along the way. They spent a night in Las Vegas. Earl and Barbara even made love. It felt like a second honeymoon, prompting Barbara to wonder out loud, "Why do we have to separate?"

"Because we have to," Earl told her.

As soon as the family was settled in California, Earl flew back to New York. He was gone for months. The next time he visited San Jose, Barbara's uncle picked him up at the airport and was surprised to see Earl exit the plane with an Asian woman. Earl told Barbara's uncle that he had just met her on the flight and that he was going to help her find a job back in New York.

At this point it had been approximately a year and a half since Earl had first dated Kultida. After her arrival in the United States in 1968 at age twenty-five, she eventually landed a job at a bank in Brooklyn, and, according to Earl, they were married in New York in 1969.

But Barbara Woods knew nothing about her. And Barbara's uncle didn't have the heart to tell her that another woman had entered the picture.

In the spring of 1969, Barbara's health took a bad turn. She suffered severe hemorrhaging, and doctors discovered fibroid tumors. Scheduled to undergo a hysterectomy, Barbara pleaded with Earl to come to San Jose. He came, but on his way he made a detour to Mexico, and he didn't reach California until four days after the surgery. That night, while Barbara was recuperating in bed at home, Earl informed her that he had obtained a divorce in Juárez, alleging "the incompatibility of temperaments between the spouses." Barbara was speechless. She would later write in her memoir that she and Earl woke the children, told them that their parents were no longer married, and then tried unsuccessfully to get them to stop crying. Earl then walked out on Barbara for good.

It turned out that Earl had not actually secured the divorce he sought. On August 25, 1969, two days after Earl returned from Mexico, the US Consulate declined to validate the paperwork, stating, "The Consulate assumes no responsibility for the contents of the annexed document, nor the validity of the document or for its acceptability in any state in the United States."

At this point, Barbara was unaware of the Consulate's opinion and of anything that had transpired between her husband and Kultida. All Barbara knew was that she had had enough. On August 25, 1969—the same day the US Consulate had declared Earl's Juárez divorce invalid—she began divorce proceedings in San Jose, citing "extreme cruelty" and "grievous mental suffering." More than two years later, on February 28, 1972, the Superior Court of California determined that "the parties are still married and . . . neither party may remarry, until a final judgment of dissolution is entered." The court later issued that judgment, officially recognizing the divorce of Earl and Barbara Woods, on March 2, 1972. But by that time, Earl and Kultida had been married for almost three years, and Barbara had a better handle on what had been going on behind her back.

"I question the LEGALITY of that marriage," Barbara Woods said in a subsequent court filing. "This man was a BIGAMIST according to California laws. All this was a COLD, CALCULATED plan. There has been FRAUD perpetrated from the very beginning."

In response to those charges, Earl filed a sworn declaration. In it, he stated: "We obtained a divorce in Mexico sometime in 1967. I remarried in 1969." This was not true. A certified copy of the judgment of divorce in Mexico shows that Earl Woods sought a divorce there on August 23, 1969, two years after he claimed he had done so. Plus, the State of California subsequently ruled that he had remained legally married to Barbara Woods until 1972. But Earl wasn't concerned. "I don't know anything about California. I didn't live in California," he said years later. "I do not consider myself a bigamist."

Earl Woods had little interest in having a child with Kultida. After being an absentee father throughout much of his military career and then walking out on their mother, he had finally started to reconnect with his kids. After retiring from the military at age forty-two, Earl took a job procuring parts for defense contractor McDonnell Douglas in Long Beach, California. Under the terms of his divorce from his ex-wife, the children had the option of moving in with him after graduating from high school, and both of his sons did so. A newborn didn't really fit into Earl's plans.

In most instances, Kultida honored Earl's wishes, dutifully cooking for him, cutting his hair, doing his laundry, and keeping the house. She had been raised in a patriarchal society, where 95 percent of the population was Buddhist, and women were considered inferior to men. A common expression in Thailand was that the husband was the front legs of the elephant while the wife was the hind legs, driving and supporting the choices made by the head of the family. At the same time, childbirth and child rearing were very important elements of Thai culture. Kultida eventually made Earl understand this.

"I would have been happy to be childless," Earl said. "However, in Thai culture it's perceived that a marriage is not really a marriage until they have a child."

After being married for approximately six years, Kultida, at age thirty-one, got pregnant in the spring of 1975. The newness of the relationship had worn off by then, and Earl had found a new love: golf. When an army buddy introduced him to the game, he was instantly hooked. If golf were a drug, he would have qualified as an addict. He liked it so much that it consumed him, leading him to spend far more time with his clubs than with his wife. "I realized what I'd been missing my whole life," Earl said. "I decided if I had another son, I'd introduce him to golf early on."

CHAPTER THREE

A STAR IS BORN

At 10:50 p.m. on December 30, 1975, Kultida Woods gave birth to a baby boy at Long Beach Memorial Hospital. Shortly after the delivery, doctors informed her that she would be unable to have more children, cementing her newborn as an only child.

It was clear from the outset that everything about him would be overly complicated, starting with his name: Eldrick Tont Woods. Dreamed up exclusively for their son, the name symbolized the nature of his relationship with his parents. The *E* in *Eldrick* stood for Earl; the *K* for Kultida. From the moment he entered the world, Eldrick was figuratively and literally surrounded by his parents, an attention-grabbing father on one end and an authentic Tiger Mom on the other.

Being a mother meant more to Kultida than anything. As a child she'd been neglected by her parents, left to fend for herself. She was determined to be the mother she had always wanted. That meant she would never rely on child care or work outside the home, no matter how stressed the family finances became. She would personally teach her son to read and write and multiply and divide. For her it was simple: She was dedicating her life to her only child. Her boy would know he was loved.

But Earl had no intention of calling his son Eldrick. He immediately nicknamed him "Tiger," in tribute to a comrade from Vietnam. Vuong Dang Phong was a lieutenant colonel in the South Vietnamese Army whom Earl often credited with saving his life on two occasions—once by commanding him to "freeze" to avoid a deadly strike from a poisonous viper, and another time by pushing him into a ditch in the midst of sniper fire. Even before that second incident, Earl had given Phong the nickname Tiger for his ferocious approach to combat. During Kultida's pregnancy,

Saigon fell, and the Vietnam War ended. In the aftermath, Earl lost track of his friend and feared he'd been captured and interned in a North Vietnamese camp. So, to honor him, Earl gave Phong's nickname to his baby boy.

The question of race was even more complex. Through his mother's side, Tiger was one-quarter Thai and one-quarter Chinese. Through his father's side, his genes were a mix of Native American, African American, and white. His predominant heritage was clearly Asian. But Earl had every intention of raising his boy as an African American. "The boy only has about two drops of black blood in him," Earl Woods said in 1993. "But like I told him, 'In this country there are only two colors: white and nonwhite.' And he ain't white."

Earl and Kultida brought Tiger home to a 1,474-square-foot ranch house at 6704 Teakwood Street in Cypress, a city, in 1975, of just over thirty thousand residents that bordered on Long Beach and Anaheim. Their Orange County community had long been the site of rich rural farmland known for its strawberry fields and dairy pastures. But by the seventies, Orange County had become Richard Nixon country—overwhelmingly white and deeply conservative. As best as can be determined, the Woodses were the only interracial couple in the neighborhood. Claiming they were victims of racial intolerance, they did not interact with their neighbors.

Six months after Tiger was born, Earl's daughter, Royce, graduated from high school in San Jose and moved in with them. It's unclear how Kultida felt about having Earl's children from his first marriage come and go, but Royce ended up being a big support for her stepmother. She helped keep the house and stepped in to care for Tiger when Kultida needed rest. Before Tiger learned to talk, he started calling his half-sister La La. She adored him so much that she adopted La La as her nickname.

Earl made himself scarce. He had a nine-to-five job and spent much of his free time working on his golf game. When he was home, he retreated to the garage, where he'd rigged up a net that enabled him to practice his swing at home. He put a square of carpet on the floor and hit balls from it into the net. The garage was his man cave, where he could smoke, sip a cold one, and refine his stroke. Best of all, it was a place of refuge. When Tiger was about six months old, Earl started bringing him to the garage and strapping him into a high chair. While using a 5-iron to hit ball after ball after ball after ball, Earl would talk to Tiger. Kultida sometimes would sit beside the high chair with a spoon in one hand and baby food in the other. The way she tells it, every time Earl hit the ball, Tiger would open his mouth, and she would insert the spoon. She would repeat this routine until he finished his meal. It became a nightly ritual—Earl swinging and talking, Tiger watching and listening, Kultida feeding her baby.

Neuroscientists have long studied the effects of repetition on a child's brain, especially during the first three years. The types of repetitious experience, as well as the quality of relationships, in those first few years have a powerful and lasting influence on the brain's development. For example, though television exposure levels may be high during infancy, studies have demonstrated that infants mimic far fewer actions from television than from a live demonstration. In Tiger's case, he was exposed to an extreme level of live demonstration. Based on Earl's later accounts, a conservative estimate suggests that by the time Tiger turned one, he had spent between one hundred and two hundred hours watching his father hit golf balls.

Although Tiger doesn't remember this chapter of his life, Earl provided a detailed account of what happened one day when Tiger was about eleven months old. After watching his father practice, Tiger slid down from his high chair and picked up a club that Earl had cut down to size for him to make a toy. Then he waddled to the carpet patch, stood over a golf ball, and swung. The ball landed in the net, and Earl shouted to his wife, "Honey, get out here! We have a genius on our hands."

The notion of an eleven-month-old possessing the coordination to execute a successful golf swing sounds like an embellished narrative from a bragging parent. Perhaps. After all, most children are barely able to take their first steps at nine months, and it's not uncommon for them to be at least a year old before being able to walk without toppling over. But it would be a mistake to underestimate the effect of the inordinate amount of exposure Tiger Woods had to his father's swing. At a time when Tiger was most impressionable, Earl spent an extraordinary amount of time modeling a golf swing for him.

Furthermore, neuroscientists and pediatricians agree that during the first year of life, trust develops. As one expert put it, the more love and responsiveness a caregiver extends, the more the child bonds to the caregiver. The sawed-off club that Earl created for Tiger became much more than a toy: it was a symbolic link between father and son. Instead of carrying around a security blanket or a stuffed animal, Tiger dragged a putter from one end of the house to the other. It seldom left his hand. At the same time, Tiger's mother rarely left his side, feeding him, wiping his mouth, talking to him, making him smile.

Earl would later say that his relationship with Kultida began to suffer at about the same time they discovered that their little boy had an affinity for golf. "Tida and I made a personal commitment to each other that we would devote all of our energies and finances to assure that he had the best we could give him," Earl wrote. "Total commitment! Well, something had to give, and it was our relationship. The priority became Tiger, and not each other. And in retrospect, I see that our relationship began to decline from that day on."

That's a terrible burden to place on a child. It's also not completely accurate; Earl was already neglecting his wife by that point. If anything, Tiger and his early proficiency in golf are what held his parents together. On the other hand, Earl deserves credit for recognizing so early on that his son possessed rare natural talents and abilities. As a father, he intended to do everything in his power to harness and develop those talents.

Since 1966, the Navy Golf Course (Seal Beach) has been serving military families by directing 100 percent of its profits to support morale, welfare, and recreation programs for active-duty sailors and their families. The then military-only facility featured a championship eighteen-hole "Destroyer" course measuring 6,780 yards, as well as a shorter, nine-hole "Cruiser" course that featured four par 4s and five par 3s.

The course was less than two miles away—a five-minute drive—from the Woodses' home. As retired military, Earl had playing privileges there and was a constant presence on the course. Over time, he became one of the very best players at the club. Kultida never went there until Tiger was able to come along. When he was eighteen months old, she started bringing him to the driving range to hit balls. Afterward, she would put him back in his stroller, and he'd doze off. Some days, Kultida would telephone Earl at work and hand the phone to Tiger. "Daddy, can I play golf with you today?" he would ask. Earl loved it, and he never told his son no. It was Kultida's job to get Tiger to the course. Beginning when Tiger was two years old, Earl made sure he spent two hours per day hitting golf balls. At an age when most toddlers were developing motor skills and feeling different textures by doing things like playing in sandboxes, Tiger was on a golf course with his father, developing the habit of practice, practice, practice.

Then one evening in 1978, Earl Woods made a decision that would alter the course of his young son's life. He placed a call to television station KNXT, then the CBS affiliate in Los Angeles, and asked for Jim Hill, the thirty-two-year-old sports anchor.

"My son is two years old," Earl began, "and I'm telling you right now that he's going to be the next big thing in golf. He's gonna revolutionize everything, including race relations."

It was a blunt way to open a call with a complete stranger. Deeply skeptical, Hill wasn't sure how to respond.

"What makes you say that?" he replied.

To Earl's credit, he knew how to pitch his son to the media. And he always did his homework. Hill had spent seven years as a defensive back in the NFL and loved to play golf. More important, he was an African American who cared deeply about minority youth and had been very involved in local outreach through the Los Angeles Urban League and the Los Angeles Department of Parks and Recreation. He was well aware that golf courses throughout the country had traditionally shut blacks out. Earl insisted that his son would one day open the game up to kids of color around the nation.

The next morning Hill and a camera crew pulled into the parking lot at the navy course. Earl, in a golf shirt and cap, smiled warmly and extended his hand.

"Where's Tiger?" Hill said.

"Come on," Earl said, leading him to the driving range.

As they approached, Hill recognized one of the sweetest sounds in sports—a golf club making square contact with a golf ball. He was shocked when he saw who was responsible for that sound.

"I see this little Tiger hitting golf balls straight," Hill recalled. "I mean *straight*. Not kind of straight. Straight! He was only a couple of feet tall. Yet he was hitting it fifty yards, and he was hitting the ball flush every time."

Hill was no longer skeptical.

"Hi, Tiger, how are you?" Hill said.

Silent, Tiger stared up at him.

"Can I play golf with you?" Hill asked.

Tiger nodded his head.

Hill sliced his first drive. He hooked his second one. "I'm not that good, am I?" he said, smiling.

"No," Tiger said, straight-faced.

Hill was smitten. This two-year-old possessed a swing that looked destined for the PGA Tour, yet the boy had an innocence that matched his size. The trip to Long Beach had definitely been worth it. After the camera crew got footage of Tiger driving and putting, Earl took them to the clubhouse.

"Tiger," Hill said gently, "I need you to do an interview with me."

Earl put his son on his lap and had him face Hill and the camera.

"Tiger," Hill asked, "what is it about golf that you like so much?"

Tiger sighed, tilted his head to one side, and said nothing. Hill tried the question another way. Once again, Tiger said nothing. No matter what Hill tried, Tiger wasn't talking. Finally, after a long pause and some encouragement from Earl to Tiger, Hill leaned forward. "Tiger," he said, grinning, "my career is in your hands. I need you to tell me what it is about golf you like so much."

Tiger slid from Earl's lap and sighed. "I gotta go poo-poo."

Hill cracked up. So did the camera crew.

Hill's segment on Tiger aired in Los Angeles and became one of the most memorable pieces of television news in his forty-plus years of broadcast journalism. The footage of a two-year-old swinging a golf club with such natural form and power was captivating. His miniature size juxtaposed with his perfect mechanics—turning his shoulders as he started his backswing, all the while not allowing his hips or body to slide to the right—looked like a fiction straight out of Hollywood. It was textbook form from a child too young to read. During the broadcast, Hill made a bold prediction: "This young man is going to be to golf what Jimmy Connors and Chris Evert are to tennis."

It's unclear what motivated Earl Woods to cold-call Jim Hill. Was it an irrepressible urge to show off his talented child, an innocent impulse inspired by understandable parental pride? Or was Earl more calculating than that? In his 1998 memoir, Earl wrote that he hoped his son's fame would reach across the globe and lead him back to the war comrade who was responsible for Tiger's nickname. "This was my fantasy: that this kid named after Tiger Phong would become famous one day," Earl wrote. "And my old, dear friend would read about a Tiger Woods in the news-paper or see him on television, and he would make the connection and find me."

That statement was written just after Tiger had turned pro in 1996. Un-doubtedly there were other factors motivating Earl in 1978, but this much is clear: by age two and a half, Tiger Woods showed unmistakable signs of being a bona fide gifted child, and his father had set in motion a series of events that were more improbable—and ultimately more burdensome—than anything Charles Dickens dreamed up for his fictional child protag-onist Pip in *Great Expectations*.

Soon after Hill's profile on Tiger aired on KNXT, ABC daytime tele-vision talk-show host Mike Douglas instructed his staff to book Tiger on his show. At the time, *The Mike Douglas Show* was one of the most-watched daytime programs in America. It was filmed in Philadelphia, and on October 6, 1978, with a live studio audience cheering him on, Tiger Woods scampered onto the stage wearing khaki shorts, white socks, a short-sleeved shirt with a red collar, and a red cap. His shoulders slumped forward under the weight of the miniature golf bag slung across his back. Flanked by Douglas, comedian Bob Hope, and actor Jimmy Stewart, Tiger put a ball on a tee, positioned himself, and hammered the ball into a net.

"Perfect!" Douglas said as the audience cheered and Hope and Stewart clapped.

But it was immediately clear that Tiger was uncomfortable. He tugged nervously at his left ear.

"How old are you, Tiger?" Douglas asked.

Tiger kept tugging at his ear while Earl answered for him.

Sensing Tiger's discomfort, Douglas got down on one knee, put his hand on Tiger's shoulder, and said in a soft voice, as he pointed at Bob Hope: "Do you know who this man is right here?"

Tiger said nothing and continued tugging at his ear.

"What's the man's name?" Earl said.

Tiger looked away.

"Turn around and look at him, Tiger," Earl said. "This man right here."

It was getting awkward. Hope bent over, hands on his knees, and smiled at Tiger.

"What is his name?" Earl repeated.

Tiger finally looked up at Hope, but still said nothing.

Eventually, Earl lifted him up.

"How about a putting contest with Mr. Hope?" Douglas said. "Can he putt too?"

"Oh, yes," Earl said.

Tiger placed his ball on the green about five feet from the cup, and proceeded to miss the putt. He made two more attempts, both failures. Earl placed a fourth ball at Tiger's feet and took a step back. Tiger picked it up, moved it within a couple of inches of the cup, and tapped it in. The audience erupted. Hope slapped his knee and howled. Douglas laughed so hard he dropped an entire basket of golf balls.

It's easy to see this as a funny moment, but Tiger's appearance on *The Mike Douglas Show* also revealed that he shared the textbook attributes of what child psychologists refer to as the gifted child: quiet, sensitive, isolated. There was the incessant, nervous pulling at his ear; his obvious desire to please his father; and his need to succeed, evidenced by his determination to ensure that he didn't miss his final putt. In her landmark book *The Drama of the Gifted Child*, renowned childhood researcher and psychologist Alice Miller defined *gifted child* as one who is more intelligent, more sensitive, and more emotionally aware than other children. Through decades of research, Miller concluded that the gifted child can be more attuned to his parents' expectations and will do whatever it takes to meet them, even if that means ignoring his own feelings and needs. Miller referred to a "glass cellar" as a place where a gifted child locks away his true self while trying to become his parents' ideal child.

Actor Jimmy Stewart was no child psychologist, but he had been around show business for almost sixty years and had seen his fair share of little children who had been put onto the big stage by parents who failed to recognize or appreciate the long-term consequences of early stardom. After Tiger's appearance on the show, Stewart talked backstage with Earl. Then he commented to Mike Douglas: "I've seen too many precocious kids like this sweet little boy, and too many starry-eyed parents."

———

Tiger Woods's first appearance on national television was a seminal moment. It's not an overstatement to say that a star was born that day. It could also be said that a star was born prematurely. Not even some of the greatest athletes in the world—Muhammad Ali, Pelé, Michael Jordan, Steffi Graf, Usain Bolt—had performed in front of a national audience at age two. But for Tiger, appearing in front of the camera soon became the norm, as Earl continued to generate media exposure for his son.

Before long, Earl had Tiger on *That's Incredible!*, an immensely popular reality show that featured everything from natural phenomena to high-risk stunts along the lines of juggling with knives or making a motorcycle jump over a rotating helicopter blade. At age five, Tiger was the subject of a lengthy feature on the show, but it was Earl who did all the talking on camera. With Kultida at his side and a bunch of Tiger's trophies serving as a backdrop, Earl said, "We can't dictate to him what he can be and what he cannot be. So as a consequence, what we do is we participate with him in golf. And if it was bowling, we would participate with him in bowling." He added, "Each and every one has our own life to live. And he has a choice to live his life the way he wants to live his life."

Kultida never spoke, but she gave her husband an icy glare when he pontificated about Tiger's having choices. Tiger did not have choices at that point. In fairness, no five-year-old chooses how to live life; at that age, parents make the decisions. In the Woods home, Earl called the shots when it came to Tiger and his golf game.

When Tiger was four years old, Earl decided it was time to get him a private instructor. He had set his sights on Heartwell Golf Course, a par 3 public course located just seven miles from the house in nearby Long Beach. The problem was that Earl couldn't afford private lessons for Tiger. It fell to Kultida to figure out how to do it.

Rudy Duran, a thirty-one-year-old assistant pro, ran the junior program at Heartwell. Duran had wavy black hair, a mustache, and a trim, athletic build. He was working behind the counter in the pro shop one spring morning in 1980 when he noticed a woman with a four-year-old in tow.

"My son is very talented," she said. "My husband and I would be happy if you could give him some private lessons."

Duran peered over the counter, and Tiger looked up at him. Duran had never seen a four-year-old golfer. His initial reaction was quite similar to that of Jim Hill the first time Earl called him—skeptical. But Duran didn't want to be insulting.

"Well," he said politely, "let's check him out."

Tiger followed his mother and Duran to the driving range. After Duran teed up four balls, Tiger pulled out the sawed-off wooden club that Earl had made for him. Using a ten-finger baseball grip, he swung, driving each ball roughly fifty yards with a perfect right-to-left ball flight.

Amazing! Duran thought to himself as he watched the balls in flight and studied Tiger's form. He couldn't get over the child's range of motion. He'd seen pros who couldn't swing like that.

"I'd be happy to work with your son," he told Kultida. "He can play here any time he wants."

The going rate in those days for thirty minutes of private instruction for a junior golfer at Heartwell was about $15 an hour. But Duran didn't bring it up, and Kultida never asked. Convinced that Tiger was a prodigy, Duran was eager to help him develop without financial obligations or age restrictions. He would serve as Tiger's golf instructor for six years. During that time, he never billed Earl and Kultida, and they never offered to pay him.

Tiger was instantly comfortable with Duran, who started by making him his own set of clubs. At that time, most junior clubs were like toys. But Duran used to work at a driving range where he had learned to re-grip clubs and refinish woods, skills that came in handy when trying to outfit a four-year-old. He took a set of lighter women's shafts to reduce the weight of the clubs, shortened them even more to fit Tiger's height, and then regripped them to fit his small hands.

Duran's teaching approach boiled down to letting Tiger play. He already possessed a rhythmic swing and near-perfect balance. He also finished with his weight on his left foot, facing the target. It was unheard-of to see such sound fundamentals in a child. So instead of drilling the youngster over and over, Duran simply allowed Tiger's natural abilities and his love of the game to grow organically. As a four-year-old, Tiger would play eighteen holes with Duran. He looked like a shrunken Tour pro on the course. But off the course, he would talk to his teacher about eating a Happy Meal or about *Star Wars*. Rudy quickly became Tiger's best friend outside of his home.

———

Par at Heartwell was 54. Seeking to build Tiger's confidence, Duran created what he referred to as "Tiger Par," which was 67. For example, on a 140-yard par 3, Duran figured Tiger would hit his drive about eighty yards, leaving a full 7- or 9-iron onto the green. If Tiger hit the green and holed the putt, his three would equal a birdie, not a par. In less than a year, Tiger shattered Tiger Par, shooting an eight-under 59.

Duran felt Tiger was ready for his own custom-built irons. Earl agreed, and together they approached a sales rep from a company called Confidence Golf. Tiger's reputation was already spreading through golf circles in Southern California, and the Confidence rep wanted to be associated with the kid everyone was starting to talk about. He offered to outfit Tiger with a complimentary set of new clubs.

Kindergarten was still months away, but Tiger was already starting to learn a valuable lesson: Superior athletes don't have to pay for things. Private lessons, greens fees, equipment—these expenses were part of the socioeconomics that normally limited the game of golf to kids from families that belonged to country clubs. Tiger was never going to be a country-club kid. But that wasn't going to hold him back.

Earl was always looking for ways to give his son an edge. Tiger was in grade school when his father furnished him with a cassette player and motivational self-help tapes. In addition to offering words of empowerment, the cassettes were filled with soft music and the sounds of nature, such as water flowing through a creek. In the early eighties, when other kids were listening to songs from Michael Jackson's *Thriller* on a Walkman, Tiger was filling his mind with words that were intended to make him great. He even wrote some of the messages from the self-help cassettes on a sheet of paper that he taped to his bedroom wall:

I believe in me
I will own my own destiny
I smile at obstacles
I am first in my resolve
I fulfill my resolutions powerfully
My strength is great
I stick to it, easily, naturally

My will moves mountains
I focus and give it my all
My decisions are strong
I do it with all my heart

Tiger listened to those tapes so often that he wore them out. They gave him a sense of confidence that enabled him to compete in the Optimist International Junior Golf Championship tournament in San Diego as a six-year-old. Out of 150 participants, Tiger finished eighth. All seven boys who finished ahead of him were ten-year-olds. In 1984, at the age of eight, Tiger won the boy 9–10 division. A year later, he won again, finishing fourteen strokes better than the boy who captured the age group *above* Woods.

On the golf course, Tiger was so confident that he came across as cocky, strutting and celebrating after making putts. But in school, he was afraid to raise his hand. His anxiety was so severe that he developed a speech impediment. "My stuttering was so noticeable, and it made me feel so anxious," he would later write, "that I made sure to sit at the back of the classroom hoping that my teachers wouldn't call on me."

The only time he didn't stammer in school was when he talked about golf. Even his teachers noticed that in those instances, he suddenly became confident and fluent. But when it came to any other subject, he recoiled. "My mind worked," Tiger explained, "but I couldn't get the words from my mind to my mouth. Anytime I had to speak, I stuttered so badly that I gave up."

He spent two years in an after-school program designed to help him learn to speak more comfortably, yet he continued to fight a stuttering problem all through grammar school. Golf was a double-edged sword for him. On one hand, his anxiety disappeared and his sense of self-confidence bloomed whenever he had a club in his hands. On the other, unlike team sports that facilitate interaction and communication with teammates, golf was a game that required Tiger to spend an inordinate amount of time alone. Even as he advanced through the grades of elementary school, he seldom had time to play with neighborhood kids after school.

"I do remember putting in the garage for hours as I got older," Tiger recalled. "Pop had put down the worst-looking, worn carpet on the floor, but it had what I would call lanes that were the same width as the head of a putter. I wanted to make sure that my putter moved away from the ball and inside the lane, then back to where I would hit the ball, and then moved inside and away from the lane again.

"Subconsciously, I learned that in the garage on the ratty piece of carpet," he continued. "The colors were almost blinding, yellow, green, and orange. It was putrid. My dad never used it, but I putted for hours on it."

When he wasn't with his instructor or working on his game at the navy course or putting in the garage, Tiger often retreated to his bedroom. There, he had his inspirational tapes and a dog that his parents had brought for him. It was a Labrador retriever named Boom-Boom. Alone in his room, Tiger would talk to him for hours. He never stuttered around Boom-Boom.

"He listened to me until I fell asleep," Tiger said.

CHAPTER FOUR

THE PRODIGY

Sitting on the couch in his living room, ten-year-old Tiger Woods stared intently at the television, his mother seated beside him, his father a few feet away in his chair. It was Sunday afternoon, April 13, 1986, and CBS was broadcasting the final round of the Masters. Earlier that day, as part of their father-son bonding, Tiger had played nine holes with Earl at the navy course near their home. But now he was watching forty-six-year-old Jack Nicklaus take the lead with a three-foot birdie putt on the sixteenth hole that sent the gallery at Augusta into a frenzy. "There's no doubt about it," the announcer said. "The Bear has come out of hibernation!"

Nicklaus went on to win the Masters for the sixth time that day, making him the oldest golfer ever to be awarded the green jacket and marking his eighteenth and final major championship. Tiger, at this point, had been counting his score in tournaments for about seven years. He dreamed of playing at Augusta someday. Nicklaus's historic achievement formed the basis of Tiger's first significant Masters memory. "His reactions over those last holes of the 1986 Masters made an impression on me because they were spontaneous, and they showed me how much of yourself you have to put into a shot," Woods wrote years later. "Jack was forty-six, and I was only ten, and I couldn't put it into words then. But I wanted to be where he was, and doing what he was doing."

Earl was a smoker, and when he was thinking he liked to take a long drag on a cigarette and exhale slowly. There was a lot to think about as he watched his son watching the great Jack Nicklaus on television. The scene at Augusta National, with the all-white gallery and Nicklaus's golden-blond hair, was starkly different from the one in the Woodses' living room. In 1934, the PGA of America amended its constitution to restrict its membership to "Professional golfers of the Caucasian Race." Even though that clause had finally been expunged in 1961, country clubs like Augusta remained bastions of exclusivity for whites. It was the one aspect of golf that Earl despised. Throughout his life he believed he had been denied personal and professional advancement based on the color of his skin—the pretty white girl he couldn't dance with at school; the motels in the Midwest that wouldn't give him a room when he traveled with his college baseball team; the racist colonel who blocked his advancement in the army.

"I was constantly fighting racism, discrimination, and lack of opportunities," Earl said. "There was just no chance for an intelligent, articulate black person to do anything worthwhile or participate successfully in the process of life. It was frustrating and suffocating in so many ways, particularly for someone who wanted to achieve things but wasn't given the opportunity."

Earl was determined that his son would change all that. Race wasn't going to hold him back. Tiger was going to do something worthwhile. He was going to get his opportunity. To hell with any notion of encouraging Tiger to be like Jack; Earl was grooming him to *beat* Jack.

After the 1986 Masters, *Golf Digest* published a list of Nicklaus's career accomplishments. It included his age at the time of each significant achievement. Tiger tacked the list to his bedroom wall. From that moment on, each morning when he woke up and each night when he went to bed, Nicklaus was there.

Tiger had been working with Rudy Duran for six years when Earl decided it was time for a change. Tiger was getting taller, and Earl wanted a coach who could shape his swing to his physical growth. He set his sights on John Anselmo, the head pro at Meadowlark Golf Course in Huntington Beach, about thirteen miles south of Cypress. Anselmo had taught many child prodigies from California over the years. Earl went to see him shortly after the 1986 Masters and quizzed him on his philosophy and method of teaching.

Anselmo had heard about Tiger. But it wasn't until he saw him swing that he realized he was one of a kind. "I'd never seen a child with that much ability," he said. He told Earl that the special ones required a different kind of coaching. "You don't do a lot of things," Anselmo told him.

"You just do things natural. And you grow with that natural sense. You've got to have that *feel*-sense."

Earl knew enough to know that Anselmo was the best instructor in Southern California. They reached an understanding that was similar to the one Woods had had with Duran—Anselmo didn't ask for payment, and Earl didn't offer it.

The first time Anselmo worked with Tiger, he made some immediate observations: Tiger swung on a flat plane, meaning his left arm never rose above his shoulders during his backswing, and early in his swing, Tiger's right wrist hinged. No one had pointed these things out before.

Tiger embraced Anselmo's technical approach and thrived on the new drills meant to help him improve. Carefully following instructions, he did things such as balancing on the balls of his feet and letting his arms hang down naturally. At the same time, instead of a club, he took hold of an empty driving-range basket, grasping the left side with his left fingers and the right side with his right fingers. Then he swung back naturally, the basket pushing back from the target, stretching the muscles in his back and left arm. It was a new sensation, and the start of Tiger learning a bigger, fuller athletic motion.

There was something else Anselmo noticed: Tiger was obsessed with hitting the ball far. This wasn't a technical flaw in his game; it was more of a mind-set. It wasn't something that could be corrected through drills. Nevertheless, in Anselmo's view, this had to change. Swinging too hard could destroy a talented golfer.

Tiger started meeting with Anselmo every week.

Transportation to and from golf lessons and practice fell to Kultida. She also shuttled Tiger to all his tournaments. With Earl working full-time, Tiger spent most of his time with his mom. They went everywhere together. The summer before Anselmo entered the picture, Tiger went all the way to Thailand. It was an opportunity to see his mother's homeland and learn about her religion. He even went with her to meet with a Buddhist monk. Kultida handed the monk a chart she had been keeping since Tiger's birth, tracking all his achievements through the first nine years of his life. She later recounted to a journalist what happened next.

"The monk asked me when I was pregnant, did I ask God for this boy to be born," she recalled. "I ask why. He say because this kid is special, like God send an angel to be born. He said this Tiger is a special kid. The monk don't know about golf. Monks don't watch TV. Monk said it's like God send angel. He said Tiger is going to be a leader. If he go into army, he be a four-star general."

The visit to Thailand was a formative one in Tiger's relationship with his mother. He didn't feel compelled to practice Buddhism, but he was determined to please her. Each night before bed, Kultida prayed to Buddha that in her next life, Tiger would again be her son. The head covers on his golf clubs had the Thai inscription *Rak jak Mea*, which meant "Love from Mom." "You can always count on Mom," she assured him. "Mom will never lie to you."

They logged thousands of hours in the car together, traveling to lessons, practices, and tournaments all over Southern California. When Tiger competed, Kultida walked every hole with him, carrying a scorecard and a pencil. She believed strongly in keeping score. Although pleasant and respectful toward Tiger's competitors, Kultida didn't like to see anyone beat her son. While driving him to tournaments, she shared her philosophy with him: "In sport, you have to go for the throat," she said. "Because if all friendly, they come back and beat your ass. So you kill them. Take their heart."

Off the course, Tiger knew the rules:

1. Education before golf.
2. Homework before practice.
3. No back talk.
4. Respect your parents.
5. Respect your elders.

On the course, he had only one rule: play without mercy.

It was an unusually hard-edged mentality on the junior golf circuit. But in 1987, at age eleven, Tiger entered thirty-three junior golf tournaments and won every one of them. "There's no feeling I've found that matches the feeling that I've beaten everybody," Tiger said. "Second place is first loser."

The evening hours were reserved for Earl. Most nights, after Earl got off work, Tiger met him at the navy course, where they would play together until dark. Being alone on the course with Pop was his favorite thing to do. He considered that his "peaceful" time. On rare occasions, when Earl would arrange it, someone would join them for a round.

One day, when Tiger was twelve years old, they were joined by Eric Utegaard, the commanding officer of a navy destroyer. Back in 1969, Utegaard was the first member of the Naval Academy to earn All-America status since the beginning of the navy's golf program in 1909. He'd made arrangements to play a round with Earl and Tiger. He also brought along a friend, Jay Brunza, PhD, a navy captain who had worked with the academy's golf team.

"What do you do for a living?" Earl asked Brunza.

Brunza explained that he was a psychologist who had been on the faculty at the Naval Academy in Annapolis, Maryland. More recently he had been with the pediatric oncology unit at Bethesda Naval Hospital, where he worked with children suffering from cancer and other life-threatening illnesses and diseases. When a child faced radiation treatment for leukemia, for example, Brunza would help him or her focus on alternative thoughts—something he called "attentive awareness." He essentially used a form of hypnosis to help his patients visualize how to deal with discomfort. On a lighter note, Brunza was a very good golfer, and he had worked as a sports psychologist for the navy's golf team.

Utegaard offered to play with Earl, and he suggested that Tiger be paired with Brunza in their foursome. Tiger immediately started talking trash to Brunza, who gave it right back to him. Tiger liked that, and he appreciated that Brunza could play. Throughout the round, Earl noted that there was an affinity between them. Afterward, he pulled Brunza aside.

"Would you help me give Tiger the kind of advantage that a lot of country-club kids get?" he asked. "Would you work with him?"

Tiger had already spent over a year working with Anselmo to improve his balance. Brunza started driving up on weekends from San Diego to teach Tiger how to visualize shots. At the outset, he gave Tiger cassette tapes containing subliminal messages that were custom-made for him. The two did breathing and visualization exercises together, in which Tiger learned to take a deep breath and hold it, and then exhale slowly while settling over a shot. It was a way of putting him at ease. Then Tiger changed his approach to putting. Instead of putting to the cup, he started visualizing a picture around the hole and putting to it. Brunza was using a blend of hypnotic techniques that he'd been using with cancer patients for years.

"The hypnotic element is that absorption," Brunza explained. "You think you lose control with hypnosis, but you don't. It's actually a heightened state of awareness and absorption. I taught Tiger a level of real focus technique, a creative awareness that you work into your nature."

After each session, Brunza sent Tiger home with a list of things to work on. He never had to tell him to practice. "Tiger was one of the best students ever," Brunza said. "A very creative and gifted child."

Like any kid, Tiger liked toys and games. But equipment fascinated him— the grips on clubs, the smooth, shiny surface of the shaft on a driver, even the smell and texture of the soft leather on a new golf bag. He took exceptional care of every item he owned, from his golf shoes to his golf balls to the covers on the heads of his clubs. Anselmo noticed this and decided to introduce Tiger to one of his former students, twenty-five-year-old Scotty Cameron.

When Cameron was a boy, he and his father started experimenting with putters in the family garage. At first they were just tinkering, but soon the garage morphed into a workshop. When Cameron and his father weren't on the golf course, they were in the shop, wrapping grips, shaping club heads, and designing putters for what they referred to as "field tests." It didn't take long for Cameron to realize that he wasn't going to make it as a pro and that his real gift was handcrafting putters. In his early twenties, he moved out of the garage and into a studio, where he could produce elite clubs with state-of-the-art tools.

Tiger was in awe when he saw Cameron's work. Despite being thirteen years younger than Cameron, Tiger spoke his language. As for Cameron, the future, he felt, was in making putters that would end up in the hands of a golfer who would revolutionize the game. Tiger started using Cameron putters.

At twelve years old, Tiger Woods was a boy surrounded by adults. He had the top golf coach in Southern California. He had a military-trained sports psychologist who often doubled as his caddie at junior tournaments. He had a true craftsman custom-making putters for him. His equipment—right down to his bag—was noticeably superior to that of other kids his age. And he had two parents—sometimes outfitted in "Team Tiger" T-shirts—whose lives were consumed with giving their son every advantage necessary to beat the wealthier country-club kids he was up against. When he stepped onto the course at a junior tournament, the other kids were intimidated by him.

Yet when Tiger looked in the mirror, he saw himself as small and scrawny. He was convinced that he wasn't tough enough, so he turned to his father for help.

Earl put him through what he called Woods Finishing School: using psychological warfare and prisoner-of-war techniques that he had once taught to soldiers, Earl broke his son down in an attempt to toughen him up.

"The psychological training that my father used inured me to whatever I might have to deal with in golf," Tiger later said. "He taught me to be completely aware of my surroundings, while maintaining complete focus on the task at hand."

Earl would later brag to golf writers that he would jingle the change in his pocket when Tiger was putting, or he would cough or drop his golf bag during Tiger's backswing. "It was psychological warfare," Earl wrote in his memoir. "I wanted to make sure he would never run into anybody who was tougher mentally than he was, and we achieved that."

The stories, when told by Earl and others, sounded benign—just one more ingenious lesson passed from a father to a son. In reality, as Tiger would reveal long after his father's death, some of Earl's tactics, under today's standards, bordered on abuse.

"My dad deliberately used a lot of profanity when I was hitting balls, all the time, and throughout my swing," Tiger said. "'Fuck off, Tiger,' he would sometimes say. . . . It was 'motherfucker' this, 'you little piece of shit,' or 'How do you feel being a little nigger?'—things of that nature.

"He constantly put me down," Tiger recalled. "Then, when I really got mad, he would say, 'I know you want to slam down that club, but don't you dare do it! Don't you dare!' He would push me to the breaking point, then back off. Push me to the breaking point, then back off. It was wild."

We may never know how Tiger really felt at age eleven, twelve, or thirteen as he was repeatedly called those demeaning names by his father. But in 2017, at age forty-one, Woods said this about the experience: "I needed him to push me to the edge of not wanting to continue, because I had to learn to block out any feeling of insecurity. We had a code word that I could use whenever I thought I couldn't take it anymore. But I never used the code word. I was never going to give in to what he was doing. I was a quitter if I used the code word. I don't quit."

The code word that Tiger never uttered was *enough*.

Earl's approach was a huge departure from anything Tiger had previously experienced. Rudy Duran and John Anselmo had always focused on building up his self-confidence. And Dr. Brunza was an extremely sensitive, mild-mannered teacher who didn't raise his voice. His whole approach was to put Tiger at ease. Earl, on the other hand, tried to make him feel insecure.

At the time, no one but Tiger knew what Earl was up to. "He had trained me to be what he sometimes called a 'cold-blooded assassin' on the course, by applying more of the principles he had learned and used while in the military," Tiger admitted in 2017. "I needed this training if I was going to be able to deal with life as a professional golfer, with life as the supposed 'black hope' in the game . . . and of whom big things were expected. . . . I entered every tournament to win, and I expected to win."

It was harsh—but it worked. Tiger simply overwhelmed the competition on the Southern California junior circuit. Even at the Leyton Invitational in Yorba Linda, California, an elite tournament that attracted the finest players in the region, he absolutely dominated. Tom Sargent, one of the most honored teaching professionals in Orange County, was the head pro at Yorba Linda Country Club. He knew nothing about Earl's methods, but he'd been watching Tiger for years and had gotten to know Kultida pretty well. They frequently spoke at tournaments, and Kultida would even call Sargent on occasion to compare notes afterward. Sargent felt that she had as much to do with Tiger's success as anyone.

"Tida is a force," Sargent said. "And you really don't want to stand in her way. I say that in a positive way. Tiger was surrounded by toughness. Let me put it this way: You wouldn't dare fuck with her son. You'd get your ass kicked."

Sargent had been hired as a private instructor for Bob May, an upperclassman at nearby Lakewood High School, who was considered the top college prospect in Southern California. Two coaches in particular—Wally Goodwin at Stanford and Dwaine Knight at UNLV—were pursuing May and would regularly check in with Sargent for updates on his progress. But Sargent had watched Tiger consistently dismantle older, bigger kids. At one point, Sargent told both Goodwin and Knight that they should keep an eye on a twelve-year-old named Tiger Woods. He was, in Sargent's estimation, a decade ahead of the other kids.

In the spring of 1989, Tiger came home from middle school and found a letter from Wally Goodwin addressed to him. The letter mentioned Tom Sargent and made clear that Stanford was interested in Tiger as a prospective member of the golf team. NCAA rules prohibited college coaches from contacting high school athletes between their freshman and junior years, but there were no rules forbidding coaches to write to middle school students—nor were there any regulations preventing a middle school kid from writing to a coach.

On April 23, 1989, Tiger wrote back to Goodwin:

Dear Coach Goodwin,

Thank you for your recent letter expressing Stanford's interest in me as a future student and golfer. At first it was hard for me to understand why a university like Stanford was interested in a thirteen-year-old seventh grader. But after talking with my father I have come to better understand and appreciate the honor you have given me. I further appreciate Mr. Sargent's interest in my future development by recommending me to you.

I became interested in Stanford's academics while watching the Olympics and [Debi] Thomas. My goal is to obtain a quality business education. Your guidelines will be most helpful in preparing me for college life. My GPA this year is 3.86 and I plan to keep it there or higher when I enter high school.

I am working on an exercise program to increase my strength. My April USGA handicap is 1 and I plan to play in SCPGA and maybe some AJGA tournaments this summer. My goal is to win the Junior Worlds in July for the fourth time and to become the first player to win each age bracket. Ultimately I would like to be a PGA

professional. Next February I plan to go to Thailand to play in the
Thai Open as an amateur.

I've heard a lot about your golf course and I would like to play it
with my dad sometime in the future.

Hope to hear from you soon.

Sincerely,
Tiger Woods
5'5" /100 lbs

Privately, Goodwin suspected that Tiger hadn't written the letter on his own. There are other verifiable instances when Earl told Tiger what to say in his letters, and this letter, in particular, appears to have been dictated by Earl. It was too polished and calculated for a thirteen-year-old. But Goodwin didn't care. He was so pleased that he shared Tiger's letter with his team and bragged about how well it was crafted. The way he looked at it, Stanford had gotten a leg up on all the other colleges that would eventually be recruiting this kid.

The summer of 1989 marked a turning point for Tiger and his family. Although he was only thirteen, everyone agreed that he was ready to start competing in national junior golf tournaments. This prompted a change in parental roles. Earl retired from his job at McDonnell Douglas, which enabled him to go on the road with Tiger. Meanwhile, Kultida would remain at home to take care of the house and the dogs. Tiger's first event was the Big I National Championship, the nation's largest junior golf tournament. He would be up against all the top junior golfers in the country—Justin Leonard, David Duval, Notah Begay III, Chris Edgmon, Patrick Lee, and many others. In all, there were 155 participants. Tiger was the youngest.

The tournament was held at the Texarkana Country Club in Arkansas, and tournament officials had placed the junior golfers in private housing for the weekend. But Earl made it clear that he wanted no part of that. He didn't want his son to stay with other people. Tiger, he told the tournament chair in a phone call, would be staying in a hotel, away from everyone else. He wanted to keep his son focused.

On the first day of the tournament, Tiger looked like a child among teenagers. But he shot a 71 and cruised to a three-way tie for first place. He easily made the cut, and on the third day, when the juniors were paired with PGA Tour pros, he found himself playing with twenty-three-year-old John Daly, a rough-and-tumble young gun known for being the longest hitter on the Tour. As soon as the round started, Daly began blasting balls over trees with his driver and hitting sand wedges to par 5s. Woods resisted the temptation to show off his power, instead remembering to follow Anselmo's advice about not overswinging. After nine holes, he led Daly by two strokes. Determined not to get embarrassed by a thirteen-year-old, Daly buckled down on the back nine. Still, with three holes to play, Tiger was in position to beat or tie him. It wasn't until Tiger bogeyed two of his last three holes that he finally ended up losing the round to Daly by two strokes. But he finished second overall in the tournament, making him the youngest player ever to finish in the top five.

The fact that Tiger had nearly beaten Daly was the talk of the tournament, and it triggered speculation about when he might turn pro. Tiger remained mum. Earl, on the other hand, went out of his way to tell reporters that Tiger was free to be whatever he wanted to be. "If he wants to be the head fireman in Memphis, Tennessee, that's fine with me," Earl told one journalist. "There are no expectations or inherent pressure on him to become a pro."

That fall at Orangeview Junior High, Tiger was undoubtedly the most gifted athlete in the school. Yet he didn't play football, basketball, soccer, or baseball—at least, not officially. "In junior high he did it secretly," one of his closest friends recalled. "He wouldn't tell his dad."

Tiger couldn't join other sports teams, but he couldn't resist competing on the playground. In one instance he was playing football during recess when he fell and scraped his knee while leaping to catch a pass. He made a big deal out of what appeared to be a relatively minor abrasion.

"Oh, man!" he said, inspecting his knee.

"Don't worry," one of his friends said. "It's not that bad."

"You don't understand," Tiger told him. "My dad is going to kill me. I'm not supposed to be playing football on a playground."

CHAPTER FIVE

WHO IS TIGER WOODS?

Tiger entered Western High School in Anaheim in the fall of 1990. At fourteen, he stood five feet nine, weighed 120 pounds, and could drive a golf ball almost three hundred yards off the tee. Only a handful of pros hit the ball farther. He was the top junior player in Southern California, and every major college with a top-ranked golf program was eyeing him. Golf writers were already opining on when he would turn pro.

Western High's golf coach, Don Crosby, felt like his fledgling golf team had won the lottery when Tiger arrived. But school officials had no idea that incoming freshman Eldrick Woods was being touted as the future of golf. Months before school started, the district was considering a modest boundary change that would have put Tiger's home just outside the Western High district. In an urgent meeting with Western High's principal, Crosby unfurled a map and drew a circle around the parcel of land at the corner of Teakwood and Chestnut Streets in Cypress.

"Whatever you do this summer," Crosby told the principal, "don't lose that tract."

"Why?" the principal asked.

"Because a kid named Tiger Woods lives there."

The principal looked up from the map and stared blankly at Crosby. "Who is Tiger Woods?"

Students didn't know Tiger either. His circle of friends was limited to three guys—Alfredo Arguello, Mike Gout, and Bryon Bell. Tiger had known Arguello the longest. They'd met in second grade and been friends ever since. They even played on the same youth soccer team. But in all that time, Arguello had seen the inside of Tiger's house only once. Gout was a year older than Tiger and lived a few doors down from him. And then there was Bell, a kid known as a brain. Tiger had met him in junior high. He also played golf, and would become the second-best player on Western High's team.

By the time they got to high school, Woods, Arguello, and Bell were like the Three Musketeers. All of them were in AP and honors classes together. Arguello was a top student in the freshman class. Woods and Bell were right behind him. They were nerds in every sense of the word, competing against each other for the best grades. They knew they weren't part of the popular crowd, which consisted of jocks and cheerleaders, but they had already figured out where they were headed in life.

"Alfredo," Woods would say, "you're going to be my attorney."

"And I'm going to be your doctor," Bell would chime in.

Outside of school, Tiger had one more friend—twenty-four-year-old Joe Grohman, the assistant pro at the navy course. They had met in 1989, shortly after Grohman started working there. In the summer leading up to his freshman year at Western High, Tiger often averaged more than ten hours per day on the practice range. Grohman was also there every day, and he started looking after Tiger like an older brother. It intrigued him that Tiger was far more inclined to practice than to play a round of golf. One afternoon he finally brought it up.

"Why don't you play the course more?" Grohman asked.

"I like practicing better," Tiger told him.

It would not be an exaggeration to say that Tiger spent more than five hundred hours practicing during the summer months before his freshman year, not including the hundreds of additional hours he spent participating in tournaments. Extreme practice habits were neither new nor challenging for him. "The first thing I taught Tiger, aside from the love of the game of golf, was the love of practice," Earl said. "When he was real small, people would ask him, 'How did you get so good, Tiger?' And he would answer, 'Practice, practice, practice.'"

Practicing golf was never a chore or something Tiger felt obligated to do. He looked forward to being alone on the range or the course with his clubs. They were, in a sense, an extension of his creative genius. In his book *Outliers*, Malcolm Gladwell looked at the careers of gifted geniuses—Bill Gates, Mozart, Bobby Fischer, the Beatles—and concluded that preparation habits played a bigger role in their extraordinary achievements than innate ability did. Using Gates and the Beatles as test cases, Gladwell looked at how much time they had spent practicing and preparing in their youth. Gates, for example, logged more than 1,500 hours on a mainframe computer during a seven-month span in eighth grade, and averaged twenty to thirty hours a week teaching himself to program. Similarly, Paul McCartney and John Lennon started playing together in high school, a full seven years before they made it big, and performed live together an estimated 1,200 times before the Beatles played their first concert in America. Gladwell coined the phrase "the 10,000-hour rule" to explain the effort that separated the greats from everyone else. "The people at the very top don't work just harder or even much harder than everyone else," Gladwell wrote. "They work much, *much* harder."

Tiger started working on his craft much earlier than Gates or McCartney or Lennon. When he was six months old, barely old enough to sit up, he spent countless hours strapped in a high chair, watching his father practice his swing. By the time he was two, according to Earl, Tiger was spending two hours per day hitting golf balls. At that rate, Tiger would have reached ten thousand hours by age fifteen. But by age five he was spending far more than two hours per day practicing golf. By that point, he was performing on television and playing in tournaments. It's probably a conservative estimate that Tiger Woods had already spent more than three thousand hours playing and practicing golf by the time he appeared on *That's Incredible!* at age five. To put this in perspective, it's estimated that McCartney and Lennon achieved ten thousand hours of practice by the time they were twenty. Bill Gates hit the ten-thousand mark around the time he turned twenty-one. Tiger Woods had probably accumulated ten thousand hours playing and studying golf by the time he was twelve.

Right before the start of Tiger's freshman year in high school, Grohman nicknamed him Champ. It never quite caught on. But Grohman always referred to him that way, and Tiger liked it. He also appreciated some straightforward advice that Grohman gave him about girls: Avoid them. Golf required an inordinate amount of time, and a girlfriend was nothing more than a distraction. "The woods are full of guys who were phenomenal until they met a girl," Grohman told him.

Tiger wasn't worried. No girls were paying attention to him anyway. They were interested in football players. They were the guys who got the girls, not him. Girls at school didn't even know Tiger's name. Early on in high school, Woods was interviewed by a reporter for *People* magazine who asked him if it was hard missing out on so many childhood experiences—specifically, the fact that Tiger didn't have a girlfriend. "I couldn't fit her in," Tiger said, adding, "This is better than childhood."

This was playing golf.

Tiger was about a month into his freshman year when Earl received a phone call from Jaime Diaz, a senior writer for *Golf Digest*. Diaz expressed an interest in meeting Tiger and perhaps profiling him for the magazine. Earl suggested they start by playing a round of golf together. Diaz agreed to fly to LA.

Meeting a journalist wasn't Tiger's idea of fun. He had never been particularly keen on talking to strangers who carried pens, notepads, and handheld recorders. His dad had been arranging interviews for him since he was two years old, and by fourteen he was sick and tired of it. But on a Saturday morning in the fall of 1990, he dutifully went with Earl to Coto de Caza Golf & Racquet Club, a private course in Orange County, to meet Diaz.

Looking down at his feet, Tiger mumbled hello when Diaz introduced himself. Diaz didn't bother trying to make small talk. They went straight to the first tee and started playing. After a few holes, Tiger started warming up to Diaz. He seemed different from other journalists. For one thing, most golf writers were white, and Diaz was a pleasant exception. He could also play—always a plus in Tiger's book. After the round, Tiger and Earl joined Diaz for a meal at Sizzler. The conversation quickly turned to the media.

"So who are the assholes?" Tiger blurted out in between bites.

Pretty cynical for a fourteen-year-old, Diaz thought, but he kept it to himself. "I think you have to figure everybody out yourself," he told Tiger. "I find some guys difficult to deal with, another guy finds him to be a favorite."

Tiger nodded.

"So I just say have an open mind and don't go in like everybody's trying to screw you," Diaz continued.

Earl chimed in that he had taught Tiger to answer only the question that is asked and never to elaborate.

It was clear that Tiger possessed a fairly sophisticated understanding of the media and how it worked. He knew all the golf writers by name, and he was well read. Diaz was invited to the house to meet Kultida. By the time he left town, he was on a first-name basis with everyone. It was the start of a unique relationship that promised to benefit both him and the Woods family.

Tiger grew up about forty miles from the ultraexclusive Bel-Air Country Club in west Los Angeles, but he'd never been there before the spring day in 1991 when he arrived to watch Jack Nicklaus put on a clinic. The club was impressive. It was impossible not to admire its lush green fairways and crystal-clear swimming pools. Club members included Ronald Reagan, Richard Nixon, Bing Crosby, Jack Nicholson, and Clint Eastwood. Only recently had the first black golfer been admitted to the membership.

At one point, Nicklaus called on Tiger to demonstrate his swing. As a fifteen-year-old being ballyhooed as "golf's great black hope," Tiger felt the eyes of everyone at the clinic shift from Nicklaus to him. It was a feeling he had experienced many times previously when entering country clubs. Privately, he referred to it as The Look, which he compared to the feeling of walking into a prison with everybody staring at him.

On this occasion, the feeling was even more pronounced. Weeks earlier, African American taxi driver Rodney King had been savagely beaten by four white police officers after a high-speed chase that ended nearby in the San Fernando Valley. Amateur video showed Taser wire on King's body as he was down on the ground being clubbed with batons, stomped, and kicked in the head and neck. The chilling video led to the arrest of all four officers and triggered a national conversation on police brutality and race in America.

Remaining poised, Woods demonstrated his flawless swing. After a few swings, Nicklaus stopped him. "Tiger," he said, grinning, "when I grow up, I want to have a swing as pretty as yours."

The Bel-Air crowd laughed. Although Nicklaus delivered the praise with a touch of self-deprecating humor, it was a rare display of public validation from the game's greatest golfer to the child prodigy who had been anointed his successor. Parents of other kids at the clinic looked at Tiger with a mix of awe, envy, and wonder.

Over the next three months, as Tiger's freshman year came to a close, he lived up to the hype. At the California high school championships in May, he outperformed juniors and seniors to win the top individual honors. In June, he won the Los Angeles junior championship. In July, despite being one of the youngest in the fifteen-to-seventeen-year-old age group, he won the Optimist International Junior Golf Championship in San Diego. Then it was on to Bay Hill Country Club in Orlando, where he won the US Junior Amateur Championship, making him the youngest—and first black—winner in the forty-four-year history of the event.

"Son," Earl told him, "you have done something no black person in the United States has ever done, and you will forever be a part of history."

Tiger felt good. His string of machinelike victories during the summer of 1991 had clearly established him as the top junior golfer in the country. In August, the *New York Times* declared in a bold headline, "Fore! Nicklaus Beware of Teen-Ager." The story was written by Jaime Diaz, who had moved to the *New York Times*. "I want to be the Michael Jordan of golf," Tiger told Diaz. "I'd like to be the best ever."

Dina Gravell was one of the prettiest girls at Western High. A cheerleader, she had blond hair, blue eyes, and slender legs. The sixteen-year-old junior was also a diligent student and a good athlete, playing on the varsity tennis and soccer teams. In her big circle of friends—mainly comprising athletes and cheerleaders—she never intersected with Tiger. She'd never even heard of him. But Tiger certainly noticed her when she ended up in his advanced accounting class at the start of his sophomore year.

Although he was a year behind her, they were the top two students in the class. After about a month, the teacher pulled them both aside and asked if they would tutor a classmate who was struggling. At the first session, Tiger said little, deferring to Gravell. When he finally chimed in, he was very good at explaining things. It was obvious that he was smart, but Gravell also recognized that he was different. Unable to quite put her finger on it, she chalked it up to the fact that he was basically a nerd. She figured Tiger would benefit from meeting a few more kids.

"Hey, you should come out with us sometime," she said after one of the tutoring sessions. "You know, go to a football game."

He wasn't sure what to say.

"Have you been to a game?" she asked.

"Not really."

"Come with us."

The invitation triggered some social anxiety. Tiger didn't know the kids Gravell knew. His world was golf, studying, and his close circle of guy friends. He liked it that way. Going to a game with Dina would be uncharted territory, way outside his comfort zone. Yet he liked the fact that one of the best-looking girls in the school was paying attention to him. His buddies would never believe it. On Friday night, he sat with Gravell and her friends in the bleachers. He was two months shy of his sixteenth birthday, and it felt good to be out. Shortly after the opening kickoff, Gravell turned to him.

"So what do you do?" she said.

"I golf."

"What's that?"

"Well, it's a sport."

"I know *that*. But, like, old people golf. Why are *you* doing that?"

He laughed. "Well, I like it."

"Huh."

"And I'm kinda good at it."

She didn't ask any more questions about it, and he didn't elaborate. Gravell had no idea that Woods was a certified star. A week earlier he had been profiled in *People* magazine. He was a household name to sportswriters from Los Angeles to New York. But he mentioned none of that. Sitting in the stands amid a sea of teenagers on a Friday night, he was perfectly content to be an invisible star. The fact was that, at Western High, Dina Gravell was more famous than Tiger Woods.

A couple of weeks later, Gravell invited Tiger to another football game. They arrived together, and when they met up with her friends, one of the girls whispered, "Hey, it's that golf guy."

Tiger said nothing and took a seat directly behind Gravell in the bleachers. He didn't know her friends, and he wasn't particularly interested in letting them get to know him. While Gravell talked to them, he watched the game. At one point, she leaned back, resting her arms on his legs and using his knees to support her back while she carried on a conversation with her girlfriends seated on either side of her. For Woods, it was as if an electric current was flooding through his body; he could barely focus on the game. Afterward, when they were alone, he confided in her.

"I was dying when you touched my legs," he told her.

She laughed. "I just leaned back," she said.

The silence that followed said a lot. He had fallen hard for her. It went beyond her being gorgeous. He could talk to her. She listened to him. The fact that he was famous and an elite golfer didn't matter to her. She didn't even know about that side of him. Everyone else he met was interested in him because of his talent. She cared about him as a person.

Gravell felt something too. The more time she spent around him, the more she adored him. He was so different from all the other boys. So many of the jocks were loud, prone to bragging, and constantly showing off. Tiger never said anything to anyone, and he never talked about himself. "He didn't try to be popular," she recalled. "He didn't try to stick out. He was just a gentleman. He minded his own business and did his own thing. I guess that's what attracted me to him."

With the holidays approaching, Gravell invited Tiger to her home to have dinner with her parents. He said yes, but he felt uncomfortable. What was he supposed to say to her parents? He kept his head down for most of the evening, saying very little. But he complimented Mrs. Gravell on her cooking and thanked her for having him over. In the dark about Tiger's golf exploits, Gravell's parents concluded that Tiger was a very shy, polite kid. They told him he was welcome at their home anytime.

Shortly after that, Tiger invited Gravell to his home to have dinner with his parents. The moment she entered the house, Gravell was struck by the trophies. They were everywhere—on tabletops, on shelves, even on the floor. There had to be a hundred of them. Plus, there were framed copies of newspaper stories about Tiger.

"You were in *People*?" she asked, amazed.

"Have you heard about the time he was on *That's Incredible!*?" Earl asked.

She had no idea what he was talking about.

Earl played a recording for her. Tiger wasn't interested. But Gravell couldn't believe her eyes. The guy she had developed a crush on had been on national television at age five?

Earl corrected her: Tiger was on national television at age two!

What? Gravell didn't get it. Why hadn't Tiger mentioned any of this to her?

There was a lot he hadn't told her about himself.

Kultida made a sensational chicken dish for dinner. Tiger had never brought a girl home before, and his mother went out of her way to make Dina feel welcome. After the meal, all Tiger wanted to do was introduce Dina to his new puppy.

It didn't take Tiger long to decide that he liked hanging out with Gravell at her house more than being at his house. He started going there after golf practice. More and more, he ate dinner with her parents, and they welcomed him like one of the family. On weekends, he and Gravell would stay up late watching television, and after her parents went to bed they would make out on the sofa.

Tiger celebrated his sixteenth birthday in Florida. He was there for International Management Group's Orange Bowl Junior Classic. After the tournament, he headed for the home of Mark O'Meara. It was all arranged by IMG agent Hughes Norton and IMG founder Mark McCormack. Both men had been courting Tiger long before most people recognized his potential. Woods realized that he would eventually be represented by IMG. He also knew that it was the biggest, most powerful sports agency in the world of golf. But he didn't know the agency's backstory or the full scope of the arrangement IMG had made with his father.

Mark McCormack had been a fiercely competitive golfer at the College of William & Mary in the late 1940s and early '50s. After graduating, he attended Yale Law School and served in the US Army before practicing law in Cleveland. He quickly figured out a way to combine his legal career with his passion for golf. He had been organizing exhibitions for pro golfers when he came up with a bigger and more lucrative idea—negotiating contracts for them. In the late 1950s, the purses on the PGA Tour barely reached $2,000, and it was virtually unheard-of for a professional golfer to have a contract with an equipment manufacturer. Golf was a sport played by the rich, but no one looked at it as a sport that was going to *make* anyone rich. Not until McCormack came along.

On January 15, 1959, McCormack convinced twenty-nine-year-old golfer Arnold Palmer to sign with him. Palmer had grown up in a mill town in Pennsylvania. Humble, handsome, and charismatic, he was the son of a greenskeeper. In McCormack's mind, Palmer was the ideal golfer to expand the appeal of the game to the middle class. Before long, McCormack had left his law firm and started an agency that he later renamed International Management Group. He eventually signed Jack Nicklaus and Gary Player and built IMG into a sports agency and marketing juggernaut. With Mark McCormack and IMG handling the contracts and endorsement deals for the biggest names in the game, Cleveland became a destination city in the golf universe.

In 1972, Hughes Norton joined IMG. When he arrived, he possessed degrees from Harvard and Yale. He was aggressive and sophisticated and had a reputation for being a tough negotiator. The one thing Norton wasn't known for was humility. He also had a vindictive streak, and he could be a bully. But McCormack and Norton were exceptional at two things: identifying talent, and leveraging that talent into lots of money for IMG. When they first got wind of Tiger Woods, they were convinced that he could revolutionize the game, in much the same way Arnold Palmer had done three decades earlier.

It's unclear exactly when IMG made its first overture to the Woods family, but Earl Woods once claimed that Hughes Norton entered the picture when Tiger was just five years old. In the book *His Father's Son: Earl and Tiger Woods*, author Tom Callahan reported that Norton had heard about Tiger when he was a toddler and showed up at the Woods home in Cypress. Tiger rode his bicycle out front while Earl and Norton talked.

"I believe that the first black man who's a really good golfer is going to make a hell of a lot of money," Earl reportedly told Norton.

"Yes, sir, Mr. Woods," Norton said. "That why I'm here."

Norton declined to answer any questions about his relationship with the Woods family. But he said in an email that he was "with Tiger and his family" for ten years, suggesting that their relationship began in 1988. At that point, Tiger was almost thirteen. Before his death in 2003, Mark McCormack confirmed that IMG had engaged with Earl Woods while Tiger was young. "I had a number of meetings with his father when [Tiger] was still an amateur, talking what-if-this, what-if-that," McCormack told British journalist Howard Sounes, author of *The Wicked Game*. "You certainly really knew he was someone who was going to be a factor in golf."

Much has been written about how the so-called handshake deal between McCormack and Arnold Palmer changed the economics of golf. By the time McCormack and Norton were romancing Earl Woods, however, IMG was an international powerhouse representing hundreds of athletes around the world. The sports agency had advanced well beyond handshakes. Plus, IMG viewed Tiger Woods as potentially bigger than any other athlete represented by the firm. He was far too valuable to risk letting him get away.

At the time, the Woods family could not afford the tens of thousands of dollars that were necessary to fund Tiger's extensive amateur travel schedule. According to court records from that time period, Earl's annual income was just over $45,000, and his monthly expenses were in excess of $5,800. Earl was essentially paying for Tiger's travel and tournament expenses with credit cards and what he later referred to as a "revolving home equity loan," which he described as money borrowed against the family home each summer, only to be somehow paid back every winter. Bottom line, the family needed money, and IMG provided it. In a big way.

According to a senior IMG executive who worked with McCormack, in or around the summer of 1991, the agency started paying Earl Woods $50,000 per year as a "junior talent scout." That figure squares perfectly with what Earl revealed two years later during an interview on ABC's *Primetime Live*, saying that he was spending $50,000 a year on Tiger's amateur career.

IMG vice chairman Alastair J. Johnston was the head of IMG's world golf operations in the early nineties. In response to a September 2017 email requesting comment on the $50,000 figure, Johnston replied: "At this stage I can't confirm details. I know that IMG did provide compensation to Earl Woods to work as a talent scout on the junior golf circuit, but I do, however, recall (because it was very important) that we did indeed discuss with the USGA who proactively engaged with IMG on this particular arrangement to ensure that the association with Earl Woods did not breach any of their rules or regulations pertaining to Tiger's amateur status."

The amount of money IMG stood to make by representing Tiger Woods was potentially record-setting. In that respect, the decision to pay Earl five figures annually to be a talent scout was a modest investment. For his "talent scouting," all Earl had to do was deliver one golfer—his son. Everything IMG did was calculated to make sure that happened, includ-

ing introducing Tiger to Mark O'Meara when Woods was in town for the
IMG tournament.

O'Meara resided in Isleworth, a 606-acre gated community within the
town of Windermere, about ten miles west of downtown Orlando. Norton asked O'Meara to spend a little time with Tiger, show him around,
play a round of golf. Perhaps they would hit it off. That was the hope,
anyway.

Tiger was instantly impressed with Isleworth. It was very different
from Cypress. He passed through a security checkpoint to enter. A private
police force patrolled the neighborhood. There were about two hundred
homes, and they were all immaculate. Actor Wesley Snipes and superstars
Ken Griffey Jr. and Shaquille O'Neal lived in Isleworth. O'Meara's house
was across the street from the golf course—which Arnold Palmer had
designed—not far from the clubhouse. There was a lot to like.

Tiger played eighteen holes with O'Meara. They talked about a range
of subjects, and O'Meara gave him some simple advice: "Have fun," he
told Tiger. "There's no rush to get to the Tour."

Afterward, they hung out at O'Meara's home. Tiger spent most of the
time talking to Mark's wife, Alicia, regarded as one of the most beautiful
wives on the Tour, who made Tiger feel at home and introduced him to
her two children. It appeared that Mark had a perfect life. He played golf
for a living, lived in a beautiful home, and had a gorgeous wife and two
cute kids. And the atmosphere in the house was laid-back. Tiger could get
used to that.

After Woods left, Mark turned to Alicia.

"What did you think of him as a person?" he asked.

"I think he's an incredibly gifted kid," Alicia said.

"You really think so?"

"Absolutely!"

Mark didn't follow; Alicia, after all, hadn't seen Tiger play golf. How
would she know whether he was gifted? But she hadn't been referring to
golf when she said *gifted*. Alicia had served on a local board of education
and had been around plenty of teenagers. Tiger seemed so much more
mature than the other teenagers she knew. He looked her in the eye when
he spoke. He had interesting things to say. He had great presence. He was
unusually charismatic. There was something about him that made it impossible to look away from him.

"But can he play golf?" Alicia asked.

Mark raised his eyebrows and nodded. "This kid can play."

When Tiger returned to Cypress, he was officially old enough to drive. He put his golf bag in the back of his used Toyota Supra and drove to Dina Gravell's house.

"You should come to the driving range with me," he told her.

"What's that?" she said.

He laughed. Suddenly she sounded like the innocent, naïve one. Rather than explain, he told her to hop in.

When they arrived at the navy course, Tiger ran into Joe Grohman.

"Hi, Champ," Grohman said.

Joe took one look at Gravell and knew that Tiger had ignored his advice. But inside, he was smiling. The Champ had gone from no girlfriend to a blond bombshell. *Typical Tiger*, he thought. *From zero straight to one hundred miles an hour.*

Grohman welcomed Gravell to the course, and Tiger led her to the driving range, where he teed up a ball and sent it sailing.

"Whoa!" she said, her head popping back with the sound of the club striking the ball. While he put on a display over the next thirty minutes, she kept repeating, "Whoa!" It was as if Tiger had ducked into a phone booth, removed his glasses, and emerged a superhero. His entire demeanor changed when he had a club in his hands. He walked with his head up. He stood taller. He brimmed with confidence. *Wow! Who is this guy?* she thought. At school he was so quiet that he rarely spoke to fellow students. On the course, he was talking confidently with adults.

Tiger took the time to explain things to her—the grip of the club, the trajectory of the ball, the placement of his feet. It was all very technical, but he made it understandable. He made it cool.

"I just didn't think of golf as a sport," Gravell said. "I thought of it as a recreational activity for older people."

Tiger couldn't help laughing at her. She was clueless when it came to golf, and she had no idea what his life was like outside of school. They both appreciated the sudden role reversal. At Western she got a kick out of his unfamiliarity with the whole social scene. Now it was his turn to teach her a few things. The navy course, he insisted, was nothing. It was just a

place to practice. To really get a glimpse of his world, she needed to come
to a tournament.

"What goes on there?" she asked.

"You'll see."

He always felt nervous on the first tee. But this was different. More intense.
As he reached into his bag and pulled out his driver, Tiger felt like he had
a sudden case of rigor mortis. He struggled to grip the club. Breathe, he'd
been taught. Just breathe. It was Thursday morning, February 27, 1992,
and Tiger should have been sitting in his geometry class at Western High in
Anaheim. Instead, he was forty-two miles away on a cliff in Pacific Palisades,
seventy feet above the first fairway at Riviera Country Club, preparing to
tee off in the opening round of the Nissan Los Angeles Open. The first hole
was 501 yards away. But that wasn't what had him anxious. He could always
handle distance. Great expectations were his burden. And at that moment,
the expectations were greater than ever. This was his first PGA Tour event.

Barely two months past his sixteenth birthday, he was the youngest
player to ever appear in a Tour event. The other 143 golfers were pros. An
army of journalists, photographers, and television cameramen were on
hand. They were all there to see him. Spectators lined up six deep around
the tee.

Wearing a white cap, a short-sleeved striped shirt, and pleated pants,
Tiger swung, launching his ball over the cliff. With the sun shining on
him, the six-foot-one, 140-pound high school sophomore stood like a
statue—his hips open, his spine twisted, his club behind him. He held his
form until his ball dropped from the sky 280 yards away. A collective roar
echoed from the crowd. Trailed by security guards, Tiger immediately
started walking toward the fairway, television cameras in his path.

The bodyguards added another element to the circus atmosphere
swirling around Tiger. They had been assigned to him after tournament
chairman Mark Kuperstock had exercised his right under what's known
as a sponsor exemption to invite someone—in this case, Tiger—who
hadn't qualified for the tournament to participate. As a result, Kuperstock
received an anonymous call from a man who didn't like the fact that the
tournament had given an exemption to a "nigger." Tiger also received a
death threat. But the fans lining the fairway adored him.

"You the kid!" one fan shouted, in a variation of the usual cry of "You the man!"

"He's the next Jack Nicklaus, maybe better," another spectator said.

"There walks the future of American golf," said another.

His nervousness dissipated and he shot 72 on the day, finishing one over par and eight shots behind the leader. He would end up missing the cut, but by the end of the second day, every pro knew Tiger Woods was the real deal. Golf writers ignored the leaderboard in order to talk to him. Fans adored him. People wanted pictures, autographs, a chance to touch him. It felt so invigorating to be the center of attention. He could do no wrong.

Dina Gravell didn't know what to say. Walking the course with Kultida had been a surreal experience. What had happened to that nerdy kid she had first encountered five months earlier in an accounting class? With a golf club in his hand, Tiger looked so invincible, so strong. Flashing a magnetic smile, he faced network television cameras and zoom lenses from *Sports Illustrated* with confidence. He never flinched as distinguished men, attractive women, teenagers, and little kids shouted his name. *Wayne's World* was the number one movie in the country that week, but Gravell came to the sudden realization that Tiger's world was more exciting than anything Hollywood could dream up, and so much bigger than anything going on in the hallways at Western High, where the so-called cool kids looked at him as just that golf guy. To the rest of the world, Tiger Woods was the man.

After he finished his final round, Tiger was eager to talk to Gravell, but first he had to talk to *Sports Illustrated*.

"I think these were the best two days of my life," he told the magazine. "I really do. Even when I hit a bad shot, people clapped."

Three days later, Tiger led the Western High golf team in its season opener against Gahr High in Cerritos. There was no press, no crowd; not even his parents or Gravell were there to watch. Tiger dominated, but it was pretty anticlimactic after playing in a PGA Tour event. High school, on many levels, limited his creativity. He was made for a much bigger stage.

Afterward, he went to Gravell's house, where her parents greeted him with hugs and high praise. They had followed the LA Open in the paper and on the local news. Plus, Dina hadn't stopped talking about it for the past three days. Tiger loved being around the Gravells and the way they so easily showed affection. They were always like that, and he wasn't used to it. His home had a much colder feel. There was no embracing, and words of affection were seldom exchanged between his parents or given to him. That was one reason Tiger preferred hanging out at Dina's place to bringing her to his house.

Once Tiger and Dina were alone, she said she'd been thinking about something since seeing him play. The simplest way to say it was that the Tiger she knew at high school wasn't the Tiger she saw at the tournament. One walked with his head down, rarely talked, and appeared socially awkward; the other was confident, strong, and in control. He seemed like two different people.

Tiger had never heard that from anyone, and he wasn't sure what to say in response. She had essentially challenged him to ask himself *Who am I?* It was a question that required some serious introspection, and he could tell that she wanted him to share his feelings. But he wasn't comfortable doing that. He didn't even know *how* to do that. One of the unspoken rules in his family was that they didn't reveal or share emotions with one another. His parents simply didn't talk to each other or to him about their feelings, about matters of the heart, or about any subject that required them to open up. Tiger would later describe this as "one of our deals of being a Woods."

Rather than trying to explain any of this to Dina, he simply avoided her observation, preferring instead to contemplate a more comfortable subject—his future. It looked like a big open road, and he couldn't wait to get on it. For the first time, however, he was considering the prospect of having someone along for the journey. Dina had cared about him as a person before she'd known that he was talented and famous. She was also the first person who had shown him physical affection. He wasn't yet ready to open up to her, but he wanted her at his side.

CHAPTER SIX

THE NEXT LEVEL

John Merchant was used to calling the shots. The sixty-year-old lawyer wore dapper suits, sat on the board of directors of Connecticut's largest bank, and had recently been appointed by the governor to head the state's Office of Consumer Counsel. From behind his desk at the State Capitol in Hartford, he directed multiple divisions of state attorneys. But on a picture-perfect day in late July 1993, Merchant was on a golf course in Portland, Oregon, some three thousand miles from home. Wearing khaki pants and a short-sleeved golf shirt that accentuated his white mustache and graying, neatly trimmed afro, he emerged unnoticed from the Field House at Waverley Country Club. It was the first day of the US Junior Amateur Championship, and the normally serene setting was bustling with people. Stopping to survey the pristine grounds, Merchant couldn't help grinning and asking himself, *How did I get here?*

It was a journey that had begun three years earlier, when golf faced a moral crisis sparked by Hall W. Thompson, a prominent Alabama businessman who had built the Shoal Creek Golf and Country Club near Birmingham. Shoal Creek was chosen to host the PGA Championship in August 1990. But in June of that year, Thompson had talked to a reporter at the *Birmingham Post-Herald* who asked about Shoal Creek's membership policy—it welcomed Jews and women, but excluded blacks. "We don't discriminate in every other area except the blacks," Thompson said.

His answer prompted an immediate backlash. The Southern Christian Leadership Conference threatened to picket the tournament. Corporate sponsors such as IBM pulled more than $2 million in commercial advertising from the television broadcast. Newspapers and media outlets throughout the country started looking into membership policies. The

Charlotte Observer published a report indicating that seventeen golf clubs that were host sites for PGA Tour events had all-white memberships. And another published report suggested that three out of four of America's private golf clubs had membership policies similar to Shoal Creek's.

After insisting he'd been misquoted, Thompson nonetheless apologized. But by that point, the PGA Tour had found itself at the center of a fast-moving firestorm over racism. The president of the USGA, Grant Spaeth, acknowledged that the organization routinely held championship tournaments at clubs that prohibited black membership. "So however distressing one finds this firestorm," Spaeth told the *New York Times*, "I conclude without question that open debate and decision making is long overdue, and we are thus provided the opportunity to sort things out fully and fairly."

In 1991, in the aftermath of Shoal Creek, John Merchant received an unexpected phone call from S. Giles Payne, a Connecticut lawyer who had long been involved with the USGA. Merchant and Payne were old friends and occasional golfing partners, but it had been a few years since they had spoken. Payne cut to the chase, asking Merchant if he had any interest in joining the USGA's executive committee. Flattered, Merchant laughed and admitted that he wasn't really sure what the executive committee was or did. Payne explained that it was the USGA's sixteen-member governing body, responsible for setting the rules of golf and regulating the equipment used throughout America and Mexico. Seats on the committee were highly coveted and typically went to individuals with wealth and influence.

Merchant was intrigued. He wasn't that wealthy, and his sphere of influence was limited to legal and banking circles in Connecticut. But he knew the deal. The bottom line was that in its ninety-seven-year history, the USGA had never had an African American on its executive committee. Shoal Creek had made it embarrassingly clear that the leadership needed to diversify. The executive committee was seeking a person of color, and Merchant seemed ideal. He had been the first black to graduate from the University of Virginia's law school, back in 1958. He was the first, and at the time, only person of color to become a member of the highly exclusive Country Club of Fairfield in Connecticut. And he was the first black to serve on the board of directors at Connecticut's largest bank. He also happened to be a very good golfer.

The process of vetting, formal nomination, and approval took more than a year. But by 1993, Merchant was in place. He had just one concern: "I don't want anybody at the USGA to think that I'm a fucking token!" he said.

Despite his government obligations as Connecticut's chief lawyer for consumers, Merchant determined that he would go to as many junior golf events as possible to get up to speed in his new role. The junior amateur in Portland was the first. Unfamiliar with the course, he decided to look around. His first observation was that there were no people of color in sight. Then he spotted a black man sitting at a table beneath an umbrella on a patio just off the course. Merchant approached, and the man looked up from his drink.

"I'm John Merchant. I'm with the USGA Executive Committee," Merchant said.

"Earl Woods," the stranger said. "Sit down."

Moments later, a waiter appeared.

"I'll have what he's drinking," Merchant said, nodding at Woods.

The two men spent the next hour getting acquainted. Earl said that his son was in the tournament, but he never specifically mentioned Tiger's name, nor did Merchant make the connection that Earl's son was Tiger. Instead, the conversation focused largely on race and golf. Woods was impressed with Merchant's accomplishments in academia, law, banking, and business. He also made a mental note that Merchant was a two-time club champion in Connecticut. Always on the hunt for anyone who could help advance Tiger's career, Earl had yet to come across a black man who was as smart, accomplished, and good at golf as John Merchant. They exchanged phone numbers and agreed to stay in touch.

Tiger ended up winning the tournament, coming from behind in dramatic fashion to defeat Ryan Armour by making birdies on his final two holes. It was his third US Junior Amateur victory and his eighteenth consecutive victory in junior amateur matches, boosting him to a 22–1 match-play record in four US Juniors. By the time Tiger walked off with the trophy, John Merchant had put two and two together—the man he'd sipped drinks with was Tiger's father. When he got back to Connecticut, Merchant telephoned Earl and congratulated him on his son's remarkable achievement. Earl insisted that they meet at the next tournament, and Merchant agreed. They had a lot more to talk about.

———

Throughout his junior year of high school, Tiger was inundated with scholarship offers. Every top program in the country wanted him. But after visiting UNLV, he came away convinced that Las Vegas was the place for him. He loved the facilities and the climate. The campus was close enough to home—roughly 270 miles away—that he could drive there in less than five hours. Plus, the city had a great vibe. For him, it seemed like the ideal place to go to school. His parents, however, were dead set on Stanford. Academically, the university was right up there with Harvard and Yale, which was important to Kultida. And from a golf perspective, Stanford had one of the top programs in the country.

Everyone, including Stanford's head coach, Wally Goodwin, assumed Tiger was going to go to Stanford. Dina Gravell was one person Tiger felt comfortable talking to about his dilemma. They had become inseparable, and she had chosen to remain at home for her freshman year of college, enrolling at Cypress Community College, to remain with Tiger during his senior year of high school. He told her that he wanted to go to UNLV, but he didn't want to go against his parents or the plan.

Little by little, Tiger had been opening up to Dina, hinting at some of the pressures he felt at home. Gravell wasn't surprised. She'd seen enough to know that Tiger's upbringing had been very different from hers, and more difficult. One time they'd been out having some mischievous fun with friends—toilet-papering houses in the neighborhood—and when they reached Tiger's house, Kultida scolded him in public. "What were you thinking?" Kultida said in a stern voice as Tiger's friends looked on. Then there was Earl, who was constantly singing Tiger's praises to the press, building him up. Gravell didn't want to complicate things.

"Whatever you decide," she told him, "we'll get through it."

Tiger faced another big decision—whom to turn to for a swing coach. Earlier in the year, John Anselmo had been diagnosed with colon cancer and was forced to take a break from teaching while undergoing treatment. Tiger had worked with him for seven years. During that time, he had won his record-setting three straight US Junior Amateur titles, established himself as the top high school golfer in the state of California, and become the most dominant junior golfer in the country. Anselmo hoped to resume coaching Tiger once he regained his strength, but Earl had already been thinking that his son needed someone else to prepare him for turning pro. And he had a specific person in mind.

Claude Harmon Jr., known simply as "Butch" on the PGA Tour, had golfing royalty in his blood. His father, Eugene Claude Harmon Sr., won the Masters in 1948. Butch went on to become the director of golf at Lochinvar Golf Club, an exclusive all-male club in Houston. He was also Greg Norman's swing coach, and in 1993 Norman had the smoothest swing on the PGA Tour.

While Tiger was in Houston to compete in his first US Amateur in August 1993, he paid a visit to Lochinvar. Its relatively small membership included former president George H. W. Bush, gas and oil barons, CEOs, and a number of pro athletes. At Harmon's invitation, Tiger agreed to put on a little exhibition. For Tiger, it was more like an audition. Millionaires who owned private planes, oil rigs, and ranches the size of Rhode Island stopped and admired as Tiger shaped shots around trees with precision and launched golf balls more than three hundred yards through the air. His raw talent and creativity impressed Harmon, but it was the speed and power of Tiger's swing that left the most lasting impression. The adjective that came to mind was *violent*. Tiger swung so violently that he had raw spots on his forearm from the friction created by their rubbing together on his release.

"What's your go-to shot when you aren't swinging well?" Harmon asked.

Tiger shrugged and kept hammering shots off the tee. "Swing as fast as I can, unleash everything I have through the ball," he said. "Then I go find the ball and hit it again."

In other words, Harmon realized, Tiger didn't have one particular shot that he relied on when he really needed to place his ball in a specific location—no three-quarter shots, no knock-down shots, no punch shots: just power. Yet he'd won three straight US Juniors, clearly demonstrating that he knew how to score and how to win. It was almost frightening to contemplate how lethal Tiger would be when he added an array of finesse shots to his repertoire.

The following night, Earl telephoned Harmon from his home in Cypress and asked a direct question: "Will you help take Tiger to the next level?"

Harmon had been hoping Earl would ask. For the previous twenty-four hours, all he'd been able to think about was the prospect of coaching Tiger. He told Earl he was in, and he agreed to waive his $300-an-hour fee. "I know you guys don't have any money, so I'm not going to charge you anything," Harmon told Earl. "But when the day comes and he turns pro and becomes a superstar—and I'm sure he will—I'll send you a bill."

"Deal," Earl said.

Tiger was on the same page with his father when it came to hiring Harmon. But he wasn't talking to Earl or his mother about college. Discussion in the Woods home was so rare that even Tiger's parents didn't know which way he was leaning. Kultida placed an urgent call to Wally Goodwin and hinted that he should make a last-ditch home visit. Goodwin assured her that wasn't necessary.

"I think Tiger and I have cleared up every question," he told her.

"Well, you better come down," she said.

Goodwin didn't like the sound of that. A couple of nights later, he showed up at Tiger's home. Tiger said nothing as Goodwin joined the family for an informal pizza dinner at a card table that was set up in the living room. The atmosphere was awkward, to say the least. With Earl and Kultida struggling to make small talk, the meal felt more like a funeral than a social dinner. Finally, Tiger looked at Goodwin with a somber expression.

"Coach, I have something for you," he said. Then he reached under his chair and retrieved a UNLV golf hat.

"Tiger, what are you doing?" Goodwin said.

Looking him in the eye, Tiger said nothing.

"You didn't ask me to come all the way down here to show me that hat, did you?" Goodwin continued.

Tiger reached under his chair and pulled out a USC golf hat.

Goodwin wasn't amused. "Okay, Tiger," he said, wiping his mouth and getting up from the table.

"No, Coach," Tiger said. "Wait."

Perturbed, Goodwin paused while Tiger reached under his chair and retrieved a third hat. It was red and had an S on it. Without saying a word, he put it on.

Days later, on November 10, 1993, Tiger made it official, signing his letter of intent to attend Stanford. He told the press that it was a straightforward decision.

"The reason I chose Stanford is to better myself as a person," he said. "There's more to life than just playing golf and hitting this little white ball around. My family's always raised me that way. School has always been the number-one priority in our family."

Privately, he rationalized his decision to Dina.

"I don't know how long I'm going to be in college anyway," Tiger told her. "I guess I can just suck it up wherever I go for a while."

Tiger took Dina to his senior prom, but it felt different from when they'd gone to her prom the previous year. In many ways, things had changed. Tiger no longer passed unnoticed through the hallways of Western High. His circle of friends hadn't expanded, but everyone respected and admired him. His classmates even voted him "Most Likely to Succeed." Everything seemed to be falling into place for him. After graduating with a 3.8 GPA, he was immediately going on the road for the summer to play in amateur tournaments. Then in the fall it was off to Stanford on a full-ride scholarship. After that, he would be on the PGA Tour. His life was already neatly mapped out. There were no stop signs, no red lights, no speed limits.

Dina's situation was much more tenuous. She was still living at home, working a minimum-wage job, and attending community college. It felt like she was stuck in neutral, especially when she compared herself to Tiger. But they never talked about her future. Tiger figured she would simply go where he went. But Dina was never comfortable with the spotlight that was always on him. She seldom went to his tournaments because she didn't like the environment. Besides, she couldn't get near him. He was always inside the ropes, and she was lost in the crowd. She couldn't help wondering if she was really cut out for the life that awaited Tiger. Shortly after Woods graduated, Dina told him that she had decided to move to Las Vegas. Her aunt lived there and had offered her a room until she sorted out her future. If nothing else, she needed to get away from Cypress for a while.

Tiger didn't understand. He wanted Dina to remain in Southern California. But Dina didn't see the point. It wasn't as if Tiger was going to be around. He was leaving for college in Palo Alto at the end of the summer. In the interim he would be on the amateur circuit. Either way, they were going to be apart.

"If we really love each other," she told him, "we'll come back to each other."

John Merchant reveled in the distinction of being the first black member on the USGA's executive committee. It gave him a platform to advance his favorite cause—minority participation in golf. Merchant had spent most of his adult life being the only African American on the courses he played, and he would often wonder how to change the situation. His position with the USGA finally afforded him an avenue to help introduce more inner-city youth to the game he had grown to love. It also didn't hurt that word of his personal connection to Earl and Tiger Woods was starting to get around.

In the year since he'd met Earl Woods, he had become like a godfather to Tiger. They had played plenty of rounds of golf together, and Tiger liked to pick Merchant's brain on a range of topics outside of golf. They even traveled together when Tiger played in amateur tournaments. Merchant was under the impression that Earl and Tiger had the best father-son relationship he had ever witnessed. They could finish each other's sentences. Recognizing that Merchant had a lot to offer, Earl increasingly turned to him for advice.

All of this put a little swagger in Merchant's step at the State Consumer Counsel's office in Hartford and at the Country Club of Fairfield, where he liked to brag about Tiger, who spent the summer of 1994 on a tear, winning the Pacific Northwest Amateur, the Southern California Amateur, and the Western Amateur. While Merchant reveled in the ride, a staff attorney in his office at the State Capitol filed an ethics complaint against him, accusing him of using his state office to conduct USGA business—specifically, attending golf tournaments on state time. The Office of State Ethics and the office of the Auditors of Public Accounts launched an investigation, which turned up evidence linking Merchant to Earl Woods.

Tiger likely knew nothing about Merchant's ethics probe, or that his name had surfaced in it. During the summer of 1994, he was preoccupied by a far more devastating discovery: His father had cheated on his mother. Earl had been unfaithful to Kultida for years. Young women would call the house and ask to speak with Earl about private golf lessons. Kultida knew what was going on. Although she and Earl hadn't been intimate in a long time, she remained married to Earl for Tiger's sake.

Earl's womanizing was well-known to his extended family. His own sister, Mae, who loved Earl dearly, famously quipped: "Oh, Lord, if he had been my husband, I'd have shot him." Earl was actually proud of the way he behaved around women and called himself a player, not a cheater. "From all signs, he wasn't ashamed of it," Tom Callahan said. "In fact, he was proud enough of his playing equipment (justifiably) that, if he knew who was at the front door, he didn't mind coming straight from the shower naked." Kultida had thus far managed to keep all of this from Tiger. But Earl had secrets that even Kultida didn't know about, some of which were aggravated by his vices—alcohol, tobacco, and pornography. His habits drove a wedge between him and his family.

On Tiger's seventeenth birthday, the family celebrated by going out for dinner. Some of Kultida's relatives joined the festivities, which amounted to an evening of celebrating Tiger's many achievements and his future. Earl had driven his own car to the restaurant. When everyone headed home, he made a pit stop at a convenience store, emerging with a brown paper bag containing a bottle of Colt 45 and a porno magazine, both of which he consumed alone.

But when Earl retired and began accompanying Tiger to tournaments around the country, it became harder and harder to hide his ways. Tiger soon figured out what was going on.

The family creed was to say nothing—part of being a Woods was keeping secrets all in the family—but eventually Tiger couldn't take it anymore. One night he picked up the phone and called Gravell in Las Vegas. Sobbing, he revealed that his father—his idol—had been unfaithful. Struggling to elaborate, he just cried. In a series of calls that stretched over a period of weeks, Tiger continued to lean on Gravell for support.

He was conflicted over his relationship with his father. He loved him and considered him his best friend, yet he hated some of the things he did. The outspoken comments and grandiose predictions about Tiger's future were embarrassing enough. But Tiger particularly disdained the way that his father had treated his mother. Tiger wanted them to be a family, but he was coming to the realization that they were never going to be one in the traditional sense.

Gravell finally gave him some advice.

"You can't live with these secrets and this pressure," she told him. "You need to have a conversation with your dad. You need to figure out what you really want."

Tiger had finally opened up to Gravell, but opening up to his father was out of the question. They could talk about golf and sports and other mundane subjects, but not about matters of the heart. That just wasn't done.

Tiger was loath to share anything personal about himself with the press, including his goals. He had a lengthy list of them, but his silence on the subject would eventually lead to what he described as a major misconception by the media—that his primary goal was to win more major championships than Jack Nicklaus. Nicklaus's eighteen major championships, however, were not Woods's primary focus. It was age, not numbers, that mattered most to Tiger.

"It was the first time he broke 40, the first time he broke 80, the first golf tournament he ever won, first time he ever won the state amateur, first time he won the US Amateur, and the first time he won the US Open," Tiger explained on the eve of his fortieth birthday. "That was it. That was the list. It was all age-related. To me, that was important. This guy's the best out there and the best of all time. If I can beat each age that he did it, then I have a chance at being the best."

One of the goals on Tiger's list—to become the youngest player ever to win the US Amateur—was front and center at the end of the summer of 1994. Nicklaus had won it when he was a nineteen-year-old junior at Ohio State University in 1959. Tiger was determined to win the US Amateur as an eighteen-year-old yet to enter college. He'd spent a year working with Butch Harmon, dialing down his swing a bit and learning to hit the ball pin-high. "Butchie harped at me to understand how to hit the ball pin-high," Woods explained. "That didn't mean flag-high. Pin-high meant whatever you decided was your number, not necessarily where the flag was. If the flag was 164 yards, maybe I'd want to make sure my ball carried 160 yards to keep it short of the hole and leave myself an uphill putt."

The long hours Tiger put in with Harmon made him a much more complete golfer, and much harder to beat. Yet as the final round wore on at the TPC at Sawgrass in Ponte Vedra Beach, Florida, on August 24, 1994, Tiger appeared destined to come up short in his age-related quest to beat Big Jack. With just thirteen holes to play, he trailed twenty-two-year-old Ernest W. Kuehne III, otherwise known as Trip, by six holes. In order to win, Tiger would have to mount the greatest comeback in US Amateur history.

But when Tiger looked at Kuehne, he saw more than an opponent; he saw an enemy. A two-time state champion in high school, Kuehne had roomed with Phil Mickelson at Arizona State during his freshman year before transferring to Oklahoma State, where he became an All-American. He was an aspiring pro who didn't know what it was like to be hungry.

One year earlier, when Tiger had participated in the Byron Nelson Classic in Dallas, he and Earl had stayed with Kuehne at his family's home in Texas. It dwarfed the Woodses' tiny ranch house in Cypress, and being there for a few days demonstrated what Earl had always preached—that golf was a game played by privileged white people. Trip's father, Ernest II, was a prominent attorney who owned two banks and was CEO of an oil company. He made a point of taking Earl and Tiger to see the facility where Trip and his other two children received private golf lessons from an instructor named Hank Haney. Tiger had little interest in meeting Haney or seeing the facility. He was aware that there were fundamental differences between him and Trip, starting with the way they had learned to play the game, and he didn't like having it rubbed in his face. Neither did Earl. Toward the end of the stay, Trip's father asked Earl, "How can you afford to do all this stuff as a retired military guy?" It infuriated Earl, who took it as an insinuation that a black man couldn't keep up.

Trip Kuehne had learned golf the traditional way—through years of membership at a country club. His father really wanted him to be a pro and pushed him hard in that direction, but Trip had plenty of other options and advantages—the finest schools, financial backing, connections. If golf didn't work out, he would do just fine in finance or business.

Tiger, on the other hand, had learned to play on public courses, and his biggest influence was his father, whose very unorthodox methods in-stilled in him a killer instinct—a mean streak—of the sort that one might expect to find in a boxer. His father was no CEO. His mother was an im-migrant from a distant land. His family had little money and few con-nections. Their only real chance for upward mobility rested squarely on Tiger's golf game.

So at the US Amateur at Ponte Vedra Beach, Tiger wasn't just out there to beat Trip Kuehne; he wanted to beat everything Trip stood for. He wanted to prove to the country-club set that he was better than them.

With his father, John Merchant, and Butch Harmon looking on, Tiger chipped away at Kuehne's lead on the back nine, playing more aggres-sively on each hole as Kuehne became increasingly tentative. With two holes left to play they were all square, and what had seemed impossible ten holes earlier suddenly seemed inevitable as Tiger stepped to the tee on the famed seventeenth hole. Facing the most intimidating par 3 in the world—an iconic island green surrounded by water and connected to the course by a long, narrow neck of grass—Tiger chose the highest-risk shot imaginable. With 139 yards to the hole, he aimed straight for the pin and hit a towering tee shot that landed just to the right of the flag and bounced into the rough, seemingly on its way into the water. But the groans from the gallery turned to euphoric cheers as the ball inexplicably spun back and eased to a stop two feet from the water's edge and fourteen feet from the cup. By the time the cheering had stopped, Tiger was on the island green, standing over the ball with the water at his back. Only the sound of a distant great egret broke the silence as his putter tapped the ball, sending it arcing toward the cup. Initially frozen still, Tiger clenched his right fist and started skipping to his left even before his ball dropped into the cup. Then he punched the sky with a vigorous uppercut. "Yeah!" he yelled, his feet shuffling left to right.

It was a defining moment. Tiger Woods—putter in his left hand, right arm bent at the elbow to form a perfect L-shape—clenched his fist as his white shoes glided over the silky green turf. He had pulled ahead of Kuehne for the first time all day. One hole still remained, but Tiger knew it was over, and he knew that Kuehne knew it too. Moments later, he stood over Kuehne's shoulder as the All-American missed a four-foot putt on the eighteenth hole. Woods won two up.

Tiger had beaten Nicklaus's record as the youngest US Amateur champion, and he'd done it by mounting the greatest comeback in tournament history. And he was the first African American ever to win the tournament.

The promise of greatness was beginning to take hold.

"It's just the start," Earl boasted. Tiger had barely picked up the trophy, and Earl was already talking to a reporter from *People* magazine. "I've seen him accomplish these things his entire life," he continued. "Since the age of eight, he's been the number-one golfer in the world. . . . He's still the same old Tiger and will always be. When he gets a little cocky, I say, 'You weren't shit before. You aren't shit now. And you'll never be shit.'"

After transcribing his interview, the *People* reporter transmitted it to his editor, who decided not to print the quotations from Earl. Instead, those controversial statements ended up in a thick manila file labeled TIGER WOODS. The omission of Earl's statements from the public record helped preserve the budding image of him as a father who was selflessly dedicated to his son's happiness and success.

Fortunately for Tiger, the media had no appetite for probing what was behind Earl's outlandish statements and focused instead on Tiger's remarkable victory at the US Amateur. His achievement landed him on the front page of the *New York Times* and *USA Today*. *Sports Illustrated* dubbed him "The Comeback Kid." Jay Leno and David Letterman wanted him on their shows. Even President Bill Clinton sent him a congratulatory letter.

Back home, Cypress presented Tiger with a key to the city. The ceremony took place at the Cypress Golf Club, where Tiger addressed a crowd of local dignitaries.

"This thing tonight is unbelievable," he told them. "Here I am, only eighteen years old, and I'm getting a key to the city? I'm very fortunate to have the City of Cypress do something like this for me. I've been very fortunate to have great parents who love me to death."

But not everyone back home was happy for Tiger. His burgeoning celebrity status rubbed a few people the wrong way, especially at the navy course, where he'd practiced throughout his youth and had enjoyed special privileges. For years, assistant pro Joe Grohman had been quietly allowing Tiger and Earl to golf for free, and they were given golf carts and offered tokens for range balls without paying as well. These were the perks that came with being revered. But some members of management began to resent them.

According to Grohman, a couple of weeks before the US Amateur, Tiger received a letter from the course manager outlining "numerous complaints" from members and informing him that he would be required to start carrying a receipt for his green fees on him at all times and to provide it upon request. Shocked, Tiger told Grohman he couldn't believe some members had complained. Neither did Grohman. He believed the club and course manager simply made up the letter to make Tiger feel unwelcome.

Things finally came to a head about a week after Tiger won the US Amateur. He was in his customary spot on the far right side of the practice range one afternoon when Grohman approached on a golf cart.

"Hey, Champ," he said. "Have you seen any guys out here hitting balls into the neighborhood?"

"Yeah, I saw a couple of guys," Tiger replied. "They walked down past the maintenance shed."

Tiger didn't think much of it as Grohman sped off in that direction. He was unaware that moments earlier, a woman had called the pro shop and complained to Grohman about golf balls being launched from the course into her neighborhood. A few minutes after Joe drove off, Tiger was interrupted again, this time by the cart manager. With little explanation, he kicked Tiger off the course. Livid, Tiger gathered his equipment and headed home.

When Grohman returned to the pro shop after unsuccessfully searching for the culprits, he encountered the other assistant pro in tears. He told Grohman that the cart manager had thrown Tiger off the course.

Pissed, Grohman confronted the guy, a Marine.

"What did you do?" he demanded.

"A neighbor lady called and said, 'A black kid is hitting balls into the houses,' so I kicked him out."

"Bullshit!" Grohman yelled. "I took that fucking phone call!"

Tiger was in the kitchen with his parents when Grohman showed up at the front door. Earl invited him in, and after listening to Kultida rail,

Grohman offered to place a call to an African American three-star general, a club member who was in command at the nearby naval base.

"No," Earl told him. "That won't be necessary."

"Goddamn navy!" Kultida said. "Fuck the navy. We don't need the navy."

Nothing unified Earl and Kultida like the sense that their son had been slighted.

"I was prepared to identify the navy course as the place where Tiger grew up playing," Earl said. "They forfeited that right."

Tiger didn't say a word. In two weeks he was heading to Stanford. It was time to move on.

CHAPTER SEVEN

THE AMATEUR

Of Earl's three children from his first marriage, Tiger had the best relationship with Earl's daughter, Royce. In the fall of 1994, Royce was thirty-six years old and living in Cupertino, not far from the Stanford campus. A few days before Tiger was due to arrive in Palo Alto, he called her.

"You still want your house?" he said.

She immediately started laughing. Back when he was three years old, Tiger had promised to buy her a house when he became rich. Every couple of years, Royce would jokingly remind him of his commitment. But it had been quite a while since she'd last teased him about it.

"Yeah," she said jokingly.

"Well, then could you do my laundry for four years?" Tiger asked.

She laughed again.

But he wasn't joking. Sensitive to the fact that Stanford was an elite school and that he had a certain image to uphold, Tiger wanted someone to launder and iron his clothes. These were things that his mother had always done for him. If Royce was willing to do them, he would buy her a new home when he turned pro.

It was an offer she couldn't refuse.

Tiger's first day of classes at Stanford was September 28, 1994. He declared economics as his major, with an emphasis on accounting. But he scarcely had time to meet his professors. He arrived in Palo Alto a few days in advance; checked into his new home—room 8 in Stern Hall; met his roommate, Bjorn Johnson, a long-haired engineering major; picked up his class schedule—calculus, civics, Portuguese cultural perspective, and history from late antiquity to the 1500s; then got on a plane to France. As the winner of the US Amateur, he'd been selected to represent the United States in the World Amateur Team Championship in Versailles. It was the first indication that Tiger was not going to have a traditional college experience.

When the American team arrived at the tournament, the foreign press encircled Tiger as he stepped from the team van. A mob of fans descended on him as well. Cameras clicked and flashed, reporters shouted questions, and fans screamed his name, but the mass of people parted like the Red Sea in *The Ten Commandments* as Tiger made his way to the clubhouse. During the tournament, record-breaking crowds packed the galleries and followed him from hole to hole. Tiger drew more spectators than all the French golfers combined.

During his nine-day stay in France, Tiger helped his teammates outplay the other four-man teams hailing from forty-four countries. The Americans finished first overall, eleven strokes ahead of second-place finishers Great Britain and Ireland. It marked the first time the Americans had won the tournament in twelve years. Tiger finished with the sixth-best overall individual score in the field. And it was clear that his star power reached across the Atlantic Ocean to Europe: The French sports daily *L'Équipe* called him "Tiger la Terreur" (Tiger the Terror), and *Le Figaro* compared him to another child prodigy—Mozart. No American celebrity since Jerry Lewis had been so celebrated by the French media.

Classes had been under way for two weeks when Tiger returned to Stanford on October 10. The Bay Area was swept up in the San Francisco 49ers' quest for a fifth Super Bowl. The man most responsible for assembling the 49ers' dynasty was legendary coach Bill Walsh, who had begun his college head-coaching career at Stanford in 1977 before taking over the 49ers in 1979. Then, after retiring from coaching in the NFL, he had returned to lead Stanford's football program again in 1992.

Tiger had long admired Walsh and his reputation as a "genius" coach, so he went to pay him a visit. Without an appointment, he greeted Walsh's secretary and entered the coach's office. Walsh was thrilled to see him.

Walsh and Woods were both very private individuals with cerebral approaches to their respective sports. Introverts to the extreme, they were more at ease by themselves than in the company of others. Both also had trouble making friends. But that day in Walsh's office, they instantly connected. They were both perfectionists, with similar organizational qualities. Walsh was as interested in learning from Tiger as Tiger was in learning from him.

Walsh encouraged Tiger to drop in anytime—no appointment necessary. Tiger took advantage of the offer, and they started meeting regularly for lengthy conversations. Before long, Walsh did something with Woods that he had never done with any of his football players: He gave Tiger his own personal key to the weight room. No other student-athlete on the Stanford campus had such a key. Within a month, Woods was practically living in the weight room. Other members of the golf team purposely avoided weights, but Tiger lifted more than some members of the football team.

From the moment he arrived in Palo Alto, Tiger had been trying to convince Dina Gravell to move to the Bay Area and attend San Jose State. She was still very much in love with him and wanted to be near him, but she preferred to avoid the whole celebrity scene that continued to grow around him. The last time she had gone to a tournament, she was approached by a reporter, which made her very uncomfortable. Tiger had done his best to shield her, consistently refusing to reveal anything about his girlfriend other than to say she was from his hometown and didn't much care for golf. He wouldn't even say her name. Still, Dina didn't want to leave Vegas. Instead, Tiger convinced her to enter into a pact that they would talk by phone every day. Some days he would call just to tell her he'd had a bad day. Other nights he would talk about the stress he was under at Stanford. But most of the time, he talked about his parents. The situation at home was making it nearly impossible to enjoy his time at school.

While Tiger was away at Stanford, John Merchant started staying in his bedroom whenever he traveled to Southern California to visit Earl. After a couple of stays in the Woods home, it became clear to Merchant that there was a problem between Earl and Kultida. He had been on the road with Earl enough times to see and hear things that led him to believe the marriage was shaky, but he'd figured it was none of his business and hadn't said a word to Earl about his behavior. But when he was in Earl's home, Merchant witnessed things that he could no longer ignore. He'd had it with Earl's foul-mouthed abuse of Kultida, the way he would tell her to "shut the fuck up."

One night during Tiger's freshman year, Merchant finally confronted Earl. "I don't care what you do when I'm not here and the door is closed," Merchant told him. "That's none of my business. But if I don't speak up, my mother will rise up out of her grave and slap the shit out of me if I allow you to continue to verbally abuse your wife as you do in my presence. So stop it, please!"

Merchant figured that if Earl behaved this way in front of him, he no doubt did the same or worse in front of his son; what bothered Merchant most was the effect this would have on Tiger. He knew how much Tiger revered and loved his father, and seeing his father mistreat his mother was bound to do long-term damage.

"Fans of golf and Tiger Woods see only the positive of the father-son relationship and the accomplishments of the son," Merchant explained. "But Tiger's greatest fan, without any question, was his mother. She went to all the tournaments. She walked around the fucking golf courses everywhere he played. She wore the hat. Talk about worship—she loved that boy beyond belief. But Earl treated her like dirt, and it pissed me off. It really did."

The family dysfunction at home weighed heavily on Tiger at college. His parents desperately needed space. They needed separation. But their ability to live apart was restricted by finances: they had virtually no savings, and Earl had retired early to invest all his time in Tiger's amateur career. Until Tiger turned pro, they were stuck living together in a cycle of acrimony and bitterness fueled by Earl's abuse of alcohol and his wandering eye.

Tiger's closest friend on the Stanford golf team was Notah Begay III, a full-blooded Native American who had been the best player on the roster until Woods arrived. Begay had an infectious smile and a great sense of humor. He quickly nicknamed Tiger "Urkel," ribbing him for his resemblance to Steve Urkel, the geeky kid with big round eyeglasses on the sitcom *Family Matters*.

Begay had a serious side too. When Stanford was invited to participate in the prestigious Jerry Pate National Intercollegiate tournament at

Shoal Creek Golf and Country Club, Begay talked to Tiger about the social implications of playing at the course whose racist membership policy
had been the catalyst for a national discussion on race. It had been four
years since the club's founder, Hall W. Thompson, had made his infamous
statement about his club's exclusion of blacks. Begay told Tiger that winning at Shoal Creek would be a slap in the face to those who thought
minorities were inferior.

Tiger didn't see it that way, but he also didn't feel like explaining himself to Begay—nor did he want to discuss the matter with the press. When
the *New York Times Magazine* asked him if racist policies at certain clubs
provided him an added incentive to win at Shoal Creek, Tiger gave a one-
word answer: no. It was a direct repudiation of his father's view. Earl insisted that Shoal Creek's history did, in fact, give Tiger added incentive. "It
provides drive," Earl told the magazine. "It provides inspiration. It provides motivation. It provides toughness."

Earl consistently tried to inject a racial angle into Tiger's golf narrative.
Right after Tiger won his first US Amateur, Earl compared him to boxer
Joe Louis. "Louis was the catalyst that gave black people pride," Earl said.
"He kept us going despite all the racism. It's repeating itself now with
Tiger. Black people from all over the country tell me how proud they were
to watch Tiger perform in the US Amateur."

But when it came to social activism, Tiger didn't want to be that guy
his father was always talking about. As an eighteen-year-old college freshman, he preferred to avoid controversy. It was tiring to always be compared to his father's heroes.

Other than being a world-class athlete, Tiger had very little in common with Joe Louis, who enlisted as a private in the army right after the
US declared war on Germany. He was the heavyweight champion of the
world at that time, and he was beloved by both whites and blacks. When
questioned about joining a racially segregated army, Louis said: "Lots of
things are wrong with America, but Hitler ain't going to fix them." Louis
never shied away from using his celebrity platform to discuss racism, but
Tiger had no taste for it. "The only time I think about race is when the
media ask me," Tiger told a journalist around that time.

Kultida blamed Earl for putting Tiger at the mercy of unwarranted expectation and scrutiny by constantly placing him on a pedestal. Whenever
Earl told the press that Tiger was like this civil rights leader or that athlete

who broke color barriers, Kultida referred to the pontifications as "Old Man bullshit." Tiger was vulnerable, and in her mind, Earl was exacerbating her son's vulnerability. As far as Kultida was concerned, all of Earl's talk about Shoal Creek was just more Old Man bullshit.

When the Stanford team arrived at Shoal Creek, civil rights leaders and protesters were outside the gates. But Tiger walled himself off from all the distractions and dominated the tournament, leading Stanford to victory. After sinking his final putt on the eighteenth green to finish two strokes ahead of the field, he encountered Hall Thompson.

"You're a great player," Thompson said. "I'm proud of you. You're superb."

Tiger didn't have much to say to Thompson. Afterward, when the press asked him about the significance of winning at Shoal Creek, Tiger ignored the implication of the question and talked about the course.

"It's absolutely awesome," he said. "This course was [built] before Nicklaus went crazy with his designs. It's pretty flat and straightforward, and not so diabolical around the greens, except at eighteen. That's the way I like it."

When a reporter pressed him about the social significance of winning at Shoal Creek, Tiger brushed him off. "The significance to me is our team won," he said. "And I also happen to be the individual champion."

Though Tiger would bask in his victory, he was finding that he could not keep a low profile, even though he wanted to. Back at Stanford, at 11:45 one night, Tiger called 911 and reported that he'd been robbed at knifepoint about thirty minutes earlier in a parking lot across the street from his dorm. He was alone in his room when Deputy Ken Bates from the Stanford Police Department arrived to take his statement. Tiger told him that he had spent the evening in San Francisco attending a celebrity dinner with Jerry Rice and other members of the San Francisco 49ers. Then he'd driven back to campus and had just exited his vehicle and remotely activated his car alarm when an individual grabbed him from behind, put a knife to his throat, and said, "Tiger, give me all you got." According to Woods, he wasn't carrying a wallet, but his attacker removed from around his neck a gold chain worth $5,000 that had been given to him by his mother. He also demanded Tiger's Casio wristwatch, then punched Tiger

in the jaw with the same hand that was holding the knife, knocking him
to the ground. His assailant then fled on foot. The only description Tiger
could provide was that the attacker was a male about six feet tall, wearing
dark clothes and white shoes.

Three more officers and a police sergeant knocked on the door of every
dorm room that had windows overlooking the lot where Tiger said he
was assaulted. No one had seen anything. Deputy Bates examined Tiger's
jaw and neck, and, according to his report, found no skin redness and no
scratches. He also looked inside Tiger's mouth and found no visible signs
of trauma or contusion. Tiger followed the officers to the parking lot. The
area was well lit, and Tiger's vehicle was parked beneath a double-headed
street lamp. The lot was located right along a main thoroughfare that had
a fair amount of pedestrian, car, and bicycle traffic. At the officers' request,
Tiger pointed out where he had been knocked down. The dried leaves on
the asphalt were undisturbed. After conducting a second inspection of
Tiger's jaw and finding no evidence that he'd been struck, Deputy Bates
handed Tiger his business card and advised him to call if he remembered
anything else regarding the incident. In his report, Bates made no attempt
to explain the whereabouts of Tiger's wallet or the fact that it—and, presumably, his driver's license—were not on him when he got out of his car
after driving home from San Francisco.

Tiger told Bates that he didn't want anyone to know about the incident. When asked why, Woods said he preferred not to elaborate. Coach
Goodwin showed up right after the police left. He'd been notified of the
incident and wanted to check on Tiger. As soon as the coach left, Tiger
called Gravell in Las Vegas. He was crying when she answered the phone.

"What happened?" she asked.

"I just got mugged," he said.

"Oh, my God! Call the police!"

"I just talked to the police."

Gravell tried not to get hysterical.

"I'm okay," Tiger told her. "I'm just really scared. I don't know if I can
do this anymore."

It was well after midnight, and Tiger had an exam in the morning,
but he kept Gravell on the phone for a long time. He didn't want to talk
about the incident. He wanted to talk about all the pressure he was under.
Stanford was a lot harder than high school. The media interest in him was

relentless. His parents weren't getting along. He felt like he had to turn pro to support them. At least two more times he repeated that he didn't think he could keep going.

"I'm not a kid anymore," he said.

The next morning, while Tiger was taking a final exam, Kultida picked up the phone and called John Strege at the *Orange County Register*. He had been covering Tiger longer than anyone, and was on good terms with the family. Kultida often called him just to talk. Strege was under the impression that she was lonely, but it immediately became clear that this call was different. There was a sense of urgency in her voice as she reported that Tiger had been robbed and beaten at Stanford.

Strege was suspicious and couldn't help thinking, *College freshman, might have been drinking, might have been embarrassed.* But he wasn't about to question Kultida. He called the Stanford Police Department and got the chief to confirm that a student had, in fact, reported being robbed at knifepoint the previous night. He also spoke to Earl, who provided more details. The next day, Strege's story appeared in the *Register* under the headline "Woods Attacked, Robbed at Knifepoint." Earl Woods was the only person quoted.

In response to Strege's story, Stanford took the extraordinary step of going against its policy of not releasing the names of students who are crime victims. On December 2, the university issued a news release: "Golfer Woods Issues Statement on Robbery." It included Tiger's only public comments about the incident.

I was not beaten, and I was not injured. I immediately reported the robbery to the police, and I did not seek medical treatment. My jaw was just sore, so I took some aspirin.

People get mugged every day, and mine was just an isolated incident. I just want to move on from this, bury this in the past. I just want to get through my finals, enjoy a great Christmas, and then come back.

Tiger hoped the story would die after he issued a statement, but Earl wasn't done talking. He told the *Los Angeles Times* that Tiger had sustained a blow, but that the incident hadn't affected his feelings toward Stanford. "He was just in the wrong place at the wrong time," Earl said. By the following day, the incident prompted a headline in the *New York Times*: "Golfer Woods Is Mugged."

Desperately in need of an escape, Tiger couldn't wait to get away for the holidays. But before leaving Stanford, he underwent surgery to remove two cysts on the saphenous vein on his left knee. It marked the first of what would be many surgeries over the course of his career stemming from excessive wear and tear on his body. During this first procedure, the doctor discovered substantial scar tissue. Tiger insisted he'd had a bad knee since childhood. "It's because of stuff I did as a kid," he said. "Wiping out on skateboards, crashing on dirt bikes, jumping off things. I banged it up pretty bad." Interviews with friends and family provide no indication that Tiger skateboarded or rode a dirt bike, much less crashed on them. In any case, the surgery left a long scar behind his knee. Weeks later, the sutures were removed, and he was outfitted with a big brace. When Tiger asked if he was free to play golf while wearing a brace, the doctors advised against it. His response to the doctor's advice was a preview of things to come.

"I said the heck with it," Tiger explained, "and went out and played with my dad at the navy course."

While home for the holidays, instead of taking it easy, Tiger returned to the course he'd been kicked out of a few months earlier. Earl thought it was a bad idea to try playing so soon after the knee surgery, but Tiger talked him into letting him tag along in the golf cart. When Earl wasn't looking, Tiger teed up a ball, blasting a shot right down the middle of the fairway. Asked how his knee felt, Tiger insisted it felt fine. In truth, he was in agony. The swelling was so bad that he could see skin coming through the brace. Determined to keep playing, he kept restrapping the brace tighter and tighter.

"The pain was excruciating," Tiger said of the experience. "And I was dying on the inside."

Yet he managed to shoot 31 on the front nine, which was six under par. At that point, he'd finally had enough.

"You know what, Dad?" he said. "I'm done. I'll just rest it from here."

Despite being in agony, he stayed with Earl for the final nine holes, riding along in the golf cart, his knee elevated and packed in ice. He never let on that he was in pain. *The mind*, he told himself, *is a powerful thing.*

By April 1995, Tiger was ranked number two in the country among all college golfers and was named a First-Team All-American. By virtue of having won the US Amateur Championship the previous summer, he automatically qualified for the Masters, despite the fact that he was still in college. In the midst of the Stanford golf season, he flew to Augusta.

Golf World and *Golfweek* magazines enlisted Tiger to keep "Masters Diaries" of his experience. He had plenty to write about. From the moment he arrived, the galleries were swelling with African American spectators. Everywhere he went, children and teenagers—white and black, rich and poor—lined up to get his autograph. Despite being physically fatigued and mentally exhausted from a grueling week of exams, he was the only amateur golfer to make the cut, and he finished tied for forty-first place, awing spectators and seasoned pros with his poise and power.

His average driving distance—311.1 yards—was the longest in the field. Davis Love III was second, averaging 306.5 yards. But the moment that made pros and spectators stand up and take notice took place after the third round of the tournament. Tiger was on the practice range beside Davis Love III, who would go on to finish second overall. The longest hitter on the tour in 1994, Love pulled out his driver, and spectators started cheering and yelling. They wanted to see if Love could drive a golf ball over the fifty-foot-high netting at the end of the range, some 260 yards away. The netting was there to prevent balls from landing on a main road that ran adjacent to the course.

Love made two attempts, but both hit the net.

"Should I try?" Tiger said.

Love nodded.

Tiger pulled out his driver, which revved up the spectators. Then he crushed a cannon shot that soared over the net and kept on going. Fans were in a frenzy, and every pro on the range stopped to admire the shot. The moment he hit the ball, it was clear to everyone that golf was going to be a different game from then on.

Tiger had barely returned to Palo Alto for the final term of his freshman year when Coach Goodwin asked to see him; there was some trouble with the NCAA. The problem started with those tournament diaries that Tiger had published with *Golf World* and *Golfweek*. The NCAA deemed his writings "a promotion of a commercial publication," which put Tiger in violation of NCAA rules. Stanford also questioned where he got the irons he had used for the final round of the Masters. Tiger's answer: they belonged to his new instructor, Butch Harmon. Stanford wanted to know why he had used Maxfli golf balls rather than the Titleist balls provided by the university. Tiger's answer: Greg Norman suggested he try them.

In the end, Stanford suspended Tiger from the team for one day for writing the diaries. He was not reprimanded over the clubs or the balls. Privately, Tiger was furious. As far as he was concerned, he had done nothing wrong, and he didn't appreciate being interrogated. But he said nothing. Earl, on the other hand, issued a not-so-subtle threat. He hinted to *Sports Illustrated* that "Tiger might leave school early if such annoying NCAA scrutiny" continued.

Tiger wasn't used to his parents' visiting Palo Alto, but they decided to come up for the American Collegiate Invitational a couple of weeks after the Masters. Tiger telephoned Dina in Las Vegas with a simple plea: "Come to Palo Alto. Please?"

Without sharing details, he made it clear that he needed her.

On the same day that 168 people were killed and 680 more were wounded in the Oklahoma City bombing, Dina packed her suitcase with enough clothing for a long weekend trip. The next day, after a short flight, she checked into a hotel room that Tiger had reserved for the two of them in Palo Alto. Television monitors everywhere were tuned to coverage of the search for the terrorists who had detonated a truck full of explosives outside the Alfred P. Murrah Federal Building. Tiger, however, was preoccupied with his own situation. It was more of the same things he'd been talking about with Dina for months—his parents' dysfunctional relationship, the pressure he was feeling. As usual, she listened. Then they spent the night together.

The next day, Dina met up with her parents, who had flown up from Southern California at the last minute to see her and Tiger. The first round of the tournament was uneventful. Tiger played well, and Dina watched from afar with Tiger's stepsister, Royce. Dina had always liked Royce, who went out of her way to treat Dina like a sister. Royce also shared Dina's aversion to crowds and celebrity.

It had been months since Dina had seen Tiger's parents. When she approached them at the tournament, they turned away and walked off as if she weren't there. They didn't even acknowledge her. That evening she related the incident to Tiger. He downplayed it, insisting they probably just hadn't seen her.

On the second day of the tournament, Tiger abruptly quit playing on the eleventh hole, complaining of shoulder pain. After huddling with the medical staff, he informed Dina that he was heading to the hospital for an MRI.

"Do you want me to come with you?" she said.

"No, no," he said. "Go with your parents, and we'll just meet up later. I'll call you."

"I love you," she said.

"I love you," he replied, kissing her good-bye.

Five hours passed without a call from Tiger.

Dina was in her parents' hotel room when the front desk notified her father that an item had been left for him. It was around nine p.m. Intrigued, Dina's father went downstairs and discovered Dina's suitcase and an envelope with his daughter's name on it. He brought them back to the room and handed them to her.

Confused, Dina looked at her father. The suitcase was the one she had brought with her from Las Vegas. How had it gotten there? She'd left it at the hotel across town where she was staying with Tiger. She opened it and discovered that all her belongings had been packed—cosmetics, toiletries, jeans, shoes, bras, underwear. She shook her head. What was going on?

She opened the envelope that had come with the suitcase. It contained a handwritten letter. The familiar handwriting sent a chill down her spine.

Dina,

My shoulder is O.K., it's just a strained and overused rotator cuff. The reason for writing this letter is to inform you of my absolute

anger and disappointment in you. Today, I heard from my parents
that you were telling everyone in the gallery who would listen
that you were "Tiger's girlfriend." Then you have the nerve to tell
me in the clubhouse that when a reporter asks who you were, you
responded with "just a friend." My parents, Royce, Louisa, and
myself never want to talk or hear from you again. Reflecting back
over this relationship I feel used and manipulated by you and your
family. I hope the rest of your life runs well for you. I know this is
sudden and a surprise, but it, in my opinion, is much warranted.

Sincerely,
Tiger

P.S. Please mail my necklace that I gave you to me when you get
back home. Don't show up at the tournament tomorrow because
you are just not welcomed.

Trembling, Dina handed the letter to her mother. None of it made
sense. She hadn't approached anyone in the stands. She'd avoided people. Royce could attest to that. Besides, how would Earl and Kultida have
known what she'd done in the stands? They'd avoided her for two days.
And what did he mean when he said he couldn't be in this relationship
anymore? They'd been together for almost four years! They were best
friends. They shared everything with each other. He was the first person
she'd been intimate with. Neither of them had been with anyone else.

Wiping tears from her cheeks, she called Royce.

"I just got this letter from Tiger," she said. "I don't understand."

"He's gone, Dina," Royce said softly.

"I just want to talk to him."

"You're not going to be able to talk to him."

"I don't understand!"

"I'm so sorry. I'm not allowed to talk to you anymore."

Not allowed? Who said so? What was going on?

Dina hung up and buried her face in her hands. Her mother handed
the letter to her husband and wrapped her arms around Dina. Her daughter didn't deserve to be treated this way. It galled her that Tiger's parents
had accused her daughter of being something other than his best friend.

"You don't need that in your life," she told Dina.

Dina just sobbed.

The next day, the team physician told Tiger that his MRI had revealed scarring in his right rotator cuff, which Tiger attributed to a high school baseball injury. "I played baseball and threw my arm out," Woods said. "I had a tear in my rotator cuff, so I had to stop that."

Tiger's medical team accepted his explanation. But it was a curious diagnosis, given that Tiger didn't play high school baseball. In fact, there's no evidence that Tiger was a member of any sports team besides the golf team. "As I started junior high," he later wrote, "Mom and Pop told me I had to choose one sport." Yet over the years he made multiple references to playing baseball and running track and cross country at Western High. But one Western coach recalled that Woods had wanted to join the track team as a 440 runner, and when he was told it would require six-thirty-a.m. workouts three days a week, he dropped the idea. And Tiger's coach, Don Crosby, confirmed that Woods definitely did not play any other sports in high school. Meantime, the medical team at Stanford made no mention of whether Tiger's aggressive new weight-lifting regimen might have played a role in his shoulder injury.

While Tiger met with the medical staff, Dina boarded a plane back to Las Vegas. Woods had just cut off his best friend and first true love and lover, a girl who had befriended him in an accounting class, introduced him to her friends and family, stayed in Cypress after graduating from high school just to be near him, and held in confidence everything that he had ever told her. But Tiger's parents were done with her. They didn't want anyone to hold their son back. And Tiger wasn't going to fight that battle, not even for the love of his life. He didn't call Dina the next night, or the night after that. Once he had ended the relationship, he never spoke to her again.

Eight months passed. Then one day, Tiger wrote Dina a letter.

I am truly sorry for what I did to you and your family. I regret the actions I took. I know that was not the way it should have ended, for that I am truly sorry. I really hope you have moved on and found someone who will make you happy in every way because

you certainly deserve it. I wish you the best in whatever you do.
Good luck.

Warmest regards,
Tiger

He never received a response from her. The way he had broken things off was so jarring that Dina felt like her best friend had suddenly died. She was convinced Tiger's parents had put him up to it.

"I think his parents felt I was going to interfere in his life," she said. "I would never have done that. I loved him too much for that."

CHAPTER EIGHT

RICH FRIENDS

On April 17, 1995, Connecticut's Office of State Ethics issued a press release saying it had found probable cause to support the allegation that John Merchant had violated state law by failing to take full vacation days or personal leave days when traveling out of state to attend golf tournaments in his capacity with the USGA. In the ongoing investigation, Merchant had also acknowledged using his secretary, office telephone and fax machine, and state-issued car for personal business. A hearing before a judge trial referee had been set for later in the year. At the same time, a lawsuit alleging that he had retaliated against the whistleblower in his office was advancing in federal court. Merchant wasn't too concerned; he was satisfied he hadn't done anything wrong. And he and Earl Woods were on to much bigger things.

But Earl had a problem. When Tiger had entered Stanford, IMG had stopped paying Earl $50,000 per year to be a talent scout, concerned about NCAA rules that strictly prohibited payments to family members as possible inducements to sign with an agent. "My recollection is that his relationship with IMG terminated when Tiger went to college at Stanford, because any association would have breached NCAA regulations," said Alastair Johnston, IMG's former head of worldwide golf operations, in an email.

Pressed to come up with money to fund Tiger's aggressive tour schedule on the amateur circuit during the summer of 1995, Earl approached Merchant for help. Together, they came up with a clever idea: they would leverage Tiger's celebrity status by offering well-heeled members of exclusive country clubs a chance to golf with him in exchange for a contribution to the cause. They would also invite minority children from nearby cities to participate in clinics with Tiger. Since Tiger's amateur status prohibited him from receiving payments, the contributions would actually go to Earl, who would give a speech prior to any round of golf with Tiger. Merchant could think of no better place to implement the plan than in his own backyard—Fairfield, Connecticut, home to two of the most affluent zip codes in the United States. It also had two prestigious golf courses: Brooklawn Country Club and the Country Club of Fairfield. Merchant liked to say that it was easier to get into Augusta than it was the Country Club of Fairfield. But as the club's first black member, he had no fears about getting Earl and Tiger in for a day. "You don't want to start an argument with the colored guy," he said with a smile.

In mid-June, Tiger was scheduled to play in the US Open at Shinnecock Hills Golf Club in Southampton, New York. Fairfield is a short distance across Long Island Sound from Southampton. Merchant lined up a clinic for minority youth with Tiger at Brooklawn and an exhibition with him at the Country Club of Fairfield. Then, during the same week that state officials notified him a hearing was being scheduled in his ethics case, Merchant telephoned General Electric CEO Jack Welch for funding.

Welch and Merchant were more than acquaintances. They had both joined the Country Club of Fairfield in the same year, and they were friendly enough that Merchant reached out to Welch directly for support for his bold initiative. He offered Welch a chance to play a round with Tiger. A day after their conversation, Merchant received a call from an individual at the GE Foundation.

"Mr. Welch asked me to call you," the caller began. "We can help, providing your budget doesn't exceed $10,000."

With the cost of the event covered, Merchant went after individual donors. On April 24, he wrote individual letters to forty-four CEOs, bankers, and other corporate titans in Fairfield County. One of the recipients was John Akers, former CEO of IBM, who sat on the board of directors at the New York Times Company. Merchant sent the letter to Akers's home in Westport, Connecticut.

April 24, 1995

Dear John:

On the morning of June 19, 1995, Tiger Woods will conduct a golf clinic for minority youngsters, and others, at Brooklawn Country Club. The General Electric Foundation has graciously consented to underwrite the clinic, which is being co-sponsored by People's Bank and Hall Neighborhood House in Bridgeport.

Following the clinic, Hall Neighborhood House has invited Earl Woods to address a group of fifty to sixty persons at the Country Club of Fairfield. Earl Woods will share some of his experiences in fathering and raising his son at lunch scheduled at 12 noon at the Country Club of Fairfield.

After lunch and the talk by Mr. Woods, eleven (11) foursomes are invited to play a round of golf at Fairfield and attend a short reception following the round.

You are cordially invited to participate in the lunch, golf and the reception. Also, while it is not necessary, if you care to contribute to the honorarium to be given Earl Woods for his talk, you may do so by sending a restricted grant to Hall Neighborhood House.

I sincerely hope that your schedule will permit you to be present at the Country Club of Fairfield to hear Earl Woods and to play a round of golf. Both Earl Woods and Tiger will join us for golf and the reception. Please indicate on the enclosed postcard your acceptance not later than May 15, 1995.

Sincerely,
John F. Merchant

Merchant and Earl didn't stop there. With Tiger scheduled to participate in the Northeast Amateur Invitational in Rhode Island in late June, they figured they should try the same approach there. A day after sending letters to prospective Connecticut donors, Merchant sent a memo to a leading Rhode Island businessman with ties to the Northeast Amateur.

FROM: JOHN F. MERCHANT
SUBJ: EARL WOODS SPEAKING

The enclosed letter was sent to forty-four (44) golfers who, along with about a dozen non-golfers, are invited to lunch at the Country Club of Fairfield to hear Earl Woods speak. Earl will be presented with an honorarium for speaking and this fact does not affect Tiger's amateur status in any way.

On the morning of June 19th, Tiger will give a clinic for minority youngsters, and others, at Brooklawn Country Club. In the afternoon, I have invited Tiger to play a round of golf with me and Jack Welch (GE CEO whose foundation will underwrite the clinic costs).

The memo and the attached letter was intended to suggest a blueprint for doing something similar in Rhode Island. Across the top of the faxed documents read the words "SENT BY: STATE OF CONNECTICUT." While state investigators were preparing a case against Merchant, they had no idea that he had moved on to more ambitious efforts to generate funds for Team Woods. The USGA, on the other hand, could only hope that none of this leaked to the press. One recipient of Merchant's letter faxed a copy to USGA executive director David Fay, along with a memo dated May 5, 1995:

TO: DAVID FAY
SUBJECT: EARL WOODS

David, I am sending this to you, not to expose these activities of John Merchant, but more for you to advise me further on what I can do ethically within any written or non-written code of the USGA.

John sent to me . . . the enclosed memo which outlines something he would like me to do.

I am always a soft touch to help an Amateur player. Would it be, in your judgment, improper for me to make a contribution to the Connecticut event? I am a bit torn since I know whatever I do for Earl Woods, it is like putting money in Tiger's pocket, and that should not be the spirit of all of this.

Pending your response, I may call John and say I would be willing to talk to a banker and see if they want to enter into a loan with this young man. People borrow money for their college education, and is this any different?

Fay was used to being asked to weigh in on whether Earl was operating within the guidelines of amateur golf. As far back as 1991, Fay had consulted with Earl on the various rules. Later, when agent Hughes Norton came up with the idea of putting Earl on IMG's payroll as a talent scout, the agency's CEO, Mark McCormack, urged Earl to meet face-to-face with Fay. The USGA determined that IMG could pay Earl as long as he wasn't designated an agent. The USGA also permitted Earl to negotiate with Nike and Titleist. Essentially, the organization was willing to look the other way because it wanted Tiger to keep participating in the US Amateur tournaments.

"If you ask me," Fay said, "Earl always had his son's best interests at heart, and he received good counsel from a number of quarters, including the USGA."

The best counsel that Woods received came from Merchant, whose primary concern was that Earl liked to run his mouth and might draw unnecessary scrutiny by saying too much. "I told Earl, 'People are paying attention. You better keep your mouth shut.'"

Merchant had essentially memorized the USGA rule book, and he deftly maneuvered Earl and Tiger to remain in compliance. He may have pushed the envelope, but he never crossed the line. When a corporation offered its private jet to fly Tiger from Long Island to Connecticut for the minority golf clinic at Brooklawn Country Club after the US Open, Merchant nixed it, determining that it would jeopardize his amateur status. But he allowed Tiger to accept a complimentary car ride—including tolls—because the rules didn't forbid it.

Still, Fay couldn't help noticing that Merchant's ethics controversy with the State of Connecticut was drawing more and more attention, none of which reflected well on the USGA.

When Tiger arrived at his first US Open, he went to the press tent at Shinnecock and left a one-page statement on the table. It read: "The purpose of this statement is to explain my heritage for the benefit of members of the media, who may be seeing me play for the first time. It is the final and only comment I will make regarding the issue. My parents have taught me always to be proud of my ethnic background. Please rest assured that is, and will be, the case. Past, present and future. The various media have portrayed me as African-American, sometimes Asian. In fact, I am both."

It was an odd way of introducing himself to the reporters covering the PGA Tour. Worse, when reporters tried to engage him, Tiger had little to say. Part of that was his personality, but most of it was a result of being raised to distrust the press. His father fancied himself a media expert, and he taught Tiger to keep reporters at arm's length and never reveal himself when doing interviews. It drove Merchant crazy to see Tiger come across so poorly, especially when he had so much charisma and charm. But rather than say anything to Earl, Merchant chose to bite his lip.

In the opening round, Tiger shot a 74, four over par. The only other amateurs in the tournament—Chris Tidland and Jerry Courville—shot 70 and 72, respectively.

"It wasn't my fault," Tiger said afterward. "I didn't make bogeys due to bad ball striking. I just couldn't make my putts."

His second round didn't start much better. He was seven over par for the tournament and looking like he wouldn't make the cut when he approached the fifth tee. Then he spotted Earl standing behind the gallery ropes. With Earl looking on, Tiger hit his ball into the rough. When he emerged from the high grass, he told his partners Ernie Els and Nick Price that he had to withdraw, saying he had sprained his wrist and "couldn't hold on to the club with normal grip pressure."

The *New York Times* reported that Tiger Woods left the US Open with his wrist taped and that he would require treatment. The folks whom John Merchant had lined up at Brooklawn and the Country Club of Fairfield started asking questions. They figured the clinic and the exhibition would be called off. Merchant told everyone not to worry.

Founded in 1895, Brooklawn Country Club was one of the first clubs to gain membership in the United States Golf Association. Redesigned by renowned golf course architect A. W. Tillinghast and steeped in tradition, its par 71 course featured sculpted, tree-lined fairways and heavily bunkered greens. More than a hundred inner-city youth who had been bused in from nearby Bridgeport sat cross-legged near the sixteenth green, gazing up at Earl, who opened the clinic by telling them how important it was to practice with a purpose. Then Tiger stepped up to an auxiliary tee with an iron in hand, and the real show began.

"Tiger," Earl said, "I want you to hit a fade at those trees and bring it back into the center of the fairway."

Tiger struck a high, sweeping shot that hugged the tree line on the left before cutting right and landing exactly where Earl had commanded.

"Now, Tiger," Earl said, "I want you to hit toward the right trees and draw it back into the middle."

Again Tiger swung, and the ball did exactly as Earl had instructed. One by one, the mouths of the Bridgeport youths opened.

"Now, Tiger," Earl said, "I want you to hit a stinger to the same spot."

Tiger blasted a low-flying bullet not ten yards off the ground that nestled up next to the other balls. Dozens of mouths popped open. Even the adults on hand for the exhibition looked on in wonder. "You could have thrown a blanket over those three balls," said Athan Crist, a longtime member and club historian who witnessed the display. "You know what it's like when you're a kid and you're watching magic tricks? That's exactly what it was like."

The clinic went on for nearly forty-five minutes, with Earl barking out orders and Tiger responding on command: a sand wedge to the base of a tree; an 8-iron to the same spot; and on and on, Tiger never missing once. For his final trick, Tiger pulled out a 3-wood and drove the seventeenth green more than three hundred yards away. Then he put his club in the bag and faced the kids.

A child raised his hand and asked, "Tiger, what was your best score?"

Earl answered the question.

Another child raised his hand. "Tiger, what's your favorite club?"

Earl answered again.

A third child's hand shot up.

"Yes," Earl said, acknowledging the boy.

The boy pointed at Tiger and said, "Does he talk?"

Tiger wasn't thrilled about doing exhibitions and clinics. He had just come off a grueling stretch, during which he lost fifteen pounds after a bad bout of food poisoning in the middle of the Pac-10 tournament, followed by a frustrating second-place finish to Oklahoma State University at the NCAA Championships in Columbus, Ohio. Upset with his performance during the first round at Ohio State's 7,109-yard Scarlet Course, Woods slammed his club into the turf after a poor shot on the twelfth hole. Moments later, after another disappointing shot, he broke his wedge by slamming it into his bag. His outburst drew a rare warning from NCAA officials. Still, he carried Stanford through the later rounds and almost single-handedly delivered the championship. But his twenty-five-foot putt for birdie on the eighteenth hole of the final round grazed the cup, forcing the first sudden-death round in the ninety-eight-year history of the tournament. On top of all this, he finished his freshman year with a 3.0 GPA, pledged Sigma Chi, and did well on his final exams.

More than anything, he needed a break, but there was no time for that. His summer was booked solid with amateur events, and the exhibitions Merchant had lined up were covering all of Tiger's travel expenses and entry fees. At the Country Club of Fairfield, he and Merchant were paired with the club pro and the eight-time club champion for eighteen holes. As reliable as Old Faithful, Tiger's command performance awed spectators and put a big smile on Merchant's face. But after the round, Tiger made himself scarce at a private reception in his honor in the dining room overlooking the eighteenth green. While his dad and Merchant downed cocktails and held court with club members, Tiger slipped out and went to a putting green, where he practiced putting for two hours in silent solitude.

Sitting in the back of a rental car, Tiger passed through a black, wrought-iron security gate and was ferried past leafy oak and maple trees before easing to a stop at a gigantic wood-shingled home situated on the eighth hole at Point Judith Country Club in Narragansett, Rhode Island. The house belonged to club member Tommy Hudson, who had agreed to let Tiger and his team—Earl, Merchant, and sports psychologist/caddie Dr. Jay Brunza—use the place during the 1995 US Amateur, being held twenty-five miles away at the Newport Country Club. Everything—the house, the food, greens fees, transportation—had been arranged by Ed Mauro, past president of the Rhode Island Golf Association. Nobody was more connected—or more gracious—than Mauro, whom Merchant had called months earlier with a request for accommodations.

Tiger followed Mauro inside the house and chose his bedroom. He could walk out the back door and step onto the course. He had stayed in a lot of homes while on the amateur circuit, but this one offered everything Tiger was looking for in a future residence: security, seclusion, and a golf course for a backyard.

Mauro invited everyone to his home for a barbecue. Some of Mauro's extended family attended, eager to meet Tiger. Weary from always being the center of attention, Tiger quietly slipped into the house. Looking for a place to disappear, he drifted into the den, where he unexpectedly encountered Mauro's fifteen-year-old grandson, Corey Martin, who had been forced by his mother to go to the barbecue. Corey, bored, had made a beeline for his grandfather's den and turned on the television. Totally disinterested in golf, he had never heard of Tiger Woods, nor did he realize that Tiger was the guest of honor. He just figured Woods was some teenager who had ended up at his grandfather's barbecue.

"Hey, what's going on?" Corey said.

"What are you watching?" Tiger asked.

"*The Simpsons*," Corey said.

Tiger took a seat, and Corey fetched a couple of bowls of ice cream. While they laughed at the antics of Bart and Homer, Corey made small talk, asking Woods where he was from and what he was doing in Rhode Island. Tiger quickly realized that Corey didn't even know he was a golfer. His naïveté allowed Woods to drop his guard, and he admitted to Corey that he wished he could dye his hair purple just to rile people up.

After about thirty minutes, a couple of Mauro's younger grandchildren entered the den. They knew nothing about Tiger either. They just thought he was big and handsome and funny. Stretched out on the floor in front of the television, he let the kids recline against him as if he were a giant pillow. One of them nodded off with her head resting against him.

The approach to the Newport Country Club is a bit like coming upon the set of *Downton Abbey*—majestic, with a breathtaking sense of grandeur built with old money. The club was established in 1893 after Theodore Havemeyer, whose family owned the American Sugar Refining Company, convinced some of the wealthiest men in America at the time—John Jacob Astor, Perry Belmont, and Cornelius Vanderbilt—to purchase a 140-acre farm overlooking the ocean. Two years later, in 1895, the Newport Country Club hosted the first US Amateur Championship and the first US Open. For the one-hundredth anniversary of the US Amateur, the tournament had returned to its birthplace.

By this time Tiger had already visited many of the greatest courses in America, but this was his first trip to Newport. From the balcony off the second-story locker room in the clubhouse, he could look out over the first fairway and see all the way to the water. It was a view normally reserved for members of a very exclusive club. Although he wasn't a member, Tiger did receive exceptional treatment.

Early in the week, club pro Bill Harmon, Butch's brother, offered to familiarize Tiger with the course. It was one of the perks of working with Butch. There were things, Bill insisted, that Tiger needed to know before playing there. For starters, the wind off the water would swirl and unexpectedly change directions. He would have to learn to control his ball in the wind. Also, Newport didn't irrigate its fairways, relying instead on natural growth. The result was a hard, dry surface, especially in the summer. On a wet course, Tiger would be able to use his driver to hit bombs, knowing the ball would sit down where it landed. But the ball responds much differently on a dry course. And there had been very little rain in Newport that summer.

"So, for example," Harmon told him, "on the third hole, which is 340, if the wind is behind you, hit a 2-iron or a 3-iron and just get it up there. Take your par and move on. Do *not* try to bury this hole."

But the most important advice Harmon gave Tiger was about the greens, which had settled over the previous hundred years, resulting in some deceptive breaks. "They don't break the way they look," he explained. "There's no way you can read them correctly the first time." Eager to learn anything that would give him an edge, Tiger watched as Harmon showed him at least two or three putts on every green and on certain pin placements. To Harmon's amazement, Tiger adapted quickly, studying the unique way the ball broke on each green, cataloging that information in his head, and adjusting his approach accordingly.

They were joined by Butch, who had flown in from Texas for the tournament. Tiger had been working with Butch Harmon for two years at that point, refining his swing and learning new shots. One of the shots Harmon had been teaching him was the knockdown, a low-flying punch shot used mainly for control in windy conditions. Tiger had yet to try the shot in a tournament setting, but Harmon insisted that, to win at Newport, it would be critical for him to use it. "There are holes on the golf course where you're going to need that shot," Harmon assured him.

Tiger arrived at the Newport Country Club with a police escort for the start of the final day of match play. The crowds had swelled to the thousands, and John Merchant had voiced concerns about Tiger's safety. Looking straight ahead, Tiger didn't say a word as his security detail cut a wedge through the throng of people who had turned out to see him. With Jay Brunza at his side, Tiger stepped to the first tee, just off the east end of the clubhouse. Spectators packed the second-story balcony overlooking the tee. Hundreds more wrapped the green. Tiger relished the opportunity to make history by becoming just the ninth player to win back-to-back amateur titles.

The one man who stood in his way was George "Buddy" Marucci, a forty-three-year-old Mercedes-Benz dealer from Pennsylvania. Marucci played like a man with nothing to lose. Tiger trailed him by one after the completion of the first eighteen holes.

With a couple of hours to go before the start of the final round in the afternoon, Tiger retired to the clubhouse. While Marucci showered and joined club members for lunch, Tiger isolated himself. On a couch outside the ladies' locker room, he put his head back and closed his eyes. For an hour he spoke to no one, choosing instead to practice the mind-relaxation exercises Brunza had taught him. When he emerged for the final round, he had on a bloodred golf shirt, a red-brimmed Stanford cap, and a no-nonsense, steely stare.

Marucci opened the second half of match play by winning what amounted to the nineteenth hole to go two up. By the time Tiger stepped to the eighteenth tee for the thirty-sixth and final hole, he was leading Marucci by one. Using a 2-iron, he drove his ball over a fairway bunker, leaving himself about 140 yards to the hole. He faced a big decision. Marucci's ball was already on the green in two, and he would have a twenty-three-foot birdie putt that could force sudden death. Tiger's shot was uphill, a situation that called for a pitching wedge or a 9-iron. Instead, Tiger asked Brunza for his 8-iron. It was time to attempt the knockdown shot he'd been working on all summer with Butch Harmon.

Tiger lifted his ball over the flag, dropping it fourteen feet behind the hole. But the backspin, coupled with the terrain, drew the ball all the way back to within eighteen inches of the cup. The crowd erupted, but no one was more excited than Tiger. Moments later, his putt was conceded and he won, winning his second consecutive US Amateur title. After a long, tearful embrace with his father, Tiger yelled to Butch Harmon.

"Did you see it, Butch?" Tiger shouted. "I did it! I did it!"

"I told you you could, Tiger!" Harmon said. "I told you you could."

"Butch, I really did it! I actually did the one you taught me!"

When he was handed the Havemeyer Trophy, Tiger smiled and held it over his head. "This one should be dedicated to the Brunza family," he said, turning toward his caddie. "This one's for you, Jay."

Brunza started crying. A month earlier, his father had passed away. The fact that Tiger remembered Brunza's father in such a triumphant moment was a thoughtful gesture. It was a standout moment for Tiger, appearing humble in the aftermath of such a significant achievement.

Afterward, in the merchandise tent set up in front of the clubhouse, Tiger was surrounded by tournament officials, senior club members, Butch and Bill Harmon, and *Sports Illustrated* writer Tim Rosaforte, who was on hand to chronicle the historic moment. Earl was there too. But on his way to the tent he had wandered into the country-club bar and downed a few drinks. Butch Harmon poured champagne into the Havemeyer trophy, and everyone applauded. Tiger didn't drink from it, but Earl did. Then he took the trophy from Tiger.

"How do you like this, Bobby Jones?" Earl said, hoisting the trophy above his head as if it were his. "A black man is the best golfer who ever lived."

Everyone stopped clapping, and an awkward silence amplified Earl's voice.

"Bobby Jones can kiss my son's black ass," he continued.

Tiger's youthful smile quickly faded as he stood stoically beside his father during the two-minute rant. Observers stared down at their feet in stunned disbelief. At nineteen, Tiger had just won his second-straight US Amateur in dramatic fashion, and what should have been a moment of pure joy for him and unspeakable pride for his father had been tarnished by an outburst of anger, resentment, and bitterness. As Earl wound down by predicting his son would have a bigger impact on golf than Jack Nicklaus, Bill Harmon reached into his pocket and rubbed a round chip between his index finger and thumb. A recovering alcoholic, Harmon was celebrating the third anniversary of his sobriety that day. Hours before the start of the final round of the tournament, he had gone to a meeting, where he received his three-year chip. Looking at Earl, he saw something familiar. "That's how I acted when I was drinking," he thought to himself. "Boy, this is all I need to know about being on the right path."

Tim Rosaforte faced a dilemma. If he wrote verbatim what Earl had said, the ramifications would potentially be devastating for Tiger. In addition to being difficult to explain to the general public, Earl's racially inflammatory comments could unfairly stigmatize his son, prompting corporate America to hesitate when considering whether to sign him as a spokesman once he turned pro. Instead, Rosaforte handled the situation with class, choosing not to complicate Tiger's future. His piece, titled "Encore! Encore!," appeared in *Sports Illustrated* days later. It began with the scene in the merchandise tent:

> *"I'm going to make a prediction," Earl Woods said Sunday night, as champagne both tingled and loosened his tongue. "Before he's through, my son will win fourteen major championships."*
>
> *America's most prominent golf father clutched the Havemeyer Trophy, from which he was drinking, and looked around the empty merchandise tent near the clubhouse of the Newport (RI) Country Club. The handful of friends and autograph seekers laughed and cheered. His son, nineteen-year-old Tiger Woods, smiled too—but bashfully. It's embarrassing when Dad blurts out your own secret thoughts.*

After graciously thanking everyone at the Newport Country Club, Tiger got into the back seat of a vehicle being driven by Brunza. Earl was in the passenger seat. Clutching the trophy, Tiger said little on the drive back to the house in Point Judith. Then Earl announced that he needed to relieve himself. After crossing the Jamestown Bridge, Brunza pulled into a convenience store parking lot. Earl had been inside for a few minutes when Tiger entered and found his father hitting on a young woman who was working behind the counter. He was creating a scene, but Tiger knew what to do.

"Pop, c'mon," Tiger said quietly. "You can do better than that."

Then he led his father back to the car, never criticizing him.

It would not be the last time that Tiger filled the role of the father and Earl the role of the son.

CHAPTER NINE

RAMPING UP

It had been a very long summer, almost all of it spent on the road. The more Tiger saw of the world, the more he realized that Stanford was a utopia. It wasn't the real world, which was precisely why he wanted to spend more time there. After a turbulent freshman year, Tiger was relieved to be back in school for his sophomore year. His golf game was certainly ready for the PGA Tour, but mentally and emotionally he wasn't prepared to live the life of a pro. Not yet, anyway.

School was the one place other than a golf course where Tiger felt mentally engaged and intellectually challenged. The classroom at Stanford was like a cerebral contest among him and his peers. All he had to do was look around the classroom, and his desire to excel kicked in. Plus, Stanford was on the cutting edge of things that mattered to him. It was one of the first schools in the country to offer email addresses to its students, and some of the Stanford faculty consulted for the internet companies that were shaking up Wall Street. Many of the e-companies and venture-capital firms supporting them were within driving distance of campus. As an economics major, Tiger had classes with professors who were knowledgeable about the online revolution. All of this fostered his interest in finance and business and got him thinking more and more about the economics of golf, and what it would be like to be incorporated.

Classes had barely resumed when Tiger got a call from Arnold Palmer. He was playing in a seniors' event in Napa, California, about an hour-and-a-half drive from Palo Alto, and he invited Tiger to meet him for dinner at the Silverado Resort and Spa. Tiger got into his Toyota, his golf clubs in the back, and started driving fast. He never worried about his speed. He didn't have time to worry about rules. He was on his way to dine with one of the greatest golfers of all time. *How cool is that?* he thought.

Tiger had met Arnold once before, back in 1991, at Palmer's Bay Hill Club in Orlando. But this was different. They talked for nearly two hours over a steak dinner. Much of the conversation centered around life off the course. For instance, Tiger wanted Palmer's advice on how to deal with fans (although he would go on to ignore pretty much all of it). They spent most of the time, however, talking about the pros and cons of turning professional. The evening marked the beginning of a friendship. Palmer was one of the few people Tiger truly admired, and Palmer genuinely cared about Tiger.

Two weeks later, Coach Goodwin pulled Tiger aside. He'd heard about the dinner, and he had just one question: "Did you pick up the tab?"

Silly question, Tiger thought. *I'm a nineteen-year-old college student. Palmer is, well, Palmer. Of course I didn't pick up the tab.*

That led to an even sillier question: How much was the dinner?

This whole line of questioning seemed ridiculous. It wasn't as if Tiger examined the check. He had never even seen it.

Goodwin called the NCAA, which determined that the rule prohibiting student-athletes from receiving benefits or gifts based on their status or reputation had been violated. Until he reimbursed Palmer for the meal, Tiger would be ineligible to play. Incensed, Tiger called his parents. Within hours, a $25 check went to Palmer, who then had to fax an endorsed copy of it to the NCAA.

Tiger was fed up with the NCAA, but he let his parents deal with the situation. Kultida again turned to John Strege at the *Orange County Register*. "This is not fair, not for a kid who's trying to set an example for kids who want to follow him by staying in school," she said. "They're trying to drive him out of school."

Earl went even further, blasting the NCAA and the university. "This is the perfect opportunity for Tiger to say, 'Kiss my yin yang,' and to leave school," he said. "Everybody would understand. They [the NCAA and Stanford] just went too far. The irony is that Tiger genuinely likes Stanford and wants to go to school.

"He would be in line to make no less than $25 million [from endorsement contracts]," Earl continued. "Tiger really doesn't need the NCAA, and he doesn't need Stanford. He could leave and be infinitely better off. It sounds like harassment to me. The kid is desirous of following the rules, but sometimes he can't understand the rules."

Once again, something that otherwise would have remained private became very public because of his parents' interference and the media's interest in him. On October 20, 1995—one day after Kultida called Strege about the Arnold Palmer dinner—the following headline appeared in the *Orange County Register*: "NCAA Driving Wedge in Woods' College Career?" It was immediately picked up by other news outlets. When the story broke, Tiger was in El Paso, on his way to winning the Savane College All-America Golf Classic in a playoff. When a reporter asked if NCAA scrutiny might prompt him to leave school early, he sent a subtle message.

"I don't think it would," Tiger said. "But you never know. It's annoying."

He was more than annoyed; he was fed up with the threats of being declared ineligible for doing something as innocent as having dinner with Arnold Palmer. Once he made his displeasure known, it didn't take long for Stanford and the NCAA to back down.

"It's all cleared up," Goodwin told the *Register*. "There's no suspension."

One of the things that Tiger loved most about Stanford was that it shielded him from the public and allowed him to work on his golf game in solitude. The school allowed him the privilege of at-will access to a state-of-the-art weight room, and he never had to compete for time on the practice green. He spent more hours practicing than the rest of the team combined. Plus, Butch Harmon was always just a phone call away. One day, while struggling to master a new shot he wanted to add to his repertoire, he telephoned Harmon, voiced his frustration, and asked for advice.

Harmon laughed. "You're at Stanford," he said. "Why are you on the practice range hitting fucking golf balls? You should be out there getting fucking girls."

Tiger was adept at many things—playing video games, reciting lines from *The Simpsons*, math—but establishing relationships with girls was definitely not one of them. Since ending the only meaningful relationship he'd ever had with a girl, he hadn't started seeing anyone else. The most confident guy on the golf course was a horrible dancer, an awkward talker, and a social misfit around women.

Tiger didn't say much about his situation to Butch Harmon. But during his sophomore year he opened up about it to Jaime Diaz. By that point he had known Diaz for almost seven years, and the comfort level between them was sufficient to let Tiger drop his guard. "I'm not pulling any pussy," he told Diaz.

He said it so cavalierly that it left a lasting impression. "He talked about it that way," Diaz recalled. "He was trying to compensate for not having any game with women, not being attractive to women. He made jokes."

Diaz had been around Earl enough to recognize that Tiger was starting to sound more like his father. "It was just Earl's whole macho ethos toward women," Diaz explained. "You bang as many as you can and then leave them behind."

One thing Tiger discussed with Diaz on numerous occasions was the fact that his increasing fame was exposing him to many more women. Everywhere he went—tournaments, restaurants, airports—women were, if not coming on to him, at least coming *up* to him. College girls, opponents' girlfriends, married women—all types. They wanted their picture taken with him. They wanted his signature. They wanted to put their hands on him just so they could say they'd touched Tiger Woods. He would enter a country club, and the most beautiful woman in the room—the one with red fingernail polish, gold around her neck and wrist, and a big diamond on her finger—couldn't stop staring at him. At his age, no other golfer generated so much interest from women.

"I don't have to work for it," Tiger told Diaz. "I don't have to have any game."

"Be careful out there," Diaz warned, tongue firmly in cheek.

"Don't worry," Tiger told him. "I put on two rubbers."

Diaz was no prude, but he couldn't help noticing the manner in which Tiger increasingly referred to women and his manhood. "Everything was about banging women and showing what a man he was," Diaz recalled. "But it wasn't like he was *doing* it. He was *talking* about it. He knew it was coming his way."

Tired and struggling to make ends meet, Earl Woods sat in his worn-out chair in his cramped living room one day in January 1996. With a pencil and paper, he formed two columns—one for a list of tournaments Tiger needed to enter in the upcoming year, and the other for the anticipated costs of travel and other related expenses:

The NCAA Finals (Chattanooga, TN)	$1,710
The US Open (Detroit, MI)	$2,480
The Northeast Amateur (Rumford, RI)	$1,230
The Scottish Open (Scotland)	$5,850
The Western Amateur (Benton Harbor, MI)	$2,970

On and on it went. By Earl's calculations, there were more than ten critical tournaments, and it fell to him to figure out how to come up with the money. Another year at Stanford meant another year of the dog-and-pony show—hitting the country-club circuit in an effort to raise money to keep the amateur train on track. Things would be a hell of a lot easier if Tiger simply turned pro. The minute that happened, they would be printing money. PGA Tour winnings. Endorsement deals. Licensing agreements. What would it be like to drive a brand-new car, to fly first class, to never have to worry about a mortgage payment or credit card bill or greens fee? And that wasn't all: There would finally be enough money to get Kultida her own home. The day-to-day battles inside the family house on Teakwood Street would end. He could live the way he wanted to live, and Kultida could live comfortably elsewhere. Living expenses would disappear. He could even pick up a six-figure salary working for his son. There were so many possibilities.

Earl had long insisted that money wasn't a factor in Tiger's decision-making process. "There are no expectations or inherent pressure on him to become a pro," Earl told the *Los Angeles Times* in 1992. "There's no financial pressure on him to turn pro, or provide for Dad's welfare. I'm set for life."

But at sixty-three, Earl longed for the one thing that had forever been out of reach: financial security. In need of help, he picked up the phone and called John Merchant.

Merchant was dealing with his own situation. On January 24, 1996, the State of Connecticut determined that he had violated state law by using his state office for financial gain, unilaterally determining that it was in-appropriate to claim work time when he was out of state to attend golf tournaments in his private capacity for the USGA. He was facing a civil penalty of $1,000 and had been ordered to cease and desist from violating the code of ethics. It was front-page news in Connecticut. Insisting that his only mistake was failing to file a form documenting that all the work he did for the USGA was done on vacation time, he paid the fine and told the commission, "Kiss my ass!"

But he also had an even bigger problem: During the Office of State Ethics investigation, Merchant had acknowledged doing golf business on his government computer. Specifically, he claimed he had typed letters in his role as "organizer for a golf clinic featuring US Amateur golf cham-pion Tiger Woods." This admission prompted investigators to subpoena files on Merchant's computer.

Despite all of this, Merchant agreed to help Earl find the money to fund Tiger's tour schedule for the year. With a motto of "Anything for Tiger," Merchant went to work. A few days later he called Earl back with news that he had found a source: an individual whom Merchant described as a "good friend" whom he had "known forever" had offered to finance what he figured would undoubtedly be the final year of Tiger's amateur golf career. The individual was quite familiar with the NCAA rules forbid-ding the payment of student-athletes, but he also recognized that Tiger's family didn't have the means to pay for all the travel expenses associated with touring. He offered to fund Tiger on one condition—he didn't want the money being traced back to him. No one but Merchant was to know he had given money to Tiger. Not even Tiger.

"So," Merchant instructed Earl, "I need you to send me a budget for the year."

At the beginning of February, Merchant received the following hand-written letter in the mail:

January 28, 1996

John,

Attached is Tiger's schedule for 1996 and the expense budget estimated & prepared. Note that hotel accommodations are estimated at $90 per night. Hope this arrives in time for your use.

I've got a lot of things to talk to you about so if you have the time, give me a call.

Sincerely Your Friend (I think)
Earl

The cover letter included a separate document titled "1996 EXPENSE BUDGET." It listed the eleven tournaments Tiger needed to enter, along with the dates, locations, entry fees, airfare, hotel, and meals associated with each one. The grand total: $27,170.

Merchant forwarded the budget to his friend. Within weeks, the transaction was complete. "I saw to it that my guy gave me the money," Merchant said. "And I got it to Earl. And Tiger participated in the tournaments."

The USGA preferred not to confront Merchant and his financial dealings with the Woods family. But it could no longer ignore the controversy swirling around him in Connecticut. The atmosphere was so charged that even Governor John Rowland had weighed in, writing a highly publicized letter that accused Merchant of flagrantly violating public confidence and threatening him with criminal prosecution. Most of Merchant's problems stemmed from his relationship with Earl and Tiger, but that relationship meant more to him than anything else. He had established himself as Earl's go-to guy for all matters legal and financial. With Tiger dominating the amateur golf world, Merchant relished his position as chief advisor and problem-solver for the Woods family. It was an arrangement that fueled his ego and gave him a feeling of being untouchable. So when the governor joined the calls for Merchant to step down as the state's Consumer Counsel, he became more defiant. "No motherfucker tells me what to do," Merchant boomed while reflecting back on that experience in 2015. "You can discuss it with me. But you don't tell me what to do."

After watching the way things were playing out in Connecticut, the USGA decided it did not want to get into a similar scrum with Merchant. Hoping to avoid having to force out the first and only black member to serve on the executive committee, the USGA transitioned him away from the committee by supporting the creation of the National Minority Golf Foundation. Merchant was named its executive director.

Earl liked the fact that Merchant was put in charge of the advancement of minority golf. Together, he figured, they would be able to make serious inroads. But in February 1996, right after Merchant rounded up the money for Tiger, Earl's priorities were elsewhere. He placed another call to Merchant.

"Look," Earl told him, "I don't know what Tiger is going to do. But in case he turns pro, I want everything in place."

Those last five words—*I want everything in place*—were the signal to Merchant that he no longer needed to worry about the State of Connecticut, the USGA, or anything else. He was about to become the personal attorney for Tiger Woods. In the interim, he agreed to be Earl's attorney and to lay the groundwork for Tiger to turn pro. It was understood that Earl didn't have the money to pay Merchant's retainer. Instead, Merchant agreed that he would be compensated later, once Tiger joined the PGA Tour. There was a lot to do in the interim: Tiger needed to sign with an agent; he had to line up a financial advisor; he needed an attorney to help him with estate planning. There would be endorsement deals to negotiate, contracts to sign, a house to purchase. Two houses, in fact—one for Tiger, and one for Kultida.

It was way too much for Earl to contemplate, let alone manage. Nor did he have the financial and legal expertise to guide Tiger through the process. One of his biggest concerns was making sure that sports agent Hughes Norton didn't take advantage of Tiger. Norton had negotiated multimillion-dollar contracts on a regular basis, and he had been aggressively courting Tiger through Earl for years. Earl never told Merchant about the tens of thousands of dollars that Norton and IMG had been funneling to him for being a "talent scout." But he let Merchant know that Norton would be Tiger's agent when the time came.

"You should talk to Hughes first," Earl told Merchant. "Start with him."

Merchant telephoned Norton to set up a face-to-face meeting. Norton had never met Merchant, but Merchant explained that he was Earl's attorney and was helping Tiger with the transition. They agreed to get together. Before hanging up, Merchant had one question: "Just curious, Hughes. What kind of commission do you charge for someone of Tiger's ilk?"

Norton was smart enough to know that Merchant was very new to the business. "Our usual fee is twenty-five percent," he said.

"Hughes, I don't think there's any reason for us to meet."

"What? Why?"

"Let me tell you something," Merchant said. "You don't know me. I don't know you. But I'm sure you know that Lincoln freed the slaves. And I'm not about to let you enslave Tiger with that ridiculous commission."

"Well," Norton asked, "what did *you* have in mind?"

"I hadn't really thought about it," Merchant said. "But somewhere around five percent."

After some back-and-forth, IMG agreed to take something less than the industry-standard 20 percent agent's cut on a sponsorship deal. It was a confrontational start to a relationship between the man Earl had chosen to be Tiger's agent and the man he had chosen to be Tiger's lawyer. Things were going exactly according to plan.

When Tiger showed up at the NCAA golf championship at the Honors Course Club outside Chattanooga in the spring of 1996, he already knew he had won the Jack Nicklaus National Player of the Year Award for being the top college player in the country. His presence completely overshadowed the heavily favored Arizona State team, with its brash group of suntanned, cigar-smoking players. A record fifteen thousand tickets had been purchased for the championship, and the NCAA had issued 225 press credentials, shattering the previous record of 80, which had been issued the year before, when Tiger was a freshman. The crowd and the press were there for one reason, and it wasn't to watch Arizona State.

Tiger didn't disappoint. He easily won the NCAA individual championship, making him the first Stanford golfer to do so in more than fifty years. It capped a remarkable sophomore season in which he:

- Won the Pac-10 Championship with a record-breaking eleven-under-par 61 in the first round.
- Won the NCAA West Regional.
- Set a single-round course record at the NCAA Championships by firing a five-under-par 67 in the second round, while finishing the tournament three under par.

- Ended the season with the lowest scoring average in collegiate golf and ranked number one in the Rolex/Nicklaus Individual Rankings.

As much as he had grown to love living in the bubble of Palo Alto, Tiger realized that, from a golf perspective, he had nothing left to prove by remaining in college. He was far and away the most dominant college player in the country. Although he still had two years to go to complete his degree in economics, he knew that a fortune the likes of which would stir envy in a Silicon Valley CEO awaited him. He didn't want the press to know what he was thinking, but he had his father to take care of that.

"I know it sells newspapers and magazines," Earl told *Sports Illustrated* around the time of the NCAA Championships. "I won't make the decision. Tiger will make the decision on his own, but [if he decides to turn pro] then he's going to have to justify it to me. I'll fire my best shots at him. I've been rehearsing my speech for six months. I'll deal with all the rationales, all the justifications, all the questions. If he still says he wants to turn pro, I'll support him one hundred percent."

Earl, of course, was just doing what he did best—laying on the bullshit. The decision had long since been made, and he was relieved and thrilled that Tiger was turning pro. One of Tiger's biggest concerns was figuring out how to take care of his parents. For answers, he turned to John Merchant.

"I recommended how much he should pay his mother and how much he should pay his father," Merchant said. "Six figures for Mom and an unlimited credit card. I think his dad would get twice what his mom was getting. So if Mom was getting $100,000, Earl was getting $200,000."

When he was a boy, Jim Riswold was a huge sports fan. He grew up collecting baseball cards. To him, the most interesting part of the card wasn't the photo on the front or the statistics on the back; it was the little cartoon on the reverse side. That was where you learned about a player's personal life. Ted Williams, for example, was a fighter pilot who served in two wars. Williams's fighter-pilot status, Riswold later learned, was what's known in the advertising world as his "unique selling proposition"—the fact that made him different from other ballplayers.

After college, Riswold took a job at Wieden+Kennedy, an ad agency in Portland, Oregon. The firm was small—Riswold was its eighth employee—but one of its clients was Nike. Riswold was soon assigned to work on the Nike account. Specifically, he was responsible for creating an advertising campaign for the company's Bo Jackson cross-training shoes. It was an opportunity for Riswold to showcase his gift for mingling pop culture with the principles of advertising. With Jackson's uniqueness as a two-sport athlete playing professional football and baseball, Riswold created the "Bo Knows" slogan, and he wrote the ad that featured baseball star Kirk Gibson saying, "Bo knows baseball," football star Jim Everett saying, "Bo knows football," and blues legend Bo Diddley saying, "Bo, you don't know diddly." This commercial and the related ads that followed turned Bo Jackson into the "most persuasive athlete in television commercials," according to a survey conducted by a New York advertising research firm in 1990.

Nike founder and CEO Phil Knight quickly recognized that Riswold was a star. In 1992, Riswold wrote the "Instant Karma" Nike ad that was set to the number one single of the same name by John Lennon. Then he was assigned to work on a Michael Jordan commercial. A voracious consumer of movies and music, Riswold had seen the cultural touchstone film *She's Gotta Have It*, starring Spike Lee, who also directed the film. From that, Riswold dreamed up the idea of pairing Lee—as the Mars Blackmon character from the movie—with Michael Jordan in commercials. Riswold's underlying story line was that Blackmon was so in love with his Air Jordans that he refused to take them off, even when he had the chance to sleep with the woman of his dreams.

By 1996, Riswold was a certified rock star in the world of advertising, the go-to guy when Nike needed to create an ad campaign for a star athlete. In July of that year, he got a call from Joe Moses, a senior executive at Nike. Moses didn't bother to say hello.

"He's ready to be a pro," Moses told Riswold. "We've got a world-changer here."

Riswold knew exactly who Moses was talking about, and he knew just what to do—start working on the Nike commercial that would introduce Tiger Woods to the world. Over the next couple of weeks, Riswold met directly with Phil Knight and a small number of others at Nike. The whole initiative was very hush-hush. A decision was made early on to use only existing footage for the commercial: there would be no new shooting. The responsibility for writing the copy fell to Riswold. A low handicapper in his own right, he couldn't stop thinking about the fact that golf was a pretty stuffy game. The commercial needed to show that Tiger was going to open new doors and change the face of the sport.

Every morning, Riswold would go for a six a.m. walk through his neighborhood, a tree-lined enclave on the southeast side of Portland. One morning in late July, an idea popped into his head: *I am not a token! No, that's not it,* he thought. *Too heavy-handed.* Then another theme came to mind, along with a set of words. As soon as Riswold got home, he wrote them down. By the time he started assembling video footage to accompany the words, he knew he had something groundbreaking.

Before heading to Portland, Oregon, for the 1996 US Amateur, Tiger told Coach Goodwin that he would be back at Stanford in the fall. But everything was hotwired for him to turn pro right after the tournament. John Merchant and Hughes Norton had worked out their differences and settled on a commission percentage for IMG that would save Tiger about $5 million in the initial deals. IMG had big endorsements in the works. Nike was poised to unleash a massive print and television advertising campaign. The shoe and apparel giant even had a private jet standing by to whisk Tiger to Milwaukee for his first tournament as a pro. A small handful of trusted journalists, including Jaime Diaz and John Strege, had been told weeks earlier that the decision was made and Tiger would announce he was turning pro right after the US Amateur. But they were also threatened with permanent excommunication from the Church of Woods if they breathed so much as a word of the news before getting clearance from Earl.

"Earl said, 'You can't write it until I let you write it,'" Strege said years later. "So we were sitting on this bombshell story, as golf goes, and couldn't do anything with it. It was a terribly awkward situation."

With a big assist from Kevin Costner, golf was on a lot of people's minds when Tiger Woods swaggered into the Pumpkin Ridge Golf Club northwest of Portland in mid-August. *Tin Cup* was the number one movie in the country, and its hardscrabble story line of a gifted golfer whose bright future is derailed by his rebellious nature and bad attitude provided a perfect contrast to Woods, whose gilded image had been so carefully crafted since childhood. The entourage that accompanied Tiger to the US Amateur created the obvious impression that he was about to forfeit his final two years at Stanford. Besides his parents, there were his sports psychologist, Dr. Jay Brunza; his personal attorney, John Merchant; his agent-in-waiting, Hughes Norton; and his swing coach, Butch Harmon. The CEOs of Tiger's future corporate partners were also on hand: Phil Knight of Nike and Wally Uihlein of Titleist. Still, a headline in the *New York Times* read: "The Question for Woods: Is It Time to Go Pro?"

Tiger had no doubt what his future held: he would be a professional golfer and a millionaire many times over by the end of the weekend. But there was one item of unfinished business. Nobody had ever won three consecutive US Amateur titles. Bobby Jones, considered the greatest amateur of all time, had managed to win two straight titles on two separate occasions, but never three in a row. Tiger wanted to put an exclamation point on his amateur career by surpassing Jones and going where no one else had gone. That, he figured, was the ideal way to end one chapter of his life before moving on to the next.

Through the first few rounds of the tournament, Tiger had more trouble dodging questions about his future than dispatching his challengers. On day three of match play at Pumpkin Ridge, he found himself cornered by *ABC World News Tonight* correspondent Carol Lin. He wasn't in the mood to talk about his future.

"I like being in school," Tiger told Lin, repeating the party line. "Unfortunately, that's not what the public wants to hear. That's not what you guys in the media want to hear."

"What do you think we want to hear?" she said.

"You want to say I'm turning pro tomorrow. But that's not what the issue is here. The issue is my happiness."

That afternoon, Tiger faced a familiar foe in the semifinals—his Stanford teammate Joel Kribel. They had been roommates on road trips that year, and Kribel considered Tiger a friend. But Tiger didn't believe in friendships when it came to competition. He barely spoke to Kribel while beating him to advance to the final.

Wearing black shades and a white sun hat with a blue bandana that said NIKE, Phil Knight liked what he saw. He was walking the fairway when Carol Lin caught up to him and pressed him on the subject of whether Tiger would turn pro.

"What does he have to lose by staying in school?" Lin asked.

Knight smiled. "Millions of dollars."

The finals were set. Tiger's opponent was Steve Scott, a nineteen-year-old rising star about to enter his sophomore year at the University of Florida. Tiger knew very little about him. The year before, Scott had reached the quarterfinals of the US Amateur in Newport, and he had finished in the top ten at the NCAA Championships in June.

But the thing that stood out most about Scott was his nineteen-year-old caddie, Kristi Hommel, an athletic blonde with long hair that she kept in a ponytail. Hommel was a member of the Florida Southern golf team, and she'd been Scott's girlfriend since they'd met in a high school parking lot one afternoon after golf practice. As Scott marched through the first five rounds of match play at Pumpkin Ridge, Hommel became the darling of the tournament. Everyone from the NBC broadcast team to random fans were smitten with the way she handled the bag, cheered on her boyfriend, and exhibited exemplary sportsmanship to Scott's opponents.

All these feel-good vibes suddenly evaporated, however, when Tiger walked to the first tee on Sunday morning. People were lined up twelve-deep to watch him. The fairways were jam-packed. The crowds at the Witch Hollow course had swelled to fifteen thousand.

"All these people," Kultida said, "they are here to see my Tiger."

The event felt more like a coronation than a golf tournament.

Feeling suddenly like they were two people against the world, Hommel looked Scott in the eye and told him she believed in him. He then proceeded to reel off six birdies in the morning round.

Each time Tiger made a clutch shot, Scott told him, "Good shot."

Tiger, without making eye contact, simply said, "Thanks." When Scott made a good shot, Tiger said nothing. He didn't even nod.

"He never said 'Good shot' to Steve once in the round," recalled Hommel. "Whatever. That's fine. He was—what did his dad call him? A trained assassin."

Tiger was fuming by the end of the first half of the thirty-six-hole final. He found himself five down to Scott. Spectators were dumbfounded.

NBC couldn't believe it. Golf writers were scratching their heads. Tiger had won thirty consecutive matches leading up to the US Amateur. Suddenly, it looked like he might actually lose.

During the ninety-minute television break before the start of the final round, Tiger cursed himself. When he finally calmed down, he sought counsel from Harmon, who made a few tweaks to his posture, and from Brunza, who helped bring his mind back into focus.

Meanwhile, like two kids on a date, Scott and Hommel used the break to shop for souvenirs at the merchandise tent, purchasing a couple of shirts and hats, mementos to help them remember the week. Unlike Woods, Scott didn't feel the need to practice between rounds. His formula was working, and he had no plans to change it. That said, he knew Woods was going to make a run. He just didn't know when.

Tiger showed up for the afternoon match in a new set of clothes: white shoes, brown pleated pants, a bloodred shirt, and a black cap. He shaved three holes off Scott's lead in the first five holes. At the turn, Scott's lead was down to one.

Sensing that he was going to get steamrolled if he didn't do something, Scott delivered in dramatic fashion on the very next hole, a 194-yard par 3. With his ball sitting in heavy greenside rough, he executed a delicate downhill flop shot that found the hole. The gallery erupted as Scott jumped up and down, pumping his fist in the air. Suddenly, his lead was back to two.

But not for long. On the next hole, Woods made a putt he had no business making, a big thirty-five-foot breaker for eagle that, after Scott answered with a birdie, closed the gap back to one and had the crowd going wild. History was on the line, and everyone wanted to see it get made—the massive throng, NBC, Nike, IMG.

"Tiger Woods was this golf machine, and not really a golf-*er*," said Hommel. "It was just the two of us against this machine."

The sixteenth hole on the Witch Hollow course at Pumpkin Ridge is a 432-yard par 4. Scott's third shot from a greenside bunker landed ten feet from the cup. At this point, Woods was two down with three holes to play. Having outdriven Scott by fifty yards, he spun a wedge to within six feet of the hole, his ball coming to a stop right in Scott's putting line. Tiger put down his coin to mark his spot and picked up his ball. Scott asked him to slide his marker over, and Tiger did. Then Scott made his putt for par, forcing Woods to make a six-footer to win the hole.

As Scott walked off the green, out of the corner of his eye he noticed where Woods was replacing his ball. Somehow, in a rare lapse of concentration, Tiger had forgotten that he had previously moved his mark. He was about to putt from the wrong spot. If you play from the wrong spot in match play, you automatically lose the hole.

With Woods about to make a monumental mistake, Scott uttered seven words that would have made the game's Scottish ancestors proud: "Hey, Tiger, did you move that back?"

Woods immediately paused, stood up, and reset his ball to the correct spot. He then made his putt, cutting Scott's lead to one with two holes to play. It was a history-altering moment. If Scott had simply remained quiet and allowed Tiger to mistakenly putt from the wrong mark, the Ninety-Sixth US Amateur would have gone the other way right then and there, with Scott ahead by three and just two holes left to play. But Scott didn't want to win on a technicality. He wanted to win with his clubs.

Walking away from the hole, Tiger didn't acknowledge what Scott had done. Didn't say thank you. Didn't say a word.

To Scott and Hommel, that came across as cold and heartless. But Woods wasn't out to play nice or make friends. Tiger's mental approach was what gave him the absolute assurance that he was going to beat Scott. His approach had also started to wear down Scott's confidence. After a clutch birdie putt by Tiger on seventeen, they ended the second eighteen holes all square and headed to sudden death, where Scott finally cracked. On the second playoff hole, Tiger stared at Scott as his eight-foot putt for par lipped out. Then, with Hommel struggling to hold back tears, Tiger stepped up and sank a tap-in to take his third straight US Amateur. Raising his arms in triumph, he soon felt his mother hugging him and kissing his cheek. Her embrace lasted just three seconds. Then he was enveloped by Earl, who was sobbing. With television cameras zooming in, Tiger embraced his father for thirty-two seconds, a virtual eternity on network television. Kultida literally circled her husband and son as NBC's boom microphone picked up Earl's sobs and moans.

Steve Scott waited patiently to offer his congratulations. Finally, Tiger hastily shook Scott's hand before NBC's Roger Maltbie, microphone in hand, stepped between them. "Tiger, a place in golf history," he said. "Up-hill battle all the way."

"Oh, it was. I got off to a horrible start this morning. I didn't really have it. And this afternoon I knew what I had to do because I've been there before. It's just a matter of going out there and doing it. I didn't make any putts until the very end when I guess I really needed them. It's just a hard-fought battle all day."

Then Maltbie turned to Scott, who praised Tiger for his win. While Scott spoke, Tiger barely looked at him, and never even cracked a smile.

During the awards ceremony, Tiger thanked the people of Portland but never once acknowledged Scott. It was Me, Me, Me. Perhaps his mind was elsewhere. He had just won an unprecedented third-straight US Amateur, after all.

But there was no time to savor it. Maltbie, like everyone else, was already looking ahead. "Well, Tiger," he said, "we gotta ask the question. What does this do to your feelings as to whether you'll turn pro or stay in school?"

"I really don't know right now," he said. "I just know one thing: I'm gonna celebrate like hell tonight."

Tiger made a call to his coach, Wally Goodwin, at home back in Palo Alto. He had barely said hello when Goodwin cut him off. "Tiger, I know why you're calling me," he said. "You don't have to go any further."

So Woods didn't. The unspoken message was obvious: his days at Stanford were over.

"Good luck," said Goodwin.

"Thanks, coach," Tiger said. "I'll see you."

In keeping with his pattern of abrupt good-byes, Tiger didn't inform the captain of his team, Eri Crum. "It's the one thing I don't love about Tiger," Crum said. "There was a disappearance. There wasn't a 'Hey, guys, this is what I'm going to do. I loved being here with you. Good luck.' It was just, he was done and moved on."

Crum liked Tiger and said he was a good teammate, but Woods was often distant. "We all wanted to be friends with him because we admired his golf skill," Crum said. "But there was never a deep friendship that made him feel the need to do that. He was hard to get to know. If he wasn't as good as he was, he wouldn't be considered a great friend."

Tiger's lack of sentimentality and personal connection to others can be traced directly to his mother. "I am a loner, and so is Tiger," Kultida said. "We don't waste time with people we don't like. I don't have many close friends. Never have. I'm independent and strong-willed. That way, you survive." Kultida took that attitude to the golf course. She preached "kill them" and "take their heart" when it came to her son's golf opponents. Tiger's stirring comebacks against Ryan Armour, Trip Kuehne, and Steve Scott seem to have derailed their PGA aspirations. As well as they played—and they all played their hearts out and were quite talented—none of them ended up making a mark on the PGA Tour.

Steve Scott went on to be a three-time All-American golfer at the University of Florida. In 1999, he was the number-one-ranked amateur in the country. That same year, he turned pro and married Kristi Hommel. The wedding took place on the eighteenth green at TPC Eagle Trace, a private golf club in their hometown of Coral Springs, Florida. They both cried when they exchanged vows. Scott said that marrying Hommel was the smartest decision he had ever made.

Five years later, he made another big decision—to walk away from the grind of the Canadian and Nationwide Tours and focus on raising their two children. He turned toward instruction and eventually became the head PGA professional at Paramount Country Club, a few miles outside New York City. He and Kristi celebrated their eighteenth wedding anniversary in 2017.

Scott's relationship with Hommel had been cemented in the epic battle against Tiger. In 2016, to mark the twenty-year anniversary of the 1996 US Amateur, they took their children to Pumpkin Ridge to show them where they had had their moment. The four of them posed for a selfie on the tenth hole, where Scott had made his famous flop shot.

As part of their visit, GOLF Films did a piece commemorating the match between Woods and Scott. Only then did Woods finally admit he had forgotten to move his marker back, and praised Scott for his sportsmanship. "For him to do that was pretty remarkable," Tiger said in the film. Twenty years after the fact, the Scotts were grateful for the admission but had long since gotten over the slight.

"We really started Team Scott at the US Amateur at Pumpkin Ridge," Scott said. "We've gone on to have a great life. I think I'm walking proof that you can win in life without winning."

Ryan Armour also had to get used to not winning. After his heart-breaking loss to Tiger at the 1993 US Junior Amateur, Armour bounced around various pro tours for two decades, but he never won a tour event until October 2017, when he captured the Sanderson Farms Championship in Jackson, Mississippi.

Perhaps no amateur loss was more life-altering than the one suffered by Kuehne. Despite being groomed for stardom from an early age, he did some soul-searching and determined he was not really wired to win at the pro level. He loved golf, but decided he didn't want to make it his life. Instead, he pursued an MBA at Oklahoma State University, fell in love with a girl from a small Oklahoma town, got married, had a son, and started his own hedge fund in Dallas. After losing to Tiger Woods, Kuehne became the first All-American in twenty-five years not to pursue a pro golf career after college. He never watched the video clips of their historic match.

The sun had set on the day of Tiger's historic third-straight US Amateur win. The crowds had disappeared. Pumpkin Ridge Golf Club was a virtual ghost town. Only the staff and the television satellite trucks remained when Tiger Woods entered a private room in the clubhouse. His parents, Hughes Norton, and Butch Harmon filed in behind him. Nike CEO Phil Knight greeted them with a smile. Tiger didn't recognize the stranger standing beside Knight—a forty-year-old man in a polo shirt and jeans. He had a VHS cassette in his hand.

"This is Jim Riswold," Knight said. "He's written some ads for me."

Tiger stared at him, unaware that Riswold was the creative genius behind Nike's most iconic television commercials. Tiger had grown up with those ads and thought they were the coolest commercials on television.

"This may be the finest ad he's ever done for me," Knight continued.

Without saying a word, Riswold inserted the tape into a VCR and pushed play. Suddenly, Tiger saw himself on television, walking in slow motion at Pumpkin Ridge, driver in hand, a crowd around him. The words *Hello world* appeared as a choir chanted and drums beat softly. It was a powerful sensory experience that triggered goose bumps and an adrenaline rush. A collage of black-and-white photos and grainy videos from Tiger's childhood and amateur career followed. There were no voices in the entire commercial—only the text that Riswold had written and cleverly overlaid on the images:

I shot in the 70s when I was 8.

I shot in the 60s when I was 12.

I won the US Junior Amateur when I was 15.

Hello world.

I played in the Nissan Open when I was 16.

Hello world.

I won the US Amateur when I was 18.

I played in the Masters when I was 19.

I am the only man to win three consecutive US Amateur titles.

Hello world.

There are still courses in the US I am not allowed to play because of the color of my skin.

Hello world.

I've heard I'm not ready for you.

Are you ready for me?

Just before fading to black, the "Just do it" slogan and a red Nike swoosh logo appeared. The commercial was fifty-seven seconds long.

Silent, Tiger stared at the dark screen while his parents and everyone else stared at him. It was a lot to absorb. In high school, kids had viewed him as a nerd. The football players hadn't considered him an athlete. The girls hadn't even seen golf as a sport. He'd been looked at as a nonathlete—a "wuss"—for playing it. What would all those kids think now? At age twenty, he was about to join a very exclusive club of athletes with their own Nike commercials: Michael Jordan, Charles Barkley, Bo Jackson, and Andre Agassi. In terms of edginess and drama, Tiger's commercial topped them all.

"Can I fuckin' see it again?" Tiger said.

Riswold breathed a big sigh of relief, rewound the tape, and proudly hit play.

After Tiger watched it a second time, Riswold explained that the only thing left to do was edit the music.

"That's the greatest fucking golf ad I've ever seen," Harmon chimed in.

Energized, Tiger was ready for the future, and Phil Knight's private jet was ready to take him there.

CHAPTER TEN

HELLO WORLD

Nike planned to roll out the "Hello World" commercial on CBS and ESPN during the Greater Milwaukee Open, which would be Tiger's first golf tournament as a professional. Sitting in a hotel room in Milwaukee, Tiger was surrounded by bags of Nike gear—shirts, hats, shoes, sweat pants—and documents to sign. The first one was a retainer agreement drafted by John Merchant. It designated Merchant as Tiger's lawyer and authorized him to act on his behalf. The next one, dated August 26, 1996, was a declaration of domicile, which changed Tiger's official residence from California (a state with a 9.3 percent income tax in 1996) to Florida (a state with no state income tax). Tiger listed his new address as 9724 Green Island Cove in Windermere, a two-bedroom golf villa owned by IMG, which now officially represented him. IMG's CEO Mark McCormack personally called the PGA of America and dictated a short statement saying that Tiger Woods was officially turning pro.

In an instant, everything had changed. Tiger no longer had to look to his father to figure out travel schedules, hotels, and budgets. Suddenly he was surrounded by lawyers, agents, and corporate heavyweights who made sure everything was taken care of for him. They were big golf fans and couldn't wait to see him perform. "The world has not seen anything like what he's going to do for the sport," said Phil Knight. "It's almost art. I wasn't alive to see Claude Monet paint, but I am alive to see Tiger play, and that's pretty great."

While Tiger prepared for his pro debut, the final numbers were still being negotiated on his new endorsement deals with Nike and Titleist. One morning, Tiger was with his father in his room when Norton came in to share some news. He'd spent a long night negotiating, and he had Nike's final offer: $40 million for five years. The gold-standard endorsement deal in golf at that time was Greg Norman's arrangement with Reebok—a reported $2.5 million per year. Norton was giddy over what Nike was offering Tiger.

"Over three times what Norman gets!" Norton said with pride.

Tiger and Earl just looked at him.

"Guys, do you realize that this is more than Nike pays any athlete in salary, even Jordan?"

"Mmm-hmm," Tiger mumbled.

"That's *it*? 'Mmm-hmm'?"

More silence.

"Let me go through this again, guys," Norton said.

Tiger listened while Norton walked him through the numbers one more time: Nike had agreed to pay him $6.5 million per year for five years, with a $7.5 million signing bonus. In exchange for that, he would be required to film commercials, appear in photo shoots, make appearances, and wear swoosh-adorned shoes and apparel. Nike was also going to design a new line of Tiger Woods clothing.

"Guess that's pretty amazing," Tiger said.

Earl said nothing, but privately he groused. No matter how much money Tiger received, Earl thought it wasn't enough.

The next day, Norton came back with Titleist's final offer—$20 million for five years. Tiger would use the company's clubs and balls, wear its gloves, and have its name emblazoned on his bag. Titleist was also offering to design an exclusive Tiger Woods line of equipment. He would do commercials, photo shoots, and appearances for the company.

Tiger had Merchant scrutinize every contract put in front of him. On paper, he was suddenly worth $60 million. "I just got rich," Tiger told Merchant, "but I don't have five cents in my pocket."

Merchant called his banker in Connecticut and directed him to overnight Tiger a credit card with a $25,000 limit.

Tiger had come to see Merchant as a problem-solver, and Merchant relished the role. But he preferred to think of himself as someone who could help Tiger avoid problems before they arose. He felt the job of a good lawyer was really to anticipate potential trouble and offer advice on how to navigate around it. In Tiger's case, he worried about those who might try to use him, and with that in mind, he warned Tiger to avoid two particular athletes: Greg Norman and Michael Jordan.

"I don't happen to have a lot of respect for Greg Norman as a person, because Greg will take advantage of you to keep his name in the paper," Merchant opined to Tiger. "He's on the downside, and you're on the up."

Merchant felt even more strongly about Jordan. "Michael can play basketball as well as anyone who's ever played the game," he told Tiger. "There isn't anything else that Michael is good at doing. Nothing! And he's had too many years of being out there in public. So he's going to try to use you."

Tiger listened but didn't say much. Whether or not Merchant was right, keeping Norman at arm's length wouldn't be difficult, but Jordan was another story. Tiger had idolized him throughout his teenage years, and now he and Jordan were the top two athletes under the same Nike umbrella. Not only was it exciting that he shared Jordan's elite status but Phil Knight even saw Tiger as Jordan's equal. When asked whether Tiger was comparable to Jordan, Knight said flatly: "You bet your ass." And shortly after Merchant warned Tiger to avoid Jordan, the world's most famous athlete publicly stated that his "only hero on earth is Tiger Woods." It was a pretty heady compliment for a twenty-year-old.

Tiger wasn't sure he could avoid Jordan. Nor did he want to.

Legally, Tiger was too young to drink or rent a car. But with two strokes of a pen, he had secured $60 million before playing his first round of golf as a pro. No athlete in the history of American sport had accumulated so much wealth so fast. Making good on his promise to his half sister, Royce, for doing his laundry for four years at Stanford, he telephoned her two years early from Milwaukee and sent her into a state of hysteria when she picked up: "Go find your house." Then, wearing a green-striped polo shirt, Tiger stepped to the podium inside the press tent at the Milwaukee Open. Pausing, he looked at the throng of media and grinned. Earl sat behind him in a cushioned, high-backed chair.

"I guess, hello, world," Tiger said, smiling.

The media didn't get the reference, and Tiger didn't bother bringing them up to speed. They would figure it out soon enough when Nike began its advertising blitz. Reading from a prepared statement, Tiger paid tribute to his parents, telling them he loved them and praising them for all the sacrifices they'd made to get him to this point. With Kultida noticeably absent, Tiger reached back and clutched his father's hand. Then he fielded questions.

"What would make this a successful tournament for you?"

"A victory."

"Nothing less?"

"In my life I've never gone to a tournament without thinking I could win. I've explained that to you guys before. That's just the mind-set I have."

Over a twenty-minute period, he told reporters that he had no fear about turning pro, he had no intention of sharing his goals with anyone, and he actually enjoyed the mobs and all the attention.

"Tiger, not too many people begin with a news conference like this," a reporter said. "How are you going to keep your head on?"

"How'm I gonna do that?" he said, grinning. "I'm gonna play it one shot at a time. And I'm gonna have one hell of a good time."

Sometime after the press conference, two-time US Open champion Curtis Strange, who was working for ABC, asked him what he expected when he first teed it up as a professional. Tiger repeated what he had already said—that he entered every tournament to win.

"You'll learn," Strange told him.

Tiger shrugged off Strange's skepticism. He knew what he was capable of.

At 1:36 p.m. on August 29, 1996, Tiger Woods hit his first shot as a pro, driving it 336 yards straight down the middle of the fairway at Brown Deer Golf Course. And with that swing, the most publicized debut in American sporting history was under way. Legendary sportswriter Leigh Montville compared it to the Beatles' first concert in the US at Shea Stadium. Record crowds turned out in hopes of seeing Tiger do something magical, something electrifying.

And he didn't disappoint. On the final day of the tournament, Tiger stepped to the par 3 fourteenth tee and launched a shot that traveled 188 yards, took a couple of hops, and rolled into the cup. The hole in one sparked a thunderous roar from the gallery, and the crowds lining the fairway sent cheers echoing across the course as Tiger walked from tee to green, beaming and tipping his cap. Then he retrieved his ball and tossed it into the crowd, touching off another loud, prolonged outburst from fans. It was exhilarating to be so good.

Despite finishing tied for sixtieth place and earning just $2,544, Tiger absolutely dominated the headlines, thanks in large part to his new Nike commercial. As Riswold had hoped, the ad's racially charged message hit a nerve. Golf pros and golf writers saw the ad as disingenuous and questioned its accuracy. Were there actually courses in America that would not let Tiger Woods play because of the color of his skin? A columnist from the *Washington Post* put that question to Nike. The company conceded that no such place existed, adding that the words in the ad weren't intended to be taken literally. That response only fueled the controversy.

Nike didn't mind all the fuss. Market research revealed that the company's core demographic—consumers between ages eighteen and twenty-nine—thought the ad was "very effective," and the phrase *Hello world* instantly became part of the American vernacular. The commercial ended up being nominated for an Emmy.

But Tiger wasn't prepared for the backlash. Some pros on the Tour quietly took potshots at the ad for being so sensationalized. Such criticisms were no doubt fueled by envy. Nonetheless, they stung Tiger, who was the newest and youngest face on the Tour. In an interview with ABC News's *Nightline* during the tournament, he tried to defend the commercial. "I feel it's a message that has been long awaited because it's very true," he said, "and being a person who is, I guess, how you could say, non-wanted, I had experienced that, and the Nike campaign is just telling the truth."

"What do you think that America's not ready for?" he was asked in a follow-up question.

"That's why the ad is very good," Tiger said. "You've got to think about it. Nike ads don't think for you. They'll make you think a certain way. You have to think for yourself."

One problem was that Tiger hadn't had much opportunity to do any thinking for himself before the commercial began airing. Swept up in the experience of seeing himself in such an edgy Nike ad, he hadn't contemplated how it might be interpreted. He really hadn't had time to contemplate anything. The entire week had been a blur.

There was another problem: everyone who covered golf knew that Tiger had been previously on record as saying, "The only time I think about race is when the media ask me."

Suddenly, he was being asked on national television to explain himself in the context of a commercial about race.

"What's your message?" he was asked on *Nightline*.

"I'm not going to tell you," he said. "That's very private."

Tiger also wasn't prepared for the criticism generated by his father's actions. Earl had taught Tiger to say very little to the press, but he rarely practiced what he preached. After Tiger ably handled his introductory press conference before the start of the Greater Milwaukee Open, his dad hung around the press tent and started spouting the gospel according to Earl.

"There is no comprehension by anyone on the impact this kid is going to have, not only on the game of golf, but on the world itself," he said. Earl went on to compare Tiger's killer instincts to those of a "black gunslinger." "He'll cut your heart out in a heartbeat and think nothing of it," he said. These statements only stoked resentment toward Tiger, who already faced a monumental task—he had just seven tournaments left in the 1996 season to try to earn his card to qualify for the 1997 PGA Tour. "It'll be very difficult for Tiger to make $150,000 [in that amount of time]," said fellow pro Justin Leonard. "That's a lot of pressure riding on a twenty-year-old's shoulders."

Leonard was putting it kindly. Some members of the national press were more direct. After Tiger's debut in Milwaukee, sportswriter John Feinstein wrote a feature story on Woods in which he labeled Earl "a pushy father" in "pursuit of publicity for himself and every dollar possible." Feinstein also went on *Nightline* and compared Earl to Stefano Capriati, the infamously overbearing father of teenage tennis star Jennifer Capriati. "Like Stefano," Feinstein said, "Earl hasn't had a full-time job since 1988, 'sacrificing' to be at his son's side. Earl Woods says he won't travel full-time with Tiger. That would be a bonus."

Feinstein's words infuriated Tiger, who felt like he was getting hit from all sides. In his view, criticizing his parents was an unpardonable sin, something he took personally and would keep fresh in his memory. Yet on September 16, 1996, after spending the first three weeks on the PGA Tour with his father at his side, Tiger said good-bye to Earl and put him on a flight back to Los Angeles. Then he got on a chartered flight with Hughes Norton and Norton's associate at IMG, Clarke Jones. A short time later, they landed in Binghamton, New York, and Tiger checked into his own room at the Regency three days before the start of the B.C. Open at Endicott. It marked the first time that Tiger had been separated from his father while on the road.

Lonely and bewildered, he welcomed the opportunity to hang out with Jaime Diaz, who was covering Tiger for *Sports Illustrated*. To Tiger, Diaz felt more like a family member than a journalist. They were making small talk in Tiger's hotel room when Norton showed up. He was fresh off a conversation with Mark McCormack, and Norton had a proposition for Tiger to consider.

"Mark thinks you should do a book," Norton said. "Just like Jack did. Just like Arnie did."

Tiger was blindsided. *A book?*

He'd been a pro for a whopping three weeks. He hadn't even won anything yet, and was still trying to qualify for the 1997 Tour. What was Hughes thinking?

"It could be an instruction book," Norton continued. "It could be a biography."

Diaz didn't say anything, but it sounded to him like Norton hadn't just come up with this idea overnight. This had been in the works.

"So what do you think?" Norton pressed.

Tiger didn't know what to think. He was a golfer, not a writer. And an autobiography went against his nature. He didn't even like telling the press what he had eaten for breakfast, never mind going on for hundreds of pages about his life.

"Arnie did it?" Tiger asked.

Norton nodded.

"And Jack did it?"

Norton nodded again.

"So who would write it?"

"I don't know," Norton said, turning to Diaz. "Jaime?"

Diaz looked at Norton and then at Tiger. He'd never written a book, but he was immediately intrigued by the prospect of teaming up with Tiger on a big project. After some more back-and-forth, Tiger reluctantly agreed to go forward with the idea. He at least liked the thought that Diaz would be involved. Norton told Diaz to come up with a number.

From a financial standpoint, Norton's idea was smart. Tiger was riding a wave, and it was a good time to approach the fickle publishing industry, which was keenly interested. The book proposal touched off a bidding war between several top New York City publishing houses. In the end, Warner Books won an auction by agreeing to pay $2.2 million for a two-book deal: an instructional book that Tiger would write right away, and an autobiography that he would write years down the road. From IMG's perspective, this was a good thing. A couple more million dollars had been added to the bottom line.

But Earl wasn't happy. He had already secured his own book deal with HarperCollins, and he was angry when he learned that IMG had persuaded Tiger to do a book. It went without saying that Tiger's book might undercut sales of Earl's. Plus, Earl thought that every business opportunity for Tiger should be run past him first. Hughes had violated a cardinal rule by going directly to Tiger.

Citing exhaustion, Tiger abruptly withdrew from the Buick Challenge in Pine Mountain, Georgia, on September 25, 1996, one day before it started. He was scheduled to be honored as the college golfer of the year for the 1995–96 season at the annual Fred Haskins Award dinner during the tournament, but instead of attending, Tiger went home. More than two hundred guests were in town for the dinner, which had to be canceled. Once again, John Feinstein pounced.

"When you are the game's Next One and you know your presence in a tournament has been promoted, you really should show up," he wrote. "And when the sponsors of a major college golf award have scheduled their awards dinner to suit you at a time and place where you have told them you will be, you don't blow off the dinner and go home."

Tiger couldn't stand Feinstein, and he had no trouble dismissing him. But he also received unexpected criticism from fellow pros, which he couldn't shrug off. Tom Kite said he couldn't remember being tired when he was twenty. Peter Jacobsen said it was no longer appropriate to compare Tiger to Nicklaus and Palmer, because they never walked out on people. The words that stung the most came from Palmer himself. "Tiger should have played," Palmer told a reporter. "He should have gone to the dinner. The lesson is you don't make commitments you can't fulfill unless you're on your deathbed."

I thought those people were my friends, Tiger thought after reading the barrage of criticism. Alone and feeling like a target, he suddenly missed Stanford and the cocoon that it had provided. Everyone was beating him up for pulling out of a tournament and skipping a dinner, but no one knew what he was dealing with back home.

For twenty years—his entire life—he and his parents had lived together in the same house in Cypress. But now Tiger had moved out, and
his parents were splitting up. John Merchant had been tasked with finding
a new home for Kultida, one that was big enough to accommodate her
relatives when they visited from Thailand. He had located a 4,500-square-
foot house with five bedrooms and six baths in a gated community in Tustin, California, for $700,000. Tiger had agreed to pay for it, and the closing
had been set for early November. The situation between his parents was
more bewildering than anything he was encountering on the Tour, but he
wasn't about to admit that. Better to just take the heat for bailing at the
last minute.

On October 6, one week after skipping the Haskins dinner, Tiger won
his first PGA Tour event, outdueling Davis Love III at the Las Vegas Invitational. The pace of his success was mind-boggling. In just his fifth PGA
tournament he had emerged victorious.

"Did you *ever* see yourself doing this so soon?" a journalist asked.

"Yeah," Tiger said matter-of-factly. "I kind of did."

Hughes Norton pointed to the win as proof that Tiger had done the
right thing by bowing out of the Buick Challenge, but that didn't change
the fact that he'd left sponsors and hundreds of people high and dry, or as-
suage the hard feelings because of it. One of the hardest things for Tiger to
do was admit wrongdoing and apologize. But something had to be done.
Golf writer Pete McDaniel, who was working with Earl on his forthcoming book about raising Tiger, was assigned to ghostwrite an apology for
Woods.

No golf writer knew more about the history of African Americans in
golf than McDaniel. And although Tiger wasn't the first black golfer, he
was the first game-changer, the one who was shattering the glass ceiling.
With that in mind, McDaniel was eager to help Woods navigate the rough
waters. He crafted an apology, and it appeared under Tiger's byline in a
column published in *Golf World* days after his win in Vegas. "I didn't even
think about the dinner," it read. "I realize now that what I did was wrong.
Even though I know I did the right thing in getting away, I should have
stayed long enough to attend the dinner and then go home. But hindsight
is 20-20."

The piece did the trick. The people in charge of the Fred Haskins
Award banquet rescheduled it for early November, and Tiger and Earl

flew back to Georgia to attend. Tiger was gracious and humble in his acceptance remarks. But Earl's introductory speech left a much bigger impression. Choking back tears, he said:

> *Please forgive me, but sometimes I get very emotional when I talk about my son. My heart fills with so . . . much . . . joy when I realize that this young man is going to be able to help so many people. He will transcend this game and bring to the world a humanitarianism which has never been known before. The world will be a better place to live in by virtue of his existence and his presence. I acknowledge only a small part in that, in that I know I was personally selected by God himself to nurture this young man and bring him to the point where he can make his contribution to humanity. This is my treasure. Please accept it and use it wisely. Thank you.*

The entire audience rose to its feet in applause as Tiger put his arms around his father.

Tiger was still smarting from the fallout of missing the Haskins dinner when he won his second PGA Tour event, beating Payne Stewart head-to-head to win the Walt Disney World/Oldsmobile Classic by one stroke. The $216,000 purse raised Woods's earnings to $734,794 in his extremely shortened season, qualifying him for the 1997 Tour. Remarkably, he had won two of his first seven professional tournaments.

After his obligatory press conference, however, he was in no mood to talk to reporters in a less formal setting. When a few of them trailed him to the locker room in hopes of getting a few more quotes, Tiger instructed the security guards not to allow any media inside, and the press was promptly told to leave. But under PGA Tour rules, the locker room had to be accessible to the press. Wes Seeley, who was in charge of PR for the Tour, told security to open it. "The Tour makes the rules, not the kid," Seeley said. "Regardless of what he and his people think, he's not the fifth Beatle."

But he had become the rock star of golf. His fame was transforming the game and wreaking havoc on the rules of etiquette at tournaments. The crowds at his first seven Tour events were twice or, in some instances, three times the normal size. Fans were trampling over the ropes to get to him. Women were approaching him on the range and proposing marriage. More than once he had had to escape to the clubhouse after playing to evade overzealous spectators. David Letterman and Jay Leno were clamoring to have him on their shows. Bill Cosby was willing to compose an episode of the *Cosby Show* around Tiger just to get him to appear on the top sitcom on television. *GQ* was offering to put him on the cover. Pepsi was ready to put up big money for him to film a commercial. Everyone, it seemed, wanted a piece of Tiger. It had gotten to the point that whenever he saw Norton approaching, he knew that this guy or that guy wanted to know when they could interview him.

"Tell them to kiss my ass!" he would tell Norton.

"All right," Norton would say. "And after that, what should I tell them?"

"Tell them to kiss my ass again!"

By the time he arrived in Tulsa, Oklahoma, for the Tour Championship at the end of October, Tiger had had it with all the pestering and intrusiveness of the press. Nobody realized this more than Earl, who was traveling with him. On the evening after the first round, Earl was in his hotel suite enjoying a cigarette when *Newsweek* senior writer John McCormick knocked on the door, introduced himself, and talked his way inside. But after explaining that his magazine wanted to do a feature on him and Tiger and put them on the cover, McCormick hit a wall. Earl said he wasn't interested, which meant Tiger wasn't interested. Determined to change Earl's mind, McCormick pulled out his wallet.

"Look," he told Earl, "I'm going to show you the reason I really want to do this story."

"Money?" Earl said.

"No, this," McCormick said, removing a photograph of his two little boys and handing it to Earl. "That's why."

Earl had developed a soft spot for children. Despite being wary, he ended up talking to McCormick for three hours, filling the reporter's notebook with plenty of quotes and anecdotes about Tiger. It was midnight by the time McCormick finally left Earl's room. About two hours later, Tiger was awakened by a phone call from his mother, who informed him that Earl had just been taken to the hospital in an ambulance after experiencing chest pain. Roughly ten years earlier, Earl had undergone a quadruple bypass in response to arteriosclerosis stemming from cholesterol buildup. Knowing his father's history, Tiger went directly to the hospital, where doctors had administered an EKG and given Earl medication to stabilize the situation.

"It'll be okay," he told Tiger. "Don't worry about it. Go on out and play."

Tiger didn't say anything, but he was too worried about the health of his sixty-four-year-old father to concentrate on golf. After spending the rest of the night at the hospital, Tiger shot a 78 the next day, his worst round since turning pro. "I didn't want to be here today," he said afterward, "because there are more important things in life than golf. I love my dad to death, and I wouldn't want to see anything happen to him."

He ended up finishing the tournament tied for twenty-first at eight over par. Weeks later, he visited Earl in Cypress. While Tiger was in town, Earl agreed to another interview with McCormick. This time he went to Earl's home, where he hoped to also talk to Tiger. Ten minutes, he told Earl, would suffice. Without making any promises, Earl called Tiger and handed the phone to McCormick, who made his pitch.

"No," Tiger told McCormick.

"Okay, just to be clear," McCormick said, "this is a story about your dad and how he raised you. I'm not trying to do a cover story about you."

"No," repeated Tiger.

McCormick was taken aback. "He wasn't unpleasant," McCormick recalled. "It was just *no.*"

Although Tiger wasn't interested in being on the cover of another national magazine, his corporate sponsors liked the idea. So he reluctantly agreed to pose with Earl for a *Newsweek* photographer. A few weeks later, they appeared together on the cover—Tiger wearing Nike gear and holding a Titleist golf club, Earl wearing a Titleist hat—under the headline "Raising a Tiger: The Family Story Behind Golf's $60 Million Prodigy." The nine-page article portrayed Tiger as "so gracious that he signs autographs for half an hour after tourney rounds" and "gives clinics to inner-city kids." It also claimed, without any evidence, that Tiger had endured "years of racist treatment at golf courses." But the thrust of the story arose from a question: "How did the parents pull it off?"

In other words, how did Earl and Kultida raise such a "fine young man"?

"Every move has been calculated to make him the best person he can be," Earl told *Newsweek*. "You have your priorities. Your priority is the welfare of the child first. Who he is, and what is going to make him a good person, has priority over making him a good athlete."

Earl's comments were self-serving. But from a marketing standpoint, Nike and Titleist could not have been happier. Even the photographs taken by *Newsweek* were carefully staged to feature Nike gear and Titleist equipment while simultaneously projecting Tiger and his family as idyllic. One image in particular portrayed Earl and Kultida standing side by side, smiling, arms around each other as if in a state of marital bliss. It was taken outside the family home in Cypress, which Kultida had just moved out of to live on her own.

Although he never talked to *Newsweek*, Tiger was always willing to do everything his powerful sponsors wanted from him. "But there won't be much more than that," Tiger said at the time. "I have no desire to be the king of endorsement money."

IMG, however, was determined to change his mind.

Tiger knew he needed advice on what to do with his money. He also knew that finance and investment strategy weren't his father's strong suits. Instead, Tiger turned to John Merchant, whom he was looking to more and more for advice. Merchant's first call was to his old friend Giles Payne, a superb attorney specializing in estate planning and trusts. Payne had been responsible for getting Merchant onto the USGA executive committee, and Merchant couldn't think of anyone more qualified than Payne and his partners at Brody Wilkinson, a boutique law firm based in Southport, Connecticut, to guide Tiger through the complicated opportunities and pitfalls presented by instant wealth. Payne and his law partners Seth O. L. Brody and Fritz Ober—both of whom were also exceptionally skilled— began working with Tiger right after he turned pro. On November 19, 1996, the firm created Tiger Woods, Inc., a Connecticut-based nonprofit that designated Tiger as chairman and Earl as president.

Weeks later, Tiger's new team of Connecticut lawyers were summoned to Florida to meet with him and his corporate partners Nike and Titleist. The group arrived at Bay Hill Club & Lodge in Orlando feeling triumphant. The joint marketing influence of both companies was paying off in spades. In addition to the *Newsweek* cover story, Nike had just aired another tour de force commercial written by Riswold—"I Am Tiger

Woods"—that featured one child after another, most of them minorities, staring into the camera while repeating the phrase "I am Tiger Woods." With everything clicking, Tiger and his team planned to spend two days mapping out plans for how to fund Tiger's newly formed nonprofit, as well as discussing ways to use it as a vehicle to expand golfing opportunities among minority youth.

Before getting down to business, the group played a round. Tiger was paired with John Merchant, and they joked and ribbed each other for eighteen holes. Tiger could not have been happier with Merchant's contribution during his transition from amateur to pro. Merchant had been watching Tiger's back at every crucial step, and he had brought in a team of financial and legal advisors that Tiger fully trusted. As a gesture of how much he respected Merchant, Tiger asked him to run the strategy session that was scheduled for later that evening. It was a responsibility that Merchant gladly accepted. After all, he had hand-picked half the men who would be seated around the table.

But after leaving the course, Merchant first met up with Earl for a drink. Both men were feeling on top of the world. One drink led to a second, and then a third. Before long, they had each downed five martinis. By the time Merchant and Earl wandered into the conference room for the appointed six p.m. strategy session, both were hammered.

Merchant found his seat between Wally Uihlein, the CEO of the Acushnet Company (corporate parent of Titleist), and Craig Bowen, the first African American sales rep for Titleist. Merchant had introduced Tiger and Earl to Bowen back when Tiger was still in high school, and that introduction had gone a long way toward cementing Tiger's decision to sign with Titleist. It had also paved the way for Titleist to help write the bylaws of Tiger Woods, Inc. Others at the table included Phil Knight; Fritz Ober; Giles Payne, whom Merchant affectionately referred to as Tiger's "money man"; and Earl.

Once everyone was present, Merchant opened the meeting by talking about Nike, which was going to help fund Tiger's foundation with $1 million of his $40 million contract. But Merchant, his tongue loosened by alcohol, objected when he learned that Earl would be in charge of overseeing the distribution of the money for "junior golf efforts." As far as Merchant was concerned, putting Earl in charge of $1 million was a license to steal.

"This is not how it should be," he boomed. "I don't give a shit how important Earl is. He can't deal with junior golf all by his damn self. Just because Nike throws money at him, that ain't gonna get it done. Earl could take that money and spend it."

A deafening silence fell over the group. Instead of spelling out his vision for how to help advance the cause of minority golf in the United States, Merchant had created an incredibly awkward situation. The meeting was abruptly adjourned. Without saying a word, Tiger got up to leave.

Craig Bowen followed him out. "Tiger," he said, "you all right?"

"No, I'm not all right. I know my dad, and I know John. This is not going to be good."

It was obvious that Merchant and Earl had both had too much to drink. The thinking was that it would be better for them to sleep it off and get a fresh start the next day, but there were two things about Lt. Col. Earl Woods that were in play: he never remembered to say thank you, and he never forgot a slight. He had a very cold, ruthless side. Tiger once said that his father could "slit your throat and then sit down and eat his dinner."

When everyone reconvened in the conference room the following morning, there was a table with breakfast food. Refreshed, Merchant set his briefcase down at his seat between Bowen and Uihlein and headed to the table for a cup of coffee. Earl intercepted him and asked him to step outside the room. Then he fired Merchant.

Dumbfounded, Merchant just stared at his friend. After all they'd been through together? After all the money he'd raised to finance Tiger's amateur career? After all the pro bono work and all the trouble he'd been through with the State of Connecticut? After everything he'd done to set Tiger up with the lawyers from Brody Wilkinson? *What the fuck?*

"It's one of the hardest things I've ever had to do," Earl said, feigning pain.

"Why?" Merchant whispered.

Earl said nothing.

"What's the problem?" Merchant pressed.

Still nothing.

Merchant felt like the room was spinning. He couldn't get his bearings. Effective immediately, he was no longer Tiger's attorney.

Without saying another word, both men returned to the conference room. Earl sat down and ate his breakfast, while Merchant picked up his briefcase and walked out. Within an hour, he had checked out of his room and left for the airport.

It was an awkward situation for Merchant's trusted friends Giles Payne and Fritz Ober, but they took over all of Tiger's legal and business affairs. As Tiger's new personal attorneys, they stepped in right away and helped execute a deed that transferred a property in Isleworth from IMG to Tiger, listing Tiger's mailing address as 135 Rennell Drive, Southport, Connecticut (the address of his new law firm). They would also go on to establish the Tiger Woods Revocable Trust, which named Earl and Tiger the sole trustees.

Retaining Brody Wilkinson was the single most important piece of advice that Merchant ever gave to Tiger. The firm would go on to handle Tiger's resources for decades, enabling him to build a vast fortune and avoid the mistakes made by so many celebrated athletes who earn millions in their early twenties only to end up broke after retirement.

Two weeks later, Merchant received an envelope in the mail from Earl. It contained a check for two weeks' severance pay. He sent it back with a message: "Shove it up your ass!"

Merchant figured he would never get to the bottom of what had truly motivated Earl to fire him. But months later, he ran into Kultida at a golf tournament. The two of them had always gotten along well, and she seemed truly remorseful that he was no longer a part of Tiger's life. In a private conversation, she confided her thoughts on the matter—namely, that Tiger had always listened to Earl. His whole life was listening to Dad. And suddenly he had started to listen to somebody else on matters of finance and investments. The competition bothered Earl. "The parent always wins," Kultida told Merchant.

Merchant never heard from Tiger again. The last words Tiger ever said to him were spoken as they were walking off the eighteenth green at Bay Hill, when Tiger looked at him, smiled, and said, "I love you, man."

CHAPTER ELEVEN

MASTERFUL

On a sunny Monday morning, Tiger Woods was inside his mother's new luxury home in Tustin, California. It was January 13, 1997, and a shiny new Mercedes was parked in the driveway. Tiger had won it, along with $216,000 in first-place prize money, the day before at the Mercedes Championships at La Costa Resort and Spa in Carlsbad. Figuring his mother could use a new luxury car to go with her new house, he told her the Mercedes was his gift to her. And why not? Kultida had devoted her life to her son, and that devotion had played a critical role in elevating him into some rare air. Two weeks earlier, on his twenty-first birthday, Tiger had received the ultimate gift—*Sports Illustrated* had put him on the cover of its year-end issue, naming him the 1996 Sportsman of the Year, the youngest athlete ever to win the honor.

Tiger hadn't been the only world-class athlete to make his professional debut in 1996. Eighteen-year-old Kobe Bryant joined the Los Angeles Lakers; twenty-two-year-old Derek Jeter started with the New York Yankees; and fourteen-year-old Serena Williams had played in her first professional tennis tournament at the end of 1995. Each would go on to become superstars in their respective sports. But in 1996, Tiger shot past them and everyone else like a comet, instantly establishing himself as a game-changer on the PGA Tour and the most compelling athlete in America. In his first seven tournaments, he finished sixtieth, eleventh, fifth, third, first, third, and first. His top-five finishes in his last five tournaments were unheard-of for an experienced pro, never mind a rookie. He led the Tour in driving average (302.8 yards); birdies per round; and eagle frequency, averaging one every fifty-seven holes. After just seven events, he had catapulted to twenty-fourth on the Tour's money list.

Tiger also instantly began changing the cultural norms of the game. Overnight, crowd sizes at tournaments doubled and tripled, thanks in large part to an infusion of minorities of all ages and swarms of youths of all races who had suddenly become interested in golf. The PGA Tour's television ratings went through the roof, and Tiger had single-handedly shoved the NFL and the NBA off the front page of the sports section, prompting seasoned sportswriters to ask (in print): "Is this really happening?" But Tiger had also become a household name in the pages of news publications like *Time*, *Newsweek*, the *Washington Post*, and the *New York Times*. It seemed like he was making history on a daily basis. Even longtime Tour pros were admitting publicly that he looked like the greatest golfer in the game. Unquestionably, Tiger's arrival was the most successful debut in the history of golf. And he'd started the new year by picking up right where he left off, winning the first PGA Tour event of the 1997 season. Maybe Nike was right after all: perhaps the golf world wasn't ready for Tiger.

But as he sat in his mother's house that Monday morning in January, Tiger faced expectations that went far beyond his sport. He'd started the 1997 season with his third PGA Tour victory, yet it had been expected. Being named Sportsman of the Year, like so many other aspects of his life, came with a downside: even greater expectations. When *Sports Illustrated* selected Tiger for the coveted honor, the magazine asked senior writer Gary Smith to author the story. Smith had no background or interest in golf per se. His expertise was crafting penetrating human-interest profiles. Toward the end of 1996, Smith spent a little over a week following Tiger on the Tour and talking to him about his life. But his perception of Tiger really took shape when he talked to Tiger's father.

"Tiger will do more than any other man in history to change the course of humanity," Earl told Smith.

Intrigued, Smith asked the logical follow-up: Was Earl referring to sports history? Did he mean more than Joe Louis, Jackie Robinson, Muhammad Ali, and Arthur Ashe?

"More than any of them, because he's more charismatic, more educated, more prepared for this than anyone," Earl said.

Anyone? Smith asked. What about Nelson Mandela, Gandhi, or Buddha?

"Yes, because he has a larger forum than any of them," Earl said. "Because he's playing a sport that's international. Because he's qualified through his ethnicity to accomplish miracles. He's the bridge between the East and the West. There is no limit, because he has the guidance. I don't know yet exactly what form this will take. But he is the Chosen One. He'll have the power to impact nations. Not people. Nations. The world is just getting a taste of his power."

Smith's story—"The Chosen One"—would go down in the annals of sports journalism as one of the most heartfelt cautionary profiles of a modern-day athlete. It defined Tiger Woods as "the rare athlete to establish himself *immediately* as the dominant figure in sport." But it also raised a haunting question: "Who will win? The machine . . . or the youth who has just entered its maw?"

A maw, of course, is the jaws or throat of a voracious animal—and nobody fed the beast quite like Earl Dennison Woods. In a *Sports Illustrated* profile that should have celebrated his son's historic debut, Earl used the pages of the sports industry's leading publication to pile more impossible expectations on Tiger than had any previous parent in the history of sports. Unlike the other pushy parents behind so many talented athletes, Earl wasn't satisfied with Tiger reaching the top of his sport. He wanted his son to eclipse mankind's most prominent spiritual leaders.

From the time he was old enough to walk, Tiger had been told by his parents that he was different, special, chosen, a genius—and he had been treated accordingly. Through his adolescent years, he had never worked a day in his life other than on his golf game; never mowed lawns, delivered newspapers, or pumped gas. Nor did he do household chores. He wasn't expected to take out the trash, do the dishes, or cook for himself. He was so pampered that he had never even had a babysitter. Not once. All of this was due to the fact that his parents thought he was going to do incredible things on the golf course. Once he did them, then and only then would he be able to do what his father had constantly told him he was born to do— change the world. For years, Tiger had internalized the pressure that came with such outsize expectations. But Earl had upped the ante by making his grandiose pronouncements in *Sports Illustrated*.

Tiger was often put in awkward situations by things his father said. In this instance, sportswriters familiar with the family dynamic were saying that the Old Man had finally gone too far, that he was off the rails. Some were snickering. Others genuinely felt bad for Tiger. His swing coach, Butch Harmon, was outright fed up, insisting, "Earl is getting out of control." But Tiger stood by Earl, responding the way he always did—by internalizing and accepting. *None of this is scary*, he told himself. *I can handle the burden.* He'd been programmed to think that way, to never admit to being weak. In all those times when his father put him through hell, using prisoner-of-war training tactics to toughen him up and beating him down with insulting names and racist taunts, Tiger had never once uttered the code word *enough*—nor would he utter that word now. Rather, he fell back on what he knew. "I *am* the toughest golfer mentally," Tiger told Smith.

That was Tiger's mind-set when he exited his mother's home that January morning and climbed into the back of a limousine, where forty-three-year-old Charles P. Pierce was waiting. It surprised Pierce that Tiger was alone. There was no PR person from IMG to monitor the interview. Pierce was writing yet another profile of Tiger, this one to accompany Tiger's appearance on the cover of an upcoming issue of *GQ*. Every bit as much a journalistic heavyweight as Gary Smith, Charlie Pierce was a prolific writer with a reputation for iconoclastic insight and irreverent prose. He had already made up his mind that Tiger possessed the most perfect golf swing ever witnessed, that he was the best golfer under age thirty who had ever lived, and that he was going to win more major championships than Jack Nicklaus. But not for a second did Pierce believe a word Earl Woods had said in the *Sports Illustrated* article, in particular the stuff about knowing God's mind. Or, as Pierce put it, "I do not believe that Earl Woods could find God's mind with a pack of bloodhounds and Thomas Aquinas leading the way."

Tiger knew a lot less about Pierce than Pierce knew about him. But when Pierce brought up the *Sports Illustrated* piece during the limo ride to a studio in Long Beach, Tiger downplayed it. "I think that the *SI* article went a little too deep," he said. "As writers go, you guys try to dig deep into something that's really nothing."

During the photo shoot, Tiger was assisted by four beautiful women who were there to dress him in stylish outfits. While a fashion photographer clicked away, Tiger had fun with the flirtatious women, telling them jokes. The Little Rascals are at school, he told them, and the teacher wants them to use specific words in sentences. "The first word is *love*. Spanky answers, 'I love dogs.' The second word is *respect*. Alfalfa answers, 'I respect how much Spanky loves dogs.' The third word is *dictate*. There's a pause in the room. Finally, Buckwheat puts up his hand. 'Hey, Darla,' says Buckwheat. 'How my dick ta'te?'"

The women laughed. The flirting escalated. Tiger told more jokes. And Pierce wrote it all down. As the shoot wound to a close, Tiger asked the women why lesbians always get where they're going faster than two gay guys. Then he answered his own question: "Because the lesbians are always going sixty-nine." More laughter. More note-taking by Pierce.

"Hey," Tiger said, looking at Pierce, "you can't write this."

"Too late," Pierce said.

Even that drew laughs. But Pierce wasn't kidding.

During the limo ride back to his mother's house, Tiger, yawning, looked at Pierce and asked, "Well, what did you think of the shoot?"

Pierce didn't say what he really thought—that Tiger was the most charismatic athlete alive, and that his image on the cover of *GQ* would get him laid 296 times over the coming year. Instead, he was more interested in hearing what Tiger thought of it.

"The key to it is to give them a time and stick to it," Tiger said. "If I say, 'I'm there for an hour,' I'm there, on time, for an hour. If they ask for more, I say, 'Hell, fuck no.' And I'm out of there."

Pierce noted that too. He noted everything Tiger said while they were together. None of it seemed to faze Tiger, who had places to go, people to meet, appearances to make.

Even at midnight, Tiger drew a crowd. When he and his mother touched down in Bangkok, Thailand, in early February, the airport was overrun with fans. Four of the country's five television stations broadcast the moment live. Nike sponsored the trip, thinking Tiger's presence in the Asian golf market was a potential gold mine. Just for appearing in the Asian Honda Classic, Tiger received $448,000. He picked up another $48,000 for winning by ten strokes. While in his mother's homeland, he had a private audience with the country's prime minister, met with prominent business leaders, and was toasted at various private parties and receptions before taking off for Melbourne, where he pocketed another $300,000 for appearing in the Australian Masters. By PGA Tour standards in 1997, the sums for these non-Tour appearances were staggering. So was the travel. It was all part of building Tiger's global brand.

Earl didn't make the trip to Thailand. After his episode in Tulsa, doctors performed an angiogram, which revealed that he had a number of damaged or blocked arteries. In addition to being told to make some serious lifestyle changes that included a new diet and giving up cigarettes and alcohol, Earl was scheduled for triple bypass surgery. The procedure took place at UCLA Medical Center at the end of February, and Tiger cleared his schedule to be there. Due to complications, Earl was in the intensive care unit, where he was heavily medicated. Tiger was watching the heart monitor one day when Earl flat-lined. "He told me later that, in that moment, he felt a surge of warmth, and felt he was walking into the light," Tiger recalled. "But he decided he didn't want to go to the light."

For the first time, Tiger caught a glimpse of what life would be like without his father. Although he didn't say anything to Earl when he made a full recovery, Earl knew what his son was feeling. "Tiger is not one to over-emotionalize things," he said shortly after he left the hospital. "Neither am I. We don't have to. We just touch, and it's all said."

Shortly after his return to the Tour in March, Tiger was at the Bay Hill Invitational, about to play the second round, when he first saw himself on the cover of *GQ*. The picture was good—he was smiling and looking dapper in a sharp suit and tie. But the headline was ominous: "The Coming of Tiger Woods, Sports' Next Messiah." *This might not be good*, he thought. He opened the magazine and saw the title of the story: "The Man. Amen." Beneath it in big bold letters were the words "In the Book of Saint Earl of the Woods, let us now turn to the next chapter, verse 1997, in which the presumed messiah—halo, swoosh and all—is revealed to be, gasp! a 21-year-old kid."

Unable to remember everything he had told Pierce—it had been two months since the interview, a virtual eternity in Tiger's fever-pitched life—he started reading. The piece opened with an irreverent joke, followed by a scene from the limo ride back to Tiger's mother's house. During the ride, Tiger had engaged in conversation with the limo driver. "What I can't figure out," Tiger said to the driver, "is why so many good-looking women hang around baseball and basketball. Is it because, you know, people always say that, like, black guys have big dicks?" *This is definitely not good.*

Tiger couldn't believe that Pierce had put that in his story. Those words were spoken to the limo driver, not to the reporter. All his off-color jokes were in the story too, along with an acknowledgment by Pierce that Tiger's jokes about blacks, gays, lesbians, and Buckwheat asking a girl how his dick tasted were no different from those told by most twenty-one-year-olds sitting around a keg in a frat house on a Saturday night. Then Tiger read this line about himself: "He tells jokes that are going to become something else entirely when they appear in this magazine, because he is not most 21-year-olds."

Feeling like he'd been sucker-punched, Tiger scolded himself. *How could I have been so stupid?* he thought.

Within twenty-four hours, IMG issued a press release. "It's no secret that I'm twenty-one years old and that I'm naïve about the motives of certain ambitious writers," Woods said in the statement. "The article proves that, and I don't see any reason for anyone to pay $3 to find that out. It's easy to laugh it off as juvenile and petty, except for the attacks on my father. I don't understand the cheap shots against him."

Pierce's piece had exposed the folly in the narrative Earl had constructed for his son. It also wounded Tiger. Already suspicious of the media, Tiger saw the *GQ* piece as proof positive that journalists could not be trusted. Rather than reexamining his own behavior or the role that IMG had played in setting up the ground rules that had left him alone with Pierce, Tiger doubled down on his determination to wall himself off. The experience cemented the policy Earl had been advising all along when it came to dealing with reporters—just answer the question; never say a word more. Going forward, Tiger would not veer off script again. There would be no more joking around, no more letting anyone with a pen or a microphone remotely close to his real thoughts or feelings.

Tiger also seemed to maintain a mental list of reporters that he perceived were out to get him, an enemies list of sorts. Charlie Pierce no doubt joined John Feinstein at the top. For Pierce, it didn't matter; he didn't cover golf. But for all the journalists covering the PGA Tour, the *GQ* piece changed the dynamic. It validated the contempt that Earl and Kultida harbored toward anyone who dared to write critically about their son. No one understood this better than Jaime Diaz.

"His parents hated it when Tiger was criticized," Diaz said. "That was, in their mind, the press being against them. Earl fostered that, and Tida took that view too. She was very black-and-white about who was on her side. She would tell me: 'You cross me, and that's it.' There was always a guillotine with the Woods family."

Tiger's new home inside the gates of Isleworth in Windermere, Florida, was a welcome refuge. In addition to the privacy, one of the things Tiger liked most about his new address was its proximity to Mark O'Meara. He and his wife, Alicia, and their two children—Michelle, age ten, and Shaun, age nine—lived a few doors down from Tiger. Overnight, Tiger became the fifth member of the O'Meara family. He spent more time with them than he did in his own home.

A family man and a consummate pro, Mark O'Meara had a profound impact on Tiger, taking him under his wing the same way Payne Stewart had mentored O'Meara back when he was a fresh face on the Tour himself. They were, in many respects, an odd couple. White and balding at forty years of age, O'Meara was practically old enough to be Tiger's father. His idea of a good time was finding a productive fishing hole. Yet Tiger did everything with him—watched sports on television, went to the movies, and even went fishing. Primarily, though, they played a lot of golf together at the Isleworth Golf & Country Club, where Tiger gave O'Meara a daily dose of his competitive juices as they battled in one practice round after another. There wasn't much O'Meara could teach Tiger about golf, but by being around O'Meara so much, Tiger could see the important role family played in Mark's career. Alicia and the children were an integral part of O'Meara's success.

It was clear to Woods that O'Meara was an exceptional player—the guy had won tournaments all over the world—but O'Meara had never managed to win a major championship. One day, Tiger asked him why. He wanted to know the factors that had kept O'Meara from beating the best when it mattered the most. O'Meara said he wasn't sure. But playing around Tiger had kindled a competitive fire in him. He wanted what Tiger had—a killer instinct and the confidence to close out a win.

Tiger, on the other hand, wanted what O'Meara already had—a beautiful wife with blond hair, two kids, a Porsche, and a big luxury home that dwarfed his current two-bedroom villa. From Tiger's vantage point, off the course, O'Meara had it all. He had certainly chosen well when he married Alicia. Besides being one of the most attractive wives on the PGA Tour, she created an ideal environment at home, and she welcomed Tiger into it. Even when Mark wasn't around, Tiger would routinely open the front door and yell: "What's for dinner?" She always set an extra place at the table for him. The O'Meara home was very different—much more casual—than the one Tiger had grown up in. Alicia and the kids often wore bathing suits around the house, going back and forth from the pool. They ordered from Domino's. Everyone went to the movies together. Unlike the tightly wound environment of Tiger's childhood, the O'Meara house was laid-back and fun—and no one expected anything from him. He was free to be himself.

On the Friday before the start of the sixty-first Masters, Tiger and O'Meara played a practice round at Isleworth. They made a friendly wager on the match. Shooting ten under par through one nine-hole stretch, Tiger was talking shit and having fun getting deeper and deeper into O'Meara's wallet. With six holes to play, Tiger drove a tee shot down the fairway, and a massive white plume appeared in the distance. O'Meara knew what it was—the space shuttle *Columbia* had just launched. But Tiger had never witnessed a launch. A chill swept over him as he took a seat in his golf cart and watched the boosters come off. As far back as early childhood, he had been interested in the space program. He'd read about NASA and its missions. Awed, he stared into space contemplating the scientists who were behind the shuttle launch. *What an accomplishment!* he thought. *Here I am playing golf while seven astronauts have just taken off in a space shuttle.* He suddenly felt small by comparison.

O'Meara couldn't help marveling as he watched Tiger. Here was a twenty-one-year-old kid who was about to play in his first major championship tournament as a professional, with virtually every golf writer in the country picking him to win. Moreover, like it or not, Woods was carrying a huge social burden heading into the Masters, where the cofounder of the tournament had once said, "As long as I'm alive, golfers will be white, and caddies will be black." It wasn't until 1975 that Lee Elder played in the Masters, the first black golfer to do so. He endured taunts and voices from the gallery saying things like "He shouldn't be here." And it wasn't until 1990 that Augusta National finally allowed a black man to join the club. Only seven years had passed since then, and the hype Tiger had generated was unprecedented. And yet Tiger was looking into the sky, fascinated by space travel, wondering about a shuttle that would transport a satellite into orbit around the Earth.

Exhilarated, Tiger stepped out of his golf cart and played six scintillating holes to finish the round with a final score of 59. It was the best round he had ever played, and O'Meara sensed that he had witnessed a prelude to history.

A couple of days later, they flew together to Augusta. On the short flight, Tiger turned to O'Meara. "Do you think it's possible to win the Grand Slam?" he asked.

O'Meara hesitated, sensing where Tiger was going with this line of questioning. The Grand Slam was golf's Holy Grail. No one—not even Nicklaus or Hogan—had come close to winning the Masters, the US Open, the British Open, and the PGA Championship in a single season.

"Unrealistic," O'Meara said finally.

Tiger didn't say much more on the subject. He wasn't interested in whether it was realistic. He was driven by the impossible. He wanted the Holy Grail, and he believed he could get it.

It had been only six weeks since his triple bypass, and Earl was still on strict orders not to travel. But he was determined not to miss what he believed would be Tiger's greatest performance to date, and so he decided to go to Augusta. By the time he arrived, he was worn out and ailing—but he was there. Staying in a house with Kultida and Tiger and a couple of Tiger's friends, Earl spent most of his time in bed, which is where he was on the night before the first round of play.

Concerned more about his father than himself, Tiger grabbed three balls and a putter and went to Earl's bedside. Then he got into his putting stance and asked his father if he noticed anything.

"Your hands are too low," Earl said. "Lift them up. Get that little arch in your hands like you always do."

Tiger was no longer a little boy in need of his father's instruction. At twenty-one, he was the most talented golfer on earth. What he needed was to feel the bond with his father that had been forged through countless hours playing golf together at the navy course back home. He could visualize the trees there, and he remembered the quiet evenings that were connected to golfing with Pop.

The next morning, April 10, 1997, as Tiger approached the first tee, it was already obvious that the sixty-first Masters would be a game-changer. Walking alongside him was his new caddie, Mike "Fluff" Cowan, sporting long gray hair and a bushy white mustache that made him look like the actor Wilford Brimley.

In every imaginable way, Tiger and Fluff were an unlikely pair. Tiger listened to R&B and rap, favored perfectly pressed clothes, and lived in a gated community. Fluff worshiped the Grateful Dead; wore frumpy, shaggy outfits; and was something of a vagabond, known to have lived in his car in earlier years. They had come together after Tiger won his third US Amateur in August of the previous year.

Tiger had had to scramble to find a caddie before his debut at the Greater Milwaukee Open, and he called Cowan. Despite being relatively unknown on the Tour, Cowan certainly had bona fides as a caddie. After starring on the golf team at William Penn College in Iowa, he had briefly returned home to Auburn, Maine, and worked as an assistant pro at a country club before finding his way to the Tour as a caddie in 1976. There he hooked up with Peter Jacobsen, a telegenic star who won six Tour events over a nearly twenty-year period with Fluff on his bag. The two of them were quite close, but Jacobsen had hurt his back earlier in the summer of 1996 and was sidelined. Tiger told Cowan he was turning pro and asked if he would caddie for him during his final seven tournaments of the year.

Fluff agreed to help, but only until Jacobsen was healthy enough to tee it up again. Tiger admired Cowan's loyalty and agreed. But while carrying the bag for Tiger at Milwaukee, Fluff had one "holy shit" moment after another as Tiger hit off the tee. He likened it to being next to a NASA launchpad. By the time Tiger had gotten his first two Tour victories, Cowan realized that Woods was making history, and he had the best seat in the house. He called Jacobsen, thanked him profusely for having treated him like a king for two decades, and told Tiger he would be his permanent caddie. It was a decision that would thrust Cowan into the spotlight and turn him into the most popular caddie on the PGA Tour— and make him a part of history. The sight of a young black golfer and an older white caddie standing on the first tee at Augusta was a complete role reversal, a vivid illustration that everything was changing.

Tiger was so amped up that he drove his first tee shot left, into the trees. He started the sixty-first Masters with a bogey, and things unraveled from there. He bogeyed the fourth and fifth holes too. Angry, he questioned himself: *What is going on?* Then on nine, he bogeyed yet again. Through the opening nine holes, he shot a four-over-par 40. Feeling the weight of everyone's eyes upon him, Tiger walked off the ninth green furious and bewildered. In the back of his mind he knew that skeptics were already predicting the tournament was over for him. The highest score ever recorded on the first nine by a Masters winner was 38. Tiger was in trouble.

"We've only played nine holes," Cowan told him. There was plenty of time to turn things around.

One thing Tiger appreciated most about Fluff was his go-with-the-flow approach. He always seemed to know what to say, and what not to say. At that moment, the last thing Tiger needed was additional tension.

Silent, he ignored the crowds that were urging him on as he walked toward the tenth tee. Deep inside his own head, trying to figure out what he was doing wrong, he drew strength from the prisoner-of-war techniques his father had put him through when he was eleven and twelve years old. It had felt so brutal back then, but Earl had told him time and time again that if he was going to become the great black hope of golf, he had to learn to block out any feelings of insecurity. Faced with the prospect of crumbling halfway through the opening round, Tiger zeroed in on the task at hand.

On the tenth tee, he pulled his 2-iron from his bag. Fluff liked the selection. Then Tiger hit a blistering shot down the fairway. *There!* That was it—the same feeling he'd had at Isleworth the week before when he'd shot 59. With a sudden uptick in his pace, Tiger walked to his ball in the fairway and, with an 8-iron, hit it to within fifteen feet of the cup before closing out the hole with a birdie putt. *Okay, this is it,* he told himself. *I'll be fine.*

His mental approach had made a complete reversal. On the back nine he shot a six-under 30, ending the day in fourth place, just three strokes behind the leader.

"The mental training for golf that my dad had put me through proved itself during that short walk from the ninth green to the tenth tee," he would later say, "and was completely vindicated by the way I played on the back nine."

Immediately after the first round, Tiger went to the practice range. He wanted to ingrain the feel of the swing he'd had on the back nine for the next round. Fluff Cowan and Butch Harmon watched him hit one perfect shot after another. Neither of them said a word. They didn't have to. There were still three rounds to play, but the sixty-first Masters was won in that lonely walk from the ninth green to the tenth tee on Thursday. From that moment on, Tiger ran away from the field.

On day two, he took sole possession of first place with an eagle on thirteen that sent a thunderous roar cascading across Augusta. He shot 66 on the day. Then on day three he shot 65, missing only one green and one fairway, giving him the largest fifty-four-hole lead in the history of the Masters. He was nine shots ahead of the field. He looked as though he were playing against old men. As he walked the course, he was greeted by screams of "Tiger! Tiger!" from waves of young fans who had never heard of Bobby Jones, Byron Nelson, or Ben Hogan. Consciously trying not to look anyone directly in the eye, he tipped his cap to what seemed like one giant blur of thousands of faces. He had never dreamt it would feel so magical.

On the night before the final round, Tiger was back at the house, contemplating what was ahead. *A nine-shot lead with one round to go*, he thought. *It would be a nightmare to lose such a lead.* Only one year earlier, Greg Norman had melted down in the final round, blowing a six-shot lead to lose the Masters. If he lost a nine-shot lead, Tiger knew, the failure would follow him the rest of his career. He couldn't let that happen.

After everyone else had gone to bed, Tiger went to Earl's bedroom to check on him. Earl was exhausted, but Tiger knew he would find him awake. Ever since Tiger was a kid, they had always talked through the final round of a tournament before going to sleep. And more than ever, Tiger wanted to hear what his father had to say. The last eighteen holes, Earl told him, would be the most difficult he had ever faced. His message was direct: don't get lackadaisical.

The next day Earl was too weak to leave the house. Knowing his father would be watching on television, Tiger wanted nothing more than to make him and his mother proud. But to do that, he needed to create some emotional distance. *I need to be that cold-blooded assassin*, he told himself.

When he arrived at Augusta, the magnitude of the moment sank in. He was about to become the youngest golfer to win the Masters. *Could this really happen?* he asked himself. It was an invigorating question, one that seemed to have gripped the entire country. A record forty-four million Americans tuned in to watch the final round of the Masters on CBS. That represented a 65 percent increase over the previous year.

Wearing a red shirt with a white Nike swoosh, Tiger walked up to the first tee shortly after three p.m. and entered his bubble of concentration. He remained there until he retrieved his ball from the ninth hole and began the short walk toward the tenth tee. This time it felt very different from the way it had three days earlier. With sixty-three holes behind him and just nine to go, he had built an insurmountable lead. As he approached the tenth tee, he allowed his mind to go to his dad, whom he visualized back at the house, watching on television. He thought of his mother, who he knew was walking the course as she had done for just about every tournament round he had played since he was a boy. With the two of them he had sat in the living room at age ten, watching Jack Nicklaus win the 1986 Masters on television, and dreamed of doing that. Here he was, eleven years later, and Jack Nicklaus was now elbowing his way through the masses of spectators, trying to get a glimpse of Tiger. The dream was fulfilled. The only question remaining was whether he could break the tournament record for the lowest score of all time.

No matter how weak he felt, Earl wasn't going to miss the moment. Rallying, he got out of bed, dressed, and had one of Tiger's friends drive him to the course in time to see the finish. He was waiting at the eighteenth green, where he watched Tiger on a small television monitor as he made his way up the eighteenth fairway.

Only fifteen months removed from being a teenager, Tiger walked through two massive columns of fans who closed in on him as he made his way to the green. It was an intoxicating rush to be on the edge of history. His final shot—a five-footer for par—sent the gallery into a frenzy as Tiger reacted with a right-arm uppercut. He hugged Cowan, then made a beeline for his ailing father and threw his arms around him. Kultida, beaming with pride, watched her son and husband embrace.

"We made it," Earl sobbed. "We made it. We made it."

Tiger didn't want to let go.

"I love you, son," Earl whispered, "and I'm so proud of you."

Those words were so rare and so cherished that Tiger wept in his father's arms. Finally, Kultida joined the embrace. The three of them were united, expressing affection. It may have been the happiest moment of Tiger Woods's life.

CHAPTER TWELVE

MANIA

Tiger's record performance at Augusta ranked as one of the most phenomenal moments in sports history, right up there alongside Cassius Clay upsetting Sonny Liston for the heavyweight boxing championship; Bob Beamon shattering the world long-jumping record by nearly two feet when he leaped 29 feet 4⅜ inches to win the gold medal at the Mexico City Olympics; and Secretariat winning the Triple Crown with his victory at the Belmont Stakes by an incredible 31 lengths. The sheer number of records Tiger had tied or set was mind-boggling:

- Youngest winner at twenty-one years, three months, and fourteen days (old record: twenty-three years, four days, by Seve Ballesteros in 1980)
- Lowest seventy-two-hole total—270 (old record: 271, by Jack Nicklaus in 1965 and Raymond Floyd in 1976)
- Largest margin of victory—twelve strokes (old record: nine strokes, by Jack Nicklaus in 1965)
- Lowest final fifty-four holes—200 (old record: 202, by Johnny Miller in 1975)
- Lowest first fifty-four holes—201 (tying the record set by Raymond Floyd in 1976)
- Lowest middle thirty-six holes—131 (old record: 132, by Nick Price in 1986)
- Most under par on back nine—sixteen under (old record: twelve under, by Arnold Palmer in 1962)
- Largest lead after fifty-four holes—nine strokes (old record: eight strokes, by Raymond Floyd in 1976).

More important than all the official records was another achievement: Tiger was the first golfer of African American heritage to win a major golf championship. That single accomplishment, more than anything else, would change his life in ways that were impossible to prepare for. Those changes began as soon as he stepped off the course at Augusta. Moments after signing his scorecard, Tiger spotted Lee Elder. Now sixty-two, Elder had been forty years old when he became the first black man to play in the Masters, the year Tiger was born. Stopping to hug Elder, Tiger whispered in his ear: "Thanks for making this possible." Elder melted into tears as he watched Tiger walk off to Butler Cabin for the traditional televised presentation of the green jacket. Grinning, Tiger held out his arms as Nick Faldo, the previous year's champion, slipped the coveted sports coat on him. The process was repeated moments later at the victory ceremony on the practice green behind the first tee, where Tiger noticed the abundance of black people from the Augusta staff who had left their posts and assembled on the lawn and the verandah on the second floor. It struck Tiger then that the barrier had been broken. Overwhelmed, he took the microphone and looked at the vast audience.

"I've always dreamt of winning the Masters and coming up eighteen like I did with the lead," he said. "I never thought this far through the ceremony."

The audience laughed, and a huge smile swept across Tiger's face.

"Last night my pop and I were talking," he continued. "He said, 'Son, this will be probably one of the hardest rounds you've ever had to play in your life. If you just go out there and be yourself, it will be one of the most rewarding rounds of golf you've ever played in your life.' And he was right."

Security guards then escorted Woods to the media center, where a throng of reporters were waiting. En route, Tiger got word that President Bill Clinton had called Augusta and was waiting on the line for him. That was his life now—a call from the president. Tiger ducked into a little room near the press area and listened as the president congratulated him on his win. He also invited Tiger to be his special guest at Shea Stadium. To mark the fifty-year anniversary of Jackie Robinson's breaking the color barrier in major league baseball, he was being honored on Tuesday night during a Dodgers-Mets game. Robinson's widow, Rachel Robinson, would be there. It would be an amazing moment, the president figured, for the young golfer who broke a color barrier at Augusta to be on hand to pay tribute to the man whom many viewed as the most important African American athlete in history. President Clinton even offered to send an air force plane to pick Tiger up.

Everything was happening so fast. Tiger breezed into the interview room wearing his green jacket, then quickly changed into another jacket and tie for the winner's dinner at the Augusta National clubhouse. Earl went back to the house to rest, and Tiger went to the dinner with his mother and Hughes Norton. Club members rose to their feet, along with all the other past winners and their spouses, as Tiger entered the dining room. At the back of the room, all the black staff—the cooks and waiters and busboys—set down their dishes and trays to clap louder and longer than the dinner guests. Bridging two worlds, Tiger paused, acknowledged the staff, and took his seat at the head table beneath a portrait of President Eisenhower.

By the time the dinner ended, Augusta looked like a ghost town. The tens of thousands of spectators were gone, and it was hard to find signs that only hours earlier it had been the site of one of the biggest sporting events in American history. Tiger piled into a Cadillac courtesy car with his mom and his friends, popped in a CD by the hip-hop group Quad City DJ's, cranked up "C'mon N' Ride It (The Train)" to full blast, and drove down Magnolia Lane with the windows down.

No Masters winner had ever left Augusta in such style.

The next morning, Tiger woke up with a headache and flew to South Carolina for the grand opening of an Official All-Star Café in Myrtle Beach. It was an obligation that had come with a new sponsorship deal he'd recently signed with Planet Hollywood, which owned the cafés. After being mobbed by fans, Tiger huddled with Hughes Norton, who had been deluged with phone messages. Some of them were from corporations seeking sponsorship deals with Tiger—fast-food chains, beverage companies, consumer products manufacturers, breakfast cereal makers, credit card companies, car companies; the list went on and on. With so many top brands now clamoring for Tiger, IMG urged him to expand his portfolio. Reluctantly, he authorized Norton to pursue a deal with American Express and said he wanted a deal with a watchmaker, a car company, and a video game company. That was it. No fast-food companies, no sugary sodas.

Most of the other messages Norton had to discuss with Tiger were from the media. David Letterman and Jay Leno wanted him to appear. Tiger said no. A bunch of newspapers and magazines wanted to talk to him. Tiger said no to them too. The big question was what to do about President Clinton's invitation to join him in New York the following evening. It wasn't every day that the leader of the free world offered to send an air force plane for you. But Tiger had planned to fly to Cancún for a much-needed escape. It would have been easy enough to delay his departure by a day to attend the Robinson event. But Tiger took it as a slight that the president had failed to include him in the earlier round of invites that went out to other notable black athletes. So his attitude toward Clinton, according to a source close to Tiger, was simple: Screw him. Tiger wasn't changing his plans, not even for the president. Norton said he would handle it, and Tiger boarded a plane for Mexico, where he hung out on the beach for four days, eating and drinking and celebrating with a couple of buddies from high school and college.

He was off the grid, but his fame was sweeping the globe. His Masters victory was being hailed in Europe, Asia, and Australia. At the same time, his decision to skip the Jackie Robinson ceremony was causing an uproar in the United States. Norton was fielding testy calls from journalists, such as this exchange with John Feinstein.

"Are you kidding me?" Feinstein said.

"He's tired," Norton said.

"He's always tired. This is the president of the United States and Jackie Robinson's widow. You go."

"He doesn't see it that way. He sees it as a last-second invitation, and he had plans."

"'Last-second'? He only won the Masters on Sunday. Were they supposed to know in advance he was going to win?"

No golf writer had gotten under Tiger's skin more than Feinstein. His criticism of Earl in his columns and on *Nightline* had roiled Woods more than anything that anyone had ever written about him or his golf game, and Earl was so furious that it was all he could do to refrain from taking matters into his own hands and getting physical with Feinstein.

Norton used intimidation of a different sort. Prior to the Masters, he called Feinstein and demanded a face-to-face meeting with him; his editor at *Golf Magazine*, Mike Purley; and the magazine's editor in chief, George Peper. The meeting took place over breakfast at Augusta, and Norton showed up with his IMG colleague Clarke Jones. It got off to a bad start when Jones demanded to know the identity of Feinstein's unnamed sources.

"Clarke, if I wanted you to know that, I'd have used their names in the magazine," Feinstein said.

"Well, I want to know right now!" Clarke said.

"Can't have everything you want in life, Clarke," Feinstein retorted.

Then Norton jumped in, suggesting that if Feinstein didn't cooperate, Tiger might decide to sign a contract as a "playing editor" with *Golf Digest* instead of *Golf Magazine*. At the time, Tiger was in talks with both publications.

Norton's not-so-subtle threat brought the breakfast to an abrupt and ugly end as Feinstein turned to his editors and said, "If you want to stay and eat with these two assholes, go ahead. But I have better things to do than listen to this crap."

A week later, Feinstein hammered Tiger for skipping the Jackie Robinson celebration at Shea Stadium. It became clear to Tiger that if he wanted Feinstein to back off, he was going to have to take matters into his own hands. He sent word through a PGA Tour PR rep that he wanted to meet with Feinstein. But with everything else that was going on in his life, he had to postpone the showdown.

Tiger flew straight from Cancún to the Nike offices in Beaverton, Oregon. By the time he landed, his decision to snub the president had reached beyond the sports pages and was making headlines in Washington. Maureen Dowd, the *New York Times* political writer with a reputation for skewering presidents and senators, wrote a column titled "Tiger's Double Bogey." In it, she suggested that Tiger was more interested in money than in honoring Robinson. "It is perplexing why a young man with such a long 'shelf life,' as his agent puts it, could not have paused on the merchandising mania for a couple of days."

Eventually, Tiger would come to the conclusion that he had made a mistake. But years would pass before he would get around to writing a letter of apology to Rachel Robinson. At twenty-one, he still had some growing up to do.

One day after the Dowd column ran, Tiger got word that fellow golfer Fuzzy Zoeller had made some racially insensitive comments about him during the final round of the Masters. A reporter for CNN's *Pro Golf Weekly* had interviewed Zoeller while Tiger was working his way through the back nine on the final day. By that point it was a foregone conclusion that he would win, and the reporter asked Zoeller what he thought about Tiger. "He's doing quite well," Zoeller said. "Pretty impressive. That little boy is driving well and he's putting well. He's doing everything it takes to win. So, you know what you guys do when he gets in here? You pat him on the back and say congratulations and enjoy it and tell him not to serve fried chicken next year [at the Champions Dinner that the winner would host the following year at the Masters]. Got it?" Zoeller then paused, snapped his fingers, turned away from the camera, and then turned back to add: "Or collard greens. Or whatever the hell they serve."

The comments aired on CNN one week after Tiger had won the Masters and were instantly compared to Los Angeles Dodgers executive Al Campanis's infamous interview with Ted Koppel in 1987, where he mused that blacks "may not have some of the necessities to be, let's say, a field manager or perhaps a general manager." A former teammate of Jackie Robinson's, Campanis was the general manager of the Los Angeles Dodgers when he made that statement, and it ended up costing him his job. Zoeller's comments brought many of the same old stereotypes back to the forefront of the news, presenting Tiger with another critical decision: How should he respond?

Tiger was familiar with Zoeller's reputation as a joker who made light of everything. *He couldn't have meant anything ugly*, Tiger thought. At the same time, he wondered why Zoeller had said those words as Tiger was approaching his historic victory. *His comments had a racist tinge*, Tiger thought. *Would it matter if he meant what he said as a joke? If he had, it sure didn't come across as funny.*

Confused and angry, Tiger initially chose to say nothing. When Zoeller reached out to him by phone, Tiger didn't call him back. In a public statement, Zoeller apologized, claiming that his comments weren't intended to be racially derogatory. "It's too bad that something I said in jest was turned into something it's not, but I didn't mean anything by it, and I'm sorry if I offended anybody. If Tiger is offended by it, I apologize to him too."

As Zoeller's statement got picked up by media outlets, Tiger flew to

Chicago and sat for an interview with Oprah Winfrey that was set to air later in the week. He was joined onstage by his father. Tiger anticipated questions about race, but Oprah surprised him by reading aloud a letter that Earl had written to him.

> Dear Tiger, you are my little man. You are my treasure. God gave you to me to nurture and to grow and to develop. I always have had your interests first and foremost in my life, and it always will be so. In fact, you mean more to me than life itself. I can remember when I taught you that it was okay to cry. That men can cry. It was not a sign of weakness, but a sign of strength. . . .
>
> I pass on all my abilities to share and to care to you. I realize that you have an infinitely higher capacity and capability to perpetuate this philosophy in our day's world. I trust that I have given you the guidance and love in which you can then execute that mission. What God has in mind for you, I don't know. It is not my call. It is my job to prepare you. I trust that I have done the best job that I can. I know you will give it your all and that you will be my little man forever. Love, Pop.

Tears streaming down his cheeks, Tiger wiped his eyes. He almost never allowed himself to show emotion, but for the second time in eight days he was crying on national television. It was no doubt an unusual and overwhelming experience. Earl didn't often express love and affection within the walls of his home—yet here he was doing it with Oprah in plain view of the millions of people watching from their living rooms.

Oprah also raised the subject of Tiger's heritage, asking him if it bothered him to be referred to as African American. "It does," Tiger said. "Growing up, I came up with this name: I'm a Cablinasian." It was a term that Tiger and some friends had coined when he was attending Stanford. "I'm just who I am," he told Oprah. "Whoever you see in front of you."

Tiger didn't think he was disrespecting blacks, nor was he trying to alienate anyone. But his comments were proof that he was still learning how to navigate the thorny subject of race in America. His views on a variety of important social issues were nowhere near as advanced as his golf game. He had been under the influence of his father's opinions for so long that there hadn't been enough time for his own to evolve, and the spotlight afforded him no margin for mistakes. Even before his interview with Oprah ran, two days after the taping, the Associated Press in Chicago previewed the segment under the headline: "Tiger Woods Doesn't Want to Be Called African-American." The story landed the same day that K-Mart announced it had dropped Fuzzy Zoeller for making racially insensitive remarks about Tiger.

Just when it looked like he was getting past the Jackie Robinson fiasco, Tiger was thrust back into an even sharper debate about race. NPR went to Harlem and did a whole show based on the slogan "I am Tiger Woods." Congress announced it was holding hearings to explore how the federal government defines and measures race and ethnicity in preparation for the next US Census, and some lawmakers were advocating for a new "mixed race" category. *Time* magazine ran a five-page spread titled "I'm Just Who I Am," quoting Tiger. The piece included a big photo of Tiger and his parents. Dealing with all this was a lot more taxing than mastering the game of golf.

Tiger reluctantly issued a statement on Fuzzy Zoeller, saying his attempt at humor was "out of bounds." But he himself had never apologized to African Americans for his own out-of-bounds jokes that had been published in *GQ*, an inconsistency that *New York Times* columnist Dave Anderson immediately pointed out in a column titled "Tiger Woods Also Needs to Apologize for Distasteful Jokes." Tiger was starting to feel like a piñata, getting hit on all sides, no matter what he said. By the time a reporter from *USA Today* raised, yet again, his decision to turn down President Clinton, asking what the reason was, Tiger unloaded.

"Well, one is I had planned my vacation already," Tiger said. "And, two, why didn't Mr. Clinton invite me before the Masters? If he wanted me there, I think it would have been best if he would have asked me before."

Yet in the midst of all the criticism, Tiger's popularity soared. A *Wall Street Journal*/NBC News poll published weeks after the Masters found that Tiger had shot past Michael Jordan as the most popular athlete in America. Only 2 percent of respondents gave Tiger a negative rating, and, according to the poll, he was more popular than Norman Schwarzkopf and Colin Powell the week after the Gulf War ended. Tiger even had a 74 percent positive rating among southern whites. "Only Robert E. Lee ever got a bigger number from the white South," the lead pollster said.

The results reinforced a powerful truth—in the eyes of fans, winning and greatness in athletics overshadow frailties in human character. All that talk about distasteful jokes in *GQ* and snubbing the leader of the free world and missing Jackie Robinson's commemoration and distancing himself from his African roots was just noise. People didn't really care what Tiger had to say about social issues or whether he considered himself black or Asian or Cablinasian. His athletic dominance was every bit as entertaining as Babe Ruth's had been in the twenties. Every time Tiger had a club in his hands, audiences were riveted. They expected something magical to happen, and more often than not, it did. That was all that really mattered.

CHAPTER THIRTEEN

CHANGES

Tiger's life was evolving so fast that he couldn't escape the feeling of being constantly off balance. As an introvert, he bristled under the strain of a microscope that seemed to get stronger and more intrusive by the day. Everywhere he went—the mall, fast food restaurants, movie theaters—sparked a small riot. Between autographs, photographs, and the endless line of interruptions, he found it exhausting to be out in public. Side doors and back entrances became his entries and exits of choice. In hopes of clearing his head, he took a month off following his victory at Augusta. But the golf course was the only place where he felt comfortable and completely in control, and in mid-May he returned to the Tour at the Byron Nelson Golf Classic in Dallas. Interest in him was so fervent that the tournament was forced to cut off ticket sales after one hundred thousand one-day passes and fifty thousand weekly passes were sold.

Determined and confident, Tiger started strong. But in the early rounds, he felt that something wasn't right with his swing. He was still playing better than everyone else, but he was winning with his putting and his short game. Things felt slightly off-kilter with his ball striking, especially off the tee. Concerned, at the end of the third round he called Butch Harmon, who immediately drove up from Houston so they could work on his swing before the final round.

On Sunday, despite going head-to-head with a Game 7 playoff contest between the New York Knicks and the Miami Heat on television, the Byron Nelson experienced a 158 percent jump in viewership from the previous year. More than eighty-five thousand fans jammed the grounds of the Four Seasons Resort to watch Tiger. Feeding off the crowds, he ended the day the same way he started it—two strokes ahead of everyone else.

As he walked off the eighteenth green with another victory notch in his belt, he received a hug from the Duchess of York, Sarah "Fergie" Ferguson, who had flown over from England to walk the course with Tiger's mother. The win pushed Tiger to number one on the PGA Tour money list for the year, with almost $1.3 million in just eight starts. He was the youngest player in history to earn $1 million in a season, and the first to surpass $2 million in overall career earnings. He'd achieved the milestone in fewer events than any golfer in Tour history. It hadn't even been a year since Tiger had turned pro, and it already seemed like everyone else was playing for second place. Like Jack Nicklaus, he *expected* to win. Now, with Big Jack in the twilight of his storied career, Woods was in a league of his own.

But Tiger couldn't stop worrying about his swing. He went to Golf Channel headquarters in Orlando and watched the tapes of his performance at Augusta. He found more than a dozen things he wanted to change. The position of the club at the top of his swing—aesthetically, it could be better. His short irons—he couldn't judge them particularly well. His movement off the ball—it was beautiful, but the club was across the target line, pointing well to the right of the spot he was aiming at. Plus, his clubface was closed down. His list of grievances went on and on. *God almighty*, he thought.

Harmon, however, wasn't concerned when he looked at the tapes. It was true that Tiger's club was slightly shut at the top, and his hands were opening up a bit on the follow-through. But he had won the Masters, the Byron Nelson, and a handful of other tournaments. He had the sweetest swing on the Tour. Why mess with success?

"I want to change this," Tiger said. "I want to do it now."

Harmon could hear the determination in his voice. It wasn't up for debate. So he suggested a more methodical approach: "We can do it a little bit at a time," he said.

"No," Tiger insisted. "I want to do it all right now."

Harmon was in awe. None other than Jack Nicklaus himself had described Tiger's Masters triumph as perhaps the finest tournament performance in PGA Tour history. Yet Tiger wanted to completely revamp his swing—not make subtle adjustments but tear it apart and construct a new version from the ground up. That realization raised some frightening possibilities. It also begged the question: What drives Tiger Woods?

Part of the answer resides in an observation that Kultida once made about her husband. "He couldn't relax," she said of Earl. "Searching for something, always searching, never satisfied." With Earl, the trait of never being satisfied—with one woman, with one drink, with any amount of money—led to some compulsive behaviors that had consequences for both his wife and his son. Tiger, to a certain degree, had inherited his father's restlessness. But at age twenty-one, his chronic dissatisfaction centered almost entirely on his performance. Beating other golfers or winning tournaments was never going to be enough for Tiger Woods. Even being ranked number one in the world didn't bring satisfaction. Golf, for him, was always so much more than a game.

"I was in it to find the answer to one question: How good can I be?" Tiger explained years later. "I suppose I was searching for perfection, although that's not attainable in golf except for short stretches. I wanted total control of my swing, and, hence, the ball."

The quest for total control led him to form some compulsive habits of his own. By the spring of 1997, Tiger was consumed with practicing and working out. A typical practice day for him entailed hitting six hundred balls, working on his short game and putting, playing a round (sometimes on his own), and working out in the gym for two to three hours. "That was the life I wanted," he said.

In her book *Just Can't Stop: An Investigation of Compulsion*, longtime science writer Sharon Begley references a growing body of scientific evidence that concludes compulsions are responses to anxiety. "Compulsions come from a need so desperate, burning, and tortured it makes us feel like a vessel filling with steam, saturating us with a hot urgency that demands relief," Begley writes. "They are an outlet valve, a consequence of anxiety as inevitable as burst pipes are a consequence of water freezing within a building's plumbing." Specifically, Begley cites creative geniuses like Ernest Hemingway, who felt so compelled to write every day that he once remarked: "When I don't write, I feel like shit." Hemingway's drive may have come from a dark, tortured place, but, as Begley points out, it drove him to "literary immortality."

Tiger Woods had developed habits that put him on a path toward golfing immortality. It would not be inaccurate to say that when he didn't practice, he felt like shit. The joy he derived from winning tournaments was always fleeting. Even shattering records at Augusta wasn't enough.

"I didn't care that I won by twelve shots," he later admitted. "I knew what I needed to do, Butchie knew what I needed to do, and, above all, I wanted to do it. I thrived on working on my swing. I was addicted to staying on the range for hours."

As a practical matter, changing a swing that virtually everyone envied as the greatest in golf was bizarre and risky. Harmon warned Tiger that until he perfected his new swing, he would very likely see a drop-off in his performance. He might not win another tournament for quite some time. Tiger's willingness to go along with Harmon's plan to create a new swing floored his coach. It's common for elite athletes to constantly look for ways to maintain their edge and refine their skills, but there was no precedent for an athlete at the top of a sport to step down from the pinnacle for a prolonged period of time in hopes of getting better. In so many ways, Tiger was mature far beyond his years when it came to golf. He was also a risk-taker. Abandoning the swing that had enabled him to conquer Augusta at age twenty-one would expose him to harsh criticism and force him to endure something he wasn't used to—losing again and again.

But it might also propel him to immortality. Sure, he could win the Masters, but Augusta happened to be perfectly suited to his strengths. In order to win the US Open, the British Open, and the PGA Championship, he knew he needed more control off the tee. The fairways at those tournaments weren't as forgiving as Augusta's. "I needed to tighten my swing if I was going to have a chance of winning them," he said. "I needed a swing that I could trust 100 percent."

And he wanted the Holy Grail.

On the eve of the Western Open on July 2, 1997, Tiger treated Mark O'Meara to dinner and a movie—*Men in Black*. O'Meara couldn't help wondering what was up, because normally Tiger never paid for anything. Whenever they went out, O'Meara always picked up the tab. But Tiger was in a celebratory mood. He was the number-one-ranked golfer in the world, and he was about to do something radical that might change that. But first, he planned to tee it up one more time with the swing that had gotten him to the top.

On the first day at Cog Hill Golf & Country Club outside Chicago, tournament organizers had to turn people away after sixty thousand fans showed up. It was Michael Jordan's town, but Tiger clearly owned it for four days. Feeling rested for the first time in weeks, he never doubted that he was going to win. By the end of the third round, the other golfers had come to the same conclusion when Tiger was tied for the lead. He had already established a reputation for not relinquishing leads. That proved to be true once again, and by the fifteenth hole of the final round he had the victory firmly in hand.

An estimated fifty-five thousand people packed the eighteenth fairway to witness his final hole. As soon as his second shot was airborne and Tiger started to walk toward his ball, thousands of fans—many of them teen-agers—broke through the ropes in a spontaneous eruption of joy. "They can't hold us back!" someone yelled. Unfazed and smiling, Tiger walked carefree down the fairway, leading the masses in a scene that looked like something out of a Frank Capra film. Then, after tapping in his final putt, he hurled his ball into the gallery.

The Western Open was Tiger's fourth victory on the PGA Tour in 1997. He admitted afterward that he hadn't played his best golf, but he had won by using what he called his greatest weapon: "my creative mind." It was a subtle way of saying that when he put his mind to it, he should be able to win. Earl was blunter: "If Tiger shows up with his A game, I don't care what game those other guys have. Tiger's going to win. It's that simple."

Earl was right. But Tiger knew something that even his father didn't yet understand. When he left Chicago, he would walk away from the swing that had taken him to the top. He wouldn't win again until May 1998. And it would take twenty-two months for him to master his new swing. For a guy whose favorite word was *compete*, Tiger was about to hit a mental wall that would test his resolve to stick with the belief that he was doing the right thing for the long run.

CHAPTER FOURTEEN

EXPLOITED

Right after turning pro, Tiger had made it clear that while he would do everything that Nike and Titleist required of him, he didn't want to do more endorsement work than that. But the lure of easy money was too strong to resist, especially for IMG. Tiger was the sports agency's most prized commodity, and Norton was working to open up as many revenue streams and capture as many commissions as possible. Earl approved of Norton's approach, and Tiger went along with it. First it was the Planet Hollywood deal, aligning Tiger with the company's All-Star Cafés; then came the rush of endorsement opportunities following the Masters. On May 19, 1997, one day after winning the Byron Nelson, Tiger flew to New York to announce his new sponsorship deal with American Express.

The financial services giant had gone all-in, paying Woods $13 million over five years—including $5 million up front—with another $1 million donated to Tiger's foundation to benefit minority golf. A dedicated American Express financial advisor was added to Tiger's team of lawyers and accountants. He also received an American Express Centurion Black Titanium card, typically offered only to members who charged upward of $450,000 per year on their cards. At twenty-one, he may have been the youngest person in the world with a Black card, and its annual $5,000 fee was waived. American Express felt it had secured the ideal global personality to help market its products to consumers in Asia and South America, where growth was occurring in both golf and credit cards. "In Tiger Woods, we have a representative who has captured the imagination of many different kinds of people," said company president Kenneth I. Chenault. "It's hard to visualize anyone he wouldn't appeal to."

A little over a week later, Rolex announced it had signed an endorsement deal with Tiger, paying him a reported $7 million over a five-year period. The company planned to repurpose its Tudor brand of watches in order to market them to a younger generation of consumers. The new watches would bear Tiger's name, and he would appear in television and print advertising campaigns.

At the same time, Earl was cashing in on Tiger's success. His book *Training a Tiger: A Father's Guide to Raising a Winner in Both Golf and Life* was published by HarperCollins in early April 1997. The initial print run was seventy thousand copies. The day after Tiger won the Masters, the publisher called for a second printing of twenty thousand copies. Then Earl went on the *Oprah Winfrey Show*, which led to more talk-show appearances, where he continued to emphasize his role in Tiger's success.

"He has to have someone to talk to and to reach out to and a shoulder to lean on," Earl told Charlie Rose. "You saw it on the eighteenth green at Augusta on the final day, when he was on my shoulder. That's home. That's his comfort zone."

"And his mother?" Rose asked.

"His mother to a degree," Earl said. "Mother is mother. But in our family, there is Father."

Earl's book ended up selling more than 233,000 copies in hardback and almost 60,000 copies in paperback. It was so successful that he signed a contract to write a follow-up book titled *Playing Through: Straight Talk on Hard Work, Big Dreams and Adventures with Tiger.* It would come out in the spring of 1998.

IMG was happy. Earl was happy. Tiger was feeling stressed out. He certainly didn't mind the money that was pouring in. After earning $13.1 million in the abbreviated 1996 season, he took home $21.8 million in 1997, and the majority of it—$19.5 million—was from endorsements. But everyone was pulling at him. On top of all the time commitments to his corporate partners, he was being pressured to get busy writing his instructional book for Warner Books. The publishing house had already paid him a substantial advance, and it was itching to take advantage of Tiger's red-hot name by getting the book onto the shelves.

"I don't have time for this shit!" Tiger snapped at Jaime Diaz, who had been talking to Norton about writing the book with him.

With everything else that was going on, Tiger had soured on the idea of writing an instruction book, and he certainly didn't want to think about an autobiography. Plus, Earl had gotten angry when he discovered that Norton had pitched Tiger's book idea without clearing it with him first.

The whole publishing business was starting to turn Tiger off. It felt like more and more people were trying to make money off him. Even before he had won the Masters, *Sports Illustrated*'s Tim Rosaforte published *Tiger Woods: The Making of a Champion*. Then, after the Masters, John Strege's book *Tiger: A Biography of Tiger Woods* came out, infuriating Tiger. To him, it seemed like everyone who got close to him was exploiting his fame for profit.

"People have something to gain off of me instead of just being a good friend," he said at the time.

Strege saw it differently. He had started covering Tiger for the *Orange County Register* back when he was a young teen. Due to his close relationship with the family, he had approached Earl in September 1996, right after Tiger turned pro, and told him that he wanted to write a book. Earl gave Strege his blessing, and Kultida even gave him access to the scrapbooks she had compiled over the first twenty years of Tiger's life. In less than three months, Strege banged out a 238-page book. But when it came out, he got the cold shoulder. He sent a copy to Earl and Kultida, but they never responded. Hughes Norton stopped taking his calls too. Norton's secretary finally informed Strege that he'd been cut off from the family. Strege even wrote a favorable column about Tiger for *Golf Digest*, but when one of the magazine's photographers approached Tiger on Strege's behalf in hopes of reviving the friendship, it didn't go well.

"John Strege wrote a pretty good column about you," the photographer said. "Did you see it?"

"Fuck John Strege!" Tiger told him.

After years of a close relationship, one in which the Woods family regularly called on Strege for help and to get stories about Tiger strategically placed in the paper, Strege never heard from the Woodses again. Tiger, in particular, ostracized him. "It occurred to me that to be his friend, you had to be his friend exclusively on his terms," Strege concluded.

In between rounds at the 1997 Masters, Tiger played *Mortal Kombat*, a fantasy fighting video game that was notorious for its bloody violence. Its particularly graphic finishing moves—known as "fatalities"—were instrumental in prompting the creation of a rating system for video games. *Mortal Kombat* was just one of several games that Tiger indulged in on and off the Tour. At one point, he spent an entire week hidden away in his Isleworth home, lying on the couch, playing video games. In terms of endorsements, the one deal that Tiger genuinely wanted was a partnership with a video-game company. But that had become another source of frustration.

In the summer of 1997, a small team from EA Sports met with Tiger and Norton in Isleworth. At that point, EA—with its cocky slogan "If it's in the game, it's in the game"—was the eight-hundred-pound gorilla in video games. Riding the wave of *Madden NFL* and the global success of FIFA soccer, EA had a business model that aggressively targeted teenage boys and what it liked to call "the fraternity couch," where all college guys were equal, no matter their size or success with women. The company had long held the exclusive PGA Tour license, but that franchise was floundering, sitting a distant fourth on the EA pecking order behind Madden, FIFA, and NHL hockey. From a gaming standpoint, the PGA Tour's conservative mind-set and its middle-aged demographic didn't connect with EA's target audience.

But then came Tiger Woods, looking like a potential white knight armed with the kind of image that would retrofit the game to appeal to youth. Nevertheless, when Norton reached out to EA, its executives weren't convinced that Tiger was a legitimate gamer and felt that there could be no fooling the target audience, guys who live, breathe, and play video games on a daily basis. So before being willing to put up millions of dollars to hire Tiger as a spokesman, EA's team wanted to test his bona fides in the clubhouse at the country club near his home.

He didn't disappoint. When asked what kind of games he played, Tiger was exact. "I don't play a ton of sports games," he told them. "I like driving games. I like shooting games. *Need for Speed. Mortal Kombat.*"

Tiger was also versed in the design of the games, and he made it clear that if he signed on to endorse a golf game for EA, he would insist on being involved in the details. He wanted the game to be authentic.

Tiger's answers were exactly what EA had hoped to hear, and when Norton started pushing for a deal, EA was ready to sign. But the negotiations stalled because of a contract dispute between IMG and Nike, one that boiled down to a single subclause regarding Tiger's "interactive rights": Nike owned them, and wanted to sell them to EA to help offset the millions they were paying Woods.

Mike Shapiro, the Tiger Woods brand manager at Nike, said Norton didn't realize this until he pointed it out to him. Norton and his team at IMG had brilliantly orchestrated a remarkable number of deals for Tiger in a very short time. Many of them were complicated, and none more so than the Nike agreement. In the hundreds of pages of terms negotiated on Tiger's behalf, IMG seemed to have overlooked this critical provision.

Norton wanted a face-to-face meeting with Shapiro, who agreed to come to Cleveland. He had barely sat down in IMG's conference room when Norton started in on him. "As far as Team Tiger is concerned," Norton told him, "we retained those rights."

"Read the contract," Shapiro said.

"I read it," Norton said. "We own the rights."

"That's not an objective interpretation," Shapiro said flatly. "It says we have . . . video game rights."

The meeting was tense, and it ended badly.

A small man with a huge ego, Norton relished a good fight, whether it was squabbling over the tiniest detail with his ex-wife in divorce court or holding the line on a subclause in a client's contract. In many ways, Norton's personality shaped the way he went about trying to maximize endorsement opportunities for his superstar clients. But he suddenly found himself in a standoff with Tiger's biggest corporate partner. Nike's lawyers held their ground, and Mike Shapiro wasn't the least bit intimidated by Norton's tactics. Before joining Nike, Shapiro had been the vice president of business affairs at Turner Sports, where he negotiated telecast rights with the NFL, NBA, PGA Tour, and Major League Baseball. Prior to that he'd been general counsel of the San Francisco Giants. He knew contracts, and he knew rights. There would be no endorsement deal between Tiger and EA without Nike's approval.

The acrimony between Norton and Shapiro drove Tiger up the wall.

"What's going on?" Tiger asked Shapiro. "Can't you just work this fucking thing out?"

"Well, Hughes and I have different opinions on things," Shapiro told him.

"Well, fuck that," Tiger said. "Just work it out. Hughes is bad-mouthing you. You're bad-mouthing him."

Norton ended up losing the argument, but he exacted revenge by playing hardball with Tiger's time. Tiger's eventual deal with EA guaranteed that the video-game company would have two or three days with Tiger each year for marketing and design development, the latter requiring green-screen motion-capture photography and dozens of on-course shots. Norton, according to Shapiro, made it difficult for EA to get onto Tiger's calendar. When dates finally opened up, the shoots were conducted on Tiger's turf and run with military efficiency from dawn to dusk. If EA had three hours blocked to shoot a TV commercial in which Woods had eight lines, once those lines were done to Tiger's satisfaction, the shoot was over. Tiger also said no when EA's marketing team wanted gamers to drive the ball 500 yards off the tee. "I can hit it 340 with the wind," Tiger told them. "Not 500."

In 1998, EA released the game *Tiger Woods 99 PGA Tour Golf*. It was a runaway success.

Nike had big plans for Tiger. In hopes of leveraging its star athlete to expand the company's brand in the lucrative Asian market, it created the Tiger Woods Invitational tournament in Tokyo, which took place in early November 1997. The tournament featured Nick Price, Mark O'Meara, and Shigeki Maruyama, and it marked Tiger's first trip to Japan. Massive crowds turned out to see him play. But from the moment he arrived, he was weary and aloof.

A week earlier, he had wrapped up the PGA Tour for the year with a twelfth-place finish in the Tour Championship. The week before that, he had crapped out at the Las Vegas Invitational thanks to a terrible third round. Earlier in the summer he had finished nineteenth at the US Open, twenty-fourth at the British Open, and twenty-ninth at the PGA Championship. Golf writers were already starting to suggest that he was in a slump, and more than one tour pro was whispering that golf's great new hope was human after all. Some of them seemed to find satisfaction in his struggles. "Tiger is proving to be a lot like everybody else on the PGA Tour," quipped Greg Norman at the end of the 1997 season. "Tiger got off to a phenomenal fast start. But he's come back to reality, and he's just another golfer out there."

Word had gotten around that Tiger was working on his swing, but he'd been customarily secretive about it. No one realized that he had abandoned his championship swing and was learning an entirely new approach. Nor did guys like Norman appreciate the demands that came with the kind of stardom that reached far beyond the world of golf.

Wishing he could just disappear, Tiger had reluctantly agreed to sit for a thirty-minute on-camera interview with Fox Sports, which had purchased the US rights to the Tokyo event. He was so reluctant to do the interview that it took the network a month of negotiations to settle on a time and location, but it was finally set for a Friday night in a Tokyo hotel. That afternoon, as Tiger was sitting in a helicopter at the tournament course, waiting to be ferried back to Tokyo for the interview, a woman climbed on board. Looking out the window, Tiger paid no attention to her.

"Hi, Tiger," she said. "I'm Deb Gelman, and I work with Nike."

Tiger turned and looked at her. "Hi," he said. "I'm Jose Cuervo." Then he turned and continued to stare out the window. He didn't say another word on the flight.

Gelman worked as a producer for Nike Sports and Entertainment, the company's newest division. One of her jobs was to make sure Woods showed up for the interview. At the hotel, Tiger went with her to the penthouse suite, where he sat down with Roy Hamilton, a former first-round pick of the Detroit Pistons who had become one of the most prominent African Americans in sports television.

Tiger wasn't interested in pleasantries. The clock started ticking the moment he entered the room, and precisely thirty minutes later, he stood up and removed the microphone that had been clipped to his shirt. Fox had set up a table with memorabilia—pin flags, posters, and such. Hamilton asked Tiger if he would mind signing some things. Without saying a word, Tiger walked past the table and left the room.

To those present, he came across as cold. But he was constantly being asked to autograph collector's items. Fans at tournaments had gotten so aggressive that he'd been cut under the eye on a couple of occasions when stray pens were pushed in front of his face. No matter where he went in public, he was stopped by strangers who wanted signatures and photos. The cumulative effect of this barrage forced him to put up some boundaries. At tournaments he tried to accommodate children, but even there he was leery of memorabilia hounds who would use kids as runners to get things signed that would then be sold in stores and at shows. At events that were organized by his corporate sponsors, Tiger signed anything and everything, spending more time than most athletes interacting with the people in attendance. But the table full of memorabilia at the hotel in Tokyo didn't fit into that category. His deal with Fox said nothing about signing flags and balls and programs. So he didn't.

The following morning, Tiger was scheduled to appear at a golf clinic prior to the final round. But he failed to show, disappointing hundreds of kids. Instead, he arrived at the course just in time to play. It appeared that he had had too much to drink the night before and was still feeling the effects. He asked a friend if he had any breath mints or gum.

"I do," Gelman chimed in.

"Meet me on every tee and every green on every hole," Tiger told her.

It was the first time he had spoken to her since the initial meeting on the helicopter. But for the next eighteen holes, Gelman was suddenly Tiger's best friend. When the round was over, he didn't say thank you or good-bye. He just disappeared.

"He struck me as so unhappy," Gelman said in 2015. "Everyone wanted a piece of him. He was so wary. It was very evident he didn't trust anyone not in his inner circle."

On Monday, January 5, 1998, Tiger was in San Diego, preparing for the Mercedes Championships. He also saw an opportunity to take up some unfinished business: John Feinstein was in San Diego too. He was conducting interviews with PGA Tour pros for his forthcoming book *The Majors: In Pursuit of Golf's Holy Grail.* Tiger sent word to him that he wanted to meet that night at a seaside restaurant. Before Feinstein arrived, Tiger asked for a corner table, and he was sitting there when Feinstein showed up.

"Couldn't wait to see me, huh?" Feinstein said, trying to break the ice with a joke.

"Actually, I'm just hungry," Tiger said flatly, choosing not to see the humor.

They didn't exactly hit it off. But over a long dinner, they hashed out their differences, especially Feinstein's comparison of Earl Woods to Stefano Capriati.

"I really don't think your dad is different than any other pushy, grab-the-bucks father," Feinstein told him. "Except for one thing: you're his son. So I give him some credit for your genes, because you're smart enough and tough enough to deal with everything he's pushed on you and still be a great player. Most kids aren't that way. I think you've succeeded in spite of your father, not because of your father."

Showing no emotion, Tiger defended Earl. He also pushed back when Feinstein pointed out that Earl had written a book that bragged about how he had created Tiger.

"He just did that because so many people asked him, 'How did you do it?'" Tiger said. "He figured it was easier to write a book than to try to answer the question a million times."

"Really?" Feinstein said. "Then why did he write the second book?"

Tiger stared at Feinstein. Then he laughed and said, "Good one."

The back-and-forth was like a chess match; Tiger was looking for weakness and finding little. He brought up the breakfast at Augusta when Feinstein had walked out on Norton and Jones. "I have to admit, you surprised them," Tiger said. "I think they figured going to your boss would get your attention."

Feinstein explained that he didn't really have a boss; he made most of his money from writing books, not covering golf for *Golf Magazine*.

Tiger eased back in his chair. "So that's it," he said. "You really don't need any one job?"

"No, I don't," Feinstein said.

"Makes it tougher to intimidate you, doesn't it?"

At the end of the night, Feinstein thanked Tiger for arranging the dinner. "You don't need me to like you or to write or say good things about you," Feinstein said. "You're Tiger fucking Woods. I think it says a lot about you that you did this. And I learned a lot tonight, not just about why we disagree on things but also about who you are."

Nodding, Tiger said, "What'd you learn about me?"

"That you're smarter than I thought you were."

Before parting, Feinstein told Tiger that he had a mini-book about him coming out in a few weeks. "I'll get you a copy as soon as I have one," he said. "It basically says the same things about your dad that we discussed tonight."

"I probably shouldn't read it, then," Tiger said.

"Probably not. But I don't want you to be blindsided by it. I'll stick it in your locker when I get it."

It seemed as though any ill feelings between them had been aired and resolved; at least, that was how Feinstein felt. He and Tiger continued to exchange friendly hellos when they would see each other at tournaments, and eventually Tiger acceded to Feinstein's request to do a sit-down interview for *The Majors*. At Tiger's suggestion, the interview was scheduled for the end of the year in Atlanta, during the Tour Championship.

But Tiger was a lot like his parents when it came to grudges. *Forgive* and *forget* were not part of their vocabulary. Earl never forgave a slight, and neither did Tida. Similarly, Tiger had a hard time letting go. Two months after the dinner in San Diego, Feinstein placed a copy of his new mini-book in Tiger's locker during a tournament. As he had warned, the book defended his previous articles comparing Earl Woods to Stefano Capriati. "The comparisons are legitimate," Feinstein wrote. "Both fathers willingly turned their children into meal tickets long before they had turned pro. . . . The only job Earl Woods has held since 1988 was the one provided for him by Hughes Norton and IMG."

The passage delivered a fresh blow to Earl's dignity. Nothing angered Tiger like public criticism of his father. The other thing he couldn't stand was people profiting off him, especially journalists. Feinstein, in Tiger's eyes, had managed to do both.

CHAPTER FIFTEEN

INSTINCTS

The week of the 1998 Masters, Tiger appeared on the cover of *Sports Illustrated*, posing with a 650-pound white Bengal tiger named Samson. The exotic beast, along with another tiger of the same size named Dimitri, had been flown to Isleworth for a photo shoot in the country club's posh ballroom. The magazine had pitched the idea of photographing Tiger with a couple of genuine adult male tigers to Hughes Norton, who had serious reservations: if something went wrong, the consequences could be horrific. As it turned out, right before Tiger arrived, something did go wrong—Samson lost his footing on the canvas that had been hung for the photo backdrop and got spooked. The animal darted across the room, causing *SI*'s creative director to bolt for the door. Norton was not pleased to see the tiger still growling when Woods walked in. But Tiger went right up to Samson, and the animal immediately calmed down. David McMillan, the tigers' handler, was amazed.

"That young man projects supreme confidence like no one I've ever seen," he told the magazine. "You can't fake that with a big cat. Samson sensed no weakness or fear in Tiger, just power and inner peace."

The encounter spoke volumes about Tiger's ability to mask his true feelings. For his entire life, he'd been disguising his emotions from friends, from opponents, from the media. Even an animal that thrived on instincts had misread Woods. The truth was that in April 1998, the circumstances of Tiger's life were giving him very little inner peace. While posing for the cover with the tigers, Woods was dealing with death threats. It was part of the ugly consequences of extreme fame. He never talked publicly about the threats, nor did he report them; but on the eve of the '98 Masters, he disclosed the situation to Mark and Alicia O'Meara.

They immediately invited Tiger to stay with them at Augusta; he could lie low, and no one would know his whereabouts. For twenty years, O'Meara had rented a home from Peggy Lewis, a local schoolteacher in Augusta who, like many people in the area, supplemented her income by making her house available for the week of the Masters. There was an extra bedroom.

Tiger took them up on the offer.

Standing six feet one, Tiger arrived at the 1998 Masters weighing 170 pounds, a twenty-pound increase from his weight at the '97 Masters. The extra weight was all muscle. He'd been spending an inordinate amount of time in the gym, power lifting. Although he already hit the ball harder and farther than anyone on the Tour, he craved more explosiveness off the tee. In his words, he wanted to "really tear through the ball from the top of his backswing." Through personal study, he concluded that he should develop his fast-twitch muscles by lifting heavy weights at a fast pace and supplementing his weight training with a lot of sprinting. He also developed his slow-twitch muscle fibers by doing long endurance runs and alternating his fast-pace lifts with slower-pace lifts. Often that meant two workouts a day. Bench-pressing 225 pounds and squatting more than 300 pounds, he had a physique that was unlike that of any other golfer on Tour. He was starting to look like a defensive back in the NFL.

But Tiger was tired. He'd spent the entire week before the Masters resting up in Isleworth, and it had helped to a certain extent—he played consistently in the tournament, shooting 71, 72, 72, and 70. It was a far cry from his performance a year earlier, but not bad for being in the midst of learning a new swing. He hung around the top of the leaderboard all weekend and ended up finishing tied for eighth place.

O'Meara, on the other hand, played the best golf of his life and captured his first major championship. It was a poetic moment when Tiger, as the defending champion, placed the green jacket on his best friend on the Tour. They had played countless hours of golf together over the previous eighteen months, and Tiger's influence had inspired O'Meara to elevate his game. O'Meara said he was channeling a bit of Woods when he birdied three of the final four holes to secure his first major.

Back at the rental house, an atmosphere of euphoria set in. Never expecting her husband to win, Alicia hadn't packed any formalwear. Peggy Lewis gathered up shoes and a dress and raced back to her home to help Alicia get ready for the Champions Dinner. While Mark and Tiger got ready, Alicia and Peggy went next door to iron the dress and have a glass of wine with the neighbors. After a few minutes, Tiger entered the house next door to Lewis's in search of Alicia. *Oh my God!* Lewis thought. She knew Tiger was staying in her home, but she had yet to meet him. Excited, she stood and extended her hand.

"Hi, Tiger, my name is Peggy Lewis. You're staying in my house next door."

Without saying a word, Tiger ignored Lewis's hand, turned to Alicia, and asked when they were leaving.

Everyone stopped talking and looked at Lewis as she sheepishly withdrew her hand.

Alicia looked at Tiger. "I'll be over in a few minutes," she said.

Humiliated, Lewis quietly sat down as Woods walked out, never acknowledging her.

Tiger was pleased for O'Meara, who would go on to win the British Open a couple of months later. Meanwhile, his own game was rounding into form. In February, he had stormed back from an eight-stroke deficit in the final round to win the Johnnie Walker Classic in Thailand. Even though Tiger had come up short at the 1998 Masters, he was a more complete player than he'd been a year earlier. In addition to being the second-longest player on Tour, he had become much straighter. And he had quietly risen to second in scoring average. But it had been nine months since he'd won a PGA Tour event, and he was sick of hearing "What's wrong with Tiger?"

Harmon kept reminding him that the only question that mattered was "Are you on track?" And from Harmon's perspective, the answer was a definite yes. It was misleading to say Tiger was in a slump; it just appeared that way after such a dazzling start to his career. If anything, Tiger was a victim of his own success. He had set the bar so high that anything short of victory was deemed a failure. Behind the scenes, he had replaced his grip-it-and-rip-it approach with a more controlled swing that was intended to lower his trajectory. In a further effort to lower the flight of his ball, he had also switched to a graphite-shafted driver. His posture was different too. All these changes went largely unnoticed, but Harmon could see what was coming. Tiger's swing overhaul was right on schedule, and the results were impressive. He had to keep reminding himself, *This kid is only twenty-two years old!*

In May 1998, Tiger won the BellSouth Classic, giving him his first Tour victory in ten months and reinforcing in his mind that he was on the right track.

Outside the ropes, however, he wasn't as sure of himself. After so many years of having parents who tightly controlled everything, Tiger was now learning life's lessons on his own. Other than Harmon, O'Meara was the one guy Tiger looked to for guidance. O'Meara urged him to try to be more approachable. Most people just wanted the thrill of being able to say, hey, Tiger Woods said hi to me or looked me in the eye, he said.

But it wasn't easy for Tiger to connect with strangers. He had enough trouble connecting with the other guys on Tour. As a result, he spent a lot of time by himself. At a press conference following a tournament in 1998, Tiger was asked point-blank: "Do you feel alone?"

"No," he said abruptly. "I've got a lot of good friends. Trust me."

He did have a social life. At that time, he was playing golf with Kevin Costner, Glenn Frey, and Ken Griffey Jr. There was an endless list of celebrities and television personalities who wanted to be around him. But his relationships with actors, rock stars, and other elite athletes were more a result of him being the alpha male in the fraternity of fame. When it came to having someone he could actually go to for sound, unfiltered advice about life and the challenges he faced, Tiger essentially had the O'Mearas. They were the ones who were most likely to tell him what he needed to hear, as opposed to what he wanted to hear. But even with Mark, Tiger held back. He would seek his advice on the business side of golf, and talk about sports, fishing, and the Tour. But when it came to life and matters of the heart, Tiger was never comfortable around men—not even Mark.

He would, however, occasionally drop his guard around Alicia. It helped that she never told him how to live his life, almost never talked to him about golf, and was not the least bit dazzled by his celebrity status. She also sensed that he needed to be around people, and that he didn't really have anyone else. In particular, his fame made it very difficult to find a girl that he could trust. One evening, Tiger accompanied Mark and

Alicia to a party at the home of tennis pro Todd Woodbridge in Isleworth. At one point, Tiger and Alicia ended up alone at the punch bowl.

"How do you know who you can trust?" Tiger said quietly.

"You don't," Alicia said.

Her answer intrigued him.

"You just have to trust your instincts," she continued. "It's hard, because you're in this little bubble. You're going to have to reach out. You have to have relationships in your life."

Her words stuck with him. Later that summer, Tiger went to a party at the University of California, Santa Barbara, where he had agreed to go on a date with a twenty-year-old student named Joanna Jagoda. Born in Poland and raised in the San Fernando Valley, Jagoda was a political-science major who had her sights on law school. A blonde who had been a cheerleader in high school, Jagoda soon became a familiar sight on the PGA Tour. Despite suddenly being in the bright spotlight that was trained on Tiger, she discreetly avoided the press and maintained a low profile. By the latter part of the 1998 season, she was traveling with Tiger, and eventually moved into his Isleworth home.

Mark and Alicia adored Joanna, who quickly became a leveling influence in Tiger's life. Shortly after she showed up, Tiger decided to take control of the decision-making process in his business affairs. From the beginning, the triangular relationship with his father and Hughes Norton had worn on him. In the summer of 1998, the three of them appeared on the cover of *GolfWorld* under the headline "The Father, Son, and Holy Ghost." Norton's ego was outsize to begin with, and had only gotten bigger when Tiger came along. In their short time together, Norton had secured roughly $120 million in endorsement deals for Tiger. It was unprecedented. His corporate partners included Nike, Titleist, Planet Hollywood, American Express, Rolex, EA Sports, Asahi, Cobra, *Golf Digest*, Unilever, and Wheaties. The list just kept growing, and that was part of the problem. Mondays were essentially the only days on which Tiger had any free time, and increasingly IMG was filling that time with sponsorship commitments that generated hefty commissions for the agency.

In October 1998, less than two months after Norton was referred to as a deity in *Golf Digest*, Tiger decided that he no longer wanted him as his agent. In October 1998, barely two years after turning pro, Tiger fired him.

The *Los Angeles Times* broke the news, reporting: "This week, Norton was downgraded from Holy Ghost to just plain ghost."

The move was a blow to Norton's ego, one that forced him to admit that he hadn't seen it coming. "It's hard to understand the decision Tiger has made," Norton said. He added, "He earns more per endorsement than any other athlete in the world, including Michael Jordan."

Norton was proud of the job he'd done for Tiger. But Norton was viewing his dismissal through the prism of money and deals, and Tiger saw things differently. More important, Mark O'Meara's view of Norton had changed. "Hughes was a hard-driven guy," O'Meara explained. "He would go for the jugular. I wanted an agent who was a little less confrontational and a little more professional." Nobody on Tour had more influence over Tiger than O'Meara, and once he said good-bye to Norton, it was only a matter of time before Tiger did the same. As it was, Tiger had never really connected with Norton, who had been handpicked by Earl. More and more, Tiger saw the agent as working for his father, not him. The decision to break with Norton was part of Tiger's effort to become his own man.

At first, Earl argued to keep Norton.

"He's been good to us," he told Kultida. "Let's give him another chance."

"No," Kultida said. "Tiger don't like Hughes. He don't want to be with Hughes. I don't like Hughes. He gotta go."

Once Norton's dismissal became public, Earl tried to appear as though he'd been behind the decision, telling the press that Norton had "overcommitted" Tiger. The truth was that, other than Tiger's book deal with Warner Books, Earl had been involved in every endorsement that Norton had pursued on Tiger's behalf.

But Tiger would almost never publicly acknowledge fault in his father. Although he no longer allowed anyone—including Earl—to tell him what to do, he remained intensely protective of his father's reputation. When Earl made an ugly comment about the people of Scotland in the lead-up to the British Open, Tiger insisted that his father had never made the statement, despite the fact that a reporter had it on tape. Tiger added, "My dad didn't mean any harm if he did say it, but I don't think he even said it." Similarly, the more he thought about it, Tiger just couldn't bring himself to sit for the interview he had promised to John Feinstein. So a few days before the start of the 1998 PGA Championship in Washington State, Tiger was on the putting green at Sahalee Country Club when he dispatched an IMG employee to track down Feinstein. A few minutes later, Feinstein showed up. "Heard you were looking for me," he said.

Tiger looked up and nodded. "Look, I'm sorry about this, because I feel like I made a commitment, but I just can't do the thing with you in Atlanta for your book."

"Okay. Is there a particular reason?"

"Yeah. I just can't get past what you've said and written about my father."

Feinstein didn't get it. His book had been out for five months. Besides, they'd been over this stuff.

"I thought we talked all that out in San Diego," Feinstein said.

"I thought we had too. But I just can't get past it," Tiger said.

After cutting ties with Norton, Tiger was ready to leave IMG altogether. But then CEO Mark McCormack stepped in and suggested that Tiger meet with a couple of young, up-and-coming agents, including one who, unlike the others he'd dealt with at the agency, had not been born into privilege.

Mark Steinberg grew up in Peoria, Illinois, and earned a spot as a walk-on on the University of Illinois basketball team that in 1989 made it to the Final Four. After law school, he interned at IMG before being hired. His main assignment was to recruit players in women's golf, and his first big break came in 1993 when he signed Michelle McGann and Karrie Webb. The following year he hit the equivalent of a hole in one when he brought Annika Sörenstam into the IMG fold. A year later, Sörenstam won the US Women's Open, putting herself and Steinberg on the sports-marketing map.

Tiger agreed to meet with Steinberg. After the meeting, Steinberg explained his philosophy about time management: "There is only so much these players can do, and there is only so much time in a day," he said. "One of the challenges is creating the most efficient schedule for Tiger."

Tiger had found the man he was looking for—a guy in his early thirties who'd played competitive sports in college and was just as interested in being Tiger's friend as he was in being his agent.

The sudden presence of Steinberg and Joanna Jagoda were a stark signal from Tiger that he was shedding his past and forming a new inner circle, starting with two people from his own generation. Jagoda was a tempering influence, bringing a sense of calm to Tiger's frenetic lifestyle. It was not uncommon for them to spend their nights at home, and he went out of his way to protect her privacy. "She's his secret weapon, and he's not about to throw her to the wolves of the golfing circuit," a Tour source said.

But Steinberg's experience with women's golf had not prepared him for the madness that surrounded his new client. Shortly after taking over as Tiger's agent, Steinberg traveled with him to England. The two of them were exiting a restaurant in London when the paparazzi pounced, shouting questions while their cameras clicked in rapid succession. Shell-shocked, Steinberg jumped in front of Tiger and started flailing his arms and trying to shield Tiger's face. While Steinberg looked like he was dancing on hot coals, Tiger calmly walked through the onslaught and ducked into the back seat of his car. Steinberg rushed around to the other side and got in.

Tiger reached across the seat and put his arm around him. "Let's just understand," Tiger said. "My life is crazy. Welcome to my world. You're going to have to calm down a little bit."

CHAPTER SIXTEEN

I GOT IT

Tiger Woods had never needed any external motivation, but he was getting a big dose of it from David Duval. While Tiger continued to reconstruct his swing, twenty-six-year-old Duval won four PGA tournaments in 1998, finishing the year ranked number one on the lists of scoring-average and money-list leaders. Tiger ranked number two and number four, respectively, on those lists. And although he still clung to the number one ranking as the top golfer in the world, Duval had moved up to number three. In the minds of some golf writers and analysts, Duval was on his way to eclipsing Tiger as the game's top player.

Tiger would never admit it publicly, but Duval was on his mind. In press conferences, he broke down Duval's play, and he could describe Duval's shots in intricate detail. The golf writers had been clamoring for a rivalry, and Duval emerged as the best candidate to challenge Tiger's supremacy, especially after he kicked off the 1999 season by winning the Mercedes Championships and, two weeks later, the Bob Hope Chrysler Classic, where he shot a record 59 in the final round. Those two wins pushed him past Tiger in overall Tour victories—nine to seven—and knocked Tiger out of the number one overall ranking.

The mounting debate over who was the preeminent golfer came at a time when Tiger was thinking seriously about making another major change in his team. Heading into the Buick Invitational at Torrey Pines in early February, Tiger asked his closest high school friend, Bryon Bell, to caddie for him. Tiger had remained close to Bell through college and his first couple of years on the Tour. It was Bell who had been instrumental in introducing Tiger to Joanna Jagoda.

After Tiger struggled through the first two rounds at Torrey Pines, narrowly making the cut, Bell knew exactly what to say. "You are so talented that if you play well, there's no one who can beat you," he told Woods. "Now go out and put up a number."

On Saturday, Tiger shot 62, a record on the demanding South Course, and his lowest round as a pro. It catapulted him past the forty-one players who'd been ahead of him, landing Tiger atop the leader board by one stroke. He maintained that momentum on the final day, holding on to his lead and capping things off with an eagle putt on the last hole. It had been nine long months since his last PGA victory. Instead of his trademark uppercut, he simply raised his arms the way a marathon runner does at the end of an exhausting race. After hugging Bell and handing him his putter, Tiger received the trophy and held it up to an enthusiastic round of applause.

Then Tiger was approached by Rick Schloss, who put his arm around him and introduced himself as the media director for the tournament.

"Is it okay if we take you to the Century Club Pavilion, take some photos with the VIPs, and then go to the media center?" Schloss said.

"Sure," Tiger told him. "No problem."

"I'll take the trophy," Schloss said, reaching for it.

"No," Tiger said. "I just beat 155 guys. *I'll* take the trophy."

It was unheard-of for the winner to carry the trophy from one stop to the next following the tournament. But Tiger wasn't about to let it out of his hands. His adamancy was an important clue to what makes Woods tick. Money didn't motivate him, nor did fame; he played for the hardware—the win. He'd been that way from the very beginning. As far back as age three, when he competed in his first golf competition—a local pitch, putt, and drive contest for kids ten and under—he finished second and had his pick of the prizes: a toy, a piece of golf equipment, or a trophy. He ignored the toys and chose the biggest trophy available, one that came up to his shoulders. By the time Woods reached high school, trophies and plaques lined his childhood home, and his parents showed them off whenever anyone visited. Likewise, Tiger prominently displayed his PGA Tour trophies in his house and liked to show them off when visitors came over. He always cared more about collecting trophies than making friends. Above all, Woods was a scorekeeper, and trophies symbolized wins—and wins denoted dominance.

When Tiger walked out of the Lodge at Torrey Pines and climbed into the back of a courtesy car, he was still carrying the trophy.

Tom Wilson, the executive director of the tournament, turned to Schloss.

"Where's the trophy?" Wilson said.

"Tiger's got it," Schloss told him.

Wilson raised his eyebrows. The trophy was supposed to remain with the tournament, not go with the winner.

"In that car," Schloss continued, pointing.

Wilson approached the vehicle and opened the rear passenger's side door.

"Hey, Tiger," Wilson said with a friendly grin. "We need to get the trophy back."

Tiger stared at him with an expression that said, *What the fuck?*

Wilson went on to explain that Woods was holding the perpetual trophy, the one that never leaves the tournament.

"We're going to send you a replica with the newspaper clippings and a whole book in a couple of weeks," Wilson continued.

Tiger said nothing as Wilson waited. Reluctantly, he finally handed it over. This trophy, in particular, symbolized a feeling he hadn't experienced in a long time—winning. It was a feeling he wanted to hold on to for as long as he could.

A week later, Fluff Cowan was back on the bag when Tiger showed up at the Nissan Open in Los Angeles. But Tiger kept his own yardage book and eyeballed his own putting lines. Publicly, Tiger insisted there was no problem between him and his caddie. "People are blowing the situation way out of proportion," he said on his website.

But privately, Tiger wasn't happy with Cowan. He had become something of a distraction, a celebrity more recognizable than 90 percent of the players on Tour. That was a problem. So was Cowan's decision to date a girl less than half his age, and his willingness to star in a hilarious series of ESPN "This Is *SportsCenter*" commercials. Tiger had started calling Cowan "a Deadhead with a yardage book."

Cowan's biggest mistake, however, had nothing to do with his choice in women or his fifteen minutes of fame. Twice during the 1998 season, *Golf Digest's* Pete McDaniel had gathered four of the top caddies on the Tour for a roundtable discussion. At one point during those discussions,

Cowan broke a cardinal rule for caddies by disclosing how much Tiger was paying him: $1,000 a week, plus 10 percent of wins. Aghast at the breach of professional protocol, the other caddies pressured Cowan to tell McDaniel he hadn't meant to say what he said. "Nah," Cowan said nonchalantly. "It's fine." Only it wasn't.

During the Nissan Open, *Golf Digest* published the issue containing Cowan's disclosure about his compensation, and Tiger hit the roof. He nearly won the tournament, finishing tied for second, but as soon as it was over, he asked Butch Harmon to recommend a few possible replacements for Cowan. Harmon offered just two names: Tony Navarro and Steve Williams.

Navarro wasn't available; he was caddying for Greg Norman, and when Harmon approached him, he made it clear that Norman had been too good to him for him to consider leaving him. That left Williams, a blunt-speaking, physically imposing thirty-four-year-old New Zealander who had begun caddying at age six. By fifteen he worked full-time for five-time British Open champion Peter Thomson, and then went on to caddie for Greg Norman and, eventually, Raymond Floyd. On tour, Williams was virtually without peer in club selection, yardage, and, even more important, his willingness to call his man off a club or shot.

Liking what he heard, Tiger urged Harmon to see if Williams was interested. On the eve of the Doral-Ryder Open in Florida, Harmon walked up to Raymond Floyd on the putting green and broached the possibility of his caddie going to work for Tiger. At that point, Floyd had won twenty-six tournaments with Williams at his side, but Floyd was fifty-six years old and playing primarily on the senior tour.

"Well, let me think about it," Floyd told Harmon.

But Tiger wasn't in the mood to wait. The next morning, he called Williams in his hotel room.

"It's Tiger Woods here," he said.

Thinking it was a prank call, Williams hung up without saying a word. Tiger called back, and Williams hung up again.

On his third attempt, Tiger blurted out: "No, no, it really is Tiger." Williams didn't hang up this time.

"I've parted ways with my caddie," he continued. "And I want to know if you'd like to caddie for me."

It was a pivotal moment for Woods, another crossroads. He had a new girlfriend who was starting to bring stability to his life off the course. He had a new agent who had seized control of his schedule and was quickly earning the nickname "Dr. No" for his fierce protection of Tiger's time. And he was on the cusp of completing his swing overhaul with Butch Harmon. The one thing Tiger lacked was a caddie with a strong presence who had the foresight to recognize what was happening on the course and the backbone to express his opinion on club selection, especially in pressure situations.

Intrigued, Williams drove directly to Isleworth at the conclusion of the Doral tournament. He vividly recalled the first time he had laid eyes on Woods; it was during a practice round at the 1996 Masters. Tiger was the reigning US Amateur champ and was grouped with Greg Norman, Fred Couples, and Raymond Floyd. Williams was on Floyd's bag that chilly morning when Tiger blew his drive way past the fairway bunker on the 575-yard, par 5 second hole. Dumbstruck, Norman, Couples, and Floyd watched in silence as Tiger's ball continued flying, looking as if it might never land. Williams was so impressed that for the first and only time in his life, he asked for an autograph. Tiger obliged, signing his scorecard at the end of the round. Almost exactly three years later, Williams rang Tiger's doorbell.

"Come on in," Tiger said. "But can you wait a minute? I've just got something I need to finish."

Tiger led him to a big-screen television, plopped down in his seat, slipped into a trance, and finished his video game.

Then the two men got to know each other. When Tiger asked Williams his approach to caddying, Williams gave him an earful. He had caddied on every continent and in nearly a hundred countries, and he didn't believe in simply carrying a bag and spilling out yardage. He saw himself as part strategist, part psychologist, and part mathematician, as well as a walking encyclopedia of each course and its quirks.

Williams could not have been more different from Cowan. A former rugby star in his native New Zealand, he was the only caddie on the PGA Tour who was more muscular than Tiger. They were both fitness fanatics, and Williams could easily double as Tiger's workout partner. He also had an air of arrogance, making it clear that he wasn't afraid to get in someone's face if they were giving Tiger a hard time. But when it came to the media, Williams knew his place—out of the spotlight.

Tiger hired him on the spot. The next day, Mark Steinberg released a statement to the media on Tiger's behalf: "I appreciate the support which Fluff has provided and recognize the contributions Fluff has made to my success as a professional. But it is time to move on, and I feel confident we will remain friends."

On May 13, 1999, Tiger shot 61 in the opening round of the Byron Nelson Classic. Afterward, he phoned Butch Harmon. The moment Harmon picked up, Tiger announced, "I got it!"

Harmon knew exactly what he meant. He listened to the enthusiasm in Tiger's voice as he stood in his new School of Golf in Henderson, Nevada, where a photo of Tiger wearing the green Masters jacket hung on the office wall. It was inscribed "To Butch, Thanks for all the hard work and patience, but more importantly thank you for making my dreams come true." It had been twenty-five long months since that moment. In the interim, the number one golfer in the world had transformed himself into an entirely different player. He'd adopted a fresh set of mechanics, ones that had felt utterly foreign to him when he started. But now there was a beautiful geometry to his swing, as elegant as it was violent.

"It's all starting to feel natural to me," Tiger told Harmon.

Harmon was so happy that he had trouble coming up with words. A month earlier, Tiger had slipped to number two in the world rankings; after forty-one weeks in the top spot, he'd been ousted by David Duval. With four tournament wins in the first four months of the 1999 season, Duval was on a hot streak. But Tiger had kept his focus on the long haul, convinced that he was on the cusp of doing things far more impressive than winning the Masters.

Tiger finished seventh at the Byron Nelson. Shortly afterward, he leased the Orlando Magic's team plane and flew an entourage of thirteen people to Germany for the Deutsche Bank-SAP Open in Heidelberg. It wasn't a PGA Tour event, but it was an opportunity to compete against five of the top ten players in the world. Plus, German billionaire Dietmar Hopp, cofounder of the global software company SAP, offered Tiger an estimated $1 million appearance fee.

By the time his plane touched down, Tiger had fallen to third place in the world rankings, behind Davis Love III and Duval. That was about to change, though. Tiger dominated from start to finish in Heidelberg, putting on a clinic and shooting 273 to win going away.

Two weeks later, he went to Jack Nicklaus's hometown and tore up the course at Muirfield Village Golf Club, shooting a 69 on the final round to finish fifteen under for the tournament. In winning the Memorial, Tiger overwhelmed the field with the length of his shots, but it was his masterful iron play and putting that stood out most. It was a statement to the skeptics and the naysayers.

He'd been telling golf writers for the better part of two years that he was making changes to his game and that it was going to take time. He knew what people were saying—*Tiger is just making excuses.* The steady drumbeat of stories about his being in a slump were eventually replaced by stories about Duval's surpassing him. But now the back-to-back wins confirmed what he had told Harmon. He felt unbeatable. But he wasn't about to let anyone else know how good he felt.

Shortly after collecting the trophy, he joined Jack Nicklaus at the post-tournament press conference. "The great thing is my game is starting to come around," Tiger said. "I'm starting to understand how to play the game of golf a little bit better than I had before."

Starting to understand how to play? It was an ominous warning to everyone else on the PGA Tour.

"I've never seen this way of playing before," Nicklaus chimed in. Then he turned to Tiger. "You're twenty-three now?"

"Uh-huh," Tiger said.

"Most players at twenty-three don't have that kind of imagination, and never had to have it," Nicklaus told the press. "As far as he hits it, there's no reason for him to ever bother practicing his short game. But he has. And that's why he's winning."

"In this day and age, Jack," a reporter asked, "with his body and physical ability, would you play the way he plays?"

"I don't know if anybody can play the way he plays," Nicklaus said. "He has the ability to do things that nobody else can."

Mark Steinberg saw something that concerned him: Tiger's image. When Steinberg was alone with his client, Tiger was funny, personable, and a pleasure to be around. But to the public, he came across as inaccessible, an island unto himself. "Yes, you're a superhuman golfer," he told Tiger. "But we want people to know the twenty-three-year-old in you."

In the spring of 1999, Nike joined the effort to rebrand Tiger by producing a lighthearted commercial featuring him at a driving range with a bunch of everyday golfers who suddenly start driving the ball three hundred yards merely by being in Tiger's presence. Then, once Tiger walks off the range, everyone reverts to being hacks, hooking and slicing shots wildly and hitting trees. It was the most humorous ad Nike had conceived for Tiger.

During a break in the filming, Tiger started killing time by bouncing a golf ball on the head of his sand wedge. Nike had hired Hollywood director Doug Liman, whose movies would include *The Bourne Identity* and *Edge of Tomorrow*, to direct the commercial. Amazed at Tiger's ability to essentially play hacky sack with a golf ball and club, Liman grabbed a camera and asked Tiger to keep juggling for twenty-eight seconds, the length of a commercial. With the camera rolling, Tiger failed in his first three attempts. When Liman jokingly accused Tiger of choking, he glared—and then put on a show, bouncing the ball up and down on the face of his club while transferring the club from his left hand to his right and maneuvering the club behind his back and between his legs. Then, all in one motion, he flipped the ball in the air, wound up, and smacked it out of the air like a baseball. It was a masterful display of artistry that only Tiger could pull off. When Liman replayed the clip, he noted the time counter at the bottom of the frame as Tiger finished his impromptu performance: twenty-eight seconds.

The scene was so authentic that Nike decided to air the unedited footage as a commercial. It ran for the first time during the NBA Finals and instantly became one of the most iconic Nike commercials of all time.

Meanwhile, IMG wanted to turn Tiger into a prime-time television star. The task fell to senior executive Barry Frank, who had negotiated record-setting television rights deals and represented some of the most powerful voices in sports television. As a result, IMG had given Frank free rein to create and sell a new genre of made-for-TV sports programming that turned weekend viewing patterns upside down. *Superstars, World's Strongest Man, Survival of the Fittest,* and *The Skins Game* were just some of the shows he had a hand in developing. Always on the lookout for what he liked to refer to as the "Next Big Thing," Frank was watching Tiger

Woods in 1999 when he dreamed up his most ingenious creation yet: *Monday Night Golf.*

The concept was simple: put the game's brightest and most charismatic star on television on a weeknight in a one-on-one competition. IMG also represented David Duval, whom Tiger had just leapfrogged in the world rankings to reclaim the number óne spot. Frank couldn't think of a better prime-time production than the top two golfers in a three-hour match-play event.

To ensure an eleven p.m. finish time on the East Coast, Frank went looking for a host venue on the West Coast. The Sherwood Country Club in Thousand Oaks, California, put up $1 million in prize money, and Motorola signed on as a main sponsor for $2.4 million more. Disney-owned ABC sold more than $2 million in additional advertising, providing Frank with more than enough money to light the last three holes on the course, guarantee $1 million to Tiger for participating, and set the prize money at $1.5 million. They called it "Showdown at Sherwood."

The Tiger-Duval rivalry was hyped for television, but the two golfers had become friends earlier that summer when they had spent time practicing together in Las Vegas and then flew together with their girlfriends on a private jet to a tournament in Maui. Before the British Open, they also traveled together to Ireland, where their friendship deepened. Tiger genuinely liked Duval and didn't feel threatened by him. Woods was the number one golfer in the world, and Duval was number two. And everyone, including the laid-back Duval, recognized that the talent gap between number one and number two was substantial.

For Tiger, the prime-time television exposure was a big deal. PGA Tour events were always broadcast during the daytime on weekends, so this would give him the chance to test the sport's mettle in a weeknight slot, up against sitcoms, dramas, and news shows. It would also satisfy golf fans who had been clamoring for Tiger and Duval to face off. But it was more than a show to Tiger; in his mind, there were no exhibition games. Not in video games, not in pickup basketball, and certainly not in golf.

On August 2, 1999, he edged Duval on prime-time television, making sure that everyone knew he was the best golfer in the world. The show pulled a television rating of 6.9, making it the second-highest-rated golf event of the year, behind the Masters but beating the US Open and the British Open. It also beat all the Monday night competition except for

CBS's *Everybody Loves Raymond* and *48 Hours*. The event was so successful that IMG and ABC decided to make it an annual event.

Fresh off his victory over Duval, Tiger arrived at the PGA Championship at Medinah Country Club in Illinois, which was the longest course in major championship history at the time. Ninety-four of the top one hundred players in the world turned out for the tournament, the last major championship of the millennium.

Sergio García, a nineteen-year-old first-year pro, raced out to a first-round lead, shooting a 66. Tiger outplayed him in the second round, but they both shot 68 in the third round, setting up a showdown on the final day. At the time, García was almost universally viewed as a petulant young punk who was long on talent but had a short fuse. Tida had taken to calling him "Crybaby." After a round, she was known to say: "What Crybaby shoot today?" But with Tiger leading by five strokes with seven holes to play, García mounted a fearless charge. After making a long birdie putt at the par 3 thirteenth hole to close within three shots of Tiger, he glared at him, as if to say: *I'm coming for you.*

"Did you see that?" Steve Williams said.

"Yes," Tiger said. "I did."

Three holes later, García scissor-kicked his way up the fairway after a miraculous recovery shot—with his eyes closed at the moment of impact, no less—from the base of a tree that reached the green at sixteen. Sprinting up the fairway after his ball, he suddenly stopped, closed his eyes, shook his head, and put his hand over his heart. The gallery loved it. Tiger's lead remained at one.

Exhausted, Tiger told himself as he reached the seventeenth hole that he had to dig deep and play two of the best two holes of his life in order to fend off García. And he did, sinking a very difficult putt on seventeen and hitting a perfect tee shot on eighteen to set up his winning birdie putt. As his ball dropped into the cup and the crowd roared, Tiger took a deep breath, exhaled, and slumped his shoulders forward, wincing and staring blankly at the green. It had been 854 days since he had won his first major championship. Finally, he had two. Finally, he was back on top of the mountain.

Coming off the green, he encountered García.

"Sergio, great playing, man," Tiger told him as they hugged. "Great playing! Great playing. Good job."

This was a new Tiger Woods. In 1997 when he won the Masters, he was routinely driving the ball 320 yards off the tee. With his new swing, he was averaging right around 300 yards. With a little less length, he had become much more accurate. His swing used to be powerful and pretty but sometimes unpredictable under pressure. He had beaten the youthful García with a swing that was simply perfect, without any idiosyncrasy.

For the remainder of the season, Tiger was virtually untouchable, winning the NEC Invitational, the National Car Rental Golf Classic, the Tour Championship, and the WGC-American Express Championship in succession. At the tender age of twenty-three, he had more shots in his repertoire than anyone on Tour. Yet when he needed to intimidate an opponent, he could always remind them that he still possessed far more power than anyone in the game. Nowhere was that more evident than in the final event of the 1999 season in Spain: with the American Express Championship on the line, Tiger stepped to the first tee in the sudden-death playoff and launched a 344-yard bomb. Challenger Miguel Ángel Jiménez gazed in awe as the ball cruised down the fairway as if it were turbocharged.

Tiger finished the season with eight PGA Tour wins. Only ten players had ever won eight tournaments in a season, and Woods was the first one to do it since Johnny Miller in 1974. His four straight victories closing out the season matched a record set by Ben Hogan in 1953. In addition to winning another major, he had won a European Tour event and finished in the top ten in sixteen of his twenty-one PGA Tour events. And since placing the telephone call to Butch Harmon back in the early part of the summer, Tiger had won eight of the eleven tournaments he'd entered.

Tiger's 1999 season belongs in the same conversation with what many consider the three greatest golf seasons in history, the so-called Holy Trinity—Byron Nelson's eighteen wins in 1945; amateur Bobby Jones's Grand Slam in 1930; and Ben Hogan's three major championships in 1953. But all three took place in a different era, when the competition was much leaner. To put Tiger's season in context, Jack Nicklaus said it was superior to any season in his career. Without question, Tiger had put together the greatest season of the previous forty years.

The dramatic changes in Tiger's game coincided with equally significant changes in his personal life. His penchant for fast food had been replaced by a growing habit of eating yogurt and fruit. He traded in his Levi's jeans for Armani slacks. Previously, his favorite word had been *compete*; in 1999 it became *balance*. He smiled more, frowned less, and was getting along with the media. He even took the time to write an apology letter to Jackie Robinson's widow, Rachel. "Whatever you may think of me," he told her, "I admire what your husband did, and I know he was an even better person than athlete. He will always be one of my heroes."

Some of his fresh outlook was a residual effect of all the time he'd spent around Mark and Alicia O'Meara. His refreshed inner circle had a big influence too. Steve Williams had his back at all times. Joanna Jagoda had graduated from college midway through the year and was at his side on and off the Tour, moving to Isleworth and establishing herself as a classy figure who had a breezy way of keeping Woods grounded. And Mark Steinberg, whom Tiger referred to as "Steiny," had played a vital role in helping Tiger retake control of his life off the course.

Unlike his predecessor, Steinberg was fiercely protective of his client's time. With a litany of corporate suitors hoping to sign Tiger as a pitchman at the end of the year, Steinberg inked a deal with General Motors, who would pay Tiger $25 million over a five-year period to endorse the automaker's Buick line. It marked Tiger's first new product deal in two years. The only other deal that Steinberg executed was a contract renewal with Japan's Asahi, which had enlisted Tiger to help sell its coffee drinks. Steinberg said no to every other opportunity. For the first time, Tiger felt like he had an agent who was working strictly for him.

"He's so well-liked, bright, and enjoyable to be around that we could probably capitalize on five to ten deals right now," Steinberg said at the time. "But Tiger doesn't want to do that."

Simultaneously, Earl's influence had begun to fade. He and Tiger were still close, but the days of having to go through Earl to get to Tiger were over. Steinberg was the new gatekeeper, and Harmon had fully supplanted Earl as Tiger's golf sage. In 1999, Earl attended very few tournaments, and when he did show up, he remained in the background. The most visible illustration of how things had changed occurred as Tiger left the eighteenth green after winning the PGA Championship in Chicago. First, he hugged Steve Williams. Then he received a hug from his mother. The longest, most emotional embrace was reserved for Butch Harmon on the edge of the green. Then Tiger hugged and received a heartfelt kiss from

Joanna Jagoda, who then turned to embrace Mark Steinberg as Tiger went off to sign his scorecard.

Earl was nowhere to be found.

Tiger celebrated his twenty-fourth birthday over dinner with family and a few friends at a hotel in Scottsdale, Arizona, on December 30, 1999. Afterward, he retired to bed early. The low-key evening was a rare opportunity to reflect on his momentous year, a year that had changed him. Tiger had always felt like an outsider, as a member of the only family of color in his Cypress neighborhood, as a middle-class golfer competing against country-club kids, as a geek in high school who didn't play a "real" sport, and as the youngest player on the PGA Tour, and the one with the biggest endorsement deals and the most powerful swing. Race factored heavily into why he didn't fit in, but so did his peculiar personality and a golf swing that seemed, as far back as age two, supernatural. By the end of 1999, however, Tiger was no longer on the outside looking in; he *was* the inside. He had taken the torch from Jack Nicklaus as golf's supreme talent, and he had taken the torch from Michael Jordan as the world's most famous athlete.

All of this had started to sink in earlier in December, when he attended the *Sports Illustrated* 20th Century Sports Awards, a black-tie event at Madison Square Garden billed as "the most august collection of athletes ever assembled." Celebrities from Al Pacino and Billy Crystal to Whitney Houston and Donald Trump turned out as the sports industry honored the greatest athletes of the century. At one point, Tiger appeared onstage with Muhammad Ali, Michael Jordan, Bill Russell, Jim Brown, Pelé, Joe Montana, Wayne Gretzky, Billie Jean King, Jack Nicklaus, Kareem Abdul-Jabbar, and a handful of others.

For Tiger it was a high point, a moment he viewed as one of the greatest in sports history. At the same time, he felt uncomfortable amid such a distinguished group. He was the youngest athlete, and he couldn't escape the feeling that he hadn't accomplished enough to justify being included. But he had always been much older than his years, and he was starting to believe he did belong among the legends he'd grown up idolizing.

With a new year dawning, he couldn't resist looking forward to even greater frontiers. His sights were on immortality, and in golf that meant winning the four major championships in the same year—the Grand Slam—a feat no one had ever accomplished in the modern age. Tiger's resolve to win the Grand Slam had been solidified two months earlier on October 25, 1999, when forty-two-year-old Payne Stewart died in a tragic accident. Stewart had been on his way to the Tour Championship in Houston when his Learjet lost cabin pressure and crashed in a field in South Dakota.

Tiger couldn't sleep after learning that Stewart was gone. They were neighbors in Isleworth, and the two of them had recently taken a fishing trip to Europe with Mark O'Meara. Word of Stewart's sudden passing cast a pall over the entire PGA Tour, but Tiger took it particularly hard. *I just saw him the other day*, he thought. *It's hard to believe he's not going to be here.*

While a lot of players shed tears, Tiger grieved differently. Rather than dwelling on the loss of a friend, he focused on his positive memories of the man who famously wore golf knickers. He told himself that Stewart was in a better place, one where there were no struggles, one where he was happy and peaceful. *Maybe Payne will be like a guardian angel to all of us*, he thought.

When he won the Tour Championship, Tiger held up the trophy and fought back tears as he looked heavenward and said a final farewell to his friend. Then he did the only thing he knew how to do—turned his focus to his golf game and how to improve it. He wondered how far he could go, and he told himself: *Anything is possible.*

CHAPTER SEVENTEEN

ANY QUESTIONS?

One day around this time, Tiger Woods and Butch Harmon were alone on the driving range at La Costa Resort and Spa in Carlsbad, California, wrapping up a lengthy practice session. The sun was setting, and every element of Tiger's form—the takeaway of his arms, the plane of his swing, the angle of his clubface, his downswing, his follow-through, his sequencing—was textbook perfect. There wasn't anything Harmon could nitpick. But he sensed Woods was getting a little lax, so he resorted to a familiar trick.

"I got something you can't do," Harmon said.

Those six words always got Tiger's attention. He hated to lose. To anyone. At anything.

A small gate at the back right corner of the range, approximately 250 yards away, had been left open. The opening was just wide enough for a range cart to pass through.

"I have a hundred that says you can't hit it through that gate," Harmon said. "I'll give you three balls."

Without saying a word, Tiger reached for a club. On his first attempt, he smoked the ball the length of two and a half football fields, sending it right through the center of the six-foot gap in the towering fence. Then he turned to Harmon with a smile, put out his hand, and said, "Is that the gate you're talking about, Butchie?"

Harmon handed him $100.

No one in the history of golf—not even the great Ben Hogan or Jack Nicklaus—possessed Tiger's ability to focus and execute difficult shots. Few people understood that fact about him better than Harmon. They'd worked together since Woods was seventeen. Since then, they had overhauled Tiger's swing twice. In the first instance, he dialed back the power of his swing off the tee and added an array of new shots to his game. With those changes, he went on to win three straight US Amateurs and turn in a record-setting performance at the '97 Masters. The second rebuild was even more radical, essentially starting over to construct a new swing that better suited his body.

Woods was the rare athlete who liked to practice as much as he liked to play, whose obsession with perfection and ability to perform without fear gave him an intimidating psychological advantage. Harmon had the sense that in the year 2000, the golf world was going to witness something unprecedented.

The Mercedes-Benz Championship in Maui was the first tournament on the 2000 PGA Tour. Tiger won it by sinking a forty-foot birdie putt on the second sudden-death hole to defeat Ernie Els. The win pushed his streak to five straight Tour wins, giving him the longest winning streak of any golfer in forty-two years. Next up was the AT&T Pebble Beach Pro-Am, where he trailed by seven strokes with nine holes to play before mounting an inconceivable comeback to defeat Matt Gogel and Vijay Singh by two strokes. In tournament after tournament, Tiger was doing the unthinkable.

With six straight victories, Tiger's streak was second only to Byron Nelson's eleven consecutive wins in 1945. It was silly, in many respects, to compare Woods's run with Nelson's. In 1945, America was at war, and golf was still in its infancy as a professional sport. The purses were nominal—Nelson earned a total of $30,250 for his eleven victories—and the audiences were tiny. Conversely, Tiger was competing against a slew of extremely talented pros, and the stakes were much, much higher. Nonetheless, Tiger was furious with himself when he finally lost, finishing second to Phil Mickelson at the Buick Invitational in mid-February. He knew he was better than Mickelson, and it galled him that he, of all people, had ended the streak and denied him the opportunity to beat the ghost of Byron Nelson. But none of that disappointed Tiger as much as his performance at the 2000 Masters. Determined to win four straight majors, he shot a surprisingly poor 75 in the first round at Augusta and ended up in fifth place, six shots behind eventual winner Vijay Singh. "For some reason, the golfing gods weren't looking down on me this week," he said afterward.

For virtually every other pro, such deep disappointment would have undermined an entire season. But not for Woods. He fed off the adrenaline rush that came from failure, backed by an unquenchable thirst to do things that had never been done in his sport. To him, a golf course was a canvas, and his equipment—mainly his clubs and golf ball—were his artistic instruments. Far more than any other golfer, Tiger obsessed over ways to enhance the tools of his trade.

One of those moments of obsession occurred on Sunday, May 14, 2000, at the Four Seasons Resort in Irving, Texas. Tiger had just shot a sizzling 63 in the final round of the Byron Nelson Classic, finishing ten under par and one stroke behind the winner. Despite a magnificent performance, Woods was alone in his room, stewing because he felt he should have won, when he received a text message just before seven p.m.: "Hey, nice playing today." It was from Kel Devlin, Nike's global director of sports marketing.

Tiger and Devlin, the son of Australian great Bruce Devlin and a scratch player in his own right, had been working closely together over the previous nine months. During that period, Tiger had been quietly testing a synthetic golf ball called the Tour Accuracy that Nike Golf was developing with Bridgestone, a golf-equipment manufacturer based in Japan. In 2000, virtually every golfer on tour, including Tiger, was using a ball whose cover was made of balata, a natural substance culled from rubber trees in Central and South America. The balata ball had a liquid core with rubber bands wrapped around it. Nike's potentially game-changing ball featured a solid, molded core injected with synthetic compounds, including polyurethane. The ball's design allowed it to maintain its velocity at its apex, minimizing the adverse effect of rain and wind.

Tiger had been using a Titleist ball since turning pro in August 1996, but, test by test, he was moving closer to switching to Nike. The last test session had been held in March, after which Tiger said he would feel more comfortable if he had one final opportunity to test the ball. But that would have to wait until after the PGA Championship at the end of the summer. In the meantime, Devlin knew a testing blackout period was in place.

But after losing by one stroke at the Byron Nelson, Tiger decided to speed things up. The start of his next tournament, the Deutsche Bank–SAP Open in Germany, was just four days away. Why not conduct the final ball test there?

Twenty minutes after reading Devlin's text, Tiger called him. It was just after five p.m. out west, and Devlin had just sat down for dinner with his family at his home outside Portland. He put down his glass of wine to take Tiger's call.

"Can you meet me in Germany Tuesday morning?" Tiger asked.

"I guess I can. Why?"

"I want to put the ball in play."

Devlin figured Tiger was messing with him. "Quit yanking my chain," Devlin said.

"No, I'm serious," Tiger said. "If I'd had my ball, I'd have won by six this weekend."

The words *my ball* were music to Devlin's ears. "You're dead fucking serious, aren't you?"

Before hanging up, Tiger asked him to bring five dozen balls to Germany.

Moments later, Devlin's phone rang again. This time it was Mark Steinberg, who cut to the chase: "Is this even possible?"

Devlin was wondering the same thing. Tiger's request created a logistical nightmare. Devlin was in Oregon. To make it to Germany on time, he would have to immediately pack and head to the airport in hopes of catching a red-eye and a series of connecting flights. The balls presented an even bigger challenge: they were at a Bridgestone manufacturing facility in Japan, where it was already early Monday morning. They would have to be retrieved, but even then there wasn't sufficient time to get them into Devlin's hands. Someone was going to have to hand-deliver them to Hamburg in less than twenty-four hours. But Devlin didn't bother trying to explain any of this to Steinberg. Tiger expected results, not excuses.

Devlin placed an urgent call to Bob Wood, president of Nike Golf, and told him that Tiger wanted to resume testing Nike's Tour Accuracy right away. Wood, a renowned inspirational leader who played a mean Fender guitar and often preached that *fuck* was the most underappreciated word in the English language, was ecstatic.

"Fuck!" he said. "No fucking way!"

"I'm serious. Tiger wants us in Hamburg. Now!"

Wood wanted Devlin in Hamburg too. But he knew of only one way to get the balls there in time.

"Call Rock," Wood said.

Rock Ishii was a scientist and engineer for Bridgestone. Affectionately known as the Maharishi Rock Ishii, he was the genius behind the design of the Tour Accuracy. He was dead asleep at his home in Japan when Devlin woke him up.

"Can you get to Hamburg with Tour Accuracy?" Devlin said.

"What are you talking about?" Ishii said.

"Tiger wants to put the ball in play. He wants you to bring five dozen balls."

Fifteen minutes later, Ishii was in his car, speeding to the plant to retrieve the balls. He called Devlin from the road. "There's a flight that leaves Narita later this morning. I'll be on it."

Back in Dallas, Tiger was on the runway, about to take off for Orlando, when his phone buzzed. It was Devlin.

"I'll have the balls," he said. "Where do you want me to meet you?"

"Meet me on the first tee," Tiger said. "Nine o'clock Tuesday morning. Steiny will arrange everything."

Tiger's initial willingness to start testing a Nike ball had evolved out of the two Nike commercials that aired the previous summer—the one with the hackers suddenly being able to drive the ball three hundred yards like Tiger, and the impromptu one of Tiger bouncing a ball on his club. The ads roiled Titleist, and in June 1999, its corporate parent, the Acushnet Company, sued Nike in the US District Court in Boston, accusing the shoe and apparel company of deceptive advertising. Acushnet claimed that Nike had improperly induced Tiger to appear in a television commercial that endorsed Nike golf balls and Nike golf equipment, both of which violated Acushnet's exclusive contract with Tiger to use Titleist golf balls and equipment. In both Nike commercials, Tiger had used a Titleist club and ball, but both commercials concluded with the Nike Golf logo, prompting Titleist to demand that the ads be taken down, because "many tens of millions" of people might think that Tiger had switched to Nike equipment.

The suit was eventually settled, and Steinberg renegotiated Tiger's contract with Titleist, enabling him to use a Nike ball. But the lawsuit effectively marked the beginning of the end of Tiger's relationship with Titleist. Before taking off for Germany, he called Titleist CEO Wally Uihlein and told him he was going to use the Nike Tour Accuracy ball for the first time at the Deutsche Bank–SAP Open.

It was raining and windy when Steve Williams arrived on the first tee at the Gut Kaden Golf Club in Alveslohe, outside Hamburg, a little before nine in the morning. Figuring the ball test was off due to the weather, he nonetheless knew that Woods would still practice. Nothing got in the way of that. Williams was shielding Tiger's golf bag from the elements when he spotted Devlin and Ishii approaching. Devlin was holding an umbrella. Ishii was cradling boxes containing dozens of balls.

Williams was surprised to see them.

"We're here for the ball test," Devlin told him.

"It's not the best day to do it," said Williams, who was still not convinced that Nike's ball was better than Titleist's.

Thirty seconds later, Tiger approached, wearing a TW cap and a smile. The bad weather was just what he wanted—ideal conditions to scrutinize the speed, flight, and spin rate of the balls.

As rain beat down, Woods set his Titleist ball on the tee and aimed a drive down the left edge of the fairway. The wind pushed it into the right rough. Then he hit Nike's Tour Accuracy ball on the same exact line. It was as if the wind and rain had stopped. The ball moved just three yards and finished left of center of the fairway. Williams was impressed. This pattern was repeated through the first nine holes.

By the time Steinberg showed up late on the front nine, Tiger was convinced he had made the right decision to use the Nike ball the next day in the pro-am. The ball's performance in the wind had even convinced his skeptical caddie.

"I guess we're changing balls," Williams said.

When Tiger returned from Germany a week later, he used the Nike ball at Muirfield Village, Nicklaus's signature course in Dublin, Ohio, and won the Memorial Tournament by six shots. It was his nineteenth PGA victory, and he did it in such convincing fashion—finishing nineteen under par—that Nicklaus quipped: "He's making mincemeat out of golf courses."

Afterward, Tiger huddled with Steinberg. The US Open was two weeks away, and Woods had decided to switch permanently to the Tour Accuracy ball. But he wanted to personally break the news to the president and the sales force of Nike Golf. Nike was gearing up to go all-in with Tiger and its new golf products, and he wanted to give them a boost of momentum. Steinberg said he would make the arrangements.

On June 1, 2000, Nike Golf held its semiannual footwear and equipment sales meetings at the Sunriver Resort in Oregon. That night, about two hundred employees from the US, Canada, and Europe gathered in the conference center. Nike Golf president Bob Wood was on the stage, outlining the company's strategy and sales goals for the upcoming 180 days. Images of various products flashed on giant screens behind him. Neither Wood nor anyone in the audience knew that Tiger was backstage, in a private room with Steinberg, Devlin, and Nike CEO Phil Knight.

Suddenly, Tiger emerged from behind a curtain at the side of the stage. Carrying a large framed picture of himself holding the Memorial trophy, as well as a signed glove and the Nike ball he had used to win the tournament, Tiger walked toward Wood. The audience spotted him and started pointing and whispering. Wood, known for his captivating speeches and unaware of Tiger's presence, couldn't figure out why everyone was distracted. Then Tiger appeared next to him.

"What the fuck are you doing here?" Wood said.

The audience roared.

Grinning, Tiger presented Wood with the framed picture. "Before we get started," he said, "I just want to tell you and everyone here that I've decided to switch permanently to the Nike Tour Accuracy ball."

With one sentence, Tiger sent the sales force into a frenzy. Everyone rose to their feet and started jumping up and down, hooting and hollering. They ended up partying until dawn.

For the one-hundredth US Open at Pebble Beach, NBC deployed forty-seven cameras—nearly double the standard number—to track Tiger from the air and from the water as well as from the course. On June 14, the day before the opening round, Woods was scheduled to be on the first tee at seven a.m. for a practice round. But a memorial ceremony had been scheduled at the same time on the eighteenth green to honor the tournament's defending champion, Payne Stewart. In a scene reminiscent of a twenty-one-gun salute, more than forty golfers lined up and hit golf balls into the sunlit Carmel Bay on the command of "Ready, aim, fire." Stewart's wife, Tracey, choked back tears as several thousand fans looked on. Tiger chose not to attend. In his mind, there was no need to show up, and it wasn't a difficult decision. He had given his condolences privately to Tracey Stewart. The public ceremony, he determined, was mainly a show for golfers to hit balls into the water, and he had no interest in being part of it. Showing up would have been detrimental to his preparation for the Open.

As his fellow golfers gathered to mourn the loss of a friend, Tiger worked his way through his practice round with Mark O'Meara. Afterward, he spent an additional two and a half hours on the putting green, making subtle adjustments to his posture and his release. Then he worked on his swing. Throughout the day, celebrities—a famous athlete, a television star, a member of the national media—tried to say hello. But he had no interest in making small talk.

When Tiger was in tournament mode, he let nothing distract him—not even questions from reporters who were worked up about his absence at Stewart's service. After all, it wasn't as if Tiger were the only one who had chosen not to attend. Jack Nicklaus hadn't shown up either, but no one was hounding him with questions about his decision. O'Meara, who had been as close to Stewart as anyone, had also skipped the service to play with Woods. Tiger didn't see the need to justify his actions to anyone.

Eleven hours after his early-morning tee time, Tiger was finally ready to call it a day. Butch Harmon was used to Woods's extreme practice habits. As he watched Tiger walk off the practice green on the eve of the tournament, he thought to himself: *No one else stands a chance tomorrow.*

Tiger felt the same way. That night, alone in a dimly lit room, Woods sat with his yardage book. Eyes closed, he visualized the first tee. From there, he played every shot in his mind, one by one, all the way through the eighteenth hole. Then he went to sleep. The next day, he shot 65 in the opening round. With three rounds still to play, everyone else already recognized that they were playing for second place. On Friday, while unusually strong winds wreaked havoc on the field, Tiger expanded his lead, playing as if his ball were impervious to the weather, driving his tee shots with precision and making birdie after birdie. But a late-afternoon start time and various weather delays forced tournament officials to suspend play after Tiger finished the twelfth hole.

He returned to the course early Saturday morning to finish the second round. It was around eight a.m. on the West Coast when he stepped to the eighteenth tee with a commanding eight-stroke lead. Then he hooked his tee shot into Carmel Bay.

"Goddamn you fucking prick!" Tiger barked.

NBC's microphones picked up the outburst.

"Whoa!" said NBC commentator Johnny Miller.

"Well, no commentary necessary," said analyst Mark Rolfing.

In golf circles, it was no secret that Tiger had a colorful mouth and a hot temper. But it was jarring to hear him let loose on national television. In parts of the country, NBC had preempted Saturday-morning cartoons to provide live coverage of the Open. Upset viewers started calling NBC and the USGA to complain.

Sports journalist Jimmy Roberts was working his very first event for NBC Sports that weekend, and had been assigned to interview Tiger after the round. Roberts had first interviewed Woods in 1996 for ESPN's *SportsCenter* on the eve of the US Amateur, and he had a good rapport with him. After that first interview, Roberts had informed Tiger that he couldn't stay for the tournament. He had to get back to New York to be with his wife, who was pregnant with their first child and undergoing some medical tests.

"Isn't it traditional to stay for the actual tournament?" Tiger quipped with a smile.

Roberts laughed.

A week later, when Tiger made his pro debut at the Greater Milwaukee Open, Roberts covered the tournament for ESPN. Despite being mobbed by reporters and fans, Woods spotted Roberts and went out of his way to speak to him privately. "How's your wife?" he asked.

Roberts was touched. Ever since then, a mutual fondness had existed between them.

As Tiger came off the eighteenth hole at Pebble Beach, Roberts planned to ask him about his cursing after the wayward tee shot. But he didn't want to blindside Tiger on live television, so instead of waiting for Woods to come up to the tower to be interviewed, Roberts went down to meet him and give him a heads-up.

With an eight-stroke lead after two rounds of play, Tiger had a smile on his face and Joanna Jagoda at his side as he came off the course and said hello to Roberts.

"Look," Roberts said, "I've got to ask you about what happened on eighteen."

The smile instantly fell from Tiger's face. He had just finished a remarkable round of golf and was on target to win the US Open by a record margin, and Roberts wanted to talk about four-letter words? Seriously? Virtually everyone on the pro tour, including some of the journalists who covered it, used similar language, but they didn't have microphones, as Harmon said, "shoved up their ass all the time."

Roiled, Tiger didn't say any of this to Roberts. Instead he just gave him a death stare.

Roberts didn't understand the pushback. From his perspective, the question would give Tiger an opportunity to apologize for a slipup and acknowledge that he was so competitive that he sometimes lost his temper.

"He's absolutely right," Jagoda said to Tiger. "Go upstairs and answer those questions."

Aggravated, Woods followed Roberts.

"You didn't finish thirty-six holes the way you would have liked to," Roberts said on the air. "And, in fact, you appeared to get pretty angry on the tee there."

"Yeah, I got a little angry," Tiger said. "I kinda let the emotions get the better of myself. I hit a bad shot. I was trying to hit a nice little straight ball out there, and I hit a pull hook. And I guess got a little upset. I'm sorry I did get upset, but I think anyone in that situation would get a little perturbed at themselves. Unfortunately, I let it voice out loud. But I collected myself, stepped up there, and just ripped the next one. I wish I could have hit that first one the way I hit the second one."

Woods was furious over the question, but he had no intention of voicing his dissatisfaction to Roberts. Unlike his outspoken father, Tiger shied away from confrontation. "I learned to let my clubs do the talking, as my mom always advised me," he said. "She taught me to be strong, and the more I said, the worse the situation would be. If I was going to let my clubs do the talking, Mom said, I might as well beat the other guys by as many shots as I could. There was a difference between winning and beating. I wanted to win, sure, but I also wanted to win by as many shots as possible. My mom liked me to 'stomp' on the other players, to use her word." He seemed to feel the same way about Roberts.

On Sunday, Tiger began the final round eight under par, ten shots ahead of his nearest competitor. It was the largest lead in the history of the tournament, but he wasn't satisfied. Determined to shatter the course record, his goal on Sunday was to play a bogey-free round. He did just that. By the time he reached the final hole, he felt calm and completely at ease with himself. He blushed as everyone on the fairway bowed as if paying tribute to royalty. He shot a 67 and won by a record fifteen strokes.

As he made his way to the trophy presentation just off the eighteenth green, NBC cut to a commercial. Jimmy Roberts was standing by. In what would be to that point the most visible piece of television in his career, he was doing the trophy presentation. Millions would be tuning in.

Seconds before Roberts was to go on the air, Harmon grabbed him by the arm. "What are you trying to prove?" he asked. "Why in the fuck are you asking these questions?" Harmon was still furious over the previous day's interview about Tiger's on-air cursing. "That's bullshit!" Harmon told him. "We thought you were a friend."

Roberts was shaken. *Holy cow,* he said to himself. *What was that all about?*

Jimmy Roberts had apparently become one of Tiger's enemy journalists.

But none of Tiger's feelings toward Roberts were on display when he entered the post-victory press conference at Pebble Beach clutching his newest trophy. After praising his own ability to make some "big par putts" in what he blithely downplayed as a "pretty good week," Woods was asked whether his record-shattering victory had solidified him as the King of Golf.

"The records are great, but you don't really pay attention to that," Tiger said. "But you don't really understand exactly what you've done until time passes. And I'll appreciate this win a lot more in the future than I do right now, because I'm too close to the moment. . . . The only thing I know is I got the trophy sitting right next to me."

CHAPTER EIGHTEEN

TRANSCENDENCE

Golf writers, seasoned pros, and historians universally agreed that Tiger's fifteen-stroke victory at the 2000 US Open was the single most dominant performance in golf history. In the 370 previous majors, no one had won by such a wide margin. It was a feat that eclipsed everything else going on in the world of sports. That same week, Kobe Bryant and Shaquille O'Neal led the Los Angeles Lakers to an NBA championship, but it was Tiger who garnered the biggest headlines and graced the cover of *Sports Illustrated*.

Days later, Tiger was in Las Vegas, working on his swing with Butch Harmon. That evening, they went out for a quiet celebratory dinner at The Palm at Caesars Palace. They reserved a private room in the back of the restaurant, out of sight of the packed house. When Woods got up to leave, a few patrons spotted him and immediately stood and applauded. The commotion drew the attention of others, and soon everyone in the restaurant stood, clapping and whistling. Touched and slightly embarrassed by the ovation, Tiger stopped. Usually he received ovations on the course, where he could rely on his equipment to do the talking. Tipping his cap or holding up his ball after nailing a putt always pleased the crowd. But he had nothing to hold on to in the middle of a jam-packed restaurant. He simply nodded and smiled, prompting a crescendo of cheers. Everywhere he went, he was the man of the hour.

With three of the four major golf championship trophies now perched on Tiger's mantel, talk of his winning the career Grand Slam in Scotland was in full froth. In July, a record 230,000 fans flocked to the Old Course at St. Andrews—the birthplace of golf—in hopes of witnessing history.

Tiger was playing so flawlessly that it almost seemed unfair to the competition. "He has raised the bar to a level that only he can jump," Tom Watson said during the British Open. "He's something supernatural." Throughout the weekend, Woods played that way. At St. Andrews, he was the only player to go through all four rounds without hitting a ball into one of the course's 112 bunkers. On the final day, Tiger was paired with his friend David Duval. For the tournament, he beat the number two golfer in the world by twelve shots, finishing a record nineteen under par.

Long before the end of the final round, it was a foregone conclusion that Tiger was on his way to becoming only the fifth player in history to win all four modern major championships, joining Gene Sarazen, Ben Hogan, Gary Player, and Jack Nicklaus in golf's most exclusive club. At twenty-four, Tiger had become the youngest to achieve the career Grand Slam.

In a moment of jubilation, fans breached the security cordon at the eighteenth fairway, overwhelming Her Majesty's marshals in a stampede that made it appear as though the crowd were carrying Tiger to the final green. The Brits and Scots were paying tribute to the sheer brilliance that stemmed from a lifetime spent largely alone, mastering the use of woods and irons to control a ball with machine-like precision.

As the masses lined the eighteenth fairway and cheered Tiger's greatness, Tida cried with joy. Throughout her marriage, her role in Tiger's success had always been overshadowed by Earl's. He was the one who wrote the books and pontificated to the press and mugged for the cameras. But while Earl, in computer terms, may have wired Tiger's circuits, it was Tida who did the vital coding. She was most responsible for Tiger's mental programming, his killer instinct. More than anyone else, she understood the price her son had paid. From the time Tiger was a toddler, Tida had walked hundreds of miles across the world's golf courses with him. And after walking all seventy-two holes at St. Andrews, Tida was completely undone as she watched thousands of fans cheering for her Tiger. At that moment, everything she had been through seemed worth it.

Tiger wasn't prepared to see his mother with tears in her eyes. He had never seen her cry at a golf tournament. After collecting the trophy, making the rounds at St. Andrews, and talking to the press, he met his mother on the curb outside the hotel. She was traveling home separately. "Bye, Mom," he said. "I love you."

She hugged him.

"See you when I get back," he said. Then he climbed into the back of a vehicle that took him to the nearby Royal Air Force base, where a private jet was waiting to take him home to Isleworth and the new, nearly eight-thousand-square-foot luxury home on Deacon Circle he had purchased two weeks earlier for $2.475 million.

A couple of years after Tiger had turned pro, Alicia O'Meara introduced him to her Orlando-based scuba diving instructor, Herb Sugden. After learning of Sugden's reputation for being a rigorous and demanding teacher, Tiger hired him and started taking basic lessons in the swimming pool behind his Isleworth home. "He was an exceptional student," Sugden recalled. "He worked at it and never tried to cut corners. When I corrected him, he would say 'Okay' and go back and get it right. He became an excellent diver."

It didn't take long before Sugden felt Tiger was ready to transition from the pool to Divemaster—a term reserved for divers just beneath the instructor level—in a little over a year, becoming qualified to lead other certified divers on dives. Before long, the ocean became his biggest passion. The ocean floor was the one place on earth where no one recognized him and no one wanted anything from him. Alone among the fish, he once confided to a friend, he felt more at peace than he did anywhere else.

After returning home from the British Open, Tiger took off for the Bahamas and disappeared beneath the sea. In addition to exploring coral reefs, he also took advantage of the opportunity to sharpen control over his nerves. When he encountered a giant fish, he learned how not to let his heart rate go up. This skill went a long way toward allowing him to control his heart rate when he had to make a crucial putt.

While Woods sought refuge in the ocean, Tiger Mania reached a fervor that surpassed even the frenzied aftermath of his 1997 Masters win. In mid-August, he simultaneously appeared on the cover of *Time* and was the subject of a twelve-page profile in the *New Yorker* titled "The Chosen One." American Express aired a commercial—"Tiger Woods in Manhattan"—showing him blasting golf balls through Central Park, over the Brooklyn Bridge, and down the middle of Wall Street. And everyone on the Tour—players, caddies, swing coaches—recognized that Tiger had established himself as the best—or damn close to it—in every single aspect of the game. Driving, ball striking, short game, putting, scoring—he didn't have a weakness. By the time he showed up at the PGA Championship at Valhalla Golf Club in Louisville at the end of August, some of the top caddies thought Tiger had become so good that it was unfair. Things had reached a point where everybody was intimidated by him. Even seasoned pros were unnerved when paired with him, especially on Sunday.

But after leading throughout the tournament and entering the final round atop the leaderboard at thirteen under par, Woods was paired with a man who was not intimidated. To most golf fans, the name Bob May meant little. But Tiger knew him well. In the mideighties, May had been the best junior golfer in Southern California. Woods was ten at the time and had already won two Junior World titles, and he studied the junior golf rankings the way some kids memorize the stats on the back of baseball cards. May had never won a major championship on the PGA Tour, but the thirty-one-year-old was ranked forty-eighth in the world and was an exceptional iron player. Tied for second, he was just one shot behind Woods.

At the start of the round, Tiger turned to Steve Williams and whispered: "This guy won't back down."

May had spent a sleepless Saturday night in his hotel room, telling himself over and over: *Play the course, not the man. You can't control what Woods is doing. He's the longest hitter in the world. He's going to play a different course than you. Play the golf course. It's the only thing you can do.*

It all felt right to May until Woods stepped up to the first tee, a dogleg left known as "Cut the Corner," and unleashed a missile over a sixty-foot-tall stand of trees as if they were shrubs. When the ball finally stopped rolling, it was at least fifty yards past May's drive. To the sold-out gallery, it looked like today would be another walk in the park for Tiger. Surely this guy May would fold under the pressure.

Instead, one of the classic duels in major championship history unfolded.

At the end of regulation, Woods and May stood tied at a PGA Championship record eighteen under par. Both men had shot 31 on the back nine, each contributing to a highlight reel of extraordinary shot-making and clutch putts. On the final hole, Woods had faced a treacherous eight-foot putt to extend the match—and possibly to collect his third straight major. After draining it, he turned to Williams and said, "Stevie, my mom could've made that putt. I'm Tiger Woods—I'm supposed to make that putt. It ain't no big deal, Stevie."

May felt the same thing. No big deal. Given the stakes, he was playing the best round of golf in his life—a final-round 65—and he had a chance to win, especially after Tiger pushed his second drive of the three-hole playoff deep into a cluster of trees.

For any other golfer on the PGA Tour, the only option was a low-risk chip-out back onto the fairway, and an almost guaranteed bogey. But Tiger's creative mind imagined something else entirely—a punched 8-iron bullet under the trees and onto a cart path, where it bounced over the rough and rolled into a swale behind the green.

Off the cart path? May was so stunned that he wondered whether Tiger had done that intentionally.

He had. And, moments later, after he parred the last two playoff holes to edge May by a single stroke, Woods joined Ben Hogan as the only player in history to win three professional major tournaments in a single season. In a breathtaking nine-week span, Woods had won the US Open, the British Open, and the PGA Championship, completing what golf writers universally consider the greatest summer in the history of the sport.

The only thing as remarkable as Tiger's trifecta was the fact that his father wasn't around to witness any of it. The father who never missed his son's major championships was nowhere to be found, yet Earl still managed to draw attention to himself by criticizing Venus and Serena Williams in *Sports Illustrated*. Two weeks before Tiger's victory at the British Open, twenty-year-old Venus had also made history by winning Wimbledon, joining Althea Gibson, who won it in 1957 and '58, as the only African American women to do so. In a moment of youthful exuberance, Williams had bounced up and down on the court and then gone into the stands, climbing over spectators to embrace her eighteen-year-old sister, Serena, the reigning US Open champion, and her father, Richard Williams, who had taught his daughters the game.

The Williams sisters' rise in the world of tennis had some notable parallels to Tiger's ascent. In addition to the obvious race corollary, there was the presence of a controversial father whose unusual methods sometimes caused awkward and embarrassing moments. With Tiger and Venus simultaneously making headlines on both sides of the Atlantic, Earl Woods was asked if he had ever met Richard Williams.

"I've never met him, and I don't want to meet him," Earl said. "I don't think much of the way he's handling his daughters. He's not allowed them to reach their full potential. He's not allowed them to have competent professional instruction. It's almost like watching Tiger play if he'd never gone to Butch Harmon. I heard Venus say [after winning Wimbledon], 'I get to buy myself a watch.' I thought, How sad. Twenty years old? Now I can buy a watch? All you have to do is listen to them. You can hear the girlish attitude and the girlish conduct. These girls are not on the road to maturity. They're in a time warp. I feel sorry for them."

Earl made these comments at a time when he had essentially disappeared from Tiger's side. His absence at all three major championships fueled speculation that there had been a falling out between him and Tiger.

"I raised Tiger to leave me," Earl said in 2000, adding: "We don't have to communicate with each other to validate our relationship."

Earl always had an answer, but this one didn't add up, especially since he'd given a different explanation to a different reporter that summer: "I don't go to tournaments anymore because I get mobbed and can't see any golf."

The real reason for Earl's sudden absence during the crowning moments of his son's career was much more complicated. It started with the fact that Tiger had spent his entire life seeking his father's approval, and he had always shared the stage with Earl. By 2000, Tiger was his own man, weary of some of Earl's antics and no longer interested in sharing the stage with him or anyone else.

At the same time, Earl was no longer making any effort to camouflage his vices. He had no intention of tempering his drinking, nor was he cutting back on smoking, despite his heart problems and the warnings from his doctor. It had long aggravated Tiger that his father failed to curtail his nicotine intake despite his heart condition. A couple of years earlier at a private dinner, Earl pulled out a cigarette only to have Tiger take it, crush it in his hand, and toss it in an ashtray. He then bent over and whispered in Earl's ear, "Knock this stuff off, Pop. I need you."

But there were much bigger issues. It had been four years since Tida had moved out, and Earl had filled the void by hiring a bevy of women—

mostly blondes and brunettes, most of whom were young enough to be
Tiger's sister—to service his needs. As the President of ETW Corp., Earl
had his own executive assistant. He also had a personal assistant, traveling assistant, foundation assistant, cook, personal trainer, dog trainer,
massage therapist, housekeeper, and even a pedicurist. According to one
of them, a few of these women were employed by Tiger's corporation but
some were not and were paid in cash, their unspoken job description to
do whatever it took to please Earl.

Tiger, by this time, was well aware that his father had repeatedly been
unfaithful to his mother over the years. Plenty of other people associated
with the PGA Tour had also begun to assume as much. As early as 1998,
Earl had stopped trying to be discreet about his interest in other women.
That year, he brought a younger woman with him to the Presidents Cup
in Australia.

But by 2000, Earl had largely stopped showing up at tour events, and
the scene at Tiger's childhood home had gotten out of hand. Women came
and went. Pornography played steadily on the television. Sex toys were
stuffed in drawers, and sexual favors were performed at Earl's request. "It
was a house of horrors," recalled a former employee. "Every drawer. Every
cabinet."

Tiger typically called ahead when he was coming to town to visit Earl,
and the women always cleaned the place up before he arrived. By now, he
had a complicated view of his father, but he would never let anyone know
how he really felt inside. It was as if there were some deep scarring in there
that he didn't want anyone to see—not even his father, whom he so often
referred to as his "best friend."

In 2000, Tiger was no longer afraid to say he was too busy to take a
call from Earl. And when he changed his cell phone number, which he
frequently did, Earl was no longer the first person to get the new number.
Tiger's silence wounded Earl. "My dad and I don't talk as much," Woods
said in the midst of his historic run. "He's doing his thing. I'm doing my
thing."

Although Tiger was spending a lot more time with his mother and his
girlfriend, he went to see Earl shortly after winning the US Open at Pebble Beach. When he arrived, he found his childhood bedroom virtually
unchanged. The Obi-Wan Kenobi poster still hung on his closet door, and
his list of Jack Nicklaus's achievements remained on the wall. Yet the en-

vironment in the house had changed. The only sign of Tida, for example, were the containers of food and pre-cut fruit that she would deliver for Earl a couple of times a week.

At sixty-eight, Earl was badly overweight and spent most of his time in his chair. Tiger got him out of the house by taking him to nearby Big Canyon Country Club in Newport Beach, which had made Tiger an honorary member. There were a lot of personal things they could have discussed that day, such as the way a husband treats his wife. But how many sons are willing to go there with their fathers?

In a quiet moment on the course, Earl did bring up one question: "Do you want me to be around more?"

"I'll be all right, Pop," Tiger said.

Earl got the message.

CHAPTER NINETEEN

COLD

One week after winning the 2000 PGA Championship, Tiger found himself on the eighteenth fairway at the famed Firestone Country Club in Akron, Ohio. It was the final round of the WGC-NEC Invitational, and Tiger was running away with the tournament. With just one hole to play, the outcome had long been decided; the only question was whether Tiger could actually find the eighteenth green. Earlier, storms had forced a three-hour stoppage in play, delaying the finish. By the time play continued, a foggy gloaming had set in, obscuring the flag waiting some 167 yards away. Visibility was so poor and the fog hung so low that Woods had to crouch down to the ground to gauge the lie. To reach his goal of finishing twenty-one under par, Tiger would literally have to take a shot in the dark.

He had grown up playing in the twilight with his dad, often finishing his final two or three holes in the dark. But this was Firestone, not the navy course back home. The situation was a perfect metaphor for this stage of Tiger's career: mere mortals were no longer a challenge; he was competing against the gods now, Mother Nature herself. Woods lived for these moments. They were chances to put his entire artistry on display. With crickets chirping and fans in the gallery holding up flickering lighters, Tiger took dead aim with an 8-iron. A flurry of camera flashes from around the eighteenth hole created a strobe effect as his ball fell from the darkened sky and landed two feet from the hole, igniting a thunderous roar that echoed down the fairway. "How 'bout that?" he said, grinning and slapping hands with Steve Williams. Then walked toward the green, holding his putter in the air as if it were a scepter and he a king.

For folks watching on television, the scene was so surreal that it was tempting to wonder if the shot was a make-believe television stunt. Even the CBS Sports broadcasters couldn't believe their eyes.

"Oh no, you can't do that," Jim Nantz cried out.

Moments later, Tiger tapped in his birdie putt to finish at twenty-one under par, the lowest score in tournament history and eleven strokes ahead of his nearest competitors. It was his eighth PGA Tour victory of the year.

Fourteen days later, Tiger was again on the seventy-second hole in fading light—only this time he was clinging to a one-shot lead in the final round of the Canadian Open at Glen Abbey outside Toronto. Thanks to an errant tee shot, he found himself in the middle of a yawning bunker, 213 yards from the flag, trees right, and virtually nothing but a huge body of water standing between him and the green. In Shakespearean terms, if the shot in the dark at Firestone was *Hamlet*, what happened next—a flushed 6-iron over two hundred yards of water, landing two feet past the pin—was *Macbeth*, another towering accomplishment.

These shots were so dramatic that they easily overshadowed the aspect of Tiger's personality that most accounted for his outlier status: his mind. During his epic run of major championship victories and jaw-dropping shots from the latter part of 1999 through the end of 2000, Tiger's concentration day in and day out was so focused on making shots that it's difficult to put into words. It's best illustrated by a sequence that took place at the Canadian Open, just moments before Tiger hit the miraculous 6-iron over water. For his tee shot on eighteen, there was total silence as he began his backswing. Then, right in the middle of his downswing, a fan shouted "Tiger!" In that instant, Tiger brought his 125-mile-per-hour club head speed to a screeching halt, freezing his driver just inches from the ball. No one else in the world could stop his driver so close to the ball. His mental control over his physical abilities was unparalleled.

At this point, it hardly mattered that he walked away with another win and simultaneously held the US, British, and Canadian Open titles. Every week, a fresh form of genius seemed to emerge. Having already sped past the career Grand Slam—at age twenty-four, the youngest in history to do it—he had far surpassed what he'd done in 1999. Everyone on the PGA Tour knew that if Tiger played his best and they played their best, Tiger would win. More important, Tiger *knew that they knew it.* "He's limitless," Mark Steinberg said at the time. "He's a transcendent athlete, finally being recognized as the greatest on the planet, and he has anywhere from twenty to forty years left."

In a fevered attempt to leverage Tiger's success, Steinberg was in the process of reevaluating all existing contracts with Woods's corporate partners. In 2000, Tiger earned an estimated $54 million from endorsements. To put that in context, the most that Michael Jordan ever made off the court in a single year at that point was $45 million. But Steinberg believed that Tiger was worth still more—much, much more, especially when it came to Nike.

Woods was now the most photographed athlete—perhaps even the most photographed entertainer—in the world. And Nike was the only brand that was visible on Tiger in all of those photographs. Even when he appeared in commercials for other companies, he always wore Nike; from the hat on his head to the shirt on his back to the shoes on his feet, Tiger was a walking billboard for the swoosh. In Steinberg's mind, that made the endorsement all-encompassing in a way that Woods's first Nike contract didn't adequately reward. Steinberg was also well aware that the company was benefiting from what Nike insiders liked to call the halo effect—Tiger's significant impact on Nike products beyond golf.

The two sides had been negotiating a new deal for eighteen months, and in mid-September of 2000, they finally came to an agreement on a $100 million endorsement contract. It was the richest deal of its kind in the history of sports.

"A lot of people have compared Tiger to Michael Jordan," said Bob Wood, the president of Nike Golf. "But one thing that makes them different is that the career of a professional golfer is so much longer than the career of a basketball player. The earning power of a professional golfer is far greater over the course of a lifetime. We're looking forward to extending our relationship with Tiger over the duration of his career, which will extend for the next twenty to twenty-five years and beyond."

It was clear that Nike had come around to Steinberg's way of thinking and was going all-in. The company also hoped that Tiger would lead its charge into the hypercompetitive golf-equipment business. Bob Wood knew that the first groups on the golf course early on Saturday mornings, the low handicappers and influencers at their clubs, didn't talk about their shirt or shoes on the first tee; they talked about their driver and ball. Tiger's switch to the Tour Accuracy ball at Pebble Beach had given Nike instant credibility among the five million or so hard-core players in the US and millions more around the world. And tens of thousands of pro shops and retail accounts that had previously been reluctant to embrace a "shoe company" with a limited foothold in the sport were now interested in Nike's ball and equipment.

Just a couple of years earlier, in the fall of 1998, Nike's nascent golf business had been losing about $30 million a year on about $130 million in sales. Prior to Woods's record-setting win at the US Open in 2000, less than 15 players in an average 156-man field were playing with solid-construction balls. But after Pebble Beach, virtually everybody on the Tour wanted to try the Nike ball. Tiger had single-handedly broken Titleist's long-standing stranglehold. Suddenly, Nike found the door to a potential 10, 12, or even 15 percent market share to be wide open.

Similarly, Tiger's other partners—General Motors, American Express, General Mills—were all willing to bend over backward to keep him happy. Even the Walt Disney Company, which almost never hired celebrities or athletes to endorse its products, was preparing a five-year, $22.5 million offer to entice Tiger to appear in commercials for the company's theme parks, as well as to endorse merchandise and make appearances on Disney's ABC and ESPN channels.

Tiger's halo effect was also clearly evident on the PGA Tour's negotiations with its network partners and tournament sponsors. When Woods turned pro in 1996, total purses amounted to $68 million per year. By 2001, the number had swelled to $175 million. In 2003, it would jump to $225 million.

But perhaps the biggest indication of Tiger's ability to draw ratings was the *Monday Night Golf* matchups that IMG had put together with ABC Sports. The second installment, billed as the "Battle at Bighorn," pitted Tiger against Sergio García at the luxurious Bighorn Golf Club in Palm Desert, California, near the end of the 2000 season. The head-to-head contest drew a Nielsen rating of 7.6, the highest in the series. Remarkably, nearly eight million viewers tuned in on a Monday night in late August to watch García and Woods compete in prime time. But when García edged Tiger by a single shot to claim the $1 million prize, Woods was so upset that the future of the series was in jeopardy.

Losing out on a million bucks was one thing—the blow was softened by his guaranteed $1 million appearance fee—but Tiger didn't like for his status to be threatened. The last thing he wanted was to give García the slightest hope that he could beat him when it counted, on Sunday in a major. So he told IMG's Barry Frank, the creator of *Monday Night Golf*, that he was done. Finished. Quitting the series.

Frank had played more than his fair share of hardball at negotiating tables around the world. He knew bullshit when he heard it, and this was no bullshit. Woods was the drawing card. Without him, *Monday Night Golf* was history.

But Frank hadn't negotiated record-breaking rights deals without having a flair for the dramatic and knowing how to keep a card or two in his back pocket. He played those cards now with Woods and Team Tiger. What about a change in format? Frank suggested. Mixed teams? Four-ball instead of match play? "That way," he told Woods, "if you don't win, it's not your fault."

Eventually, Tiger agreed to a new format that ensured none of his rivals would have a chance to beat him one-on-one in prime time. The next year, Tiger and Annika Sörenstam edged David Duval and Karrie Webb in nineteen holes. Then, in 2002, Tiger and Jack Nicklaus defeated García and Lee Trevino 3 & 2. On it went. IMG and ABC profited, and so did Tiger. Over the course of seven years of *Monday Night Golf* matches, Frank estimated that Tiger earned at least $10 million in prize money and guarantees from the show.

Frank never expected to be loved by Tiger, but he wanted to be liked, and, more than anything, to be respected. In an interview at his home in Connecticut in the summer of 2015, Frank made clear that Woods had never been unkind or rude, and never owed him anything. But at the same time, Frank said they had never shared what he called an intimate moment, such as a celebratory drink or lunch, and Woods had never once offered a single word of thanks for everything Frank had done for him. Sitting on the back deck of his sprawling ranch home, Frank was asked if Woods respected him. A long pause ensued before Frank, who was celebrating his eighty-third birthday, answered.

"No," he finally said. "I think I was just another Jew doing what he was paid to do. That I owed him more than he owed me."

It was no surprise that the 2000 season ended with Tiger earning every conceivable honor and award, including being named *Sports Illustrated*'s coveted Sportsman of the Year for the second time in five years. This time the magazine's profile was written by Frank Deford, who was considered a legend of sports journalism and was the first sportswriter to be awarded the National Humanities Medal. A colleague once referred to him this way: "Frank Deford with a pen in his hand is like Michael Jordan with a basketball and Tiger Woods with a driver."

With pen in hand, Deford made this observation about Woods at the end of his brilliant year: "Tiger is such an extraordinary champion and so widely admired that we have granted him a sort of spiritual amnesty. His persona is still insulated by his deeds, his misjudgments by his youth. Sometime soon, though, we will weary of the tedium of his persistent success and start peering more deeply into that heavenly smile and those steely eyes. Won't we?"

At that time, the only person peering deeply into Tiger's steely eyes was Joanna Jagoda. Earlier in the year, rumors had circulated that they were getting engaged, a prospect Woods quickly shot down when a golf writer raised it. "It's not true," Tiger said. "I'm here to tell you that right now. Let's put an end to this crap right now."

Jagoda remained at Tiger's side as he won his three major championships during the summer. But in the fall of 2000, she went her own way, enrolling in law school at Pepperdine and quietly disappearing from Tiger's life. Months later, it became public knowledge that they had split. After law school, Jagoda went to work for Bear Stearns & Co., Inc., before joining JPMorgan Chase, where she rose to the position of vice president and assistant general counsel.

Jagoda has never publicly discussed her relationship with Tiger, or what prompted their breakup. But by all accounts, everyone who was close to Tiger at that time—Mark and Alicia O'Meara, Butch Harmon, Mark Steinberg, and others—adored her. She had, in many ways, the perfect temperament for Woods. In public, she always conducted herself with grace and dignity, interacting affably with everyone from officials and fellow golfers on the PGA Tour to Tiger's corporate partners. A conservative dresser who smiled easily and had a friendly disposition, she also connected with fans. Privately, she was discreet, avoiding the spotlight and politely declining interview requests.

She also wasn't afraid to tell Tiger when she thought he was out of line or when he needed to do things that he would have preferred to avoid, such as talking to fans or engaging with the press.

"She was good for Tiger," said Alicia O'Meara. "If she didn't agree with something he said, she would politely say, 'I see it this way.' He had so many years of everybody telling him yes. When you're a celebrity, people tell you what you want to hear. She wasn't that kind of person."

In one sense, Jagoda was similar to Tiger's first love, Dina Gravell. Both women truly loved Tiger, but neither of them cared much for the lifestyle that came with his excessive fame. As he had with Gravell, Tiger shared parts of himself with Jagoda and had moments of intimacy, but there were aspects of his life that he kept from her—including the fact that he was getting more and more attention from other women. As a result, he was gaining confidence, and his expectations of who he wanted on his arm were changing.

Once the relationship was over, Tiger never looked back.

Two things coincided with Joanna Jagoda's departure from Tiger's side: he failed to win any of the first six tournaments he entered in 2001, and he became a lot surlier, especially toward the press. He was in a particularly foul mood with the media prior to the start of the Bay Hill Invitational in mid-March, if for no other reason than that he was sick and tired of any suggestion of a "slump." For the most part, the golf press danced around the word, but Tiger knew what everyone was thinking and went out of his way to remind the writers that his scoring average through the first six tournaments in 2001 was actually *better* than it had been in 2000 when he was winning tournament after tournament. Talk of a slump, he made clear, was just idiotic.

"Does it bug you that we make it a story line, 'My God, he's gone six events and he hasn't won, what's wrong with the guy?'" asked one reporter.

"Well, it's annoying because of the fact that if you think that way, then you really don't understand the game of golf," Tiger said.

In his mind, one of those lacking such understanding was Jimmy Roberts, his former friend and now—in Tiger's eyes—foe, ever since the unwelcome question about Tiger's cursing on live television during the US

Open in 2000. A week before Tiger got to Bay Hill, Roberts had done a piece for NBC essentially defending Woods, artfully equating Tiger's "slump" to the Beatles' not having a number one record for a few months. That Roberts was supporting him made no difference to Tiger; he hated having the word *slump* applied to him in any context.

So when Roberts asked Woods if, in effect, he was a victim of his own success, Woods gave him essentially the same "you don't understand the game of golf" answer—only it wasn't an insult in the isolated confines of a press tent: the exchange took place in front of millions of viewers on national television.

To put it mildly, Roberts was none too pleased. *You're not even listening*, he thought. *You don't even get it.*

Tiger won at Bay Hill, but he wasn't about to let go of his animus toward the media—and especially toward Roberts. The next week, at The Players Championship, Woods had another tense exchange with Roberts following an early round. *Golf World* columnist John Hawkins was standing nearby. "Don't worry, dude," Hawkins told Roberts from across a rope line. "You keep on asking those good questions."

Roberts took one look at Hawkins and told him what he thought of him and the rest of the fawning reporters who had long treated Woods as though he were labeled "Handle with care."

"Let me ask you something," he said. "When the *fuck* are you guys going to start asking him those good questions?"

Hawkins paused and looked down before responding. "Good point," he said. "Because we've all been kissing his ass for years now, and we still don't get anything interesting."

On Monday, after taking possession of The Players Championship trophy in the rain-delayed event, Woods once again faced Roberts, this time on the eighteenth green. Expressing congratulations, Roberts attempted a generic question.

"Some slump," Tiger said, completely ignoring what Roberts was saying.

Roberts tried again, but Tiger cut him off. "Means the slump is over," he said. Moments later, with Roberts in midsentence, Woods walked off, leaving Roberts standing alone on live television.

Weeks later, Roberts approached Tiger privately in hopes of having a man-to-man talk to resolve any misunderstandings. But Woods brushed him off. He wanted nothing to do with Roberts.

"I've thought a lot about him over the years, because we've had some serious ups and downs," Roberts said in 2016. "There's more 'fuck you' in Tiger Woods than in any athlete I've ever covered. In those days, it felt like a one-way street with him. He demanded respect but wasn't willing to offer any in return. He burns with hate toward people that he feels have wronged him or are not on his side."

With the slump talk officially dispatched in the most ignominious manner, the 2001 story line shifted to gentler and more familiar terrain—the Masters. Would Woods be able to make it four majors in a row? If so, would that qualify as a Grand Slam, despite the fact that they were not won in a single calendar year? Woods made it clear that if he held all four major championship trophies at the same time, the media could call it whatever it wanted—Grand Slam, Tiger Slam, or Some Other Slam. That was his answer.

At Augusta, it's the back nine on Sunday where the tournament often divides. By the eighteenth tee, Woods had pushed Phil Mickelson aside and was one stroke clear of David Duval, who had torn up the course earlier with seven birdies in the first ten holes. On the green in two, Woods was twelve feet from a two-putt par and carving his name deeper into the history of the game. Instead, he dropped the putt for birdie. Then he walked to the side of the green and buried his face in his hands.

"I just started thinking, you know, I don't have any more shots to play. I'm done—I won the Masters," he said afterward. "It was just a weird feeling, because when you're focused so hard on each and every shot, you kind of forget everything else. When I didn't have any more shots to play, I started to realize what I had done, and I started getting a little emotional."

With his Masters win, he simultaneously possessed the four most prestigious trophies in golf—the US Open, the British Open, the PGA Championship, and the Masters—and proudly displayed them on the mantel above the fireplace in his home. There had never been a human being on the planet who had won all four tournaments in succession.

Soon after winning his second Masters, Woods was back on the range at Isleworth with O'Meara. While they practiced, Tiger chose to voice one of his favorite complaints—his loss of privacy.

"You whine all the time about wanting privacy," O'Meara told him. "You gave all that up."

Woods didn't want to hear it, but O'Meara wasn't about to let up on his friend.

"You're one of the most famous people in the world," he continued. "People feel like they own a part of you. That's the price to be paid."

Woods said nothing.

"Now, I can help you with that," O'Meara said.

"You can?" Woods asked.

"Walk away," O'Meara said. "Just walk away. Give it all up. Take your money and run."

But Woods knew that would mean walking away from the one thing that gave meaning to his life, symbolized by the shiny trophies that decorated his home. At twenty-four, he already had five majors in his pocket, a milestone that Nicklaus didn't achieve until he was twenty-six. Woods wasn't about to give up the fame either; as much as he hated being a public figure, he loved what that status afforded him: the hip Nike commercials; the American Express Centurion Black card in his wallet; the Rolex on his wrist; the luxury home in Florida; the bachelor pad in Newport Beach; private planes, limousines, and security guards; his face on Wheaties boxes, billboards, and magazine covers throughout the world. The adulation was intoxicating.

Yet he was inescapably lonely.

After the round, Tiger invited O'Meara over to his place. He wanted to show him the latest addition to his mantel. O'Meara watched as Tiger spent time taking pictures and lining up the glittering symbols just so. In a way, they were his best friends, the objects he'd devoted his life to acquiring.

Joanna Jagoda had treasured the trophies almost as much as Tiger did, but since she was out of the picture, there was no longer anyone special for him to share his successes with.

But that was about to change.

CHAPTER TWENTY

IN THE BUBBLE

As Tiger's private plane made its descent into Las Vegas in the dark, the cluster of new megaresorts below came into view. The Mirage, Bellagio, Luxor, Mandalay Bay, the Venetian—their shimmering lights seemed to be winking at him.

For Tiger, Vegas had become a familiar place, a home away from home. He frequently went there to work with Butch Harmon, who had relocated his golf school to nearby Henderson. Tiger's trainer, Keith Kleven, an acquaintance from his Stanford days who was helping him build up his endurance, strength, flexibility, and speed, also lived there. But by the summer of 2001, Woods's primary purpose for going to the desert was to escape. His destination of choice was the MGM Grand, and he had a system that enabled him to get there without detection.

It helped that Tiger never traveled with a huge entourage. Upon arrival, he would step from his private plane into a limo that delivered him to the Mansion, an ultraexclusive Italian-themed enclave of twenty-nine villas tucked behind the MGM. Using a secluded alley entrance, Tiger would duck into an elevator that took him to a private floor, where his luxury suite awaited. Once inside, he could stay for days, and no one in the outside world would know he was there. A personal VIP host was at his service, ready to deliver most anything upon request—fine cuisine, a corner table, endless rounds of free drinks, exotic women, and, most of all, absolute discretion. That's what made Vegas so attractive. It was his private playground, a place where he could indulge without fear of scrutiny, what locals called being "in the bubble."

When it opened in the spring of 1999, the Mansion was billed as an invitation-only high-rollers' paradise promising "beyond attentive" service and absolute privacy. It was just what Tiger craved, and he had no trouble gaining access to it. Villas were doled out like four-carat diamonds, reserved for "whales"—casino-speak for gamblers with credit lines of $100,000 and above.

Tiger wasted little time becoming a whale. He'd always been a numbers guy, and he easily took to gambling in the late nineties when he started betting $100 a hand at blackjack and established a $25,000 credit limit that steadily increased over time. After a few years, Woods would routinely play $20,000 per hand, often on two or more hands at a time. His credit line at the MGM reached $1 million; only about a hundred gamblers in the country had that kind of limit.

Unlike a lot of celebrities who went to casinos to party, Tiger approached gambling the way he approached golf. He was there to win, and he often did. Industry insiders in Vegas referred to Tiger as "a sharp," meaning he took a very smart, calculated approach to his bets and consistently won more than he lost. He thought nothing of walking away with half a million in winnings, and he didn't chase big losses.

Tiger had gotten his first taste of the town as a high school recruit who was seriously considering enrolling at UNLV. But he'd been a geek then, and not about to dabble in the city's pleasures. A few years later, he celebrated his twenty-first birthday at the MGM, and he was much more experienced in the ways of the world by that point. But it wasn't until NBA superstars Charles Barkley and Michael Jordan entered the picture that Tiger's eyes were really opened to what Sin City had to offer a world-class athlete.

Tiger met Barkley in Orlando in 1996, when the two of them played golf together for the first time. Barkley was twelve years older than Tiger, but they became fast friends, often hanging out together at casino resorts. Barkley taught Tiger to loosen up and enjoy the fruits of celebrity.

"I would always say, it doesn't do any good to be Tiger Woods if you're not going to fucking enjoy being Tiger Woods," said Barkley. "Part of being great is you have to enjoy it."

Tiger didn't need much convincing, but he didn't know how to go about doing it. He simply lacked the requisite set of social skills. On top of being intensely introverted, Tiger had spent most of his life within the protective cocoon built by his parents. His adolescent years were so tightly controlled that he was afforded few opportunities to experience life outside of golf and school. In the rare instances when he dared to break the rules set by his parents, he paid for it. "Mom beat the hell out of my ass," Tiger once told a reporter. "I've still got the handprints."

"The expectations in that house and the pressure in that house were just so intense," said one of Tiger's best friends from that time. "I felt sorry for him."

One result of the way he was raised was that Tiger never disobeyed. He was determined not to do anything that might tarnish the gold-plated image that his parents had worked so hard to cultivate. Earl, in particular, had hyped his character so much that Tiger feared getting caught doing anything questionable. Now, a dozen major corporations had constructed endorsement campaigns around Tiger's clean-cut reputation. Meeting Charles Barkley in 1996 was like finding a long-lost older brother who initiated him into a different side of life.

In some ways, Sir Charles was a perfect role model: He was beloved everywhere he went, but especially in Vegas. A big-time gambler, Barkley had a reputation for handing out hefty tips that endeared him to bellmen, valets, bartenders, and caddies. He talked to all of them as if they were his friends.

Michael Jordan provided an entirely different example. Tiger initially met Jordan in passing, running into him numerous times right after he turned pro, but the first time they spent any quality time together was in 1997. After attending a Bulls game at the United Center, Woods sped off with Jordan in his Porsche to Lake Michigan. That night they spent hours on a luxury casino boat. It was the beginning of a relationship that was cemented by their mutual love of golf and gambling. Despite stern warnings from his then attorney John Merchant, Tiger started calling Jordan a couple of times a week for advice. "I guess he looks at me as kind of a big brother," Jordan said at the time. "He's got a lot to deal with. He's twenty-two years old, but people want to project him to be older. Just because he hits the ball nine miles and wins the Masters by twelve strokes, he's supposed to have all the answers. He's supposed to be perfect. That's not fair."

One of the areas where Jordan exerted some influence early on was Tiger's natural inclination toward solitude. "His first instinct at being in the spotlight was to become a recluse," Jordan said. "Well, that's wrong. Believe me, I know. You can't just go to the golf course and when you're done go back and lock yourself in your hotel room. I've been there; it's miserable. You can't just stare at the TV. You lose your sense of society. You're not living life."

Perhaps it was inevitable that Tiger would turn to Jordan. There was no other athlete alive who had experienced the same level of fame. The two of them essentially belonged to their own exclusive club. As a result, Jordan exercised considerable influence over Tiger's attitude toward fame, women, and power.

"We call each other brothers because Michael is like the big brother," Woods said. "I'm like the little brother. To be able to go to a person like that who has been through it all—and has come out of it just as clean as can be—that's the person you want to talk to. And on top of that, he's one great guy."

Tiger's view of Jordan wasn't universally shared by the working class in Vegas. They found him to be an aloof, arrogant star who embraced the word *entitled* with a capital *E*. You didn't have to travel far to find stories of Jordan's barely tipping or altogether stiffing caddies, locker-room attendants, card dealers, and bartenders, or of his driving his tricked-out North Carolina–blue golf cart down the middle of a fairway at Shadow Creek, music blaring as he blew by one foursome after another while yelling, "Hurry the fuck up! You guys are slow as fuck!"

In the words of one Vegas insider, "A complete fucking asshole."

But Vegas being Vegas, Jordan's boorish behavior never leaked out. "Everybody protected Michael back then because he was the best ever," said one Vegas source. "Nobody ever talked about Michael. Nobody ever told on Michael. Everybody was scared of Michael. And Tiger learned from him."

By the time Jordan entered the picture, Tiger's attitudes toward money and people were already well ingrained. Even when a meal was free—and it almost always was—Tiger rarely left a decent tip. And as far as tipping doormen, bellmen, and valets? It got to the point where PGA Tour representatives were often quietly leaving $100 tips on Tiger's behalf with locker room attendants at Tour stops to keep his parsimonious ways out of the press. For Tiger, even the most basic human civilities—a simple hello or thank you—routinely went missing from his vocabulary. A nod was too much to expect. Tiger didn't learn all of this behavior from Jordan. If anything, this sense of entitlement had been originally

authored by Earl. Tiger's relationship with Jordan simply provided re-
inforcement.

"When Tiger got famous, he got mean," said a former nightclub owner.

When it came to women, Tiger's head didn't turn easily—at least, not
when he was on the golf course. He was once asked by a writer how he
managed to avoid getting distracted by the unusual number of "golf bun-
nies" behind the ropes at his tournaments. He replied that he didn't notice
them. His focus, he said, was on getting his ball in the hole. Even when a
young model who worked as a lap dancer stripped naked and ran onto the
eighteenth green to dance in front of Tiger at the British Open in 2000,
he remained locked in, prompting a Scottish police officer who took the
woman into custody to remark: "Tiger did not respond to her at all. His
concentration is astounding."

But that all changed at the British Open the following year, when Tiger
noticed a striking twenty-one-year-old blond nanny with fellow pro Jesper Parnevik and his wife, Mia. Up to that moment, Phil Mickelson's wife,
Amy, who had formerly been a cheerleader for the Phoenix Suns and who
had appeared in the *Sports Illustrated* swimsuit issue, was generally considered the most striking woman on the PGA Tour. But the Parneviks'
nanny was going to make everyone forget about Amy Mickelson. In a very
brief encounter, Tiger said hello, and she introduced herself as Elin. Smitten, he was eager to learn more about her.

Elin Maria Pernilla Nordegren was born in Stockholm on New Year's
Day in 1980. Her identical twin, Josefin, was born minutes later. Elin
and her sister were raised in the coastal town of Vaxholm. Their father,
Thomas Nordegren, was one of Sweden's most accomplished journalists.
Their mother, Barbro Holmberg, was a highly educated social worker.
When Elin was six, her parents divorced. Her father eventually moved to
Washington, DC, to cover the White House for Swedish National Radio.
Her mother went on to work for the Swedish government, where she rose
to a cabinet-level position as minister for migration.

When Elin was nineteen, she was contacted by Bingo Rimér, a prominent
fashion photographer who did work for Scandinavian *Playboy*. Rimér, who
fancied himself Sweden's answer to Hugh Hefner, had seen a candid photo
of Elin and instantly thought she had the potential to be a top model. After

tracking her down, he convinced her to sit for a couple of photo shoots. One of his pictures of her in a bikini ended up on the cover of the magazine *Café Sport*. But Elin had no real interest in modeling and instead enrolled at Lund University, one of Sweden's top schools, to study psychology.

During the summer after her freshman year, she took a job at a clothing boutique in Stockholm, where, a few weeks later, Mia Parnevik went shopping and encountered her. The Parneviks had four young children and were looking for a new nanny, and Mia was instantly struck by Elin's friendly nature and ease around kids. Shortly after that chance encounter in the boutique, Elin quit her summer job in Sweden and moved to Florida to be the Parneviks' nanny, taking up residence in the family's three-thousand-square-foot guesthouse. The first time she accompanied the Parneviks to a tournament was to the 2001 British Open.

Life-altering chance encounters were the norm for Elin Nordegren, but when she bumped into Tiger Woods in Scotland, she had no interest in a relationship with him. A short while later, he reached out through an intermediary and asked her out, but she found his approach odd and off-putting. Besides, she had a steady boyfriend back in Sweden and wanted nothing to do with a famous athlete. She wasn't about to be a trophy girlfriend. She turned him down.

By this time, it was rare for anyone to say no to Tiger. The fact that Elin did said everything Tiger needed to know about her. "I resisted his courting for a long time," Elin once said. "I was not an easy catch."

But Tiger persisted, regularly texting her and calling the house, sounding nervous whenever Jesper would answer the phone. Once he got to Nordegren, though, Tiger turned on the charm. He made her laugh and showed her a good time. She felt safe around him. By the fall, he had won her over, and they started seeing each other. Initially, it was all very hush-hush. Tiger didn't want anyone to know—at least, not yet. "When she started dating Tiger, it was like there was an unwritten agreement that she wouldn't say anything to anyone," a Tour insider said. "She became like Greta Garbo."

Publisher Larry Kirshbaum was getting concerned. Shortly after turning pro, Tiger had signed a $2 million contract with Warner Books to write an instructional book on golf and an autobiography later on. After waiting for four years for the first book, Kirshbaum invited Mark Steinberg to his office to make clear that he wanted Tiger's book out in time for Christmas 2001. It was the agent's first meeting with Kirshbaum, one of the most powerful people in publishing. When Steinberg stepped into his office, he immediately noticed some University of Michigan regalia prominently displayed on Kirshbaum's desk.

"Don't tell me you're a Wolverine," Steinberg said.

"Well, where are you from?" Kirshbaum snapped. "Slippery Rock College?"

"I'm a Fighting Illini," Steinberg said proudly.

Without saying another word, Kirshbaum turned, knelt down, and started messing with the stereo he kept on the bottom shelf of his bookcase. His behavior puzzled Steinberg, but Kirshbaum had a plan. Well aware that Steinberg had played on the Illinois team that lost a heartbreaker to Michigan, 83–81, in the Final Four in 1989, he played "The Victors," the most well-known fight song in history. As Steinberg cupped his ears, Kirshbaum cranked up the volume on what amounted to fingernails on a chalkboard for any Big Ten rival.

"I can't take this anymore," Steinberg said. "I'm going. I'm leaving."

They both had a big laugh. And Kirshbaum got what he wanted—a commitment from Steinberg to get Tiger to deliver. He suggested using Tiger's columns from *Golf Digest* as the basis for the book, and recommended that some of the editors there could interview Tiger to enhance the narrative. It all sounded good to Kirshbaum.

By the summer of 2001, Steinberg had made sure that Tiger delivered, turning in his long-awaited book *How I Play Golf*. At Steinberg's urging, Warner Books used an image of Tiger in his latest Nike gear on the cover. The book was slated for publication in the fall, but Kirshbaum faced a quandary after the 9/11 terrorist attacks—should he delay publication? The concern was that there might be little appetite for a golf book while the country was in mourning. But Kirshbaum ended up sticking with the publication date. On October 9, 2001, Tiger's book went on sale and became an instant best seller, moving almost one million copies in hardback alone. His popularity was at an all-time high, and it seemed that everything he touched turned to gold. "We were in it for over $2 million for two books," Kirshbaum said. "But it turned out to be cheap in the end because the instructional book was such a huge success."

And Warner still had an autobiography from Tiger to look forward to down the road.

At the end of December 2001, Nordegren returned to Stockholm for the holidays. While she was home, she went to see Bingo Rimér and told him about her budding romance with Tiger Woods. Rimér had become a confidant, and she let him know that she would soon need to have him release some images of her to the media—but only specific ones that she personally approved.

While Elin was overseas, Tiger went to Vegas, where he remained for a VIP bash celebrating the grand opening of Light, an upscale nightclub inside Steve Wynn's Bellagio hotel. Tiger's go-to guy at the Mansion had set him up with an all-expenses-paid comp.

Previously, Tiger had hung out with Barkley and Jordan at places like Drink or the bar at P.F. Chang's. Light, however, was a whole new scene, the kind of place that literally put the "sin" in Sin City. It catered to a young, hip crowd with money to burn, and offered—for a $300 fee— premium white-glove treatment and a chance to party with A-list stars. With little more than a nod, a VIP could have his host escort a woman from the dance floor and discreetly deliver her to his table. Light's runaway success spawned similar nightspots such as Pure, Tao, and Jet, each trying to be more exclusive and seductive than the last. But the opening of Light marked the first time that the casino industry had embraced an upscale nightclub that catered to the rich and famous, and it quickly became Tiger's late-night destination of choice. "It was absolutely crazy, out of control," said one longtime Vegas insider who partied at the club alongside Woods.

One night not long after the grand opening, Tiger and another high-profile athlete had settled into their VIP table, in a back corner just off the dance floor, when they noticed a couple of attractive young women partying at a nearby table. A request was made, and a VIP host approached the ladies with the magic words: "Tiger Woods would like you at his table." The brunette and her blond friend got up as if shot out of a cannon. Later, they accompanied Tiger and the other athlete up to a suite at the Bellagio, where the group stripped down and slipped into a hot tub. At one point, Woods took the brunette by the hand and led her out of the hot tub. Avoiding the various bedrooms, he instead walked her straight into a closet and had his way with her in the dark. The rough nature of the encounter shocked the brunette. She left wondering why he couldn't have at least taken her to a bed.

Starting in 1998, each year during the week of the Masters, Tiger stayed with Mark and Alicia O'Meara at the Augusta-area home of Peggy Lewis. He liked it there for a number of reasons: It was out of the way and afforded great privacy, plus O'Meara always paid the rent. And when O'Meara failed to make the cut, he would leave town on Friday night, meaning Tiger had the place to himself for the remainder of the weekend.

In 2002, Woods chose to stay at Lewis's place again, and this time he brought Elin along. Two weeks earlier she had stepped into the limelight for the first time, quietly cheering him on at the Bay Hill Invitational in Orlando. But Tiger was still trying to keep a lid on their relationship, and Lewis's home provided the cover he was looking for. After O'Meara missed the cut and left town, Tiger and Elin were alone at Lewis's place. They didn't venture out, choosing instead to eat in and remain out of sight.

On Saturday, Tiger woke up at four thirty a.m., his focus squarely on the fact that he trailed the leader, Vijay Singh, by six strokes. He went out and shot a 66, blowing past Singh to take the lead at eleven under. Then, on Sunday, he fended off Singh and three of his closest rivals—Els, García, and Mickelson—and, for the second straight year and the third time in six years, won the Masters. The other players were reluctant to admit it, but they were intimidated by Tiger and the murderous way he went about knocking them off, one by one, in big tournaments.

At age twenty-six, Tiger had won seven majors faster than anyone in history. Perhaps even more telling, he had never finished second in a major—meaning that when he was in contention in the final round, he simply didn't lose. In contrast, Jack Nicklaus had six second-place finishes in a major championship by the time he was twenty-six years old.

But this latest victory lacked the emotional exuberance of the 1997 win or the historical significance of that of 2001. This time it felt almost routine, as if he were just going about his business, systematically checking off another item on his growing list of achievements. The energetic fist-pumping had been replaced by long, silent stares.

At the press conference afterward, Tiger was asked: "Can you please share with us how you plan to celebrate and with whom tonight?"

But Tiger had no intention of sharing his plans. "You know," he said, "right now, I'm going to a dinner here, the Champions Dinner. I think when I get home, I've got to pack up my suitcase and get ready for my flight. But I will celebrate. I'm not going to tell you how, but I will celebrate."

It must have been some celebration, because the next day when Peggy Lewis returned to her home, it was a wreck. Shaving cream was smeared on the bedroom and bathroom walls. Plates with partially eaten food were left under Tiger's bed. The kitchen looked as though it had hosted a frat party. Lewis ended up staying in a hotel that night while a cleaning service restored her home. A few weeks later, she got her phone bill and discovered more than $100 worth of long-distance calls had been made to Sweden and England during the weekend of the Masters. Fed up, Lewis did something she'd never done—she placed a call to Tiger's office.

It was bad enough that Tiger had never paid her for the use of her home or left her a tip, but what really upset her was his basic lack of respect and appreciation. Year after year she would return home to find her personal property damaged or destroyed, none of which Tiger had apologized for or offered to replace. When Tiger's assistant got on the phone, Lewis unloaded.

"He's not allowed in my house again," Lewis told her, launching into a list of grievances that ranged from small (one year she found her nicest white comforter covered in bloodstains and balled up in the corner of Tiger's room) to expensive (in 2001, she had to replace a brand-new dining room table after someone—she suspected Earl Woods—had left cigarette burns all over the surface). When the O'Mearas heard about the table incident, they purchased a new one for her. The only year Lewis's home hadn't been damaged while Tiger was in it was in 2000—the year Joanna Jagoda was with him. That was also the only year Lewis had received a thank-you card. It read: "Thank you very much for sharing your lovely home. I hope to see you when I come back. Joanna." Not a word, however, from Tiger.

"I asked him one time if we should send flowers," Tiger's assistant told Lewis.

It was a little late for that.

There had been Sunday nights when Lewis had to go to a hotel because Tiger was still in her house. It irritated her that in those instances, Tiger still didn't offer to pay her expenses.

But it was the calls to Sweden that had pushed her over the edge. Tiger was the richest athlete in the world. Would it really be so difficult to leave behind some money and a note explaining they had used the phone?

"Make a copy of the bill and send it to me," his assistant said.

A few days later, Lewis received a bouquet of flowers from Tiger's office. Then, a couple of weeks after that, she received an envelope containing a photocopy of her phone bill and a check. The calls that Elin had made were highlighted in yellow. The check was for the exact amount of those calls, and not a penny more.

Tiger's inability to show gratitude, apologize, or express appreciation was rooted in his warped upbringing. His mother pampered him like a prince, and his father rarely uttered the words *thank you* or *I'm sorry*. Tiger learned early and often that his needs were all that mattered. His unapologetically self-centered attitude was critical to his success in golf, but it had an utterly devastating impact on the way people perceived him. Sadly, Woods didn't seem to care about the latter part. It didn't matter that someone like Peggy Lewis would have adored him for life if he'd simply acknowledged and thanked her.

Elin stood behind Tiger as he sat at a craps table at the Mandalay Bay Resort & Casino, a pair of dice in his hands and a stack of brightly colored chips in front of him. A sea of boisterous onlookers pressed against the outstretched arms of security guards wearing earpieces. As if alone on an island, Tiger ignored the ruckus and tossed his dice. It was nearly midnight on Friday, April 19, and he was giving Elin a little taste of Vegas before the start of his annual fund-raising extravaganza, known as Tiger Jam. Actors, musicians, and other athletes crowded around, shouting encouragement at Tiger.

Finally, Barkley showed up, drawing grins and nods with his loud commentary. "I've played with Phil and all those guys, and Tiger does things they can't do," Barkley said. "They're intimidated by Tiger. They're soft as shit. Black Jesus scares them."

Elin rolled with it. The atmosphere was a far cry from studying psychology in Sweden, but she was in love.

Soon afterward, the internet was flooded with risqué images from Elin's photo shoot with Bingo Rimér, including one particularly sultry image of her posing topless and cupping her breasts. The tabloids ran salacious headlines, referring to her as Tiger's "sexy Swede." The *New York Post* called her "a tantalizing cross between Pamela Anderson and Cindy Margolis." Back in Sweden, the tabloids got so out of hand that they ran nude images, falsely claiming that they were of Elin. Tiger responded by putting out a statement saying she had never posed nude and had no plans to do so in the future.

"One of the reasons she didn't date him right away was because she didn't want to be just a celebrity girlfriend," Rimér said. "Elin is not like that. She's a smart girl, raised in a family of intellectuals. She has dreams. She didn't want to be seen just as a decoration on Tiger's arm."

But there she was, on Tiger's arm.

CHANGES II

From the start, the atmosphere at the 2002 US Open at Bethpage Black on Long Island in New York felt more like a Giants football game at the Meadowlands than a golf tournament. The New York fans boisterously shouted, chanted, and cheered at decibel levels that exceeded anything Woods had heard in his entire career. But the loudest ovations weren't for him—they were reserved for the number-two-ranked golfer in the world, Phil Mickelson. Tiger had never particularly liked Mickelson and went out of his way to badmouth him, routinely referring to him as "Phony Phil." It was Tiger's preferred means of exerting control over a competitor while at the same time keeping as much distance as possible between them. Although Mickelson, about to turn thirty-two, had yet to win a major championship, Tiger recognized that he had emerged as a rival worth watching.

Tiger's disdain for Mickelson went beyond the ropes, though. Mickelson was a perennial fan favorite, with his everyman image, which Tiger, like many regulars on Tour, felt was artificial. Mickelson had a beautiful wife and two young children, and they were frequently around him on the Tour. In the final round at Bethpage, Mickelson had to back away from the fifteenth tee when the "Let's go Mick-el-son" chants grew too loud. It was Mickelson's birthday, and on the seventeenth tee, his fans sang "Happy Birthday" to him.

But like a well-oiled machine, Tiger led from start to finish, never allowing Mickelson to get close enough to inspire any hope. While he drew his share of cheers, Tiger didn't engage the fans as his rival did. Instead, he wore a scowl throughout on his way to capturing his eighth major championship. His dour demeanor prompted *Sports Illustrated* senior writer Michael Silver to posit afterward: "Has any pro golfer—hell, any great athlete—ever looked so grim while doing his job?"

One problem may have been boredom. It had taken Tiger just twenty-two majors to win eight times. Nicklaus, in contrast, needed thirty-five majors to collect his first eight wins. With his triumph at Bethpage, Tiger had won seven of the last eleven major championships. There was no one to really challenge him. His only source of stimulation came from his obsession with continually getting better, a compulsion at the root of a slow-forming rift between him and Butch Harmon. Personally, they still got along fine. But Tiger had lost interest in Harmon's philosophy. Essentially, Harmon felt that Tiger had perfected his swing and simply needed to maintain it with subtle refinements—an opinion that was supported by the fact that Tiger was in the midst of a 264-week run as the number-one ranked golfer in the world.

Maintenance, however, was a word Tiger hated. He was a man in constant search of something he couldn't find. It made him a hard person to be around, much less to like, even for his friends. "He was so consumed with being the greatest golfer ever; he wasn't a very social guy," said Charles Barkley. "Golf is just a game. But when your whole life revolves around how you're doing on a golf course, you're going to develop a negative attitude to a certain degree, instead of saying, 'I've actually got it pretty good.'"

Harmon more or less agreed with Barkley. The difference was that Harmon had to work with Woods, and the brunt of Tiger's obsession with perfection was felt most acutely by those who worked with him in a professional capacity. They were expected to perform at the same level of perfection that Tiger did. When that didn't happen, he could be cold and unforgiving. Two months after winning the US Open, Tiger froze out Harmon at the PGA Championship at Hazeltine. A few days earlier, Woods had telephoned Harmon with the news that their partnership was at an end. "You know, I really just want to do this on my own," he said. "Thank you for everything you've done for me, how you've helped me with my swing. But I'm going to go on my own."

Harmon was shocked that Woods had mustered the courage to make the call. "Between the ropes, he's the toughest son of a bitch to compete against I've ever seen," Harmon said in 2017. "But he's *not* good at looking you in the eye and saying something."

A couple of days after the call, Tiger was on the practice tee at the PGA Championship when Harmon showed up. Ignoring him, Tiger kept swinging. Stung, Harmon walked off. Just like that, after nine years to-gether, the relationship was over.

Harmon's departure marked the start of an unprecedented drought for Tiger. He finished second at the PGA, losing by one stroke. Thirty-four months would pass before he would win another major championship. Injury contributed to the start of the drought. At the end of 2002, Woods flew to Park City, Utah, to undergo arthroscopic surgery to remove benign cysts on his knee and drain some fluid. But during the procedure, doctors Thomas Rosenberg and Vern Cooley determined that his anterior cruciate ligament was significantly compromised. They told him he had about 20 percent of his ACL left. Tiger's question was simple: "How long will that last?" The answer was complicated. It was only a matter of time before his ACL was gone altogether, which would then require a more significant surgery. In the meantime, he was going to have to modify his approach.

Mark O'Meara owned a condo in Park City, and he had escorted Tiger to the surgery. Afterward, O'Meara and Tiger met up with O'Meara's swing coach, Hank Haney, who owned a condo nearby. The conversation quickly turned to Tiger's ACL and the challenges it posed. "I'm going to have to change my swing," he told Haney.

While sitting out the first five tournaments of 2003, Tiger aggressively rehabbed and managed to return to the Tour in mid-February at the Buick Invitational in San Diego. Despite playing in pain, Woods won the tour-nament. Then, after finishing tied for fifth at the Nissan Open, he took the WGC–Accenture Match Play Championship and the Bay Hill Invitational. Heading into the 2003 Masters, he looked primed for a third-straight green jacket. But, as was his wont, Woods was trading pain—and potentially de-bilitating injury—for the trophies that mattered most. At the same time, he had redoubled his weight-lifting routine, working out twice a day, morning and night, for as much as ninety minutes at a time. As a result, his upper body, particularly his chest and shoulders, continued to get bigger, which was affecting his swing. With Harmon no longer in the picture, Tiger was determined to figure things out on his own. On the course, he even started giving his caddie the silent treatment. On Sunday at Augusta, just three off the lead to start the round, Tiger ignored Williams's advice to use the driver on the third hole and ended up flaring his tee shot wide right, forcing him to double-bogey. In response, Tiger didn't say a word to Williams for the better part of two hours. On the ninth fairway, Williams had finally had enough.

"Pull your head out of your arse and start behaving like an adult," Williams told him. "If I'd given you the wrong club and it cost you double bogey, then fair enough, but don't hit a shitty shot and tell me it's the wrong club."

Tiger said nothing.

"Get your shit together and stop acting like a child," Williams told him.

Tiger finished tied for fifteenth.

He ended up smoothing things out with Williams, but in a larger sense, the break with Harmon was indicative of Tiger's arriving at a point where he was shedding those who had been with him the longest. Back on January 1, 1997, just months after Tiger had turned pro, Nike had assigned Greg Nared (pronounced "Nard") to be a liaison between Woods and the corporate office. Working under the umbrella of the company's Athlete Relations program, Nared was officially a business-affairs manager with Nike Golf. Unofficially, he was part of Nike's so-called guy program—a personal concierge service reserved, at that point, for just two other Nike athletes: Michael Jordan and Ken Griffey Jr. It was Nared's responsibility, as Tiger's "guy," to communicate all business-related issues involving apparel, footwear, equipment, and advertising to Woods and coordinate directly with the product teams. In addition, Nared oversaw all Nike-related appearances and scheduling for Woods, as well as for select other sponsors. It was his job to ensure that Tiger knew where he needed to be and, if push came to shove, to end an interview or photo shoot that was running past its prescribed time limit.

"Greg was the funnel for everything Tiger-related," said Chris Mike, former director of marketing for Nike Golf. "I couldn't just pick up the phone and call Mark Steinberg. Greg was the guy."

Tall, good-looking, and African American, Nared had been a starting point guard at Maryland before joining Nike. In many ways, he had the perfect temperament for his job, which landed him deep inside Woods's inner circle and, often, on the receiving end of Tiger's biting sense of humor. Woods was like a hammer and Nared his nail, constantly getting hazed by the star he was responsible for helping. Nared took everything in stride, embracing the pivotal role of navigating Tiger through the uncharted waters of extreme fame and fortune. Not surprisingly, Tiger could be demanding, especially when it came to things like selecting the perfect rainwear; it had to fit just so, and could not restrict his swing. And when there was blowback, Nared was often the recipient. At Nike, athletes of Woods's wattage were never wrong.

Through it all, Nared absorbed the blows and treated Woods like a brother. Eventually, however, the brotherly bond began to fray, especially after Woods learned the corporate ropes and his patience grew thin when it came to Nike's response to his input and needs. Within a year, Tiger decided to make a change. He left it to Kel Devlin to break the news to Nared. "It was a nightmare to tell Greg he wasn't going to be Tiger's guy anymore and have it not come from Tiger," said Devlin. "That was part of the job I did that was not fun."

Dating from his days at Stanford, there had long been a cold side to Woods; he never let anyone get too close to him. Harmon and Nared knew him as well as anyone; other than perhaps O'Meara and Steinberg, there was probably no one who spent more one-on-one time with Tiger between 1996 and 2003 than his swing coach and personal aide-de-camp. Taking them off the team was like removing the guardrails from the curves of a high-speed freeway.

Tiger still won five tournaments in 2003, but after March he managed to win only twice. He was essentially a nonfactor in all four major championships. He was out of sync, and he knew it. O'Meara knew it too, but he was searching for the right opportunity to broach the subject of what to do about it. Then, early in 2004, the two of them flew together on Tiger's Gulfstream G500 to the Middle East for the Dubai Desert Classic, where O'Meara ended a five-year winless streak with a surprising victory. As he walked off the eighteenth green following the final round, Tiger was waiting for him. "I'm as happy for you right now as you are," he told O'Meara.

Coming from Tiger, that statement had huge significance, and O'Meara knew it; Tiger seldom showed concern for others. Feeling confident, O'Meara decided to finally speak up. "Tiger," he said during the flight back, "you've got to get someone to help you with your game."

Woods almost seemed relieved. "Who should I get?" he asked.

O'Meara suggested Butch Harmon's brother, Billy.

Tiger quickly shot that idea down. Too many potential complications in hiring the sibling of his prior coach.

They kicked around a couple of other names, none of which resonated with Woods. Finally, O'Meara suggested his own instructor. "Tiger, I know Hank's my friend and I've been with him for years, but he's the best teacher in the world," he said.

"Yeah, I know," he said. "I'm going to call him tomorrow."

Hank Haney first met Tiger and Earl Woods in 1993 when they were in Dallas for the Byron Nelson Classic. Tiger was a seventeen-year-old amateur at the time, and he'd been invited to play in the tournament on a sponsor's exemption. Haney was then a private instructor for Trip Kuehne and his two siblings. Kuehne's father took Earl and Tiger to meet Haney at his training facility north of Dallas. It was a frosty introduction. Congratulating Tiger on his accomplishments, Haney extended his hand. Tiger limply shook it and said nothing. Earl seemed even less interested in saying hello to Haney.

Three years later, after Tiger moved to Isleworth, Haney started running into him on the practice range. Haney would be there working with O'Meara, and Tiger would often join them for dinner afterward. There were also plenty of times at tournaments when Harmon and Haney were with Tiger and O'Meara during practice rounds. Still, Haney never imagined that one day he would end up coaching the man he considered the greatest golfer who ever lived.

But hours after Tiger and O'Meara returned home from Dubai, O'Meara's agent, Peter Malik, called Haney and told him he was going to be receiving a phone call. The next day—March 8, 2004—Haney was having dinner with his father in Plano, Texas, when his cell phone rang. He stepped out and took the call.

"Hey, Hank, this is Tiger."

"Hey, bud," Haney said.

True to form, Tiger dispensed with any small talk. "Hank, I want to know if you'll help me with my golf game."

"Sure, Tiger, of course," he said, trying to conceal his enthusiasm.

Tiger told him he wanted him in Isleworth on Monday morning. The call lasted a mere three minutes. Thoughts raced through Haney's head: *I've won the lottery. I'm going to gain in stature. I'm going to be famous. I'm going to get to try out all my ideas on the ultimate student, and he's going to prove them so right.*

After a few minutes, he went back inside and told his father the news. A lifelong Nicklaus fan, Haney's father chuckled with pride. "You know," he said a few minutes later, "that's going to be a hard job. Are you sure you want to do it?"

A month earlier, Tiger Woods had formed a company in the Cayman Islands for the sole purpose of purchasing a 155-foot yacht. He named his new company Privacy, Ltd., and he named the yacht the same thing. According to court records, *Privacy* was "intended to be a respite for the Woods Family to relax and escape the rigors of their celebrity." At that point, the closest thing Tiger had to a family was Elin. They were living together in Isleworth and were engaged to be married. But Tiger treated the engagement like a state secret; the only people who were allowed to know about it were family and a few close friends, all of whom were sworn to secrecy.

Elin had been with Tiger long enough that the burden of fame and Tiger's obsession with privacy had begun to rub off on her. Naturally inclined to trust others, she had become much more reserved and guarded. But she trusted Tiger implicitly, and she was in awe of his work ethic. On top of the tournaments, he was constantly on the road fulfilling obligations to his sponsors, making appearances, shooting commercials, and attending functions. He had earned over $200 million in endorsement money in the three years since they had started seeing each other, and with that came enormous demands on his time; so Elin never questioned his desire to escape on a yacht. She figured he deserved *Privacy*.

One of the few people who were invited to spend time on the yacht with Tiger and Elin was Tiger's dive instructor, Herb Sugden. In addition to teaching Elin to scuba dive, Sugden offered to teach Tiger how to spearfish. But he instantly discovered that Tiger's hand-eye coordination was so exceptional that all he had to do was hand Woods the spear gun and get out of the way. "I didn't have to teach him," Sugden said. "I just showed him once how to do it, and he did it. He's a better spearfisher than I am. He was phenomenal."

Tiger liked Sugden and treated him exceptionally well. When he yearned for a greater feeling of adventure, he asked Sugden to teach him cave diving, a much riskier form of scuba diving that entailed going into underground caves that were full of water. At first, Sugden was apprehensive. "At that time, Tiger [was] at the peak of his career, winning everything," Sugden said. "Cave diving can be dangerous. You're underground and you're underwater. The only way to get air is what you got on your back. And the only way you can get out is to come back to the place you went in. You can get lost. It's a hazardous thing."

But Tiger was fearless. And just as he had with scuba diving, he soon became a fully certified cave diver as well. It helped that he possessed an unusual ability to hold his breath longer than most humans. Nonetheless, his insurance carrier didn't like the fact that he was diving in caves. In an attempt to reassure his insurer, Tiger had Sugden meet with them. "I had to go up and tell them how safe cave diving was," Sugden said.

On Monday morning, March 15, 2004, Tiger was standing in his driveway, swinging a golf club. His custom-made golf cart was parked nearby with his clubs in the back. He was waiting for Hank Haney to arrive for their first practice session. When Haney pulled up in his rental car, Tiger walked over and said hello.

"I'm looking forward to working with you," Haney said.

Tiger wasted no time before telling Haney how things were going to be done. He had observed Haney plenty of times as he worked with O'Meara, and Tiger made it clear at the outset that he disagreed with some of his methods. It was a not-so-subtle way of saying that Haney was going to have to earn his trust.

Tiger got into his cart and drove Haney toward a secluded area on the range. "I want to get more consistent in every phase," he said on the way over, "so I have the kind of game that at majors will always get me to the back nine on Sundays with a chance. I don't want to just have a chance on the weeks when I'm hot. I want to have a chance all the time."

Haney knew he was dealing with more than a world-famous golfer. He considered Tiger's mastery of every facet of the game—right down to the equipment he used—downright intimidating. For instance, according to Kel Devlin, Nike had recently shipped a box of prototype titanium drivers to Woods so he could test them. There were six in total. After putting the drivers through their paces, Tiger told Devlin that he preferred the one that was heavier than the others. Devlin informed him that all six drivers were the exact same weight. Tiger argued otherwise, insisting that one weighed more than the others. To prove him wrong, Devlin sent the drivers back to the design wizards at the Nike testing facility in Fort Worth with instructions to weigh them. They found that five drivers were exactly the same weight, but the sixth was two grams heavier. When they pulled the club apart, they discovered that an extra dab of goo had been added to the inside of the head by one of the engineers to help absorb a few floating particles of titanium. The weight of the goo was equivalent to the weight of *two one-dollar bills*. Yet Tiger noticed the difference in the way the driver felt in his hands.

With stories such as that in mind, Haney understood that it wasn't wise to consider Tiger his student. He knew Woods was testing him, and he wasn't about to get off on the wrong foot by arguing with him. As Tiger started to hit balls, they talked about the fact that he wasn't consistently able to get his upper body to rotate fast enough on his downswing. The other thing they worked on was getting Tiger's eyes to stay level through his swing. Woods's intensity on the practice range was beyond anything Haney had ever experienced. He proceeded gently through this first session.

By the time he returned home, Haney had an agreement with Tiger to continue working with him. Haney would be earning $50,000 per year—the same amount Tiger had paid Harmon—and would receive a $25,000 bonus each time Tiger won a major championship.

Later that week, Tiger played in the Bay Hill Invitational. After a strong first round, he played poorly, shooting 74, 74, and 73 to finish tied for forty-sixth place. In his press conference afterward, he said that he was very excited about what he had worked on earlier in the week and that 90 percent of his game was good. But what he said publicly was almost always different from what he really felt.

When Haney showed up at Isleworth the next day for his second round of practice sessions, Tiger was already on the range, hitting balls. He didn't look up when Haney reached the tee. Nor did he respond when Haney pointed out a few things he had noticed in Tiger's swing during the Bay Hill Invitational. A couple of compliments from Haney didn't faze Tiger either. Silence was his way of sending a message. It was also his method for assessing weakness.

"I'm not sure what you're doing here," Haney finally said. "But I guess you're trying to knock me off my spot. I know what you need to do to get better. I know what your plan needs to be. So if you're trying to knock me off my spot, it's not going to happen."

Tiger still didn't acknowledge him, but when Haney suggested some new drills, he immediately executed them with passion and precision. The practice session was solid. The next day's session was even better. But Tiger stayed in silent mode, providing instant clarity to something Butch Harmon had said to Haney the first time he saw him after being succeeded as Tiger's coach. "Hank, good luck," Harmon told him. "It's a tough team to be on. And it's harder than it looks."

The good news heading into the 2004 Masters was that Tiger was still the number one golfer in the world, and he felt no real pressure from his flanks. David Duval had been derailed by injuries. Sergio "Crybaby" García had crumbled under the bright light of expectation (just two wins in seventy-eight Tour starts). Ernie Els appeared to be on his last legs. Vijay Singh was playing well but remained something of an outlier. The only guy Woods continued to think was capable of giving him a real challenge was Mickelson, who had earned his own nickname from Tida: "Fat Boy." Despite twenty-one victories on Tour, Mickelson had also earned the dreaded Best Player Never to Win a Major label. Tiger felt that if Mickelson won just one major, the floodgates would open.

In previous years, Woods had always been the one talking trash about Mickelson. But by 2004, Mickelson had become pretty good at talking shit himself. A year earlier, he'd done just that, expressing his surprise to *Golf Magazine* that Tiger had played so well given his "inferior equipment"—a jab at Nike clubs and balls. Woods brushed it off as simply "Phil trying to be funny" and "Phil being Phil."

When Mickelson arrived at Augusta, he was eager to mix it up with Tiger. That was especially clear when Mickelson birdied five of the last seven holes, including eighteen, in the final round to finally capture his first major championship.

"I had a different feeling playing this week," Mickelson said afterward. "I didn't feel the anxiety of it slipping away, or 'How is the tournament going?' or 'Who is doing what?' It was, 'Let's hit some shots.'"

Shots were exactly what Woods *didn't* hit. After finishing back in the pack, he wasn't about to stick around and congratulate Mickelson. Instead, he disappeared with his father to the place where Earl had been stationed as a Green Beret—Fort Bragg, North Carolina. They met up with a bunch of Earl's military buddies. Drawing on his father's military contacts, Tiger spent a few days doing army special-ops training. Wearing a camouflage uniform with his name above the left pocket, Tiger did four-mile runs in combat boots, participated in hand-to-hand combat exercises, and did drills in wind tunnels. It was risky behavior, considering that he had a significantly compromised ACL, but Tiger's mind was elsewhere. Back in 1998, Earl had been diagnosed with prostate cancer, which was successfully treated with radiation. But in 2004 the cancer returned, and it was spreading through his body. He was also dealing with diabetes. Sensing that his father's days were numbered, Tiger wanted to be closer to him. The highlight of the trip was tandem-jumping with the army's parachute team. Strapped to a soldier, Tiger flung himself out of the jump plane. Exhilarated, Woods grinned as he dropped through the air. On the ground, Earl breathed with the aid of an oxygen tank as he waited in the drop zone. When Tiger landed, his father hugged him with pride.

"Now you understand my world," Earl told him.

Before leaving the base, Tiger sat with his father and listened to Earl's old army buddies tell stories about him. It was the first time that Tiger had heard about his father's heroism in combat. The more he heard, the more he longed to live up to Earl's expectations.

By the time Tiger showed up at the 2004 US Open at Shinnecock Hills, golf writers were openly talking about the fact that he was in another slump. In the previous eighteen tournaments, he'd won just two times. Even Butch Harmon publicly criticized him. "Tiger Woods is not playing well," Harmon said on television during the tournament. "He's not working on the right things in his golf swing, although Tiger obviously thinks he is."

Tiger hated it when anyone criticized him publicly. But it felt like a stab in the back to hear it coming from his former swing coach. He spent the weekend in a foul mood, barely setting foot in the locker room, avoiding everyone, and giving Tour officials the *What the fuck do you want?* look anytime they approached. Steve Williams played the role of human shield. On the very first hole of the tournament—in which Tiger finished ten-over and tied for seventeenth—Williams kicked a camera belonging to a pesky news photographer. In the final round, he confiscated an unauthorized camera from a fan—an off-duty police officer, as it turned out. Both player and caddie were at wit's end. The US Open marked the eighth consecutive major championship without a win, the longest such stretch of Tiger's career.

Afterward, Tiger was behind the wheel of his rental car, headed back to the house he had stayed in. Williams sat in the passenger's seat. Suddenly, Tiger pulled over to the side of the road and hit his caddie with the verbal equivalent of a 9-iron to the gut.

"Stevie," he said, "I think I've had enough of golf. I'd like to try to be a Navy SEAL."

Stunned, Williams searched for something rational to say. All he could think of was this: "Don't you think you might be a bit old for that?"

But Tiger was serious. He had practically worn out a Basic Underwater Demolition/SEAL Training DVD that covered a six-month training course. He had memorized every exercise, and many of the slogans on the video were ones he had started repeating as his own.

Williams wasn't the only one who was concerned. Hank Haney had been spending a lot of time at Tiger's home in Isleworth, where he had observed Woods's fixation on a video game called *SOCOM: U.S. Navy SEALs*. Wearing headphones, he would respond to orders from an animated commander. "Tiger would get totally immersed," Haney said, "sitting on the edge of the couch, as intense and focused as if he were playing in a major championship."

The sudden and intense interest in Navy SEAL training coincided with stepped-up workout routines and cardiovascular exercises. Tiger's quest resulted in additional upper-body muscle mass, which forced him to significantly modify his golf swing yet again.

One consequence of Butch Harmon's publicly chastising Tiger was that it sped up his bonding process with Haney. Whether intentional or not, Harmon's comments about Tiger were also swipes at Haney. They were both highly motivated to prove Harmon wrong, and it brought them together. After the 2004 US Open, Tiger fully embraced Haney's approach to overhauling his swing.

———

Early in the summer of 2004, the Boys & Girls Clubs honored Denzel Washington with a lifetime achievement award at a black-tie dinner held at the Waldorf Astoria hotel in New York City. The guest list was a virtual Who's Who of the Hollywood and sports industries. Tiger blew off the dinner, choosing instead to attend the after-party in Denzel's suite. A couple of days later, he was with Elin at the clubhouse at Isleworth when he ran into a neighbor who had attended the dinner at the Waldorf. She knew Tiger had been invited, and she wondered why he'd skipped it. He explained that he'd gone to the after-party. Elin had no idea what Tiger and their neighbor were talking about. Finally, she looked at Tiger and said, "You were in *New York*?"

There were a lot of things Tiger didn't tell Elin, especially when it came to his whereabouts and the women he met on the road. His secret life in Las Vegas and all the temptations that besieged him begged the question: Why get married?

The answer may lie in the fairy-tale life that Woods desired—a heart-stopping wife and adorable children living with him in the six-bedroom mansion on Deacon Circle that he had purchased four years earlier. It was the image that he saw in the marriage between Mark and Alicia O'Meara. For Tiger, Elin Nordegren represented the key piece of that puzzle—blond, beautiful, and adoring. They would live happily ever after, right down the street from the O'Mearas.

There was another important factor: Elin was the first woman who fully measured up to the lofty expectations of both Earl *and* Kultida. Tiger had been in love before, and he'd been very close to more than one woman who would have been much more likely to try to rein in his vices and insist that he stay on the straight and narrow. But it soon became clear that he wanted it both ways—the picture-perfect marriage and the freedom to walk on the wild side. In that respect, he was a lot like his father—but with one big difference: unlimited opportunity.

On October 5, 2004, Tiger and Elin exchanged vows in Barbados at the ultraexclusive Sandy Lane Resort. To ensure ultimate privacy, Tiger spent a reported $1.5 million to rent the entire resort for the week, filling the time with fishing, boating, golf, and snorkeling. On the night of the wedding, the island sky was ablaze with a spectacular display of fireworks. Only family and close friends were invited. Tiger spent his nights sitting around with his father and Michael Jordan and Charles Barkley, smoking cigars and talking about glory days. Meanwhile, Kultida beamed. At age twenty-eight, her son was now a man in the fullest sense. Soon, she hoped, there would be a grandchild.

Just before Christmas of 2004, Tiger and Elin went on their first getaway as a married couple, flying to Park City for a week of skiing with the O'Mearas and the Haneys. For years, Tiger had been telling O'Meara he was going to try skiing. Now that he was married to an advanced skier who playfully bragged that she was much better than he was at the sport, Tiger was determined to show her that skiing was a lot simpler than golf. But he had one condition for going on the trip: he didn't want to be seen with a ski instructor.

O'Meara promised to take care of everything. He talked to his friend Karl Lund, one of the top instructors in Utah. Lund had taught both of O'Meara's children to ski, and he was very connected at the luxurious Deer Valley Resort. At O'Meara's request, Lund talked to the resort and made special arrangements for Tiger to receive lessons outside the normal course of business. There would be no reservations and no payment. Lund would simply meet Tiger on the slopes and ski with him for the day.

The mere fact that Tiger was going skiing with his swing coach was a graphic illustration of how much things had changed. When Butch Harmon was his swing coach, he used to bar Woods from shooting jump shots by himself for fear that he might jam a finger. Now Haney and O'Meara were encouraging Tiger to try downhill skiing. It was clear that Tiger had accepted Haney into his inner circle, viewing him as a friend. The feeling was mutual.

The next morning, Tiger showed up on the slopes wearing a bulky knee brace. It had been almost two years to the day since his last knee surgery. His SEAL training exercises and intense weight-lifting regimen had been putting increased stress on his troubled left knee, but he wasn't going to let that slow him down on the slopes.

At first, he resisted any instruction. "Don't worry," he told the group. "I'll be fine."

He started out slowly on the bunny slope. With Elin cheering him on, he soon moved off the beginner hill. After a short break for lunch, Tiger decided to try a more advanced run. Haney watched in fear as Tiger rapidly gained speed. Lund and O'Meara were partway down the slope when Woods flew by them. They estimated his speed at close to forty miles per hour, and he was completely out of control. "Holy shit!" Lund said, taking off after him.

Tiger was balanced on his skis just enough to pick up speed and hung on for dear life as he headed straight for some aspen trees. "Turn! Turn!" everyone screamed.

Suddenly, at the last second, Tiger turned just enough to avoid the trees, toppled, and landed flat on his back between two trees. Frightened, Lund skidded to a stop beside him.

Out of breath and feeling exhilarated, Tiger looked up at him.

"Hey," Lund said, "are you okay with me helping you out with a few things?"

"That'd be great," Tiger said.

Lund helped him up and dusted him off. Then he started teaching some basics, such as how to turn. "Skiing is basically left turns and right turns," he said, demonstrating what he meant, and encouraging Tiger to follow. Rights. Lefts. Rights. Lefts. "That's it," Lund said. "Up on your toes. Feel it?"

"Why doesn't this fuckin' ski turn?" Tiger barked. "This fuckin' ski doesn't turn!"

"Just relax," Lund said. "Stay positive."

After more than twenty-five simple turns, Tiger had had enough. He wasn't interested in drills. He wanted speed.

But Lund wouldn't let him. "Get your shins against the front again," he said.

Tiger just glared at him. Elin was watching, and he was pissed.

"You know what?" Lund said. "A really loud FUCK YOU would make you feel better right now."

"Fuck you!" Tiger yelled.

"Do you feel better?"

Tiger grinned. "Yeah."

Lund smiled. "Now, get your shins against the front."

He lasted about ten minutes before he lost it again. He was Tiger fucking Woods! He didn't need to be taught. He knew what to do. "Fuck you!" he said to Lund again.

Determined not to let Tiger get hurt on his watch, Lund dug in, insisting that he not go downhill without learning how to turn properly.

Tiger's natural inclination was to do what's known in ski jargon as "crank and yank": basically, every time he tried to turn, his skis would end up in a V-shape, the inside leg getting in the way and needing to be yanked around to complete the turn. But due to the downhill angle, the back of Tiger's ski was catching when he tried to twist, putting tremendous strain on his knee. Aware that he'd undergone ACL surgery, Lund didn't want him to do any long-term damage to the ligaments by learning an improper technique.

The more they practiced, the more frustrated and surly Tiger became. As he finished his final run with Lund, Tiger saw O'Meara approaching. Without saying thank you or good-bye, Tiger started trudging toward the lodge.

"See you later," Lund said.

"Fuck you!" Tiger said.

Lund couldn't believe it. He was the most experienced instructor on the mountain, and he had spent the afternoon working with Tiger as a courtesy. It was a fitting end to the most frustrating year in Tiger's career. In 2004, he had won just one of the nineteen tournaments he entered. Phil Mickelson had won the Masters and was no longer afraid of him. And in September, Tiger had been toppled from the number one ranking in the world by Vijay Singh. Woods hadn't won a major championship since June 2002, and the whispers were growing louder that the Tiger era might be coming to an end. As an ailing and frustrated Woods removed his bulky knee brace in Park City, it certainly seemed that way.

On January 23, 2005, Tiger won the Buick Invitational at Torrey Pines. It was his first PGA tournament victory since he had begun working with Hank Haney ten months earlier. During that period, Tiger had once again changed his swing, making major adjustments to his grip and retooling many of the things he had worked on with Harmon. This was the third major swing change of his career, and he and Haney still had a long way to go toward calming down his swing in hopes of avoiding injury and getting the new mechanics fully refined. But a win was a great way to start the 2005 PGA Tour season.

Elin was particularly ecstatic. This was Tiger's first win since the wedding, and she had walked every hole of the final round with him.

Afterward, back at the hotel, Elin leaned against him and said, "We have to celebrate. What should we do?" She brought up the fact that when she used to work for the Parneviks as a nanny, they would throw a party every time Jesper won.

"E, that's not what we do," Tiger told her. "I'm not Jesper. We're *supposed* to win."

Elin nodded, the smile shrinking from her face. There would be no celebration.

Tiger's emotional detachment after victories was part of his formula for greatness. Even when he played flawlessly, he acted as if he had simply done okay. The best was always yet to come.

"Tiger never allowed himself to be satisfied, because in his mind, satisfaction is the enemy of success," said Haney. "His whole approach was to delay gratification and somehow stay hungry. It's the way of the superachiever: the more celebrations, the less there'll be to celebrate."

It was an attitude that kept him motivated week after week, but it took a toll on his relationships. Nevertheless, Elin quickly molded her approach to his, stifling her enthusiasm and hiding her emotions. It was the Woods way.

The one opponent who generated a different, more visceral reaction from Tiger was Phil Mickelson. He wouldn't admit it publicly, but Tiger viewed Mickelson differently after he won the Masters in 2004. He had proven himself to be a serious contender. And while Tiger was in the midst of a swing change, Mickelson saw vulnerability. Weeks after the win at Torrey Pines, Tiger ended up in a head-to-head battle with Mickelson at Doral. Woods ended up sinking a thirty-foot birdie putt on the seventeenth hole to finally put Lefty away. The win restored Tiger to the number one ranking he had briefly lost to Vijay Singh in 2004. More important, Tiger sent a direct message to Mickelson—*I'm still better than you.*

Afterward, he came as close as he would get to expressing joy after a win.

"That one meant a little more, huh?" Haney asked him.

"Oh, yeah," Tiger said. "Anytime I can beat that guy."

Still, there was no celebration.

CHAPTER TWENTY-TWO

UNPLAYABLE LIE

In the spring of 2005, Charles Barkley's *Who's Afraid of a Large Black Man?* was published. An instant best seller, the book was cowritten with *Washington Post* columnist Michael Wilbon and featured a collection of candid conversations on race with prominent figures, including Bill Clinton, Morgan Freeman, Jesse Jackson, Marian Wright Edelman, and Ice Cube. Barkley also included a chapter featuring a conversation with Woods. In it, Tiger claimed he was the target of a violent racist attack when he was five years old. This is an excerpt from what Woods said in Barkley's book:

> *I became aware of my racial identity on my first day of school, on my first day of kindergarten. A group of sixth graders tied me to a tree, spray-painted the word "nigger" on me, and threw rocks at me. That was my first day of school. And the teacher really didn't do much of anything. I used to live across the street from school and kind of down the way a little bit. The teacher said, "Okay, just go home." So I had to outrun all these kids going home, which I was able to do.*

This was not the first time Woods had told this story about his first day in elementary school. By 2005, he had been repeating it in one form or another for well over a decade. But the version that he told Barkley was the most sensational account to date. As best as can be determined, the tale was first told by Earl Woods, who shared it with *Golf Magazine* in 1992, when Tiger was sixteen years old. In that telling, Earl claimed that Tiger was the only black student at Cerritos Elementary School and that he had been tied to a tree by some older classmates. One year later, the story resurfaced in a *Los Angeles Times* profile on Tiger. From there, the story grew. In his seminal profile on Tiger Woods for *Sports Illustrated* at the end of 1996, Gary Smith wrote the following about the incident:

> *What happened was a gang of older kids seizing Tiger on his first day of kindergarten, tying him to a tree, hurling rocks at him, calling him monkey and nigger. And Tiger, at age five, telling no one what happened for several days, trying to absorb what this meant about himself and his world.*

The following year, in the biography of Tiger supported by Earl and Kultida, journalist John Strege described the incident as a "shocking introduction to racism" wherein Woods was tied to a tree by a group of older white boys, taunted with racial slurs, and pelted with rocks. Later in 1997, Woods was interviewed by Barbara Walters, who asked him about the first time he experienced any kind of discrimination. He responded by repeating the kindergarten story, but he added a new twist, saying, "I was tied to a tree by the sixth-graders and had, um, nigger written on me and rocks thrown at me, and I was bleeding all over the place and went home."

No single story fueled the Tiger Woods racial narrative more powerfully than his account of being the victim of a brazen hate crime at the age of five. But under scrutiny, the incident seems to be made up.

Low-lying and the color of creamed coffee, Cerritos Elementary School first opened its doors in September 1961. It sits alongside a five-lane boulevard right across from a local park. In 2016, when we visited the school, its two kindergarten classrooms were still housed in the far southwest corner of the building, completely separating kindergarteners from the rest of the students—just as they were on September 14, 1981, the first day of school for five-year-old Eldrick Woods. Tiger's kindergarten teacher, Maureen Decker, remembers some details from that day like it was yesterday. She also remembers twenty years later when she was watching a televised interview with Tiger and first heard him turn that day into a scene from a Spike Lee film.

"I was flabbergasted," said Decker. "I almost fell out of my chair at home when I heard him say that, because I knew it was absolutely untrue. It never happened. How did the sixth-graders get past me or the other teacher on duty? It never happened. It makes no sense that we would ever let sixth-graders come out to the kindergarten playground in the first place."

The two kindergarten classes at Cerritos were connected by a workroom for the teachers. Just outside the classrooms there was a large playground, completely fenced in. Only kindergarten students had access to the playground. In 2016, Jim Harris, the longtime director of maintenance, operations, and transportation for the Savanna School District, which includes Cerritos, provided a walking tour of Tiger's former kindergarten playground. The entire area had a concrete surface and was fully enclosed by a five-foot-high chain-link fence and a single gate. The grounds also featured two mature trees. Kindergarten students, Harris pointed out, are always supervised, especially on the first day of school, adding to the improbability of Tiger's account. "I can't understand how that could have happened," he said of the alleged incident. "The kids are very, very protected. They're so guarded."

Woods also claimed that after the incident, he immediately ran a few short blocks home. But in addition to having to leave a fenced-in area without being stopped by teachers, parents, or administrators, he would have had to cross five lanes of traffic in front of the school without raising the suspicion of a crossing guard—all of which begs the question: How did a five-year-old get tied to a tree on a concrete playground, have the word *nigger* spray-painted (or written) on his body, be pelted with rocks until he was covered in blood, untie himself, escape, and make it across five lanes of traffic while being chased by older kids without anyone's witnessing any element of this story?

There's more: In the official Tiger Woods DVD collection released in 2004, Earl Woods claimed that the incident took place in *first grade*, not kindergarten, and that Tiger didn't tell him about it for "two or three days." Earl also claimed that at his urging, Cerritos principal Donald Hill investigated the incident and provided Earl with a report, and that the kids involved were punished. Hill flatly denied Earl's account. "I have never heard of that story," he said in 2003. "Something that was that serious, I would question why didn't the father come to me and complain? . . . It certainly didn't come to my office."

In response to a specific request for any reports or documentation related to a racial incident involving Tiger Woods during either kindergarten or first grade, Dr. Sue Johnson, superintendent of the Savanna School

District, said in an email: "There are no reports of any kind related to the alleged incident."

So why tell this story if the incident never happened? Perhaps the best answer can be found in one of the more famous phrases ever to exit Earl Woods's mouth: "Let the legend grow." It was a reference to Tiger's image. Earl, who fashioned himself a media expert, knew the impact that adding an incendiary racial element would have in burnishing the story of the "Chosen One." Claims of racism and bigotry, whether real or imagined, injected a powerful element into the narrative.

When Tiger arrived at Augusta for the 2005 Masters, he hadn't won a major championship since the US Open in 2002. During practice sessions leading up to the tournament, he felt he was hitting the ball better than he had at any time previously in his life. But midway through a rain-shortened third round, he trailed Chris DiMarco by four strokes. That night, before going to sleep, Woods received a text from Haney: "All you have to do is what you're doing. There is no one here who can beat you. Even if it takes you extra holes, this is your tournament."

Tiger's relationship with Haney had crystalized. Although he rarely thanked Haney or said anything positive about his teaching methods, Woods was thriving under him. More than anything, he trusted Haney.

By the time the final round began on Sunday, Woods led DiMarco by three shots, thanks to a streak of seven straight birdies on his way to a third-round 65. But his lead had dwindled to just one as he stared down his second shot on the par 3 sixteenth, known as "Redbud." With a fourth green jacket on the line, Tiger had left his tee shot long and left of the pin, against a second cut of rough, in an area that Steve Williams had never scouted. The stage was set for one of the most dramatic chip shots in history.

Time and time again in his hotel room, alone or with friends, Woods had practiced chipping blindly over a bed into a bathroom cup. Far more often than not, he either hit the cup or dunked the shot. A wedge had come to feel like a magic wand in his hands. And like a magician unveiling his most famous trick, Woods now hit a skipping pitch that paused on a faint ball mark, the *exact spot* Woods wanted, before drawing down the slope, funneling closer and closer to the hole. The ball's progress tracked with the crowd's cheers and Verne Lundquist's classic call on television: "Here it comes . . . Oh my goodness . . ." The ball paused on the lip of the cup as if to catch its breath, its Nike swoosh perfectly on display, before toppling into the hole for a birdie. A roar thundered through the Augusta pines as Tiger smacked Williams's outstretched hand and thrust his club into the air. "OH, WOW!" Lundquist shouted. "In your *life* have you seen anything like that?"

Nobody had. The shot was a supernatural display of imagination, touch, and control that encapsulated the brilliance of Tiger Woods. As a human being, he might not have been lovable—or even likable—but as a performer, he possessed unsurpassed talents that he honed through a lifetime of practice. On Sunday afternoons, he shared his gifts with millions, enabling them to forget reality and vicariously experience thrills that were more exhilarating than anything felt in a church pew. Golf had never meant so much to so many.

The next morning, still basking in the glow of Woods's ninth major championship, Phil Knight, Kel Devlin, national sales manager Doug Holt, and three other Nike execs hopped onto Knight's plane for a champagne-soaked flight back to Portland. By Tuesday morning, Jim Riswold and his team at Wieden+Kennedy had cut three inspiring "Just Do It" commercials bereft of any artifice—just Woods, a pulse-pounding soundtrack, and Lundquist at his poetic best. One cut was then embellished with a computer-generated starburst just as a bright white ball and an iconic blue swoosh disappeared into the hole. Riswold loved that version the best, but the other two were more traditional, which was the operative word at Augusta National.

The club was allowing Nike to use footage from CBS Sports for no fee, but in exchange it wanted final approval of any ad. When the commercials made their way to Glenn Greenspan, the man in charge of communications at Augusta, he nixed the starburst version on the spot, according to Riswold. Yet the commercial that did air served as a rocket launch for Nike Golf. Tiger's unforgettable shot marked a profound moment for his biggest corporate partner.

Shortly after getting married, Woods sat for another interview with *People* magazine writer Steve Helling, who focused his attention on a single subject.

"I knew that Elin was a special woman pretty soon after I met her," Tiger told him. "I knew that she was the one for me. She's a special person, and I know how lucky I am to have her. We're at the beginning of our life together, and that's an exciting place to be."

Unlike the previous two times when Tiger had met with Helling, on this occasion, Woods asked a lot of questions. Helling had just covered the breakup of Brad Pitt and Jennifer Aniston, and Tiger wanted to know if Angelina Jolie was really the other woman. He also asked about Nicole Kidman and Tom Cruise. Woods had never met any of these actors, but he talked about them as if they were all part of the same club.

When Helling brought the conversation back around to Elin and asked why Woods had married her, he offered a superficial answer.

"I married Elin because I see a long future with her," he said.

Woods may have envisioned such a future, but his present, much like a critical part of his past, was proving to be a myth. Just months after making that statement to Helling, Tiger was back in Vegas, seated at his VIP table just off the dance floor at Light, the nightclub at Bellagio. His high school friend Bryon Bell and his Stanford friend Jerry Chang were along for the ride. Woods spotted a woman in tight jeans and a form-fitting top that showed off her figure. She was partying with friends when Tiger's VIP host approached with the magic words: "Tiger would love to meet you."

Twenty-one-year-old Jamie Jungers was a small-town Kansas girl who had come to Las Vegas in search of good times and a better life. Standing five feet nine and weighing just 105 pounds, she quickly found part-time gigs as a model, doing some charity work with a group called Angels of Las Vegas. She also landed a job in construction that put a little money in her pocket. After being pulled away from her friends and pointed toward Tiger's table, she strolled up, and Tiger greeted her.

"You're gorgeous," he said.

A few hours later, Jungers found herself more than a little drunk and alone with Woods in his suite at the Mansion. The confidence he had long displayed on the golf course had found its way into the bedroom. "It started out just making out, and then it turned very wild," she would later say about that initial encounter. "Different positions. It almost seemed like he had known me for a while, like he was comfortable with me already."

During an interlude, she asked Woods if he was married. It wasn't very often that Tiger met a woman who didn't know his marital status, but

Jungers didn't follow golf and hadn't paid attention to the tabloid coverage of his marriage to Elin. He told Jungers that his wife was back in Sweden visiting her twin sister.

Jungers left the suite early the next morning, figuring it was a one-night stand. Then her phone rang later that day.

"Hey, it's Tiger," he said. "I had a great time last night, and I'd love to see you again."

It was the beginning of an eighteen-month affair filled with passion, a cute nickname (Tiger called her "my little coffee cup"), and insight into Woods's deceptive method of operation. For starters, he gave Jungers his personal cell phone number and told her to store it under a different name. Next, Bryon Bell checked in with Jungers. He was the facilitator, the one who passed her instructions from Tiger. The first place he wanted her was in Chicago in his hotel suite. From then on, every time Tiger wanted Jungers to fly somewhere, Bell would make all the travel arrangements, always in coach. "I would always go through Bryon," Jungers said.

Woods eventually brought Jungers to his villa in Vegas, where she learned that the words "I'm Jamie, and I'm with Tiger" opened the Mansion's gate like Aladdin's cave.

Years would pass before Jungers would discover that she was just one in a parade of women Woods was using for personal gratification. Like so many, she was swept up in the thrill of secret rendezvous with the most famous athlete in the world.

When looking at Tiger's quest for sex outside of marriage, it's easy to rely on well-worn clichés such as *like father like son* or *the apple doesn't fall far from the tree*. Perhaps. But sex-addiction experts see serial infidelity in a more complex light, particularly among high-powered narcissists used to being in control. In general, they say, narcissists build a brick wall around their softhearted center and fragile self-esteem. Only after treatment do they come to realize that their vulnerability drives the addiction. What they think instead is, *I'm impenetrable*. Another factor is something called conditional worth, which is self-worth that's based on performance: the more success, the more worth, and the more pressure—pressure that seeks release. Finally, there's the hero child living the legacy of his dad, which can lead to a concept known as eroticized rage—anger funneled into sex. *I could never rage at you when I was young and you were too strong. But now I can.*

For reasons that had nothing to do with his wife, Woods was never content to stay at home. Nor did he limit his infidelity to Las Vegas: he was losing control over his impulses, straying from Elin right down the road from their idyllic home in Isleworth in Orlando nightclubs like the Roxy and Blue Martini. And just two months after Tiger and Elin were married, Club Paris opened in town. Owner Fred Khalilian paid Paris Hilton millions for the use of her name and occasional appearances. Tiger quickly became a familiar face, standing on the owner's balcony at one in the morning, overlooking a jam-packed dance floor, cocktail in hand, waiting for the waitress he fancied to get off work. Woods liked to hang with Khalilian, smoking cigars in his huge office, talking sports.

Khalilian knew celebrities, which meant he knew the shy, quiet guy sitting across from him was in pain. What he saw in Woods, he had seen in others. "I got to hang with Michael Jackson for a long time," said Khalilian. "Tiger reminded me a lot of Michael. He was that kid who never lived that childhood life. And he wanted to be bad. He wanted to do whatever he wanted. He wanted to do, in my opinion, what he thought he shouldn't do because he always had to do what he was told to do."

Yet there were no signs that his duplicitous life off the course was having any deleterious effect on his performance inside the ropes. On the contrary, Woods played some of the best golf of his life in 2005. He won six Tour events, including the Masters and the British Open, while finishing in the top four at both the US Open and the PGA Championship. He averaged a career-high 316.1 yards off the tee, second-best on the Tour; took home another scoring title; and was named PGA Tour Player of the Year for a record seventh time. On the cusp of turning thirty, Tiger had done something far more remarkable than anything that could be measured in awards or statistics. Under Haney, he had reached a turning point in his new mechanics, and for the third time in his career, he had mastered a new swing and established himself as the most dominant golfer in the world.

CHAPTER TWENTY-THREE

LOSS

Leading up to his thirtieth birthday, Tiger took an unexplained six-week hiatus from golf. During this period there was a twenty-four-day stretch—the longest in his career—when he didn't even touch his clubs. His absence during the first few tournaments on the PGA Tour schedule in 2006 coincided with a stormy transition under way in the Woods family. At issue was Earl's day-to-day care at the family home in Cypress, where he was confined as he struggled through the final stage of cancer. At the end of December 2005, Kultida had placed an urgent telephone call to Earl's daughter, Royce, saying Earl was in bad shape and desperately needed someone to be with him full-time. It was a full-blown family crisis, brought on by dysfunction and resentment.

The fact was that Earl had been receiving in-home care long before Kultida reached out to Royce. Tiger had paid for nurses to come in and administer medications prescribed for his heart, his diabetes, the poor circulation in his legs, and the complications from his prostate cancer, as well as provide other medical care. On top of that, Earl had a full-time assistant—a woman who had been at Earl's side for a number of years—to help him with everything from bathing and using the bathroom to transporting him to medical appointments. But in a fit of anger triggered by a misunderstanding concerning Earl's care, Kultida had abruptly fired Earl's assistant, whom she referred to disparagingly as a "housekeeper." She was much more than that. The woman had shepherded Earl through some of the loneliest, most uncomfortable months of his life.

Royce called the blow-up between Kultida and Earl's longtime personal assistant "a kerfuffle." That was putting it mildly. When Kultida lost her temper, those on the receiving end of her wrath would not soon forget. In this instance, the responsibility for cleaning up the mess fell to Royce, so she took a six-month leave of absence from her employment and began the process of relocating to Cypress. She moved in with her father and took over his day-to-day care in mid-January 2006.

Prior to Royce's arrival in Cypress, Tiger had spent a great deal of time at the family home on Teakwood Street during his break from golf, especially around the holidays. But he remained purposely aloof from the drama that accompanied his parents' complicated relationship. Dating back to 1996, when Kultida moved into her own place, Tiger was well aware that his father had begun hiring women to wait on him in every way. Kultida always resented these women, but Earl's home was no longer her home, and she largely chose to ignore his choice of company after the separation.

It's unclear how much Tiger knew about the details of what went on in his father's house. One individual with direct knowledge of the promiscuous atmosphere there described it as a "fucking rodeo." At one point, a young woman who showed up for a job interview wearing a super-short miniskirt and cropped halter top promptly took a seat on Earl's lap and hugged him. She was immediately hired to be his executive travel assistant. But by the end of 2005, the environment inside Earl's home had completely changed. He was virtually incapacitated at that point, and the only woman who remained a fixture in the home was the full-time assistant Kultida would soon cut loose.

Remarkably, none of the stress stemming from Earl's worsening condition seemed to adversely affect Tiger's golf game. As far back as childhood, he had always managed to thrive inside the ropes despite the dysfunction at home. His most astonishing characteristic—much more so than his ball striking or his athleticism—was his ability to compartmentalize and numb any emotional pain when he competed. When he returned to the PGA Tour at the end of January 2006, he won the Buick Invitational at Torrey Pines. A week later, he won the Dubai Desert Classic. Then he won at Doral.

Tiger's streak to start the year was made all the more impressive by the increasing complexity of his personal life. Just days before returning to the Tour and ripping off the three consecutive wins, he had paid a visit to the Naval Special Warfare Combatant-craft Crewman Training Center in Coronado, California. While there, Tiger got the VIP treatment, visiting with SEAL Team 7, watching a weapons demonstration, and speaking to a class of future SEALs in training. He told them he had wanted to be one of them when he was young. Afterward, in a private conversation with the weapons instructor, Tiger asked how the SEALs managed the stress, year after year. "It's a life," the instructor told him. "You just do it. You keep practicing."

It was a message that Tiger could relate to.

The only thing that seemed to be a consistent source of inspiration was Tiger's foundation and a new education initiative. Back on 9/11, when he was in St. Louis preparing to play in the WGC–American Express Championship, the tournament was abruptly canceled. With flights grounded, Woods rounded up a rental car and started driving toward Orlando and home. Alone on the highway for fifteen hours, he had a lot of time to contemplate what mattered in his life. With the country reeling in the immediate aftermath of the deadliest terrorist attack in American history, Tiger felt inspired to do something more in the world. He didn't have a clear vision, but he knew he wanted to focus his efforts on helping young people, and he began to see that the Tiger Woods Foundation, as then constructed, was not the best vehicle. A phone call to his father led to a brainstorming session. By the time Woods reached home, he had decided to change the focus of his foundation from golf clinics—which had become something of a circus act and had little lasting impact—and grants to community groups to something more meaningful and lasting: education. The result was a four-year effort to fund and construct the Tiger Woods Learning Center, a state-of-the-art facility focused on teaching science, technology, engineering, and math (STEM) to underprivileged children. The thirty-five-thousand-square-foot flagship building was constructed near his childhood home in Anaheim, a city with a high percentage of minority and low-income students.

With the grand opening scheduled for February 2006, Woods was looking to generate publicity. His foundation requested that former first lady Barbara Bush attend as a guest of honor, but after initially accepting the invitation, she had to cancel. Tiger's team then approached California governor Arnold Schwarzenegger, but he was unable to fit the event into his schedule. His wife, television correspondent Maria Shriver, was suggested instead, but she was not quite what the foundation was looking for in terms of star power. With time running out, Executive Director Greg McLaughlin called Casey Wasserman, a prominent entertainment and sports industry executive based in Los Angeles and the grandson of legendary Hollywood mogul Lew Wasserman. Casey, in turn, reached out to attorney Doug Band, Bill Clinton's longtime counselor. Band couldn't help seeing the irony in Tiger's asking Clinton for a favor.

"Did they tell you the story?" Band asked Wasserman.

The story, of course, involved the Jackie Robinson ceremony snub back in 1997, sparking a schism between Clinton and Woods that was later widened by a subsequent Presidents Cup incident in which Clinton walked into the US team's locker room only to see Tiger walk out. Later, Woods refused to have his picture taken with Clinton when the victorious American team visited the White House. For these reasons, Tiger was sure Clinton would never go for it. The ex-president, he insisted, hated him. Woods never let a slight go, and he assumed Clinton operated the same way.

However, after much wrangling, the former president's people came back and said Clinton would be amenable to an appearance under certain conditions: Tiger had to personally call and make the request; as an ice-breaker, he wanted to play a round of golf with Woods in Orange County when he came out for the event; and he needed a private plane to travel to the West Coast.

After several moments of whining, Tiger got over his reluctance and made the call. A gracious Clinton put him at ease, and the event and golf game were scheduled. Wasserman had already agreed to provide a private plane, so the deal was done.

"Wow, that was easy," Woods told everyone after hanging up.

On the day before the official opening of the learning center, Woods met Clinton, Doug Band, sports agent Arn Tellum, and Wasserman for the promised round of golf at Shady Canyon Country Club in Irvine. Tiger was having breakfast with McLaughlin in the clubhouse when Tellum and Wasserman approached. At that point, Woods had never met either man. Dispensing with introductions, Tiger wanted to know if the president had arrived. When told Clinton was on his way, Woods replied with a straight face, "I can't wait to talk about pussy."

The situation got even more awkward after Clinton arrived. Tiger's behavior did nothing to bridge the gap between him and Clinton. At the outset, Clinton started carrying on, monopolizing the conversation, as he was known to do, before Woods interrupted and said, "How do you remember all that shit?" Once they got onto the course, Tiger acted completely indifferent to the entire group, mostly riding alone in his cart and spending an inordinate amount of time on his phone. After finishing a hole, he would routinely exit the green while others were still putting, a major breach of golf etiquette. When the president hit a wayward drive, Woods snickered. He also told a series of off-color jokes, including his go-to "black-guy condom" knee-slapper.

"He was really obnoxious," said one observer. "It was so clear to me that day who Tiger really was. I've never seen the president more put off by a person than that experience."

To make matters worse, about a week later, Clinton's office sent a picture of Clinton and Woods on the course together and asked Tiger to personalize it and send it back to the president for framing. Whether Tiger forgot or simply ignored the request remains unclear. Many months later, a staffer for Clinton called Tiger's office in exasperation and asked, essentially, what the fuck was going on. At that point, Tiger scribbled his name on the photograph and sent it back. Years later, a longtime Clinton staffer had unpleasant memories of the entire situation. "Clinton hauled his ass out west, and you can't sign a picture? The whole experience was a lot of 'I'm Tiger Woods, king of the world, go fuck yourself.'"

In his illustrious twenty-five-year career at *60 Minutes*, Ed Bradley had profiled a wide range of subjects, from Muhammad Ali and Michael Jordan to Bob Dylan and Lena Horne to Michael Jackson. With his career winding down due to ill health, Bradley had a few major interviews left on his bucket list—one of which was Tiger Woods. Bradley and his longtime producer Ruth Streeter had courted Woods for years with no success. That finally changed when Woods, wanting publicity for his new learning center, granted a two-part profile. He agreed to be interviewed as long as the *60 Minutes* segment was built around the grand opening. Woods said no to Bradley's desire to see his yacht. He said no to Bradley's visiting his estate. And he made it clear that Elin was strictly off-limits. "He was really definite about not wanting us to meet his wife," said Streeter. "We went left. We went right. Tried everything. But he would not let us meet her."

Still, Bradley was eager to ask Tiger about other aspects of his life—the role his father had played in shaping him, how he had dealt with childhood celebrity, and his views on race. The interview took place in early 2006, and Bradley was uncharacteristically nervous.

Woods, on the other hand, showed no signs of anxiety. By then, Tiger had gone one-on-one with many skilled interviewers—Charlie Pierce, John Feinstein, Charlie Rose, Barbara Walters, and Gary Smith—and he'd been profiled countless times. The days of telling off-color jokes in the back of a limousine with a journalist or crying on Oprah's couch were ancient history. From the moment he sat down with Bradley, Woods made it clear that he had no intention of opening up about anything.

This exchange was typical of how the interview went:

> **Woods:** *I'm kind of a private person.*
> **Bradley:** *So how do you handle it?*
> **Woods:** *Try and do the best I can.*

On the subject of race, Bradley brought up the kindergarten incident, prompting a halfhearted response from Woods. "Well, they tied me to a tree. And, you know, threw rocks at me. It happened."

When Bradley asked why it happened, Woods said he didn't know. Trying a different approach, Bradley asked what his parents had said about the incident, and Tiger said he couldn't remember. Even when Bradley ventured into safe territory, such as Woods's greatness as a golfer, he churned out short sentences that relayed next to nothing.

Afterward, Bradley and Streeter rode together to the airport. En route, like an old married couple, they rehashed the interview. "We didn't lay a glove on him," Bradley said to her. "We didn't touch him."

It was a remarkable admission coming from Bradley, whose streetwise style and innate ability to connect with his subjects had established him as the most skilled interviewer at *60 Minutes*. "His best quality was that he could be spontaneous," said *60 Minutes* executive producer Jeff Fager. "No matter how the subject responded, Ed could come up with just the right next question." He had even managed to get Oklahoma City bomber Timothy McVeigh to open up about his motivation for carrying out one of the worst terrorist attacks in American history. But Woods proved to be more fiercely guarded than a man facing the death penalty. "Even at thirty years old, he was frozen and undeveloped as a person, isolated in many ways," recalled Streeter. "There was no *there* there. To be fair, I don't think Tiger was trying to hide anything from us. I think he was doing what he had programmed himself to do. There was something weird, and we couldn't unravel it."

In fact, there was a lot that Woods kept hidden from Bradley, especially with respect to his marriage and his image as a family man. "I have found a life partner, a best friend," Woods told Bradley. "You know, Elin's been incredible for me. She's brought joy and balance in my life, and we love doing things together."

In truth, by 2006, Tiger's life was anything but balanced, and nothing was more out of sync than his marriage. He and Elin were seeing little of each other, and when they *were* together in public, Tiger looked disengaged and empty. Meanwhile, he was spending much more time on the road, where he increasingly pursued other women behind Elin's back. Yet he told Bradley, "Family always comes first. Always has been in my life, and always will."

On May 2, 2006, Earl's kidneys started shutting down, and he was placed on oxygen. Tiger was with Jamie Jungers at his nearby luxury condo in Newport Beach when his mother telephoned him with the news. Woods immediately drove to the house on Teakwood, where Royce was doing all she could to keep her emotions in check. It was eminently clear that the end had arrived. Tiger spent a few hours with his dad that evening, but then he returned to his condo, where he had sex with Jungers. "I could see he was preoccupied and worried about his dad," Jungers would later say. "But when he went to bed, he still wanted to have sex as usual."

At about three a.m., Tiger was awakened by the phone. Jungers was lying next to him when he picked up and heard his mother's voice on the other end of the line. She had called to tell him that his dad had passed. Tiger didn't shed a tear, nor did he say a word. He'd known for some time that his father was dying, and now the dreaded moment had arrived. Woods hung up and stared blankly.

So much has been made of the storied father-son relationship between Earl and Tiger. It's hard to count how many times Woods has said over the years that his father was his best friend, the person who understood him better than anyone else. And the scene of Tiger in Earl's arms after winning a tournament had become so commonplace that the networks always had a cameraman ready to capture the shot at the end of their broadcasts. Yet when Earl passed, Tiger wasn't at his father's bedside but rather a few miles away, in bed with a lingerie model he had picked up in Vegas. Earl took his final breaths in the arms of his daughter, who had stayed by his side day and night for the final four months of his life.

"People are aware of how close Tiger and my father were," Royce said. "But they are not aware of how close Dad and I were. I've always been Daddy's girl. When he passed away, it was very hard. I was just lost. Very lost. He was a major, major part of my life."

Earl's death devastated Tiger as well. Although he didn't verbalize it, he had lost his best friend, his anchor, the one person who understood him the most. But Tiger didn't grieve in front of others. At a private wake and funeral service held for Earl in Southern California, people who had known him since Tiger first burst onto the national scene—guys like Joe Grohman, now the head pro at the navy course, and golf writer Jaime Diaz—were in attendance. So were some of Tiger's famous acquaintances, such as Charles Barkley and Michael Jordan, as well as Tiger's newest associates, like Hank Haney. They couldn't help noticing that Woods remained stoic when talking about his father's life. And his comments about his father were so emotionless that it was hard for some who were there to remember what he had said.

Earl was cremated, and after his funeral, the family flew on a private plane to Kansas to bury his ashes in Manhattan, the town where he had been born. Earl's children from his first marriage always assumed that he would receive a traditional headstone. They were surprised to discover long after the burial that no headstone had been ordered. To this day, the father of the wealthiest athlete in history remains buried in an unmarked grave. It's an inexplicable fact that was still a source of speculation and dismay to certain family members a decade after the fact.

"Tida handled all the burial and funeral arrangements," Royce said in 2016. "So as to why, I don't know. I don't even know if there is a reason."

Only Kultida can explain the motivation behind her decision to bury her husband in this manner, but the biggest clue may be found in a statement she made back when Earl was still alive. Referring to him, she said:

"Old Man is soft. He cry. He forgive people. Not me. I don't forgive anybody."

Kultida Woods may have spoken broken English, but she wasn't hard
to understand. And no one needed her forgiveness more than Earl. His
relationship with her began with an act of betrayal when he brought her to
America while he was still married to his first wife. Eventually, he betrayed
Kultida too. Along the way, he degraded her with verbal abuse and insults.
She bristled when Earl piled impossible expectations on their only child—
saying that Tiger had been sent by God and that he would be the most important human ever—and when he hogged the credit for Tiger's success.
If it had been up to Earl, his son would have financed the construction of
a giant monument with an inscription that said something along the lines
of "Here lies the father of Tiger Woods." But it was up to Kultida, and she
buried him in a way that would make him virtually impossible to find.
The closest Earl got to public recognition was an obituary in the *New York
Times*. The headline read: "Golf: Earl Woods, Tiger's Father, Dies."

A few weeks after burying his father, Tiger disappeared to a mountain-
ous region close to the Mexican border, outside the little-known city of
Campo. Following a winding road that passed through a stretch of barren
desert, he arrived at a remote facility called the Mountain Warfare Training Facility Camp Michael Monsoor. It was a place where the landscape
resembled Afghanistan. In an award-winning profile that appeared in
ESPN The Magazine in 2016, journalist Wright Thompson detailed what
happened there. Wearing camouflage pants and a brown T-shirt, Tiger
carried an M4 assault rifle and had a pistol strapped to his right leg as
he entered what's known as a kill house—a place where SEALs simulate
clearing rooms and rescuing hostages under extreme duress. With a SEAL
instructor running him through the house, Tiger took fire from high-
powered paint rounds that cause large bruises on impact. He also fired
at targets dressed up as terrorists with weapons. "Eventually," Thompson
wrote, "Woods learned how to clear a room, working corners and figuring out lanes of fire, doing something only a handful of civilians are ever
allowed to do: run through mock gun battles with actual Navy SEALs."

With the 2006 US Open just two weeks away, Tiger was off the grid,
handling guns and dodging mock enemy fire rather than gripping clubs

and working on his short game. Even the SEALs were a bit perplexed. One of the SEAL instructors, a petty officer whose father had also served as a Green Beret in Vietnam, pulled Tiger aside for a private conversation outside the shooting facility.

"Why are you here?" the instructor asked respectfully.

"My dad," Tiger told him, insisting that his father had told him he would be a golfer or a special ops soldier. "My dad told me I had two paths to choose from."

This was a new narrative, one that diverged quite significantly from the consistent story that Earl had told about raising Tiger. In the three books Earl published and in the countless interviews he granted over the years, there is no mention of him telling his son that he had a choice between being an athlete or a soldier, nor had Tiger ever said anything publicly about such a decision. But in the aftermath of his father's death, he had a lot weighing on his mind.

"I definitely think he was searching for something," the SEAL instructor told Thompson. "Most people have to live with their regrets. But he got to experience a taste of what might have been."

Tiger's foray with the SEALs panicked Hank Haney, one of the few people in Tiger's inner circle who had access to his schedule. Haney fired off a text message:

> With the US Open 18 days away, do you think it was a good idea to go on a Navy SEALs mission? You need to get that whole SEALs thing out of your system and stick to playing Navy SEAL on the video game. I can tell by the way you are talking and acting that you still want to become a Navy SEAL. Man, are you crazy? . . . That Navy SEAL stuff is serious business. They use real bullets.

Woods wasn't crazy. He was suffering and emotionally disoriented. Not long after vanishing into the Southern California desert with the SEALs, Tiger ended up in a nightclub in New York when he spotted a group of women. One of them, Cori Rist, a curvaceous blonde in her late twenties, caught his eye. Rist turned out to be an exotic dancer at the Penthouse Executive Club on Manhattan's West Side. Moments later, he sent an associate over to use the familiar pickup line: "Tiger would like to meet you."

As Rist approached his table, Tiger scooted over, making room for her. Then he started telling her jokes. At one point, he put the tips of his shoes together, moving his feet up and down, and asked: "What's this?"

Rist wasn't sure.

"A black guy taking off his condom," he said, laughing.

It was one of the jokes he had told the girls at the *GQ* photo shoot in front of Charlie Pierce back in 1997. Nine years later, he was using the same sophomoric humor as a substitute for conversation. One of the perks of being a celebrated athlete is that tact and personality are not prerequisites for securing female companionship.

After some drinks, he led Rist to a friend's apartment and took her to bed. They exchanged phone numbers and started sleeping together whenever he came to New York. When they were together, he would talk a lot about his father and how he'd made him the man that he became. When they weren't together, Tiger would repeatedly text her, wanting to know whom she was with. As an exotic dancer in a high-end strip club, Rist was used to possessive men. But Tiger was unusual. "He was very jealous," she said. "It was almost like high school, when you call someone all the time: 'Where are you? How do you feel about *me*?' He needed constant attention and reassurance."

He needed no such reassurance on the golf course. Six weeks after Earl's death, Tiger returned to the PGA Tour and played in the US Open at Winged Foot Golf Club just outside New York City. It was the first time in thirty-seven majors as a professional that he missed the cut. But a month later at the British Open, he finished eighteen under to win his third Claret Jug and his eleventh major championship. He played so flawlessly that his ball-striking was described by even the toughest critics as sheer perfection. His swing coach pointed to Tiger's performance at Royal Liverpool Golf Club as the greatest display of iron play he had ever witnessed. In four rounds, Tiger didn't hit a single fairway bunker. He hit driver only once in seventy-two holes.

Tiger dedicated his majestic performance to Earl, and as soon as he sank his final putt, he did something he hadn't allowed himself to do since Earl died: break down. First, he buried his face in the shoulder of caddie Steve Williams and wept as the two men stood on the green. Then he sobbed like a baby as Elin put her arms around him and he exited the course. "It just came pouring out of me," Woods said, "all the things my dad meant to me, and the game of golf. I just wish he could have seen it one more time."

The victory at the British Open marked the start of one of the most sublime runs of Tiger's career. The next week he won the Buick Open, then the PGA Championship by five strokes, making him the first player in the modern era to win more than one professional major in consecutive years. A week after that he won the Bridgestone Invitational. Two weeks later, he won the Deutsche Bank Championship. He finished the year by winning six straight tournaments, displaying absolute and utter dominance in every phase of the game. But his iron play in particular was what separated him from everyone else. "In 2006, Tiger was eight feet four inches better than the Tour average with his irons," explained Golf Channel analyst Brandel Chamblee. "That is unfathomable. A foot would separate thirty to fifty players, and Tiger was *eight feet* better than the Tour average."

Golf historians still point to Tiger's performance in 2000 as the single greatest season in golf history, but in the six years that had elapsed since then, he had become a more precise and consistent golfer. In 2006, for example, he won eight of the fifteen tournaments he entered. It was unprecedented in the modern era for a pro golfer to win more than 50 percent of the time. The most extraordinary aspect of Tiger's splendid display of victories to close out the '06 season was that his game had finally reached perfection at a time when he was struggling more than ever in his personal life.

Weeks before his father died, Tiger had been in Las Vegas to film a new commercial for Nike. It was shot by renowned cinematographer Janusz Kaminski, whose work on *Schindler's List* and *Saving Private Ryan* earned him two Oscars. Tiger dressed all in black for the shoot, which took place in a sound studio. With Woods using his driver, Kaminski filmed him face-on and from several other angles, capturing his swing from takeaway to follow-through. Then he slowed down the sequence to fifty-three seconds and added a cello solo. The commercial—titled "Swing Portrait"—was a tribute to the greatest golf swing in history.

Viewed another way, the ad ingeniously captured the dichotomy of

ursed by parents who found little in common
tion to their son, a son whose own life now
to a similar sense of desperation and sadness
fection in the game. The man most respon-
not there to shepherd his son through the
tness the culmination of triumphs that ul-
boy who had started imitating his father
toddler.

e was nevertheless the one person Tiger
star had disappeared, and Woods was
ns like never before, forcing him into
vering up more and more to maintain
han anyone realized at the time, was

TICK, TICK, TICK

Tiger Woods met Roger Federer for the first time in New York at the US Open Tennis Championships in 2006. He was in Federer's box, cheering him on, when Federer defeated Andy Roddick to capture his third-straight Open title. Afterward, the world's greatest golfer and the world's top tennis player shared a champagne toast, and Woods invited Federer to come to one of his tournaments. Federer took him up on it, and a few months later, Woods brought him inside the ropes at Doral. It was the start of a friendship facilitated by the fact that they were both generally regarded as the "best ever." It also helped that they were both represented by IMG and were the top two pitchmen for Nike.

"We could relate very much to one another," Federer said at the time. "We have a lot of expectations from everybody, so we have a lot of common ground. It's good that we kind of know each other and can talk to each other about it."

As was the case with everyone else in his life, Woods never revealed much about his friendship with Federer—or much of himself to his new friend. But professionally they shared how they changed their respective sports—Woods revolutionizing a game of skill with overpowering athleticism, Federer transforming an athletic sport with his artistic power and grace.

At the start of 2007, there was little doubt in the minds of golf and tennis fans that Woods would eclipse Nicklaus's eighteen major championships and Federer would surpass Pete Sampras's benchmark of fourteen Grand Slam titles. The only question, it seemed, was who would reach the milestone first—Woods or Federer. The odds at that point were strongly in Tiger's favor. He had already won twelve majors. Federer, who was six years younger, had won nine Grand Slam tournaments. The two men decided to enter into a friendly wager. As things turned out, Federer surpassed Sampras just two years later. Woods, on the other hand, as we all know now, will likely never catch Nicklaus. His sudden demise was something that no one saw coming, not even Woods. But the beginning of the end of Tiger's dominance as a golfer started in the most unlikely of places—in the back seat of his Cadillac Escalade, about a mile from his home.

In early 2007, Woods had no clue that his late-night ventures into the Orlando nightclub scene had long since tripped the radar of the *National Enquirer*. In major cities like New York and Los Angeles, the *Enquirer* made it its business to know what A-list celebrities were doing after the sun went down. To that end, it employed a loose network of women pretty enough to blend right in at the hottest clubs, then backed up that surveillance with various valets, bartenders, bouncers, and cocktail waitresses at hotels, restaurants, and clubs, along with a stable of young stunners who worked the private-party circuit. Everyone keeping tabs for the *Enquirer* was paid between $200 and $500 a night in cash to inform on the behavior of various actors, comedians, musicians, and politicians known to boost newsstand sales. In 2007, Woods was by no means a sales commodity on the scale of Brad Pitt or Jennifer Aniston, but a fall from grace was a fall from grace, and nobody monetized that kind of misery quite like the *Enquirer*.

The *Enquirer* was founded in the fifties by Generoso Pope Jr., a mysterious child of privilege with alleged Mafia ties who ran the publication for thirty-six years. Turning the words "Enquiring minds want to know" into a cultural catchphrase, Pope tapped into the public's fascination with blood, guts, and the bizarre. The publication hit its zenith in 1977 when it put a photo of Elvis Presley in his casket on the cover. That issue sold a record 6.7 million copies.

The publication changed considerably after Pope died and the New York–based investment-banking firm Evercore Partners absorbed the tabloid in 1999 as part of its $767 million purchase of American Media, Inc. (AMI), owner of most of the nation's supermarket tabloids and gossip magazines. Under the new leadership of editor in chief David Perel, the

Enquirer began doing more sophisticated investigations. In 2003, it broke the story of Rush Limbaugh's addiction to painkillers. Then in late 2007, it worked on a series of Pulitzer Prize–worthy stories that revealed presidential candidate John Edwards had fathered a child out of wedlock during his campaign.

Perel was a big believer in what he called "predictive human behavior," and he loved the long game. He famously preached patience when stalking a story. Never force it, he would tell his staff; the story will come to you. That is exactly what happened in the case of Tiger Woods. Sometime in 2006, the *Enquirer* received a tip that Woods was catting around Orlando. The *Enquirer* soon deployed reporters to various nightspots in the city. Club Paris owner Fred Khalilian confirmed that in '06 he was approached several times by the tabloid and offered what he said was hundreds of thousands of dollars for security footage of Woods partying inside his club. "It was all about Tiger," said Khalilian. "I told them to go screw themselves. That's not who we are. That's not what we do."

Initially, nobody in Orlando was willing to expose Woods's late-night assignations—not in 2006. Plus, Woods was very discreet when he went to local nightspots, usually remaining out of sight in restricted VIP areas and going to great lengths to avoid being seen with women in public places. But outside the club scene, he had become much more emboldened, going so far as to arrange trysts inside his gated community when his wife wasn't home.

Just when it seemed the *Enquirer* had hit a dead end in its attempt to catch Woods in a compromising position, a call came in to its tip line from a woman who claimed her daughter was having an affair with Tiger. The caller was willing to provide proof for a price. Predictive behavior, indeed.

Mindy Lawton worked as a waitress at Perkins Restaurant & Bakery, an eatery where Tiger and Elin frequently went for breakfast. For months, Lawton, dark-haired and shapely, would seat them and take their order. She made two observations: Elin always ordered for Tiger, and the two of them seldom said a word to each other. "I didn't see any signs of affection," Lawton would later say. "I figured he was in a loveless relationship with his wife."

Then one morning, Lawton felt Tiger's eyes on her. Shortly after he and Elin left the restaurant that day, the phone at the hostess station rang. Lawton picked up.

"Hi, this is Ti."

"Who?"

"Tiger. A couple of friends and I are going out tonight to the Blue Martini, and I was wondering if you would join us."

It's a scenario that's hard to fathom. An athlete of almost unimaginable stature and celebrity has a wife who is considered one of the most beautiful women on the planet—and she happens to be pregnant with their first child. Yet there he is, making a play for the local waitress who serves him and his wife breakfast. That kind of hypersexual behavior—what addiction experts call a "hijacked brain"—begins to make sense only in the context of sex addiction. Like individuals addicted to alcohol or drugs, those who attempt to fill a void or self-medicate through sex often find themselves powerless, in an unmanageable situation. At a certain point, it's not about pleasure or passion; it's simply a quest for pain relief, no matter the place or the partner.

Hours after calling Lawton, Woods had her behind the velvet rope in the VIP alcove at the Blue Martini Lounge. He also had a few of his buddies with him. Whenever he was out in public, at bars or clubs, he took care to surround himself with a few friends to engender a sense of propriety and that he was never seen alone with a woman other than his wife. When he wanted to be alone with a woman, Woods took careful steps to ensure his needs were filled away from prying eyes.

"What are you doing after?" he asked Lawton as the bar was shutting down. She had no plans, so he gave her some instructions.

At around three a.m., Woods was in his black Cadillac Escalade, parked next door to the Perkins Restaurant, when Lawton rolled up in her car. Woods had her follow him through the security gate at Isleworth and back to his house. Without turning on the lights, he took her inside. They barely made it to the couch before he removed her clothes. "We ended up doing it right there," Lawton recalled. "He was very passionate and very rough." He tugged her hair. He spanked her. Finally, they were naked in the kitchen with the lights on. After just forty-five minutes, Lawton was out the door, leaving just before the sun came up. Disheveled as a rag doll, she felt she had experienced one hell of a one-night stand.

A few hours later, Woods showed up for breakfast at Perkins. With Elin out of town, he had a couple of buddies with him. He texted Lawton after her shift ended, saying he wanted to meet again. He brought her back to his house, but this time they didn't even make it inside. While passing from the driveway through the garage, Woods grabbed Lawton by a golf cart, quickly removed her clothes, and lifted her up against the wall. A routine developed for Lawton: Meet in secret. Have sex.

Woods was taking bigger and bigger risks. Lawton, on the other hand, thought she was falling in love. She couldn't help telling family members what was happening. And that's when her mother saw an opportunity and called the *Enquirer.* In exchange for cash, she informed the supermarket tabloid of an upcoming tryst between her daughter and Woods.

Tiger was unaware that the *Enquirer* was onto him and Lawton. When Woods met Lawton in a parking lot early one morning in the predawn darkness, an experienced photographer was on the scene, snapping away. Before the brief sexual encounter, Lawton tossed something to the ground. After Tiger and Lawton went their separate ways, the photographer checked the ground around where Woods's SUV had been parked. He discovered a fresh bloody tampon. Like a police officer collecting forensic evidence, he placed it in a clear plastic bag.

As editor in chief of the *Enquirer*, David Perel was immediately briefed. He then notified David Pecker, the CEO of American Media, Inc.

"Holy shit," said Pecker. "We've got our Elvis."

Nearly one-quarter of the *Enquirer's* weekly sales occur at Walmart. Almost three-quarters of all sales are generated at chain stores. It's a readership base that doesn't play much golf and isn't particularly interested in Tiger Woods—but like many people, they're titillated by indiscretions and are definitely interested in highly successful individuals who fail. "These are people who live their lives failing, so they want to read negative things about people who have gone up and then come down," Pecker told the *New Yorker* in 2017.

After some internal discussions, Perel placed a call to IMG and left an ominous voice mail: "What is Tiger Woods's relationship, if any, with Mindy Lawton?" Then he hung up the phone.

That wasn't the only call IMG received. After Lawton informed Tiger that the *Enquirer* was aware of their affair, he put her in contact with Steinberg, who told her, "We'll take care of it."

Shortly after Perel left his voice mail, IMG called back. Careful not to overplay his hand, Perel mentioned something about photographs, but he did not elaborate. He knew, given the poor lighting in the parking lot, that the photographer had not gotten The Shot. The few photos he had taken were too dark and grainy to use in the tabloid, but this information was not shared with IMG—nor would it have put IMG at ease. The fact that the *Enquirer* was onto Woods and knew about Lawton was scary enough. The situation presented an all-out public relations crisis for both Tiger and his agency. Woods stood to earn $100 million in endorsement revenue in 2007 alone. Some of his corporate partners were certain to cancel their endorsement deals and run for the hills if Woods was caught up in a tawdry adultery scandal.

With Perel running point for the *Enquirer* and Mark Steinberg leading the discussions for IMG, lawyers and executives from both sides engaged in a series of conference calls. Neal Boulton, a corporate editor for American Media, was one of the individuals brought in at the outset. "IMG knew they had a problem to handle, and it was intense," he said. Boulton was also the editor in chief of *Men's Fitness* magazine, another American Media publication that was considered one of its crown jewels. From the start, Boulton realized that *Men's Fitness* was going to become a critical player in the negotiations that were underway between IMG and the *Enquirer.*

Woods suddenly found himself in a very unfamiliar place, as the world of tabloid journalism plays by an entirely different set of rules than that of the collegial confines of the golfing press. Steinberg and IMG immediately recognized that they weren't going to be able to talk the *Enquirer* out of publishing the story. They were going to have to give something up. Within twenty-four hours of the parking-lot encounter, an "exclusive" cover story on Woods for *Men's Fitness* was on the table in exchange for the *Enquirer* killing the story on Lawton. Boulton, for one, found it distasteful.

"I'm sitting there going, 'Whoa, whoa, whoa,'" he said. "I'm certainly no saint. I mean, I've had drug problems. But that's *nothing* compared to blackmailing the most popular athlete in the world."

In New York literary circles, Boulton was viewed as a figure torn from the pages of a Truman Capote novel. Brilliant, bisexual, and possessing a taste for drugs and self-aggrandizement, he had risen through the ranks of American Media to become corporate development editor and oversaw numerous redesigns of the *Enquirer* and other titles. Given his past, Boulton conceded that he was the last person to grab the moral high ground.

But, he said, he simply could not dig this deep into the dirt. As the negotiations between IMG, the *Enquirer*, and American Media entered their final stages, Boulton left the office on a Friday night and never returned. (David Pecker would later say that he didn't see the negotiations as blackmail since he had decided against publishing the story.)

Ultimately, the two sides executed a contract outlining the conditions of a cover story on Tiger in *Men's Fitness*. The contract is said to have covered everything from how the headline would read to the fact that there would be no hint of any sex scandal. American Media handpicked Roy S. Johnson, a former senior writer and editor at *Sports Illustrated* who had known Earl and Tiger for more than a decade, to write the story.

"I was not part of Tiger's inner circle, but I did meet Tiger on a regular basis," Johnson explained. "We stayed in touch, mostly through Earl."

Johnson said he had no idea how the cover story had come to be. His assignment was to write it—and that's what he did. He spent the better part of a full day with Tiger in Isleworth.

Woods liked Johnson, and it showed. He went out of his way to engage with him. Tiger also enjoyed showing off his physique to the photographer.

"He was jacked," said Johnson. "He had his shirt tailored so his biceps popped."

Johnson was doing double duty as the de facto art director on the shoot. At one point he wanted to capture the beautiful arc of Woods's swing. The photographer had shot Woods from all sides, but Johnson had one last request.

"Is there any way we can get it from the front?" Johnson asked Woods. "You don't have to hit the ball."

But Woods wanted to hit the ball.

"Here's what you need to do," said Woods, positioning the photographer and an assistant holding a sunshade not ten feet in front of him. "Now, don't move," he told them.

Johnson was nervous. Woods planned to launch a ball off the tee while the cameraman and his assistant were directly in front of him. And Tiger had given himself only a ten-inch window to hit through.

Woods took a full swing and hit the ball exactly where he wanted—over the parking lot and into a nearby lake. Not once; not twice; but six times.

Johnson's 3,500-word cover story hit newsstands in late June, right after the 2007 US Open. It portrayed a smiling, absolutely ripped Woods under a blaring headline in red: "TIGER! HIS SURPRISING WORKOUT: HOW HE GOT BIG." Over twelve splashy pages filled with photos of Woods working out, Johnson delivered an upbeat profile that referred to Tiger's weight-lifting levels as "off the charts" and even mentioned that he was about to become a father.

The Mindy Lawton story simply went away.

Woods had long ago learned that he was above the rules. It was a lesson his parents started teaching him at a young age, and was reinforced by his experiences as an elite golfer. As early as his sophomore year of high school, he was allowed to enter his first PGA Tournament under an exemption that was accorded him by the individual in charge of the Los Angeles Open. An *exemption* is a term of art in golf, but it was a way of life for Woods. His escape from accountability in the Mindy Lawton affair took the Rules Don't Apply to Me mantra to a perilous new level.

On one hand, Mark Steinberg's masterful handling of the *Enquirer* situation probably qualified him to be a candidate for Fireman of the Year. After all, there was no question that Tiger had been stalked by the *Enquirer*. It's also true that he had been targeted, to a certain degree, by Lawton's mother. But none of this would have been possible if not for the fact that by the summer of 2007, Woods was acting out of desperation. Although the depth of his problems may not have been known to his agent at that point, the nature of his involvement with Lawton was a big red flag. An athlete worth a billion dollars sneaking off for an early-morning quickie in a parking lot is not the behavior of a husband who has strayed. It's more like a man lost in the wilderness who desperately sends up a signal flare in hopes of being rescued.

Even before the ink had dried on the deal that IMG struck to avert the *Enquirer* story, Woods was pursuing another young woman. This time it was a twenty-one-year-old cocktail waitress from San Diego. In April 2007, Jaimee Grubbs and a group of girlfriends went to Las Vegas for a few days of fun. It seemed like the perfect way to celebrate the fact that Grubbs—a five-foot-seven, 105-pound blonde—was now old enough to drink legally. On their first night in town, they went to the nightclub Light.

Before long, a VIP host brought Grubbs and her friends complimentary drinks and led them to a table occupied by a group of men. Grubbs was stunned when she realized that Woods was one of them. She didn't know golf, but she certainly knew Tiger, and it felt surreal when he showed an interest in her. At the end of the night, Grubbs and her friends filed into a limo with Woods and his friends. After her friends were dropped off at their hotel, Grubbs was invited to Tiger's suite at the Mansion. His friends tried to persuade her to get into the Jacuzzi with them.

"No offense," she told them, "but I'm not doing the hot-tub scene with four boys and being the only girl."

That night, Grubbs fell asleep on Tiger's couch. The next morning, she awoke to the words, "Are you ready for your massage?" A massage therapist gave her the first professional massage of her life. The cost was $400, and one of Tiger's friends instructed her to sign for it and tack on a $100 tip, all of which was billed to Tiger's room. The friend then took Grubbs on a shopping spree. They drove a Rolls-Royce Phantom that Tiger had at his disposal for the weekend. That night, wearing a brand-new dress that Woods had paid for, she partied until three thirty a.m. with her girlfriends before being picked up in a stretch limo that delivered her to Woods. She ended up sleeping at his suite again, and for the second straight night Woods was a gentleman. In the morning she awoke to the sound of his voice.

"Wake up, Sleeping Beauty," he told her.

They had breakfast together in his dining room, and then he had a plane to catch. As she helped him pack, Grubbs playfully pushed him onto the bed. Woods gave her a good-bye kiss and promised to call her the next time he was in San Diego.

For Grubbs, it was like experiencing a scene from *Pretty Woman*—only this wasn't a movie, and she had no idea what she was getting into. She didn't even realize that he was married. "Never in a million years would I take him to be a ladies' man," she would later say.

Woods, by this time, was accustomed to dealing with women who were much more familiar with the ways of the world. One such woman was Michelle Braun, a notorious South Florida and Southern California madam who ran a high-end escort service known as Nici's Girls. Braun reportedly earned at least $8.5 million and employed scores of women at a time, providing Playmates, Pets, porn stars, and party girls to men who were willing to spend five and six figures for the pleasure of their company. Woods started going to Braun well before the *Enquirer* episode. According to Braun, Tiger's friend Bryon Bell usually made the arrangements, but there were times when Woods was in a pinch and, Braun said, he would make the call himself. "He'd say, 'Hey, it's Tiger. I'm going up to LA for a meeting. You got anybody in Orange County today?'"

Initially, according to Braun, Woods was interested in the clean-cut girl-next-door type, and he was paying five figures for a weekend. But after a while, Braun set him up with one of her most exotic women— Loredana Jolie Ferriolo, a former Hawaiian Tropic model and *Playboy* Playmate whose matchmaking fee ran as high as $100,000. She had been matched with some of the richest men in the world—Saudi princes, heads of state, CEOs. Ferriolo claims that Woods paid $15,000 for their first date, financed shopping sprees, and flew her to the Bahamas, Dubai, and Las Vegas for secret rendezvous.

In the midst of this chaos, Elin gave birth to a baby girl on June 18, 2007, in Florida. Hours earlier, Tiger had finished second at the US Open at Oakmont in Pennsylvania. His final putt stopped a foot short of the hole. Furious at himself, he didn't say a word as he left the course and headed for his plane. He landed in Orlando around eleven p.m. and went directly to the hospital, arriving just in time to see the delivery of his first child—Sam Alexis Woods.

She arrived thirteen months after the death of Woods's father, and her name has its roots in Tiger's relationship with Earl. From the time Tiger was little, his father had sometimes called him Sam. It was a nickname that no one except Earl used, and then only in certain situations. "When he wanted me to know that he was there, to reassure me he was behind me no matter how I did, he called out 'Sam,'" Tiger said. "He used that name off the course as well. It always made me smile."

One of the first people Tiger called to announce that he was a father was Hank Haney. Tiger looked at Haney as a true friend, though he didn't always treat him that way. But Haney and caddie Steve Williams had emerged as stabilizing influences at a time when Woods's world outside the ropes was running wild. Despite all the drama and turmoil in his personal life, Tiger played phenomenally well in 2007. Of the sixteen tournaments he entered, he won seven, including the PGA Championship, his thirteenth major. He finished first in every major category—first in scoring average, first in money leaders. He was the PGA Tour Player of the Year for a record ninth time.

But 2007 was the first time Haney started to think that Woods, as he put it, "was closer to the end of his greatness than he was to the beginning." The signs were too subtle to spot in tournaments. They were more apparent in practice sessions and in the shot-dispersion charts kept in testing sessions by the gurus at Nike Golf. "There were subtle changes below the surface," Haney said. "Tiger's work habits started to slip. There were more distractions."

The most obvious distraction was Tiger's cell phone. It was constantly blowing up with text messages and phone calls. Haney had no idea that Woods was communicating with women. He just knew that the interruptions were affecting Tiger's concentration in practice. Rather than vent directly at his pupil, Haney voiced his frustration by making fun of Tiger's outdated flip phone.

"I was always giving him shit," Haney explained. "'When are you going to get rid of that stupid flip phone?'"

Tiger had his reasons for not upgrading to a smartphone. One big benefit of a flip phone is that texts don't pop up on the screen—a feature that makes it easier to conceal incoming messages. He had lost contact with Michelle Braun by the time her home was raided by the FBI in October 2007. She later surrendered to federal authorities, who charged her with money laundering and transporting an individual from Orange County to New York City "with intent that such individual engage in one or more acts of prostitution." In 2009 she pled guilty, paid a $30,000 fine, and served time under house arrest. But by then, Woods had established a vast web of women whose names and numbers were stored in his cell phone. Jaimee Grubbs was only one of many. After initially meeting Grubbs in Vegas, Woods had her stay with him at the W Hotel the next time he was in San Diego. The more time they spent together, the more urgent his text messages became:

I will wear you out soon

Send me something very naughty

This was a long way from "Wake up, Sleeping Beauty."

The significant uptick in distractions caused by Tiger's cell phone was another red flag that his personal life was amiss, but Haney and Williams were much more concerned about something they both could see happening before their eyes—the breakdown of Tiger's body. In 2007, he was often in physical pain, and Haney and Williams both attributed it to his extreme workout regimen and fascination with Navy SEAL training.

When Tiger first participated in training exercises at Fort Bragg right after the Masters back in 2004, it was essentially a one-time experience, a chance to bond with his father at a time when Earl's health was rapidly deteriorating. But since Earl's death, Tiger's fascination with the military had morphed into an obsession. Haney believed that Tiger's interest in becoming a Navy SEAL had gotten so out of hand that it was putting his health and his game at risk. Williams had similar concerns.

But Tiger ignored them, stepping up his SEAL activities. He started training in army boots and going for military-style runs while wearing a weighted vest. And in 2007, he upped the ante, embarking on a series of SEAL trips on which he trained in parachuting and urban warfare. On one trip he visited a "Special Warfare SEALs unit" in Coronado two days before playing in his first PGA Tour tournament of the year at Torrey Pines. While there, he made connections with a number of SEALs, including one guy whom Tiger ended up hiring as his personal bodyguard. He started showing up at Tiger's home, teaching him self-defense and occasionally spending the night.

Williams, in particular, didn't like the influence Tiger's new bodyguard was having on him and feared Woods was going to get hurt during his rigorous training routines. Tiger had told both Williams and Haney that he was thinking of leaving golf to pursue a career in the military. But when Haney suggested as much to Steinberg, he was essentially told to calm down.

"He's not going to do that," Steinberg said. "There's no way. He can't. He's got obligations."

But Steinberg didn't realize what Woods was doing when he was off with the SEALs. In one three-day training exercise, he did as many as ten parachute jumps per day, and Tiger admitted to a friend that he had injured his shoulder on one jump when he collided with a partner. In another instance, Woods was doing urban-warfare training exercises when he was shot in the thigh with a rubber bullet, leaving a baseball-sized bruise. "I screwed up," he told Haney. "In a real mission, I probably would have gotten my squad killed."

My squad? Woods was sounding more and more like a wannabe SEAL and less and less like the number one golfer in the world.

One day when Haney was in Tiger's living room, Woods put his arm around Haney's neck to demonstrate a SEAL training move. "From here," Woods told him, "I could kill you in about two seconds."

Another time, he told Haney he was taking concrete steps to qualify to join the SEALs. When Haney pointed out that Tiger was thirty-one and the age limit for the SEALs was twenty-eight, Woods insisted that they were making an exception for him.

Exasperated, Haney decided to make a last-ditch effort to bring Tiger to his senses. Standing with Woods on the short-putting green at Isleworth, right next to a sand trap, he asked, "Doesn't Jack Nicklaus's record mean anything to you?"

Woods stopped, looked him in the eye, and said, "No. If my career ended right now, I'm happy with everything I've accomplished."

"Tiger, you're destined to be the greatest golfer in the world, not a Navy SEAL. You need to get that stuff out of your mind and start thinking about what you're doing here."

It didn't register.

Tiger's longtime trainer Keith Kleven had his own concerns—namely that Woods was becoming so muscle-bound that he was stressing his joints. He also was afraid that all the military training—especially the extensive pull-ups and running with weights—was putting too much strain on his shoulders and knees. Kleven shared his concerns with Haney and Williams. Haney, in turn, talked to Steinberg, who finally acknowledged that the SEAL-training routine had to be addressed.

"I'm going to have a talk with Tiger," Steinberg told Haney.

On July 30, 2007, Steinberg hosted a dinner at his home near Cleveland. Woods, Williams, and Haney attended. After the meal, Steinberg took Woods into his home office for a private conversation that lasted close to an hour. Five days later, Tiger won the WGC–Bridgestone Invitational at Firestone. Two weeks after that, he won the PGA Championship. Then he won the BMW Championship and the Tour Championship in back-to-back weekends. He closed out the year by winning seven of his final eight tournaments, finishing second in the only tournament he didn't win during that stretch. Steinberg appeared to have gotten through to Woods.

The way Tiger finished 2007 was nothing short of jaw-dropping. About to turn thirty-two, he sat with *New York Times* golf writer Larry Dorman for a profile. Dorman argued that time was on Tiger's side for him to break Nicklaus's record of eighteen major championships. Even Nicklaus was saying as much. "I would think that if Tiger stays healthy, he will break it," Nicklaus said. When compared with the performances of every great golfer who had preceded him, Tiger was indeed headed into what should have been his prime years. But Woods was unlike every other great champion. Among other things, he never allowed anyone to closely examine him or see what he was really thinking. In his profile, Dorman mentioned a website that compared Tiger to God. At a subsequent press conference, Woods acknowledged being aware of the site, but said he hadn't visited it. When asked if he was officially denying his deity, Woods smiled and said: "Man, I'm so far away from that."

IT'S JUST PAIN

Tiger had been playing with a severely compromised ACL for years. Back in 2002, at the time of his first knee surgery, doctors told him that only about 20 percent of the thick ligament connecting the thighbone and shinbone of his left leg remained intact. After playing for nearly five years on what amounted to borrowed time, Tiger felt something go in his knee in July 2007. But he chose not to tell anyone that he was hurting. His thought process was consistent with that of other elite athletes who try to play through pain: *There's a difference between being hurt and being injured. If I'm hurt, I can deal with pain. Pain is no big deal. I can block that out. But when I'm injured, my body doesn't respond.* In other words, as long as he could still compete and win, Tiger determined that he wasn't injured. He looked at his situation as if through a straw, focusing solely on the here and now.

With his body breaking down and his personal life in turmoil, Woods maintained a single-minded approach to competition, playing some of the best golf of his life. He started the 2008 PGA Tour season the same way he had ended the '07 season: winning. He won the first three tournaments he entered—the Buick Invitational, the WGC–Accenture Match Play Championship, and the Arnold Palmer Invitational. But with each tournament, the pain in his knee intensified. By the time he got to the 2008 Masters, he admitted to Hank Haney that he was hurting. At the same time, he had no intention of stopping.

"Nothing that some drugs can't take care of," he told Haney. "I'm fine."

The first reported instance of Tiger using painkillers during a tournament was in 2002, when he experienced constant aching in his knee. By 2008, the pain was more severe, and, according to his trainer,

Woods used Vicodin at the 2008 Masters to manage the extreme pain in his left knee. He finished in second place at Augusta, just three strokes behind the winner, an amazing achievement given the grave condition of his ACL. But he would have won easily if his putting hadn't been so uncharacteristically off. Putting, more than any other aspect of golf, is a function of touch and feel—both of which can be compromised by pain medication.

Two days after leaving Augusta, Tiger underwent knee surgery in Park City, Utah. "I made the decision to deal with the pain and schedule the surgery for after the Masters," Woods announced on his website. "The upside is that I have been through this process before and know how to handle it. I look forward to working through the rehabilitation process and getting back to action as quickly as I can."

But the surgery didn't go quite as planned. Orthopedic surgeons Thomas Rosenberg and Vern Cooley, who had operated on Tiger's left ACL in 2002, intended to clean up some of the damaged cartilage around his knee. It should have been a fairly simple procedure that would have alleviated pain and enabled Woods to return to the Tour in time for the US Open seven weeks later. But after scoping his knee, they made a surprising discovery: Tiger's ACL was completely torn, meaning he needed ACL ligament replacement surgery.

From a medical standpoint, it was hard to reconcile the condition of Tiger's knee with his performance. He had won nine of his previous twelve tournaments, and he'd done it with a severely compromised left knee. In the three tournaments he didn't win during that stretch, he'd finished second twice and fifth once. To put this in context, during this period, Tiger was winning more frequently than he had in 2000, when he turned in the greatest season in golf history, or in 2006 when he played the finest golf of his career.

Rosenberg's instinct was to reconstruct Tiger's ACL while the knee was open. But Woods was unconscious and had consented only to having loose cartilage removed from his left knee joint. The more extensive reconstruction procedure would force him to miss the remaining three major championships, and Rosenberg wasn't about to do it without Tiger's okay. So he left the shredded ACL alone, choosing instead to clean up the cartilage as best he could. It was a stopgap measure that would potentially enable Woods to play through the summer.

Possessing an extremely high tolerance for pain, Tiger had been able to play for approximately nine months without an ACL thanks in large part to the unusually strong muscles he had built up around his knee. Those muscles were a by-product of his weight-lifting routine. But in the aftermath of his surgery in April, those muscles naturally weakened, compromising the only remaining support around the knee. Swelling, soreness, and stiffness set in. Nevertheless, with his sights set on returning to the PGA Tour at the Memorial Tournament on May 26, Tiger resumed hitting balls in mid-May.

While practicing one day at Isleworth, he felt a crack just below his left knee. Two days later, Haney showed up in Orlando. That night—Sunday, May 18, 2008—Tiger and Elin had Haney over for dinner. When Tiger got up from the table, he immediately stopped and bent over, grimacing with his eyes closed. Worried, Haney and Elin looked at each other.

"I'm fine," Tiger said.

"Tiger, you can't even walk," Haney said. "How are you going to be able to play?"

The next day Woods was limping so badly that he decided to withdraw from the Memorial and undergo an MRI. Days later, Dr. Rosenberg and a colleague flew out from Utah to go over the results. The mood was grim as Tiger and Haney sat on a couch in Tiger's living room while Rosenberg pulled up images on his laptop and pointed to two dark lines on the screen. Tiger's left tibia, he explained, had two stress fractures right below the knee.

Silent, Tiger stared blankly at the fracture lines. The 2008 US Open was just two weeks away, at Torrey Pines Golf Course in La Jolla, California. Chiseled out of the coastal cliffs high above the Pacific Ocean, Torrey Pines boasted panoramic views and breathtaking vistas. For the average golfer, it was a paradise. But Tour pros saw Torrey for what it was at the time—two scenic municipal courses owned by the city of San Diego, one, the North course, that annually ranked among their least favorites to play. Tiger, however, loved Torrey for its wide fairways and the fact that it had virtually no out-of-bounds. At age fifteen he'd won a Junior World title there. He'd since won six PGA Tour events at the course, including four in a row from 2005 to 2008, when he opened the season by winning the Buick Invitational. And from the moment the 2008 season began, he had fixated on playing there in the US Open, more so than on the Masters or any other tournament. He wanted to win on what he considered his home course in front of fans who cheered his every move.

But a fractured tibia on top of a ruptured ACL seemed to foreclose any hope of collecting another major, prompting Haney to inquire about the standard treatment for stress fractures.

Six weeks on crutches, Rosenberg said, followed by a month of rehab.

The math was clear: Tiger's season was over. Ten weeks out of action meant he would miss the British Open and the PGA Championship too.

Tiger finally spoke up: "I'm playing in the US Open. And I'm going to win it."

His voice was defiant, and Rosenberg wasn't about to challenge him. "Tiger, you can try to play," he said. "There's not too much more damage you can do at this point. It's just a matter of how much pain you can take."

"It's just pain," Woods said, bending over to put on his golf shoes. "C'mon, Hank. Let's go practice."

Earl Woods once described Tiger as the first golfer who was a "true athlete." Those words, in Tiger's mind, meant tough, strong, and accustomed to dealing with pain the way football and basketball players did—which is to say, by ignoring it.

"That's just what we do as athletes and competitors," Tiger said. "You have to deal with it. But it's trying to get up every day and knowing you have to go into the gym and bust your butt, and it's going to hurt, and you're going to put yourself in a different place, a different state of mind. For me, I enjoyed that part of it."

On the Saturday before US Open week, Woods played nine holes with Haney at Big Canyon Country Club in Newport Beach. It was, by any measure, a disaster. Wearing a bulky leg brace that looked like something you would expect to see on an offensive lineman, Woods couldn't rotate his lower body. As a result, he sprayed shots all over the course—into the rough, over fences, into hazards. After nine holes, he actually ran out of balls. The brace was throwing off the mechanics of his swing.

"I can't play with this thing," he told Haney in frustration.

On Rosenberg's orders, Tiger had been wearing the brace for weeks. But he decided to play the final nine holes at Big Canyon without it. Haney figured that the pain of playing without the brace would finally persuade

Tiger that his goal of participating in the US Open simply wasn't realistic. But he underestimated Tiger's determination.

Without the brace, Tiger limped noticeably when he walked, but his swing improved. Although the pain level went up a few ticks, the challenge of playing with a severe physical limitation seemed to invigorate him. Over the next few days, his game got a little better with each practice session. But the more time he spent on the golf course, the more the swelling increased around the stress fractures. The stiffness was getting worse too. His physical therapist worked on him before and after each practice session, but Tiger refused to take prescription pain medication, as he had done at the Masters. He would take nothing other than Motrin or Advil to help combat the swelling, and he was determined to fight through the pain.

The PGA Tour's new drug-testing policy was set to go into effect on July 1, 2008. Sometime between the end of the 2008 Masters and the start of the US Open, Woods had his blood drawn and tested in what he told Hank Haney was a precaution against the supplements he was taking. "That's the way he framed it," Haney said in a 2017 interview. "'They're going to start testing me. You can get all kinds of false positives.' At one point he said, 'Motrin can give you a false positive for marijuana. I've got to make sure none of these supplements I'm taking have anything in them.' And then he took the [blood] test and said everything came back all fine."

The Open would be played solely on the South Course at Torrey Pines. At 7,628 yards, it was the longest in major championship history—toughened by gnarly Open-length rough, pesky bunkers, and multitiered greens. For the first time, the USGA had used the World Golf Rankings for pairings, which meant Woods, Mickelson, and Adam Scott—ranked one, two, and three in the world—would be grouped together on Thursday and Friday. Mickelson and Scott knew that Tiger was coming back from knee surgery, but no one outside of Woods's inner circle and his medical team knew that his ACL was ruptured and that his tibia was fractured in two places. Tiger wanted it that way. Mickelson and Scott, in his mind, were soft. Not real athletes. There was no way either of them would ever think about playing with a broken leg and no ACL. No other golfer would.

"Tiger knew he was climbing the biggest mountain of his career at

Torrey Pines," said Haney. "And it inspired him to an incredible achievement."

Over four spectacularly uneven days, Woods showcased the utter genius of his game, particularly his putting. Wayward drives that led to four double bogeys were overshadowed by three astounding eagles, including a sixty-five-foot downhill racer from the fringe when he really needed it on Saturday; bogeys countered by birdies; an ugly 38 on the first nine on Friday reversed by a lights-out 30 on the back; and every single day, when it counted, a barrage of gut-wrenching putts for par.

Woods held a one-shot lead over Lee Westwood and was two clear of Rocco Mediate going into Sunday. In his thirteen previous wins at major championships, Woods had never lost a major when leading after three rounds. But with three holes to play, he found himself in uncharted waters—down one to Mediate, a journeyman pro 147 spots below him in the world rankings. Westwood was still in the hunt but about to fall victim to the Tiger Effect. Everyone else within striking distance had already succumbed to the same illness, what one longtime Tour regular loosely described as a bad case of nerves and a shrinking ball sack. "That was the week when guys were so petrified of Tiger," the insider said. "Nobody had the *nuts* to get ahead of him that week."

Nobody but Rocco Mediate. With one critical putt to go, Mediate was holding his breath and a one-stroke lead at one under par, watching on television outside the scorer's shack as Woods lined up a treacherous fifteen-foot putt for birdie.

Tiger was fifteen feet away because Steve Williams had the nuts to put his job on the line. Woods had flared his second shot to the par 5 eighteenth hole into the right rough—96 yards from the green, 101 from the hole. Woods wanted to hit a fifty-six-degree sand wedge. But given the lie and Tiger's pumped-up demeanor, Williams argued for a full sixty-degree wedge, and backed the call with everything he had.

"Tiger, you have to absolutely trust me on this one," Williams said. "And if I'm wrong, fire me. I know how much this means to you, so if I'm wrong, just fire me."

Williams wasn't wrong. The shot landed about twenty feet past the hole on the right and trickled back down the slope, leaving Woods a chance for birdie to tie Mediate and force a playoff. The putt was a lot tougher than it looked. If Woods hit it too high, it would stay high. If he got it too low, it would fall off. Basically, he needed his putt to ride a ridge.

Adding to the stakes: it was late in the day, the greens were bumpy, and the ball was resting on one of the worst parts of the green. Woods told himself, *Two and a half balls outside on the right. It's going to break late. Make a pure stroke and stay committed.* So he hit it.

The putt ran the ridgeline like its life depended on it, then took a sharp left and banged into the right side of the cup. Instead of lipping out, it rattled in. Amid a roar that was heard by the hang gliders hovering over the Pacific a mile away, Tiger thrust his fists into the air and then slapped hands with Williams, the agonizing pain in his leg eclipsed by the adrenaline rush. Woods and Mediate were headed to an eighteen-hole playoff on Monday.

"Unbelievable," Mediate said to himself as he watched Woods celebrating on the monitor.

As soon as Tiger left the course, euphoria gave way to worry. He had geared himself up to play seventy-two holes, not ninety. His knee and leg felt like they had been hit with a thousand hammers. He spent the night with his physical therapist and told himself he would have to dig deeper than ever to make it through eighteen holes the next day.

During Monday's playoff round, Nike ran an ad featuring Earl Woods, as if he were speaking to Tiger from the grave. "Tiger, I promise you that you'll never meet another person as mentally tough as you in your entire life," he said. Very few people knew just how tough he would need to be that day.

For the longest time, Monday's playoff looked like a replay of the day before: all square through fourteen holes. Throughout the day, Woods resembled an aging prizefighter—knocked to his knees by pain for one swing after another, only to rise to his feet and continue to fight. It was sporting drama of the highest order. Tiger trailed by one as he and Mediate stepped to the tee at the par 5 eighteenth. And just as in Sunday's round, the best Mediate could do was par, leaving Woods a short birdie putt to force only the third sudden-death playoff in the US Open since 1954.

And that's when Mediate, a real fan favorite, finally faltered. A wayward drive on the first playoff hole at the par 4 seventh left him in an awkward lie in a fairway bunker leading to a dead pull left of the green. The best Mediate could do was a bogey 5, opening the door for Woods.

Tiger stuck a 9-iron in the center of the green from 157 yards way and two-putted for par and his third US Open Championship.

Walking gingerly off the green, he got into a golf cart with Elin. At that moment, despite a damaged knee and a fractured tibia, the future never looked brighter for Woods. He was on "the other side" now, as he liked to call it, a father for the first time. At every opportunity he talked about how he and "E" were a team in raising their daughter, Sam. Earlier in the year, Sam had crawled for the first time. Now she was walking, dragging a cut-down club around the house. This win at Torrey Pines could not have meant more. "It's probably the greatest tournament I've ever had," said Tiger.

At thirty-two, he had won his fourteenth major, a milestone Nicklaus didn't reach until he was thirty-five. Tiger was on a trajectory to annihilate all of golf's records. The next day in the *New York Times*, columnist David Brooks called Woods "the exemplar of mental discipline" and declared that he "had risen above mere human status and become an embodiment of immortal existence."

At that moment, it would have been unthinkable—preposterous—to predict that the US Open at Torrey Pines would be the final major championship in the career of Tiger Woods.

CHAPTER TWENTY-SIX

MIRACLE WORKERS

Eight days after the most extraordinary win of his career, Tiger underwent season-ending surgery at a clinic in Park City. A ligament was taken from his right hamstring and was used to reconstruct his left ACL. Afterward, he was told to remain off his left leg for two months.

"Can I do push-ups?" Tiger asked.

The answer was no.

"Sit-ups?"

No again.

"Upper-body stuff?"

Still no.

"What can I do?" Tiger insisted.

Dr. Rosenberg wanted him to rest, to give his body time to heal.

The next months were two of the most difficult of Tiger's life. The deep, throbbing, aching pain never went away. He hated the post-surgery treatment because there was no adrenaline rush. He wanted to get back into the gym, but first he needed extensive rehab. Fortunately, Team Tiger knew exactly where to turn.

By the summer of 2008, the name Dr. Mark Lindsay was being passed among elite athletes searching for state-of-the-art recovery techniques and the realignment of their bodies. A Toronto-based chiropractor known for his "magic hands," Lindsay had worked with hundreds of athletes, including tennis star Maria Sharapova, Olympic sprinter Donovan Bailey, and New York Yankees infielder Alex Rodriguez. Lindsay's method was called ART, short for Active Release Technique, a controlled but aggressive combination of neuromuscular massage and stretching designed to stimulate and release the fascia tissue beneath the skin and thereby maximize recovery and athletic performance.

"It's like playing an instrument," Lindsay once told Canadian author Bob McKenzie. "You can be superbright, superintelligent, but it has to translate to tactile, to the hands. From my own experience, getting treatments, you can tell right away when someone gets it, when someone has the touch. . . . Sometimes I think, 'This is cool—this is my job.'"

Woods had been introduced to Lindsay by professional volleyball star Gabby Reece, who had found her way to Lindsay through NFL linebacker Bill Romanowski, a four-time Super Bowl champion. In the late nineties, "Romo" was one of the first US athletes to put his faith—and career—in Lindsay's hands. He would eventually go on to play a record 243 consecutive games at linebacker before retiring from the league in 2003.

"Bottom line, Tiger's career was over if he didn't have Mark," said Romanowski. "Tiger was so locked up, his whole kinetic chain was messed up."

About six weeks after the surgery, Lindsay sent Woods to Bill Knowles, a certified strength-and-conditioning specialist with two decades of experience working with world-class athletes. Knowles's area of expertise was alpine skiing, so he knew a blown-out knee when he saw one, and what he saw with Woods was not pretty. "Let's just say the surgery was a very big surgery," Knowles recalled years later. "Not a straightforward surgery. It was a very big operation."

Woods and Knowles worked together on rehab five days a week for about six straight months—gym and pool, gym and pool, twice a day, up to two hours at a time. As Knowles reconditioned Woods's knee, he also worked on his body and mind.

In mid-October, Tiger was cleared to start swinging a golf club. Dr. Rosenberg suggested he take it slowly, but Tiger began swinging at thirty-five miles per hour. Within a month he was at sixty-five miles per hour and driving the ball 150 yards. He also stepped up his weight-lifting routine, especially for his lower body. By the end of 2008, he was doing Olympic-style lifts.

Tiger was on schedule to return to the Tour at the start of the 2009 season, but right around his thirty-third birthday, he injured his right Achilles tendon while working out. For the third time in a little over a year, one of the world's best-conditioned athletes suffered a serious injury while training.

Psychologically, the Achilles injury was a huge setback. It threatened to derail Tiger's return. Dr. Lindsay recommended bringing in another Toronto-based sports-medicine expert—Dr. Anthony Galea. Lindsay had first met Galea at the Winter Olympics in 1994, and they later shared office space for years. Galea was considered a pioneer in PRP—platelet-rich plasma therapy, a process whereby a small amount of blood is withdrawn from the injured athlete and then spun in a centrifuge, separating red blood cells from the platelets. The resultant protein-rich plasma is then injected directly into the injured area—tendon, muscle, or ligament—catalyzing the body's instinct to repair itself and accelerating the healing process.

"It's very effective," Lindsay said. "It's legal as long as you're fixing a legitimate injury. There are growth factors in the platelets—it's basically a form of stem cell, [but] it's your own tissue—no drugs, no foreign substances. It works best for hamstring tears, Achilles tears, and groin tears. That's why Tony and I worked so well together. Tony would treat the specific injury and I would work on the [body] system."

Tiger agreed to see Galea, who had to be in Tampa to treat Pittsburgh Steelers receiver Hines Ward in the lead-up to Super Bowl XLIII. Galea went directly from Tampa to Tiger's home in Isleworth.

Like Lindsay, Galea was, by 2009, seen as something of a miracle worker, the go-to guy among elite athletes for injury and recovery procedures outside the medical norm. Galea cut a dramatic figure, with his spiky black hair and feline features. His background was equally unusual. The son of a beautician and a bookkeeper, he had graduated with a medical degree from Canada's McMaster University before establishing his own clinic, the Institute of Sports Medicine Health & Wellness Centre, just outside Toronto. At forty, he divorced the mother of his four children and married a tennis pro less than half his age and fathered three more children. Galea's hobby was biblical archaeology, and he claimed to have had a spiritual awakening in an olive grove during one of his frequent trips to Jerusalem.

In their book *Blood Sport*, authors Tim Elfrink and Gus Garcia-Roberts detail how Galea "took a liking to the medical patents of a Miami-area doctor named Allan R. Dunn, whose off-label use of human growth hormone consisted of scraping away scar tissue from inflamed joints and re-filling the area with HGH." Galea had frequently cited Dunn in medical lectures, much to Dunn's dismay. "I would like to tell him to get lost," Dunn told Elfrink and Garcia-Roberts. "I don't want any part of him." But increasingly, some of the most elite athletes in the United States and Canada did.

Court documents suggest an extra incentive that Dr. Galea had avail-able to get male athletes to seek his services—access to Viagra or Cialis, for free and without fear of detection. When traveling from Canada to the US, Dr. Galea would instruct his medical assistant to prepare a "checklist" of items to enable him to treat patients: IV bags, IV tubing, ATP (Ger-man), syringes, ginseng, Nutropin, Actovegin, centrifuge, Cialis/Viagra, Celebrex. Specifically, according to the US government's 2009 indictment of Dr. Galea, he "instructed his [medical assistant] to take Viagra and Cia-lis out of their original packages and put them in nondescript pill bottles so as to make detection of them less likely during border inspections." If asked by a patient, Dr. Galea would allegedly provide Viagra or Cialis free of charge and without a prescription. "Viagra was the hook," said one ath-lete with direct knowledge of Galea's method of operation. "The closer for athletes who didn't want to go to a doctor for a prescription."

When Galea started treating Tiger, he would go to his home in Isle-worth and Tiger would lie down on a massage table in his family room. He winced as Galea placed a long needle directly into his injured Achilles tendon and injected platelet-rich plasma. The following day, Tiger's Achil-les felt better. The next time Galea returned to Tiger's home, he injected his Achilles and his knee with PRP. The doctor was living up to his repu-tation as a miracle worker.

According to court records and other sources, Dr. Galea's unique med-ical services centered around four treatments: PRP; anti-inflammatory IVs, which contained, among other things, Actovegin, an unapproved drug derived from calf's blood; injections containing Actovegin; and "in-jections containing a mixture of substances including but not limited to Nutropin, a human growth hormone, injected into the knee and admin-istered for the purpose of regenerating cartilage" and reducing joint in-flammation.

At the end of 2009, Dr. Galea told the *New York Times* that his pre-ferred treatment for knee or ACL injuries was platelet-rich plasma. In the

Times article, Dr. Galea said he had treated Woods's left knee solely with PRP using a centrifuge borrowed from an Orlando doctor—and not with unapproved Actovegin or any illegal performance-enhancing drug. He said he had treated Woods just four or five times—which turned out to be false.

According to records later obtained as part of a Florida Department of Health investigation, Galea actually made fourteen trips to treat Woods between January and August 2009, charging $3,500 per consultation plus expenses for first-class travel and lodging. Galea's total invoices amounted to more than $76,000.

There's a very good chance Galea's work with Woods would not have become public if not for the events of September 14, 2009. On that day, Galea's longtime medical assistant was crossing the Peace Bridge connecting Canada and Buffalo, New York, when she was stopped by a US Customs and Border Protection (CBP) officer and referred for a secondary inspection. During the inspection, CBP officers discovered, among other items, 111 syringes, a centrifuge machine, and a bag with twenty vials and seventy-six ampules of assorted substances and medications, including 10 mg of Nutropin (synthetic HGH) and 250 ml of Actovegin. The assistant told officers she was traveling to Washington, DC, for a medical conference, which turned out to be untrue. She was actually taking what she described as Dr. Galea's "medical kit" to DC so he could treat an injured NFL player.

Faced with criminal charges, the assistant began cooperating with agents from Homeland Security, Immigration and Customs Enforcement, and the Food and Drug Administration. She eventually turned over her BlackBerry to investigators. A month later, on October 15, 2009, Canadian police raided Galea's office, seizing an "NFL file folder" and a "professional players journal."

Galea was subsequently indicted in the US by a federal grand jury on five counts, including possession of HGH with intent to distribute and introducing misbranded drugs into interstate commerce. As part of its case, the government charged Dr. Galea with unlawfully entering the US more than one hundred times between July 2007 and September 2009 to illegally provide drugs and medical services to more than twenty professional athletes, including Woods. Billings during this more than two-year period alone amounted to about $800,000. Galea later pled guilty to one count of introducing misbranded drugs into interstate commerce and was sentenced to one day in jail and a $275,000 fine.

In an affidavit filed as part of an FBI investigation, Dr. Galea's long-time assistant appeared to contradict his assertion that PRP and Actovegin were the sole treatment options for knee injuries. She told the government, "Dr. Galea would at times inject a cocktail containing HGH into an athlete. The ... HGH injections were designed to help regenerate cartilage growth." She also told authorities that Galea had injected at least eight professional athletes—seven in the US and the other in Canada—with a mixture of substances that included human growth hormone. (In an email, an attorney for the assistant insisted that she had never witnessed Dr. Galea injecting HGH into Woods.)

A close inspection of the government's case against Dr. Galea reveals what could be construed as an attempt to conceal the exact nature and history of his treatment of high-profile athletes. Invoices from Galea routinely described his services in vague terms—"Consultation" or "Consultation/IV/Injections." Checks were written to Galea Investments Inc. and not to the doctor himself or to his health and wellness center.

In defending his use of HGH, which was legal in Canada but subject to extreme limitations in the US, Galea said he had injected the drug only in patients over forty years old as a way to improve their health and stamina. Galea admitted he had personally used HGH for ten years.

So was Woods getting some kind of pharmaceutical boost to speed his recovery from injury? One source with knowledge of Dr. Galea's treatment of Woods had no doubt. "One hundred percent," the source said. "No question."

According to the source, Galea's PRP injections into Woods's injured knee and Achilles also contained what the source described as "minuscule" amounts of both testosterone and HGH. "All of those—the HGH, testosterone, and PRP—just work together really well to create healing at that localized place of injection," said the source. "There's just not enough [testosterone and HGH], and it's so localized [that] there's just no way it would show up in a drug test. It would have been out of his system in a day. Tiger may not have known exactly what Tony was putting in there."

No question has hovered over Woods more than whether he used performance-enhancing drugs. In a 2010 survey conducted by *Sports Illustrated*, 24 percent of the seventy-one PGA Tour pros who responded said they thought Woods "used HGH or other performance-enhancing drugs." Those suspecting he used PEDs, particularly testosterone, have pointed to the muscular development of his upper body and arms beginning in the early 2000s; the need to recover from his twice-daily two-hour workouts; and his unusual—at least for golf—string of ligament and tendon injuries. Victor Conte is one of those who suspects Woods used PEDs. Conte was the man in the middle of the 2003 BALCO steroid scandal. Now owner of a thriving nutritional supplement company (SNAC, Scientific Nutrition for Advanced Conditioning), he remains a knowledgeable resource on the current state and use of PEDs.

Conte said Woods's injury history could be a sign of PEDs in the form of mineral depletion. "When you use anabolic steroids, it depletes the body of copper," said Conte. "So while you're simultaneously building your muscles with nitrogen and promoting protein synthesis from the use of steroids, you're weakening connective tissue, ligaments, and tendons. So when you describe his [injury] history, could that possibly be a result of his using anabolic steroids, and the answer is yes."

Woods has consistently and categorically denied the use of performance-enhancing drugs. "[Dr. Galea] did come to my house," Woods said at a Masters press conference in 2010. "He never gave me HGH or PEDs. I've never taken that my entire life. I've never taken any illegal drug ever, for that matter."

Dr. Galea also denies any suggestion that he was party to performance enhancement with Woods or any other athlete. "Dr. Galea at no time has ever been engaged in any performance-enhancement activity," said Galea's attorney, Brian H. Greenspan. "These sorts of innuendo of suspicion are absolutely, one hundred percent false."

Greenspan insisted that Woods had gone to Galea because he was a pioneer of PRP at the time and that Galea was a healer, not a cheater. Asked specifically if Galea had ever injected a "cocktail of healing" containing testosterone and HGH into Woods, Greenspan said Dr. Galea was unable to respond. In an email, Greenspan cited Galea's "positive regulatory obligation to maintain the confidentiality of his patients' medical records, which cannot be disclosed without their express instructions in writing."

Those who know the truth about Woods and whether he knowingly or otherwise used PEDs probably can be counted on the fingers of one hand. One of those people is almost certainly Dr. Mark Lindsay. Between September 15, 2008, and October 30, 2009, Lindsay treated Woods forty-nine times, charging $2,000 per day plus expenses, according to a Florida Department of Health investigation. He was paid a total of $118,979 for his services, including expenses. Lindsay has told friends his routine with Woods rarely varied. As soon as Tiger woke up, Lindsay would perform his specialized Active Release Techniques on him. Woods would then go to practice and work out for the next three hours and then return home for lunch, after which Lindsay would work on him again. When Tiger was preparing for a major, Lindsay would often bring his therapeutic table to the range, where he would work on Woods for an hour in between practice sessions that focused on swing mechanics.

"The goal was to create efficiency and elasticity of the complex movements using the forces generated from the ground," Dr. Lindsay explained. "The efficacy of doing this on site and interchangeably with Tiger Woods's golf swings was significant."

Lindsay's extensive treatment sessions with Woods provided unparalleled doctor-patient access during a time that some people suspect Tiger had gained an unfair advantage through PEDs. In a one-year span, from 2008 to 2009, Tiger underwent hundreds of hours of treatment at the hands of Dr. Lindsay. After initially declining to speak on the record, Dr. Lindsay— through his Toronto-based attorney, Timothy S. B. Danson—obtained a limited doctor-patient privilege waiver from Woods, authorizing him to disclose information about his treatment of the golfer and to provide his medical opinion on whether Woods used banned substances or performance-enhancing drugs. On December 17, 2017, Dr. Lindsay signed a four-page declaration witnessed by his attorney. With Tiger's consent, Lindsay provided his declaration to the authors of this book. It is the most authoritative and definitive statement to date on the question of whether Tiger Woods used performance-enhancing drugs. It reads in part:

> *During this extended period of time, I was very close to Tiger. At no time during this intensive process did I ever witness Tiger Woods take, discuss, or ask for any banned or performance-enhancing substances, nor did he even indirectly hint about the subject matter of banned substances. Anyone suggesting or implying otherwise is misinformed and wrong. To the contrary, Tiger Woods was fully committed to a proper and highly disciplined rehabilitation process.*

Tiger Woods is an exceptionally gifted, highly disciplined, and very spatially aware athlete. These qualities, along with his passion and single-minded commitment to be the best golfer of all time, are nothing short of breathtaking; they are what puts Tiger Woods in a very elite cohort of the best athletes in the history of sports. It is simply wrong and misconceived to apply normal standards of recovery and performance to world-class, elite athletes like Tiger Woods. The exceptional and unique qualities that made Tiger Woods the best elite athlete in his field are the same exceptional and unique qualities that he applied to his rehabilitation and comeback.

I have been in the practice of sports medicine for over twenty-seven years. I have treated hundreds of world-class athletes spanning eight Olympic Games and multiple professional sports disciplines. I know what muscle tone and tissue should feel like. This is critical to the proper treatment of a patient. I continue to be involved in research and stay current with the latest applicable medical literature. I understand body/muscle tone and tissue and the effects of certain drugs on tone and tissue. Tiger Woods's body/muscle tone and tissue are completely consistent with what one would expect from an elite athlete free of any performance-enhancement drugs. Stated differently, there was no evidence of rigid, stiff, and hypertonic body/muscle tone or tissue during my multiple physical examinations of Tiger Woods, which one would expect if performance-enhancing drugs were being used.

With regard to my experience described above and my direct observations and treatment of Tiger Woods, it is my professional opinion that he has not taken any performance-enhancing substances, and that the notion of taking such substances would be abhorrent and repugnant to him. Tiger Woods is truly one of the most impressive, skilled, intense, and determined athletes I have ever worked with. These are the qualities and attributes that drive his rehabilitation and comeback.

CHAPTER TWENTY-SEVEN

CRASH

It may have been the loudest cheering ever generated by Tiger Woods. At dusk on March 29, 2009, the gallery around the eighteenth hole at Bay Hill in Orlando could be heard a mile away as Tiger's sixteen-foot putt banged in, capping one of the biggest comebacks of his career. In his 239th start, Woods had won his sixty-sixth PGA Tour event. More important, the victory at the Arnold Palmer Invitational was his first tournament win since undergoing knee surgery nine months earlier. The NBC announcers referred to Tiger's performance as "magical." In this instance, adjectives like *supernatural* and *otherworldly* would not be exaggerations. It had been only three months since he had blown out his Achilles. The stress fractures in his tibia were healed, and he had a reconstructed ACL. Whatever Lindsay and Galea were doing was working. After starting the final round five strokes behind, Woods had come roaring back, demonstrating more emphatically than ever that he remained the greatest individual performer in all of sports.

As Woods walked off the green to the chant of "Ti-ger, Ti-ger, Ti-ger," he was greeted by the King, Arnold Palmer.

"What did I say to you last year?" Palmer asked him. "I said Earl would have loved it. He would have loved it."

Woods smiled and thanked him. It felt exhilarating to be back on top.

In Tiger's career, the year 2009 will forever be remembered for what happened to him off the course—a mysterious motor vehicle accident, followed by the exposure of an infidelity crisis so big that he would never again be looked at in the same light. But his spectacular fall from grace would not come until the end of the year. Prior to that, Woods played some of the most remarkable golf of his life. He ended up winning seven of the nineteen tournaments he entered that season. In sixteen of those tournaments he finished in the top ten. He was first in birdie average, scoring average, iron play from 175 to 200 yards, and greens in regulation; he topped the money list with more than $10 million; and he finished the year ranked number one in the world. It was also the year that he became the first athlete in history to exceed $1 billion in career earnings. By every visible measure, Tiger Woods was alone at the pinnacle of professional sports, the most talented golfer to ever play the game, the greatest athlete of his generation, and the richest athlete of all time.

But Woods was living in denial, deceiving himself and those closest to him. In February, he and Elin had welcomed their second child, Charlie Axel Woods, into the world. It should have been an occasion of immense joy, a family milestone that could have inspired Woods to spend more time with his wife and children. Many of the game's greatest golfers experienced at least a modest decline in their competitive edge after children came along and priorities changed. "When I was younger, before I had children and money, all I wanted to do was play golf, work at my golf, get better at my golf," Tom Watson said. "But when the children came, my time with them was very important to me. I definitely lost some edge." Woods, on the other hand, never lost his competitive drive to dominate his sport, to win every time he stepped onto a golf course. At thirty-three, he was untethered from his family by a narcissism that fed his self-destructive addictions to bodybuilding, painkillers, sleeping pills, and sex.

His upbringing, so critical to his development into a machine-like athlete, forever stunted his ability to form—much less maintain—the kind of intimate relationship with a spouse that is built on self-sacrifice, loyalty, trust, and selflessness; nor was he equipped to cope with fatherhood. He loved his children, but his lifestyle virtually assured that he would be an absentee dad.

In June 2009, Woods was in New York City to attend yet another promotional event, this time for EA Sports. The video-game maker was rolling out a new product, and Tiger was on hand for the launch. Afterward, on the same day that Michael Jackson died after fatally overdosing on a cocktail of pain and sleep medications, an obviously worn-down Woods talked to *People* magazine writer Steve Helling. The subject quickly turned to parenting. "My dad passed away before Sam was born," Tiger told Helling, "so I didn't have a chance to talk to him about being a father. I regret that. I will always regret that. I think of him every day. He taught me everything. I hear his voice."

There is a lot to unpack in that statement. Woods, who started taking Ambien to combat sleeplessness back when his father was dying, was still in the grip of insomnia. Racked by regrets stemming from the loss of his father and his own perceived inadequacies as a dad, Woods desperately missed communicating with his best friend. But the saddest part of Tiger's statement wasn't *what* he said but *who* he said it to. Instead of opening up to his wife or a genuine friend, he was talking to a writer at a celebrity magazine. It was an indication that by 2009, Woods was more alone than ever. Yet he was signaling that he needed help.

On the same day that Tiger talked to Helling, he met up with his friend Derek Jeter. They ended up at a Manhattan nightclub with three women in their twenties. One of the women in the group was Mark O'Meara's niece, Amber Lauria. Tiger had known Lauria since 1997, when they were introduced to each other at O'Meara's home. Woods had spent countless hours with Lauria at Isleworth and around Orlando during her teenage years. From the beginning, their bond was more like a brother-and-sister relationship than a friendship. By 2009, Lauria had graduated from college and was working at Fox News, and they would meet up from time to time when Woods was in New York. He also communicated with her frequently by phone and text.

After Earl died, Lauria said, her conversations with Tiger took on a more depressing tone. From that point on, he seldom seemed happy.

"He looked at me like a family member," Lauria said. "But I remember thinking he's in a really bad spot to be calling and crying and being this upset for this long. That's when I really started seeing a big change in him. He would just go to a dark place." Lauria admired Elin and remembered thinking, *I wish Elin were here with him at a time when he's so upset.* But she also recognized that it wasn't practical for Elin to be on the road with Tiger. She had two young children at home.

Lauria agreed to meet up with Woods at the nightclub because she still cared about him as a friend. "He was alone, and he needed people around him," she said. Still, it was clear that things were amiss. "I said to him, 'I'm here for you, but you should be with your wife or calling your wife. I know you're traveling. But what's going on?'"

Emotionally, Woods was adrift, constantly moving from city to city, hooking up with one woman after another. Most of the women whose names and numbers filled his cell phone directory were ones he had met in nightclubs and casinos. He persuaded one after another to believe that she was his only mistress. All of these women—the ones he paid and the ones he picked up—were women he could control. For the most part, they were younger than he was, less sophisticated, enamored of his status, and in the dark about his exploits. It was a situation that made it easier to maintain his secret life.

But during his visit to New York City that week in June 2009, he met a woman who represented something different. Thirty-four-year-old Rachel Uchitel, a glamorous beauty, had grown up a child of privilege in Manhattan. Well-educated and possessing a degree in psychology, she first encountered fame after the 9/11 terror attacks. The *New York Post* ran a photo of her weeping while holding a picture of her missing fiancé, who worked in the World Trade Center, and the image was distributed around the world via the internet. Uchitel went on to become a television producer at Bloomberg before transitioning to VIP hostess/manager at high-end nightclubs from the Hamptons to New York to Las Vegas, earning high praise for her people skills and attention to detail. Uchitel gained another measure of fame when it was reported that she'd had an affair with actor David Boreanaz. She also knew Derek Jeter.

Woods was taken with Uchitel. She was a year older than he was, and she lived a lifestyle that was more akin to his than the other women he knew. She was a jet-setter, accustomed to flying around the world and running in the same circles as celebrities and CEOs. By the time Tiger left New York, he'd added Uchitel to the directory on his phone, and she'd added him to hers, under the code name Bear.

Uchitel started flying down to Orlando, where Tiger would put her up in a condo near his home. When Woods arrived, he would close the blinds. They would stay up watching late-night comedy on television. And despite being plagued by insomnia, Tiger didn't have trouble going to sleep when he was with Uchitel. Their sexual intimacy and mutual familiarity with grief—he was still suffering from the loss of his father, and she had lost her fiancé in an act of terrorism, as well as her father to a cocaine overdose—enabled them to bond in a way that provided a deeper element to their relationship. On one occasion, while with Uchitel in the Orlando condo, Tiger said, "This makes me so happy." It was a sad admission, considering he was practically around the corner from his home, where Elin was taking care of their newborn son and two-year-old daughter, blissfully unaware.

At this point, Hank Haney didn't know what was going on either, but he recognized a drop-off in Tiger's practice hours and in his effort. "There were times at Isleworth," Haney said, "when I'd say, 'Where is he?' I mean, he'd say he's going to the store and be gone for an hour or two. Or Elin would be out of town, and he'd be getting ready to go out. 'Where are you going?' I'd ask. And he would make up some story about how he was going over to Bryon Bell's house. I could tell he was lying."

Yet it never crossed Haney's mind that Woods might be meeting up with other women. Haney was around Tiger more than almost anyone, and he said he never witnessed any flirting, never mind infidelity. "I never saw him with anybody," Haney said. "I'm the kind of friend that if I saw something, I would say something. Steve Williams was the same way."

The one thing that Woods couldn't hide from Haney and Williams was his increasingly surly behavior on the golf course. Almost immediately after Woods returned to the Tour in 2009, both his swing coach and his caddie started seeing red flags about his emotional state. The first one went up at the 2009 Masters. After playing poorly at Augusta, Woods went on a rant to the press: "I fought my swing all day and just kind of Band-Aided it around, and almost won the tournament with a Band-Aid swing." Without naming Haney, Woods had given him a backhanded insult, igniting rumors that Haney was on the verge of being fired.

Haney responded with an email to Woods: "You didn't make any friends or fans with the way you acted at the Masters. You just looked stressed and pissed the whole time you were there."

It became even clearer that Woods was reaching the end of his emotional rope at the 2009 PGA Championship at Hazeltine National Golf Club outside Minneapolis. After scores of 67 and 70 in the first two rounds, Woods held a four-shot lead going into the third round. He appeared to be well on his way to closing to within three majors of Nicklaus's record. But in Friday's post-round press conference, an enterprising reporter summoned the courage to inquire if Woods ever felt he had choked in a major.

Furious, Woods just stared him down.

Finally, moderator Kelly Elbin broke the awkward silence. "We'll take that to be a no?" he said.

"Be creative," Woods finally said to the reporter. "You usually are."

But the question would prove prescient.

After the third round, Woods maintained a two-stroke lead, and the outcome seemed like a foregone conclusion. Tiger had never lost a major when leading after three rounds. He entered the final round two strokes ahead of South Korea's Yang Yong-eun, better known as Y. E. Yang. Yang, who was thirty-seven, hadn't picked up a club until he was nineteen, and hadn't broken par until he was twenty-two. Earlier in the year, Yang had been forced to sink a seven-foot putt on the final hole of the last day of qualifying school just to make the Tour. He had a grand total of one victory on the PGA Tour. He was the longest of long shots to beat Woods.

All day long, Woods and Steve Williams barely said a word to Yang, employing the kind of gamesmanship—isolation, slow play, crowding—Tiger was famous for. But Yang never got rattled. After twelve holes, he had pulled even with Woods. On thirteen, Woods stuffed a 3-iron from 248 yards to within eight feet of the hole. When Yang buried his tee shot in a greenside bunker, it appeared a birdie-bogey swing was in the works and Woods was on his way to his fifteenth major. But then Yang hit the shot of his life, blasting out of the bunker to twelve feet. Moments later, he snaked in a tough putt for par.

Still, all Woods had to do to stay even with Yang was make an eight-foot birdie putt, the kind he'd dropped hundreds of times under pressure. Only this time, the unthinkable happened. Woods missed. His putt burned the left edge of the cup and failed to fall. The look on Woods's face was a mix of anger and disbelief.

Inside the clubhouse, players—many of whom had crumbled in similar pressure-packed situations against Woods—were jumping up and down on a couch, cheering Yang on, hoping somebody, anybody, even the South Korean son of a vegetable farmer, would finally slay the dragon.

With five holes still to play, Woods had plenty of time to overtake Yang. But something was amiss; the failure to drop the kind of putt he hadn't missed, even under pressure, in two decades had shaken something loose in Tiger. When Yang chipped in for eagle on the next hole, Woods never recovered, missing two more critical, makeable putts on the last four holes. He ended up losing to Yang by three strokes. His perfect record of 14–0 in winning majors after holding or sharing the third-round lead was broken.

Steve Williams later told a friend that he thought the loss of the PGA

Championship to Yang was the first crack in the armor. It was the beginning of what he called the Snowball Effect. In his 2006 book *Golf at the Top*, Williams described the effect as an unexpected moment that "allows a flash of self-doubt to enter the conscious mind and then to penetrate all the way to the imagination." Then, having opened a wound in the most sensitive part of the brain, the person begins to "listen more and more closely to the negative interpretations the imagination is placing on events and project them onto the next shot and the next round and the next tournament."

In other words, when you miss once when it really counts—like an eight-foot birdie putt late at the PGA Championship—the dark whispers in your mind grow louder and louder. As summer turned to fall, Woods was hearing such whispers seemingly at every turn. Weeks after losing to Yang at the PGA, he came unglued at the Deutsche Bank Championship in Massachusetts, throwing his driver in a fit of anger. Then at the Australian Masters in November, he lost his temper again. After a bad tee shot, he threw his club down with such force that it landed in the gallery. It could easily have injured someone.

Hank Haney was watching the outburst on television and thought to himself, *This is a troubled guy.*

The problems in Australia ran deeper than Haney or Williams ever imagined. Back on August 29, Woods had sent a series of dark, denigrating texts to porn star Joslyn James, another mistress, that signaled his state of mind:

4:08 p.m.	Hold you down while i choke you and Fuck that ass that i own.
4:10 p.m.	Then im going to tell you to shut the Fuck up while i slap your face and pull your hair for making noise.
5:00 p.m.	I really do want to be rough with you. Slap you around
5:15 p.m.	I want you to beg for my cock. Kiss you all over to convince me to let you have it in your mouth
5:26 p.m.	Next time i see you, you better beg and if you don't do it right i will slap, spank, bite and fuck you till mercy

In October, he was texting Jaimee Grubbs, the cocktail waitress from San Diego: "I will [see] you Sunday night. It's the only night in which I am totally free."

If that wasn't enough, Woods was reportedly hooking up with a twenty-seven-year-old marketing manager for a Las Vegas nightclub, confiding to her that he wasn't happy in his marriage and telling her how much pressure he felt.

In the middle of October, Woods was back at it with Grubbs, hoping to arrange a rendezvous in Newport Beach. But on the 18th, he texted:

Change of plans. Meet me at the island hotel. It's a little safer. Got us a room for the night. Room 905. It's on the east side of fashion island.

Then he followed up with further instructions:

It's under the name Bell—Mr. and Mrs. Bryon Bell.

At the same time, Woods was arranging a rendezvous with Rachel Uchitel.

Acting on a tip, the *National Enquirer* was hot on Tiger's trail once again. Back in 2007, it had seemed like a coup when IMG and sophisticated lawyers managed to squelch the *Enquirer* story about Woods and the pancake-house waitress in Orlando. But after that great escape, Tiger overlooked the fact that tabloids are like sharks that can detect prey from the scent of a single drop of blood in the water. Once Woods was wounded in '07, the *Enquirer* never stopped tracking him—and after Uchitel entered the picture, the chase was on. The tabloid staked out her apartment and waited to see what would happen.

"It just became, well, let's follow her," said a source at the *Enquirer*. "Following people looks good on TV, but in real life the success rate is, like, two percent. Amazingly, this actually worked out all the way right up to the room."

The room in question turned out to be a suite on a special floor at the Crown Towers in Melbourne, Australia, where Woods was staying during the Australian Masters. Uchitel was headed there after receiving this email from Bryon Bell: "Here are the details for all the flights. Sorry for all the changes. I look forward to meeting you tomorrow."

Bell was a critical cog in the setting up and maintaining of the secrecy of Tiger's trysts. But this time a surveillance team photographed Uchitel's arrival at the Melbourne airport and hotel. Then, as she entered an elevator on her way to the thirty-fifth floor, an *Enquirer* reporter slipped inside and confronted her as she walked to Woods's suite. At first Uchitel denied any connection to Woods, but the futility of that approach quickly became apparent. She eventually returned to the US, leaving Team Tiger to sort out how to handle its most explosive scandal to date.

While performing a staggering juggling act in his private life, Tiger won the Australian Masters by two strokes and pocketed a $3 million appearance fee. Afterward, he talked at length with Australian golf writers about the nuances of shot-making. "I felt this was a tricky golf course in a sense," he said. "It's not overly long, but you can hit marginal shots and have them in pretty bad spots. You had to make sure that you understood where to miss the golf ball. That's one of the things that I love on a golf course—it gets fast like this, and you have to maneuver the golf ball correctly."

Woods's press conference was an insightful illustration of the compartmentalization performed by a man living a double life. At a time when he was careening toward a steep cliff that threatened to expose his duplicity and ravage his marriage, he calmly talked about the thrill he derived from shaping a shot away from danger zones. Immune for so long to the responsibilities of everyday life, Woods had, no doubt, developed a gaping blind spot that covered the consequences of his narcissistic ways, enabling him to believe he could cheat on his wife with impunity and forever escape detection.

On the other hand, it's also possible that the high-stakes risks he was taking with so many women—arranging clandestine trysts and lying about his singular devotion to each woman on his overgrown list of paramours—may have breathed oxygen into his creative genius as a golfer. Perhaps Woods had scaled Everest so many times as an athlete that he was forever searching for external sources of adrenaline rushes—deep-water diving, Navy SEAL training, extreme workouts. The women in his life, in that respect, were just another way to fill a void and satisfy an urge. As strange as it may sound, Tiger played some of his best golf in the years when his life was most out of control. It was as if the chaos in his life outside the ropes propelled his play on the course to new heights.

But on the flight home from Melbourne, a feeling of foreboding set in. Back in Isleworth, he confided to a fellow pro: "I think I'm about to come out on the wrong side of a big media story."

Complicating matters was the fact that despite her attempts at discretion when confronted by the reporter in Australia, Uchitel had previously disclosed details of her affair with Woods to other people, one of whom had passed a polygraph and sold her story to the *Enquirer*.

Woods tried to get the story killed. "We probably heard from every lawyer Tiger's ever employed in his life," said a source at the *Enquirer*.

This time, however, there would be no deal to save him from exposure. With his gold-plated, family-friendly reputation facilitated by the likes of Nike and Disney and American Express, Woods was too alluring a target. For the better part of four years, he'd managed to elude the *Enquirer*. But now the superhero-like athlete with the magnetic smile that appeared on everything from Wheaties boxes to airport billboards was finally locked in the tabloid's crosshairs.

"You don't go in until you have the smoking gun, and then it really doesn't matter what they say," a source at the *Enquirer* said. "Then it's like, 'Go ahead and sue me.' And we'll sue you for malicious prosecution."

When it became apparent that even the combined forces of IMG and a platoon of high-priced lawyers were not going to be able to derail the story, Woods and his team started circling the wagons. Mark Steinberg telephoned Hank Haney, who was on his way to China to establish a junior golf academy. "Hank, I want to give you a heads-up," Steinberg told him. "There's going to be a story coming out about Tiger and this girl. It's not true. Everything is going to be fine. But if anybody asks you about it, don't say anything."

Steinberg also sent a text to Steve Williams: "There is a story coming out tomorrow. Absolutely no truth to it. Don't speak to anybody."

It fell to Woods to convince his wife. He told her the tabloid story was a lie, that there was no affair between him and Uchitel. But on Monday, November 23, in advance of publication, the Uchitel exposé began circulating on the internet. It contained a quote attributed to her that read like a dagger directed at Elin: "It's Tiger Woods. I don't care about his wife! We're in love."

Blindsided, Elin didn't know what to believe. It was the week of Thanksgiving, and little Charlie had just learned to walk and was starting to say his first words. For Elin, these were monumental milestones of joy. But the suspicions in her mind were making it impossible to focus on anything else. In need of someone to confide in, she called the one person she trusted above all—her identical twin, Josefin. They had been best friends since childhood. Elin knew Josefin would know what to do. After obtaining a Master of Laws from the London School of Economics and Political Science, Josefin received her law degree in Sweden and joined the American-based firm McGuireWoods LLP. When Elin called her, Josefin was working out of the firm's London office, where she specialized in mergers and acquisitions. She immediately came to her sister's aid, providing emotional support and advice.

With the situation worsening, Woods took the extraordinary step of arranging a phone call between Elin and Uchitel, who corroborated Tiger's account that there had been no sexual relationship between them. Unconvinced, Elin wanted to see Tiger's phone. Afraid that she would find out about the other women in his life, Tiger frantically tried to cover his tracks. He left an urgent voice mail with Jaimee Grubbs: "Can you please take your name off your phone? My wife went through my phone and may be calling you. So if you can, please take your name off . . . [and] just have it as a number on the voice mail. You've got to do this for me. *Huge.* Quickly. All right. Bye."

The following day, the *Enquirer* landed on supermarket racks in the Orlando area. It was the day before Thanksgiving, and the "World Exclusive" headline "Tiger Woods Cheating Scandal" splashed across the cover intensified the already dire atmosphere in the Woods home. The tension was amplified by the fact that Tiger's mother was visiting for the holiday. Nothing triggered anxiety in Woods like the fear of disappointing his mother, and nothing had ever disappointed Kultida more than family betrayal—first when her parents abandoned her, and then when her husband was repeatedly unfaithful. It was overwhelming to contemplate how she would react to the realization that her son had far eclipsed his father in the infidelity department.

The holiday provided a false appearance of reprieve. The *Enquirer* story got very little play elsewhere. But Tiger's cell phone was an explosive electronic record of his illicit affairs. His device had also become another addiction. On Thanksgiving Day, Woods couldn't resist texting multiple women, including Grubbs. In a short exchange, he wished Grubbs a happy Thanksgiving, and she replied, "u too love."

At the same time, Elin remained fixated on Tiger's phone. After he fell into an Ambien-induced sleep on Thanksgiving night, she searched his text history. She found one from him that said: "You are the only one I've ever loved." He had not sent that text to her.

Unsure of the recipient's identity, Elin sent a text to the person from Tiger's phone. It read, "I miss you. When are we seeing each other again?" Before long, a reply came back. While her husband slept, Elin called the mysterious number, and Uchitel picked up. Immediately recognizing her voice, Elin lost it.

In the intense moments that followed, Woods awoke and emerged from his home barefoot in the middle of the night and got into his SUV. Speeding out of his driveway, he lost control, clipping a hedge and swerving into his next-door neighbor's yard, driving over a fire hydrant and plowing into a tree. When police arrived after responding to a 911 call from Tiger's neighbor, they found that the windows on both sides of the back seat of his vehicle had been smashed out with a golf club that had been swung by Elin.

Renowned marriage therapist Esther Perel has worked with hundreds of couples who have been shattered by infidelity. "Few events in the life of a couple, except illness and death, carry such devastating force," Perel said. In her best-selling book *The State of Affairs: Rethinking Infidelity*, Perel explains that the agony suffered by a betrayed spouse goes much deeper than just a violation of trust. "It's a shattering of the grand ambition of romantic love. It's a shock that makes us question our past, our future, and even our very identity. Indeed, the maelstrom of emotions unleashed in the wake of an affair can be so overwhelming that many psychologists turn to the field of trauma to explain the symptoms: obsessive rumination, hyper-vigilance, numbness and disassociation, inexplicable rages, uncontrolled panic."

In the case of Tiger Woods, it would be an understatement to say that Elin's discovery of his infidelity unleashed a maelstrom of emotions. As Woods lay unconscious on the road at 2:25 a.m. on November 27, 2009, blood on his teeth and lips, he finally appeared as he truly was—a vulnerable, fragile, deeply wounded person. In shock, Elin tended to the man who had broken her heart—placing a pillow under his head, slipping socks on his feet, covering him with a blanket, and pleading with him to open his eyes. Frantic, Kultida ran from the house, yelling, "What happened? What happened?" Soon police officers and paramedics were on the scene, asking the same question. As Tiger was placed on a gurney and rolled toward an ambulance, he momentarily opened his eyes and tried to speak. His lips moved, but there were no words. Then his eyes rolled back in his head, as if he were dead. Elin screamed and Kultida wept as the medics closed the doors and the ambulance lights slowly faded into the Florida night.

FIRESTORM

How did I get here?

For Woods, it was a question that extended beyond the walls of the ER at Health Central Hospital. When he woke up there on the morning after Thanksgiving, his world was upside-down. What had started out as a desperate attempt to keep a secret from his wife had spiraled into a full-scale crisis. Suddenly, he had to worry that the whole world might discover his secrets.

Bewildered, he was surrounded by medical personnel. They checked his vital signs, cleaned and stitched the laceration on his lip, and drew his blood. There were monitoring devices to track his blood pressure and heart rate, hospital charts to note his progress, and an attending nurse asking how he was feeling. Accustomed to being in control, Tiger found himself out of his element, completely in the hands of others.

Outside the hospital room, two police officers assigned to investigate the crash were waiting, hoping to talk to him. They were also interested in the results of his blood test. Elin had already provided them with two bottles of pills—the sleep aid Ambien and the painkiller Vicodin—that she said her husband was taking. The question was whether the contents of those bottles had played a role in the crash. Meanwhile, television crews were assembling in the parking lot.

Over a period of hours, as his vital signs stabilized and it became clear that his injuries were not serious, Woods yearned to return to the place he had fled in the middle of the night. At one p.m. he got his wish. Ten hours after being admitted to the ER, he was discharged from the hospital.

As Tiger returned home, his impounded Cadillac was photographed and searched by investigators. They recovered only one item—an out-of-print science book by British astronomy professor John Gribbin titled *Get *a Grip on Physics*. As a kid, Tiger was interested in space and often read about NASA's missions. As an adult, he still liked reading about science. Partially covered by shards of broken glass, the physics book was evidence of innocence lost, but it didn't help explain why Woods managed to hit so many objects in the mere 150 feet he traveled from his driveway to his neighbor's front yard. Hours after Tiger settled back into his house, the Florida Highway Patrol released the accident report, informing the media that the crash remained under investigation and that charges could be filed. "We don't believe it's a domestic issue," a police spokesman told the media, stoking rumors to the contrary.

Also that afternoon, Tiger's spokesman issued a very short statement saying Woods was in good condition. The notion that he was in "good" condition was a farce. The truth was that he had never been in a more precarious place. In addition to being the subject of an investigation that threatened to put his personal life under a microscope, Tiger's wife no longer trusted him and felt betrayed by the people around him. So she had turned to her family, especially her sister. Appreciating the gravity of the situation Elin faced, Josefin called Richard Cullen, the managing partner of her law firm, with a simple plea: "Can we help my sister?"

Cullen had worked on both the Watergate and Iran-Contra investigations, and he served on President George W. Bush's legal team during the recount following the 2000 election. After a stint in law enforcement as US Attorney for the eastern district of Virginia and as that state's attorney general, Cullen went on to represent large multinational corporations under investigation by the US Department of Justice and the SEC. His law firm, with offices in the United States and Europe, did not specialize in family law, but Cullen was a master tactician whose specialty was solving complex business problems that often put powerful corporations at odds with government entities. In many ways, he possessed the perfect skill set for the task at hand. Elin was in uncharted waters. Still reeling from the realization that the man she loved had been unfaithful, she nonetheless had the presence of mind to recognize that potentially ending a marriage with the richest athlete in the world was not going to be a typical divorce case. It would be more like the breakup of a very powerful business—only there were two young children involved, and Elin wanted to make sure that whatever she did was in the best interest of the kids.

Convinced that she had found the right team to advise her, Elin ended up retaining McGuire Woods. With Cullen and his Richmond-based partner Dennis Belcher leading the legal team, three other lawyers were assigned to assist Elin—the firm's corporate partner in London, a third partner in the firm's Virginia office, and Josefin. For the first time in their marriage, Tiger wasn't the only one with a team of high-powered lawyers and advisors.

A few hours after Tiger left the hospital, two police officers knocked on his front door. Elin answered and invited them in. When they asked to speak with her husband, she told them he was asleep and could not be disturbed. When they asked to talk with her about the crash, she said she wouldn't do that without Tiger present. She suggested they return at three p.m. the following day. Tired, she then walked off, disappearing down a hallway. Left standing alone in Tiger's home, the officers quietly let themselves out.

Woods's whereabouts on the day after the crash remain unclear. At least one published account suggests that upon being discharged from the hospital, Tiger flew to Arizona via private plane to have dental work performed. His top front tooth had been knocked out sometime after his wife had discovered the text message from Rachel Uchitel and before EMTs arrived to find him on the sidewalk beside his crashed vehicle. Multiple sources believe that a leading cosmetic dental surgeon in the Phoenix area—who declined to answer any questions—performed the surgery. In any event, Tiger had much bigger problems than a missing tooth.

No one appreciated this more than Mark Steinberg, who flew to Orlando to deal directly with the situation. From the beginning, Steinberg had hoped the story about Tiger's dalliance with Rachel Uchitel would remain confined to the pages of the *Enquirer*. As long as it was a tabloid story, he believed it wouldn't be taken seriously and Tiger would survive it. There would be damage to repair at home, but everything else would remain business as usual—his golf game, his endorsement deals, his foundation. But Steinberg had a new perspective by the time he reached Tiger's house. Woods's marriage was on the rocks, and the crash was making headlines around the globe, rendering the containment strategy much more tenuous. In the initial twenty-four hours after the accident, the public-affairs officer at the Florida Highway Patrol received no fewer than 1,600 emails from media outlets seeking information. Queries came from as far away as Mexico, Canada, Japan, and Australia. The Associated Press alone placed sixty-eight calls to the police department, requesting every-thing from documents and photographs to updates. By the time Steinberg huddled with Tiger at his Isleworth home, news helicopters were hovering overhead, and television satellite trucks were lining up outside the gates.

The press had the same questions as the police: What drove Tiger from his home at two thirty in the morning? Where was he headed? What caused him to lose control of his vehicle and hit bushes, a hedge, a fire hydrant, and a tree? What role, if any, did his wife play in the incident? And how was he injured?

Woods faced a quandary. While under no legal obligation to speak with law enforcement, refusing to answer basic questions was a surefire way to fuel speculation in the court of public opinion that he had something to hide. Normally a master craftsman when it came to shaping public per-ception, Tiger was up against a self-generated wave of external forces that was pushing him to do something he'd always managed to avoid: con-front the truth about himself. But he remained deep in denial, still lying to Elin, to his mother, and to himself. With so much more lurking behind the crash, his instinct was to hide, to wall himself off from everyone: the police, the press, the public—even his family.

Steinberg had an impossible task. He cleared Tiger's calendar. The news conference he was supposed to hold in three days in advance of a tourna-ment to benefit Woods's foundation was canceled, as was his participation in the event. Citing injuries, Steinberg also announced that Woods would not take part in any more tournaments in 2009. Then he dealt with the police. When investigators returned to Tiger's home at the time Elin had suggested, Steinberg played lead blocker, meeting them in the driveway, introducing himself as Tiger's agent, and informing them that his client wasn't feeling well. He asked to reschedule the interview, indicating that Woods and his wife would talk the following day at three p.m.

But Woods, it seemed, was never going to talk to investigators. Stein-berg retained Mark NeJame, one of the most prominent criminal-defense attorneys in Orlando, to handle the police matter. After Steinberg put the officers off for one more day, NeJame notified the Florida Highway Patrol that there would be no interview with his client and Mrs. Woods. Instead, NeJame said he would provide a copy of Tiger's driver's license, along with his vehicle registration and proof of insurance.

On November 29, officers went to Tiger's home for the third time, where they met NeJame and obtained the motor vehicle documents. While there, they noticed security cameras in the driveway and asked Ne-Jame if they could obtain copies of the surveillance video from the night of the crash. Later that day, NeJame's office notified the police that Woods was unable to obtain any video recordings from the surveillance cameras. In other words, forget about it.

That afternoon, as the number of satellite trucks parked outside the gates of Isleworth was starting to look like a fleet, Tiger posted a statement on his website:

> Although I understand there is curiosity, the many false, un-founded, and malicious rumors that are currently circulating about my family and me are irresponsible.
>
> My wife, Elin, acted courageously when she saw I was hurt and in trouble. She was the first person to help me. Any other assertion is absolutely false.
>
> This incident has been stressful and very difficult for Elin, our family, and me. I appreciate all the concern and well wishes that we have received.
>
> But I would ask for some understanding that my family and I deserve some privacy no matter how intrusive some people can be.

It was hard to believe that it had been only thirty-six hours since the crash. For Woods, it surely seemed like weeks. His wife still didn't know the half of it, and there was nothing worse than the anxiety that the rest of his secrets would come out. For days, his infidelity had smoldered like a small brush fire, contained to the pages of tabloids and gossip websites—but the stonewalling of law-enforcement officials by Team Tiger was fanning the controversy, threatening to push it past the fire line and into the mainstream media. By Sunday, the *New York Times* ran the headline "What Is Woods Hiding?" Reuters and the Associated Press were digging too. Network news reporters were also on the case. The situation was incendiary.

Steinberg had cause for panic as well. The focus of the press coverage was shifting more ominously to Tiger's credibility, which was the bed-rock of his value to his corporate sponsors. Collectively, they were paying Woods more than $100 million annually to pitch their products. A headline in the *Times* suggesting Tiger was hiding something from law enforcement was a threat to his bottom line. CEOs were willing to ignore the gossip rags, but they all read the *Times*. If the story continued to expand, Tiger's sponsors were going to start getting restless.

The day after Woods issued the statement on his website, the local state's attorney's office denied a request from the police for an investigative subpoena. The subpoena was intended to seek the medical results of the tests performed on the blood drawn from Tiger while he was hospitalized, but investigators had insufficient information to support the request. So on December 1, just four days after his release from the hospital, Woods was issued a traffic citation for careless driving and ordered to pay a $164 fine. More than a hundred reporters and cameramen jammed into the department's Orlando headquarters for a press conference, at which the department announced that the case was closed. Afterward, Tiger's lawyer spoke to the media. "We are pleased with the outcome," NeJame said. "It's over."

But the trouble was really just beginning. All the maneuvering by Team Tiger during the aftermath of the crash was as effective as using a blanket to smother a forest fire—and if the *Enquirer* story about Tiger's affair with Rachel Uchitel was the match that set the blaze, the crash was ten gallons of gasoline thrown onto it. NeJame had spared Tiger from a police investigation, but there was no escaping the public relations flames. Less than twenty-four hours after the Florida Highway Patrol closed its case, the new issue of *Us Weekly* hit newsstands. The cover featured an idyllic picture of Tiger and Elin with the headline "Yes, He Cheated." The article detailed Tiger's lengthy affair with cocktail waitress Jaimee Grubbs, who reportedly received $150,000 for her story. Grubbs told the magazine that she'd had twenty sexual encounters with Woods. She also claimed she had more than three hundred racy text messages from him, along with a voice mail he had left her just prior to the crash. A link to the voice mail on *Us Weekly*'s website went viral, and NeJame's phone started ringing.

With a second mistress identified, Woods hurriedly posted an apology on his website. "I have let my family down, and I regret those transgressions with all of my heart," he said. "I have not been true to my values and the behavior my family deserves. . . . But for me, the virtue of privacy is one that must be protected in matters that are intimate and within one's own family."

Nike immediately made clear that it was standing by Woods, issuing a strong statement that he and his family had the company's full support. But Tiger's other corporate partners were more guarded. Gatorade said, "Our partnership continues," a tepid endorsement that left out the obvious words *for now*. A Gillette spokesman was even more circumspect, saying: "At this time, we are not making any changes to our existing marketing programs." With Tiger's nine-figure annual endorsement money hinging on the words *at this time*, Steinberg and Tiger's lawyers faced some daunting questions: How many more women were out there? And with tabloids willing to pay for stories, what was it going to take to persuade mistresses to remain quiet?

The one they feared most was Uchitel. In the aftermath of the crash, she had hired famed attorney Gloria Allred, who scheduled a press conference for her in Los Angeles. The last thing Woods needed was a tearful Uchitel talking to a sea of reporters. The press conference was promptly canceled when Tiger's lawyers reached out to Allred. Uchitel subsequently appeared on the cover of the *New York Post* under a bold headline: "TIGER'S GREEN FEES: Megabucks to Hush Up Rachel—& Millions to Keep Wife." Although terms were not disclosed, it would later be reported that Woods had paid $10 million to Uchitel in exchange for a comprehensive confidentiality agreement that prohibited her from saying anything whatsoever about him.

It seemed like every move Tiger made, even the ones intended to ensure confidentiality, was leaking out to the public. One day after Uchitel was in the news, Mindy Lawton went public about her sexual encounters with Woods, claiming that he had refused to wear a condom. This touched off a new round of criticism by pundits who accused Woods of putting Elin's health at risk.

Before the accident, Elin had been stunned by the discovery that her husband had cheated on her. But the subsequent litany of new revelations in the aftermath of the crash left her in a state of shock and disbelief. "I felt so stupid as more things were revealed," Elin said. "How could I not have known anything?"

The feelings of embarrassment were overwhelming. This wasn't one affair, nor was it two or three; Tiger was a serial philanderer. *How could I have been so deceived?*

Her sister and her mother traveled from Europe to stay with her and lend support to her and the children. They had to remind Elin that for the previous three years—during the height of Tiger's infidelity—she had been through two pregnancies and was going to school at night to complete her degree in psychology. The reality was that she had been consumed with raising children and furthering her education, and therefore rarely traveled with Tiger. Nor did she have any reason to suspect that anything was amiss in their marriage; she had always been relentlessly loyal to Tiger and their children, and she fully trusted that he was equally faithful to her and the kids. Shortly after her mother arrived from Sweden, Elin confided to her that she had always been inclined to believe the good in people, but she feared she had lost that. "The word *betrayal* isn't strong enough," Elin said. "I felt like my whole world had fallen apart."

By Friday, December 11, the number of mistresses who had come forward had reached fourteen. That afternoon, Tiger announced that he was stepping away from professional golf. "I am deeply aware of the disappointment and hurt that my infidelity has caused to so many people, most of all my wife and children," he said in yet another statement on his website. "I would like to ask everyone, including my fans, the good people at my foundation, business partners, the PGA Tour, and my fellow competitors, for their understanding. . . . After much soul-searching, I have decided to take an indefinite break from professional golf. I need to focus my attention on being a better husband, father, and person."

So much of Tiger's value to corporate America rested on his image as an elite athlete with a sparkling reputation. But that reputation had now been trashed. For twenty-one consecutive days, Tiger appeared on the cover of the *New York Post*, surpassing the previous record of twenty consecutive covers devoted to the 9/11 terrorist attacks. His scandal was regular fodder for late-night comedians. And one day after Tiger had announced that he was taking a hiatus from golf, *Saturday Night Live* lampooned him in a sketch called "Mistress #15." Tiger's sponsors didn't find any of this funny. Accenture became the first sponsor to cut all ties with Woods, who had been the face of the company since 2003. From the start, Accenture bet big on Woods, and now, at $7 million a year, it was among his largest sponsors. Its omnipresent "Go On. Be a Tiger" ads and their successors had helped transform the former Andersen Consulting into a corporate titan with 177,000 employees across fifty-two countries and a market cap of $26 billion. In 2008 alone, Accenture had spent $50 million in advertising, with Woods far and away the predominant image. "Tiger was a powerful device for our advertising, there's no doubt about it," company spokesman Fred Hawrysh told the *New York Times*.

Was. Now he was history.

"After careful consideration and analysis, the company has determined that he is no longer the right representative for our advertising," Accenture said. Within hours of ending its sponsorship, Accenture had replaced Woods's face on the company website with the image of an anonymous skier. A day later, all signs of his connection to the company had been scrubbed from the New York office, a purge that swiftly moved to marketing and promotions departments around the world.

Two days after Accenture dropped Woods, the *Times* published a front-page story revealing that federal authorities were looking into whether Tony Galea had dispensed performance-enhancing drugs to athletes, and that Galea had treated Woods at his home multiple times in 2009. Right after the Galea story landed, the *Wall Street Journal* reported a substantial accounting of the backroom deal among American Media, Team Tiger, and *Men's Fitness* to bury the Mindy Lawton story back in 2007.

Like a wildfire burning out of control, the scandal was spreading and consuming everything in its path. One by one, Tiger's sponsors separated from him. AT&T severed its relationship; Procter & Gamble scaled way back; and so did Swiss luxury watchmaker Tag Heuer. In the end, only Nike and EA Sports decided to stand by their man. The EA decision had gone all the way to chairman Larry Probst and the company's board of directors—EA's long-standing partnership with Woods balanced against the weight of damaged goods. The video-game maker had weathered a number of storms with Steinberg, mainly Tiger's refusal to share a cover with any other golfer. At one point, the marketing side had pitched a "Young Guns" concept to Steinberg as a way of introducing some rivals and juice into the game. Absolutely not, they were told—Tiger has to sit alone on the altar. Now EA sensed a business opportunity. "The pendulum swung back our way from a power standpoint, and I know we got some concessions that we'd been wanting," said Chip Lange, vice president of marketing for EA at the time. First and foremost was the ability to supplant Woods's top billing on products in favor of an emerging Rory McIlroy.

It had been more than three weeks since his release from the hospital, and Tiger still hadn't left his home. Aside from Steinberg, Woods had cut off contact with his friends and closest associates. O'Meara sent texts and emails but got no reply. Haney sent texts. Williams left messages. Barkley waited for a call. Under siege and too embarrassed to face friends, Tiger ignored them.

The combination of Tiger's silence and the reports in the media baffled his friends. In December, Haney ran into Barkley and asked him, man-to-man, if he'd had any idea that Tiger had been seeing so many women. "Charles," said Haney, "I want you to be one hundred percent honest with me."

"Hank," replied Barkley, "let me ask you a question. I spent ten to fifteen days a year with Tiger. You spent two hundred days a year with Tiger. If you didn't fucking know, how in the fuck am I going to know?"

Haney even reached out directly to Elin, hoping to assure her that he'd had no prior knowledge of Tiger's affairs. More important, though, he wanted to express his support. Friends like Haney and O'Meara and Williams adored and admired Elin, and it upset them that Tiger's behavior had caused her so much pain and public humiliation.

For her own reasons, Elin remained mum too. Naturally shy with a preference for privacy, she turned inward, determined not to share her feelings with anyone other than her family and a few close friends. The pain and sadness was beyond anything she had ever experienced. During the day, she tried to conceal her grief from the children, hoping to shield them from the turmoil in their home. But the stress of trying to hold everything together was taking a toll. She was losing weight. Insomnia heightened her anxiety. There was so much to sort out. Raising the children in an intact family, she believed, was ideal for their upbringing. But was that even possible anymore?

The one thing that was clear was that she needed space from Tiger while she figured things out. In mid-December she packed up her belongings and the children's things and moved into an unfurnished rental house about a mile from Isleworth. With Christmas days away, she managed to put up a tree. But this was not the way she had imagined spending Charlie's first Christmas—surrounded by boxes in a strange place with borrowed furniture. Staring blankly, she was sitting at a table when three-year-old Sam approached and put her little hand on her mother's cheek.

"Mommy, where is your boo-boo?" Sam asked in Swedish.

"Mommy's boo-boo is in her heart right now," Elin told her. "But it will be better."

"Can Sam kiss it and make it better? Or maybe popcorn will."

The departure of Elin and the children forced Tiger to do something he'd always managed to avoid—confront the truth about himself. He had a serious problem, and he needed professional help. Losing corporate sponsors was one thing; losing his family felt entirely different. In a few weeks' time, the carefully crafted image that had taken thirteen years and hundreds of millions of dollars to build and maintain had been obliterated by his addiction to sex. Without treatment to get the addiction under control, there was no chance of his marriage surviving. Desperate to hold on to Elin, he agreed to check himself into a facility right after Christmas.

Elin supported his decision. For the sake of the children, she also agreed to spend Christmas Day with him. Then she took the kids to Europe to get away from all the craziness and to spend some time with her family.

Once his family had left the country, Tiger felt the loneliness really set in. A few days earlier he had received a text message from Haney. It read: "I just wanted you to know that I will always be your friend, bud. I am sure you feel bad about everything that has happened. The fact is that everyone makes mistakes and you can't undo something that has already been done. . . . If I can ever help in any way, I am always available. I just wanted you to know that I am thinking of you. Hang in there."

After Christmas, Tiger finally called Haney. It was the first time in six weeks that he had spoken to him. "God, the media is pounding me," Tiger said. "They're such vultures."

It was a brief conversation, and Woods revealed nothing about his situation or his feelings. His voice was flat, his tone subdued. Without elaborating, he ended the call by telling Haney, "I'm going to be gone for a while."

Haney wasn't sure what that meant, but he decided not to ask.

CHAPTER TWENTY-NINE

THE RECKONING

The campus of Pine Grove Behavioral Health & Addiction Services is tucked between buildings that house everyday businesses on Broadway Drive in downtown Hattiesburg, Mississippi. Right after the holidays, Tiger walked through the doors and checked into the facility's sex addiction treatment program, known as Gratitude. He surrendered his cell phone and was shown to the place that would serve as his temporary home for the next forty-five days—a tiny, sparsely furnished cottage with a bed and a dresser. There was no television, no computer, no internet. The bathroom was shared. Curfew was ten p.m., followed by bed check at three a.m. Access to pills for pain and sleep was restricted. There were at least a dozen other patients on the grounds with Tiger, but none of them was undergoing such a drastic change in environment. For Tiger, a billionaire who had always lived by his own rules, this went way beyond confining.

The Gratitude program was the brainchild of Patrick Carnes, PhD, who first introduced the term *sexual addiction* into the medical lexicon in 1983 based on behavioral patterns he had witnessed among men in pain. Dr. Carnes wrote *Out of the Shadows: Understanding Sexual Addiction*, a pioneering work on the subject. "As children," Carnes said, "sex addicts grow up in environments where there is a classic 'elephant in the living room' syndrome: everyone pretends there is no problem, although there is a huge issue interfering with everyone's lives. In such a situation, children learn very early with everyone pretending there is no problem."

Tiger's treatment was based on Dr. Carnes's well-established research showing that most sex addicts come from families in which addiction is already present and members are "disengaged" from one another, where there is little sharing or intimacy. Children in these homes learn that mistakes are not acceptable and that it is not safe to trust others. Secrets, Carnes said, become more important than reality. In such situations, Carnes believed, sex addiction—like addiction to alcohol, compulsive gambling, nicotine, or drugs—is an illness of escape, the alternative to letting oneself feel hurt, betrayed, and, most of all, lonely.

Tiger's father was addicted to nicotine and alcohol, and he'd been a perpetual skirt chaser. Tiger himself was burdened with impossible expectations, and he had always had a hard time trusting anyone. He was compulsively secretive, and loneliness marked his life from his earliest days of elementary school through college and into his days on the PGA Tour.

Sex therapists look for addictions that are carried from parent to child: it could be drinking, it could be drugs, it could be living without boundaries. "That's the nature of dysfunctional homes," explained Bart Mandell, a Certified Sexual Addiction Therapist (CSAT-S) who was the first therapist in New York State to be trained and certified by Dr. Carnes. "Behavior is learned. Somewhere along the line it had to be downloaded on a hard drive from somewhere."

As part of his first week in treatment, Tiger underwent a comprehensive diagnostic assessment. It included a brief physical and medical history, followed by a psychiatric evaluation and psychological testing. Perhaps the most valuable diagnostic tool was something called the Sexual Dependency Inventory, or SDI, which gathered information on various sexual behaviors, fantasies, and interests. As part of that assessment, Woods had to put together a time line from childhood to the present day detailing every sexual experience and encounter he could remember, including what his family had taught him about sex and sexual development. Many of the four-hundred-plus questions on the survey were probing and precise: about frequency of masturbation, whether or not he had ever been caught, sexual secrets, desires.

The purpose of this highly invasive assessment was very deliberate. Over time, extensive research has yielded clues regarding the commonalities of sex addicts—none more prevalent than childhood trauma. "The family dynamic is critical," said Monica Meyer, PhD, a licensed psychologist and the clinical director of the Gentle Path program at The Meadows in Arizona who now works with Dr. Carnes. "On average, most sex addicts come from family systems that were rigid and disengaged. What that means is that they have strict rules in their family but not a lot of warmth or closeness. You can have a lot of structure in a family and a child can thrive as long as they know that structure comes from a warm place of love and caring. Without the warmth or closeness, the structure is just cold and . . . militant."

After Tiger completed all the tests and the results were evaluated, he was given a specific treatment-and-recovery program custom-made for him. At that point, most of the treatment was delivered in group therapy, an approach that was intended to make it near impossible for Tiger to hide his pain for long.

"Recognition of childhood trauma is often a big ah-ha moment in treatment," said Dr. Meyer. "Sometimes this may involve holding your parents accountable. The hero in the family struggles with this because the hero's job is to represent the family well, not expose the family's secrets. It can be difficult for someone in the role of family hero to tell the truth about their family and allow themselves to have emotion about their parents' behavior because they're so loyal."

Like so many powerful men, Woods was used to being in control. The idea of losing control, of being honest about his sexually addictive self, meant breaking down a brick wall. But in group therapy sessions with six to eight people in a room sharing stories of shame and addiction, Woods soon discovered there was little tolerance for "addict speak"—excuses and rationalizations for the narcissistic nature of his behavior.

By design, about twenty-eight days into treatment, many of the principles of the 12-step program at the heart of Alcoholics Anonymous were introduced. Only this time, the Big Book, as it's known in AA, was green, not blue. Still, the message was unmistakably the same: *Admit you are not in charge. You are powerless over your sexual urges and behavior. Your life has become unmanageable. You need to look to a higher power greater than yourself for help.*

"The First Step is about getting in touch with your vulnerability and the need for help," said Dr. Meyer. "If you're on top of the world, manipulating everything, deceiving all of these people, then admitting you're powerless over your sexual urges and behavior and that your life is unmanageable is crucial to being willing to accept help in recovery."

It was only now that Woods was ready for the penultimate week of his treatment—and a dramatic confrontation with Elin hidden under the benign title of "Family Week." From the moment he entered Gratitude, Tiger knew full disclosure would be part of his recovery. But now, in the accountability statement he would soon read to Elin, he was actually admitting he was a sex addict and identifying and listing every single betrayal he could remember—the illicit phone calls, texts, and gifts. The lies. It's not uncommon for men of power and means to list more than one hundred such sexual encounters on their statements. As part of holding himself accountable, Woods also wrote down how his addiction had impacted his life and that of his wife. All week he worked on his words with his therapist and practiced in front of his group. Was he being honest? Making eye contact? Showing legitimate regret?

Elin loved to write. As a child growing up in Sweden, she dreamed of being a journalist like her father. Back then, it would have been impossible to imagine that she would one day live through the most sensational infidelity scandal in contemporary American history, much less write about it. But while Tiger was in treatment, Elin wrote extensively in her journal. She had moved past the stage of shock and disbelief to anger and depression. She had been through hell, and putting her thoughts down on her laptop was a good way to vent her frustration. Words were insufficient to describe the depth of her pain, but the adversity had made her stronger. She drew on that strength as she traveled to Hattiesburg for the official start of Family Week, an integral part of Tiger's treatment at Pine Grove.

Upon arrival, Elin attended several lectures on sex addiction and addiction in general. Then came the hard part—Accountability Tuesday. After not having seen Tiger for a month, she sat with him as he spent a solid hour telling her the truth about his secret life. Therapists were also present, watching for signs of stress or explosive outbursts of anger and advising deep breaths, as a seemingly endless betrayal of vows was laid bare. The biggest reason Elin had fallen for Tiger was that they had so much fun together. Her wedding day was one of the happiest days of her life. That seemed so long ago. The sheer number of women and the variety of locations was too much to grasp: luxury hotel suites, empty parking lots, even *in their home*. After this brutal session, Elin left the room and joined other women who had just been through the same experience. They were all trying to process what they had heard.

Addicts often speak of a profound emotional release once all the lies are exposed. Not so for the wives or significant others; for them it's like being stabbed in the back and the heart at the same time. Therapists have a phrase for it: *posttraumatic stress*. (In 2011, Dr. Meyer said, Gratitude made adjustments to the manner in which full disclosures were processed based on new research demonstrating the need for additional support and preparation focused on the traumatized partner receiving this information.) At one point, Elin was asked to prepare an impact statement, explaining how Tiger's infidelity humiliated and devastated her, as well as how it ravaged their marriage.

For Woods, it was excruciating to hear. "I betrayed her," he said. "My dishonesty and selfishness caused her intense pain. My regret will last a lifetime."

One of Tiger's hardest days in treatment was February 8, 2010, when his son, Charlie, turned one. Alone in his room, Tiger was overcome by regret that he feared would stay with him for the rest of his life. "I missed my son's first birthday," he said. "I can't go back to where I was. I want to be part of my son's life and my daughter's life going forward."

He vowed that he would never miss another birthday.

Gratitude forced Tiger to take a hard look in the mirror and confront the fact that he had been living in a world of denial, repeatedly deceiving himself and the people he loved most. While he took affirmative steps to acknowledge the pain and heartache he'd caused his wife and family, the tabloids continued to dog him. His whereabouts and the nature of his treatment were supposed to be confidential, but halfway through his six-week stay at Pine Grove, RadarOnline.com, a sister publication of the *National Enquirer*, reported that he was getting treatment at the Mississippi facility. But that was only the beginning. The *Enquirer* quickly launched a full-scale operation in Hattiesburg. Using Google Earth, the tabloid scoped out an aerial view of Pine Grove, then used a whiteboard to diagram every entrance and exit before determining where the tabloid's photographers could legally shoot. "Basically," said a source, "it came down to one position." That position turned out to be straight across from the main gate. So twenty-four hours a day, seven days a week, the tabloid stationed one incredibly relentless photographer with a long lens on public property and waited. He spotted his target one day as the gate was opening, when Woods—dressed in a baseball cap and black hoodie—exited a building, drink in hand. The *Enquirer* snapped the photo. It would later accompany a report in the tabloid alleging that while enrolled in Gratitude, Woods confessed to cheating with as many as 120 different women.

The merciless pursuit by tabloid journalists was mortifying. Even in a treatment facility he couldn't escape. It was as if publicly shaming Tiger had become a blood sport.

On February 15, 2010, Woods completed his inpatient treatment and returned to Isleworth. Three nights later, he walked out of his home and crossed the street to the practice range. It had been almost three months since Tiger had touched a golf club. Using a sand wedge, he hit golf balls and watched them disappear into the darkness. Undoubtedly, he wished he could similarly disappear, just fade away into the night.

Being in treatment had been the worst experience he'd ever had, the hardest thing he'd ever done. It felt horrible, and after all that, he wasn't convinced that Elin was buying the idea of therapy anyway. She was so wounded that it was hard to know exactly what she thought, other than the fact that she wanted him to stop playing golf for two years. She had made that very clear.

But golf was the one thing in his life that gave Woods a sense of purpose. Inside the ropes was the only place where he really felt in his element. More than ever, he longed to get back there. However, in addition to Elin's opposition, Tiger faced an even bigger hurdle that stood between him and a return to the PGA Tour—a public apology. Steinberg had assembled a crisis-management team to help him navigate through the fallout from the scandal, especially the potential impact on fund-raising for his foundation. The team was telling Woods that before he could think about playing golf again, he had to publicly acknowledge his mistakes, apologize, and ask for forgiveness.

The head of Tiger's crisis-management team was Ari Fleischer, the former White House press secretary for President George W. Bush. After leaving the West Wing, Fleischer went on to form his own communications and media strategy firm, advising high-profile clients. One of his clients was baseball slugger Mark McGwire, who faced a steroids scandal. As part of McGwire's return to baseball as hitting coach for the St. Louis Cardinals, he finally admitted his use of performance-enhancing drugs throughout his career—although he claimed he'd done so for health reasons—including during the 1998 season when he blasted a then-record seventy home runs. In coming clean, McGwire had spoken from the heart. Fleischer had some tough advice for Woods: "If the things you say and believe are sincere," he said, "America is a very forgiving place. If you screw up, people are more than willing to forgive. But you have to be sincere."

Fleischer faced his biggest pushback from Steinberg. Schooled in West Wing politics, Fleischer knew control when he saw it. He found Steinberg to be one of the most controlling people he had ever met. Everything involving Tiger had to be authorized and packaged in a particular way. "I had to fight through that to get Tiger to apologize, which he ultimately did," Fleischer said, "but it was tough sledding."

As Woods stood alone in the dark hitting balls on the eve of his scheduled public apology, he was still extremely uncomfortable with the idea of standing up in front of the whole world to talk about being repeatedly unfaithful to his wife. It was humiliating enough to endure six weeks of sex addiction treatment. Plus, his mistakes had already been put on full display in every media format—print, television, radio, and, especially, the internet.

Nevertheless, the following morning, Woods appeared at PGA Tour headquarters in Ponte Vedra Beach, Florida. The mood was somber when Tiger entered a room where three rows of wooden chairs had been arranged in the shape of an arc. Writers from three news services—the Associated Press, Reuters, and Bloomberg News—sat among members of Tiger's corporation, Tiger's friends and business partners, Notah Begay III, and a representative from Nike. Kultida sat in the front row. Elin did not attend.

Wearing a dark sport coat, an open-collared shirt, and an unfamiliar expression of trepidation, Tiger stepped to a lectern and faced the music. "Good morning, and thank you for joining me," he began.

It was eleven a.m. on February 19, 2010, and for the next thirteen mesmerizing minutes, Americans everywhere stopped what they were doing. People in airports, bars, and hotel lobbies stared at television screens. In Times Square, crowds watched live on a giant screen. Twenty-two broadcast and cable networks broke into their regular programming with special reports on his speech. Roughly thirty million viewers tuned in on television, twelve million more on radio. Websites slowed or crashed. At a nearby resort hotel, some three hundred media members from as far away as Japan and Australia packed into two overflow ballrooms to watch on closed-circuit television.

"Many of you in this room are my friends," Woods said. "Many of you in this room know me. Many of you have cheered for me or you've worked with me or you've supported me. Now every one of you has good reason to be critical of me. I want to say to each of you, simply and directly, I am deeply sorry for my irresponsible and selfish behavior I engaged in. I had affairs. I was unfaithful. I cheated."

Reading from a prepared statement, Woods looked and sounded robotic. But he was doing something that took much more courage than all of his greatest shots combined.

"I knew my actions were wrong," he continued, "but I convinced myself that normal rules don't apply. I never thought about who I was hurting. Instead, I only thought about myself. . . . I thought I could I get away with whatever I wanted. I felt I had worked hard my entire life and deserved to enjoy the temptations around me. I felt I was entitled. . . . I was wrong. I was foolish. I don't get to play by different rules. . . .

"My failures have made me look at myself in a way I never wanted to before," he said. "It's hard to admit I needed help. But I do."

Looking on, Kultida repeatedly dabbed her eyes. From the time Tiger was a toddler, she had been there to cheer him on. She'd walked over a thousand miles and traversed the most storied golf courses in the world to watch her son achieve greatness. At the same time, she was a member of the parental team that had helped build the crushing weight her son had been hauling around his entire life. Everything imprinted on him, all the software in his head, was the stuff he had downloaded from his parents. Until rehab, there was no deprogrammer in his life.

Ideally, parents put an emphasis on helping a child become well-rounded, popular for the right reasons, friendly, respectful, appreciative. But Tiger got little of that. Instead, Earl and Kultida created an alternative universe for their son, one where they were in control and he was the little boy emperor who was going to be the best in the world at one thing. In the process, they took away some of Tiger's humanity and replaced it with skills. It was a parenting approach that worked for Earl and Kultida in spite of their dysfunctional marriage. Even after they split up after Tiger turned pro, they remained a controlling presence in his life. All Woods had to do was see his father or his mother on the golf course, and it was like the remote control was there. As a result, Tiger developed into the greatest golfer who ever lived, a virtually unbeatable machine—but at the same time, he didn't know how to love and be loved as a human being. The adoration he experienced was always tied to golf and performance.

But as Kultida cried while watching her son say to the world "I need help," she loved and adored him for his character. Nothing he had ever accomplished on a golf course brought her as much pride as the way he was fighting through all the adversity in his personal life. Everyone has secrets and weaknesses and makes mistakes, but it was rare to see someone of Tiger's stature endure such a public onslaught of criticism and humiliation for his indiscretions. His willingness to acknowledge his vulnerability and say that he needed help showed immense courage. Bill Clinton, Eliot Spitzer, and Kobe Bryant also faced infidelity scandals; none of them was as forthcoming as Woods.

"I am so proud to be his mother, period," Kultida said after Tiger's apology. "He didn't do anything illegal. He didn't kill anybody."

In his statement, Woods made veiled references to his time in treatment, set no timetable for his return to golf, spoke of "losing track" of what he had been taught about Buddhism by his mother, and made clear that his priority was repairing his marriage. He said he and Elin had begun to discuss the damage caused by his behavior but made no promises as to what the future might hold. "As she pointed out to me," said Woods, "my real apology to her will not come in the form of words. It will come from my behavior over time."

Woods also lashed out at the media, slamming reports that Elin had attacked him in the early-morning hours of November 27. "It angers me that people would fabricate a story like that," Tiger said. "She never hit me that night or any other night. There has never been an episode of domestic violence in our marriage. Ever."

As he wrapped up, Tiger appeared to speak directly to Elin. He didn't expect her to love him as unconditionally as his mother did. All he could hope for was a chance to make amends for the pain he had caused her. "There are many people in this room and there are many people at home who believed in me," he said. "Today, I want to ask for your help. I ask you to find room in your hearts to one day believe in me again."

"Good job."

Tiger looked at the two-word text message and felt grateful. It was from Hank Haney. After the press conference, when Woods was alone, he called Haney to say thanks. "I learned one thing for sure," he said. "When I play golf again, I'm going to play for myself. I'm not going to play for my dad, or my mom, or Mark Steinberg, or Steve Williams, or Nike, or my foundation, or you, or the fans. Only for myself."

Up to that moment, Woods had never acknowledged that he had played for his parents or anyone else. The familiar narrative from childhood through college and his amateur career had been that his parents had never pushed him to play golf, but Tiger always worked excessively hard to please his parents and earn their love. Golf was his vehicle. His victories were the only things that brought out hugs and tears from his father. Golf was the one thing that kept his parents together. But now with his own family in ruins and his personal reputation in tatters, Tiger was finally asking himself some difficult questions about his upbringing and his motivations.

"Anyway," he told Haney, "I have a lot of work to do."

He pivoted away from an uncomfortable subject to a familiar one— golf. He told Haney he had gone to the practice range the night before. "First swings since all this shit happened," he said.

"So how did you hit them?"

"Oh, they were solid."

His swing was one of the few precious things he had left. Elin had taken the children and moved out. Most of his corporate sponsors had abandoned him. He'd cut off contact with almost every one of his friends. What else was there to do but get back to work?

One week after his public apology, he called Haney again and told him he wanted him to come to Isleworth. He was ready to start rebuilding his game. "You can stay in the house as long as you want," Tiger told him. "It's just me."

CHAPTER THIRTY

CONSTANT STATE OF SHAME

The house no longer felt like a home. Elin and the children were living elsewhere. Butcher paper covered the windows, preventing anyone—especially tabloid photographers—from seeing inside. Self-help books littered the kitchen counter. It had been a month since Tiger had completed inpatient treatment for sex addiction. Now his days consisted of lying low. He was exercising on his own, hitting golf balls by himself, getting most of his meals from the clubhouse, and going to bed early. He was in marriage counseling and receiving outpatient treatment for sex addiction. He was also meditating on a daily basis in an attempt to reconnect with his Buddhist roots and get himself in the right mind-set to work through a very difficult reconciliation process with his wife. *I need to do these things*, he told himself.

For so many years, Tiger had always had IMG, Steinberg, and Nike to take care of everything for him. They told him where he needed to be and made sure he got there. In the time slots that weren't spoken for, Tiger was free to plan and indulge in his clandestine affairs with women. The scenario was both an addict's dream and a recipe for disaster. After years of lying to others and lying to himself, he emerged from treatment a changed man, more committed to being honest with himself and the people around him. But he faced a totally unfamiliar situation: for the first time in his life, his time was all his own. He had no tournaments to play in, no commercials to shoot, no appearances to make. His indefinite break from the game was intended to give him time and space to get a firm grip on his addiction, regain control of his personal life, and try to salvage his marriage.

Tiger was trying, but he was living in a constant state of shame. Although he wasn't particularly religious, he viewed his infidelity and the lies he had told to conceal it as "personal sins." In an attempt to seek redemption, he had confessed to those he loved most, chiefly his wife, along with his children and his mother. There was a certain liberating aspect to those grueling private conversations. Conversely, public confessions about personal sins were demoralizing. Even after making his mortifying public apology at Tour headquarters, Tiger was still dogged by journalists in search of skeletons from his past, none more determined than Mark Seal. In a two-part exposé in *Vanity Fair* titled "The Temptation of Tiger Woods," Seal not only named names and spared none of the sordid details but his reporting was also accompanied by risqué photographs of Tiger's paramours.

The worst part was that it seemed like Woods would never escape his past. Shortly after he got out of treatment, Tiger was confronted by one of his longtime neighbors, a twenty-two-year-old college student who was home on spring break. She was distraught and anxious. Approximately a year earlier, in the spring of 2009, Tiger had taken her to his office about a mile from his home and had sex with her. She was looking for closure.

Woods had known the young woman since she was fourteen. Her family lived in Isleworth, and her father, a successful Orlando businessman, had long admired Tiger. The one-time sexual encounter changed all that, causing heartache within the family, which fulminated anger and disdain toward Tiger. Initially enamored by the attention from the world's most famous athlete, the twenty-one-year-old nonetheless felt guilty immediately after the encounter. The crib in Tiger's office was a painful reminder that Elin had just had a baby. So when Tiger reportedly sent his young neighbor racy texts in hopes of hooking up again, she ignored him. Then, when reports surfaced of Tiger's multiple affairs with other women, the woman felt used. "I just wanted to dig a big hole, crawl in, and die," she reportedly told a friend.

She was more direct with Tiger. "I feel extremely violated by what you did to me," she told him.

Tiger said he was sorry.

But he suddenly faced a much harder situation—what, if anything, should he say about the matter to Elin? During treatment, Tiger had admitted to an overwhelming number of affairs with women he'd met around the world, but he hadn't told Elin about the girl next door. It was painful enough—for him and for his wife—to talk about affairs that involved porn stars, lingerie models, party girls, high-priced escorts, and pancake-house waitresses, but they both recognized that it was a vital step on the long and tortured path to reconciliation.

Tiger realized that his prospects of remaining married to Elin were tenuous at best. The only factor that weighed in his favor was Elin's desire to raise the children in an intact family. The children remained her priority, and her desire to do what was best for them was the driving force behind her effort to reconcile with Tiger. Any mention of his dalliance with a girl in the neighborhood would surely push Elin past the point of no return.

From Tiger's perspective, after everything else he had dumped on Elin, telling her about the neighborhood girl seemed like pouring salt on an open wound. His wife's heart was already broken. What good would be served by adding to her misery?

Whether motivated by selfish reasons, noble ones, or some combination of the two, Woods decided not to say anything to Elin. It was a decision fraught with danger and trepidation.

For his entire career, Tiger had remained aloof on the PGA Tour, an almost mystical presence, distancing himself from players, fans, and the golf press. The time off from the sport changed his perspective and helped him realize how much he missed what he had always taken for granted. He also missed the competition. In mid-February 2010, he started hitting balls again. Then, in early March, he resumed working on his game with Hank Haney. Being on the range with Haney felt like old times. At that point it was an easy decision: forget the hiatus. He was returning to the PGA Tour.

On March 16, 2010, Tiger issued a statement announcing that he was playing in the Masters the following month. "The Masters is where I won my first major, and I view this tournament with great respect," he said. "After a long and necessary time away from the game, I feel like I'm ready to start my season at Augusta."

Hank Haney was surprised by the announcement and immediately thought Tiger was coming back way too soon. They had practiced together for only a week prior to Woods's deciding to play in the Masters.

Tiger was still spraying the ball all over the place. His game was a long way from being tournament-ready. Besides being rusty, he looked lost and helpless on the golf course, like a man weighted down with the worries of the world.

In Haney's mind, Tiger was setting himself up for failure. Augusta, after all, was the ultimate stage, and the spotlight on him would be brighter than ever. Sean McManus, the president of CBS News and CBS Sports, had predicted that Tiger's return to professional golf after the scandal would be the single biggest media event in the past ten to fifteen years, outside of Barack Obama's inauguration.

But Tiger's mind was made up. Nobody understood what it was like to be in his shoes. His life was in ruins, his messy past complicating and dictating his future. The one surefire place where he could establish some normalcy and do something that he felt good about was inside the ropes, even at the risk of alienating Elin, who wanted him to take a much longer hiatus from the game. There, over the course of four days and seventy-two holes, the rules would be different. In golf, the past is the last hole, the present is the current shot you face, and the future is the next one after that. Eager to get back to his comfort zone, Tiger summoned Steve Williams to Isleworth. It was time to get ready to go to Augusta.

When Williams arrived at Tiger's home on April 3, he had a lot to get off his chest. After the scandal broke, Williams had repeatedly asked Team Tiger to release a statement clearing him of any involvement. Instead he got the silent treatment. Then one mistress, cashing in on her five minutes of fame, insisted she had met both Williams and Tiger in Las Vegas, creating the inference that Williams had known about Tiger's adultery and covered it up. This unsubstantiated rumor spun itself into news in Williams's native New Zealand and soon splashed around the world. In rehab, Woods had finally communicated with Williams in the form of an email, apologizing for his actions. Later, he called Williams's wife, Kirsty, in an effort to smooth things over at home, but it was too little, too late. Kirsty had long considered Elin one of her best friends, and she wasn't persuaded by Tiger's words. In the meantime, doubts lingered about how much Steve knew. The bottom line was that Tiger's infidelity had damaged Williams's reputation in New Zealand and strained his marriage.

Tiger was well aware that he had disappointed Williams. He also knew that it was on him to clear the air with his longtime caddie. But when

Williams entered his home, Tiger was preoccupied. After a less than enthusiastic greeting, Tiger said they would talk later. In the meantime, he insisted he had to run out.

This didn't sit well with Williams. He had a long list of grievances that he wanted to air, and he'd been assured by Steinberg that Tiger would have a face-to-face conversation with him once he got to his house. Frustrated, Williams was in a foul mood hours later when he and Haney joined Tiger for a practice round at Isleworth. "I don't even know why we're going to Augusta," Williams told Haney. "He can't make the cut hitting it like this. It's horrible."

Haney didn't disagree. But he also realized that Tiger's mind was made up. So on the eighteenth fairway, he pleaded with Tiger to at least modify his swing path, sacrificing some distance off the tee in hopes of minimizing the degree to which his shots were going off-line. "Tiger," he told him, "you have no chance the way you're swinging."

Tiger finally made peace with Williams the next day on the way to the airport. Behind the wheel and wearing a pair of wraparound shades, Tiger never took his eyes off the road as Williams vented, telling Woods that his actions had put him and his family in a difficult position and that he was going to have to earn back his respect. It was pretty clear that Williams didn't feel appreciated after all his years of loyalty and service. Going forward, Williams said he wanted three things from Tiger: some verbal communication of appreciation, a pay raise, and an apology.

The request for a salary increase bugged Woods, but he considered Williams a great friend, someone who had remained loyal to him through a very rough patch. Plus, he needed Steve back on the bag, and he didn't want any more friction between them. While Tiger mended fences with Williams, he had more pressing matters to worry about. The *National Enquirer* had found out about his affair with the college student at Isleworth. One of the girl's friends had talked to the tabloid, which was planning to break the story during the Masters. At the same time, Woods had to gear up for his first press conference since the crash. He was scheduled to take questions from the press at Augusta, and he was dreading it. Writers from around the world would be in attendance, and they weren't coming to ask him about golf.

Basketball fans had embraced Kobe Bryant when he led the Lakers to an NBA championship after being accused of rape. Football fans had welcomed back Michael Vick when he turned in the best season of his career after serving twenty-one months in federal prison for his role in a dog-fighting ring. Mark Steinberg believed that golf fans would forgive and forget Tiger's indiscretions too. The key, he told Tiger, was to perform well.

The discussion about Bryant and Vick took place inside Tiger's rental home in Augusta, where Woods huddled with Steinberg to prepare for his press conference. Tiger fielded hypothetical questions and worked on his responses. Then, at two p.m. on the Monday before the start of the Masters, he entered the jam-packed media center at Augusta National and took a seat beside Craig Heatley, the chairman of the Masters Media Committee.

"Ladies and gentlemen, good afternoon, and a very warm welcome to you all," Heatley began. "I would also like to welcome Tiger Woods, our four-time Masters champion. Tiger, we are delighted to have you here with us."

Going in, Tiger didn't know what to expect; but as he looked around, he suddenly felt at home. He knew the room like the back of his hand. So many of the faces were familiar. In therapy he had learned a new phrase: "Are you open?" Tiger faced the throng of reporters and decided to be more open than he'd ever been with them.

"What I've done over the past years has been just terrible to my family," Tiger said. "And the fact that I won golf tournaments I think is irrelevant. It's the pain and the damage that I've caused, you know, my wife, my mom, my wife's family. My kids, going forward, are going to have to . . . I'm going to have to explain all of this to them."

This was better theater than golf or anything else on television in the middle of the day on a Monday. The networks cut into their regularly scheduled programs to carry the press conference live. It also aired live on the Fox News Channel, CNN, ESPN, and a variety of other cable stations and was streamed live around the world. With no prepared statement or notes, Tiger spoke from the heart, then took a barrage of questions about sensitive personal matters that would have been unthinkable to bring up before the scandal—performance-enhancing drugs; his relationship with the recently arrested Dr. Anthony Galea; Vicodin; Ambien; the state of his marriage; the police report detailing his car crash; his affairs; and the nature of his inpatient treatment.

Woods refused to say the words "sex addiction," and he politely declined to answer one question: What was he in treatment for?

"That's personal, thank you," he said. But he dealt with everything else head-on, stating the following:

- He had never used performance-enhancing drugs, and he had only received PRP treatment from Dr. Galea.
- He had been contacted by federal authorities who were conducting a criminal investigation into Galea, and he was cooperating fully.
- He used Vicodin and Ambien, but he had not undergone treatment for addiction to either one.
- Rehab was brutal; his treatment was ongoing; Elin would not be attending the Masters; and he was doing everything possible to hold on to his family.

"What's been the most difficult thing for you to deal with?" a reporter asked toward the end.

"Having to look at myself in a light that I never wanted to look at myself in," Tiger said. He pledged to tone down his angry outbursts when things didn't go his way on the course, and to show more appreciation to fans. "I need to be a better man," he said.

This was Tiger 2.0: uncharacteristically forthcoming, contrite, remorseful. The greatest athlete in the world had never looked so vulnerable, so human. Steinberg, Haney, and Williams couldn't help wondering how all this would affect Tiger's play. Intimidation—the steely glare, the cold demeanor, the machine-like approach—had always been one of his best weapons. Would the reformed Tiger still have his competitive edge?

Woods was more worried about how he would be received by the fans. Would they give him dirty looks? Heckle him? Or just gawk at him? Large crowds gathered to watch him play a practice round, following him from hole to hole, cheering him on and offering words of encouragement. The warm reception seemed to influence his play. Haney saw a noticeable uptick in the quality of Tiger's swing and his focus. Even Williams felt the positive energy. The fans were clearly behind Tiger. For the first time in a long time, he was smiling. Augusta felt like a refuge.

Or so it seemed.

After serving as the president and CEO of the Atlanta Committee for the 1996 Olympic Games, Billy Payne was named chairman of Augusta National Golf Club in 2006. One of his duties was to deliver an annual address on the eve of the Masters. It was a long-standing tradition, affording the head of America's most prestigious golf club to weigh in on the state of the game. But when Payne faced the golf writers on the day before the start of the 2010 Masters, he went off script and publicly scolded Tiger.

"He forgot in the process to remember that with fame and fortune comes responsibility, not invisibility," Payne said. "It is not simply the degree of his conduct that is so egregious here; it's the fact that he disappointed all of us and, more important, our kids and our grandkids. Our hero did not live up to the expectations of the role model we saw for our children."

It was one thing for pundits, newspaper columnists, and talk-show hosts to pontificate about Tiger's misdeeds; that sort of thing happened so routinely that Tiger was practically numb to it. But to have the head of Augusta publicly chastise the number one player in the world on the eve of the most prestigious tournament on the PGA Tour was stunning. Payne spoke for the entire membership at Augusta, and he didn't hesitate to lecture Woods about his future.

"Is there a way forward?" he said. "I hope yes. I think yes. But certainly his future will never again be measured only by his performance against par, but measured by the sincerity of his efforts to change. I hope now he realizes that every kid he passes on the course wants his swing but would settle for his smile."

Payne had never previously commented on a golfer's behavior off the course, nor had his predecessor. It simply wasn't done.

Normally, no one outside of the golf press paid much attention to the chairman's state of the union address. But word of Payne's rebuke of Tiger instantly became a national story. Even the foreign press covered it.

Tiger heard about Payne's comments while he was on the course. Asked what he thought of Payne's insistence that he had disappointed everyone, Tiger took it in stride. "I disappointed myself," he said, leaving it at that.

It hurt to hear that he had let children down and failed to live up to expectations. Tiger didn't exactly need to be reminded. But even in private, he didn't feel like talking about it.

"Man, how about Billy Payne?" Haney said on the car ride back to the house.

"Yeah," Tiger said.

That same evening, the following headline appeared on the *National Enquirer's* website: "Tiger Woods Sex Romp with Neighbor's Young Daughter." "Shockingly," the website teased, "Tiger's sexual advances started in his car, only yards from where the golfer's devoted wife, Elin, was home, ending with a two-hour sex session on the couch in Tiger's private office. To see exclusive pictures of Tiger's young beauty, run—don't walk—to get the new *Enquirer* before it sells out! Plus! Shocking XXX details of his tawdry texts you won't find anywhere else!"

Like wildfire, the story went viral. *Deadspin* and the *Huffington Post* soon posted photos of Tiger's neighbor, and the *Daily News* and *New York Post* ran scandalous headlines: "Tiger Bedded Neighbor's 21-Year-Old Daughter." For Elin, this appeared to be the tipping point. Around the time that news of Tiger's affair with the neighbor became public, she came to the conclusion that ending the marriage was better for the children than staying together without trust or love. She informed Tiger in no uncertain terms that their union was over. She wanted a divorce.

Earl Woods used to tell his son that no man he ever faced would be mentally stronger than he was. He made sure of it, using some techniques that were not designed for a boy. Insulting him—"Motherfucker." Breaking him down—"You little piece of shit." Pushing him to the edge—"Little nigger." In an attempt to toughen up his son, Earl treated him like a soldier in boot camp. But he was right about the end result: no golfer in the history of the PGA Tour matched the sheer willpower of Tiger Woods. Never was that more apparent than at the start of the opening round of the Masters on April 8.

A sea of humanity jammed the area surrounding the first tee. Patrons packed the grounds all the way back to the clubhouse. Inside, Tiger waited. The crowds had been nice to him in the practice rounds, but what would they think of him now? Suddenly, the door opened and Tiger emerged. Anxious but determined, he looked straight ahead and walked through a human tunnel of people who were close enough to touch him. The sound of clapping and cheers rippled from the clubhouse to the tee and down the fairway. "Tiger!" "Welcome back!" "We're with you."

Instead of blocking out the crowd as he'd done his whole career, he smiled widely and nodded as he worked to keep his emotions in check. After months of being beaten up and beating himself up, he was at a place where he was accepted, among people who loved him for his talent. Then the crowd went dead silent as Tiger stood over his ball, preparing to take his first competitive swing in 144 days. Everyone—the writers, the other golfers, the television executives at CBS and the other networks that broadcast golf, Phil Knight and the folks at Nike, the millions watching from home, and the thousands of fans hovering around him—was wondering the same thing: After such a precipitous fall from grace, can Tiger Woods still generate the magic?

The silence was broken by the whipping sound of his driver and the sonic boom of his clubhead colliding with the ball. His ball soared straight and true, finally dropping down in the center of the fairway. It was a perfect shot that launched a cascade of cheers. He was back.

Pleased, Tiger handed his club to Williams, and the two of them started down the fairway, propelled by the applause of the gallery. Overhead, a low-flying plane pulled a banner that read TIGER: DID YOU MEAN BOO-TYISM? Even Buddhism, apparently, was fair game for mocking. But Woods could take the heat—he always could—as long as he was competing. As he hammered tee shots and sank putts through his opening round, Nike aired a jarring new commercial that featured Tiger somberly staring into the camera as if facing his father. Like a voice from beyond the grave, Earl speaks to him: "Tiger, I am more prone to be more inquisitive . . . to promote discussion. I want to find out what your thinking was. I want to find out what your feelings are. And did you learn anything?" The camera zoomed in on Tiger's eyes as the screen faded to black and the Nike swoosh appeared.

For a man who craved privacy, Woods's sins were on full display, and his road to redemption would be trudged under the weight of public spectacle. "My regret will last a lifetime," Tiger later wrote.

Yet amid all the swirl, Tiger shot a scintillating 68 on the first day, the lowest he had ever shot in the opening round of the Masters. He followed that up with a 70 in round two, leaving him just two shots behind the leader heading into the weekend. Through the first two rounds he had smiled more at fans, hugged fellow golfers, and slapped the hand of his caddie more than in his previous sixteen Masters tournaments combined.

Williams welcomed Tiger's sunny disposition, but as he walked with Woods and Steinberg from the media center after the second round, he listened as Steinberg told Tiger that if he wanted to win, he had to "stop being a nice guy" and go back to the old Tiger. "I couldn't believe my ears," Williams later recalled. "After all that Tiger had been through, and the fact that he had made a public commitment to be a less snarling and aggressive Tiger . . . his main advisor was telling him the opposite."

It was a turning point for Williams. He had been looking at the Masters as a proving ground for Woods, a chance to demonstrate that he could be more tolerant, more appreciative, and less hostile. Suddenly, it felt like Tiger was being encouraged to scrap that. "Right then," Williams later wrote, "something inside me changed. A brick in the foundation of my relationship with Tiger had been pried loose."

Twenty-four hours later, Haney had an eerie premonition: *This will be the last time I ever work for Tiger Woods.* The feeling came after Woods shot 70 again on Saturday, leaving him just three shots behind Phil Mickelson and four shots behind the leader, Lee Westwood. Astonishingly, after everything that had happened, with one round to go, Tiger was well within striking distance. He was right near the top of the leaderboard and in position to win his fifth Masters, yet he was fuming as he made his way to the practice range afterward.

"I hit it like shit," he complained.

On the contrary, Tiger had hit fifteen of eighteen greens on Saturday. He was playing superbly. But when Haney tried to boost him up, Tiger lashed out. The bottom line was that he had lost ground to Mickelson and Westwood, and Tiger blamed his predicament on his swing, which came across as him being pissed at Haney.

The next day, Tiger showed up for the final round in a foul mood. His marriage was imploding, the tabloids and late-night comedians were pillorying him again, and fucking Mickelson was playing like he didn't have a care in the world.

During warm-ups, Haney watched in silence as Tiger hit one low shot after another. He looked defeated. Finally, Haney stepped in. "You just have to get the ball up in the air," Haney told him. It was a familiar phrase between them, one that Haney had used for years whenever he wanted Tiger to open his clubface to increase the trajectory upon impact. Woods had always responded affirmatively to the instruction. But this time he looked at Haney and said, "What do you mean by that?" Then he resumed hitting low. It was as if he wasn't even trying.

In that instant, something snapped inside Haney. The job no longer seemed worth it. Emotionally, he felt exhausted. Steinberg had told him more than once that Tiger considered Hank one of his best friends, but it didn't feel that way. Even after treatment, Woods didn't seem capable of reciprocating the graciousness that Haney was extending to him. As Tiger hit some final putts and started toward the first tee, Haney stepped to him.

"You know what we talked about. Do that, and you'll be all right."

Tiger nodded.

"Good luck," Haney said.

That would be the last thing Tiger ever heard from Haney on a golf course as his coach.

Tiger eagled two holes during the final round, but Mickelson parred his first seven holes and pulled away from the field to win his third Masters. Tiger finished five shots back, tied for fourth. "Good job!" Williams told him as they exited the eighteenth green to the cheers of the gallery. "Good job!"

It was more than a good job—only three players in the world had played better. None of them was trying to concentrate while the world crashed down around him. Williams was truly impressed. But Tiger had his life to get back to. He was in no mood to talk to anyone. He wasn't going to congratulate Phil. He wasn't going to thank people. He didn't have anything to say to Haney. Elin wasn't around.

Steinberg's phone rang. It was Haney. "Mark, I'm finished," he told him. "I've had enough."

"Hank, you can't do this," Steinberg said. "You can't do this to him. This is the toughest time of his life."

Haney just listened.

"You understand him," Steinberg pleaded. "He needs you. Whatever you do, don't abandon him now."

SEPARATION

Tiger had spent six years with Hank Haney. During that period, from March 2004 to April 2010, he played in ninety-three PGA tournaments and won thirty-one times, including six majors. It was a remarkable run, during which Tiger won 33 percent of the time. By comparison, in a little over seven years under Butch Harmon, Tiger had won nearly 27 percent of the time, taking 34 of the 127 PGA tournaments he entered, including eight majors. Woods and Harmon had spent more years together, resulting in more majors, but Woods and Haney had had a success rate that was unparalleled in the annals of golf. During that period, Tiger had come to trust Haney more than almost anyone else in his life outside of his family and Mark Steinberg. But the meltdown of his marriage and the disintegration of his reputation had a lot of unintended collateral damage. Haney was among the casualties.

Shortly after the 2010 Masters and his conversation with Steinberg, Haney reluctantly agreed to try to stick it out with Woods. Taking Steinberg's plea to heart, Haney took the time to write a candid, five-page email to Tiger, proposing a plan for going forward. He copied Steinberg on the email. Given that Haney had just threatened to quit, he figured his long missive would draw a thoughtful response from Tiger. It didn't. Tiger never responded.

After the Masters, Woods had bigger priorities than Haney's feelings. He was dealing with divorce lawyers, financial advisors, and questions about custody. On top of everything else, another woman had come forward. This one was claiming that Tiger was the father of her child. Needless to say, working his way through Haney's five-page email wasn't on top of Tiger's to-do list. It wasn't until two weeks later, on the eve of the Quail Hollow Championship in Charlotte, that Tiger finally got around to calling Haney. He never mentioned the email, launching instead into the allegations about him being the father of another woman's child. Insisting her time line was off, Tiger said the claim couldn't be true.

As usual, the conversation was all about Woods and never got around to what was on Haney's mind. This had been the case throughout their relationship, but in this instance it irritated Haney more than ever. At a time when Haney really needed Tiger to recognize his concerns about their partnership, he didn't.

Without Haney around, Tiger played poorly in Charlotte, shooting a 79 on Friday, his highest score on the Tour since 2002. He ended up missing the cut. A week later, Woods withdrew in the final round of The Players Championship, complaining of neck pain. Once again, Haney wasn't there, and once again, Tiger was off. "Hey, Tiger!" a young kid yelled as Woods headed toward the clubhouse. "Say so long to that number-one ranking. Kiss it good-bye!"

Whatever magic Tiger had mustered for the Masters had quickly vanished. A month into his comeback, his swing was off, and he was distracted, impatient, and unable to make the clutch shots and critical putts that had long defined his game. Suddenly, he no longer looked like a superhero on the golf course. He looked beatable. Other players sensed it, and so did the fans.

Meanwhile, he left his swing coach hanging. No dialogue. No calls. Nothing.

Fed up, Haney was determined not to be pushed aside the way Butch Harmon had been years earlier. *You're not blowing me off,* he thought. *Fuck you!*

On the morning after Tiger pulled out of The Players Championship, Haney wrote a statement explaining why he was quitting as Tiger's coach. He sent it to Jim Gray at Golf Channel and asked him to hold it for a few hours. Then he texted Tiger, saying they needed to talk. "I can't talk today," Tiger texted back. "I'm with my kids."

Despite the fact that he and Elin were proceeding toward a divorce, Tiger was spending as much time with his children as possible. In one respect, he was making up for lost time; but on a deeper level, the guilt he felt when he had missed Charlie's birthday during treatment served as a constant reminder that he no longer wanted to put anything—not even his career—ahead of his children.

Oblivious to the fact that Haney was quitting, Tiger was surprised when he got a second text from him. "If anybody should understand the value of friends at this point in their life, it should be you," Haney wrote. "I feel like I've been a great friend to you. I don't think I've gotten that in return."

Haney had always been ultrasensitive to criticism about Tiger's swing. In this instance, Woods thought Haney was once again overreacting to things that commentators had said about his game during the last tournament. He had no sense that Haney's frustration went much deeper than that. "Maybe it's time that we just take a little break," Tiger texted.

Without consulting his agent or his wife or anyone else, Haney replied with a message that was intended to cut the cord for good. "Tiger, I appreciate everything you did for me, the incredible opportunity I had to work with you," he said. "I can't tell you how grateful I am for the opportunity, but it's time for you to find another coach."

Still, Tiger wasn't hearing him. "Thanks, Hank," Tiger texted. "But we're still going to work together."

"No we're not," Haney said. "It's finished. Done. Over. I'm no longer your coach."

Seconds later, Tiger texted: "We'll talk in the morning."

That afternoon, Woods did a telephone press conference in which he reiterated that Haney was still his coach and that they had a lot of work to do. On the verge of losing his family and isolated from so many of his friends, Tiger seemed unable to come to grips with the fact that Haney was leaving him too. But by the end of the day, he had to face reality when Golf Channel read Haney's statement on the air: "I have informed Tiger Woods this evening that I will no longer be his coach," he said. "Just so there is no confusion, I would like to make clear that this is my decision."

What followed was a classic illustration of the adage that breaking up is hard to do. First Steinberg called Haney and told him that Tiger would be releasing his own statement that claimed their parting was a "joint decision." Angry, Haney called the move "bullshit" and threatened to go public and call Tiger's statement a lie if he issued it. Haney's stance prompted Steinberg to modify Tiger's statement to say "Hank Haney and I have agreed that he will no longer be my coach." Right after it was issued,

Tiger called Haney and thanked him for being a great coach and a great friend. "You know," Tiger told him, "we're still going to work together."

Haney was baffled. "Tiger, if you ever want me to watch you or help you with an opinion, as a friend I'll be happy to do it. But we're not going to work together. I'm never going to be your coach again."

"We're still going to work together," Tiger said.

Haney chuckled. "No, we're not," he replied.

Days later, Haney was interviewed on Golf Channel by Jim Gray, who asked him if he had ever known of Tiger taking performance-enhancing drugs. Haney said he believed that Tiger never took PEDs. "The only thing I knew about was his issue with sex addiction," Haney said.

Tiger wasn't pleased. Right after the interview, he shot Haney a text: "Thanks for telling everyone that I was in sex-addiction treatment."

Steinberg was more outspoken. Fuming, he telephoned Haney. "How could you do that?" he yelled. "How could you say that? How can he raise any money? This will kill his foundation."

"I didn't mean to hurt him or cause him any problems. I apologize if I did," Haney said.

"You better not be doing any more interviews," Steinberg threatened.

"Mark, you don't control me anymore. I'm going to talk to who I want to talk to."

For nearly fifteen years, Tiger relied on Peter Mott and his boutique law firm in Southport, Connecticut, to oversee his complex estate planning and provide legal advice on his personal and business empire. There was scarcely an investment decision or property acquisition or significant financial transaction that Tiger executed without the advice of Mott and his partners. One of the best decisions Tiger ever made was to listen to John Merchant back in 1996 when he advised him to retain Mott's firm. Now it fell to Mott to guide Tiger through the most important transaction of his life: his divorce from Elin.

By 2010, Tiger had earned well over $1 billion through golf and endorsement deals. His net worth was estimated to be in the range of $750 million. He owned homes and real estate in different parts of the world, some of which were jointly owned by Elin, along with other personal property. Since Florida law required an equitable division of property or assets, there was a lot to sort out.

But Tiger had no interest in a contested divorce. Both he and Elin were unified in their desire to do what was best for the children, and that started with an amicable separation. So on a hot summer day, Woods and his lawyers met with Elin and her lawyers to negotiate the terms governing the custody of the children. Under the circumstances, it was a remarkably cordial session. Tiger made it clear that he wanted to meet the needs of Elin and the kids.

After the session, he and Elin signed a Marital Settlement Agreement over the Fourth of July weekend. It included a parenting plan spelling out the shared custody of the children, as well as a stipulation entitling Elin to over $100 million. The plan was for Tiger to move into the nine-thousand-square-foot home that he and Elin had purchased on Jupiter Island, Florida, for $40 million back in 2006. At the time of purchase, they had planned to eventually move the family from Isleworth to Jupiter, but now Elin and the children would look for a home of their own in nearby North Palm Beach.

For Tiger, the divorce was devastating. The scope of what he had squandered was staggering. When he met Elin, her physical beauty was so breathtaking that people had trouble seeing past it. Fluent in two languages and exceptionally smart, she had career aspirations. But at twenty-one, she put her ambitions aside, moved to the United States, and vowed to spend the rest of her life with Woods, for better or for worse. She channeled all her talents and energy into raising their children, and all the while, she never had eyes for anyone but Tiger—until Tiger broke her heart. Now, the most beautiful woman he'd ever laid eyes on was no longer Mrs. Woods. When the court in Bay County, Florida, granted the Final Judgment of Dissolution of Marriage on August 23, 2010, Elin dropped her married name and had her maiden name restored: Elin Maria Pernilla Nordegren.

For Elin, the divorce was liberating. In the weeks leading up to it, the stress was so bad that her hair started falling out, but she emerged from the ordeal stronger than ever. Although the family she had so badly wanted for her children was a thing of the past, she wasn't feeling sorry for herself. She was free from the stifling demands of the PGA Tour. She no longer had to live with the oppressive corporate structure that had coalesced around her husband over the years. And the hidden burdens of being Tiger's wife had been lifted. At thirty, she was a single mother with dreams of her own. With her newfound freedom, she decided that the first thing she was going to do was set the record straight in terms of what she'd been through.

In the entire time that Elin had been with Tiger—roughly three years as his girlfriend and almost six years as his wife—she had never granted an interview. The idea to do one after the divorce was something she had gotten from her lead attorney, Richard Cullen. In an arrangement brokered by Cullen and the general counsel for AOL–Time Warner, Elin spent nineteen hours over the course of numerous days talking to *People* magazine feature writer Sandra Sobieraj Westfall. The exclusive interviews took place at Elin's home and led to a cover story titled "My Own Story." In it, Elin took the high ground, saying nothing negative about her ex-husband but being open and honest about the pain and disappointment.

"Forgiveness takes time," she said. "It's the last step of the grieving process. I am going to be completely honest and tell you that I am working on it. I know I will have to come to forgiveness and acceptance of what has happened for me to go on and be happy in the future. And I know I will get there eventually."

The World Golf Rankings are updated weekly, but between June 12, 2005, and October 30, 2010, the number one ranking never changed. Tiger occupied that spot for an unprecedented 281 consecutive weeks. That streak came to an end on October 31, 2010, when he slipped to number two, surpassed by Lee Westwood. By that point, Tiger hadn't won a PGA Tour event in well over a year, and the warm reception he had received from fans and fellow golfers six months earlier at Augusta seemed like ancient history. Fans were heckling him. Rivals no longer feared him. He had lost his wife. He had lost his coach. He had lost his swing. And he was about to lose his caddie.

Not long after his split with Haney, Tiger asked Canadian-born Sean Foley to be his new swing coach. A certified golf geek, Foley was at the forefront of a new wave of instructors who embraced an emerging technology called TrackMan, a Doppler radar–like device that measures the collision of the ball and the club and tells you every single parameter from the path of the club to the trajectory and spin of the ball. One day early on, as Foley used biomechanical terms like "fascial chains" and "kinesthetic submodalities" to explain his philosophy to Tiger, Steve Williams couldn't help thinking how bizarre everything he was saying sounded. For Williams, the arrival of Foley was the writing on the wall: Tiger wasn't the same, and neither was the friendship and the trust that had once existed between them. Together, Williams and Tiger had won seventy-two tournaments, including thirteen majors. But ever since Tiger's return to the Tour, the chemistry that Williams had once enjoyed with him was gone. Woods's choice of a new swing coach with a radical approach only made matters worse.

In 2011, Tiger's swing and health consistently deteriorated. At the Masters, he injured his left Achilles tendon while hitting from an awkward stance. The injury forced him to withdraw from the Wells Fargo Championship a month later. Then, in mid-May, he withdrew from The Players Championship after shooting an abysmal 42 on the front nine. He was diagnosed with an MCL sprain in his left knee to go along with the Achilles injury.

Nine days before the US Open at Congressional Country Club, Tiger announced he was pulling out of the tournament due to injuries. Within hours of withdrawing, he got a call from Williams, who explained that Adam Scott needed a caddie for the Open and had inquired about Steve's availability. Williams told Tiger he wanted to do it.

"No problem," Tiger told him.

But after hanging up, Woods thought about it and changed his mind. Scott was an opponent, and he didn't like the idea of his caddie helping an adversary. So he had Steinberg send Williams a text questioning the request.

Angry, Williams called Woods. He'd already given Scott his word that he would caddie for him. It was a one-time deal. And he wasn't going back on his word.

Tiger relented, but he wasn't pleased.

The rift between Woods and Williams emerged as Tiger was also on the outs with IMG. His longtime agency had decided in May that it was parting ways with Mark Steinberg, whose employment contract was up for renewal at the end of June. Conflicting reports were published, some claiming that Steinberg was fired for poor performance or for his singular devotion to Woods, while others indicated that the two sides were not able to come to terms on a new contract. But as far as Tiger was concerned, Steinberg had done a masterful job representing him since taking over as his agent in 1999. More specifically, no one had been more loyal to him during the infidelity scandal and its aftermath than Steinberg. So when Steinberg left IMG to join Excel Sports Management, Tiger announced on June 6, 2010, that he too was leaving IMG to join Excel. It was the same week that Williams told Woods he was going through with his decision to caddie for Adam Scott at the US Open.

Scott played poorly at the Open, missing the cut. Two weeks later, however, when Scott learned that Tiger would also be sitting out the AT&T National, he again asked Williams to be on his bag. The AT&T was a tournament that Tiger hosted. Some of the proceeds went to benefit his foundation. For personal and professional reasons, he put his foot down, telling Williams that if he caddied for Scott, they were finished.

"Then we're done," Williams told him.

Williams had always been the rare person in Tiger's inner circle who always spoke his mind. He had never been intimidated by Tiger. And his patience with Woods had grown increasingly thin in the wake of the scandal. Without hesitation, he told Scott he would be on his bag for the AT&T. After the final round, Williams agreed to meet with Tiger in a boardroom at Aronimink Golf Club, just outside Philadelphia.

Woods was leaning back in a chair with his feet up on the table—a favorite power move of his father's—when Williams walked in. Williams quickly determined that it was a waste of time to vent his anger. Why bother? Instead, he wished Tiger luck. Tiger did the same. Like so many of the meaningful relationships in his life, this one ended coldly. There was a firm handshake, but there was also a lot of pent-up frustration in both directions. Tiger believed that Williams had been bad-mouthing him behind his back, an absolute no-no for a caddie; and Williams felt like he'd been jerked around by Tiger. (Williams declined to discuss his employment by Woods, citing a nondisclosure agreement.)

In late July, right after the British Open, Woods announced on his website that Williams would no longer be his caddie, saying it was "time for a change." The next day, Williams issued a statement: "After 13 years of loyal service, needless to say this came as a shock. Given the circumstances of the past 18 months working through Tiger's scandal, a new coach and with it a major new swing change, and Tiger battling through injuries, I am very disappointed to end our very successful partnership at this time."

Tiger had helped make Williams a rich man. Reportedly, Williams earned $12 million in eleven-plus years of caddying for Tiger—yet Williams would later write in his memoir that at times he felt like he was Tiger's "slave," an incendiary comment that was more an indication of the rocky nature of their breakup than a reflection of reality. But in August 2011 at the Bridgestone Invitational, Tiger and Williams were adversaries. Back from injury, Tiger finished tied for thirty-seventh, while Adam Scott won the tournament by four strokes. It was the first win for Scott with Williams on his bag. Afterward, in a rush of excitement, Williams tweeted: "THIS is the greatest win of my career."

The message to Tiger was clear: Stick it up your *arse*.

Two months later, Tiger hired forty-seven-year-old veteran caddie Joe LaCava to take over his bag. A steadying presence, LaCava was a classic New Englander—tough and deeply loyal. But when Tiger looked around, he saw only one person still standing with him from his inner circle: Steinberg. It was becoming fashionable to say that Tiger had lost his edge, that the aura of invincibility that had surrounded him for his entire career was gone. In 2011, recurring injuries limited him to playing in just nine Tour events, and toward the end of the season, after finishing tied for thirtieth in the Frys.com Open, Tiger saw his world ranking fall all the way to fifty-two. He knew there were not fifty-one golfers in the world who were better than he was. There wasn't *one* golfer who was better than he was. Steiny agreed. Tiger just needed to get healthy.

ONLY HUMAN

Heading into 2012, Tiger had not won a PGA Tour event in well over two years. Since returning to the Tour in April 2010, he had played in twenty-seven tournaments without a victory. It didn't help that he was in the midst of overhauling his swing for the fourth time in his career; and on top of that, his new swing coach, Sean Foley, was suggesting radical changes that critics contended were sapping Woods of his innate feel for the game and contributing to a rash of injuries. Pain in his neck, back, knee, and Achilles had forced him to withdraw from numerous tournaments. But the overarching problem with Tiger's game was in his head. His killer instinct was gone.

Tiger's mind-set had always been what separated him from everyone else. Players flat-out feared him. He had the biggest muscles, the fastest swing speed, the best overall game, the bodyguards, the toughest caddie, the biggest corporate backers, the shrewdest agent, the most money, the prettiest wife; it was all part of the outsize image that he leveraged to intimidate opponents. But the infidelity and cheating scandal and his very public divorce had wiped out that aura of invincibility. It was as if the spell he'd long held over his adversaries had finally been lifted. Suddenly, they looked at him differently. Everyone did. Tiger was still the most talented golfer to ever play the game, but he was also fallible, a human being with weaknesses and frailties.

Thanks to therapy, Tiger had also begun to look at himself in a more realistic light. His parents had raised him to believe he was "the Chosen One" and trained him to be a "cold-blooded assassin." But fame had been thrust on him at a very early age, skewing his perspective and damaging him in ways that were impossible to predict and that took years to manifest. In other words, the seeds of his self-destructive, addictive habits were planted long before his marriage to Elin. It took treatment to get him to realize that certain aspects of his life had been a lie.

While treatment helped him put things in perspective, it also left scars. Tiger looked back on his time in therapy as "horrible," summing it up as "the worst experience" he'd ever been through. It was an ordeal that broke him down in ways that affected the mental aspects of his game, wreaking havoc on his self-confidence and leaving him vulnerable in the eyes of those whom he had dominated for so many years.

Treatment also taught Tiger something that changed his modus operandi when it came to women—that he could no longer randomly have sex with someone unless he genuinely felt something for that person. Otherwise, he would be putting himself in serious jeopardy. On an intellectual level, this was easy to understand—but on a practical level, Tiger was facing a monumental challenge. As the world's most celebrated athlete, he had become accustomed to casual sex with lots of partners. "I ran straight through the boundaries that a married couple should live by," he said. "I thought I could get away with whatever I wanted to. I felt I had worked hard my entire life and deserved to enjoy all the temptations around me. I felt I was entitled. Thanks to money and fame, I didn't have to go far to find them."

Suddenly he was being advised to do two things that didn't come easy to him: show restraint, and pursue a meaningful, healthy relationship with a woman. It was a tall order. "There are some girls who are going to be after me even more now," he had confided to Hank Haney shortly after he completed the Gratitude program. "Especially the wild ones."

His situation made for a lonely, treacherous, and at times impossible existence. Back when Tiger first started dating Elin, journalists described her as living a "fairy-tale life" on account of winning over golf's most eligible—and richest—bachelor. But that narrative was wrong from the start. "People think it's like a Cinderella story for her, but Tiger is the one who got the catch," Mia Parnevik told *Sports Illustrated* back in 2004. "With the weird lifestyle he leads, he might never have met a nice girl. He's lucky he found Elin. I mean, can you imagine how empty his life was before she came along, just hitting golf balls all day long?"

In hindsight, Parnevik's assessment seems prescient. Ten years after meeting Elin, Tiger had essentially reverted to hitting golf balls all day long, and the notion of establishing a new relationship with a so-called nice girl seemed like a pipe dream. Avoiding women altogether, it appeared, was the safest course. Golf, on the other hand, was the one thing that gave him a sense of purpose, a reason to get out of bed every day. He still thrived off the competition, which helped explain his determination to grind away at refining his swing and his drive to keep playing through pain. At the tail end of 2011, he felt like he was finally turning a corner when he finished the year by winning the annual tournament that helped benefit his foundation—the Chevron World Challenge at Sherwood Country Club. Although it wasn't an official PGA Tour event, the tournament provided him a much-needed victory, boosting his confidence heading into the 2012 season. Physically, he was feeling better too. For the first time in a long time, things were looking up. Then he got hit with something he never saw coming.

In January, Tiger heard that Hank Haney had written a book—*The Big Miss: My Years Coaching Tiger Woods.* It was due to come out right before the 2012 Masters. *Hank wrote a book?* Stunned, Tiger immediately questioned Haney's motives. *Why didn't Hank mention this?*

Tiger wasn't the only one who was upset. Steinberg was furious. Airing private moments and conversations between a swing coach and a golfer violated an unspoken cardinal rule within the world of golf. It just wasn't done. Worse, Haney didn't give Tiger the courtesy of a heads-up. The blindside was proof of the bad blood that existed between Haney and the duo of Woods and Steinberg. "I didn't inform them of anything," Haney later explained. "I had nothing in my contract that said I couldn't [write the book]."

Given Tiger's obsession with privacy and his penchant for requiring people who worked for him to sign confidentiality agreements, it was mystifying that Haney was free to write about things he had witnessed and heard during his extensive one-on-one time with Woods. Even his publisher had trouble believing that he wasn't under any legal restrictions. His editor at Crown repeatedly asked him to verify that he had not signed a nondisclosure agreement. Haney consistently assured them he had never been asked to sign one. "Steinberg screwed up," he said.

Tiger and Steinberg viewed Haney's book as an act of betrayal. Of course, it paled in comparison to the betrayal of extramarital affairs and sophisticated attempts to cover them up. Nevertheless, Haney's book promised to wound Tiger, exposing a rift that might have been avoided if Tiger had been more demonstrative in showing gratitude. Simple gestures of appreciation and empathy would have gone a long way with Haney, but Tiger didn't do show-and-tell with his feelings. When he ended relationships with people, he forgot them. In Haney's case, almost two years had passed since they parted ways. In that entire time, Tiger never once called just to say hello or see how Haney was doing. The last words he spoke to Haney were: "I know we'll always be friends." To Haney, that was really code for "Don't say anything." He decided to break the code.

Adding insult to injury, Haney had chosen Jaime Diaz as his collaborator. No golf writer had known Tiger longer or understood him and his family better than Diaz. He had spent significant time in Tiger's family home, traveled abroad with Kultida, and been Tiger's choice to help him write his golf instruction book. As far as Woods was concerned, Diaz's involvement with Haney's book was one more betrayal.

At the end of February, *Golf Digest* published the first excerpt from the book. It focused on Tiger's obsession with becoming a Navy SEAL in 2007, claiming his military-style training exercises put his body at risk of injury. The claims sparked headlines and debate. Even the SEALs came under fire, facing questions about whether they had, in fact, allowed a civilian to train with them. "I can confirm in 2006 he fired weapons at one of our ranges," a SEAL spokesman told CNN. It's important to remember that at this point, the public was not aware of Tiger's military fixation. Haney was essentially outing him.

With controversy brewing, Steinberg went after Haney, calling his approach "armchair psychology." In a statement, Steinberg said: "Because of his father, it's no secret that Tiger has always had high respect for the military, so for Haney to twist that admiration into something negative is disrespectful."

Criticizing Haney's book before it was even on sale only fueled interest in it. During a press conference prior to the start of the Honda Classic at the end of February, Tiger was peppered with questions about the SEALs. One by one, he brushed the inquiries aside, until Golf Channel contributor Alex Miceli pushed back, asking if Tiger actually considered joining the SEALs.

"I've already talked about everything in the book," Tiger said tersely. "I've already commented on everything."

"Then I must have missed you answering that question," Miceli said.

"Well, I've already commented on the book," Tiger snapped. "Is that in the book? Is that in the book?"

Miceli said he hadn't seen the book. He'd only read the excerpt.

"You're a beauty," Tiger said, using his go-to code word for *asshole*. "You know that?"

It was the kind of cold putdown that Tiger was known for. But in a move that would have been unheard-of before the crash, Miceli didn't back down. Saying that Steinberg's statement suggested the excerpt was erroneous, Miceli pressed to know whether what Haney had written was true.

Furious, Tiger glared at him for five long seconds. "I don't know," he finally said, breaking the awkward silence. "Have a good day."

Haney's book was an instant best seller, shooting to number one on the *New York Times* list. The fact that someone from the inner circle had dared to write what he had seen and heard while in places such as Tiger's home caused a sensation. Journalists who covered the Tour couldn't resist reading it. Players couldn't stop talking about it. Caddies and swing coaches were whispering. Haney had covered everything from Tiger's relationship with his wife to the way he treated people one-on-one. He even took some swipes at Steinberg. But Woods played through all the noise. On March 25, 2012, he won the Arnold Palmer Invitational at Bay Hill, his first PGA Tour victory since the BMW Championship back in September 2009. He followed that up with an abysmal performance at the Masters, and then was forced to miss a few tournaments due to pain. But in June and July—sandwiched between a poor showing at the US Open—he won the Memorial and the AT&T. By early July 2012, Tiger had climbed back to the number two ranking in the world. Only Luke Donald was ahead of him.

In the midst of what looked like a resurgence in his game, Tiger met twenty-seven-year-old Olympic skier Lindsey Vonn. A friend of Tiger's who worked at his foundation introduced them. Leery of women since undergoing sex addiction treatment, Tiger was immediately at ease around Vonn. Despite meeting countless women in his life, Tiger had almost certainly never met one who had as much in common with him as Vonn. Pushed by her father, she was on skis at age two and was skiing year-round by age seven. As a teen, she moved with her mom to Vail, Colorado, to train and ski exclusively at the elite Ski & Snowboard Club Vail. Her high school years were very nontraditional; taking classes online in order to accommodate her intense training schedule, Vonn did not attend dances, do sleepovers, or meet friends outside of the skiing world. By sixteen, she had started racing on the professional World Cup circuit. She went on to win a record eight World Cup season titles in the downhill discipline and became the first American woman to win an Olympic gold medal in downhill skiing.

Tiger greatly respected Vonn for her talent. He also admired her dedication. A typical day for Vonn consisted of six to eight hours of training. She lived to ski. Yet despite her dominance in her sport, Vonn struggled with her self-image. Growing up, she was self-conscious about her body, fearing that she stood out for the wrong reasons—too tall and too muscular. And while she was arguably the best female skier in the world, she never got comfortable with fame. The one place she felt totally confident was on a mountain, where she was fearless.

In many ways, Woods and Vonn were kindred spirits. For the first time, Tiger had encountered a woman who had the same sort of tunnel vision he did. Vonn's mentality enabled her to understand Woods in a way other women simply couldn't. "He just wanted to win," she said, summing him up. "And he wanted to be the greatest." It sounded simple, but Vonn knew from firsthand experience that Tiger's drive fueled his preoccupation with the conditioning of his body and the performance of his game. To others, Tiger appeared selfish; to Vonn, he looked familiar. Elite athletes—especially those who play individual sports—have to be self-centered.

Tiger and Vonn had something else in common: they were both rebounding from broken marriages. A few months before meeting Tiger, Vonn and her husband—the first man she had ever seriously dated—initiated divorce proceedings. The divorce was messy and took more than a year to finalize. But in Tiger she found someone to trust, someone to talk to, someone she felt safe with. Over the latter part of 2012, Tiger and Vonn quietly built a healthy friendship. By the time Vonn's divorce was official in early 2013, Tiger saw her as more than a friend. She had met Tiger's children and easily connected with them. Even Elin liked Vonn, particularly because of how much the children enjoyed being around her.

For the first time since the crash, there was a woman in Tiger's life who cared about him.

On February 5, 2013, Tiger was at home, and his television was tuned to the FIS Alpine World Ski Championships in Austria, where Vonn was competing in the super giant slalom, or super-G, race. A super-G course requires skiers to make turns past widely set gates while racing at speeds that are much higher than those reached in giant slaloms. On the women's side, Vonn was the top super-G racer in the world and was favored to win the competition. With his personal chef, his housekeeper, and his five-year-old daughter, Sam, in the room, Woods watched Vonn fly down the course in Schladming at nail-biting speed, when suddenly Vonn's knee buckled and she went hurtling over the tips of her skis, sprawling down the mountain in a horrific crash. Writhing in pain, Vonn screamed so loudly that her cries were heard on television. It was a scream, Tiger feared, that might haunt his daughter. He quickly asked his housekeeper to take Sam out of the room.

Intimately familiar with excruciating knee pain, Tiger didn't need to watch replays of Vonn's crash to recognize that she was in really bad shape. Feeling helpless, he watched as medics airlifted her to a nearby hospital, where doctors delivered a grim prognosis. Her anterior cruciate ligament and her medial collateral ligament were torn. She also had fractured the upper part of her tibia. It was hard to predict when Vonn would ski again.

Determined to do all he could, Tiger dispatched his private plane to transport Vonn back to Colorado for surgery. He also saw her during pre-surgery and assured her that everything was going to be okay. The hardest part, he knew, would be post-surgery. "It's going to hurt," he told her. "It's just going to hurt, and you're going to put yourself in a different place, a different state of mind."

Vonn's accident was a pivotal event in their relationship. Shortly after the surgery, they decided to announce their relationship on Facebook, where they posted pictures together. Then Tiger made a formal announcement on his website: "Lindsey and I have been friends for some time," he wrote in March 2013. "But over the last few months we have become very close and are now dating. We thank you for respecting our privacy."

Heading into the 2013 Masters, Tiger was heavily favored to win. He had opened the season by taking the Farmers Insurance Open, the WGC–Cadillac Championship, and the Arnold Palmer Invitational, which enabled him to reclaim his place as the number-one-ranked player in the world. It had been a long, rocky road, but Woods was back on top. For golf and the networks that broadcasted the PGA Tour, this was very welcome news.

With the hype surrounding Tiger's quest for a fifth green jacket at a fever pitch, Vonn accompanied Woods to Augusta, marking the first time that they had stepped out in public as a couple. She watched the tournament with Steinberg as Tiger got off to a fast start, shooting a two-under 70 in the first round. In the second round, he electrified the galleries, making birdie after birdie as he surged to the top of the leaderboard. On a day with gusting winds, Tiger was the only player in the field without a bogey. But the 2013 Masters will long be remembered for what happened to him on his third shot on the par 5 fifteenth hole in the second round.

After slicing his drive into the trees and punching his way out with a shot that left his ball eighty-five yards from the hole, Tiger used a wedge to attack the pin. The shot was very near perfect, striking the flagstick just two feet above the ground. But when the ball caromed off the flagstick, it bounced backward and rolled down the slope and into the pond in front of the green. Bad break. And given the circumstances—Tiger was tied for the lead while chasing his fifteenth major championship—it may have been the worst break of his career.

Ticked off, he stared ahead, expressionless. *Now what?*

Under the rules of golf, Tiger knew he had three options: play a ball from the left edge of the fairway, about forty yards short of the green, from an area known as the drop circle; chart an imaginary line from the hole to the spot at which his ball entered the water and drop a new ball as far back along the line as he desired; or drop a ball "as nearly as possible at the spot from which the original ball was last played."

In the past, Steve Williams would have weighed in with advice. But Tiger's new caddie, Joe LaCava, stood still while Tiger walked toward the green. Looking over the drop area, he ruled out the first option. It would have had him hitting into the grain. *Tough shot,* he thought. Option two didn't look promising either—dropping his ball along the imaginary line left him too little green to work with. It was going to have to be option three.

He turned and walked back up the fairway toward the divot hole that marked the original spot he had just hit from. Still ticked off about his bad luck, he didn't want to hit from the same spot. *I need to take some yardage off this shot*, he thought.

Without consulting LaCava or asking a rules official to oversee his ball placement, Tiger dropped his ball two yards behind the divot. It was a clear violation of the rule requiring him to drop his ball "as nearly as possible" to the spot his original ball had been played from. Two inches behind the divot was one thing; two yards was another story. But his two playing partners and their caddies were waiting up by the green, too far away to notice. From eighty-seven yards away, Tiger fired a shot that landed on the green, bounced, and spun to a stop four feet from the hole. It couldn't have worked out better. Moments later, he tapped in his putt to make bogey—a great outcome under the circumstances. He finished his round with a 71, just three strokes behind the leader. Heading into the weekend, he was in an ideal position to make one of his trademark runs.

In a post-round interview with ESPN, Tiger was asked about the drop on fifteen. Always eager to discuss his performance, he elaborated.

"I went back to where I played it from, but went two yards farther back, and I tried to take two yards off the shot of what I felt I hit," Tiger said. "And that should land me short of the flag and not have it either hit the flag or skip over the back. I felt that was going to be the right decision to take off four [yards] right there. And I did. It worked out perfectly."

His comments immediately touched off chatter on Twitter and ignited a controversy on the internet. That evening, CBS broadcaster Jim Nantz telephoned the tournament's Competition Committee chairman, Fred Ridley, and told him about Tiger's comments. Ridley had a certified mess on his hands, and Nantz didn't know the half of it. It turned out that Ridley had been made aware of Tiger's infraction very shortly after it happened. David Eger, one of golf's preeminent rules experts, had detected Tiger's infraction while watching the Masters on television from his home in North Carolina. He immediately reached out to tournament officials to alert them. "The thing I saw immediately was there was no divot hole [near his ball] when he played his fifth shot," Eger told golf writer Michael Bamberger, who, along with Alan Shipnuck, wrote the definitive account of the episode. "I realized he had played from the improper spot—there was no doubt it was a penalty." Prompted by Eger's message, Ridley had gone to the tournament headquarters while Tiger was still on the course and reviewed video of Tiger's drop. Despite visual evidence that Tiger's ball was not placed "as nearly as possible" to the divot, Ridley chose not to take any action, enabling Tiger to finish the round and sign his scorecard. Now that Woods had publicly admitted to dropping his ball two yards back, his scorecard was incorrect—and signing an incorrect scorecard is grounds for disqualification, the very thing that Eger had been trying to avert with his urgent message.

Sensing a fast-approaching storm, Ridley returned to Augusta after talking with Nantz. Huddling with other tournament officials, he reviewed more video. Meanwhile, Nantz went back on the air, reporting that Tiger's drop was "a developing story." Twitter, by this point, was blowing up. Tournament officials and CBS executives were scrambling. It was after midnight when Tiger was awakened by an urgent text from Steinberg. Ridley wanted to see him first thing in the morning.

Woods was in trouble of his own making, but so was Ridley. It didn't help that the tournament was already getting bad press for penalizing Guan Tianlang, a fourteen-year-old prodigy from China who earned an invitation to the Masters by winning the Asia-Pacific Amateur Championship. Guan played remarkably well in the first round at Augusta, finishing just three shots behind Woods. In the second round he was fighting to make the cut when he was assessed a one-stroke penalty on the seventeenth hole for slow play, an outrageous decision considering how notoriously slowly the rounds are played at Augusta; yet Guan was the first player in tournament history to be penalized for his pace. Even other golfers, including his playing partner, Ben Crenshaw, came to Guan's defense. But when Tiger was asked about the harshness of Guan's penalty, he replied: "Well, rules are rules."

The question was whether Ridley would now apply that standard to Woods. Doing so would require him to disqualify the number one player in the world while he was perched near the top of the leaderboard at Augusta. To fail to do so would open him up to charges of favoritism.

Tiger arrived at Augusta at eight a.m. on Saturday to meet with Ridley, who was accompanied by Augusta chairman Billy Payne. While they huddled, commentator Brandel Chamblee opened his morning broadcast on Golf Channel by reminding viewers that Bobby Jones once called a penalty on himself during the 1925 US Open, which caused him to lose by one stroke. "It is incumbent on Tiger Woods to call this penalty on himself and disqualify himself for signing an incorrect scorecard," Chamblee said, wagging his finger at the camera. His comments reflected the sentiments of many among the golf press.

But Tiger maintained that he didn't intentionally break the rules. "At hole #15, I took a drop that I thought was correct and in accordance with the rules," he wrote on Twitter. "I was unaware at that time I had violated any rules. I didn't know I had taken an incorrect drop prior to signing my scorecard."

Nor was Ridley inclined to follow the letter of the law. Instead, behind closed doors, he invoked a rule dating back to 1952 that reads, "A penalty of disqualification may in exceptional individual cases be waived, modified or imposed if the Committee considers such action warranted." The exceptional individual case was that Ridley had failed to intervene when originally made aware of Tiger's rule violation. That didn't excuse the incorrect drop, but Ridley's inaction had paved the way for Tiger to sign an incorrect scorecard. Hoping to put the matter to bed, Ridley imposed a two-stroke penalty for the improper drop, effectively changing Tiger's second-round score from 71 to 73. Woods was allowed to remain in the tournament.

"We got a two-stroke penalty," he matter-of-factly told Joe LaCava after meeting with Ridley. "And we're going to have to work that much harder to get back in this thing."

But it wasn't that simple. Ridley's decision instantly came under fire, and Tiger's unwillingness to disqualify himself triggered even more outrage. "He will never live this down," Chamblee said on Golf Channel. Other pros immediately chimed in, including two Hall of Famers. Calling the situation "dreadful," Nick Faldo publicly called on Tiger to do "the real manly thing" by acknowledging that he broke the rules and withdrawing. Greg Norman tweeted, "It's all about the player and the integrity of the game. Woods violated the rules as he played #1 carries a greater burden. WD for the game."

Once again, Tiger was at the center of a scandal—only this time the setting was inside the ropes, and his integrity as a professional was being called into question. He had endured months of headlines referring to him as a cheater for what he'd done behind his wife's back, but he had never been characterized as a cheater in golf. He didn't see himself that way, and it was painful to think that others did. Nevertheless, he wasn't about to give in. After sending out a tweet of his own—"I understand and accept the penalty and accept the Committees' decision"—he stepped to the first tee at 2:10 p.m. on Saturday as a man in the eye of a raging storm. The familiar weight of so many eyes resting on him returned.

Meanwhile, Lindsey Vonn was getting a taste of what it was like to be the girlfriend of Tiger Woods. The spotlight she had been under as the top female skier in the world was like a flashlight compared to the noonday sun that was Tiger's limelight. Her admiration for him increased.

With the rest of the tournament overshadowed by controversy, Tiger didn't play as sharply as he had in the first two rounds. Instead of claiming another green jacket, he ended up finishing tied for fourth. It's unclear how much, if at all, the situation affected his performance, but it was no doubt hard to ignore the spirited celebration of caddie Steve Williams high-fiving Adam Scott as he captured his first Masters.

For Woods, the most complicated chapter in the history of golfing jurisprudence didn't end at Augusta; rather, it stuck to him like a scarlet letter. The next time he hit a ball into the water—in May at The Players Championship—NBC broadcaster Johnny Miller questioned the location of his drop. Then, five months later at the BMW Championship in Lake Forest, Illinois, he was penalized again, this time during the second round for failing to report that his ball had moved while he was clearing away a twig under a tree behind the first green—only this time, the infraction was captured by a videographer working for PGA Tour Entertainment. Before Tiger signed his official scorecard at the end of the round, he was stopped by Slugger White, the vice president of competition at the PGA Tour, who showed him the video evidence of his ball moving. From White's perspective, it was clear that Woods—due to the position he was in, looking down at the ball at the time—could not have seen the subtle movement. But when confronted with the visual evidence, Tiger still didn't want to accept that his ball had, in fact, moved ever so slightly.

"How's that?" he said to White, insisting that his ball had remained in its original spot.

White and Tour officials replayed the video for Woods, who only became more adamant. After a heated discussion, Tiger was assessed a two-shot penalty, turning his double-bogey on the first hole into a quadruple bogey and changing his overall score for the round from 70 to 72. While addressing the media afterward, Woods didn't back down.

"After seeing the video, I thought the ball just oscillated, and I thought that was it," Woods said. "I thought that was the end of the story. But they saw otherwise. We had a very good discussion, and we'll end it at that. . . . I was pretty hot because I felt like nothing happened.

"They replayed it again and again," he continued, "and I felt the same way. I'd worked my tail off, and to go from five behind to seven behind was tough."

Few criticized Woods for failing to initially recognize his ball's movement, but he came under intense scrutiny for denying what was plainly visible on the video. His use of the word *oscillated*—a term in physics that means to vary in magnitude or position in a regular manner—prompted Brandel Chamblee to insinuate that Tiger was a cheater. "He lost the Tour wives after the 2009 adultery scandal," Chamblee said in 2017. "He lost the locker room after the BMW tournament. They assumed Tiger would call the penalty on himself. When he didn't, they looked at him as a cheater."

After Chamblee wrote a controversial column on Golf.com in which he gave Tiger an F for being "a little cavalier with the rules," Steinberg told ESPN that he was giving some thought to legal action. Days later, Chamblee acknowledged that he had "gone too far" and apologized to Tiger on Twitter. "What brought me here was the realization that my comments inflamed an audience on two sides of an issue," he said. "Golf is a gentleman's game, and I'm not proud of this debate. I want to apologize to Tiger for this incited discourse."

Woods wasn't interested in an apology. "All I'm going to say is I know I'm going forward," he told reporters. "The whole issue has been very disappointing, as he didn't really apologize and he sort of reignited the whole situation."

Even at the height of his infidelity scandal, Tiger's reputation as a professional had remained above reproach, but the 2013 Masters and BMW Championship tarred it with a big black brush. At the same time, there were also signs of another gathering storm, starting with his back tightening up during the final round of the 2013 PGA Championship in August. Two weeks of stiffness in his back then extended to his neck, prompting Tiger to only chip and putt on the back nine during the pro-am at the

Barclays. He blamed a soft mattress in his hotel room. A few days later, during the final round of the tournament, a violent back spasm dropped Tiger to his knees following a shot.

It was becoming apparent that there was a serious problem with Woods's back that was compromising his play. Somehow, despite a wooden swing, a cranky back, and a "cheater" label hanging over him, Tiger managed to win five PGA tournaments in 2013, and he ended up being the Tour's top money earner, second in scoring, and Player of the Year. He also maintained his number one ranking. But 2013 proved to be more of a belated encore performance to his brilliant career than a prelude to a return to glory.

The quality that Lindsey Vonn most admired in Woods was his mental toughness. His example is what helped her get through rehab. The mental exercise, Tiger assured her, was dealing with the day-to-day, trying to make progress without having any setbacks. He hated treatment; lying on a table while someone worked on him did nothing to get his adrenaline going. Rehab, on the other hand, was like training. It hurt like hell, but his attitude was: *Experience the pain.*

Determined to ski in the 2014 Olympics, Vonn adopted Tiger's approach. Pushing herself, she was back on skis just ten months after tearing two ligaments in her right knee and fracturing a bone. But in November 2013 she retore her surgically repaired knee in a training crash, tumbling headfirst at 60 miles per hour.

Devastated, Vonn went into panic mode. "What do I do?" she pleaded. Her dream of skiing in the Winter Olympics in Sochi was dead.

Tiger got her through those dark days. But two months after Vonn announced she was withdrawing from the Olympics, in January 2014, Woods's deteriorating physical condition forced him to pull out of the Honda Classic. The spasms and lower-back pain just wouldn't let up. A week later he made it through the Cadillac Championship at Doral, but the pain was so bad by the end of the tournament that he shot a 78 on the final day, the highest score of his career in a final round. Ten days later he pulled out of the Arnold Palmer Invitational due to persistent back pain. But the incident that convinced him he was really in trouble happened at his estate in Jupiter.

While practicing on the minicourse that effectively served as his backyard, Tiger hit a flop shot over a bunker and instantly felt like he had
pinched a nerve. He went down as though he'd been shot. There's pain,
and then there's *pain*; this was the latter. Unable to move, he lay helpless
on the ground, fearing for the first time that his career might be over.
With no cell phone on him, all he could do was hope that someone would
find him.

Finally, his daughter, Sam, strolled outside, looking for him.

"Daddy, what are you doing lying on the ground?" she said.

"Sam, thank goodness you're here. Can you go tell the guys inside to
try to get the cart out to help me back up?"

"What's wrong?" she said.

"My back's not doing very good."

"Again?"

"Yes, again, Sam. Can you please go get those guys?"

CHAPTER THIRTY-THREE

POINT OF NO RETURN

Lying facedown and motionless on an operating table in Park City, Utah, Tiger closed his eyes. A surgeon preparing to make a small incision in his lower back stood over him. It was March 31, 2014, and Woods was desperate for relief—desperate enough to go under the knife. A damaged disc was pressing on a nerve in his lower spine. As far back as childhood, Tiger had been generating tremendous torque with his violent swing. It was the energy source behind the dazzling power of expression that he used to tell the world *There isn't anyone like me.* The net result of that excessive rotation—combined with two decades of relentless weight lifting, long-distance running, and more recent intense SEAL training—had finally caught up to him. If Tiger's spine was the operating system for the most majestic swing in golf, microdiscectomy surgery—a procedure to remove the herniated portion of a lumbar disc that presses against a nerve root—was akin to defragging a hard drive in hopes of making that operating system run smoothly again. The question was whether it would work. When he came out of surgery, he was advised to give things time to heal.

But taking time for healing was never Tiger's strong suit. After each knee surgery he consistently beat the recovery clock, powering through rehab and returning to competition at a pace that defied the medical community's timetables for typical patients. He figured he could do the same thing after back surgery. On June 26, 2014—less than three months after the procedure on his spine—he was in Maryland for the Quicken Loans National, insisting he was fit to play. He finished the first two rounds seven over par and ended up missing the cut. A month later, he slogged through the British Open, finishing in fourth-to-last place, *twenty-three strokes* behind the winner. Then he failed to make the cut at the PGA Championship, limping so badly that he barely completed the second round. Looking feeble, he finally acknowledged that his ailing back needed more time to heal and strengthen. One week after the PGA, Woods shut things down for the rest of the year. In just seven official events in 2014, he had two withdrawals, two missed cuts, and five finishes of five over par or worse.

The 2014 season was a bust. It was also a preview of things to come. At thirty-eight, Tiger still looked like the most physically imposing, well-conditioned athlete on the PGA Tour—but that was when he stood still. When he swung, he looked wounded. In addition to limiting his rotation, nagging back and nerve pain was causing him to alter his swing. Hoping to sort things out before the start of the 2015 season, he started by parting ways with his swing coach, Sean Foley. "This is the right time to end our professional relationship," Tiger said on August 25, 2014, announcing the split on his website.

The decision wasn't surprising. Since hiring Foley in the summer of 2010, Woods had once again rebuilt his swing, adopting Foley's highly technical philosophy. But in their four years together, Tiger never came close to winning another major championship and had the lowest winning percentage of his career (14 percent), capturing just eight of his fifty-six events with Foley. Under Hank Haney, Woods won 33 percent of his Tour starts. It's not altogether fair to compare the Foley era to the Haney era, given that Woods was much more injury-prone under Foley and had only two seasons—2012 and 2013—in which he managed to play a full schedule. During that brief span, Woods did regain his place as the number one golfer in the world by applying Foley's approach; nevertheless, some golf analysts suggested that Foley's methods made him more susceptible to injury. Publicly, Woods shot down this theory. When he let Foley go, he avoided casting aspersions, choosing instead to express gratitude and give compliments. "Sean is one of the outstanding coaches in golf today," Woods said. "And I know he will continue to be successful with the players working with him."

With Foley out of the picture, Woods said he was in no hurry to find a new coach, but in fact he was anxious to find a fresh approach. His former Stanford teammate Notah Begay III introduced him to Chris Como, a thirty-seven-year-old graduate student who was finishing up a master's degree in biomechanics at Texas Woman's University. Hiring Como certainly qualified as a new approach. It also begged the question: What can the most naturally gifted golfer in history learn from someone whose entire coaching résumé consisted of working with three guys named Aaron Baddeley, Jamie Lovemark, and Trevor Immelman? But Tiger wasn't really looking for a swing coach. Como's specialty was applying the laws of mechanics to human movement in an effort to improve performance and reduce injury. Woods hired him as his swing "consultant."

Tiger was convinced that he needed to get back to fundamentals. One of the first things he did with Como was break out some old VHS tapes of his days with Butch Harmon. Together, they spent hours watching and critiquing his old form. Then they set out to rebuild his swing for what amounted to the fifth time in his career. Como's techniques were a big change from what Foley was teaching, but by the end of the year, Tiger's swing speed and driving distance were reaching numbers he hadn't touched since 2000.

"Chris wanted to get Tiger's swing as close to [that of] his junior golf days as possible," said Golf Channel analyst Brandel Chamblee. "It was a more upright swing, with lateral movement and a right shift. The biggest change was that Chris was not as arrogant or as linear as Foley. It was almost like Sean wasn't ready for the things that he was given. Now Sean has changed the way he teaches. He's a marvelous teacher now, but at the time he wasn't ready, and it led to Tiger's downfall."

Woods had it all planned out. He would make his return to the PGA Tour at the Phoenix Open at the end of January 2015. That same weekend, the New England Patriots would be facing the Seattle Seahawks in Super Bowl XLIX in nearby Glendale, Arizona. Figuring it would be a great way to cap off the weekend, Tiger secured tickets to the game, planning to go directly from TPC Scottsdale to University of Phoenix Stadium. After a five-month layoff, there was a lot to look forward to.

But first, Woods made a spur-of-the-moment trip to Italy, where Lindsey Vonn was competing in a World Cup ski event. Following a long road back from injuries, Vonn looked poised to win again and to capture the all-time world record for women's World Cup titles. Tiger decided to surprise her by showing up for her big moment. After taking a private jet to Italy and a helicopter to the Cortina d'Ampezzo resort in the Dolomite mountains, he went incognito—wearing a hood, dark shades, and a black-and-white mask emblazoned with a toothy skull—to make his way through the crowds without detection. When Vonn finished 0.85 seconds ahead of her closest challenger, Woods was there to greet her.

"No way!" she said. "I can't believe you came!"

"I told you," he said.

She threw her arms around him and kissed him while he still had the scarf-like mask over his lips. The fact that he had come all that way just to see her final run down the mountain meant the world to her. But his presence quickly overshadowed her record-setting victory. Although Tiger went out of his way to avoid the media during his brief time at the event, an Associated Press photographer snapped a picture of him with his mask lowered. It revealed that Tiger was missing one of his top front teeth. The British tabloids had a field day, resurrecting old rumors that Elin had allegedly broken his tooth by throwing a cell phone at him after discovering his infidelity back in 2009. Woods did end up getting a root canal on his top tooth, and he did wear a false tooth, but he had always vehemently denied that Elin had struck him.

Nevertheless, with Tiger's missing tooth creating headlines across the globe, Mark Steinberg issued a statement insisting that Woods's tooth was accidentally knocked out by a photographer while watching Vonn celebrate her victory. "During a crush of photographers at the awards podium at the World Cup event in Italy, a media member with a shoulder-mounted video camera pushed and surged toward the stage, turned, and hit Tiger Woods in the mouth," Steinberg said. Tiger's account became an international controversy when race organizers in Italy refuted Steinberg's statement, claiming Woods was nowhere near the photographers at the finish area and had been whisked away on a snowmobile after requesting extra security. "I was among those who escorted him from the tent to the snowmobile, and there was no such incident," said Nicola Colli, the secretary general of the race organizing committee. "When he arrived, he asked for more security, and we rounded up police to look after both him and Lindsey."

By the time Woods got to Phoenix, newspapers from the *Washington Post* to the *New York Daily News* were questioning Tiger's version of events. But he was focused on his return. The Phoenix Open is consistently the most boisterous, well-attended event on Tour, annually drawing over half a million spectators. Two days before the start of the tournament, Tiger was greeted by massive crowds that showed up to cheer him on during a nine-hole practice round. Buoyed by the overwhelming support, he mingled with fans, signing autographs and posing for pictures. In the pre-tournament press conference, he was relaxed, joking with reporters and reminiscing about playing in Phoenix earlier in his career. But the conversation quickly shifted to his tooth when a reporter asked, "Tiger, can you take us through what happened to your tooth a couple weeks ago?"

He confidently offered a lengthy explanation of how he was still wearing his mask when he ended up standing amid a pool of photographers after Vonn's race. "The dude with one of the video cameras on his shoulder, who was kneeling right in front of me, stood up, turned, and caught me square in the mouth," he said, pointing to his teeth. "So he chipped that one and cracked the other one. So I'm trying to keep this thing on so the blood's not all over the place."

He went on to say that after breaking his tooth, he couldn't eat or drink until he returned to the US and saw his dentist. "Jesus, the flight home was a joke," he said. "I couldn't eat. I couldn't drink . . . I couldn't have anything touch it. Even breathing hurt."

The more he tried to explain it, the more unbelievable it sounded. He was standing in a sea of photographers, bleeding "all over the place," yet not one photographer managed to take a picture of him at that moment? No one—not even Vonn—said they saw Tiger bleeding after the event.

"What does it feel like to have so many people not believe in your story?" another journalist asked.

Tiger shrugged and smiled. "You guys . . . It's just the way the media is. It is what it is."

"It's not just the media," the reporter said.

"It's just what it is," said Tiger, shrugging.

It was all smiles until play started; then things went downhill fast. He bogeyed his first two holes and was four over after just four holes. In blue slacks, a white belt, and a fitted pink Nike shirt that showcased his physique, Tiger was the sharpest-dressed guy in the field, but his short game looked trashed thanks to a bad case of the "chip yips," a golf term for repeatedly flubbing short shots due to jitters. By the second round, golf writers were asking "Who is this guy?"—and they weren't referring to Chris Como. Facing a thirty-five-foot pitch on the fourth green, Woods hit the ball forty-seven feet *past* the target. On fourteen, his attempt at a thirty-one-yard chip traveled just nineteen yards. And on fifteen, he found himself forty-eight feet from the hole, but after two shots he had advanced the ball only twenty-three feet. The baffling bladed shots sent shock waves through the crowd. Never coming close to making the cut, Woods finished the second round with two double bogeys, a triple bogey, and six bogeys on his way to a jaw-dropping eleven-over-par 82. It was one of the most shocking performances in golf history.

Yet Tiger's attitude afterward was almost as puzzling. He was actually smiling and joking with the press. It was so out of character that a reporter asked how he could be smiling after what had just happened. "It's golf," Tiger said. "We all have days like this."

The fact was that Tiger had *never* had a day like that. His second round at the 2015 Phoenix Open ranked as his single worst round of golf in 1,109 starts in his PGA Tour career. This was no off day—it was a complete meltdown.

Struggling to make sense of it, one reporter asked the question on everyone's mind: "Have you had any discomfort in your back? How did it hold up today?"

"I'm fine," Tiger said, looking him in the eye. "That's not an issue anymore."

He then went straight to his plane and flew home. There was no point in hanging around Phoenix for the Super Bowl. He had work to do.

Heading into the 2015 season, Tiger was playing his familiar shell game with the press, telling everyone that his back was pain-free and that any drop-off in performance was due to the fact that he was still adjusting to his swing change. Tiger being Tiger, golf writers gave him the benefit of the doubt. That was about to change.

One week after Phoenix, Tiger went to Torrey Pines for the Farmers Insurance Open. To longtime observers, his unsteady gait and aged look set off alarms. So did his attempt during a practice round to *putt* a ball out of heavy rough around a green. After warming up for the opening round, he stood around for nearly two hours, waiting for a heavy fog to lift. Once he finally teed off, he immediately started doing things that defied the eyes, like spraying drive after drive into adjacent fairways. Plus, he was having trouble bending over to retrieve his ball from the cup. Just eleven holes into the first round, after playing his last hole like a 20-handicapper,

Woods informed his playing partners that he was done. He wished them luck. A longtime member of Tiger's personal San Diego Police Department security detail, officer Deborah Ganley, pulled up in a golf cart to escort him off the course. Tiger slumped into the front seat, and Ganley promised to go slowly to protect his balky back. "I'm okay," he told her. "I'm okay."

No one believed that. For the second consecutive tournament, the best player in the world looked like he'd forgotten how to play golf. A bad back was the only thing that remotely made sense, although a fractured psyche was another plausible explanation. By the time the golf cart reached the players' parking lot, a mob of reporters and cameramen was waiting to question him. Downplaying the disaster that all of them had just witnessed, Woods said that his back had stiffened up during the fog delay and he was never able to get loose. "It's just my glutes are shutting off," he said. "Then they don't activate, and then, hence, it goes into my lower back. So I tried to activate my glutes as best I could in between, but they never stayed activated."

His explanation quickly became a punch line. Golf publications ran headlines such as "Tiger Woods Blames a 'Deactivated' Butt for His Latest Injury." And his backside was trending on Twitter with the hashtag #glutesshuttingoff. "He's become the butt of bad jokes #Glutes #Tiger," tweeted golf writer Robert Lusetich.

Tiger had been mocked before, but his game had never been the subject of ridicule. After seeing him grimace with each swing and walk gingerly from point A to point B, even the adversaries that he'd been dominating for years felt sorry for him. "As competitive as we are, we don't want to see anyone suffer like that," Ernie Els said following Tiger's early exit at Torrey Pines.

Nobody was more disappointed than Tiger himself. His pride was hurting as much as his back. Enough was enough, he decided. Days after blaming his glutes, he decided to take a step back. "My play, and scores, are not acceptable for tournament golf," he said on his website. "I enter a tournament to compete at the highest level, and when I think I'm ready, I'll be back."

Frustrated, he disappeared from the Tour for the next two months. He didn't surface again until the 2015 Masters. When he arrived, Lindsey Vonn and his two children were with him. The only silver lining in his struggles was that he had someone at his side who understood what he was going through. Tiger had watched Vonn fight through post-surgery setbacks. Her unrelenting desire to dominate her sport was something he rarely saw in another human being, and it was one of the things he loved most about her. Together, they'd been spending a lot of time in the gym, pushing each other to get healthy. It was clear during the annual Par 3 Contest early in the week at Augusta that Vonn was like a full member of Tiger's family. She walked with Tiger as Charlie and Sam caddied for him. More than any of his previous girlfriends, Vonn seemed capable of handling the spotlight that constantly shined on Woods, keeping her focus on him and his children. "They're great kids," she told a reporter. "I love them."

Huge crowds followed Woods through the first round at Augusta. From the outset, he played much better than he had in February. He also looked different. He had lost weight since the beginning of the season and appeared more flexible. His smile had returned too. He even shared a few laughs with his old friend Mark O'Meara. "Hey," O'Meara told him, "your boy's going in this summer. I expect you to be there." Woods knew what he meant: O'Meara had been selected for the World Golf Hall of Fame. The induction ceremony was later in the year at the British Open at St. Andrews. By telling Tiger he had better be there, O'Meara was extending an olive branch, letting him know that he was willing to look past the fact that Woods hadn't called him since the crash. It was time to let bygones be bygones.

Through the first three rounds at Augusta, Woods looked more like his old self, shooting 73, 69, and 68. He was competing. When asked how he had turned things around and gotten himself in shape to compete at the Masters, he quipped, "I worked my ass off." His motivation was what it had always been—winning. But now he had an added incentive: The last time he won the Masters, in 2005, his children weren't born. Now they were six and seven. He wanted nothing more than for them to see their dad put on a green jacket.

But Tiger couldn't keep up on Sunday, especially after he tweaked his wrist while swinging his club partway through the round. His seventh-place finish—his best performance since his back surgery thirteen months earlier—was a little souvenir in a terrible year. But he couldn't ignore the fact that he still finished thirteen shots behind the charismatic winner, twenty-one-year-old Jordan Spieth. Ten years had now passed since Tiger's last Masters victory. At thirty-nine, he was watching a player nearly half his age put on the green jacket. Time was not on his side.

After the Masters, Woods disappeared again. This time he had a personal issue to deal with—the abrupt end of his relationship with Vonn. After three great years together, on May 3, 2015, he announced on his website: "I have great admiration, respect, and love for Lindsey, and I'll always cherish our time together. She has been amazing with Sam and Charlie and my entire family. Unfortunately, we lead very hectic lives, and are both competing in demanding sports. It's difficult to spend time together."

On the same day, Vonn said essentially the same thing on her Facebook page: "Unfortunately, we both lead incredibly hectic lives that force us to spend a majority of our time apart."

Woods and Vonn had successfully insulated their relationship from public inspection. Now that it was over, they weren't about to explain why. But it was more complicated than busy schedules, which are an inherent part of being an elite athlete. Vonn had proven to be an ideal partner who fit into Tiger's complicated life. She loved him. She loved his children. And she got along amicably with Elin; they had even been together with Tiger at one of the kids' tee-ball games just before the breakup. But now Lindsey was gone. When pressed for an explanation, she took the high road. "Jumping into a relationship right away after getting a divorce was probably not the smartest move on my part," she said. "I don't regret anything. I loved Tiger, and I had an amazing three years with him. But it was a learning experience as well. With every relationship, you learn what you need and what you want in a partner."

One of the things that Tiger had always liked about being a golfer was that it was so compatible with his personality, requiring him to spend countless hours in solitude on the practice range and the practice green. "We can be loners and never see anybody," he said in 2015. But being alone depressed Vonn, and it took a toll on Woods too. For the first three days after Vonn left, he didn't sleep.

Still in a funk a month later, Tiger played in the Memorial Tournament. His third-round performance was so bad—a thirteen-over-par 85—that it topped his second-round disaster at the Phoenix Open, giving him a new career low. Then he broke another personal record, finishing with a combined score of 302, the worst seventy-two-hole mark of his professional career. Each tournament, it seemed, saw him setting a new personal record for worst performance ever. At the US Open the unraveling continued: in the worst thirty-six-hole performance of his pro career, he shot a combined 156, shanking shots, swearing at himself, and slamming his clubs into the ground. He even had his club fly out of his hands and land roughly twenty feet behind him after a poor swing. At one point, the television announcers were so baffled by what they were seeing that they were speechless. "I don't know what to say," one of the broadcasters said on the air. "I really don't know what to say."

Woods could no longer deny the obvious: returning from back surgery was not the same thing as coming back from knee surgery. Nerve damage was much more debilitating than joint damage. Whether an optimist or an illusionist, he kept insisting that he was making progress, but in reality, he was making matters worse by trying to play when he wasn't healthy. One moment on the second day of the US Open summed up the state of Tiger's career at that point: On the first hole, he had jerked a drive that landed his ball in the rough on a steep hill. As he tried to position himself over the ball, he lost his footing and landed flat on his backside. It was a classic laugh-or-cry moment. Woods was too exasperated to do either.

Mark O'Meara was inducted into the World Golf Hall of Fame in a ceremony at St. Andrews on July 13, 2015, a few days prior to the start of the British Open. For Tiger's onetime best friend on the PGA Tour, this was a cherished moment, the capstone of his career. At fifty-eight, O'Meara walked onto the stage at Younger Hall to rousing applause, accepted his trophy, and delivered a heartfelt acceptance speech. Other than family, there was no one he had hoped would attend more than Woods, his longtime practice partner who had inspired and propelled him to his only two major championships. O'Meara even went so far as to place a follow-up call to remind Woods to come. Twenty-one Hall of Fame golfers were in the audience that night. But Woods, who was in town to play in the Open, didn't show up.

In his seventeen-minute speech, O'Meara personally thanked Hank Haney for "changing my life" and Tom Watson for being "an incredible inspiration to me." He singled out Palmer and Nicklaus as "the greats." But he made no mention of Tiger. Long after the lights had dimmed on that exceptional evening, O'Meara summed up his deep disappointment in Woods. "Sooner or later you have to be a human being," he said in 2016, his voice trailing off. "I don't know. It's not the same. I wish it was." A year later, thinking back on that night, he added: "It's just very disappointing. It wasn't about me. It would have done him good to be there."

For being such an important figure in the lives of so many, Woods seemed to always fall short in his personal relationships. It was the curse of genius. His mind was always consumed by his own quests. In 2015, his only goal was to make it to Sunday. It was all he could do to finish tournaments. Heading into the British Open, he was facing a vexing question: Would the old Tiger ever return? "I know some of you guys think I'm buried and done," he told the press prior to the start of the tournament. "But I'm still right here in front of you. I love playing. I love competing. And I love playing these events."

Under the circumstances, this may have been the most revealing statement Tiger Woods ever uttered. His body was begging him to stop competing, but he didn't know how. As a young boy, he was given the code word *enough* by his father and told that all he had to do was say it when he could no longer take the adversity being set upon him. Afraid of being a quitter, Tiger never used the E-word as a kid. As a thirty-nine-year-old man, he still feared quitting. If he stopped competing, then what? Of course, he had two beautiful children that he could spend more time with. He had a highly successful foundation that was changing the lives of tens of thousands of underprivileged kids. He even had a thriving golf-course design business—TGR Design—that was gaining recognition with an award-winning course in Texas and had projects under way in Florida, Missouri, Cabo San Lucas, the Bahamas, Dubai, and China. But none of those things could fill the void that would form when he no longer had events to play. The secret to Tiger's dominance was that he was the most one-dimensional human being on the PGA Tour. The game was his life. He wasn't prepared for life without the game.

After a hellish opening round on the Old Course at St. Andrews—a course on which he'd twice won the British Open—Tiger once again missed the cut. His frail performance and early departure cast a pall over the event. The writing was on the wall. By now, Woods was ranked 254th in the world and was dropping like a rock. The last time he'd been ranked that low was at the Quad Cities Open in 1996, right after he turned pro.

"The end is here for one of the greatest golfers who ever lived," declared sports columnist Joe Posnanski after watching Woods at the British Open.

Tiger played in just three more tournaments in 2015, his last one—the Wyndham Championship—at the end of August. Then, on September 18, he underwent a second microdiscectomy surgery. Neurosurgeon Dr. Charles Rich, who had operated on him in March 2014, removed a disc fragment that was pinching a nerve. This time, Dr. Rich deemed the surgery a "complete success." But in the weeks that followed, the pain was so debilitating that one month later Tiger had to have another procedure—his third back surgery in eighteen months—to relieve the discomfort. When he woke up, Tiger faced a new normal: immobility coupled with powerful prescription drugs intended to deaden pain. He could barely get out of bed, and like a prisoner stuck inside his waterfront fortress on Jupiter Island in Florida, he had nothing to do but think. One thought in particular consumed him:

I may never play again.

CHAPTER THIRTY-FOUR

INTO THE ROUGH

Tiger had just started walking again. It had been two months since his third back surgery, and the most he could manage was about ten minutes on the beach. Then he would have to return to the house and lie down, passing the time watching television. The one thing he hated watching, however, was golf. After a lifetime as the center of attention, he didn't have it in his DNA to be a spectator. And now that his life revolved around pain and the attempt to manage it, seeing others compete only added to the misery.

There are serious downsides to being the best in the world at something: no other life experience compares to the thrill and personal satisfaction derived from performing at the peak of greatness, but, inevitably, performance starts to slip. The fingers of a renowned concert pianist begin to move a tad slower. The voice of a world-famous opera singer develops a tremor. A gold-medal sprinter loses a step. In Tiger's case, his body had finally succumbed, beaten down by an iron will programmed to never say *enough*. Even after being sidelined by a dozen serious injuries and seven surgeries, he had repeatedly come back too soon, playing through pain with a single goal in mind. "There's no sense in going to a tournament if you don't believe that you can win it," he said during one of his attempted comebacks. "That is the belief I've always had, and that's not going to change."

But at the end of 2015, Woods was on the cusp of turning forty and, like so many people who reach mid-life, his beliefs were changing along with his body. He had trouble getting out of bed in the morning. Walking was a chore. Bending over to tie his shoes was agonizing. *I've had a good run*, he thought. *Having it all end because of injuries is not what I want to*

*have happen, and it's not what I'm planning on having happen. But if it
does, it does.*

That was Tiger's attitude as he sat in his new restaurant, The Woods
Jupiter, near his home days before his fortieth birthday. A bag of ice on his
back, he met with longtime Canadian journalist Lorne Rubenstein for a
rare one-on-one interview.

"Do you have any recovery goals?" Rubenstein asked.

"There's no timetable," Woods said. "And that's a hard mind-set to go
through, because I've always been a goal setter. Now I had to rethink it,
and say, Okay, my goal is to do nothing today. For a guy who likes to work,
that's a hard concept for me to understand.

"I've learned a little bit of it," he continued. "I know that, one, I don't
want to have another procedure. And two, even if I don't come back and I
don't play again, I still want to have a quality of life with my kids. I started
to lose that with the other surgeries."

Rubenstein's questions covered a wide range of subjects, but in many
of Tiger's answers, he kept referring to his children. This was a milestone
of a different sort for Woods; immobility forced him to contemplate the
end of golf and the start of something more lasting. He was particularly
frustrated by a recurring scene that had been playing out in his home.
One of his children would say, "Daddy, let's go play," and Tiger would say,
"Daddy can't move."

Fatherhood and the desire to grab on to the years he had left with his
kids seemed to be weighing on Woods like never before. His most treasured childhood memories were the times he spent alone with his father
on the golf course. Similarly, his favorite thing to do with his own children
was to teach them to play sports. The fact that he couldn't even kick a
soccer ball around the backyard with his kids was depressing. "The most
important thing," Tiger told Rubenstein, "is that I get to have a life with
my kids. That's more important than golf. I've come to realize that now."

Nevertheless, the transition from being one of the world's most singu-
larly focused athletes to spending a life doing something else—even something as noble as parenting—was fraught with restlessness and longing.

"Are you able to keep a sense of peace?" Rubenstein asked.

"I would have to say that, probably, my only peace has been in between
the ropes and hitting the shots," Woods admitted.

Woods was so uncharacteristically introspective with Rubenstein that

Time magazine published a lengthy transcript of their conversation under the headline "Tiger's Private Struggles." Woods also chose Rubenstein to help him write a book commemorating the twentieth anniversary of his historic win at the Masters. With the publication of *The 1997 Masters: My Story* scheduled to coincide with the 2017 Masters, Woods spent considerable time with Rubenstein, sharing memories and telling stories. To the delight of his publisher, Woods wrote about his stuttering as a child and the fact that it took him two years of working with a speech therapist before he learned to speak comfortably, and about the pressure of being the so-called black hope of golf. He also talked candidly about his father's deliberately using demeaning profanity to toughen him up. Reflecting back on that period of his life, Tiger defended his father's methods, crediting Earl for teaching him how to be a champion. He decided to use his book to praise his father and to let the world know how much he loved his parents.

Although Woods talked to Rubenstein a great deal, he was off the grid for much of 2016, in too much pain to play in tournaments or make many public appearances—nor did he reach out when the people closest to him were suffering. When his longtime friend Glenn Frey, front man for the Eagles, unexpectedly passed away early in the year, Tiger didn't contact the family or send any kind of condolences. His silence, according to a close friend of Frey's, left the family puzzled and hurt. The Eagles, after all, had supported Tiger's foundation from the very beginning, headlining the first Tiger Jam fund-raising event in Los Angeles in 1998. And Frey also performed at several Tiger Jams in Las Vegas, helping to raise millions of dollars for Tiger's charity over the years.

Similarly, when Lindsay Vonn suffered a gruesome injury while training in Colorado in November 2016—shattering the humerus bone in her right arm, requiring emergency surgery—Tiger didn't reach out to her either, despite the fact that his former lover had suffered nerve damage that left her fearing she may never ski again. Although Tiger's silence toward the Frey family and Vonn may appear callous, it's plausible that he was simply consumed by his own personal struggles with chronic pain and insomnia, relying more and more on powerful medication for relief.

According to the Institute for Medicine, more than 100 million Americans suffer from chronic pain, and the mental health implications can be devastating and frequently misinterpreted. "Pain sufferers often are misdiagnosed, misunderstood, and miserable," explained Rachel Noble Benner, a mental health counselor and researcher with Johns Hopkins University. "Their identities may be significantly altered because they cannot engage in activities they once enjoyed. . . . I have worked with people who had full, rich lives as corporate leaders, athletes, and professors before their chronic pain. However, by the time I saw them, they were isolated, overmedicated, and depressed, and they believed their lives were devoid of meaning."

Tiger's identity had always been defined by his position on a leaderboard. One of the teachings his parents had drilled into him was that winning is what matters, yet Tiger found himself in the midst of the most fallow period of his career—a four-year stretch in which he would not win a single golf tournament. Floundering, he tried to find purpose through his foundation and other business ventures, but nothing filled the void left by his inability to compete. Plus, for a man who guarded his privacy so tightly, Woods missed the camaraderie of the Tour. When he was approached to serve as a vice-captain of the US squad at the 2016 Ryder Cup at Hazeltine, he jumped at the opportunity.

Historically, Woods had a surprisingly poor record in Ryder Cup competition. Many believed that his 13–17–3 overall record reflected his lack of enthusiasm for the team spirit of the event, and, in truth, he had always been aloof from his teammates. But as vice-captain, he spent hours talking strategy by telephone with team members like Brandt Snedeker leading up to the tournament. Guys who had never heard a word from Tiger were suddenly getting peppered with calls. It was so unusual that they were laughing about how engaged he had become. "For the first time with everybody," one source said, "he was completely a locker-room guy."

On picture day, five chairs were set up as two players sat on either side of Captain Davis Love III and the rest of the 12-member squad gathered around. Woods got so caught up in the moment that he was oblivious to the fact that the photographer was politely waiting for him to step out of the frame. Tiger, it seemed, believed he was part of the team, and no one on the US contingent had the heart to tell the greatest golfer of all time that he didn't belong, leaving the photographer to deliver the news. "Ah, Tiger," he said diplomatically, "could you just go off to the right there?" Not quite getting the message, Woods took a few steps but remained in the shot. Taking it all in, US team members whispered and elbowed each other like second graders until someone finally mustered the nerve to speak up.

"Tiger," came the words, "you're not on the team. Please go stand over there with the other coaches."

Everyone cracked up as a huge grin swept across Woods's face. All week, the game's young guns had been in awe of him, but suddenly Tiger came across as just one of the guys. They had never seen him appear so human. "It just made you love the guy," one said.

More than ever, Tiger missed being part of what he liked to refer to as "the fight." He hated that his body was holding him back. Despite three back surgeries and a long layoff, he was still in an inordinate amount of pain. Some days, even lying down hurt. It was maddening. Against his better judgment, Woods decided to attempt a comeback at the Farmers Insurance Open in late January 2017—but the impact of swinging his club generated sharp nerve pain, and he shot a 76 in the opening round and failed to make the cut. After seventeen months away from the PGA Tour, it looked like his playing days were coming to an end.

Still, he soldiered on, traveling to the Middle East for the Dubai Desert Classic. This time the long flight did him in, exacerbating his back spasms and forcing him to withdraw after the first round. By the time Woods arrived in Southern California to host his tournament—the Genesis Open—in mid-February, he could barely walk. Right before the start of the tournament, Tiger attended a private luncheon at Hillcrest Country Club in Beverly Hills. His condition startled the crowd. "If you didn't see him from the front, you would have thought he was a ninety-year-old man, the way he was shuffling," said one Hillcrest club member who was present.

Following the luncheon, Woods cautiously made his way to an adjacent room, where some Hillcrest members were waiting for him and his golf course design team to make a final presentation. Entering the room, Tiger had trouble navigating a few small steps. He was in such bad shape that he had to walk up the steps *backward*. Even more troubling was the look of his eyes—glassy and bloodshot. "He was way, way, way overmedicated," observed one eyewitness.

The next day, Woods canceled his Genesis tournament press confer-

ence, citing doctor's orders that he "limit all activities." After two tournaments in which he'd failed to get past the second round, Tiger shelved his
comeback. Other than a round of media appearances in New York City
to promote the release of his new book in March, he remained out of the
public eye until April and the Masters. Despite resting his back for nearly
two months and doing everything possible to get himself ready to play,
he couldn't tolerate the pain when he swung the club. Nevertheless, he
made the trek to Augusta and attended the Champions Dinner, where he
sat next to Mark O'Meara. They hadn't spoken since Woods had failed to
show up at O'Meara's induction into golf's Hall of Fame, nor had Tiger
responded to texts from O'Meara leading up to the Masters. But being
back at Augusta with his old friend gave Woods a moment of joy. He cherished the fact that after all these years, O'Meara still called him "the Kid."

"I love you," Woods told O'Meara.

He meant it, but O'Meara wasn't sure what to think. He probably
knew Tiger better than anyone on Tour, and yet he never felt like he really
knew his friend. Like Hank Haney, O'Meara couldn't help wondering why
Tiger seldom extended the simple courtesies, such as returning a text message or being the one to call and check in. He just seemed to inexplicably
go dark for long periods of time—but whenever Woods saw O'Meara at
a tournament or somewhere else, he authentically reacted as if he were
reuniting with a long-lost brother.

O'Meara asked how he was feeling. "Good days and bad days," Woods
said. Then he dropped his guard, telling O'Meara that his back was killing
him, and adding that he believed his work with Sean Foley had aggravated
the situation. The frank conversation reminded O'Meara of the way they
talked during a round of golf when they were neighbors in Isleworth. It
reminded O'Meara how much he, in turn, loved Woods.

A day later, O'Meara did a brief interview with Golf Channel anchor
Rich Lerner following the final practice round. Asked by Lerner how Tiger
was doing, O'Meara wasn't about to reveal what Woods had told him. Instead, he kept his answer vague, mentioning that he had sat next to Tiger
at the Champions Dinner and that his friend had "good days and bad
days." That night, O'Meara woke up around two a.m., needing to use the
bathroom. As he got out of bed, he noticed his phone lighting up. Woods
was texting to say that he loved O'Meara like a brother but would appreciate it if he did not discuss his health with the media.

Publicly acknowledging vulnerability, even when it was painfully obvious, went against everything Woods believed. Privately, however, he was at the end of his rope. He had tried every nonsurgical route to alleviate the pain in his lower back—rehabilitation, medications, injections, restricting his activities—but nothing had worked. Unable to live with the pain any longer, he consulted a specialist and weighed his options. He knew that the L5/S1 disc in his lower back had severely narrowed, resulting in sciatica and burning back and leg pain. His best hope was a minimally invasive surgery known as anterior lumbar interbody fusion, otherwise known as a spinal fusion. It entailed removing the damaged disc and re-elevating the collapsed disc space to normal levels, which might allow one vertebra to fuse to the other. The ultimate goal was to relieve pressure on the nerve, affording it the optimal opportunity to heal.

"If you're going to have a single-level fusion, the bottom level is the best place for it to occur," explained Dr. Richard Guyer of the Center for Disc Replacement at the Texas Back Institute.

On April 20, 2017, Woods had the surgery, which Dr. Guyer declared a success. If everything went according to plan, Tiger would gradually begin rehabbing until the area was completely healed, and then he would begin workouts geared toward helping him return to competitive golf.

One month after his fourth back surgery, Woods wrote an unusually wordy blog post expressing his regrets for missing his annual Tiger Jam at the MGM Grand and thanking the many celebrities who had shown up to make the weekend a success. "It has been just over a month since I underwent fusion surgery on my back," he wrote, "and it is hard to express how much better I feel. It was instant nerve relief. I haven't felt this good in years." After elaborating on why he opted for fusion surgery, he praised his doctors and said his prognosis for returning to golf was positive. "There's a long way to go, but as I said, words cannot convey how good it feels to be pain-free."

He posted that statement on May 24, 2017. Five days later, Woods took a potentially lethal cocktail of drugs—Dilaudid, a controlled substance prescribed for severe pain; Vicodin, another powerful opiate used for pain relief; Xanax, an antianxiety medication also used to help treat sleep deprivation; THC, the active ingredient in marijuana; and Ambien, an anti-insomnia medication—and lost consciousness while behind the wheel of his Mercedes sports car. Shortly after two a.m., an officer from the Jupiter Police Department pulled up behind Tiger's car, which was stopped in the right-hand lane in the 2900 block of Military Trail, just south of Indian Creek Parkway. Both tires on the driver's side were blown out, and the rims were damaged. The right blinker was flashing, the brake lights were illuminated, and the engine was still running.

After activating his flashing red-and-blue lights and turning on his dashcam, the officer approached the passenger side and shined his flashlight through the window, observing Woods, whose eyes were closed. Tapping on the window, the officer jarred him awake and gave instructions to put the vehicle in park and turn off the engine. Dazed, Woods struggled to fully open his eyes as he fumbled for the button to lower the window while the officer repeatedly asked him to put the car in park. Finally complying, Tiger managed to find his license and hand it to the officer, who examined it. Woods was fifteen miles from home, but he was heading in the opposite direction.

"Where were you coming from?" the officer asked.

"Jupiter," Woods said.

"Where were you going?"

"Jupiter," he repeated, starting to nod off again.

As the officer returned to his cruiser to run Tiger's license, Woods leaned back against the headrest and closed his eyes. Moments later, a second officer approached the driver's side of the Mercedes, asking Woods where he was coming from.

"LA," he said this time, adding that he was on his way to Orange County.

The officer informed Tiger that he was in Florida, not Southern California.

The officer asked Woods to step out of the car, and he leaned on the door to steady himself. Noting that Tiger's shoes were untied, the officer asked if he wanted to tie them. When Woods explained that he couldn't bend down that far, the officer observed that his speech was slurred, and his eyes were so droopy that he could scarcely keep them open. All the while, the dashcam video was running. Swaying and using his arms to balance himself, Woods failed a series of standard roadside sobriety tests.

Once the greatest athlete in the world, he was now unable to walk in a straight line.

"Sir, I want you to go ahead and place your hands behind your back," one officer said, as the other applied handcuffs.

Tiger's arrest for driving while impaired took place the day before Memorial Day, a slow news day. By midday Memorial Day, his mug shot—droopy eyes, scruffy face, disheveled hair—had set the internet ablaze. The *New York Post* and the *Daily News* put it on their front pages with an identical bold headline: "DUI of the Tiger." Other headlines were equally merciless: "Watch the Birdie! Bleary-Eyed Tiger Woods Doesn't Look to Be in Championship Form in His Mug Shot"; "Master of His Own Demise"; "Catatonic."

After spending the night in the Palm Beach County Jail, Woods was released around noon. Later that day, a spokesman issued a statement: "I understand the severity of what I did, and I take full responsibility for my actions. I want the public to know that alcohol was not involved. What happened was an unexpected reaction to prescribed medications. I didn't realize the mix of medications had affected me so strongly."

The fact that he had recorded 0.00 for alcohol on a breath test was beside the point. The urine sample he provided after his arrest confirmed that Woods was living in what some experts refer to as "a new kind of jail for the opiate age." By combining the opiates Vicodin and Dilaudid with the powerful sedatives Xanax and Ambien, plus THC, Woods had put his life at risk—not to mention the lives of other motorists—when he got behind the wheel. Vicodin, for example, can cause respiratory distress and death when taken in high doses or when combined with other substances. And Xanax can impair memory, judgment, and coordination. Taken together, they can suppress breathing and lead to a high risk of addiction, overdose, and impairment.

Woods certainly wasn't alone. Drug overdoses are now the leading cause of death among Americans under fifty, with overdose deaths totaling 52,404 in 2016, the most in US history. But it's safe to say that no other individual struggling with an addiction to prescription drugs did so under more scrutiny and with more public humiliation than Woods.

With news agencies seeking access to details about Tiger's arrest, authorities in Florida released extensive video of him stumbling through his roadside sobriety tests and talking incoherently while in police custody. The footage aired on CBS, ABC, NBC, Fox, and CNN, and on a host of news websites. More than a million viewers watched clips on YouTube.

Tiger needed help, not ridicule and condemnation—and not long after his arrest, he received a call from Olympic swimmer Michael Phelps. Along with winning twenty-eight Olympic medals, Phelps was twice arrested for DUI and spent eight weeks in a treatment facility seeking help for anxiety and depression. After his release from The Meadows in Arizona, Phelps devoted himself to helping others deal with the stigma of addiction and mental illness. "I want to be able to get out in public and talk and say, 'Yes, I've done these great things in the pool, but I'm also a human,'" Phelps said. "I'm going through the same struggles as a lot of . . . people." One of the people Phelps had helped was Tiger's close friend Notah Begay III, a recovering alcoholic who reached out to the swimmer. From Begay's perspective, Phelps was one of the few people in the world who had the credibility and experience to reach Tiger at such a critical time.

Phelps looked at Tiger's arrest through a unique lens. "I feel like that's a massive scream for help," he said.

The first time Woods spoke to Phelps, the phone call lasted two hours. It was the beginning of an important new friendship, facilitated by other friends who cared deeply for Tiger. Begay and Phelps had both walked the road of treatment and recovery, and together, they joined forces to offer a lifeline to a man drowning in pain and despair. "We weren't looking at trying to salvage a golf career," Begay said. "We were trying to salvage someone's life and future."

CHAPTER THIRTY-FIVE

MAKING THE CUT

Tiger beamed as his ten-year-old daughter, Sam, and eight-year-old son, Charlie, posed for pictures with Lionel Messi, the greatest soccer player in the world. It was a private moment of parental pride, the kind of which most moms or dads could only dream. Since both of his children played soccer, Tiger had arranged a private audience for them with Messi while his Spanish club, FC Barcelona, was in Florida for a preseason match in July 2017.

"Isn't it neat to meet a living legend?" Tiger said to his kids.

"Yeah," Sam said. "We live with one."

Her response drew laughs. It also got Tiger thinking seriously about the fact that his kids had never seen him play in his prime. Sam was around when her dad won the last of his fourteen major championships, but she was too young to remember. And Charlie was still a toddler when Tiger won his last PGA Tour trophy at the 2013 WGC-Bridgestone Invitational. *How great would it be to have one of them carry my bag in a tournament?* Woods wondered. *Imagine what it would be like for them to see me win again.*

Imagination had always set Woods apart from everyone else: he didn't just conceive impossible shots and unprecedented performances, he willed them into reality. One of the most devastating effects of being derailed by years of chronic pain was that it robbed Tiger of his creative genius. But now that he was three months removed from spinal fusion surgery, Woods was experiencing one of life's greatest feelings—freedom from pain. For the first time in a long while, he had his mobility back.

He'd also been through treatment for misusing prescription drugs. In the wake of his arrest and public humiliation, Woods had quietly checked himself into a clinic in June. During inpatient care, he got his reliance on pain medication under control. It had taken being lost on the side of a road just fifteen miles from home to convince him that he needed help. "I'm proud of him," Mark Steinberg said after Tiger entered treatment. "He's going to get himself right to be able to essentially lead a healthy lifestyle."

Steinberg, like others who were concerned for Woods, was focused on Tiger the human being, not Tiger the golfer. The quiet support from friends and other elite athletes buoyed Woods, helping him to emerge from the clinic determined to finally start that delayed second chapter of his life. Perhaps the best indication that he had turned a corner came at the US Open tennis championships in New York City in late August and early September 2017, where he had gone to watch his friend Rafael Nadal. Nadal's quarterfinal match drew a flock of celebrities—Uma Thurman, Bill Gates, Leonardo DiCaprio, Jerry Seinfeld, Julianna Margulies. Woods, however, stood out as the only celebrity parent who went to the tournament with two children in tow. No longer inhibited by a damaged disc in his lower back, he was spending the kind of quality time with his children that his father had spent with him. And while his children sat with him in Nadal's box, Woods was on the verge of something far greater and more impressive than his fourteen major championships and seventy-nine PGA Tour wins: redemption.

Woods had hit rock bottom in May 2017. The Tiger Woods who stumbled and slurred his words in the police video shot during his arrest was the polar opposite of the Tiger Woods who once pumped his fist on the world's most prestigious golf courses and smiled charismatically in television commercials for the likes of Nike and American Express. During an eight-year span stretching back to his 2009 SUV crash, Woods had lost his marriage, his reputation, his iconic status, and his health. The sheer height from which he'd fallen would have destroyed most mortals—but Tiger Woods never behaved or reacted the way most people do. While Earl's methods for instilling extreme mental toughness in his child prodigy are open to questioning, Tiger did end up with an indefatigable will. He always knew he was different. He practiced longer, trained harder, and prepared more relentlessly. No one had ever been so dominant in every aspect of golf. But after his arrest, Woods became different in a new way. For once, his uniqueness had nothing to do with athleticism or talent. Instead, he was channeling all that he learned and inherited from his parents to rise up, dust himself off, and begin anew.

It started with a willingness to face his new reality. In August 2017, he entered a DUI first-offender program. Then, on October 27, surrounded by eight uniformed officers, Woods entered a courtroom in Palm Beach Gardens, Florida, accepted full responsibility for his actions, and pleaded guilty to reckless driving. He was put on probation for twelve months and required to submit to regular drug testing, complete DUI school, and perform fifty hours of community service.

The first public test came at the end of the year at the Hero World Challenge, a tournament that Woods hosts each year in the Bahamas to raise money for his foundation. Dating back to the tournament's inception in 2000, it had always been an unofficial event, a guaranteed payday that drew some of the top golfers in the world. On November 30, 2017, more top players than usual were on hand, but viewers from around the world tuned in for one reason and one reason only—to see Tiger Woods play golf for the first time since his fusion surgery. As he approached the first tee, there were almost as many cameramen as spectators. The last time he'd played competitive golf—301 days earlier—he could barely swing his club. The question on everyone's mind today was whether his surgically fused back would hold up.

As Woods prepared to tee off, he spotted Rafael Nadal. The number one tennis player in the world was vacationing with family in the Bahamas and had decided to show up unannounced to show his support. Tiger's face lit up. Then he ripped a drive that landed thirty yards ahead of the ball of his playing partner Justin Thomas. Before long, he made his first birdie. A little while later, his trademark fist pump followed a long putt for par. And in a show of solidarity, athletes from around the world chimed in on Twitter:

"It's a great day to see @TigerWoods back on the golf course!" wrote Bo Jackson.

"The wait is over. The wait is over," said Stephen Curry.

"Pumped to be watching @TigerWoods back out there!!!" Michael Phelps wrote.

Woods shot three rounds in the sixties and finished the tournament tied for ninth in an all-star field of eighteen. But by every measure, Tiger was winning at something bigger than golf. Other than taking an anti-inflammatory pill ahead of each round as recommended by his doctor, Woods was medication-free. There was no more wincing when he swung or bent over. He was all smiles after his finish on Sunday. He didn't pretend that he felt like he did in his twenties; he was honest about the fact that no one in his forties feels the way he did in his twenties. It was another admission of truth that made him increasingly relatable.

The personal struggles of Tiger Woods humanized him in ways that had never been possible during his single-minded ascent to the top of the golf world. Tiger was never going to live up to the outlandish expectation of making a greater impact on the world than Martin Luther King Jr., Gandhi, and Nelson Mandela, nor had he ever demonstrated a desire to follow in the footsteps of Muhammad Ali or Arthur Ashe when it came to activism on issues of race and social justice. As it turned out, Woods hadn't even improved the racial integration of the PGA Tour. Despite all his success, only one African American—Harold Varner III—was on the Tour at the start of 2018, and only a handful of current elite junior golfers are black. Nevertheless, Tiger's determination to fight his way back from frailties and bouts of addiction was irresistible to fans. After his performance in the Bahamas, ticket sales for the Farmers Insurance Open at Torrey Pines in late January 2018 underwent the equivalent of electric shock treatment as soon as Woods announced he would be participating in the event.

Unsure what to expect from himself, Tiger was greeted by adoring crowds that turned out to watch him play a practice round prior to the start of the tournament. During the press conference that followed, Tiger used the word *fun* no less than nine times when describing the current state of his life. "My expectations have tempered a little bit because I haven't played," he said. "I haven't played a full schedule since 2015. It's been a long time. To be honest with you, I just want to start playing on the Tour and getting into a rhythm of playing a schedule again."

This was the new Tiger Woods. At forty-two, his cheeks were thicker, and his hairline more circuitous. He was heavier and had wrinkles on his neck. But just before 10:40 a.m. on Thursday, January 25, 2018, he left the putting greens and made his way through a gauntlet of fans shouting "C'mon, Tiger! Let's go, Tiger!" Hundreds of spectators had swarmed the first tee at Torrey Pines South, with thousands more lined twenty deep along both sides of the fairway. Suddenly, an old familiar feeling returned: *Everyone is looking at me.* The other players, the packed gallery, viewers watching on television—he still had the aura. *What a great feeling!*

It may have been a Thursday morning in January at Torrey Pines, but it felt more like a Sunday afternoon in April at Augusta. Ten years earlier, on the same Torrey Pines course, Woods had won the US Open—his last major championship—while playing with a broken leg. The sport had changed so much since then. A parade of young stars—Rory, Dustin, Jordan, Rickie, Justin, and Jon—had taken their turn in the spotlight. But none of them were in Tiger's league. Consider:

Rickie Fowler had three PGA Tour wins at age twenty-seven. Tiger had thirty-four at the same age.

It took Jordan Spieth 112 Tour starts to get his tenth win. Tiger got there in 63.

Dustin Johnson won his only major at age thirty-one. At the same age, Tiger had won twelve.

As much as they liked the idea of having Woods back on Tour, none of the young guns had any idea what it was like to compete against Tiger in his prime. Meanwhile, more seasoned pros noticed one big change—Tiger's surly, stone-faced demeanor had been replaced by a smiling, engaging one. Perhaps the most telling example came on Thursday, on the par 5 thirteenth hole, after Woods somehow missed a two-and-a-half-foot putt for par. If Tiger was angry with himself, it didn't show. As he walked off the green and headed toward the fourteenth tee, he looked up and noticed the abundance of military personnel packed into the stands behind the green. A Marine in full dress had been holding the flag as players putted out. It was Torrey's tribute to a military town. Pausing, Woods acknowledged the men and women in uniform.

The gesture thrilled one longtime Tour insider. "He never, ever, ever would have done that before," the observer said. "He would have had his head down and not seen a thing. Now he was looking up and taking it all in, smelling the roses."

But could an older, transformed Woods still muster the trademark killer instinct that had enabled him to crush one pro after another for so many years? For most of the first two days, Tiger fought a driver that betrayed him on virtually every hole, only to grind his way, if not into contention, to a realistic chance of making the thirty-six-hole cut. On Friday, Woods faced a do-or-die situation, the kind of test he'd routinely aced in the past. It came on his final hole of the day, the par 5 ninth, on the tighter, tougher, redesigned North course. Woods found himself some eighty feet away from the hole in two shots. Desperately needing a two-stroke birdie to have a shot at playing on the weekend, he stalked the putt like the Tiger of old. Then he slowly drew back his putter and sent the ball streaking toward the cup before it slowly rolled to a stop a mere eight inches from the cup. Amid a chorus of cheers, he tapped in for birdie and wound up making the cut. Smiling, he removed his cap, waved to the crowd, and shook hands with his playing partner Patrick Reed.

On the same weekend when thirty-six-year-old tennis star Roger Federer further redefined the limits of age by winning his twentieth Grand Slam singles title at the Australian Open, Woods dominated the headlines by completing a PGA Tour event for the first time in nearly nine hundred days. By the time he finished his round on Sunday, the sports world was experiencing a sense of déjà vu. Final-round ratings for the CBS Sports telecast were up 38 percent from the year before, giving the tournament its best Sunday numbers in five years—since the last time Woods won at Torrey. It proved once more that as long as he's competing, Tiger is the golfer that people care about the most.

Woods's performance tempted journalists to suggest that his return to competitive golf was something of a miracle. Perhaps it was. Given the depth of his descent into a dark, cavernous hole that has swallowed so many child stars—actors, musicians, athletes—Tiger's greatest victory was not in golf but rather in his journey back into the light and, for the first time in many years, into life. A changed man, he stood poised to show his children—and a fresh generation of golf pros and fans—just what a living legend looks like.

AFTERWORD

Tiger emerged from beneath the water in the Bahamas and climbed onto his boat. Earlier in his career, scuba diving and spearfishing had been his great escape, his way to get away from it all and unwind. This time his children were with him, which made him cherish the experience on a different level. It was the summer of 2018, just days after missing the cut at the US Open. Instead of focusing on the fact that he hadn't played well, he was doing something he rarely experienced in life—enjoying the moment.

"Dad," his daughter, Sam, said, looking up at his diving gear. "I didn't think you could ever do this again."

Only a year earlier, when he was recovering from back fusion surgery and trying to cope with unyielding pain through pills, the freedom to strap on a tank of air and take a giant stride off the back of a boat and hunt grouper seemed like a distant memory. Fully aware of how fortunate he was, Woods struggled to keep his emotions in check.

Sam looked into her father's suddenly misty eyes.

"It's the seawater," Tiger said.

It was a line that would bring a smile to any father who knew what it was like to hide tears from a child.

Redemption swells the soul with gratitude in a way that is hard to put into words. He wasn't about to attempt to explain this to his kids. But he was determined to hold on to what he had. *I'm not going to screw this up,* he told himself. *I'm not going to screw this up.*

A month later, on the Carnoustie Championship course in Scotland, Tiger overcame a four-stroke deficit in the final round of the British Open. With eight holes to play, he was atop the leaderboard. There was no hesitation in his swing. No flinch in his putting stroke. No hint of nerves. Wearing his vintage bloodred shirt and black pants, he was on the cusp of pulling off the inconceivable—winning his first major in more than ten years. The roar of the crowd seemed to be propelling him.

Then his ball landed in a bunker. And after a double bogey on eleven and a bogey on twelve, he was behind his playing partner, Francesco Molinari, who went on to complete a bogey-free round. Angry at himself, Tiger knew his chance had gotten away from him. Still, he reminded himself to keep things in perspective—*I'm in the hunt at the British Open Championship!*

He finished tied for sixth, three strokes behind Molinari. It marked Tiger's best finish at a major since the 2013 US Open. Congratulating Molinari and tipping his cap to the crowd, Tiger exited the course amid rousing applause. His children were there to greet him.

"Hopefully you're proud of your pops for trying as hard as I did," he told them.

They put their arms around him and squeezed.

The desire to win still burned within him. But he no longer measured wins and losses as he had in the past. With a surgically repaired back, he was in the mix on one of golf's biggest stages. That's a W. He was loving fatherhood. That's a W. He had a new girlfriend—thirty-three-year-old Erica Herman—and they were true friends. Another W.

Given where I was to where I'm at now, I'm blessed, he told himself.

"Ti-ger! Ti-ger! Ti-ger!"

Two months later, on the final day of the Tour Championship, the massive crowds trailing Tiger could be heard all across the East Lake Golf Club just outside Atlanta. Up to this point, in seventeen tour events in 2018, he had finished in the top five four times. But had yet to win a tournament. In August he came closest, finishing second at the PGA Championship, just two shots behind winner Brooks Koepka. Experts and analysts had been weighing in on what it would take—and how much it would mean to the game of golf—for Woods to finally win again.

But when it comes to golf, the best voice for Tiger has always been the one inside him. That was especially true in 2018. After all, no one else really understood just how high of a mountain he was climbing. No champion had fallen so far, or had so much baggage to shed on his way back up. A year earlier, he couldn't even swing a club. No golfer in history, not even legendary Ben Hogan, had faced the emotional and physical trials Woods had endured. So it wasn't as if Tiger could go to someone for advice. He just had to figure it out on his own.

At East Lake it all came together. Woods put on a dazzling display of putting and ball striking, shooting a sizzling first-round 65, followed by a 68 on Friday. Then on Saturday he shot another 65, vaulting him to the top of the leaderboard by two over Rory McIlroy. On the first tee on Sunday, on arguably the toughest driving hole on the course, Woods belied his history of shaky starts and absolutely striped it with his driver, sending a clear message to the field—*I'm back!*

Some five hours later, as Tiger walked toward the eighteenth green with the lead in hand, thousands of ecstatic spectators overwhelmed security and swarmed the fairway. Trailed by a mob with smartphones raised high, Tiger smiled jubilantly as he strode toward his ball. The chaotic scene was reminiscent of when fans stormed the fairway on the final hole at Cog Hill in Chicago in 1997, following him as he raised his putter en route to victory at the Western Open.

To a certain degree, those two triumphant moments symbolized turning points in Woods's life. The victory at Cog Hill in '97 was just his fourth win on the PGA Tour, and that chaotic fairway scene represented the unofficial start of Tiger Mania, a period of his life dictated by extreme fame and celebrity. The stroll down the fairway at East Lake on September 23, 2018, looked like the arrival of a man with a new lease on life.

When Woods was at the pinnacle of his sport, he came off more like a machine than a man. He dispatched opponents with the cold precision of a trained assassin. He had a distant, surly relationship with the press. He kept fans at a distance. He was so much better than everyone else and so single-minded that spectators couldn't relate to him.

Now, at forty-two, he had formed friendships with everyone from Justin Thomas, Rickie Fowler, and Jordan Spieth to Phil Mickelson and was gracious in defeat. He joked with reporters. He went out of his way to engage with fans. The fact that his personal problems played out in public—an infidelity scandal, sex addiction treatment, divorce, the misuse of prescription painkillers, and a DUI arrest—ultimately endeared him to the public in ways that his mastery of golf never could. The fact that he endured so much—and pulled himself out of such a deep hole—created a groundswell of support from people throughout the world who now root for Tiger Woods the man, the *human* being, much more than Tiger Woods the golfer.

With millions glued to their television sets, silently cheering him on, Woods feathered a bunker shot up close to insure that he would win his first PGA Tour event in five years—in 1,876 days, to be exact. Moments later, when he tapped in his final putt, thunderous cheers shook the ground around him as he thrust his arms into the air.

"We thought we'd never see it!" NBC Sports announcer Dan Hicks exclaimed. "Tour Championship winner—Tiger Woods! A winner again!"

The ovation was so loud that it overwhelmed the television broadcasters. Tiger's eyes welled up as he looked at the thousands of spectators surrounding the green, chanting his name. He'd been famous since he was two years old. Now, finally, he was beloved.

ACKNOWLEDGMENTS

This book would not exist, certainly not in this form, without invaluable assistance from our excellent team. First and foremost, we salute Timothy Bella, an extraordinary reporter who rode shotgun with us on *The System* and assumed a similar role on this journey. Tim waded through administrative red tape to track down and obtain public records from municipal governments, state and federal agencies, courts, and police departments. He conducted a number of valuable interviews. And we nicknamed him "the people finder" for his uncanny ability to use social media and other databases to locate individuals—often within minutes of us giving him a name. He also read and annotated more than three hundred Tiger Woods press conference transcripts.

Attorneys Bruce Fay in Florida and Michael McCann in Vermont tracked down real estate records, financial documents, court records, and police reports. Legal researcher Ron Fuller in Washington, DC, mined court dockets and helped generate hundreds of pages of court cases involving Tiger Woods, his corporation, Nike, Titleist, and other individuals and entities. And Eliza Rothstein obtained sales figures on books published by Tiger Woods and Earl Woods. Dan Riemer of Revelations, Inc., in Plantation, Florida, did some valuable background work.

The *Stanford Daily* provided us with copies of every article it ever published mentioning Tiger Woods. At the same time, a research librarian at *Sports Illustrated* shipped us boxes containing hard copies of more than a thousand articles about Tiger Woods from newspapers, magazines, journals, and other periodicals. Jeff Benedict's research assistants Brittany Weisler and Mette Laurence put all these articles into chronological order and helped us construct a detailed time line of Tiger's life, a process that took more than six months to complete.

Editor Carolyn Lumsden provided us with all the articles from the *Hartford Courant* pertaining to Connecticut's various cases against John Merchant.

LTC Ben Garrett, from the US Army's media relations, helped us obtain Earl Woods's military records. And David Martin, CBS News's longtime Pentagon correspondent, helped us interpret and understand those records.

Jon Parton, editor in chief of the *Kansas State Collegian*, conducted an initial interview with Mike Mohler, sexton of Sunset Cemetery, and dug up clips and information on Earl Woods's days at K-State.

Journalists Jaime Diaz, Alan Shipnuck, John Strege, John Feinstein, Jimmy Roberts, and Wright Thompson were gracious in sharing their valuable insights. The folks at CBS Sports and NBC Sports were very helpful in providing clips and background information.

We are also grateful to: former ABC News senior producer Paul Mason, the man behind "Tiger's Tale," the first network television profile of Woods and his family, which ran on *Primetime Live* on July 15, 1993; Lance Barrow, the longtime coordinating producer of the PGA Tour Golf on CBS Sports, for his Texas-sized hospitality and access to select Tour events; Rick Schloss, the media director for thirty years at the Buick Invitational and Farmers Insurance Open at Torrey Pines; Dave Cordero, director of communications for the World Golf Hall of Fame & Museum, for the link to Mark O'Meara's 2015 induction speech; Tom Clearwater, for opening the door to certain Las Vegas insiders; Norm Clarke, Mr. Las Vegas and the man behind *NORM!*, his Vegas diary; Rick Ryan, president of the Brooklawn Country Club; Barclay Douglas Jr. and other members of the Newport Country Club; Ed Mauro; Tom Graham, of the Country Club of Fairfield; and Dr. Gary Gray, PT, FAFS®, CEO of the Gray Institute, and founding father of Applied Functional Science.

In compiling a list of sports and golf writers and analysts to thank, we begin with an apology to those we've inadvertently failed to mention. Tiger's career has been chronicled by some of the very best in the business. They are acknowledged here in alphabetical order, with their corresponding employment at the time of their work on Woods: Karen Allen, *USA Today*; Nancy Armour, *USA Today*; Michael Bamberger, *Sports Illustrated*;

Thomas Bonk, *Los Angeles Times*; Nick Canepa, *San Diego Union-Tribune*; Mark Cannizzaro, *New York Post*; Brandel Chamblee, Golf Channel; Tim Crothers, *Sports Illustrated*; Karen Crouse, *New York Times*; Tom Cunneff, *People*; Steve DiMeglio, *USA Today*; Larry Dorman, *New York Times*; Tim Elfrink, *Miami New Times*; Doug Ferguson, Associated Press; Gus Garcia-Roberts, *Newsday*; Shav Glick, *Los Angeles Times*; Hank Gola, *New York Daily News*; Bob Harig, ESPN.com; Mickey Herskowitz, *Houston Chronicle*; Tod Leonard, *San Diego Union-Tribune*; Robert Lusetich, Fox Sports.com; Jonathan Mahler, *New York Times*; Cameron Morfit, *Sports Illustrated*; Ian O'Connor, ESPN.com; Bill Pennington, *New York Times*; Bill Plaschke, *Los Angeles Times*; Rick Reilly, *Sports Illustrated*; Howard Richman, *Kansas City Star*; Mark Seal, *Vanity Fair*; Ed Sherman, *Chicago Tribune*; Alan Shipnuck, *Sports Illustrated*; Ron Sirak, Associated Press and Ronsirak.com; Gary Smith, *Sports Illustrated*; Howard Sounes, author; Gary Van Sickle, *Sports Illustrated*; Dan Wetzel, Yahoo Sports; and Michael Wilbon, *Washington Post*.

Finally, there is the publishing team, starting with our agent, Richard Pine, an incredibly smart and creative advocate and an even better friend. He was with us every step of the way on this, from idea to publication. Dorothea Halliday provided invaluable input and guidance on the narrative. Kelvin Bias was our astute fact-checker. Our editor, Jofie Ferrari-Adler, offered smart, insightful guidance that helped transform the narrative. And our publisher, Jon Karp, was a gem to work with, along with manager of copyediting Jonathan Evans and the entire Simon & Schuster team, including Julianna Haubner, associate editor; Richard Rhorer, associate publisher; Larry Hughes, associate director of publicity; Dana Trocker, associate marketing director; Kristen Lemire, managing editor; Lisa Erwin, production director; Samantha Hoback, production editor; Ben Holmes, copyeditor; Laura Ogar, indexer; Jackie Seow, cover designer; and Carly Loman, who made the pages inside this book look so clean and crisp.

NOTES

When reporting what Tiger said, we relied on statements he's made—in press conferences, in interviews, or during competitions or other events that were videotaped—and on his writings, primarily those in his book *The 1997 Masters: My Story*. We also relied on interviews with scores of individuals who recounted direct conversations with him. Similarly, when reporting Tiger's *thoughts*, we relied on statements and writings in which he discussed his thinking. We also conducted interviews with individuals with whom Tiger shared his thinking.

In instances where we've described scenes, we interviewed at least one source who was present or had firsthand knowledge of what took place. Where we've reconstructed dialogue, we always attempted to interview at least one person who was a party in the conversation, and when possible we also interviewed a witness to the conversation. Additionally, we pulled quotations and dialogue from press-conference transcripts, court records, sworn affidavits, police records, video footage, and previously published works.

Unless otherwise specified in these notes, direct quotations derive from interviews with the authors. Roughly half of those whom we interviewed asked not to be identified. While we seldom quoted anonymous sources, we found their input invaluable. We are particularly grateful to those who agreed to speak to us on the record: Al Abrams, Charles Barkley, Sharon Begley, Marian Bergeson, Neal Boulton, Craig Bowen, Dr. Jay Brunza, Ann Burger, Brandel Chamblee, Norm Clarke, Chris Coen, Victor Conte, Jerry Courville, Athan Crist, Don Crosby, Dr. Eri Crum, Tom Cunneff, Brad L. Dalton, Joe DeBock, Maureen Decker, Kel Devlin, Jaime Diaz, Peter DiBari, Ryan Donovan, Barclay Douglas Jr., Walt Douglas, Rudy Duran, Diane Euler, John Feinstein, Ari Fleischer, Barry Frank, Paul Fre-

gia, Deborah Ganley, Deb Gelman, Wally Goodwin, Tom Graham, Dina
Gravell, Dr. Gary Gray, Brian H. Greenspan, Joe Grohman, Hank Haney,
Bill Harmon, Butch Harmon, Don Harris, Jim Harris, Bruce Heppler, Jim
Hill, Lori Hintelmann, Mike Holder, Tommy Hudson, Roy S. Johnson,
Fred Khalilian, Laurence Kirshbaum, Bill Knowles, Magdalena Kochanek,
Chip Lange, Amber Lauria, David Lee, Shari Lesser-Wenk, Peggy Lewis,
Karl Lund, Robert Lusetich, Megan Mahoney, Bart Mandell, Corey Martin,
Paul Mason, Ed Mauro, Bob May, John McCormick, Pete McDaniel, John
Merchant, Dr. Monica Meyer, Chris Mike, Julie Milton, Mike Mohler, Kim
Montes, Candace Norton, Jeffrey Olgin, Alicia O'Meara, Mark O'Meara,
Dr. Barak Ozgur, Rod Personius, Charles Pierce, Curt Pringle, Dr. Keith
Pyne, T. R. Reinman, Jim Riswold, Jimmy Roberts, Bill Romanowski, Rick
Ryan, Tim Sargent, Rick Schloss, Matt Schneider, Kristi Scott, Steve Scott,
Mark Seal, Scott Seymour, Michael Shapiro, Ed Sherman, Alan Shipnuck,
Doc Sims, Gary Smith, Ruben Smith, Howard Sounes, Grant Spaeth, Lori
Spaeth, Leslie Spaulding, Ruth Streeter, John Strege, Herb Sugden, Diane
Sullivan, Gary Sykes, Tom Tait, Dr. Richard Taite, Wright Thompson, Don
Transeth, Brian Tucker, Dr. David Vail, Tom Wilson, Roy Wininger, Rick
Wolff, Royce Woods, William Wuliger, and Dennis Young.

PROLOGUE

Primary sources include research conducted by the authors in Manhattan,
Kansas, and specifically at Sunrise Cemetery, as well as interviews with Mike
Mohler, Royce Woods, Wright Thompson, and an individual at Manhattan
Monuments. We also relied on the military records of Earl Woods obtained
from the National Personnel Records Center in St. Louis, Missouri (the offi-
cial repository for military records), and records obtained from Kansas State
University and the PGA Tour.

xiv *died of a heart attack*: Frank Litsky, "Golf: Earl Woods, Tiger's Father,
     Dies," *New York Times*, May 4, 2006.
xiv *"He is the Chosen One"*: Gary Smith, "The Chosen One," *Sports Illus-
     trated*, December 1996, 33.
xiv *referred to as his "best friend"*: Tiger Woods, press conference, Memorial
     Tournament, June 1, 1999.
xiv *and "hero"*: Earl Woods, *Playing Through: Straight Talk on Hard Work,*

Big Dreams, and Adventures with Tiger (New York: HarperCollins, 1998), 1.

xiv *"I love you, son"*: CBS Sports broadcast of the Masters, April 13, 1997.

xiv *Earl's burial lot*: Sunset Cemetery Site Map, cityofmhk.maps.arcgis.com.

xiv *flying from Southern California*: Wright Thompson, "The Secret History of Tiger Woods," *ESPN The Magazine*, April 21, 2016.

xiv *ten-inch-by-ten-inch square wooden box*: Authors' interviews with Mike Mohler.

xiv *twelve inches long by twelve inches wide*: Ibid.

xvi *he was an introvert*: Tiger Woods, *The 1997 Masters: My Story* (New York: Grand Central Publishing, 2017), 179.

xviii *not allowed to look at them*: Authors' interview with an assistant librarian at Western High School.

CHAPTER ONE: THE END

Primary sources include research conducted by the authors in the community of Isleworth in Windermere, Florida, and at the Florida State Highway Patrol in Orlando; and interviews with Sgt. Kim Montes, Robert Lusetich, Steve Helling, sources at the *National Enquirer*, and residents of Isleworth. We also relied on police reports from the Florida Highway Patrol and the City of Windermere, as well as photographs and a DVD provided by the authorities.

1 *Barefoot and groggy*: Police report, Florida Highway Patrol, November 27, 2009.

1 *a locked bathroom door*: Maureen Callahan, "The Night Tiger Woods Was Exposed as a Serial Cheater," *New York Post*, November 24, 2013.

1 *It was around two a.m. on Friday*: Police report, Florida Highway Patrol.

1 *clouded by prescription drugs*: Ibid.

1 National Enquirer, *hot on his trail*: Authors' interviews with former employees of the *National Enquirer*.
Authors' note: Rachel Uchitel declined requests for comment.

1 *supermarket tabloid accused Tiger*: *National Enquirer*, November 28, 2009.

1 *after thirty excruciating minutes*: Robert Lusetich, *Unplayable: An In-*

side Account of Tiger's Most Tumultuous Season (New York: Atria Books, 2010), Kindle version.

1 *and started scrolling*: Callahan, "The Night Tiger Woods Was Exposed as a Serial Cheater."

2 *"I miss you"*: Ibid.

2 *"I knew it"*: Lusetich, *Unplayable.* Another variation, as reported in Callahan, "The Night Tiger Woods Was Exposed as a Serial Cheater," has Elin saying: "I knew it was you. I know everything."

2 *"Oh, fuck"*: Callahan, "The Night Tiger Woods Was Exposed as a Serial Cheater."

2 *"She knows," he texted Uchitel*: Ibid.

2 *the only woman he had ever truly feared*: Tiger Woods, press conference, Buick Open, August 7, 2002 ("It was my mom that I was always afraid of," Woods said. "If I didn't say please around my mom, I would be smacked").

2 *"I will beat you"*: S. L. Price, "Tiger Rules," *Sports Illustrated*, April 3, 2000.

2 *golf club in hand*: Gerald Posner, "Tiger's Thanksgiving Mystery Solved," *Daily Beast*, January 24, 2010.

3 *sped out of the driveway . . . plowing into a tree*: Florida Traffic Crash Report Narrative/Diagram, November 27, 2009.

3 *Elin shattered . . . windows*: Incident form, Windermere Police Department, November 27, 2009; and police report, Florida Highway Patrol.

3 *Kimberly Harris woke*: Police report, Florida Highway Patrol.

3 *"find out what's happening"*: Florida Highway Patrol interview with Jarius Adams and Kimberly Harris, November 27, 2009.

3 *"Tiger, are you okay?"*: Police report, Florida Highway Patrol.

3 *His teeth were bloodstained*: Incident form, Windermere Police Department.

3 *"Please help me"*: Police report, Florida Highway Patrol.

3 *"911, what's your emergency?"*: Steve Helling, *Tiger: The Real Story* (Cambridge, MA: Da Capo Press, 2010).

4 *"on the phone with the police"*: Florida Highway Patrol interview with Jarius Adams, November 27, 2009.

4 *the whites of his eyes*: Helling, *Tiger.*

CHAPTER TWO: FAMILY MATTERS

Primary sources include author visits to the Cerritos Elementary School and Tiger's childhood home and neighborhood in Cypress, California; records from the Savanna School District, Kansas State University, and the United States Army; court records from New York, California, and Mexico; books by Earl Woods, Barbara Woods Gary, and Howard Sounes; and interviews with Maureen Decker, Ann Burger, and Royce Woods.

5   *On September 14, 1981*: Email to the authors from Dr. Sue Johnson, superintendent, Savanna School District, January 8, 2016.

5   *his mother created a multiplication table for him*: Woods, *Playing Through*, 75.

6   *"Golf was my decision"*: "Tiger's Prowl: His Life," disc 1, *Tiger: The Authorized DVD Collection*, Buena Vista Home Entertainment, 2004.

7   *"old, fussy, cussy man"*: Howard Sounes, *The Wicked Game: Arnold Palmer, Jack Nicklaus, Tiger Woods, and the Story of Modern Golf* (New York: William Morrow, 2004).

7   *"He could swear for thirty minutes"*: Mickey Herskowitz, "For Earl Woods, a Loving Son Makes Every Day a Father's Day," reprinted in the *Manhattan Mercury*, June 17, 2001.

8   *"'Yeah, that's about right'"*: Ibid.

8   *like "a little dictator"*: Sounes, *The Wicked Game*.

8   *pitch and play first base*: Kansas State University records.

9   *Harold Robinson and Veryl Switzer*: Tim Bascom, "First on the Field," *K-Stater*, December 1997.

9   *first black player to make the American Legion*: Sounes, *The Wicked Game*.

9   *The team left*: Jimmie Tramel, "Tiger Was Raised by a Wildcat," *Tulsa World*, August 3, 2007.

9   *lone black player would not be allowed*: Ibid.

9   *an attractive white girl*: Larry Weigel, "Ray Wauthier and the 'Tiger' Connection," TheMercury.com, February 1, 2013.

9   *degree in sociology*: Nineteenth Annual Commencement, Kansas State College of Agriculture and Applied Science, May 24, 1953.

9   *Barbara Ann Hart, a local girl*: Barbara Woods Gary, *At All Costs: My Life with the Man behind the Tiger* (self-published, 2000).

9   *married . . . during a thunderstorm*: Ibid.

10 *Earl started to disappear*: Ibid.

10 *She felt abandoned*: Ibid.

10 *"who is that man?"*: Woods, *Playing Through*, 48.

10 *"I am to blame for that"*: Ibid., 47.

11 *an* unaccompanied tour: Gary, *At All Costs*, 64.

11 *"a stunningly attractive woman"*: Woods, *Playing Through*, 55.

11 *"this fine little thing"*: Tom Callahan, *His Father's Son: Earl and Tiger Woods* (New York: Gotham Books, 2011), 31.

11 *"I had me a date"*: Ibid.
Authors' note: Kultida Woods did not respond to our request for comment.

12 *"I felt abandoned"*: Jaime Diaz, "Tida in Thailand," *Golf Digest*, July 1, 2013.

12 *first date . . . spent in church*: Woods, *Playing Through*, 55.

12 *"there are only two colors"*: Ibid., 60.

12 *assistant professor of military science*: National Personnel Records Center, St. Louis, Missouri.

13 *psychological warfare studies*: Ibid.

13 *"I don't understand . . . You need help"*: Gary, *At All Costs*, and Callahan, *His Father's Son*, describe this dialogue in slightly different ways. We relied on both accounts for this exchange.

13 *"Maybe I do need help"*: Gary, *At All Costs*, 75.

13 *up-and-coming New York attorney*: Ibid.

13 *"the hardest thing I've ever had to do"*: Ibid., 76.

13 *"the parties hereto are now Husband and Wife"*: Agreement between Barbara Ann Woods and Earl Dennison Woods, May 29, 1968.

13 *"Woody wants a legal separation"*: Ibid.

13 *"living separate and apart"*: Ibid.

13 *"as if sole and unmarried"*: Ibid.

14 *$200 per month "for her support"*: Ibid.

14 *"Why do we have to separate?"*: Gary, *At All Costs*, 85.

14 *with an Asian woman*: Ibid., 92.

14 *in 1968 at age twenty-five*: Diaz, "Tida in Thailand."

14 *married in New York in 1969*: "Declaration of Earl D. Woods," October 2, 1995, Superior Court of California, County of Santa Clara.

14 *"temperaments between the spouses"*: "Judicial Power of the State of Chihuahua Certified Copy of Judgment of Divorce," August 23, 1969, docket 5420/969.

15 *"Consulate assumes no responsibility"*: Gori P. Bruno, Consul of the United States of America, to Earl Woods, letter, August 25, 1969.

15 *"extreme cruelty" and "grievous mental suffering"*: "Complaint for Divorce," no. 226251, filed by Barbara A. Woods, August 25, 1969.

15 *"the parties are still married"*: Interlocutory Judgment of Dissolution of Marriage, Case Number 226251, February 28, 1972.

15 *officially recognizing the divorce*: Final Judgment (Marriage) of Dissolution, filed March 2, 1972, Superior Court of California, County of Santa Clara.

15 *"I question the LEGALITY of that marriage"*: Barbara Woods Gary to the California Superior Court, letter, April 5, 1995.

15 *"I remarried in 1969"*: "Declaration of Earl D. Woods."

15 *"I do not consider myself a bigamist"*: Sounes, *The Wicked Game*.

CHAPTER THREE: A STAR IS BORN

Primary sources include interviews with Jim Hill, Rudy Duran, Royce Woods, and Jaime Diaz; books by Tiger Woods and Earl Woods; and reporting by Jaime Diaz, Gary Smith, Tom Callahan, and John Strege.

17 *unable to have more children*: Jaime Diaz, "Raising Tiger Hardly Just a Father Affair," *GolfWorld*, April 8, 2009.

17 *E in Eldrick stood for Earl*: Callahan, *His Father's Son*, 41.

17 *neglected by her parents*: Diaz, "Tida in Thailand."

17 *nicknamed him "Tiger"*: Woods, *Playing Through*, 32.

18 *one-quarter Thai and one-quarter Chinese*: John McCormick and Sharon Begley, "How to Raise a Tiger," *Newsweek*, December 9, 1996.

18 *"he ain't white"*: Bill Plaschke, "It's a New Day for Golf's Child Prodigy," *Los Angeles Times*, February 22, 1993.

18 *1,474-square-foot ranch*: Property records, Orange County Assessor's Office.

18 *he retreated to the garage*: Woods, *Playing Through*, 69.

19 *Kultida feeding her baby*: Callahan, *His Father's Son*, 41.

19 *"a genius on our hands"*: USA Today Weekend, July 24–26, 1992. Over the years, Earl told various versions of this story.

19 *sawed-off club*: Smith, "The Chosen One"; McCormick and Begley, "How to Raise a Tiger."

20   *"Tida and I made a personal commitment"*: Woods, *Playing Through*, 62.

20   *"Daddy, can I play golf with you today?"*: McCormick and Begley, "How to Raise a Tiger."

23   *"This was my fantasy"*: Woods, *Playing Through*, 39.

23   *Mike Douglas instructed his staff*: Callahan, *His Father's Son*, 42.

23   *"How old are you, Tiger?"*: Mike Douglas, *The Mike Douglas Show*, https://www.youtube.com/watch?v=o92UYBvBdMs.

24   *a "glass cellar"*: Alice Miller, *The Drama of the Gifted Child: The Search for the True Self* (New York: Basic Books, 1997).

24   *"too many starry-eyed parents"*: Callahan, *His Father's Son*, 43.

25   *"We can't dictate to him"*: *That's Incredible!*, https://www.youtube.com/watch?v=kfTY5xUFaJs.

25   *an icy glare*: Ibid.

25   *"My son is very talented"*: Rudy Duran, *In Every Kid There Lurks a Tiger: Rudy Duran's 5 Step Program to Teach You and Your Child the Fundamentals of Golf* (New York: Hachette Books, 2002).

27   *complimentary set of new clubs*: Ibid.

27   *motivational self-help tapes*: John Strege, *Tiger: A Biography of Tiger Woods* (New York: Broadway Books, 1997), 21.

28   *"I do it with all my heart"*: Ibid.

28   *"teachers wouldn't call on me"*: Woods, *The 1997 Masters: My Story*, 74.

28   *"stuttered so badly that I gave up"*: Ibid.

28   *two years in an after-school program*: Ibid., 75.

29   *"Subconsciously, I learned that in the garage"*: Ibid., 18.

29   *"until I fell asleep"*: Ibid., 75.

CHAPTER FOUR: THE PRODIGY

Primary sources include interviews with Dr. Jay Brunza, Meg Mahoney, Tom Sargent, John Strege, and Wally Goodwin; books by Tiger Woods, Earl Woods, and Howard Sounes; reporting by Jaime Diaz; and footage from CBS Sports.

30   *Woods stared intently at the television*: Woods, *The 1997 Masters*, 13.

30   *Earlier that day . . . Tiger had played*: Ibid.

30   *"The Bear has come out of hibernation"*: CBS Sports broadcast, April 13, 1986.

30 *"I wanted to be where he was"*: Woods, *The 1997 Masters*, 14.

30 *PGA . . . amended its constitution*: *Encyclopedia of African-American History* (Oxford, UK: Oxford University Press, 2009), 310. Other sources, such as Alan Shipnuck's book *The Battle for Augusta National: Hootie, Martha, and the Masters of the Universe* (New York: Simon & Schuster, 2004), indicate the change was made in 1943, not 1934.

31 *finally been expunged in 1961*: Ibid.

31 *"I was constantly fighting racism"*: Woods, *Playing Through*, 25.

31 Golf Digest *published a list*: Strege, *Tiger*, 26.

31 *"I'd never seen"*: "Tiger's Prowl: His Life," *Tiger: The Authorized DVD Collection.*

32 *"have that feel-sense"*: Sounes, *The Wicked Game*, 130.

32 *Anselmo didn't ask for payment*: Ibid., 144.

32 *Kultida . . . shuttled Tiger*: Diaz, "Raising Tiger Hardly Just a Father Affair."

32 *Tiger went all the way to Thailand*: Ibid.

33 *"he be a four-star general"*: Strege, *Tiger*, 25. A slightly different version of this story appeared in Smith, "The Chosen One."

33 *"Rak jak Mea"*: Diaz, "Tida in Thailand."

33 *"Mom will never lie to you"*: Diaz, "Raising Tiger Hardly Just a Father Affair."

33 *"go for the throat"*: Ibid. In Strege, *Tiger*, Tida is quoted as saying "Kill them" on p. 37.

33 *"There's no feeling"*: "Tiger's Prowl: His Life," *Tiger: The Authorized DVD Collection.*

34 *favorite thing to do*: Woods, *The 1997 Masters*, 21.

34 *Jay Brunza, PhD*: Dr. Jay Brunza, professional résumé.

35 *When Cameron was a boy*: Jason Sobel, "Why Any Ol' Putter Just Won't Do for Tiger," ESPN.com, April 23, 2017.

35 *Tiger started using Cameron putters*: Ibid.

36 *saw himself as small and scrawny*: Woods, *The 1997 Masters*, 98.

36 *"psychological training that my father used"*: Ibid., 102.

36 *Earl would later brag to golf writers*: Bill Fields, "Ahead of His Time," *Golf Magazine*, February 1992.

36 *"It was psychological warfare"*: Woods, *Playing Through*, 83.

36 *"Fuck off, Tiger"*: Woods, *The 1997 Masters*, 100.

37 *"I needed him to push me"*: Woods, *The 1997 Masters*, 98.

37 *code word . . . was enough*: Smith, "The Chosen One."

37 *"a 'cold-blooded assassin'"*: Woods, *The 1997 Masters*, 98.

38 *letter from Wally Goodwin*: Stanford recruiting letter to Tiger Woods, March 28, 1989.

38 *Tiger wrote back to Goodwin*: Tiger Woods to Wally Goodwin, letter, published in *Golf Digest*, October 9, 2014.

40 *playing with . . . John Daly*: "A Young Lion Named Tiger Will Play Open," *Los Angeles Times*, January 26, 1992.

CHAPTER FIVE: WHO IS TIGER WOODS?

Primary sources include research conducted at Isleworth in Windermere, Florida; court records from California and Ohio; interviews with Don Crosby, Dina Gravell, Joe Grohman, Jaime Diaz, Alicia O'Meara, Mark O'Meara, William Wuliger, Tom Cunneff, and IMG executives; transcripts of Tiger Woods's interviews and press conferences; books by Tiger Woods and Earl Woods; and reporting by John Garrity, Tim Rosaforte, Jaime Diaz, and Tom Cunneff.

42 *They had met in 1989*: Grohman Golf Gazette 1, no. 1 (April 28, 1998).

42 *"'Practice, practice, practice'"*: Woods, *Playing Through*, 74.

43 *"the 10,000-hour rule"*: Malcolm Gladwell, *Outliers: The Story of Success* (Boston: Little, Brown & Company, 2008).

43 *Grohman nicknamed him Champ*: Grohman Golf Gazette 4, no. 1 (June 2002).

44 *"I couldn't fit her in"*: Tiger Woods, interview with Tom Cunneff, *People*, August 11, 1991.

44 *"This is better than childhood"*: Ibid.

45 *to watch Jack Nicklaus*: Tim Rosaforte, *Raising the Bar: The Championship Years of Tiger Woods* (New York: Thomas Dunne Books, 2000), xi.

45 *first black golfer been admitted*: Lance Pugmire, "Private Investigation," *Los Angeles Times*, April 10, 2003.

45 *golf's great black hope"*: Larry Dorman, "A Way Out," *New York Times*, June 7, 1994.

45 *walking into a prison*: Woods, *The 1997 Masters*, 101.

45 *Rodney King . . . beaten*: Chelsea Matiash and Lily Rothman, "The Beating That Changed America," *Time*, March 3, 2016.

45 *"a swing as pretty as yours"*: Strege, *Tiger*, 40.

46 *"Son . . . you will forever be a part of history"*: Tim Rosaforte, "The Come-back Kid," *Sports Illustrated*, September 5, 1994. ("When Tiger won his first US Junior in 1991," said Earl, "I said to him, 'Son, you have done something no black person in the United States has ever done, and you will forever be a part of history.' But this is ungodly in its ramifications.")

46 *"I'd like to be the best ever"*: Jaime Diaz, "Fore! Nicklaus Beware of Teen-Ager," *New York Times*, August 1, 1991.

46 *playing on the varsity tennis and soccer teams*: Western High yearbooks, 1992 and 1993.

47 *profiled in* People *magazine*: "Tiger on the Tee," *People*, September 27, 1991.

49 *Both men had been courting Tiger*: Sounes, *The Wicked Game*, 159.

49 *McCormack . . . fiercely competitive golfer*: Matthew Futterman, *Players: How Sports Became a Business* (New York: Simon & Schuster, 2016).

50 *he could be a bully*: Complaint for Divorce, Custody, Restraining Order and Other Equitable Relief, Candace B. Norton vs. John Hughes Norton III, Court of Common Pleas, Division of Domestic Relations, Cuyahoga County, January 7, 1985; authors' interview with attorney William T. Wuliger.

50 *"I believe that the first black man"*: Callahan, *His Father's Son*, 43.

50 *"That's why I'm here"*: Ibid.

50 *"with Tiger and his family"*: Email from Hughes Norton to the authors, September 23, 2015.

51 *Earl's annual income . . . $45,000*: Earl Woods, Income and Expense Declaration, Superior Court of California, October 2, 1995 (the exact figure was $45,233.72).

51 *monthly expenses . . . $5,800*: Ibid.

51 *"revolving home equity loan"*: Woods, *Playing Through*, 100.

51 *paying Earl Woods $50,000 per year*: Authors' interview with a senior IMG executive. In a 2003 interview, Earl Woods denied receiving any salary: "You cannot buy me for the money that I got as expenses. You can't buy me for that. I'm too high-principled for that" (Sounes, *The Wicked Game*, 177).

51 *$50,000 a year on Tiger's amateur career*: "Tiger's Tale," transcript, *Prime-time Live*, July 15, 1993.

51 *"IMG did provide compensation to Earl Woods"*: Alastair J. Johnston to the authors, email, September 27, 2017.

52 *Isleworth, a 606-acre gated community*: Authors' research at Isleworth.

52 *private police force*: Ibid.

52 *"There's no rush"*: John Garrity, "You the Kid!" *Sports Illustrated*, March 9, 1992.

54 *He always felt nervous*: Tiger Woods, press conference, US Amateur Championship, August 18, 1996: "I'm always nervous. When I tee it up on the first tee, I'll be nervous, and then it will go away."

54 *case of rigor mortis*: Garrity, "You the Kid!"

54 *Tiger should have been sitting in his geometry class*: Ibid.

54 *six deep around the tee*: Ibid.

54 *an exemption to a "nigger"*: Sounes, *The Wicked Game*, 161.

54 *Tiger also received a death threat*: Plaschke, "It's a New Day for Golf's Child Prodigy."

55 *"He's the next Jack Nicklaus"*: Garrity, "You the Kid!"

55 *"when I hit a bad shot"*: Ibid.

56 *"one of our deals of being a Woods"*: Tiger Woods, press conference, British Open, July 14, 2005.

CHAPTER SIX: THE NEXT LEVEL

Primary sources include interviews with John Merchant, Jeffrey Olgin, Dina Gravell, Butch Harmon, Grant Spaeth, Wally Goodwin, Jaime Diaz, and Joe Grohman; court records from Connecticut; books by Tiger Woods, Earl Woods, John Merchant, and John Strege; PGA Tour videos; CBS Sports footage; Western High School yearbooks; USGA research; the *Stanford Daily*; and reporting by Tom Cunneff.

57 *"We don't discriminate"*: Bill Pennington, "Hall Thompson, Who Stirred Golf Controversy, Dies at 87," *New York Times*, October 28, 2010.

58 *"however distressing one finds this firestorm"*: Jaime Diaz, "Racism Issue Shakes World of Golf," *New York Times*, July 29, 1990.

58 *S. Giles Payne, a Connecticut lawyer*: John F. Merchant, *A Journey Worth Taking: An Unpredictable Adventure* (Xlibris, 2012), 335.

58 *first black to graduate*: Ibid.

58 *first black . . . Connecticut's largest bank*: Ibid.

60 *Anselmo had been diagnosed with colon cancer*: John Strege, "John Anselmo Has Died," *GolfWorld*, July 15, 2017.

61 *Harmon Sr., won the Masters*: John McCormick, "Even Tiger Needs a Trainer," *Newsweek*, December 9, 1996.

61 *Norman's swing coach*: Ibid.

61 *visit to Lochinvar*: Woods, *The 1997 Masters*, 41.

61 *raw spots on his forearm*: David Kindred, "Tiger Woods Grows Up," *Golf Digest*, April 2000.

61 *"What's your go-to shot"*: Authors' interview with Butch Harmon; Woods, *The 1997 Masters*, 55 ("Butchie asked during our first session together after the '93 Amateur if I had a go-to automatic shot when I wasn't swinging well. . . . I told Butchie that my go-to shot was what I did just about every time: swing as fast as I could, unleashing everything I had through the ball").

61 *"Swing as fast as I can"*: Ibid.

62 *$300-an-hour fee*: McCormick, "Even Tiger Needs a Trainer."

63 *Tiger made it official*: Rob Rose, "Men's Golf Team Signs Top Recruit," *Stanford Daily*, November 11, 1993.

63 *"Most Likely to Succeed"*: Western High School yearbook, 1994, 60.

63 *a 3.8 GPA*: Peter de Jonge, "Tiger Woods," *New York Times Magazine*, February 5, 1995. De Jonge reported Tiger's GPA as 3.79. Various other reports indicate that his GPA was 3.86. We went with 3.8.

64 *an ethics complaint*: Jeffrey Olgin, Letter of Complaint, June 15, 1994.

64 *launched an investigation*: Memorandum of Decision, John F. Merchant vs. State Ethics Commission, no. CV960330176, September 2, 1997.

65 *his name had surfaced*: Alan Levin, "Rowland Ousts Counsel for Golfing on State Time," *Hartford Courant*, March 7, 1996.

65 *"I'd have shot him"*: Callahan, *His Father's Son*, 96.

65 *a player, not a cheater*: Ibid.

65 *"from the shower naked"*: Ibid., 97.

66 *misconception by the media*: Lorne Rubenstein, "Tiger's Private Struggles," http://time.com/tiger/.

67 *greatest comeback in US Amateur history*: Rosaforte, "The Comeback Kid."

67 *transferring to Oklahoma State*: Ibid.

67 *Earl had stayed with Kuehne*: Hank Haney, *The Big Miss: My Years Coaching Tiger Woods* (New York: Three Rivers Press, 2012), 8.

67 *prominent attorney who owned two banks*: Joe Drape, "A Prodigy Finds Skeptics in the Crowd," *New York Times*, April 20, 1997.

68 *the highest-risk shot*: Rosaforte, "The Comeback Kid."

68 *Initially frozen still*: http://www.usga.org/videos/2013/03/04/woods -mounts-comeback-at-1994-u-s—amateur-2203223061001.html.

69 *"you'll never be shit"*: Earl Woods interview with Tom Cunneff (transcript provided to the authors by Cunneff).

69 *Clinton sent him a congratulatory letter*: Bill Clinton to Tiger Woods, letter, September 8, 1994.

69 *"tonight is unbelievable"*: Strege, *Tiger*, 78.

69 *Tiger and Earl to golf for free*: Joe Grohman, "Inside Team Tiger," *Grohman Golf Gazette* VI, no. 2 (March 2004); authors' interviews with Joe Grohman.

70 *Tiger received a letter*: Ibid.

70 *"Have you seen any guys?"*: Ibid.

70 *kicked Tiger off the course*: Ibid.

70 *"'A black kid is hitting'"*: Ibid.

71 *"That won't be necessary"*: Ibid.

71 *"Fuck the navy"*: Ibid.

CHAPTER SEVEN: THE AMATEUR

Primary sources include interviews with Royce Woods, Dina Gravell, Grant Spaeth, Lori Spaeth, Wally Goodwin, John Merchant, Jaime Diaz, John Strege, Don Crosby, members of the San Francisco 49ers organization, and the Stanford Police Department; records from Stanford University; information from PGATour.com; books by Tiger Woods, Earl Woods, and John Strege; personal correspondence between Tiger Woods and Dina Gravell; transcripts of Tiger Woods's press conferences; the *Stanford Daily*; and reporting by Jaime Diaz and Peter de Jonge.

72 *economics as his major*: "Woods to Stanford," *New York Times*, November 11, 1993.

72 *roommate, Bjorn Johnson*: Heather Knight, "Living with Summer and Tiger," *Stanford Daily*, January 11, 1995.

72 *his class schedule*: Paul Newberry, "Tiger Still on Course of History," Associated Press, October 26, 1994.

73 *Championship in Versailles*: Allyson Mizoguchi, "Tiger Woods: Just Another Frosh?" *Stanford Daily*, September 22, 1994.

73 *called him "Tiger la Terreur"*: Jaime Diaz, "Tale of a Tiger," *Sports Illustrated*, October 17, 1994.

73 *celebrity since Jerry Lewis*: Ibid.

74 *trouble making friends*: Authors' interviews with former members of the San Francisco 49ers organization.

74 *no appointment necessary*: Tiger Woods, press conference, Dubai Desert Classic, February 5, 2006 ("I had numerous conversations with the great football coach, Bill Walsh, my freshman year").

74 *wouldn't even say her name*: De Jonge, "Tiger Woods."

75 *full-blooded Native American*: Ibid.

75 *nicknamed Tiger "Urkel"*: Ibid.

76 *slap in the face*: Ibid.

76 *"It provides drive"*: Ibid.

76 *Louis, who enlisted*: "Joe Louis Departs to Finish Training," *New York Times*, June 23, 1942.

76 *"things are wrong with America"*: Ira Berkow, "Joe Louis Was There Earlier," *New York Times*, April 22, 1997.

76 *"only time I think about race"*: Smith, "The Chosen One."

77 *"You're a great player"*: Newberry, "Tiger Still on Course of History."

77 *"It's absolutely awesome"*: Ibid.

77 *"our team won"*: Ibid.

77 *Tiger called 911*: Felony Incident Report, Office of the Sheriff, County of Santa Clara, December 1, 1994. The Stanford Police Department told the authors that the 911 cassette was destroyed after three years, per department policy.

77 *dinner with Jerry Rice*: Ibid. Through a spokesperson, Jerry Rice said he had met Tiger while he was a student at Stanford, but he did not "know about this specific event." When asked, then San Francisco 49ers team president Carmen Policy could not recall a dinner event at which he met Tiger Woods in 1994.

77 *"Tiger, give me all you got"*: Supplement to Incident Report, December 2, 1994.

79 *"I was not beaten"*: "Golfer Woods Issues Statement on Robbery," Stanford News Service, December 2, 1994.

80 *"at the wrong time"*: Mike DiGiovanna, "Woods Not Seriously Injured," *Los Angeles Times*, December 3, 1994.

80 *"Golfer Woods Is Mugged"*: *New York Times*, December 4, 1994.

80 *surgery to remove two cysts*: Woods, *The 1997 Masters*, 60.

80 *"Wiping out on skateboards"*: Jaime Diaz, "The Truth about Tiger," *Golf Digest*, December 20, 2009.

80 *left a long scar*: Woods, *The 1997 Masters*, 60.

80 *"the heck with it"*: Ibid.

80 *"pain was excruciating"*: Ibid.

81 The mind, *he told himself*: Ibid.

81 *longest in the field*: Jaime Diaz, "Out of Sight," *Sports Illustrated*, April 17, 1995.

81 *Davis Love III was second*: Ibid.

81 *The longest hitter*: Ibid. (283.8 yards, according to PGATour.com).

81 *"Should I try?"*: Ibid.

82 *"a commercial publication"*: Strege, *Tiger*, 158.

82 *used Maxfli golf balls*: Ibid.

82 *Stanford suspended Tiger*: Jaime Diaz, "Out of the Woods," *Sports Illustrated*, July 17, 1995.

82 *Privately, Tiger was furious*: John Strege, "Tracking Tiger," *Sports Illustrated*, June 19, 1995.

82 *"Tiger might leave"*: Ibid.

82 *168 people were killed*: USA Today, June 20, 2001.

83 *Tiger abruptly quit playing*: Brian Lee, "Four Golfers Enough to Take a Title at Home," *Stanford Daily*, April 25, 1995.

83 *"My shoulder is O.K."*: Tiger Woods to Dina Gravell, letter.

85 *MRI had revealed scarring*: Lee, "Four Golfers Enough to Take a Title at Home."

85 *high school baseball injury*: Ibid.

85 *"I played baseball"*: Tiger Woods, press conference, Deutsche Bank Championship, September 1, 2006.

85 *"I had to choose one sport"*: Woods, *The 1997 Masters*, 22.

85 *"I am truly sorry"*: Tiger Woods to Dina Gravell, letter.

CHAPTER EIGHT: RICH FRIENDS

Primary sources include interviews with John Merchant, Rick Ryan, Athan Crist, Tom Graham, Ed Morrow, Corey Martin, Ed Mauro, Butch Harmon, Peter DiBari, Barclay Douglas, Bill Harmon, members of the Newport Country Club, and Tommy Hudson; Connecticut Ethics File, Letters; court records from Connecticut; records from Connecticut Attorney General's office, Ethics Commission, and Governor's Office; research provided by the Newport Country Club and Brooklawn Country Club; Country Club of Fairfield; the *Stanford Daily*; correspondence with David Fay and Bev Norwood; and reporting by Tim Rosaforte and Rick Lipsey.

87 *found probable cause*: Connecticut Office of State Ethics, press release, April 17, 1995.

87 *Merchant had also acknowledged*: John F. Merchant v. Office of State Ethics, no. CV960330176, September 2, 1997.

87 *"My recollection is"*: Alastair Johnston, email to authors, September 27, 2017.

90 *Norton came up with the idea*: Rosaforte, *Raising the Bar*, 51 ("Earl Woods was already on the IMG payroll, hired in a scheme devised by super agent Hughes Norton to be a 'talent scout' at AJGA events"). Authors' note: David Fay did not respond to an email request to comment.

91 *"purpose of this statement"*: Strege, *Tiger*, 115.

92 *"It wasn't my fault"*:

92 *he spotted Earl*: "Wounded Tiger," *Sports Illustrated*, June 26, 1995.

92 *Founded in 1895*: Brooklawncc.com/clubhouse/history.

93 *bout of food poisoning*: Brian Lee, "Men's Golf Qualifies for NCAAs," *Stanford Daily*, May 22, 1995.

93 *slammed his club*: Rick Lipsey, "Down to the Wire Oklahoma State Beat Stanford in the First Playoff for the NCAA Championship," *Sports Illustrated*, June 12, 1995.

93 *His outburst drew*: Ibid.

94 *first sudden-death round*: Ibid.

95 *"Hey, what's going on?"*: Authors' interview with Corey Martin.

96 *"They don't break"*: Authors' interview with Bill Harmon.

97 *Spectators packed the second-story*: USGA, Annual Report, 1995.

97 *Mercedes-Benz dealer*: Dan Gillette, "Marucci Happy to Gain a Spot in Walker Cup," *Newport Daily News*, August 28, 1995.

97 *thirty-sixth and final hole*: Jim Donaldson, "Woods Is Still No. 1 in U.S.," *Providence Journal-Bulletin*, August 28, 1995.

97 *within eighteen inches*: Brett Avery, "The Young and the Restless," *Golf Journal*, October 1995.

98 *"This one's for you, Jay"*: Pete McDaniel, "Twice as Nice," *Golf World*, September 1, 1995.

98 *father had passed away*: Ibid.

98 *wandered into the country-club bar*: Authors' interviews with Newport Country Club members.

98 *"How do you like this, Bobby Jones?"*: Authors' interviews with three individuals who were present.

98 *"kiss my son's black ass"*: Ibid.

99 "I'm going to make a prediction": Tim Rosaforte, "Encore! Encore!" *Sports Illustrated*, September 4, 1995.

99 *"Pop, c'mon"*: Authors' interview with a source who witnessed the exchange.

CHAPTER NINE: RAMPING UP

Primary sources include interviews with Butch Harmon, Jaime Diaz, John Merchant, Jim Riswold, Steve Scott, Kristi Scott, Wally Goodwin, Dr. Eri Crum, and John Strege; court records from Connecticut; personal correspondence between Earl Woods and John Merchant; footage from NBC Sports, ABC News, and Golf Films; transcripts of Tiger Woods's press conferences; and reporting by Jaime Diaz.

100 *Stanford was a utopia*: Jaime Diaz, "A Fast Study," *Sports Illustrated*, April 8, 1996 ("Stanford is like utopia. It's not the real world, which I guess is why I want to spend more time there").

100 *mentally engaged*: Ibid.

101 *$25 check went to Palmer*: Ibid.

101 *"Kiss my yin yang"*: Pat Sullivan, "My Dinner with Arnie—Woods Pays His Tab," *San Francisco Chronicle*, October 21, 1995.

103 *he formed two columns*: Earl Woods to John Merchant, "1996 EXPENSE BUDGET," letter, January 28, 1996.

104 *"no financial pressure"*: "A Young Lion Named Tiger Will Play Open."

104 *violated state law*: Memorandum of Understanding, John F. Merchant v. Office of State Ethics, September 2, 1997.

105 *violating the code of ethics*: Ibid.

105 *a criminal investigation*: Ibid.

106 *John Rowland had weighed in*: Levin, "Rowland Ousts Counsel for Golfing on State Time."

108 *IMG agreed to take*: *New York Post*, April 1997.

108 *cigar-smoking players*: William F. Reed, "In His Sights," *Sports Illustrated*, June 10, 1996.

108 *record fifteen thousand tickets*: Ibid.

108 *225 press credentials*: Ibid.

109 *"I know it sells newspapers"*: Ibid.

111 *he would be back at Stanford*: Authors' interview with Wally Goodwin.

111 *assist from Kevin Costner*: Janet Maslin, "When Golf Is Life and Life a Game," *New York Times*, August 16, 1996.

112 *"Time to Go Pro?"*: Larry Dorman, "The Question for Woods: Is It Time to Go Pro?" *New York Times*, August 18, 1996.

112 *"I like being in school"*: Tiger Woods interview with Carol Lin, *ABC World News Tonight*.

113 *kept in a ponytail*: NBC Sports broadcast.

114 *thirty consecutive matches*: Jeff Ritter, "*Golf Films* Presents 'All Square': Tiger Woods, Steve Scott, and the 1996 US Amateur," *Golf*, August 16, 2016.

114 *down to a single stroke*: NBC Sports broadcast.

115 *"Hey, Tiger, did you"*: "*Golf Films* Presents 'All Square'"; authors' interview with Steve Scott.

115 *Tiger didn't acknowledge*: Authors' interview with Steve Scott.

115 *cold and heartless*: Authors' interviews with Steve and Kristi Scott.

116 *"why you're calling me"*: Authors' interview with Wally Goodwin.

116 *"one thing I don't love"*: Authors' interview with Dr. Eri Crum.

117 *"I am a loner"*: Diaz, "Raising Tiger Hardly Just a Father Affair."

117 *"kill them"*: Ibid.

117 *"take their heart"*: Ibid.

118 *suffered by Kuehne*: Ryan Lavner, "The Amateur: Trip Kuehne's Life Without Pro Golf," GolfChannel.com, September 14, 2016.

118 *MBA at Oklahoma State*: Ibid.

118 *never watched the video clips*: Ibid.

119 *a "wuss"*: Tiger Woods, press conference, Memorial Tournament, May 30, 2011 ("Growing up as a kid, we were looked at as wusses. Guys who didn't, shouldn't be called athletes, shouldn't be considered athletes").

CHAPTER TEN: HELLO WORLD

Primary sources include interviews with Jim Riswold, John Merchant, Jaime Diaz, John McCormick, John Feinstein, Craig Bowen, Sharon Begley, Gary Smith, Larry Kirshbaum, Rick Wolff, Charles Pierce, and Mark Seal; books by Tiger Woods and John Feinstein; footage from the PGA Tour, Golf Channel, ABC News, and NBC Sports; court records from Connecticut; real estate records from Ohio and Florida; and reporting by Gary Smith, Charles Pierce, Tom Cunneff, and Jaime Diaz.

120 *bags of Nike gear*: Leigh Montville, "On the Job Training in Milwaukee: The Professional Debut of Amateur Champ Tiger Woods Was a Qualified Success," *Sports Illustrated*, September 9, 1996.

120 *changed Tiger's official residence*: Tiger Woods, Declaration of Domicile, August 26, 1996.

120 *9.3 percent income tax*: lao.ca.gov/1996.

120 *9724 Green Island Cove*: Declaration of Domicile.

120 *"see Claude Monet paint"*: Pete McDaniel, "Rare Air," *Golf World*, August 30, 1996.

121 *"three times what Norman gets"*: Smith, "The Chosen One."

121 *"Guess that's pretty amazing"*: Ibid.

121 *thought it wasn't enough*: Authors' interview with a source close to the family.

121 *"You bet your ass"*: Jaime Diaz, "Roaring Ahead," *Sports Illustrated*, September 2, 1996.

122 *"only hero on earth"*: Smith, "The Chosen One."

122 *drink or rent a car*: Montville, "On the Job Training in Milwaukee."

122 *"I guess, hello, world"*: Tiger Woods, press conference, Greater Milwaukee Open, August 28, 1996.

123 *"In my life"*: Ibid.

123 *"You'll learn"*: Woods, *The 1997 Masters*, 2.

123 *Strange's skepticism*: Ibid.

123 *straight down the middle*: Ibid.

123 *most publicized debut*: Montville, "On the Job Training in Milwaukee."

123 *at Shea Stadium*: Ibid.

124 *earning just $2,544*: Ibid.

124 *put that question to Nike*: James K. Glassman, "A Dishonest Ad Campaign," *Washington Post*, September 17, 1996.

124   *fueled the controversy*: L. Jon Wertheim, "The Ad That Launched a Thou-
        sand Hits," *Sports Illustrated*, April 14, 2003.

124   *nominated for an Emmy*: Stuart Elliott, "Disputed Commercial Wins a
        TV Award," *New York Times*, September 9, 1997.

124   *"You have to think for yourself"*: Tiger Woods, *Nightline*, August 27,
        1996.

125   *"That's very private"*: Ibid.

125   *say very little*: Smith, "The Chosen One."

125   *"There is no comprehension"*: Rosaforte, *Raising the Bar*, 64.

125   *"black gunslinger"*: Ibid.

125   *"cut your heart out"*: Ibid.

125   *"difficult for Tiger to make"*: McDaniel, "Rare Air."

125   *"a pushy father"*: John Feinstein, *One on One: Behind the Scenes with the
        Greats in the Game* (New York: Little, Brown & Company, 2011), 331.

125   *"every dollar possible"*: Ibid.

125   *"Like Stefano . . . Earl hasn't had"*: Rosaforte, *Raising the Bar*, 73.

125   *good-bye to Earl*: Jaime Diaz, "Crowd Pleaser," *Sports Illustrated*, Septem-
        ber 21, 1996.

125   *at the Regency*: Ibid.

126   *"should do a book"*: Authors' interview with Jaime Diaz.

126   *"who would write it?"*: Ibid.

126   *a bidding war*: Authors' interview with Rick Wolff.

126   *$2.2 million for a two-book deal*: Authors' interview with Larry Kirsh-
        baum.

127   *Earl wasn't happy*: Authors' interview with a source close to Earl.

127   *"should show up"*: Feinstein, *One on One*, 332.

127   *tired when he was twenty*: Smith, "The Chosen One."

127   *no longer appropriate to compare*: Ibid.

127   *"Tiger should have played"*: Strege, *Tiger*, 204.

127   *were my friends, Tiger thought*: Smith, "The Chosen One."

127   *suddenly missed Stanford*: Ibid.

128   *tasked with finding*: Authors' interview with John Merchant.

128   *4,500-square-foot house*: Assessor's records, Orange County, California,
        Parcel Number 501-181-26. According to public records, the home was
        purchased for $700,000 on November 4, 1996. Other published reports
        list the sale price of the house as $804,000.

128   *won his first PGA Tour event*: Gary Van Sickle, "Jackpot," *Sports Illus-
        trated*, October 14, 1996.

128 *"I kind of did"*: Smith, "The Chosen One."

128 *assigned to ghostwrite*: Authors' interview with Pete McDaniel.

129 *"Please forgive me"*: Smith, "The Chosen One."

129 *arms around his father*: Ibid.

129 *$216,000 purse*: Larry Dorman, "Tiger Woods Adds a Chapter to His Legend," *New York Times*, October 21, 1996.

129 *qualifying him*: Ibid.

129 *told security to open*: Feinstein, *One on One*, 333.

129 *"the fifth Beatle"*: Ibid.

130 *Bill Cosby was willing*: Smith, "The Chosen One."

130 *"Tell them to kiss my ass"*: Ibid.

130 *phone call from his mother*: Earl Woods interview with Tom Cunneff.

130 *arteriosclerosis*: Ibid.

131 *administered an EKG*: Ibid.

131 *"It'll be okay"*: Ibid.

131 *to concentrate on golf*: Woods, *The 1997 Masters*, 8. Writing about the night his father was taken to the hospital in 1996, Woods said: "I couldn't concentrate after spending the night in the hospital with my father, worrying about him, and I shot 78 in the second round."

131 *worst round since turning pro*: Larry Dorman, "Lehman in Control, But Woods Loses His," *New York Times*, October 26, 1996.

131 *"I love my dad to death"*: Ibid.

131 *Tiger wearing Nike gear*: McCormick and Begley, "How to Raise a Tiger."

131 *a "fine young man"*: Ibid.

132 *"king of endorsement money"*: Smith, "The Chosen One."

132 *group arrived at Bay Hill*: Fritz Ober, email to the authors, April 27, 2015.

133 *downed five martinis*: Authors' interview with John Merchant.

133 *both were hammered*: Authors' interview with Craig Bowen.

135 *helped execute a deed*: Warranty Deed, Cuyahoga County, Ohio, December 13, 1996.

135 *Tiger Woods Revocable Trust*: Conformity Deed, Orange County, Florida, February 14, 2002.

CHAPTER ELEVEN: MASTERFUL

Primary sources include interviews with Butch Harmon, Charles Pierce, Gary Smith, Jaime Diaz, Alicia O'Meara, and Mark O'Meara; book by Tiger Woods;

the PGA Tour; CBS Sports; and reporting by Tom Cunneff, Charles Pierce, Gary Smith, Jaime Diaz, and Rick Reilly.

136 *shiny new Mercedes*: Charles P. Pierce, "The Man. Amen," *GQ*, April 1997.

136 *Tiger had won it*: Ibid.

136 *his first seven tournaments*: Rick Reilly, "Top Cat," *Sports Illustrated*, October 28, 1996.

136 *every fifty-seven holes*: PGATour.com.

136 *twenty-fourth . . . money list*: Ibid.

137 *ready for Tiger*: Reilly, "Top Cat."

137 *his perception of Tiger*: Authors' interview with Gary Smith.

137 *"Tiger will do more"*: Smith, "The Chosen One."

138 *never worked a day*: Authors' interviews with sources close to the family.

138 *"Earl is getting out of control"*: Pierce, "The Man. Amen."

139 None of this is scary: Smith, "The Chosen One" ("I don't see any of this as scary or a burden").

139 *"I am the toughest golfer"*: Ibid.

139 *climbed into the back of a limousine*: Pierce, "The Man. Amen."

139 *"Thomas Aquinas leading the way"*: Ibid.

139 *"little too deep"*: Ibid.

140 *"The key to it"*: Ibid.

140 *touched down in Bangkok*: Jaime Diaz, "Thais That Bind," *Sports Illustrated*, February 17, 1997.

140 *Tiger received $448,000*: Ibid.

141 *doctors performed an angiogram*: Earl Woods interview with Tom Cunneff.

141 *cigarettes and alcohol*: Ibid.

141 *at UCLA Medical Center*: Woods, *The 1997 Masters*, 8.

141 *Earl flat-lined*: Ibid.

141 *"walking into the light"*: Ibid.

141 *"We just touch, and it's all said"*: Earl Woods interview with Tom Cunneff.

141 *first saw himself on the cover*: Jaime Diaz, "One for the Ages," *Sports Illustrated*, April 7, 1997.

142 How could I have been so stupid?: Diaz, "One for the Ages."

142 *It also wounded Tiger*: Ibid.

143 *Tiger asked him why*: Woods, *The 1997 Masters*, 84.

143 *O'Meara said he wasn't sure*: Ibid.

143 *Tiger . . . what O'Meara already had*: Authors' interviews with sources close to Tiger.

144 *ten under par*: Woods, *The 1997 Masters*, 5.

144 *a massive white plume*: Ibid.

144 *never witnessed a launch*: Ibid.

144 What an accomplishment: Ibid.

144 *"caddies will be black"*: Rick Reilly, "The New Master," *Sports Illustrated*, April 21, 1997.

144 *black man to join the club*: Ibid.

145 *looking into the sky*: Woods, *The 1997 Masters*, 5.

145 *fascinated by space travel*: Ibid.

145 *Exhilarated, Tiger stepped*: Ibid.

145 *weeks since his triple bypass*: Woods, *The 1997 Masters*, 8.

145 *"Your hands are too low"*: Woods, *The 1997 Masters*, 8.

146 *actor Wilford Brimley*: Rick Reilly, "What a Trip," *Sports Illustrated*, May 26, 1997.

146 *Fluff worshipped*: Ibid.

147 *so amped up*: Ibid.

147 What is going on?: Ibid.

147 *"only played nine holes"*: Ibid.

147 *great black hope*: Dorman, "A Way Out."

147 I'll be fine: Woods, *The 1997 Masters*.

147 *"The mental training"*: Ibid.

148 *Cowan and Butch Harmon watched*: Authors' interview with Butch Harmon.

148 It would be a nightmare: Woods, *The 1997 Masters*.

148 *went to Earl's bedroom*: Ibid.

148 *don't get lackadaisical*: Ibid.

149 I need to be that cold-blooded assassin: Ibid.

149 Could this really happen?: Ibid.

149 *forty-four million Americans*: Michael Starr and Richard Wilner, "CBS Breaks Record, Too," *New York Post*, April 1997.

149 *65 percent increase*: Ibid.

149 *allowed his mind to go*: Woods, *The 1997 Masters*.

149 *Nicklaus was now elbowing his way*: Reilly, "The New Master."

149 *"We made it"*: CBS Sports broadcast.

150 *"I love you"*: Woods, *The 1997 Masters*, 160. "The words kept coming

back to me for years, and they still do," Tiger wrote years later. "I will always cherish and never forget the embraces I shared with Pop and Mom behind the eighteenth green."

CHAPTER TWELVE: MANIA

Primary sources include interviews with Mike Shapiro, Chip Lange, Butch Harmon, John Feinstein, PGA Tour sources, and confidential sources; book by Tiger Woods; ABC News; and the *Oprah Winfrey Show*.

151 *sheer number of records*: PGA Tour.
152 *Lee Elder . . . first black man*: Reilly, "The New Master."
152 *"Thanks for making this possible"*: Ibid.
152 *"I've always dreamt of winning"*: CBS Sports broadcast.
152 *Bill Clinton had called*: Woods, *The 1997 Masters*.
152 *Clinton even offered*: Maureen Dowd, "Tiger's Double Bogey," *New York Times*, April 19, 1997.
153 *the black staff*: Reilly, "The New Master."
153 *Cadillac courtesy car*: Woods, *The 1997 Masters*.
153 *cranked up*: Ibid., 165.
153 *woke up with a headache*: Woods, *The 1997 Masters*, 167.
153 *Café in Myrtle Beach*: Larry Dorman, "With Woods, a Grand Slam Is No Longer a Dream," *New York Times*, April 15, 1997.
153 *signed with Planet Hollywood*: Ibid.
154 *Letterman and Jay Leno*: Ibid.
154 *Tiger said no*: Ibid.
154 *Tiger took it as a slight*: Authors' interview with a source close to Tiger. Also, Joe Drape, "Woods Has Empathy for Zoeller and a Rebuke for the President," *New York Times*, May 14, 1997.
154 *plane for Mexico*: Woods, *The 1997 Masters*, 168.
154 *eating and drinking*: Ibid.
154 *"Are you kidding me?"*: Feinstein, *One on One*, 336.
155 *"Can't have everything"*: Feinstein, *One on One*, 334.
155 *"these two assholes"*: Ibid., 335.
155 *offices in Beaverton*: Woods, *The 1997 Masters*, 168.
155 *"It is perplexing"*: Dowd, "Tiger's Double Bogey."
155 *made a mistake*: Woods, *The 1997 Masters*, 171.

155 *letter of apology*: Ibid., 172.

156 *"He's doing quite well"*: CNN, https://www.youtube.com/watch?v=9uf
pU3X-t4w.

156 *"some of the necessities"*: Ted Koppel interview with Al Campanis, *Night-line*, April 6, 1987.

156 couldn't have meant: Woods, *The 1997 Masters*, 169.

156 a racist tinge: Ibid.

156 *chose to say nothing*: Ibid., 179.

156 *"It's too bad"*: "Zoeller Apologizes for Woods Comment," *New York Times*, April 22, 1997.

157 *"'Dear Tiger'"*: *The Oprah Winfrey Show*, April 24, 1997.

157 *"I'm a Cablinasian"*: Ibid.

158 *dropped Fuzzy Zoeller*: Richard Sandomir, "Zoeller Learns Race Remarks Carry a Price," *New York Times*, April 24, 1997.

158 *"out of bounds"*: Woods, *The 1997 Masters*, 170.

158 *"Needs to Apologize"*: Dave Anderson, "Tiger Woods Also Needs to Apologize for Distateful Jokes," *New York Times*, April 27, 1997.

158 *"planned my vacation already"*: Harry Blauvelt, "Time to Return to Work," *USA Today*, May 14, 1997.

158 *"Only Robert E. Lee"*: Albert R. Hunt, "Tiger Joins with Michael in Some Very Rare Air," *Wall Street Journal*, May 2, 1997.

CHAPTER THIRTEEN: CHANGES

Primary sources include interviews with Butch Harmon, Mark O'Meara, Chris Mike, Sharon Begley, Ed Sherman, and Jimmy Roberts; books by Tiger Woods and Steve Williams; and reporting by Gary Van Sickle and Alan Shipnuck.

160 *cut off ticket sales*: Gary Van Sickle, "The Beat Goes On," *Sports Illus-trated*, May 20, 1997.

160 *slightly off-kilter*: Woods, *The 1997 Masters*, 175.

160 *drove up from Houston*: Ibid.

160 *158 percent jump*: Van Sickle, "The Beat Goes On."

160 *eighty-five thousand fans*: Ibid.

161 *the Duchess of York*: Ibid.

161 *youngest player in history*: Ibid.

161 *watched the tapes*: Woods, *The 1997 Masters*, 174.

161 God almighty, *he thought*: Gary Van Sickle, "On a Roll," *Sports Illustrated*, July 12, 1999.

161 *Harmon . . . wasn't concerned*: Ibid.

161 *"I want to change this"*: Ibid.

162 *"He couldn't relax"*: Smith, "The Chosen One."

162 *"How good can I be?"*: Woods, *The 1997 Masters*, 177.

162 *A typical practice day*: Ibid., 176.

162 *short game and putting*: Ibid., 175.

162 *"The life I wanted"*: Ibid., 176.

162 *"Compulsions come from"*: Sharon Begley, *Just Can't Stop: An Investigation of Compulsion* (New York: Simon & Schuster, 2017), 2.

162 *"I feel like shit"*: Ibid.

163 *"I didn't care"*: Woods, *The 1997 Masters*, 176.

163 *"tighten my swing"*: Ibid.

163 *dinner and a movie*: Alan Shipnuck, "Charge!" *Sports Illustrated*, July 14, 1997.

164 *fifty-five thousand people packed*: Ibid.

164 *broke through the ropes*: Ed Sherman, "The One and Only Tiger Woods Delivers," *Chicago Tribune*, July 7, 1997.

164 *"They can't hold us back"*: Ibid.

164 *Tiger walked carefree*: Ibid.

164 *"my creative mind"*: Steve Williams and Hugh de Lacy, *Golf at the Top with Steve Williams: Tips and Techniques from the Caddy to Raymond Floyd, Greg Norman & Tiger Woods* (Berkeley, CA: Ulysses Press, 2006), 52.

164 *"If Tiger shows up"*: Shipnuck, "Charge!"

164 *favorite word was* compete: Woods, *The 1997 Masters*, 227.

CHAPTER FOURTEEN: EXPLOITED

Primary sources include interviews with John Strege, Jaime Diaz, EA Sports, Nike, American Express, Deb Gelman, John Feinstein, Don Transeth, Mike Shapiro, and Shari Lesser Wenk; transcripts from Tiger Woods's press conferences; reporting by Tom Cunneff; court records in Ohio and California; and footage from PBS.

165 *paying Woods $13 million*: Richard Sandomir, "Tiger Woods Signs Pact with American Express," *New York Times*, May 20, 1997.

165 *youngest person in the world*: Authors' interview with an American Express senior executive.

165 *ideal global personality*: Stephen E. Frank, "Can Tiger Woods Sell Financial Services?" *Wall Street Journal*, May 20, 1997.

165 *"we have a representative"*: Sandomir, "Tiger Woods Signs Pact with American Express."

165 *Rolex announced*: Stuart Elliott, "Tiger Woods Signs Contract with Rolex," *New York Times*, May 28, 1997.

166 *"shoulder to lean on"*: Earl Woods, *Charlie Rose*, May 7, 1997, https://charlierose.com/videos/10188.

166 *233,000 copies in hardback*: Sales figures provided by HarperCollins in an email to the authors, June 15, 2015.

166 *"I don't have time"*: Authors' interview with Jaime Diaz.

167 *"something to gain"*: Tiger Woods, press conference, Doral-Ryder Open, March 3, 1998.

167 *"Fuck John Strege!"*: Authors' interview with John Strege.

167 *"It occurred to me"*: Ibid.

167 *Tiger played* Mortal Kombat: Notes from Tom Cunneff's interview with Jaime Diaz.

168 *"I don't play"*: Authors' interview with Don Transeth.

168 *Tiger's answers*: Ibid.

169 *"Read the contract"*: Authors' interview with Mike Shapiro.

169 *ex-wife in divorce court*: Complaint for Divorce, Custody, Restraining Order and Other Equitable Relief, Candace B. Norton v. John Hughes Norton III, January 27, 1985.

169 *"What's going on?"*: Authors' interview with Mike Shapiro.

170 *"I can hit it 340"*: Authors' interview with Don Transeth.

170 *weary and aloof*: Authors' interview with Deb Gelman.

170 *cut under the eye*: Tiger Woods, press conference, Memorial Tournament, May 26, 1998 ("They were so aggressive last year, I would come home with pen marks all over me, on my shirts, my hat; a couple of times I got cut under the eyes with pens—stray pens. People are so aggressive").

172 *too much to drink*: Authors' interview with Deb Gelman.

172 *any breath mints*: Ibid.

172 *"Meet me on every tee"*: Ibid.

172 *"Couldn't wait to see me"*: Authors' interview with John Feinstein.

173 *"Makes it tougher"*: Ibid.

174 *interview was scheduled*: Ibid.

174 *"The comparisons are legitimate"*: John Feinstein, *The First Coming: Tiger Woods: Master or Martyr?* (New York: Ballantine, 1998).

CHAPTER FIFTEEN: INSTINCTS

Primary sources include interviews with Mark O'Meara, Alicia O'Meara, Peggy Lewis, Butch Harmon, John Feinstein, and Jaime Diaz; transcripts of Tiger Woods's press conferences; and reporting by Jaime Diaz.

175 *the exotic beast*: Bill Colson, "Cover Shoot: A Tale of the Tigers," *Sports Illustrated*, April 13, 1998.

175 *serious reservations*: Jaime Diaz, "Masters Plan," *Sports Illustrated*, April 13, 1998.

175 *"That young man"*: Ibid.

176 *dealing with death threats*: Authors' interviews with Alicia O'Meara.

176 *twenty-pound increase*: Diaz, "Masters Plan."

176 *Bench-pressing 225 pounds*: Ibid.

176 *Tiger was tired*: Ibid.

177 *"What's wrong with Tiger?"*: Jaime Diaz, "Spelling It Out," *Sports Illustrated*, March 23, 1998.

177 *grip-it-and-rip-it*: Gary Van Sickle, "Training a Tiger," *Sports Illustrated*, July 27, 1998.

177 *graphite-shafted driver*: Ibid.

178 *"a lot of good friends"*: Tiger Woods, press conference, Doral-Ryder Open, March 3, 1998.

178 *Ken Griffey Jr.*: Diaz, "Masters Plan."

179 *"who you can trust?"*: Authors' interview with Alicia O'Meara.

179 *student named Joanna*: Peter Sheridan, "She's the Tiger's Meow," *New York Post*, August 2, 2000.

179 *cheerleader in high school*: Ibid.

179 *discreetly avoided the press*: Ibid.

179 *moved into his Isleworth home*: Ibid.

180 *"just plain ghost"*: Thomas Bonk, "Being Fired Is Norton's Reward for Making Woods Rich," *Los Angeles Times*, October 16, 1998.

180 *"It's hard to understand"*: Ibid.

180 *"Hughes was a hard-driven guy"*: Authors' interview with Mark O'Meara.

180 *had "overcommitted" Tiger*: Bonk, "Being Fired Is Norton's Reward for Making Woods Rich."

180 *had it on tape*: Tiger Woods, press conference, US Open, June 17, 1999.

180 *"My dad didn't mean"*: Ibid.

181 *"I'm sorry about this"*: Authors' interview with John Feinstein.

182 *"She's his secret weapon"*: Sheridan, "She's the Tiger's Meow."

CHAPTER SIXTEEN: I GOT IT

Primary sources include interviews with Tom Wilson, Rick Schloss, Mark O'Meara, Butch Harmon, Hank Haney, Barry Frank, and Al Abrams; transcripts of Tiger Woods's press conferences; books by Steve Williams; and reporting by Jaime Diaz, John Garrity, Gary Van Sickle, and David Kindred.

183 *broke down Duval's play*: Tiger Woods, press conference, the US Open, June 15, 1999.

183 *Duval emerged*: Jaime Diaz, "It Takes Two to Tango," *Sports Illustrated*, March 15, 1999.

183 *Bell, to caddie*: Jaime Diaz, "Blast from the Past," *Sports Illustrated*, February 22, 1999.

183 *introducing Tiger to Joanna*: Sheridan, "She's the Tiger's Meow."

184 *"You are so talented"*: Ibid.

184 *played for the hardware*: Tiger Woods, press conference, US Open, June 16, 2002.

184 *the biggest trophy available*: Plaschke, "It's a New Day for Golf's Child Prodigy."

185 *"Deadhead with a yardage book"*: "Tiger to Fluff: Bag It," *Golf World*, March 5, 1999.

186 *"Nah . . . It's fine"*: Authors' interview with a Tour source.

186 *Williams hung up*: Steve Williams, *Out of the Rough: Inside the Ropes with the World's Greatest Golfers* (Auckland, NZ: Penguin Random House, 2015).

186 *"I've parted ways"*: Ibid.

187 *Floyd watched in silence*: Ibid.

187 *"Come on in"*: Ibid.

188 *"I appreciate the support"*: Associated Press, "The Split Is Official: Tiger Fires Fluff," March 9, 1999.

188 *"To Butch, Thanks"*: Harry Blauvelt, "Woods: No Rest," *USA Today*, December 30, 1999.

188 *Tiger had slipped to number two*: http://www.owgr.com/ranking.

188 *thirteen people to Germany*: Alan Shipnuck, "Ich Bin ein Winner," *Sports Illustrated*, May 31, 1999.

188 *billionaire Dietmar Hopp*: Ibid.

189 *"The great thing"*: Tiger Woods and Jack Nicklaus, press conference, Memorial Tournament, June 6, 1999.

189 *"I've never seen this"*: Ibid.

189 *"I don't know if anybody"*: Ibid.

190 *"you're a superhuman golfer"*: Kindred, "Tiger Woods Grows Up."

190 *Liman grabbed a camera*: Cork Gaines, "The Amazing Story Behind Tiger Woods' Iconic Nike Juggling Commercial," *Business Insider*, December 5, 2015.

190 *Nike decided to air*: Ibid.

190 *record-setting television rights*: Tripp Mickle, "Champions: Barry Frank, the Dealmaker," *SportsBusiness Journal*, April 4, 2011.

191 *$2 million in additional advertising*: Richard Wilner, "ABC Put a Tiger in Its Tank to Break Par," *New York Post*, August 4, 1999.

191 *"Showdown at Sherwood"*: Ibid.

191 *practicing together in Las Vegas*: Kindred, "Tiger Woods Grows Up."

191 *television of rating of 6.9*: Clifton Brown, "Woods-Duval Rates a Solid Par," *New York Times*, August 4, 1999.

192 *"What Crybaby shoot today?"*: Authors' interview with Hank Haney.

192 *"Did you see that?"*: Williams, *Out of the Rough*.

192 *García scissor-kicked*: https://www.youtube.com/watch?v=ShDwNijsLww.

193 *"Sergio, great playing"*: Ibid.

193 *a 344-yard bomb*: Jaime Diaz, "A Year Beyond His Years," *Sports Illustrated*, November 15, 1999.

193 *Ben Hogan in 1953*: Harry Blauvelt, "Eye of Tiger," *USA Today*, November 8, 1999.

193 *greatest golf seasons in history*: Ibid.

193 *Nicklaus said it was superior*: Ibid.

194 *eating yogurt and fruit*: John Garrity, *Sports Illustrated*, January 17, 2000.

194 *Levi's jeans for Armani slacks*: Kindred, "Tiger Woods Grows Up."

194 *favorite word . . . became* balance: Ibid.

194 *smiled more, frowned less*: Rick Reilly, "The Promise Keeper," *Sports Illustrated*, February 21, 2000.

194   *"Whatever you may think"*: Kindred, "Tiger Woods Grows Up."

194   *Jagoda had graduated*: Sheridan, "She's the Tiger's Meow."

194   *deal with General Motors*: Gary Strauss and Bruce Horovitz, "Can Tiger Make Buick Roar?" *USA Today*, December 15, 1999; authors' interview with Al Abrams.

194   *sell its coffee drinks*: Ibid.

194   *hugged Steve Williams*: CBS broadcast.

195   *Pacino and Billy Crystal*: Ibid.

196   *Payne Stewart died*: Gary Van Sickle, "Playing with Payne," *Sports Illustrated*, November 11, 1999.

CHAPTER SEVENTEEN: ANY QUESTIONS?

Primary sources include interviews with Jimmy Roberts, Butch Harmon, Kel Devlin, PGA Tour sources, and Mark Rolfing; transcripts of Tiger Woods's press conferences; book by Tiger Woods; court records; and footage from NBC Sports.

197   *"I got something"*: Authors' interview with Butch Harmon.

198   *an inconceivable comeback*: Clifton Brown, "Woods Fashions an Unforgettable Comeback," *New York Times*, February 8, 2000.

198   *six straight victories*: Ibid.

198   *golf was still in its infancy*: John Garrity, "Mean Streak," *Sports Illustrated*, February 21, 2000.

198   *Nelson earned . . . $30,250*: Harry Blauvelt, "Nelson Rooting for Woods," *USA Today*, February 3, 2000.

199   *"Hey, nice playing today"*: Authors' interview with Kel Devlin.

201   *Acushnet Company, sued Nike*: "Nike Is Sued Over Tiger Woods Golf Ads," *New York Times*, July 9, 1999.

201   *Steinberg renegotiated*: Ivan Maisel, "A Herr Off," *Sports Illustrated*, May 29, 2000.

201   *he called . . . Wally Uihlein*: Ibid.

203   *Tiger was backstage*: Authors' interview with Kel Devlin.

203   *"What . . . are you doing here?"*: Ibid.

203   *"Before we get started"*: Michael Bamberger, "Witnessing History," *Sports Illustrated*, December 18, 2000.

203   *partying until dawn*: Authors' interview with Kel Devlin.

203 *NBC deployed forty-seven cameras*: "He's the Man," *Sports Illustrated*, July 27, 2000.

203 *twenty-one-gun salute*: CNN, transcript, June 14, 2000.

204 No one else stands a chance: Authors' interview with Butch Harmon.

204 *alone in a dimly lit room*: Ibid.

205 *"Goddamn you fucking prick"*: NBC Sports broadcast.

205 *Upset viewers*: Maggie Haberman, "Tiger's Lost Green Shot Sparks Blue Blast on TV," *New York Post*, June 18, 2000.

205 *"How's your wife?"*: Authors' interview with Jimmy Roberts.

206 *"I've got to ask"*: Ibid.

206 *"shoved up their ass"*: Authors' interview Butch Harmon.

206 *"Yeah, I got a little angry"*: NBC Sports broadcast.

206 *"let my clubs do the talking"*: Woods, *The 1997 Masters*, 22.

207 *"trying to prove?"*: Authors' interview with Jimmy Roberts.
     Authors' note: Butch Harmon disputes the "why the fuck" confrontation scene, saying something similar occurred two years earlier but with another reporter.

207 *"big par putts"*: Tiger Woods, press conference, PGA Championship, June 18, 2000.

207 *"records are great"*: Ibid.

CHAPTER EIGHTEEN: TRANSCENDENCE

Primary sources include interviews with Butch Harmon, Alicia O'Meara, Herb Sugden, Amber Lauria, Bob May, sources close to the Woods family, and Tom Sargent; reporting by Michael Bamberger, Steve Rushin, Rick Reilly, Tom Cunneff, and S. L. Price; property records from Florida; administrative records from ETW Corp.; and books by Steve Williams.

208 *quiet celebratory dinner*: Authors' interview with Butch Harmon.

208 *nodded and smiled*: Ibid.

208 *record 230,000 fans*: Steve Rushin, "Grand," *Sports Illustrated*, July 31, 2000.

209 *"He has raised the bar"*: Rosaforte, *Raising the Bar*, 31.

209 *112 bunkers*: Bamberger, "Witnessing History."

209 *Tida cried with joy*: Diaz, "Raising Tiger Hardly Just a Father Affair."

209 *"Bye, Mom . . . I love you"*: Rushin, "Grand."

210 *Royal Air Force base*: Ibid.

210 *$2.475 million*: Orange County Property Appraiser, Property Record Card, Orange County, Florida.

210 *off for the Bahamas*: Dan Goodgame, "The Game of Risk," *Time*, August 14, 2000.

210 *simultaneously appeared*: "Tiger's Tale," *Time*, August 14, 2000; "The Chosen One," *New Yorker*, August 21 & 28, 2000.

210 *American Express aired*: Joe Pytka, director, "Tiger Woods in Manhattan," June 30, 2000.

211 *never won a major*: The Louisville Slugger!, DVD, PGA Valhalla, 2000.

211 *"won't back down"*: Williams, *Out of the Rough*.

211 Play the course: Authors' interview with Bob May.

211 *"Cut the Corner"*: Masters.com.

212 *"Stevie, my mom"*: Williams, *Out of the Rough*.

212 Off the cart . . . *He had*: Authors' interview with a source close to Tiger Woods.

212 *Woods joined Ben Hogan*: The Louisville Slugger!

212 *Venus . . . winning Wimbledon*: Selena Roberts, "Venus Williams Wins Wimbledon," *New York Times*, July 9, 2000.

213 *"I've never met him"*: Rick Reilly, "An Audience with the Earl," *Sports Illustrated*, July 24, 2000.

213 *"I raised Tiger to leave me"*: S. L. Price, "Tunnel Vision," *Sports Illustrated*, April 3, 2000.

213 · *"I get mobbed"*: Reilly, "An Audience with the Earl."

213 *"Knock this stuff off"*: Earl Woods interview with Tom Cunneff.

213 *a bevy of women*: Employment records of ETW Corp.; authors' interviews with sources close to Earl Woods.

214 *women were employed by*: Ibid.

214 *brought a younger woman*: Authors' interview with a PGA Tour insider who was on the flight to Australia.

214 *changed his cell phone*: Authors' interview with a source close to Earl Woods.

214 *"dad and I don't talk as much"*: Goodgame, "The Game of Risk."

215 *food and pre-cut fruit*: Authors' interview with a source close to Earl Woods.

215 *"I'll be all right, Pop"*: Bamberger, "Witnessing History."

CHAPTER NINETEEN: COLD

Primary sources include interviews with Kel Devlin, Barry Frank, Jimmy Roberts, Mark O'Meara, Alicia O'Meara, Dina Gravell, Nike, Butch Harmon, and Amber Lauria; transcripts of Tiger Woods's press conferences; footage from CBS Sports and the PGA Tour; and reporting by Michael Bamberger.

216 *Woods had to crouch down*: Tiger Woods, press conference, NEC Invitational, August 27, 2000.

216 *shot in the dark*: Bamberger, "Witnessing History."

216 *twilight with his dad*: Tiger Woods, press conference, NEC Invitational, August 27, 2000 ("This is how it used to be. This is how I grew up playing. My dad and I . . . we used to have probably two holes in pitch black or dark").

216 *flickering lighters*: PGATour.com.

217 *"You can't do that"*: Ibid.

217 *a fan shouted, "Tiger"*: Bamberger, "Witnessing History."

217 *No one else in the world*: Ibid.

218 *"He's limitless"*: "Tiger Woods on His Way," GOLFonline.

218 *the halo effect*: Authors' interview with a Nike source.

218 *"compared Tiger to Michael"*: Clifton Brown, "Nike Deal for Woods Said to Be the Richest," *New York Times*, September 15, 2000.

219 *limited foothold*: Scorecard, "Mining Woods for Gold," *Sports Illustrated*, September 25, 2000.

219 *about $130 million in sales*: Authors' interview with Kel Devlin.

219 *$68 million per year*: PGATour.com.

219 *Nielsen rating of 7.6*: Doug Ferguson, "Prime Time Golf Turns into Big Hit," Associated Press, July 31, 2001.

220 *"it's not your fault"*: Authors' interview with Barry Frank.

220 *"just another Jew"*: Ibid.

221 *Sportsman of the Year*: Frank Deford, "Better Than Imagined," *Sports Illustrated*, December 18, 2000.

221 *"Deford with a pen"*: Authors' interview with a colleague of Frank Deford.

221 *"It's not true"*: Tiger Woods, press conference, WGC Andersen Consulting Match Play Championship, February 22, 2000.

222 *"Does it bug you"*: Tiger Woods, press conference, Bay Hill Invitational, March 13, 2001.

222 *"Well, it's annoying"*: Ibid.

223 *defending Woods*: Authors' interview with Jimmy Roberts.

223 not even listening: Ibid.

223 *"Don't worry, dude"*: Ibid.

224 *"just started thinking"*: Tiger Woods, press conference, Masters, April 8, 2001.

CHAPTER TWENTY: IN THE BUBBLE

Primary sources include interviews with Butch Harmon, Charles Barkley, Kel Devlin, Ed Sherman, Larry Kirshbaum, Rick Wolff, Peggy Lewis, Alicia O'Meara, Norm Clarke, Las Vegas sources, Mark O'Meara, and MGM sources; author visits to Las Vegas and Keith Kleven Institute; transcripts of Tiger Woods's press conferences; reporting by Mark Seal, Sandra Sobieraj Westfall, Michael Bamberger, Jaime Diaz, and Alan Shipnuck; and books by Howard Sounes and Tim Rosaforte.

226 *Kleven, an acquaintance from his Stanford days*: Teri Thompson, "Keith Kleven . . . Goes Quiet," *New York Daily News*, December 28, 2009.

226 *ultraexclusive Italian-themed*: MGMgrand.com.

226 *"beyond attentive"*: Ibid.

227 *routinely play $20,000 per hand*: Authors' interviews with Mansion sources.

227 *"a sharp"*: Ibid.

227 *twenty-first birthday at the MGM*: Jaime Diaz, "Off Like a Shot," *Sports Illustrated*, September 20, 1997.

227 *"you have to enjoy it"*: Authors' interview with Charles Barkley.

228 *"I've still got the handprints"*: Mark Seal, "The Temptation of Tiger Woods: Part II: Losing Control," *Vanity Fair*, May 2, 2010.

228 *Woods sped off with Jordan*: Allison Samuels, "Tiger's 'Brothers,'" *Newsweek*, June 17, 2001.

229 *"Michael is like the big brother"*: Rosaforte, *Raising the Bar*, 151.

229 *wasn't universally shared*: Authors' interviews with Las Vegas sources.

229 *leaving $100 tips*: Authors' interview with PGA Tour source.

230 *lap dancer stripped naked*: Andy Farrell, "Streaker and Steward Taint Tiger's Special Moment," *Independent*, July 24, 2000.

230 *"Tiger did not respond"*: Bamberger, "Witnessing History."

230 *born in Stockholm*: Alan Shipnuck, "Who Is This Woman?" *Sports Illustrated*, September 14, 2004.

230 *identical twin, Josefin*: Ibid.

230 *Thomas Nordegren . . . accomplished journalists*: Ibid.

230 *Barbro Holmberg . . . highly educated*: Ibid.

230 *her parents divorced*: Ibid.

230 *work for Scandinavian* Playboy: Ibid.

231 *magazine* Café Sport: Ibid.

231 *no real interest in modeling*: Elin Nordegren interview with Sandra Sobieraj Westfall, *People*, May 30, 2017.

231 *Mia Parnevik went shopping*: Shipnuck, "Who Is This Woman?"

231 *three-thousand-square-foot guest house*: Ibid.

231 *odd and off-putting*: Ibid.

231 *with a famous athlete*: Ibid.

231 *"I was not an easy catch"*: Sounes, *The Wicked Game*, 238.

231 *sounding nervous whenever Jesper*: Shipnuck, "Who Is This Woman?"

231 *She felt safe around him*: Elin Nordegren interview with Sandra Sobieraj Westfall.

231 *"She became like Greta Garbo"*: Shipnuck, "Who Is This Woman?"

232 *lost a heartbreaker to Michigan*: sports-reference.com/cbb/postseason /1989-ncaa.

232 *moving almost one million copies*: Bookscan.

233 *went to see Bingo Rimér*: Shipnuck, "Who Is This Woman?"

233 *she personally approved*: Ibid.

233 *Tiger's go-to guy at the Mansion*: Authors' interview with Las Vegas source.

233 *all-expenses-paid comp*: Authors viewed Tiger's comp ticket.

233 *places like Drink*: Authors' interviews with Las Vegas sources.

233 *"Woods would like you at his table"*: Authors' interview with a source who witnessed the exchange.

233 *into a hot tub*: Ibid.

234 *straight into a closet*: Authors' interview with a source familiar with the incident.

234 *Tiger woke up at four thirty a.m.*: Rick Reilly, "Killer Instinct," *Sports Illustrated*, April 22, 2002.

234 *his closest rivals*: Ibid.

234 *intimidated by Tiger*: Ibid.

235 *"Can you please share with us"*: Tiger Woods, press conference, Masters, April 14, 2002.

235 *"I will celebrate"*: Ibid.

235 *"hope to see you when I come back"*: Handwritten note from Joanna Ja-
      goda to Peggy Lewis.

236 *Elin stood behind Tiger:* Josh Elliott, "Tiger Woods in Tiger Jam," *Sports
      Illustrated*, May 6, 2002.

236 *"Black Jesus scares them"*: Ibid.

237 *internet was flooded with risqué images*: Shipnuck, "Who Is This Woman?"

237 *"sexy Swede"*: Bridget Harrison and Bill Hoffmann, "Sexy Swede Is Tee-
      Rific For Tiger," *New York Post*, May 6, 2002.

237 *"Pamela Anderson and Cindy Margolis"*: Ibid.

CHAPTER TWENTY-ONE: CHANGES II

Primary sources include interviews with Charles Barkley, Butch Harmon,
Hank Haney, Kel Devlin, Mark O'Meara, Chris Mike, Mike Shapiro, Don
Transeth, Chip Lange, Herb Sugden, Karl Lund, Peggy Lewis, residents of
Isleworth, and PGA Tour sources; transcripts of press conferences by Tiger
Woods, Phil Mickelson, and Mark O'Meara; unpublished interviews with
Tiger Woods; books by Steve Williams and Hank Haney; court records from
Florida; and reporting by Wright Thompson.

238 *"Let's go Mick-el-son"*: Michael Silver, "Halfway Home," *Sports Illus-
      trated*, June 24, 2002.

238 *"Has any pro golfer"*: Ibid.

239 *slow-forming rift*: Authors' interview with Butch Harmon.

239 Maintenance . . . *a word Tiger hated*: Haney, *The Big Miss*.

240 *undergo arthroscopic surgery*: Lee Benson, "About Utah: Dr. Vern Cooley
      Had Tiger of a Tale before He Met Tiger Woods," *Deseret News*, Janu-
      ary 29, 2012.

240 *20 percent of his ACL*: Unpublished Tiger Woods interview, obtained
      from a confidential source.

240 *"How long will that last?"*: Ibid.

240 *"change my swing"*: Haney, *The Big Miss*, 35.

241 *"Pull your head out"*: Williams, *Out of the Rough*.

241 *point guard at Maryland*: Don Markus, "Nared Doing Better Job for
      Maryland," *Baltimore Sun*, February 4, 1989.

242 *"I'm as happy for you"*: Mark O'Meara, press conference, Dubai Desert
      Classic, March 7, 2004.

242 *"got to get someone"*: Haney, *The Big Miss*, 36.

242 *"Who should I get?"*: Ibid.

243 *Haney first met Tiger*: Authors' interview with Hank Haney.

243 I've won the lottery: Haney, *The Big Miss*, 36.

244 *"intended to be a respite"*: ELDRICK "TIGER" WOODS and PRIVACY, LTD v. CHRISTENSEN SHIPYARDS LTD, Southern District of Florida, Case no. 04-61432.

245 *"working with you"*: Haney, *The Big Miss*, 42.

246 *$50,000 per year*: Ibid., 54.

247 *"Hank, good luck"*: Ibid., 53.

247 *"inferior equipment"*: *Golf*, March 2003.

247 *"Phil trying to be funny"*: Tiger Woods, press conference, Buick Invitational, February 12, 2003.

247 *"I had a different feeling"*: Phil Mickelson, press conference, Masters, April 11, 2004.

248 *disappeared with his father*: Thompson, "The Secret History of Tiger Woods."

248 *tandem-jumping*: Haney, *The Big Miss*, 138.

248 *"you understand my world"*: Thompson, "The Secret History of Tiger Woods."

248 *"Woods is not playing well"*: ESPN.com.

249 *Williams kicked a camera*: Associated Press, "Williams Blames Repeated Camera Clicks," July 1, 2004.

249 *"I've had enough of golf"*: Williams, *Out of the Rough*.

249 *video game called* SOCOM: Haney, *The Big Miss*, 78.

250 *"You were in New York?"*: Authors' interview with an Isleworth resident who witnessed the conversation.

250 *smoking cigars*: Authors' interview with Charles Barkley.

251 *wearing a bulky knee brace*: Authors' interviews with four individuals who were present.

251 *"I'll be fine"*: Ibid.

252 *"This fuckin' ski"*: Ibid.

254 *"We have to celebrate"*: Haney, *The Big Miss*, 86.

254 *"Tiger never allowed"*: Ibid.

CHAPTER TWENTY-TWO: UNPLAYABLE LIE

Primary sources include interviews with Maureen Decker, Jim Harris, Mike Shapiro, Kel Devlin, Jim Riswold, Bart Mandell, and Fred Khalilian; author visits to Cerritos Elementary School; transcripts of Tiger Woods's press conferences; footage from CBS Sports and the *Howard Stern Show*; books by Hank Haney and John Strege; and reporting by Gary Smith and Mark Seal.

255 *"I became aware"*: Charles Barkley, *Who's Afraid of a Large Black Man?* (New York: Penguin, 2005).

255 *the story resurfaced*: Plaschke, "It's a New Day for Golf's Child Prodigy."

256 *the story grew*: Smith, "The Chosen One."

256 *"shocking introduction to racism"*: Strege, *Tiger*, 18.

256 *"bleeding all over the place"*: Tiger Woods interview with Barbara Walters, May 11, 1997.

257 *"I have never heard of that"*: Sounes, *The Wicked Game*, 128.

258 *"There are no reports"*: Email to the authors from Dr. Sue Johnson, superintendent, Savanna School District, January 8, 2016.

258 *"Let the legend grow"*: Smith, "The Chosen One."

260 *"Tiger would love to meet you"*: Mark Seal, "The Temptation of Tiger Woods," *Vanity Fair*, March 20, 2010.
Authors' note: In an email Jerry Chang declined to be interviewed.

260 *"it turned very wild"*: Ibid.

261 *"had a great time"*: Ibid.

261 *"my little coffee cup"*: *Howard Stern Show*, March 10, 2010.

261 *Bell checked in with Jungers*: Seal, "The Temptation of Tiger Woods."

261 *"always go through Bryon"*: Ibid.
Authors' note: Bryon Bell did not respond to request for comment on his relationship with Woods.

261 *"I'm with Tiger"*: Ibid.

261 *narcissists build a brick wall*: Authors' interviews with Bart Mandell, CitiTherapy Counseling Services, New York.

261 *conditional worth*: Authors' interview with Dr. Monica Meyer, Gentle Path, The Meadows.

261 *could never rage*: Ibid.

CHAPTER TWENTY-THREE: LOSS

Primary sources include interviews with Royce Woods, Hank Haney, Brandel Chamblee, Ruth Streeter, Joe Grohman, Charles Barkley, Jaime Diaz, Mike Mohler, John Merchant, sources close to the Woods family, Mark Seal, sources close to President Bill Clinton and Casey Wasserman, and Tiger Woods Foundation sources; books by Tiger Woods and Hank Haney; transcripts of Tiger Woods's press conferences; CBS News transcripts; footage from ESPN; and reporting by Wright Thompson.

263 *an urgent telephone call*: Authors' interviews with Royce Woods and sources close to the Woods family.
263 *hired a full-time assistant*: Ibid.
263 *shepherded Earl through*: Ibid.
264 *Tiger was well aware*: Ibid.
264 *Kultida always resented*: Ibid.
265 *visiting with SEAL*: Thompson, "The Secret History of Tiger Woods."
265 *"It's a life"*: Ibid.
265 *driving toward Orlando*: Woods, *The 1997 Masters*, 222.
265 *call to his father*: Ibid.
265 *change the focus*: Ibid.
265 *a circus act*: Tiger Woods, press conference, Buick Invitational, January 25, 2006.
265 *thirty-five-thousand-square-foot*: Tiger Woods Foundation website.
265 *approached California governor*: Authors' interview with a source close to the Tiger Woods Foundation.
266 *hated him*: Ibid.
266 *under certain conditions*: Ibid.
266 *make the request*: Ibid.
266 *moments of whining*: Ibid.
266 *"that was easy"*: Ibid.
266 *Tellum and Wasserman approached*: Authors' interviews with sources with knowledge of what transpired that day.
266 *"talk about pussy"*: Ibid.
267 *"How do you remember"*: Ibid.
267 *completely indifferent . . . exit*: Ibid.
267 *" 'I'm Tiger Woods' "*: Ibid.

267 *Bradley had profiled*: Jacqueline Alemany, "Remembering Ed Bradley," CBSNews.com, November 9, 2009.

268 *"kind of a private person"*: "Son, Hero, Champion," *60 Minutes*, March 26, 2006.

268 *"they tied me to a tree"*: Ibid.

268 *"His best quality"*: Jeff Fager, *Fifty Years of 60 Minutes: The Inside Story of Television's Most Influential News Broadcast* (New York: Simon & Schuster, 2017).

269 *"found a life partner"*: "Son, Hero, Champion."

269 *"Family always comes first"*: Ibid.

269 *luxury condo in Newport Beach*: Jeff Collins, "Tiger Woods' Newport 'Love Lair' For Sale," *Orange County Register*, May 4, 2012. Woods reportedly purchased the two-story condo on Ocean Boulevard for $3 million in April 2004.

269 *"he was preoccupied"*: Katie Nelson, "Accenture Drops Tiger Woods," *New York Daily News*, December 13, 2009.

269 *a pair of panties*: Ibid.

269 *didn't shed a tear*: Ibid.

270 *Earl took his final breaths*: Authors' interview with Royce Woods.

271 *"Old Man is soft"*: David Brooks, "The Frozen Gaze," *New York Times*, June 17, 2008.

271 *The headline read*: Litsky, "Golf: Earl Woods, Tiger's Father, Dies."

272 *handling guns*: Thompson, "The Secret History of Tiger Woods."

272 *"Why are you here?"*: Ibid.

272 *"They use real bullets"*: Haney, *The Big Miss*, 139.

273 *"Tiger would like to meet you"*: Seal, "The Temptation of Tiger Woods: Part II."

273 *"He was very jealous"*: Ibid.

273 *single fairway bunker*: Michael Bamberger, *Sports Illustrated*, July 31, 2006.

274 *"just came pouring out"*: Ibid.

CHAPTER TWENTY-FOUR: TICK, TICK, TICK

Primary sources include interviews with Neal Boulton, Hank Haney, Roy S. Johnson, Dr. Monica Meyer, *National Enquirer* sources, Fred Khalilian, and sources close to Tiger Woods; books by Tiger Woods and Hank Haney; court records in New York; and reporting by Jeffrey Toobin, Mark Seal, and Larry Dorman.

277 *tripped the radar*: Authors' interviews with sources at the *National Enquirer*.

277 *employed a loose network*: Ibid.

277 Enquirer *was founded*: Jeffrey Toobin, "The *National Enquirer*'s Fervor for Trump," *New Yorker*, July 3, 2017.

277 *6.7 million copies*: Ibid.

278 *"predictive human behavior"*: Authors' interviews with sources at the *National Enquirer*.

278 *call came . . . tip line*: Toobin, "The *National Enquirer*'s Fervor for Trump."

279 *"Hi, this is Ti"*: Seal, "The Temptation of Tiger Woods."
     Authors' note: Mindy Lawton could not be reached for comment.

279 *a "hijacked brain"*: Authors' interview with Dr. Monica Meyers.

279 *"What are you doing after?"*: Seal, "The Temptation of Tiger Woods."

279 *He spanked her*: Ibid.

280 *the brief sexual encounter*: Authors' interviews with sources at the *National Enquirer*.

280 *"We've got our Elvis"*: Authors' interviews with Neal Boulton.

280 *Perel placed a call*: Authors' interviews with sources at the *National Enquirer*.

280 *"We'll take care of it"*: Seal, "The Temptation of Tiger Woods."

281 *$100 million in endorsement*: https://www.statista.com/statistics/411993/earnings-of-tiger-woods/.

281 *Perel running point*: Authors' interviews with sources at the *National Enquirer*.

283 *by Lawton's mother*: Toobin, "The *National Enquirer*'s Fervor for Trump" ("The tipster was Lawton's mother").

283 *April 2007, Jaimee Grubbs*: Seal, "The Temptation of Tiger Woods: Part II."

284 *"No offense"*: Ibid.

284 *"Wake up, Sleeping Beauty"*: Ibid.

284 *Nici's Girls*: "Hollywood Madam Michelle Braun Cozies Up to Federal Agents," *New York Daily News*, May 9, 2009.

284 *at least $8.5 million*: Ibid.
     Authors' note: Michelle Braun did not respond to requests for comment.

285 *"Hey, it's Tiger"*: Seal, "The Temptation of Tiger Woods: Part II."

285 *Hawaiian Tropic model*: Ibid.

285 *Woods paid $15,000*: Ibid.

285 *financed shopping sprees*: Ibid.

285 *to the Bahamas*: Ibid.

285 *directly to the hospital*: Haney, *The Big Miss*, 157.

285 *"he called out 'Sam'"*: Woods, *The 1997 Masters*, 150.

286 *"'stupid flip phone'"*: Authors' interview with Hank Haney.

286 *raided by the FBI*: Terrence McCoy, "Michelle Braun: Notorious L.A. Madam's South Florida Adventure," *Miami New Times*, May 23, 2013.

286 *She later surrendered*: Email to the authors from Thom Mrozek, a US Department of Justice spokesman, on November 17, 2017.

286 *"with intent"*: United States of America v. Michelle Louise Braun, Case no. SACR09:0068, US District Court for the Central District of California, Southern Division.

286 *she pled guilty*: Email to the authors from Thom Mrozek, November 14, 2017.

286 *"I will wear you out"*: "Text Messages Between Tiger Woods and Jaimee Grubbs," *New York Post*, December 9, 2009.

286 *"Send me something very naughty"*: Ibid.

287 *"SEALs unit" in Coronado*: Haney, *The Big Miss*, 140.

287 *"There's no way"*: Ibid.

287 *"In a real mission"*: Ibid.

288 *"career ended right now"*: Ibid.

288 *Steinberg hosted a dinner*: Ibid.

289 *"if Tiger stays healthy"*: Larry Dorman, "As Woods Enters Prime, Time Is on His Side," *New York Times*, December 13, 2007.

289 *"so far away from that"*: Ibid.

CHAPTER TWENTY-FIVE: IT'S JUST PAIN

Primary sources include interviews with Joe DeBock, Deborah Ganley, Hank Haney, and PGA Tour sources; unpublished interviews with Tiger Woods; transcripts of Tiger Woods's press conferences; books by Tiger Woods, Steve Williams, and Hank Haney; and footage from CBS Sports and NBC Sports.

290 *the thick ligament*: Haney, *The Big Miss*, 168.

290 There's a difference: Unpublished Tiger Woods interview, obtained from a confidential source.

290 *"Nothing that some drugs"*: Haney, *The Big Miss*, 165.

290 *Tiger using painkillers . . . 2002*: Diaz, "The Truth about Tiger."

291 *Woods used Vicodin*: Haney, *The Big Miss*, 165.

291 *"I made the decision"*: Associated Press, "Woods Has Surgery on Left Knee," April 16, 2008.

291 *damaged cartilage*: Benson, "About Utah."

291 *ligament replacement surgery*: Ibid.

291 *Rosenberg's instinct*: Haney, *The Big Miss*, 169–70.

292 *felt a crack*: Ibid.

293 *"I'm playing in the US Open"*: Ibid., 171.

293 *a "true athlete"*: Ibid., 153.

293 *"That's just what we do"*: Unpublished Tiger Woods interview, obtained from a confidential source.

294 *new drug-testing policy*: "A Timeline of the PGA Tour's Drug-Testing Policy," PGA.com, January 31, 2013.

294 *"the way he framed it"*: Authors' interview with Hank Haney.

294 *fractured in two places*: Woods, *The 1997 Masters*, 220.

295 *"absolutely trust me"*: Williams, *Out of the Rough*.

295 *putt was a lot tougher*: Authors' interview with Joe DeBock, head PGA professional, Torrey Pines Golf Course.

296 *one of the worst parts*: Ibid.

296 Two and a half balls: Tiger Woods, press conference, US Open, June 15, 2008.

297 *"greatest tournament I've ever had"*: Tiger Woods, press conference, US Open, June 16, 2008.

297 *"exemplar of mental discipline"*: Brooks, "The Frozen Gaze."

CHAPTER TWENTY-SIX: MIRACLE WORKERS

Primary sources include interviews with Hank Haney, Dr. Keith Pyne, Bill Knowles, Bill Romanowski, Brian H. Greenspan, and Victor Conte; unpublished interviews with Tiger Woods; transcripts of Tiger Woods's press conferences; books by Tiger Woods and Hank Haney; court records in New York;

Florida Department of Health investigation records; and reporting by Tim Elfrink, Gus Garcia-Roberts, and Don Van Natta Jr.

298 *"Can I do push-ups?"*: Unpublished interview with Tiger Woods, obtained from a confidential source.

298 *"magic hands"*: Bob McKenzie, *Hockey Confidential: Inside Stories from People Inside the Game* (New York: HarperCollins, 2014), 18.

299 *introduced to Lindsay*: Authors' interview with Bill Romanowski. Confirmed by a source close to Dr. Mark Lindsay.

299 *cleared to start swinging*: Haney, *The Big Miss*, 182.

299 *injured his right Achilles*: Associated Press, "Complete List of Tiger Woods' Injuries," April 1, 2014.

300 *platelet-rich plasma*: Arraignment and Plea, United States of America v. Anthony Galea, Case no. 10-CR-307A, US District Court, Western District of New York, 17.

300 *"It's very effective"*: McKenzie, *Hockey Confidential*, 25.

300 *a dramatic figure*: Tim Elfrink and Gus Garcia-Roberts, *Blood Sport: A-Rod and the Quest to End Baseball's Steroid Era* (New York: Plume, 2014), 125.

300 *at forty, he divorced*: Ibid., 126.

300 *Galea's hobby*: Arraignment and Plea, United States of America v. Anthony Galea, 36.

301 *"tell him to get lost"*: Elfrink and Garcia-Roberts, *Blood Sport*, 125.

301 *access to Viagra*: Indictment, United States of America v. Anthony Galea, Case no. 10-cr-00307-RJA-HBS, US District Court, Western District of New York.

301 *"Viagra was the hook"*: Authors' interview with a confidential source.

301 *on a massage table*: Authors' interview with Hank Haney.

301 *"injections containing a mixture"*: Indictment, United States of America v. Anthony Galea, 10.

301 *his preferred treatment*: Don Van Natta Jr., "Doctor Sought by Elite Athletes Is the Subject of a Doping Inquiry," *New York Times*, December 15, 2009.

302 *made fourteen trips*: Department of Health Investigative Report, State of Florida, January 7, 2011.

302 *charging $3,500*: Ibid.

302 *more than $76,000*: Ibid.

302 *crossing the Peace Bridge*: Indictment, United States of America v. Anthony Galea, 19.

302 *CBP officers discovered*: Criminal Complaint, United States of America v. Anthony Galea, Case no. 10-cr-00307-RJA-HBS, US District Court, Western District of New York, 11.

302 *Galea's "medical kit"*: Ibid., 3.

302 *raided Galea's office*: Van Natta Jr., "Doctor Sought by Elite Athletes Is the Subject of a Doping Inquiry."

302 *introducing misbranded drugs*: Indictment, United States of America v. Anthony Galea.

302 *more than one hundred times*: Ibid., 20.

302 *athletes, including Woods*: Arraignment and Plea, United States of America v. Anthony Galea.

302 *about $800,000*: Ibid.

303 *She told the government . . . "cocktail containing HGH"*: Affidavit, Justin Burnham, special agent, Immigration and Customs Enforcement; David Epstein and Melissa Segura, "The Elusive Dr. Galea," *Sports Illustrated*, Sept. 27, 2010.

303 *Checks were written*: Ibid.

303 *no question has hovered*: Tiger Woods, press conference, Masters, April 5, 2010.

303 *a 2010 survey*: "Almost a Quarter of PGA Tour Pros Surveyed by *Sports Illustrated* Think Woods Took PEDs," Golf.com, May 12, 2010.

303 *Those suspecting he used*: David Paisie, "Tiger Woods and Steroids or HGH: Could It Be True?" *Bleacher Report*, January 1, 2010.

304 *Conte . . . suspects Woods*: Authors' interview with Victor Conte.

304 *"I've never taken"*: Tiger Woods, press conference, Masters, April 5, 2010.

304 *"Dr. Galea at no time"*: Authors' interview with attorney Brian H. Greenspan.

304 *"positive regulatory obligation"*: Email from Brian H. Greenspan to the authors, October 9, 2017.

304 *treated Woods forty-nine times*: Invoices, Lindsay Sports Therapy, Inc., Department of Health Investigative Report, State of Florida.

305 *therapeutic table to the range*: Authors' interview with a source close to Tiger.

CHAPTER TWENTY-SEVEN: CRASH

Primary sources include interviews with Amber Lauria, Wright Thompson, Hank Haney, and Las Vegas sources; transcripts of Tiger Woods's press conferences; books by Tiger Woods, Steve Williams, Hank Haney, Robert Lusetich, and Steve Helling; footage from NBC Sports and the PGA Tour; reporting by Mark Seal and Maureen Callahan; and police records from the Florida State Highway Patrol.

307 *"What did I say"*: NBC Sports broadcast.

308 *first in birdie average*: PGATour.com.

308 *in New York City*: Helling, *Tiger*, xii.

308 *"My dad passed away"*: Ibid.

309 *started taking Ambien*: Tiger Woods, press conference, Masters, April 5, 2010.

310 *child of privilege*: Lusetich, *Unplayable*.

310 *earning high praise*: Authors' interviews with Las Vegas sources.

310 *Woods was taken with Uchitel*: Seal, "The Temptation of Tiger Woods: Part II."

310 *code name Bear*: Callahan, "The Night Tiger Woods Was Exposed as a Serial Cheater."

310 *"makes me so happy"*: Authors' interview with Wright Thompson.

311 *"he was lying"*: Authors' interview with Hank Haney.

311 *"never saw him with anybody"*: Ibid.

311 *"fought my swing all day"*: Ibid., 187.

311 *"make any friends"*: Ibid.

312 *"Be creative"*: Tiger Woods, press conference, PGA Championship, August 14, 2009.

312 *hadn't picked up a club*: Ian O'Connor, "After Yang Took Down Tiger," ESPN.com, August 8, 2015.

312 *sink a seven-foot putt*: Ibid.

312 *players . . . jumping up*: Ibid.

313 *the Snowball Effect*: Williams and Hugh de Lacy, *Golf at the Top with Steve Williams*, 57.

313 a troubled guy: Haney, *The Big Miss*.

313 *denigrating texts*: Josh Levin, "That's What She Said," Slate.com, March 18, 2010.

313 *"Hold you down"*: Ibid.

313 *"I am totally free"*: Radaronline.com, December 10, 2009.

314 *"It's under the name Bell"*: Seal, "The Temptation of Tiger Woods: Part II."

314 *"Here are the details"*: "Concrete Proof of Tiger's Secret Rendezvous," TMZ Sports, December 4, 2009.

315 *"a tricky golf course"*: "Tiger Woods Wins Australian Masters," *Sunday Morning Herald*, November 15, 2009.

315 *"wrong side . . . big media story"*: Lusetich, *Unplayable.*

316 *"Hank . . . a heads-up"*: Haney, *The Big Miss*, 193.

316 *"Don't speak to anybody"*: Williams, *Out of the Rough.*

316 *"We're in love"*: Seal, "The Temptation of Tiger Woods: Part II."

317 *extraordinary step*: Lusetich, *Unplayable.*

317 *urgent voice mail*: Helling, *Tiger.*

317 *"World Exclusive"*: *National Enquirer*, November 28, 2009.

317 *"u too love"*: Seal, "The Temptation of Tiger Woods: Part II." (This text has also been published in other publications.)

318 *"only one I've ever loved"*: Callahan, "The Night Tiger Woods Was Exposed as a Serial Cheater."

318 *"I miss you"*: Ibid.

318 *"Few events in the life"*: Esther Perel, *The State of Affairs: Rethinking Infidelity* (New York: HarperCollins, 2010).

318 *blood on his teeth and lips*: Police report, Florida Highway Patrol, November 27, 2009.

318 *"What happened?"*: Florida Highway Patrol interview with Jarius Adams and Kimberly Harris, November 27, 2009.

CHAPTER TWENTY-EIGHT: FIRESTORM

Primary sources include interviews with Chip Lange, Charles Barkley, Sgt. Kim Montes, Mark O'Meara, Hank Haney, and Las Vegas sources; police reports from the Florida Highway Patrol and the Windermere Police Department; Elin Nordegren's interview with *People*; and reporting by Mark Seal.

320 *two police officers assigned*: Police report, Florida Highway Patrol, November 27, 2009.

320 *two bottles of pills*: Florida Highway Patrol narrative, November 27, 2009.

320 *out-of-print science book*: Police photographs, Florida Highway Patrol.

321 *"We don't believe"*: "Tiger Woods Injured in Crash," ESPN.com, November 30, 2009.

321 *he was in "good" condition*: Larry Dorman, "Tiger Woods Out of Hospital after Car Accident," *New York Times*, November 27, 2009.

321 *"Can we help"*: Authors' interview with a source close to Josefin Nordegren.

321 *Cullen had worked*: McGuireWoods.com.

322 *officers knocked*: Florida Highway Patrol narrative, November 27, 2009.

322 *1,600 emails*: Authors' interview with Sgt. Kim Montes.

323 *news conference . . . canceled*: Joseph Berger and Larry Dorman, "Woods, Not Talking to Police, to Skip Tournament," *New York Times*, November 30, 2009.

323 *reschedule the interview*: Florida Highway Patrol narrative, November 27, 2009.

323 *NeJame notified*: Ibid.

324 *motor vehicle documents*: Ibid.

324 *surveillance video*: Ibid.

324 *"there is curiosity"*: Berger and Dorman, "Woods, Not Talking to Police, to Skip Tournament."

325 *an investigative subpoena*: Florida Highway Patrol narrative, November 27, 2009.

325 *"Yes, He Cheated"*: "Yes, He Cheated," *Us Weekly*, December 1, 2009.

325 *"let my family down"*: TMZ Sports, December 2, 2009.

325 *Nike . . . full support*: Larry Dorman, "Gillette to Limit Role of Tiger Woods in Marketing," *New York Times*, December 12, 2009.

326 *hired . . . Gloria Allred*: Seal, "The Temptation of Tiger Woods: Part II."

326 *$10 million to Uchitel*: Seal, "The Temptation of Tiger Woods: Part II."

326 *"I felt so stupid"*: Elin Nordegren, "My Own Story," interview, *People*, September 6, 2000.

326 been so deceived: Ibid.

327 *"betrayal isn't strong enough"*: Ibid.

327 *stepping away from professional golf*: Larry Dorman, "Woods Says He'll Take 'Indefinite Break' From Golf," *New York Times*, December 11, 2009.

327 *"I am deeply aware"*: Tiger Woods, statement, *New York Daily News*, December 11, 2009.

327 *Accenture became the first*: Brian Stelter, "Accenture, as if Tiger Woods Were Never There," *New York Times*, December 16, 2009.

328 *"a powerful device"*: Ibid.

328 *Galea had dispensed*: Van Natta Jr., "Doctor Sought by Elite Athletes Is the Subject of a Doping Inquiry."

328 *deal among American Media*: Reed Albergotti, "How Tiger Protected His Image," *Wall Street Journal,* December 18, 2009.

329 *"let me ask you a question"*: Authors' interview with Charles Barkley.

329 *losing weight*: Elin Nordegren, "My Own Story."

329 *Insomnia*: Ibid.

330 *"Mommy, where is your boo-boo?"*: Ibid.

330 *"just wanted you to know"*: Haney, *The Big Miss*, 195.

330 *"I'm going to be gone"*: Ibid., 196.

CHAPTER TWENTY-NINE: THE RECKONING

Primary sources include interviews with Dr. Monica Meyer, Bart Mandell, Ari Fleischer, a former Gratitude patient, and Hank Haney; and transcripts of Tiger Woods's press conferences.

331 *surrendered his cell phone*: Authors' interview with a former Gratitude patient.

331 *Carnes wrote*: Patrick Carnes, PhD, *Out of the Shadows: Understanding Sexual Addiction* (CompCare Publishers, 1983).

331 *"sex addicts grow up"*: Patrick Carnes, PhD, *Facing the Shadow: Starting Sexual and Relationship Recovery* (Wickenburg, AZ: Gentle Path Press, 2000), 1–2.

331 *little sharing or intimacy*: Ibid.

331 *an illness of escape*: Ibid.

332 *comprehensive diagnostic assessment*: Authors' interview with Dr. Monica Meyer.

334 *wrote extensively in her journal*: Elin Nordegren, "My Own Story."

334 *adversity made her stronger*: Ibid.

334 *attended several lectures*: Authors' interview with Dr. Monica Meyer.

335 *"I betrayed her"*: Woods, *The 1997 Masters*, 217.

335 *"I missed my son's first birthday"*: Tiger Woods, press conference, Masters, April 5, 2010.

335 *people he loved most*: Ibid.

335 Enquirer *quickly launched*: Authors' interview with a source at the *National Enquirer*.

336 *worst experience he'd ever had*: Haney, *The Big Miss*, 196.

336 *stop playing golf for two years*: Ibid., 197.

337 *admitted his use of performance-enhancing drugs*: Mark McGwire, statement to Associated Press, January 10, 2010.

337 *"I had to fight"*: Authors' interview with Ari Fleischer.

337 *mood was somber*: Harvey Araton, "Apologizing, Woods Sets No Date for Return to Golf," *New York Times*, February 19, 2010.

337 *"Good morning"*: Tiger Woods, statement, CNN.com.

337 *thirteen mesmerizing minutes*: Donald G. McNeil Jr., "An Apology With Echoes of 12 Steps," *New York Times*, February 22, 2010.

338 *roughly thirty million*: Helling, *Tiger*, 225.

339 *"I am so proud"*: Doug Ferguson, Associated Press, February 13, 2010.

339 *"As she pointed out"*: Woods, statement, CNN.com.

349 *"I learned one thing"*: Haney, *The Big Miss*, 197.

CHAPTER THIRTY: CONSTANT STATE OF SHAME

Primary sources include interviews with Hank Haney and Kel Devlin; transcripts of Tiger Woods's press conferences; official statements by Tiger Woods; Elin Nordegren's interview with *People*; and books by Tiger Woods, Steve Williams, and Hank Haney.

341 *Butcher paper covered the windows*: Haney, *The Big Miss*, 201.

341 *receiving outpatient treatment*: Tiger Woods, press conference, Masters, April 5, 2010.

341 *lying to others*: Ibid.

341 *lying to himself*: Ibid.

342 *"personal sins"*: Tiger Woods, statement, December 2, 2009 ("Personal sins should not require press releases").

342 *Tiger was confronted*: Chris Wilson, "Tiger Bedded Neighbor's 21-year-old Daughter," *New York Post*, April 8, 2010.

342 *had sex with her*: Ibid.

342 *"I just wanted to dig"*: Ibid.

342 *said he was sorry*: Ibid.

342 *he hadn't told Elin*: "Tiger Woods Sex Romp with Neighbor's Young Daughter," *National Enquirer*, April 7, 2010.

342 *an intact family*: Nordegren, "My Own Story."

343 *Haney was surprised*: Haney, *The Big Miss*, 205.

344 *single biggest media event*: Jonathan Mahler, "The Tiger Bubble," *New York Times Magazine*, March 22, 2010.

344 *Williams had repeatedly asked*: Williams, *Out of the Rough*.

344 *apologizing for his actions*: Ibid.

345 *assured by Steinberg*: Haney, *The Big Miss*, 209.

345 *"I don't even know"*: Ibid.

346 *The key . . . perform well*: Ibid., 211.

346 *"What I've done"*: Tiger Woods, press conference, Masters, April 5, 2010.

347 *"That's personal"*: Ibid.

348 *"He forgot"*: Billy Payne, press conference, Masters, April 5, 2010.

348 *"Is there a way"*: Ibid.

348 *"I disappointed myself"*: Haney, *The Big Miss*, 212.

349 *"Tiger's sexual advances"*: "Tiger Woods Sex Romp with Neighbor's Young Daughter."

349 *"Motherfucker"*: Woods, *The 1997 Masters*, 100.

349 *"You little piece of shit"*: Ibid.

349 *"Little nigger"*: Ibid.

350 *DID YOU MEAN BOOTYISM?*: Haney, *The Big Miss*, 213.

350 *Woods's sins were on full display*: Tiger Woods, statement, December 2, 2009.

350 *"My regret will last a lifetime"*: Woods, *The 1997 Masters*, 217.

351 *"stop being a nice guy"*: Williams, *Out of the Rough*.

351 *"couldn't believe my ears"*: Ibid.

351 *This will be the last time*: Haney, *The Big Miss*, 216.

352 *"Good luck"*: Ibid., 218.

352 *"You understand him"*: Ibid., 220.

CHAPTER THIRTY-ONE: SEPARATION

Primary sources include interviews with Hank Haney and Brandel Chamblee; transcripts of Tiger Woods's press conferences; books by Hank Haney and Steve Williams; Elin Nordegren's interview with *People*; and court records from Florida.

353   *ninety-three PGA tournaments*: PGA Tour.

353   *34 of the 127 PGA tournaments*: Ibid.

353   *five-page email*: Authors' interview with Hank Haney.

354   *another woman's child*: Haney, *The Big Miss*, 222.

354   *"Say so long"*: Karen Crouse, "Woods Withdraws from Players Championship," *New York Times*, May 9, 2010.

354   You're not blowing me off: Authors' interview with Hank Haney.

354   *"I have informed Tiger"*: Haney, *The Big Miss*, 223.

356   *never took PEDs*: Ibid., 227.

356   *"in sex-addiction treatment"*: Ibid., 227.

356   *Tiger had earned . . . $1 billion*: Kurt Badenhausen, "Sports' First Billion-Dollar Man," *Forbes*, September 29, 2009.

357   *he and Elin signed*: Marital Settlement Agreement, July 3, 2010.

357   *over $100 million*: Published reports, none of which have been confirmed, identify the amount of the divorce settlement at figures that range from $100 million to $750 million. Sources with knowledge of the settlement figure told the authors that the figure was over $100 million but not as high as $750 million.

357   *nine-thousand-square-foot home*: Sheree R. Curry, "Tiger's Jupiter Island Estate Revealed," AOL Real Estate.

357   *home of their own*: Ashley Reich, "Elin Nordegren's New Home: $12.2 Million Florida Mansion," *Huffington Post*, March 18, 2011.

357   *maiden name restored*: PETITIONER/WIFE'S PETITION FOR DISSOLUTION OF MARRIAGE, Elin Maria Pernilla Woods and Eldrick Tont Woods, Case no. 10-1709.

357   *"Forgiveness takes time"*: Elin Nordegren, "My Own Story."

357   *Fans were heckling*: Crouse, "Woods Withdraws from Players Championship."

357   *new wave of instructors*: Authors' interview with Brandel Chamblee.

359   *"fascial chains"*: Williams, *Out of the Rough*.

359   *"No problem"*: Ibid.

359   *send Williams a text*: Ibid.

360   *Steinberg left IMG*: Mark DeCambre, "Tiger Woods' Agent Sent Packing by IMG," *New York Post*, May 31, 2011.

360   *"Then we're done"*: Williams, *Out of the Rough*.

360 *feet up on the table*: Ibid.

360 *"time for a change"*: "Tiger Woods Gets Rid of Steve Williams," ESPN .com, July 20, 2011.

360 *"years of loyal service"*: Ibid.

361 *Tiger's "slave"*: Williams, *Out of the Rough*.

361 *"greatest win of my career"*: "Steve Williams Triumphs at Masters Again," Golf.com, April 15, 2013.

CHAPTER THIRTY-TWO: ONLY HUMAN

Primary sources include interviews with Brandel Chamblee and Hank Haney; an unpublished interview with Tiger Woods; transcripts of Tiger Woods's press conferences; the book by Hank Haney; a transcript of Lindsay Vonn's interview with *60 Minutes Sports*; and reporting by Michael Bamberger and Alan Shipnuck.

362 *suggesting radical changes*: Authors' interview with Brandel Chamblee.

363 *"the worst experience"*: Haney, *The Big Miss*, 196.

363 *randomly have sex*: Ibid., 205.

363 *"straight through the boundaries"*: Tiger Woods, apology, February 19, 2010.

363 *"Especially the wild ones"*: Haney, *The Big Miss*, 205.

363 *"a Cinderella story"*: Shipnuck, "Who Is This Woman?"

364 *"I didn't inform them"*: Authors' interview with Hank Haney.

364 *act of betrayal*: "Coaching, and Betraying, Tiger Woods," *New Yorker*, April 5, 2012.

365 *Tiger never once called*: Authors' interview with Hank Haney.

365 *"armchair psychology"*: Doug Ferguson, Associated Press, February 29, 2012.

365 *"Because of his father"*: Ibid.

365 *"I've already talked"*: Tiger Woods, press conference, Honda Classic, February 29, 2012.

366 *foundation introduced them*: Unpublished Tiger Woods interview, obtained from a confidential source.

367 *self-conscious about her body*: Lindsey Vonn interview with *60 Minutes Sports*.

367 *totally confident*: Ibid.

367 *divorce was messy*: Bill Pennington, "Fearlessly Forging Ahead," *New York Times*, November 15, 2015.

368 *hurtling over the tips*: Ibid.

368 *take Sam out of the room*: Unpublished Tiger Woods interview, obtained from a confidential source.

368 *anterior cruciate ligament*: Pennington, "Fearlessly Forging Ahead."

368 *ligament were torn*: Ibid.

368 *"It's going to hurt"*: Unpublished Tiger Woods interview, obtained from a confidential source.

368 *announce their relationship on Facebook*: Doug Ferguson, "Woods Made Relationship with Vonn Public to Devalue Paparazzi Photos," Associated Press, March 20, 2013.

369 *the rules of golf*: The primary sources for the account of Tiger's controversial drop shot at the 2012 Masters are Michael Bamberger, "The Story Behind Tiger's Ruling at the Masters," Golf.com, March 19, 2014; and Alan Shipnuck, "Tiger Woods and the Drop: An Inside Look at Golf's Most Controversial Pardon," Golf.com, April 24, 2014.

369 Tough shot: Ibid.

370 take some yardage off: Ibid.

370 *Jim Nantz telephoned*: Ibid.

371 *penalizing Guan Tianlang*: Nancy Armour, "Guan Receives One-stroke Penalty," Associated Press, April 12, 2013.

371 *"rules are rules"*: Tiger Woods, press conference, Masters, April 12, 2013.

372 *wagging his finger*: Authors' interview with Brandel Chamblee.

372 *"A penalty of disqualification"*: Bamberger, "The Story Behind Tiger's Ruling at the Masters"; Shipnuck, "Tiger Woods and the Drop."

373 *penalized again*: "Tiger Woods Hit with 2-shot Penalty at BMW," Associated Press, September 14, 2013.

373 *captured by a videographer*: Ibid.

373 *"How's that?"*: Ibid.

374 *"After seeing the video"*: "A Meditation on Oscillation: Woods Risks Respect of Peers by Protesting Penalty," Associated Press, September 17, 2013.

374 *"He lost the Tour wives"*: Authors' interview with Brandel Chamblee.

374 *gave Tiger an F*: "Woods Responds to Chamblee Criticism, Apology," Associated Press, October 28, 2013.

374 *thought to legal action*: Ibid.

374 *"gone too far"*: Ibid.

374 *"All I'm going to say"*: "Woods Responds to Chamblee Criticism, Apology."

375 *The mental exercise*: Unpublished Tiger Woods interview, obtained from a confidential source.

375 *He hated treatment*: Ibid.

375 Experience the pain: Ibid.

375 *she retore . . . knee*: Pennington, "Fearlessly Forging Ahead."

376 *"Daddy, what are you"*: Rubenstein, "Tiger's Private Struggles."

CHAPTER THIRTY-THREE: POINT OF NO RETURN

Primary sources include interviews with Mark O'Meara, Brandel Chamblee, and Deborah Ganley; transcripts of Tiger Woods's press conferences; and PGATour.com.

377 *disc was pressing on a nerve*: Associated Press, "Complete List of Tiger Woods' Injuries."

377 *missing the cut*: PGATour.com.

377 twenty-three strokes *behind the winner*: Ibid.

378 *just seven official events*: Ibid.

378 *"the right time"*: Ryan Lavner, "Woods Announces Split with Swing Coach Foley," Golfchannel.com, August 25, 2014.

378 *Under Hank Haney*: PGATour.com.

378 *"Sean is one"*: Lavner, "Woods Announces Split with Swing Coach Foley."

378 *master's degree in biomechanics*: Tony Manfred, "Tiger Woods Hired an Unknown Graduate Student," *Business Insider*, November 24, 2014.

379 *old VHS tapes*: Ibid.

380 *"No way"*: Josh Gardner and Lydia Warren, "Tiger Woods' Tooth Was Not Knocked Out by Photographer," DailyMail.com, January 20, 2015.

380 *throwing a cell phone*: Nathaniel Vinton, "Tiger Woods' Story about Cameraman Knocking Out Tooth Starting to Fall Apart," *New York Daily News*, January 21, 2015.

380 *"a crush of photographers"*: Fred Barbash, "The Mystery of Tiger Woods's Missing Tooth," *Washington Post*, January 21, 2015.

380 *"I was among"*: Ibid.

380 *questioning Tiger's version*: Ibid.

381 *"The dude with . . . video cameras"*: Tiger Woods, press conference, Phoenix Open, January 27, 2015.

381 *"I couldn't eat"*: Ibid.

381 *"Who is this guy"*: Will Gray, "Woods' Flaws on Full Display," Golfchannel.com, January 30, 2015.

382 *eleven-over-par 82*: Ibid.

382 *"It's golf"*: Tiger Woods, press conference, Phoenix Open, January 30, 2015.

382 *single worst round*: Gray, "Woods' Flaws on Full Display."

382 *"not an issue anymore"*: Tiger Woods, press conference, Phoenix Open, January 30, 2015.

383 *"I'm okay"*: Authors' interview with Deborah Ganley.

383 *"just my glutes"*: https://www.youtube.com/watch?v=DXR1SCZ0t7g.

383 *"a 'Deactivated' Butt"*: Brendan Porath, "Tiger Woods Blames a 'Deactivated' Butt," SBNation.com, February 5, 2013.

384 *Sam caddied for him*: Nancy Armour, "Family Fun at Augusta," *USA Today*, April 9, 2015.

384 *"They're great kids"*: "Lindsey Vonn Enjoys Hanging Out with Tiger Woods and His Kids," Golf.com, April 21, 2015.

384 *"your boy's going in"*: Authors' interview with Mark O'Meara.

384 *"I worked my ass off"*: Tiger Woods, press conference, Masters, April 7, 2015.

385 *"Jumping into a relationship"*: Pennington, "Fearlessly Forging Ahead."

385 *"We can be loners"*: Rubenstein, "Tiger's Private Struggles."

385 *he didn't sleep*: Tiger Woods, press conference, Players Championship, May 5, 2015.

385 *thirteen-over-par 85*: PGATour.com.

386 *to remind Woods*: Authors' interview with Mark O'Meara.

387 *"changing my life"*: https://www.pgatour.com/video/2015/07/13/mark-o-meara-s-2015-world-golf-hall-of-fame-acceptance-speech.html.

387 *"Sooner or later"*: Authors' interview with Mark O'Meara.

387 *"some of you guys think"*: Tiger Woods, press conference, British Open, July 14, 2015.

387 *golf-course design business*: TigerWoods.com.

388 *removed a disc fragment*: Steve DiMeglio, "Tiger Woods Has Second Back Surgery," *USA Today*, September 19, 2015.

388 *"complete success"*: Ibid.

388 *to relieve the discomfort*: Associated Press, "Complete List of Tiger Woods' Injuries."

CHAPTER THIRTY-FOUR: INTO THE ROUGH

Primary sources include interviews with Mark O'Meara, Hillcrest Country Club member, and a family friend of Glenn Frey. Also, writings by Tiger Woods, Charlie Rose's interview with Tiger Woods in 2016, Lorne Rubenstein's interview with Tiger Woods in 2016, TigerWoods.com, Tiger Woods Foundation source, *60 Minutes Sports*, PGA Tour source, Jupiter Police Department reports and dashcam video, and the *New York Times*.

389 *ten minutes on the beach*: Lorne Rubenstein, "Tiger's Private Struggles," *Time*, December 2015.

389 *"not going to change"*: John Strege, "Tiger Woods' Comeback Attempt Begins with Expectations that in a Marked Departure Do Not Include Winning," *Golf Digest*, January 24, 2018.

389 I've had a good run: Lorne Rubenstein, "Tiger's Private Struggles," *Time*, December 2015.

390 *"There's no timetable"*: Ibid.

390 *"Daddy, let's go play"*: *Charlie Rose*, PBS, October 20, 2016.

390 *"The most important thing"*: Lorne Rubenstein, "Tiger's Private Struggles," *Time*, December 2015.

391 *Tiger didn't contact the family*: Authors' interview with a family friend.

391 *Tiger didn't reach out to her either*: Lindsey Vonn interview with Sharyn Alfonsi, *60 Minutes Sports*, December 8, 2016.

391 *100 million Americans suffer*: Sam Quinones, "A New Kind of Jail for the Opiate Age," *New York Times*, June 18, 2017.

392 *"lives were devoid of meaning"*: Rachel Noble, "Chronic Pain Not Only Hurts, It also Causes Isolation and Depression," *Washington Post*, January 12, 2015.

392 *"completely a locker-room guy"*: Authors' interview with PGA Tour source.

393 *"you're not on the team"*: Ibid.

393 *even lying down hurt*: Tiger Woods, "Updates on Tiger Jam and My Recovery," *Tiger's Blog*, May 24, 2017.

393 *"the way he was shuffling"*: Authors' interview with a member of Hillcrest Country Club.

393 *"way, way overmedicated"*: Authors' interview with a person who attended the luncheon at Hillcrest Country Club.

394 *"I love you"*: Authors' interview with Mark O'Meara.

394 *the end of his rope*: Tiger Woods, "Updates on Tiger Jam and My Recovery," *Tiger's Blog*, May 24, 2017.

395 *tried every nonsurgical route*: Ibid.

395 *"the best place for it to occur"*: "Tiger Undergoes Successful Back Surgery to Alleviate Pain," TigerWoods.com, April 20, 2017.

395 *"it feels to be pain-free"*: Tiger Woods, "Updates on Tiger Jam and My Recovery," *Tiger's Blog*, May 24, 2017.

395 *lethal cocktail of drugs*: Toxicology Report, Palm Beach County Sheriff's Office, June 8, 2017.

396 *"Where were you coming from?"*: Jupiter Police Department Incident/Investigative Report/Supplemental Report, May 29, 2017.

396 *his speech was slurred*: Ibid.

397 "hands behind your back": Ibid.

397 *"Watch the Birdie"*: *New York Post*, May 30, 2017.

397 *"Master of His Own Demise"*: Mike Lupica, *Daily News*, May 30, 2017.

397 *"I understand the severity"*: Yaron Steinbuch, "New Scandal as golfer is busted on DUI rap in Fla.," *New York Post*, May 30, 2017.

397 *overdoses . . . leading cause of death*: American Society of Addiction Medicine, "Opioid Addiction 2016 Facts & Figures."

398 *"I'm also a human"*: Karen Crouse, "Michael Phelps, Counselor to the Stars," *New York Times*, September 24, 2017.

398 *"massive scream for help"*: Ibid.

398 *"salvage someone's life and future"*: Ibid.

CHAPTER THIRTY-FIVE: MAKING THE CUT

Primary sources for this chapter include the authors' reporting and observations from the Farmers Insurance Open, PGATour.com, CBS Sports Public Relations, and the *New York Times*.

399 *"meet a living legend"*: Chris Wright, "Tiger Woods Dubbed 'the Lionel Messi of Golf' by His Daughter," ESPN.com, November 29, 2017.

400 *"I'm proud of him"*: Associated Press, "Tiger Woods Seeks Help for Dealing With Pain Medication," *New York Times*, June 20, 2017.

401 *entered a DUI first-offender program*: Marc Freeman, "Tiger Woods DUI Case: Golfer Enters First-Time Offender Program," *South Florida Sun Sentinel*, October 27, 2017.

401 *fifty hours of community service*: Ibid.

402 *"tempered a little bit because I haven't played"*: Tiger Woods, PGA Tour press conference, January 24, 2018.

INDEX